Essential Latin Dictionary

Teach Yourself®

Latin–English
English–Latin

Alastair Wilson BA

Revised by Valentina Asciutti

For UK order enquiries: please contact Bookpoint Ltd, 130 Milton
Park, Abingdon, Oxon OX14 4SB. *Telephone:* +44 (0) 1235 827720.
Fax: +44 (0) 1235 400454. Lines are open 09.00–17.00, Monday to
Saturday, with a 24-hour message answering service. Details about our
titles and how to order are available at www.teachyourself.com

For USA order enquiries: please contact McGraw-Hill Customer
Services, PO Box 545, Blacklick, OH 43004-0545, USA. *Telephone:*
1-800-722-4726. *Fax:* 1-614-755-5645.

For Canada order enquiries: please contact McGraw-Hill Ryerson Ltd,
300 Water St, Whitby, Ontario L1N 9B6, Canada. *Telephone:* 905 430
5000. *Fax:* 905 430 5020.

Long renowned as the authoritative source for self-guided learning –
with more than 50 million copies sold worldwide – the *Teach Yourself*
series includes over 500 titles in the fields of languages, crafts, hobbies,
business, computing and education.

British Library Cataloguing in Publication Data: a catalogue record for
this title is available from the British Library.

Library of Congress Catalog Card Number: on file.

**First published in UK 1965 as TeachYourself Latin Dictionary by
Hodder Education,** part of Hachette UK, 338 Euston Road, London
NW1 3BH.

First published in US 1992 by The McGraw-Hill Companies, Inc.

This edition published 2010.

Previously published as Teach Yourself Latin Dictionary

The *Teach Yourself* name is a registered trade mark of Hodder Headline.

Copyright © 1965, 2003, 2010 Alastair Wilson

Typeset by Transet Ltd, Coventry, England.
Printed in Great Britain for Hodder Education, an Hachette UK
Company, 338 Euston Road, London NW1 3BH.

The publisher has used its best endeavours to ensure that the URLs for
external websites referred to in this book are correct and active at the
time of going to press. However, the publisher and the author have no
responsibility for the websites and can make no guarantee that a site
will remain live or that the content will remain relevant, decent or
appropriate.

Hachette UK's policy is to use papers that are natural, renewable and
recyclable products and made from wood grown in sustainable forests.
The logging and manufacturing processes are expected to conform to
the environmental regulations of the country of origin.

Impression number 10 9 8 7 6 5 4 3 2 1
Year 2014 2013 2012 2011 2010

Contents

Credits

Front cover: Oxford Illustrators Ltd

Foreword

This dictionary is intended for anyone with an interest in the Latin language.

This new edition of our classic Latin dictionary has been revised and now includes

- *One-, five- and ten-minute summaries of the Latin language. These short articles are intended to allow readers to come away with useful information about Latin if they have only one, five, or ten minutes available.*
- *Fifty 'author insight boxes' containing short information about elements of Latin that are difficult to grasp or that are essential for everyone to know. These can be tips to help the learner remember a particular grammar rule or key vocabulary and phrases.*

The study of a foreign language should always begin with a good understanding of the basic grammar rules of such a language; therefore, the learner should always have to hand a good Latin grammar book such as **Essential Latin Grammar**, *by Gregory Klyve, in the same series.*

Only got a minute?

Latin is an Italic language originally spoken in the region of central Italy called *Latium* (today Lazio) and the ancient city of Rome, the *aeterna urbs*. With the Roman conquest, Latin spread throughout Italy, the Mediterranean and Europe. The so called Romance languages such as Catalan, French, Italian, Portuguese, Romanian, and Spanish are descended directly from Latin; many other languages, English included, although not directly derived from Latin, have inherited and acquired much of their vocabulary from it.

Latin is a perfect language with a very precise set of grammatical rules; it is a synthetic language where affixes are attached to fixed stems of words to express gender, number, and case in nouns, pronouns and adjectives; this process is called declension. Latin nouns, pronouns and adjectives therefore decline; there are five declensions in Latin and every declension has six cases (*nominative*, *accusative*, *vocative*, *genitive*, *dative* and *ablative*); each case has a specific meaning and function. In Modern English, nouns have distinct singular and plural forms; so in a way, they *decline* to reflect their grammatical number. On the other hand, verbs are conjugated in Latin; there are four main conjugations where affixes are attached to fixed stems of verbs to denote person, number, tense, voice, mood, and aspect.

Latin is not a spoken language today but there are traces of Latin in many modern languages and in every sentence we speak. Some examples of Latin words or expressions commonly used in everyday speech are:

- *a.m./p.m.* stand for *ante/post meridiem* (before/after midday)
- *etc.* stands for *et cetera* (and other things)
- *forum* is a marketplace, the real social and political centre of a town, today commonly used to denote an online space used for discussion.

5 Only got five minutes?

Latin is an Italic language originally spoken in the region of central Italy called *Latium* (today Lazio) and the ancient city of Rome, the *aeterna urbs*. With the Roman conquest, Latin spread throughout Italy, the Mediterranean and Europe. Britain was occupied by the Romans from AD 43 to AD 410 and during this time Latin was the main language used in the island, apart from Scotland. *'Veni, Vidi, Vici'* (= I came, I saw, I conquered) is the famous sentence reportedly written by Julius Caesar in 47 BC after his expedition to Britain. However, the conquest of Britain didn't start until AD 43 with the invasion led by Claudius. Roman rule ended in AD 410 and Britain was then overrun by Anglo-Saxons in the following years, so that there was no major Latin influence on the language at this stage; Anglo-Saxon was indeed the predominant tongue. However, when Norman and Angevin kings ruled England for some 300 years, the Latin-based French was incorporated into Middle English, adding enormous richness to it. So, Latin influence was back into the English language, this time through French. The so called Romance languages such as Catalan, French, Italian, Portuguese, Romanian, and Spanish are instead descended directly from Latin but many other languages, English included, although not directly derived from Latin, have inherited and acquired much of their vocabulary from it.

Latin is a perfect language with a very precise set of grammatical rules; it is a synthetic language where affixes are attached to fixed stems of words to express gender, number, and case in nouns, pronouns and adjectives; this process is called declension. Latin nouns, pronouns and adjectives therefore decline; there are five declensions in Latin and every declension has six cases (*nominative, accusative, vocative, genitive, dative* and *ablative*). Each case has a specific meaning and function: *nominative* is the case of the subject, *accusative* is the case of the direct object, *vocative* is the case used when addressing someone, *genitive* is the case that shows possession, *dative* is the case of the indirect object and *ablative* is a case with several functions, its main meanings being 'by', 'with', 'from', 'at', 'in' and 'on'. There is also an old seventh case, called the *locative* case, used to indicate a location, corresponding to the English 'in' or 'at'. This is far less common than the other six cases of Latin nouns and usually applies to cities, small towns, and small islands, along with a few common nouns (e.g. *domi* = at home). In the first and second declension singular, its form coincides with the genitive (e.g. *Romae* = in Rome). In the first and second declension plural, and in the other declensions, it coincides with the dative and ablative (e.g. *Athenis* = at Athens). The meaning of the cases can also change when these are used with prepositions. Prepositions are short words that stand in front of a noun or pronoun to introduce an adverbial phrase; in Latin prepositions can take either the accusative or the ablative, only the preposition in can take both cases: 'in + a noun in the ablative case' means 'in', 'at', 'on', (e.g. *in schola* = at school) 'in + a noun in the accusative case' means 'into', 'onto', 'towards' (e.g. *in scholam* – into the school). The main prepositions in Latin are: a) prepositions with accusative: *in* (into), *ad* (to), *per* (through, by means of, on account of), *ante* (before), *contra* (against), *ob/propter* (because of, on account of), *post* (after), *praeter* (along, except), *prope* (near), *trans* (across); b) prepositions with ablative: *cum* (with), *a/ab/e/ex/de* (by, from, out of – de + ablative can also mean about), *in* (in, at, on). Even in Modern English, nouns have distinct singular and plural forms; so in a way, they *decline* to reflect their grammatical number. On the other hand, verbs are conjugated in Latin; there are four main conjugations (first, second, third and fourth) and a mixed conjugation (third and fourth) where affixes are attached to fixed stems of verbs to denote person, number, tense, voice, mood, and aspect. There are six tenses in Latin (i.e. present, imperfect, future, perfect, pluperfect, and future perfect), three grammatical moods (i.e. indicative, imperative and subjunctive, in addition to the infinitive, participle, gerund, gerundive and supine), three persons (first, second, and third), two numbers (singular and plural) and three voices (active, passive and deponent).

Verbs are described by their principal parts (e.g. *amo*, *amare*, *amavi*, *amatum*):

- The first principal part is the first person (or third person for impersonal verbs) singular, present tense, indicative, active (or passive for verbs lacking an active voice).
- The second principal part is the present infinitive active (or passive for verbs lacking an active voice).
- The third principal part is the first person (or third person for impersonal verbs) singular, perfect, indicative, active (or passive when there is no active forms).
- The fourth principal part is the supine form. It usually shows the neuter (*-um*) of the participle. It can also be the future participle when the verb cannot be made passive.

Latin lacks indefinite and definite articles.

Latin is not a spoken language today but there are traces of Latin in many modern languages and in every sentence we speak. Some examples of Latin words or expressions commonly used in everyday speech are:

- *a.m./p.m.* stand for *ante/post meridiem* (before/after midday)
- *etc.* stands for *et cetera* (and other things)
- *forum* is a marketplace, the real social and political centre of a town, today commonly used to denote an online space used for discussion
- *e.g.* stands for *exempli gratia* (for example)
- *i.e.* stands for *id est* (that is, namely)

10 Only got ten minutes?

Latin is an Italic language originally spoken in the region of central Italy called *Latium* (today Lazio) and the ancient city of Rome, the *aeterna urbs*. With the Roman conquest, Latin spread throughout Italy, the Mediterranean and Europe. Britain was occupied by the Romans from AD 43 to AD 410 and during this time Latin was the main language used in the island, apart from Scotland. 'Veni, Vidi, Vici' (= I came, I saw, I conquered) is the famous sentence reportedly written by Julius Caesar in 47 BC after his expedition to Britain. However, the conquest of Britain didn't start until AD 43 with the invasion led by Claudius. Britain was then overrun by Anglo-Saxons in the years following the end of the Roman rule, so that there was no major Latin influence on the language at this stage; Anglo-Saxon was indeed the predominant tongue. However, when Norman and Angevin kings ruled England for some 300 years, the Latin-based French was incorporated into Middle English, adding enormous richness to it. So, Latin influence was back into the English language, this time through French. The so called Romance languages such as Catalan, French, Italian, Portuguese, Romanian, and Spanish are descended directly from Latin but many other languages, English included, although not directly derived from Latin, have inherited and acquired much of their vocabulary from it. English has taken some of its Latin-based words direct from Latin, others through an intermediary language such as French (e.g. wine comes from vinum). Moreover, some English words look similar to Latin because both English and Latin are Indo-European languages. The Indo-European family extends from the Atlantic coasts of Europe to India. In Europe four big-groups can be detected: Hellenic, represented by the various dialects of Greek; Italic, mostly consisting of Latin; Germanic, including English, German, and the Scandinavian languages;

and Celtic, including Welsh and Irish. Latin is also the ancestor of the Romance languages, as mentioned above. So, in a way, Latin is not a dead language but it persists in all the modern Romance languages, which represent the evolution of its spoken forms.

Latin is a perfect language with a very precise set of grammatical rules; it is a synthetic language where affixes are attached to fixed stems of words to express gender, number, and case in nouns, pronouns and adjectives; this process is called declension. Latin nouns, pronouns and adjectives therefore decline; there are five declensions in Latin and every declension has six cases (*nominative, accusative, vocative, genitive, dative* and *ablative*). Each case has a specific meaning and function: nominative is the case of the subject, accusative is the case of the direct object, *vocative* is the case used when addressing someone, genitive is the case that shows possession, *dative* is the case of the indirect object and *ablative* is a case with several functions, its main meanings being 'by', 'with', 'from', 'at', 'in' and 'on'. There is also an old seventh case, called the *locative* case, used to indicate a location, corresponding to the English 'in' or 'at'. This is far less common than the other six cases of Latin nouns and usually applies to cities, small towns, and small islands, along with a few common nouns (e.g. *domi* = at home). In the first and second declension singular, its form coincides with the genitive (e.g. *Romae* = in Rome). In the first and second declension plural, and in the other declensions, it coincides with the dative and ablative (e.g. *Athenis* = at Athens). The meaning of the cases can also change when these are used with prepositions. Prepositions are short words that stand in front of a noun or pronoun to introduce an adverbial phrase; in Latin prepositions can take either the accusative or the ablative, only the preposition in can take both cases: 'in + a noun in the ablative case' means 'in', 'at', 'on', (e.g. *in schola* = at school) 'in + a noun in the accusative case' means 'into', 'onto', 'towards' (e.g. *in scholam* – into the school). The main prepositions in Latin are: a) prepositions with accusative: *in* (into), *ad* (to), *per* (through, by means of, on account of), *ante* (before), *contra* (against), *ob/propter* (because of, on account of), *post* (after),

praeter (along, except), *prope* (near), *trans* (across); b)
prepositions with ablative: *cum* (with), *a/ab/e/ex/de* (by, from,
out of – de + ablative can also mean about), *in* (in, at, on).
Even in Modern English, nouns have distinct singular and
plural forms; so in a way, they *decline* to reflect their
grammatical number. On the other hand, verbs are conjugated
in Latin; there are four main conjugations (first, second, third
and fourth) and a mixed conjugation (third and fourth; e.g.
capio) where affixes are attached to fixed stems of verbs to
denote person, number, tense, voice, mood, and aspect. There
are six tenses in Latin (i.e. present, imperfect, future, perfect,
pluperfect, and future perfect), three grammatical moods (i.e.
indicative, imperative and subjunctive, in addition to the
infinitive, participle, gerund, gerundive and supine), three
persons (first, second, and third), two numbers (singular and
plural) and three voices (active, passive and deponent). The
indicative mood is used to state something as a fact or to ask a
question. The imperative expresses a command, an order. The
subjunctive is used, among other functions, to express doubt or
unlikelihood. The infinitive can be described as a verbal noun.
It acts as a verb when it is active or passive, has a present,
future and past tense and can govern cases; it can also act as a
noun, when it is neuter and it stands in the nominative or
accusative case. The participle can be defined as an adjective
formed from a verb; there are three tenses of participle in
Latin: present, future and perfect. As adjectives, participles
agree in case, number and gender with the noun or pronoun to
which they refer. The gerundive is a verbal adjective; it is a
passive adjective, based on a verb, ending in *-ndus, -a, -um* like
a fist-and-second-declension-adjective, meaning 'to be -ed' and
frequently expressing the idea of obligation (e.g. *hoc faciendum
est* = this must be done).The gerundive usually has the agent
expressed in the dative case or *a/ab* + a noun in the ablative
case. The gerund, as much as the infinitive can be described
best as a verbal noun; it is a neuter noun, formed from a verb;
this form is never nominative and is mostly used with a
preposition. Finally, the supine is that part of a verb from
which other parts of the verb can be predicated, especially the
passive forms. Verbs can have active, passive or deponent
forms. Deponent verbs are those verbs that have a passive form

but they are translated with an active meaning (e.g. *utor* = I use); also, there are the so-called semi-deponent verbs; they adopt active forms in some tenses and deponent forms in others (e.g. *audeo* = I dare).

Verbs are described by its principal parts (e.g. *amo, amare, amavi, amatum*):

- The first principal part is the first person (or third person for impersonal verbs) singular, present tense, indicative, active (or passive for verbs lacking an active voice).
- The second principal part is the present infinitive active (or passive for verbs lacking an active voice).
- The third principal part is the first person (or third person for impersonal verbs) singular, perfect, indicative, active (or passive when there is no active form).
- The fourth principal part is the supine form. It usually shows the neuter (*-um*) of the participle. It can also be the future participle when the verb cannot be made passive.

Only the principal parts of irregular verbs or verbs with their own individual forms are given in the dictionary. Regular verbs have the following endings:

am-o, am-are, am-avi, am-atum
mo-eo, mon-ere, mon-ui, mon-itum
leg-o, leg-is, leg-i, lec-tum
aud-io, aud-is, aud-ivi / aud-ii, aud-itum

Some of the most important verbs with irregular principal parts to remember are:

- *ago, agere, egi, actum* = I do
- *augeo, augere, auxi, auctum* = I increase
- *cado, cadere, cecidi, casum* = I fall, I die
- *capio, capere, cepi, captum* = I take
- *coepi, coepisse, coeptus* = I have begun
- *credo, credere, credidi, creditum* = I believe
- *curro, currere, cucurri, cursum* = I run
- *dico, dicere, dixi, dictum* = I say
- *do, dare, dedi, datum* = I give

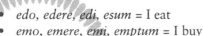

- *edo, edere, edi, esum* = I eat
- *emo, emere, emi, emptum* = I buy
- *eo, ire, ii/ivi, itum* = I go
- *facio, facere, feci, factum* = I make
- *fero, ferre, tuli, latum* = I bring
- *fio, fieri, factus* = I become
- *gero, gerere, gessi, gestum* = I do, conduct
- *iubeo, iubere, iussi, iussum* = I order
- *malo, malle, malui* = I prefer
- *maneo, manere, mansi, mansum* = I wait
- *mitto, mittere, misi, missum* = I send
- *nolo, nolle, nolui* = I do not want
- *odi, odisse, osus* = I hate
- *possum, posse, potui* = I can
- *sto, stare, steti, statum* = I stand
- *sum, esse, fui, futurus* = I am
- *tollo, tollere, sustuli, sublatum* = I lift
- *traho, trahere, traxi, tractum* = I drag
- *volo, velle, volui* = I want

Latin lacks indefinite and definite articles.

Latin is not a spoken language today but there are traces of
Latin in many modern languages and in every sentence we
speak. Some examples of Latin words or expressions commonly
used in everyday speech are:

- *a.m./p.m.* stand for *ante/post meridiem* (before/after
  midday)
- *etc.* stands for *et cetera* (and other things)
- *forum* is a marketplace, the real social and political centre
  of a town, today commonly used to denote an online space
  used for discussion
- *e.g.* stands for *exempli gratia* (for example)
- *i.e.* stands for *id est* (namely)

Introduction

The chief benefit that a knowledge of Latin confers is the ability to read the works of the Roman authors, particularly those of the Golden and Silver Ages of Latin Literature, i.e. 60 BC–AD 100. This dictionary has been compiled with this in mind, and also with an eye to the 'non-specialist'. To this end, the equivalents in the Latin–English section of the dictionary have been presented in as simple and 'modern' a form as possible, while at the same time the most important distinctions in meaning which each Latin word bears have been indicated. The vocabulary has been based on that commonly used by the authors of the period mentioned above, and a person who is acquainted with Latin grammar and the common forms of the Latin language should be able, with a little help from this dictionary, to read them without much difficulty. *Teach Yourself Latin Grammar*, by Gregory Klyve, may be of assistance to those who are not so acquainted, or whose memory has been dimmed by the passage of time.

In the English–Latin section, the Latin equivalent given is that which represents the best general meaning of the English, and which is used in that sense by a Classical author. Occasionally, however, where no exact Latin equivalent for an English word exists, it has been necessary to give a short circumlocution: in this case the phrase given is always translated into English, e.g. **disinterested** neutri favens (**favouring neither side**). Where several different meanings are borne by the same word, or where ambiguity may occur, care has been taken to differentiate between the various meanings, e.g. **order**, *nn*, (**arrangement**), ordo, *m*; (**in —**), *adj*, dĭspŏsĭtus; (**command, direction**), iussum, *n*; (**class, rank**), ordo, *m*; (**in — to**), ut.

Where fuller information is required about any of the words given in the dictionary, reference should be made to Lewis and Short's *Latin Dictionary* (Oxford University Press, 1963), available on line via the Perseus Digital Library, at **http://www.perseus.tufts.edu/**, which comprises a magnificent collection of primary and secondary Classical sources.

Advice on learning vocabulary

If you are gifted with a good memory, you will find it particularly easy to learn Latin vocabulary, especially if you try to link in your mind new Latin words and any English derivatives of them which you can think of, e.g. **mare**—sea—marine; **nauta**—ship—nautical. A high proportion of Latin words have quite common English derivatives. If you do this, not only will your interest in both languages grow, but you will begin to form an impression of the debt which our language owes to that of the Romans.

If on the other hand, you are one of those who find it difficult to make words stick, then here is a piece of simple advice – not to be despised because of its simplicity – which might help you to retain words in your memory. To learn a new word it is not only essential to find out and to understand its meaning, but also to see it working in relationship to other words, and to 'meet' it as many times as possible immediately after first acquaintance. It is therefore advisable to re-read the piece in which you originally met the word two or three times after you have learned it, and to make an effort to find the same word again within a day or two of first meeting it, otherwise you may find, on ultimately seeing it again, that it has 'gone'. Above all, try to maintain your interest in learning new vocabulary, for without such an interest no learning of real or lasting nature can take place.

Abbreviations used

( ) Brackets are used to indicate alternative forms.

See *Teach Yourself Latin Grammar*, by Gregory Klyve, for an explanation of the grammar terms used.

a, um   see adj.
abl.   ablative case.
acc.   accusative case.
acis   genitive singular ending of nouns indicating that they
atis   belong to the third declension.
adj.   adjective, **a, um, era, erum** after an adjective indicates that it declines like a noun of the first or second declensions, **e** that it declines like a noun of the third declension.
adv.   adverb. The adverb ending is often given, e.g. **e, iter, nter, um, o,** and should be attached to the *stem* of the adjective, e.g. **abditus** (*adj*); **abdite** (*adv*).

ae   genitive singular ending of a noun, indicating that it belongs to the first declension.

arum   genitive plural ending, indicating that the noun belongs to the first declension.

auxil.   auxiliary verb.

c.   common gender.

comp.   comparative adjective or adverb.

conj.   conjunction.

cris, cre   nominative feminine and neuter endings, indicating that an adjective declines like a noun of the third declension.

cl.   clause.

dat.   dative case; also some verbs take a dative case after them.

defect.   a defective verb; i.e. it has not all its parts.

demonst.   demonstrative pronoun.

dep.   see v. dep.

e   see adj.

ei   genitive singular ending of noun, indicating that it belongs to the fifth declension.

enis ⎫   genitive singular endings of nouns indicating that they
etis ⎭   belong to the third declension.

exclam.   exclamation.

f.   feminine gender.

f.pl.   feminine plural.

fut.   future.

genit.   genitive case.

i, ii   genitive singular ending of noun, indicating that it belongs to the second declension.

icis ⎫   genitive singular endings of nouns indicating that they
inis ⎭   belong to the third declension.

impers.   impersonal verb.

indecl.   indeclinable.

inf.   infinitive.

interj.   interjective.

interr.   interrogative.

irreg.   irregular verb.

is   genitive singular of noun, indicating that it belongs to the third declension.

iter   see adv.

itis   genitive singular ending of noun, indicating that it belongs to the third declension.

ium   genitive plural ending of noun, indicating that it belongs to the third declension.

loc   locative case

m.   masculine gender.

m.pl.   masculine plural.

n. neuter gender.

nn. noun.

nter see adv.

ntis genitive singular ending of some nouns and adjectives of the third declension.

num numeral.

n.pl. neuter plural.

obj. objective.

onis } genitive singular noun ending, indicating that the noun
oris } belongs to the second declension.

orum genitive plural ending, indicating that a noun belongs to the second declension.

partic. participle.

pass. a passive verb, conjugated in the passive voice only.

perf. perfect.

pers. personal.

phr. phrase.

pl. plural.

poss. possessive.

prep. preposition: the case taken by the preposition is usually indicated.

pres. present.

pron. pronoun.

pron. adj. pronominal adjective; a pronoun which declines and agrees like an adjective.

reflex. reflexive.

rel. relative.

semi-dep. semi-deponent; verbs which are deponent in some of their tenses.

sup(erl). superlative adjective or adverb.

tis } genitive singular ending of some nouns and adjs. of
tris } the third declension.

um genitive plural ending of noun, indicating that it belongs to the third declension.

ūs genitive singular ending of noun, indicating that it belongs to the fourth declension.

v. vb. verb. The conjugation to which a verb belongs is indicated by the figure 1, 2, 3, or 4. In the case of third conjugation verbs, and other verbs whose perfect stem and supine are not regular, these are given with the verb, e.g. **aboleo, evi, itum**. If none of these parts are given, it may be assumed that the verb is regularly conjugated; if some, but not all parts are given, it may be assumed that the ones not given are not in regular use.

v. dep.   verb deponent.

v.i.   verb intransitive, i.e. a verb which does not have a direct object.

v. impers.   verb impersonal.

v.i.t.   a verb which can be used intransitively or transitively. The separate uses are indicated by the use of the semi-colon, e.g. **abhorreo**, *v.i.t.*, 2, to shrink back (intransitive); to disagree with (transitive).

voc.   vocative case.

v.t.   verb transitive, i.e. a verb which has a direct object.

Alphabet

The Latin alphabet contained 23 letters:

A B C D E F G H I K L M N O P Q R S T V X Y Z

Pronunciation

Although there is not complete agreement about the way in which the Romans spoke Latin, this is one method of pronunciation which many people believe to have been used by the Romans.

Vowels

ă (short a) as in 'fat'; ā (long a) as in 'father'.
ĕ (short e) as in 'net'; ē (long e) as in 'they'.
ĭ (short i) as in 'pin'; ī (long i) as in 'police'.
ŏ (short o) as in 'not'; ō (long o) as in 'note'.
ŭ (short u) as 'oo' in 'wood'; ū (long u) as 'oo' in 'mood'.

In the dictionary ă, ĕ, ĭ, ŏ, ŭ represent the respective vowels with the combined long (macron ‾) and short (breve ˘) marks (e.g. 'ăprīcor'). This mark is used to indicate that the syllable is anceps. In Latin, vowels could be long or short; anceps syllables could be both.

Diphthongs

Two vowels pronounced together to form one sound are called diphthongs, e.g. ae, au, oe, and are pronounced as follows.

ae, as in 'ai' in 'aisle'.
au, as 'ow' in 'cow'.
oe, as in 'oi' in 'oil'.

Consonants

These are mostly pronounced as in English, but note:

c is always hard, as in 'cat'.

g is always hard, as in 'get'.

i, when it is used as a consonant, is always pronounced as 'y' in 'yellow' e.g. *iam*, 'yam'.

s is always pronounced as in 'son'.

t is always pronounced as in 'top'.

v is pronounced as 'w' in 'wall', e.g. *servi*, pronounced 'serwee'.

th is pronounced as 't' and *ch* as 'k'.

Latin–English dictionary

A

Insight

There is no **definite article** in Latin. Therefore there are no Latin words to express the English 'the'. Likewise, there is no **indefinite article** in Latin. Thus, there are no Latin words to express the English 'a' and 'an'.

ā, ăb *prep. with abl,* by (agent); from (place, time); in, at (position); since

ăbăcus, i *m,* sideboard, counting or gaming board, slab

ăbălĭēno *v.t.* 1, to estrange, make a legal transfer

ăbăvus, i *m,* great-great-grandfather, ancestor

abdĭcātĭo, ōnis *f,* renunciation of office

abdĭco *v.t.* 1, to resign

abdīco, xi, ctum *v.t.* 3 to refuse assent

abdĭtus, a, um *adj, adv,* ē, hidden, secret

abdo, didi, dĭtum *v.t.* 3, to conceal

abdōmĕn, ĭnis *n,* belly

ăberro *v.i.* 1, to go astray

ăbhinc *adv,* ago

ăbhorrĕo *v.i.t.* 2, to shrink back; disagree with

ăbi see **ăbĕo**

ăbĭcĭo, iēci, iectum *v.t.* 3, to throw away

abiectus, a, um *adj, adv,* ē, downcast

ăbĭēgnus, a um *adj,* made of fir

ăbĭēs, ĕtis *f,* fir

ăbĭgo, ĕre, ēgi, actum *v.t.* 3, to drive away

ăbĭtĭo, ōnis *f,* departure

abiūdico *v.t.* 1, to deprive by legal sentence

abiungo, nxi, nctum *v.t.* 3, to unyoke

Insight

Third declension nouns have a great variety of endings in the nominative singular. What unites them all is that the genitive singular always has the same ending (-*is*). Therefore, when learning third-declension nouns, it is essential to memorize both the nominative and the genitive singular.

abdūco, xi, ctum *v.t.* 3, to lead away

ăbĕo *v.i.* 4, to go away

abiūro *v.t.* 1, to deny on oath

ablātus, a, um *adj.* from **aufĕro,** taken away

Insight

The **ablative** is a case with many usages and meanings. The basic meanings are 'by', 'with', 'from', 'at', 'in' or 'on'. Many prepositions take the ablative determining the meaning of the noun. Many verbs are followed by the ablative case (e.g. *utor*).

ablēgātĭo, ōnis *f*, banishment

ablēgo *v.t.* 1, to send away

ablŭo, ŭi, ūtum *v.t.* 3, to wash away

ablūtĭo, ōnis *f*, ablution, washing

abnĕgo *v.t.* 1, to refuse

abnormis, e *adj*, irregular

abnŭo, ŭi, ūtum *v.i.t.* 3, to refuse

ăbŏlĕo, ēvi, ĭtum *v.t.* 2, to destroy

ăbŏlesco, ēvi *v.i.* 3, to decay

ăbŏlītĭo, ōnis *f*, abolition

ăbolla, ae *f*, cloak

ăbōmĭnor *v.t.* 1, *dep*, to wish away (being ominous)

ăbŏrīgĭnes, um *m.pl*, natives

ăbortĭo, ōnis *f*, miscarriage

ăbortus, ūs *m*, abortion

abrādo, si, sum *v.t.* 3, to scrape off

abrĭpĭo, ŭi, reptum *v.t.* 3, to drag away

abrōdo, si, sum *v.t.* 3, to gnaw away

abrŏgātĭo, ōnis *f*, repeal

abrŏgo *v.t.* 1, to repeal

abrumpo, rūpi, ruptum *v.t.* 3, to break off

abruptus, a, um *adj*, steep

abscēdo, cessi, cessum *v.i.* 3, to go away

abscīdo, cīdi, scīsum *v.t.* 3, to cut off

abscindo, scĭdi, scissum *v.t.* 3, to tear away

abscīsus, a, um *adj, adv*, **ē**, steep

abscondĭtus, a, um *adj, adv*, **ē**, hidden

abscondo, di, dĭtum *v.t.* 3, to conceal

absens, entis *adj*, absent

absentĭa, ae *f*, absence

absĭlĭo *v.i.* 4, to jump away

absĭmĭlis, e *adj*, unlike

absinthium, ii *n*, absinth

absisto, stĭti *v.i.* 3, to stand aloof

absŏlūtĭo, ōnis *f*, acquittal

absŏlūtus, a, um *adj, adv*, **ē**, discordant

absolvo, vi. sŏlūtum *v.t.* 3, to unfasten, acquit

absŏnus, a, um *adj, adv*, **ē**, discordant

absorbĕo, bŭi, ptum *v.t.* 2, to swallow up

absquĕ *prep. with abl*, without

abstēmĭus, a, um *adj*, sober

abstergĕo, rsi, rsum *v.t.* 2, to wipe off

absterrĕo *v.t.* 2, to frighten away

abstinens, ntis *adj, adv*, **nter**, temperate

abstĭnentĭa, ae *f*, self-restraint

abstĭnĕo, ŭi, tentum *v.i.t.* 2, to abstain from; restrain

abstrăho, xi, ctum *v.t.* 3, to drag away

abstrūdo, si, sum *v.t.* 3, to push away

abstrūsus, a, um *adj, adv*, **ē**, hidden

absum, esse, abfui (afui) *v.i. irreg*, to be absent

absūmo, mpsi, mptum *v.t.* 3, to take away, use up

absurdus, a, um *adj, adv*, **ē**, stupid, tuneless

ăbundans, ntis *adj, adv*, **nter**, plentiful

ăbundantĭa, ae *f*, plenty

ăbundo *v.i.* 1, to overflow

ăbūtor, i, usus sum *v.* 3, *dep, with abl*, to use up, abuse

āc *conj*, and

ăcācĭa, ae *f*, acacia

ăcădēmĭa, ae *f*, academy

accēdo, cessi, cesssum *v.i.* 3, to approach

accĕlĕro *v.i.t.* 1, to hurry; quicken

accendo, ndi, nsum *v.t.* 3, to set on fire

accensĕo, ŭi, nsum *v.t.* 2, to add to

accensus, i *m*, attendant

accentus, ūs *m*, accentuation

acceptĭo, ōnis *f*, acceptance

acceptum, i *n*, receipt

acceptus, a, um *adj*, agreeable

accessĭo, ōnis *f*, approach, increase

accessus, ūs *m*, approach

accīdo, cīdi, cīsum *v.t.* 3, to cut

accĭdo, cĭdi *v.i.* 3, to fall upon, happen

accingo, nxi, nctum *v.t.* 3, to equip, put on

accĭo *v.t.* 4, to summon

accĭpĭo, cēpi, ceptum *v.t.* 3, to receive

accĭpĭter, tris *m*, hawk

accītus, ūs *m,* summons
acclāmātĭo, ōnis *f,* shout
acclāmo *v.t.* 1, to shout at
acclīnis, e *adj,* leaning on
acclīno *v.t.* 1, to lean
acclīvis, e *adj,* uphill
acclīvĭtas, ātis *f,* ascent
accŏla, ae *c,* neighbour
accŏlo, cŏlui, cultum *v.t.* 3, to live near
accommŏdātus, a, um *adj, adv,* **ē,** suitable
accommŏdātĭo, ōnis *f,* compliance
accommŏdo *v.t.* 1, to adapt
accommŏdus, a, um *adj,* suitable
accresco, crēvi, crētum *v.i.* 3, to grow
accrētĭo, ōnis *f,* increase
accŭbĭtĭo, ōnis *f,* reclining
accŭbo *v.i.* 1, to lie near, recline at table
accumbo, cŭbŭi, cŭbĭtum *v.i.* 3, to lie near, recline at table
accŭmŭlo *v.t.* 1, to heap up
accūro *v.t.* 1, to take care of
accūrātus, a, um *adj, adv,* **ē,** prepared carefully, precise
accurro, curri, cursum *v.i.* 3, to run to
accūsātĭo, ōnis *f,* accusation
accūsātor, ōris *m,* accuser
accūso *v.t.* 1, to accuse
ācer, cris, e *adj, adv,* **ĭter,** keen
ăcer, ĕris *n,* maple tree
ăcerbĭtas, ātis *f,* bitterness

ăcētārĭa, ōrum *n.pl,* salad
ăcētum, i *n,* vinegar
ăcĭdus, a, um *adj, adv,* **ē,** sour
ăcĭes, ēi *f,* edge, pupil of eye, battle line, keeness
ăcĭnăces, is *m,* scimitar
ăcĭnus, i *m* **(um, i** *n*), berry
ăcĭpenser, ĕris *m,* sturgeon
aclys, ўdis *f,* small javelin
ăcŏnītum, i *n,* aconite
acquĭesco, ēvi, ĕtum *v.i.* 3, to rest, aquiesce
acquīro, sīvi, sītum *v.t.* 3, to procure
ācrĭmōnĭa, ae *f,* sharpness
ācrĭter *adv,* keenly
acta, ōrum *n.pl* acts, records
actĭo, ōnis *f,* act, legal action
actor, ōris *m,* driver, plaintiff, performer
actŭārĭus, a, um *adj,* swift
actŭārĭus, i *m,* notary
actum, i *n,* deed
actus, a, um see **ăgo**
actus, ūs *m,* impulse, act (of drama)
ăcūlĕātus, a, um *adj,* prickly
ăcūlĕus, i *m,* sting
ăcūmĕn, ĭnis *n,* point, sting
ăcŭo, ŭi, ūtum *v.t.* 3, to sharpen
ăcus, ūs *f,* needle, pin
ăcūtus, a, um *adj, adv,* **ē,** sharp
ad *prep. with acc,* to, towards, near (place), about (time), for (purpose)

Insight

In Latin the 'place to which' is expressed by **in/ad** with a noun in the accusative case (*ad oppidum* = to the town). The 'place from which' by **a/ab/e/ex/de** with the ablative (*ex oppido* = from the town). The 'place where' by **in** with the ablative (*in oppido* = in the town).

ăcerbo *v.t.* 1, to embitter
ăcerbus, a, um *adj,* bitter, keen
ăcernus, a, um *adj,* made of maple
ăcerra, ae *f,* incense-box
ăcervo *v.t.* 1, to heap up
ăcervus, i *m,* heap

ădaequo *v.i.t.* 1, to be equal; to make equal
ădaequo *v.i.t.* 1, to be equal; to make equal
ădămas, ntis *m,* steel, diamond
ădămo *v.t.* 1, to love deeply

ădăpĕrĭo, ŭi, rtum *v.t.* 4, to open fully

ădaugĕo, xi, ctum *v.t.* 2, to increase

addīco, xi, ctum *v.t.* 3, to assent, award

addictĭo, ōnis *f*, adjudication

addictus, a, um *adj*, dedicated

addo, dĭdi, dĭtum *v.t.* 3, to add to

addŭbĭto *v.i.t.* 1, to doubt

addūco, xi, ctum *v.t.* 3, to lead to, influence

ădemptĭo, ōnis *f*, seizure

ădĕo *v.i.* 4, to approach, attack

ădĕo *adv*, so much, so long

ădeps, ĭpis *c*, fat

ădeptĭo, ōnis *f*, attainment

ădĕquĭto *v.i.* 1, to gallop up

ădhaerĕo, si, sum *v.i.* 2, to cling to

ădhaeresco, si, sum *v.i.* 3, to cling to

ădhĭbĕo *v.t.* 2, to apply, invite

ădhortātĭo, ōnis *f*, encouragement

ădhortor *v.t.* 1, *dep*, to encourage

ădhuc *adv*, still

adiăcĕo *v.i.* 2, to adjoin

adĭcĭo, iēci, iectum *v.t.* 3, to throw to, add to

ădĭgo, ēgi, actum *v.t.* 3, to drive to, compel

ădĭmo, ēmi, emptum *v.t.* 3, to take away

ădĭpiscor, eptus *v.t.* 3, *dep*, to obtain

ădĭtus, ūs *m*, approach

adiūdĭco *v.t.* 1, to assign

adiūmentum, i *n*, assistance

adiunctĭo, ōnis *f*, union

adiungo, xi, ctum *v.t.* 3, to join to

adiūro *v.t.* 1, to swear, confirm

adiūtor, ōris *m*, helper

adiŭvo, iūvi, iūtum *v.t.* 1, to precipitate

admētĭor, mensus *v.t.* 4, *dep*, to measure out

admĭnĭcŭlum, i *n*, prop

admĭnister, tri *m*, servant

admĭnistrātĭo, ōnis *f*, aid, management, arrangement

admĭnistro *v.t.* 1, to assist, manage

admīrābilis, e *adj*, *adv*, **ĭter**, wonderful

admīrātĭo, ōnis *f*, admiration

admīror *v.t.* 1, *dep*, to wonder at

admiscĕo, scŭi, xtum *v.t.* 2, to mix with

admissārĭus, ii *m*, stallion

admissĭo, ōnis *f*, reception

admissum, i *n*, fault

admitto, mīsi, ssum *v.t.* 3, to let in, let go, incur, commit

admixtĭo, ōnis *f*, mixture

admŏdum *adv*, up to the limit, very much, nearly

admŏnĕo *v.t.* 2, to remind

admŏnĭtĭo, ōnis *f*, warning

admŏnĭtus, ūs *m*, suggestion

admordĕo, di, sum *v.t.* 2, to bite at

admōtĭo, ōnis *f*, application

admŏvĕo, mōvi, mōtum *v.t.* 2, to conduct, assault

admurmūrātĭo, ōnis *f*, murmur

admurmŭro *v.i.* 1, to murmur at

adn- see ann...

ădŏlĕo, ŭi, ultum *v.i.* 3, to grow up

ădŏlescens, ntis *adj*, young

ădŏlescens, ntis *c*, young person

ădŏlescentĭa, ae *f*, youth

ădŏlescentŭlus, i *m*, very young man

ădŏlesco, ēvi, ultum *v.i.* 3, to grow up

ădŏpĕrĭo, ŭi, rtum *v.t.* 4, to cover up

ădoptātĭo, ōnis *f*, adoption

ădoptĭo, ōnis *f*, adoption

ădoptīvus, a, um *adj*, adoptive

ădopto *v.t.* 1, to choose, adopt

ădor, ŏris *n*, grain

ădōrātĭo, ōnis *f*, adoption

ădōrĕa, ae *f*, reward for bravery

ădŏrĭor, ortus *v.t.* 4, *dep*, to attack, undertake

ădorno *v.t.* 1, to equip, decorate

ădōro *v.t.* 1, to worship, entreat

adrādo, si, sum *v.t.* 3, to shave

adsum, esse, adfui *v.i*, *irreg*, to be near

ads... see ass...

ădūlātĭo, ōnis *f*, flattery

ădūlātor, ōris *m*, flatterer

ădūlor *v.t.* 1, *dep*, to flatter

ădulter, ĕri *m*, adulterer

ădultĕra, ae *f*, adulteress

ădultĕrātĭo, ōnis *f*, adulteration

ădultĕrīnus, a, um *adj*, false

ădultĕrĭum, ii *n*, adultery

ădultĕro *v.i.t.* 1, to commit adultery; to falsify, pollute

ădultus, a, um   *adj*, grown up
ădumbrātĭo, ōnis   *f*, sketch
ădumbro   *v.t.* 1, to sketch
ăduncus, a, um   *adj*, hooked
ădurgĕo   *v.t.* 2, to press
ădūro, ssi, stum   *v.t.* 3, to scorch
ădusque   *prep. with acc*, right up to
ădusta, ōrum   *n.pl*, burns
ădustus, a, um   *adj*, burnt
advĕho, xi, ctum   *v.t.* 3, to carry to
advĕna, ae   *c*, stranger
advĕnĭo, vēni, ventum   *v.t.* 4, to reach
advento   *v.t.* 1, to approach
adventus, ūs   *m*, arrival
adversārĭus, ii   *m*, opponent
adversārĭus, a, um   *adj*, opposite, opposing
adversor   *v.* 1, *dep, with dat*, to oppose
adversus, a, um   *adj*, opposite; (of winds) contrary
adversus   *prep. with acc*, opposite
adversum   *adv*, opposite
adverto, ti, sum   *v.t.* 3, to direct towards
advespĕrascit, avit   *v. impers*, evening approaches
advĭgĭlo   *v.i.* 1, to keep watch
advŏcātĭo, ōnis   *f*, summons, legal assistance
advŏcātus, i   *m*, legal adviser
advŏco   *v.t.* 1, to call, summon help
advŏlo   *v.i.* 1, to fly towards
advolvo, vi, ūtum   *v.t.* 3, to roll, grovel before
ădўtum, i   *n*, sanctuary
aedēs, is   *f*, temple; pl. house

aedĭcŭla, ae   *f*, shrine, niche
aedĭfĭcātor, ōris   *m*, builder
aedĭfĭcĭum, ii   *n*, building
aedĭfĭcātĭo, ōnis   *f*, constructing
aedĭfĭco   *v.t.* 1, to build
aedīlĭcĭus, a, um   *adj*, of an aedile
aedīlis, is   *m*, aedile – Roman magistrate
aedīlĭtas, ātis   *f*, aedileship
aedĭtŭus, i   *m*, verger
aeger, ra, rum   *adj*, ill, sad
aegis, ĭdis   *f*, shield
aegrē   *adv*, with difficulty, scarcely, amiss, with displeasure
aegresco   *v.i.* 3, to fall ill
aegrĭtūdo, ĭnis   *f*, illness, grief
aegrōtātĭo, ōnis   *f*, sickness
aegrōto   *v.i.* 1, to be ill
aegrōtus, a, um   *adj*, ill
aemŭlātĭo, ōnis   *f*, rivalry
aemŭlor   *v.t.* 1, *dep*, to rival, envy
aemŭlus, a, um   *adj*, rivalling
aēnĕus, a, um   *adj*, of bronze
aenigma, ătis   *n*, riddle
aequābĭlis, e   *adj, adv*, ĭter, similar, uniform
aequābĭlĭtas, ātis   *f*, equality
aequaevus, a, um   *adj*, of equal age
aequālis, e   *adj, adv*, ĭter, level, contemporary
aequālĭtas, ātis   *f*, uniformity
aequē   *adv*, equally, justly
aequĭlībrĭum, ii   *n*, horizontal position
aequĭnoctĭum, i   *n*, equinox
aequĭpăro   *v.i.t.* 1, to equal; compare
aequĭtas, ātis   *f*, equality, fariness, calmness

Insight

Latin has two words that are commonly translated by 'house': *domus* and *aedes*. The fourth declension noun *domus* means 'house' as well as 'home'; the third declension noun aedes means 'house' if used in its plural form, otherwise it is translated as 'temple'. The noun *casa* which means 'house/home' in Italian, Spanish, Portuguese and Catalan means 'cottage' in Latin.

aequo *v.i.t.* 1, to equalize; match, raze
aequor, ŏris *n*, even surface, sea
aequum, i *n*, plain, justice
aequus, a, um *adj*, flat, friendly, equal, reasonable

aether, ĕris *m*, upper air, heaven
aethĕrĭus, a, um *adj*, celestial
Aethĭops, ŏpis *m*, Aethiopian, negro
aethra, ae *f*, upper air
aevum, i *n*, lifetime, generation

Insight

aequus and *equus* are pronounced the same but they are two distinct words. *Aequus* means 'even', hence the English words 'equations', 'equal', 'equality' and so on. Equus means 'horse', hence 'equine', 'equestrian' etc.

āēr, ris *m*, air
aerārĭa, ae *f*, mine
aerārĭum, i *n*, treasury
aerārĭus, a, um *adj*, of bronze, of the treasury
aerātus, a, um *adj*, bronze covered
aerĕus, a, um *adj*, of bronze
aerĭpes, ĕdis *adj*, bronze-footed
āĕrĭus, a, um *adj*, lofty
aerūgo, ĭnis *f*, rust, envy
aerumna, ae *f*, suffering
aerumnōsus, a, um *adj*, wretched
aes, aeris *n*, copper, money
aescŭlētum, i *n*, oak-forest
aescŭlĕus, a, um *adj*, oaken
aescŭlus, i *f*, oak
aestas, ātis *f*, summer
aestĭfer, ĕra, ĕrum *adj*, hot, sultry
aestĭmābĭlis, e *adj*, valuable
aestĭmātĭo, ōnis *f*, valuation
aestĭmātor, ōris *m*, valuer
aestĭmo *v.t.* 1, to value, assess
aestīva, ōrum *n.pl*, summer camp
aestīvus, a, um *adj, adv*, ē, summer-like
aestŭārĭum, ii *n*, creek, air-hole
aestŭo *v.i.* 1, to seethe, glow
aestŭōsus, a, um *adj, adv*, ē, sweltering
aestus, ūs *m*, heat, tide, rage, excitement
aetas, ātis *f*, age, lifetime
aetātŭla, ae *f*, tender age
aeternĭtas, ātis *f*, eternity
aeternus, a, um *adj, adv*, um, everlasting

affābĭlis, e *adj, adv*, ĭter, courteous
affătim *adv*, enough
affātus *partic. from* **affor**
affectātĭo, ōnis *f*, pretension, whim
affectātus, a, um *adj* far-fetched
affectĭo, ōnis *f*, disposition, whim
affecto *v.t.* 1, to strive after
affectus, ūs *m*, mood, sympathy
affĕro, afferre, attŭli, allātum *v.t, irreg*, to bring to, announce, help, produce, confer
affĭcĭo, affēci, ctum *v.t.* 3, to influence, seize
affigo, xi, xum *v.t.* 3, to fasten to
affingo, nxi, ictum *v.t.* 3, to add to, fabricate
affinis, e *adj*, neighbouring, related
affinĭtas, ātis *f*, kinship
affirmātē *adv*, explicitly
affirmātĭo, ōnis *f*, assertion
affirmo *v.t.* 1, to assert
affixus, a, um *adj*, fastened to
afflātus, ūs *m*, breath, blast
afflicto *v.t.* 1, to trouble, shatter
afflictus, a, um *adj*, damaged, prostrate
afflīgo, xi, ctum *v.t.* 3, to dash to the ground, damage
afflo *v.t.* 1, to breathe on, inspire
afflŭens, ntis *adj, adv*, nter, rich in
afflŭo, xi, xum *v.i.* 3, to flow towards, flock in
affor *v.t.* 1, to speak to, accost
affulgĕo, ulsi *v.i.* 2, to shine on

affundo, ūdi, ūsum *v.t.* 3, to pour on, in
Āfrĭcus (ventus) S.W. wind
āfui see **absum**
ăgāso, ōnis *m*, groom
ăgĕ! come on!
ăgellus, i *m*, small field
ăgens, ntis *adj*, powerful
ăger, gri *m*, field, territory
agger, ĕris *m*, mound, rampart
aggĕro, ssi stum *v.t.* 3, to convey
aggĕro *v.t.* 1, to heap up
agglŏmĕro *v.t.* 1, to add to
aggrăvo *v.t.* 1, to make heavier or worse
aggrĕdior, grĕssus *v.t.* 3, *dep*, to approach, attack, undertake
aggrĕgo *v.t.* 1, to adhere, join
aggressus see **aggrĕdior**
ăgĭlis, e *adj, adv, ĭter*, active
ăgĭlĭtas, ātis *f*, activity
ăgĭtātĭo, ōnis *f*, quick movement, contemplation
ăgĭtātor, ŏris *m*, charioteer
ăgĭtātus, a, um *adj*, driven, dogged
ăgĭto *v.t.* 1, to drive, shake, swing, torment, mock, consider
agmen, ĭnis *n*, marching column
agna, ae *f*, ewe lamb
agnātus, a, um *adj*, related (male line)
agnĭtĭo, ōnis *f*, recognition
agnōmen, ĭnis *n*, surname, additional name
agnosco, nŏvi, ĭtum *v.t.* 3, to recognize, acknowledge
agnus, i *m*, lamb
ăgo, ēgi, actum *v.t.* 3, to drive, steal, bring, do, negotiate, pass (time), act, lead (life)
ăgrārĭus, a, um *adj*, agrarian
ăgrārĭi, ōrum *m.pl*, land reformers
ăgrestis is *m*, peasant
ăgrestis, e *adj*, rural, coarse
agrĭcŏla, ae *m*, farmer, countryman
agrĭcultūra, ae *f*, agriculture
āio *v, defect*, to assert
āla, ae *f*, wing, armpit, porch
ălăcer, cris, e *adj, adv, ĭter*, brisk, vigorous

ălăcrĭtas, ātis *f*, briskness
ălāpa, ae *f*, slap
ălauda, ae *f*, lark
albārĭum, ii *n*, whitewash
albātus, a, um *adj*, clothed in white
albĕo *v.i.* 2, to be white
albesco *v.i.* 3, to become white
album, i *n*, whiteness, register
albus, a, um *adj*, white
alces, is *f*, elk
alcēdo, ĭnis *f*, kingfisher
alcўon, ŏnis *f*, kingfisher
alcўōnēus, a, um *adj*, halcyon
ālĕa, ae *f*, gambling, a game with dice, chance, hazard
ālĕātor, ōris *m*, gambler
ālĕs, ĭtis *adj*, winged
ālĕs, ĭtis *c*, bird
alga, ae *f*, seaweed
algĕo, si *v.i.* 2, to feel cold
algĭdus, a, um *adj*, cold
algor, ōris *m*, coldness
ălĭā *adv*, in a different way
ălĭās ... ălĭās *adv*, at one time ... at another time, otherwise
ălĭbi *adv*, elsewhere
ălĭcŭbi *adv*, somewhere
ălĭcunde *adv*, from somewhere
ălĭēnātĭo, ōnis *f*, transfer, aversion, delirium
ălĭēnātus, a, um *adj*, alienated
ălĭēnĭgĕna, ae *m*, foreigner
ălĭēno *v.t.* 1, to transfer, estrange
ălĭēnus, a, um *adj*, someone else's, strange, hostile, unsuitable
ălĭēnus, i *m*, stranger
ălĭēnum, i *n*, stranger's property
ālĭger, ĕra, ĕrum *adj*, winged
ălĭi see **ălĭus**
ălĭmentum, i *n*, nourishment
ălĭmōnĭum, ii *n*, nourishment
ălĭō *adv*, to another place
ălĭōqui(n) *adv*, in other respects
ālĭpēs, ĕdis *adj*, wing-footed
ălĭquā *adv*, somehow
ălĭquamdĭu *adv*, for some time
ălĭquando *adv*, at some time
ălĭquantus, a, um *adj, adv, ō, um*, somewhat, some
ălĭqui, qua, quod *pron, adj*, some, any
ălĭquis, quid *pron*, someone, something

ălĭquō   adv, to some place
ălĭquot   adj, several
ălĭquŏtĭes   adv, at different times
ălĭter   adv, otherwise
ălĭunde   adv, from elsewhere
ălĭus, a, ud   pron, adj, other, different
allābor, psus   v. 3, dep, to glide, flow towards
allapsus, ūs   m, stealthy approach
allātro   v.t. 1, to bark at
allecto   v.t. 1, to entice
allēgo   v.t. 1, to commission
allēgo, ēgi, ectum   v.t. 3, to elect
allēgŏrĭa, ae   f, allegory
allĕvātĭo, ōnis   f, raising up
allĕvo   v.t. 1, to lift up, relieve
allĭcĭo, exi, ectum   v.t. 3, to attract
allīdo, si, sum   v.t. 3, to strike
allĭgo   v.t. 1, to bind, fasten
allĭno, ēvi, ĭtum   v.t. 3, to bedaub
allĭum, i   n, garlic
allŏcūtĭo, ōnis   f, speech, address
allŏquĭum, ii   n, exhortation
allŏquor, lŏcūtus   v.t. 3, dep, to speak to, exhort, console
allūdo, si, sum   v.i.t. 3, to play, joke; sport with
allŭo, ŭi   v.t. 3, to wash against, bathe
allŭvĭes, ēi   f, pool
allŭvĭo, ōnis   f, inundation
almus, a, um   adj, nourishing, kind
alnus, i   f, alder
ălo, ŭi, altum   v.t. 3, to nourish, cherish, encourage
alŏē, ēs   f, aloe
alpīnus, a, um   adj, Alpine
alsĭus, a, um   adj, cold, chilly
alsus, a, um   adj, cold, chilly
altāre, altāris   n, high altar
altārĭa, ĭum   n.pl, high altar
alter, ĕra, ĕrum   adj, one or the other of two, second
altercātĭo, ōnis   f, dispute
altercor   v.i. 1, dep, to quarrel
alterno   v.i.t. 1, to hesitate; alternate
alternus, a, um   adj, alternate
altĕrŭter, ra, rum   adj, one or the other, either
altĭlis, e   adj, fattened, rich

altĭsŏnus, a, um   adj, high sounding
altĭtūdo, ĭnis   f, height, depth
altor, ōris   m, foster-father
altrix, īcis   f, foster-mother
altum, i   n, the deep (sea)
altus, a, um   adj, high, deep, great
ălūcĭnor   v.i. 1, dep, to wander in the mind
ălumna, ae   f, foster-child
ălumnus, i   m, foster-child
ălūta, ae   f, soft leather
alvĕārĭum, ii   n, beehive
alvĕus, i   m, salver, channel, canoe
alvus, i   f, belly, stomach
ămābĭlis, e   adj, adv, ĭter, lovable, amiable
āmando   v.t. 1, to remove
ămans, ntis   adj, fond
ămans, ntis   m, lover
ămārĭtĭes, ēi   f, bitterness
ămārus, a, um   adj, bitter
ămātor, ōris   m, lover
ămātōrĭum, ii   n, love-philtre
ămātōrĭus, a, um   adj, amatory
ambactus, i   m, vassal
ambāges, is   f, roundabout way
ambĭgo   v.i. 3, to waver, go about
ambĭgŭĭtas, ātis   f, double sense
ambĭgŭum, i   n, uncertainty
ambĭgŭus, a, um   adj, adv, ē, doubtful, changeable
ambĭo   v.i.t. 4, to go round; solicit
ambĭtĭo, ōnis   f, canvassing
ambĭtĭōsus, a, um   adj, adv, ē, embracing, fawning
ambĭtus, ūs   m, going round, circuit, bribery
ambō, ae, ō   adj, both
ambrŏsĭa, ae   f, food of the gods
ambrŏsĭus, a, um   adj, immortal
ambŭlātĭo, ōnis   f, walk
ambŭlātor, ōris   m, walker
ambŭlo   v.i. 1, to walk, lounge
ambūro, ssi, stum   v.t. 3, to singe
ambustum, i   n, burn
amellus, i   m, star-wort
āmens, ntis   adj, out of one's mind
āmentĭa, ae   f, madness
āmentum, i   n, strap
ămĕs, ĭtis   f, pole, shaft
ămĕthystus, i   f, amethyst
ămīca, ae   f, friend, mistress

ămĭcĭo, ŭi, ctum *v.t.* 4, to wrap
ămīcĭtĭa, ae *f*, friendship
ămictus, ūs *m*, cloak
ămĭcŭlum, i *n*, cloak
ămīcus, i *m*, friend
ămīcus, a, um *adj, adv*, ē, friendly
āmissĭo, ōnis *f*, loss
ămĭta, ae *f*, paternal aunt
āmitto, misi, missum *v.t.* 3, to let go, dismiss, lose
amnis, is *m*, river
ămo *v.t.* 1, to love, like

anceps, cĭpĭtĭs *adj*, two-headed, doubtful
ancĭle, is *n*, oval shield
ancilla, ae *f*, maidservant
ancŏrāle, is *n*, cable
ānellus, i *m*, small ring
anfractus, ūs *m*, circuitous route, digression
angĭna, ae *f*, quinsy
angĭportus, ūs *m*, alley
ango, xi, ctum *v.t.* 3, to strangle, torment

Insight

The perfect tense (e.g. *amavi*) has three basic meanings: a) a completed action in past time; b) an action in the past seen from the point of view of the present; c) a present state arising from past action.

ămoenĭtas, ātis *f*, pleasantness
ămoenus, a, um *adj, adv*, ē, charming
āmōlĭor *v.t.* 4, *dep*, to remove, refute
ămor, ōris *m*, love, desire
āmŏvĕo, mōvi, tum *v.t.* 2, to remove
amphĭthĕātrum, i *n*, amphitheatre
amphŏra, ae *f*, two-handled jar
amplector, xus *v.t.* 3, *dep*, to embrace
amplexus, ūs *m*, embrace
amplĭficātĭo, ōnis *f*, enlargement
amplĭfico *v.t.* 1, to enlarge
amplĭo *v.t.* 1, to enlarge
amplĭtūdo, ĭnis *f*, width, size
amplĭus *comp. adv*, more
amplus, a, um *adj, adv*, ē, ĭter, spacious, great, glorious
ampulla, ae *f*, bottle
ampŭtātĭo, ōnis *f*, pruning
ampŭto *v.t.* 1, to cut away
ămurca, ae *f*, dregs of oil
ămўlum, i *n*, starch
ăn *conj*, or: also used to introduce a question
ănăphŏră, ae *f*, recurrence
ănăs, ătis *f*, duck
ănătĭcŭla, ăe *f*, duckling

angor, ōris *m*, strangling, distress
anguilla, ae *f*, eel
anguĭnĕus, a, um *adj*, snaky
anguĭpēs, ĕdis *adj*, snake-footed
anguis, is *c*, snake
angŭlātus, a, um *adj*, angular
angŭlāris, e *adj*, angular
angŭlus, i *m*, corner
angustĭae, ārum *f.pl.*, defile, straits, difficulties
angustus, a, um *adj, adv*, ē, narrow, difficult
ănhēlĭtus, ūs *m*, panting, vapour
ănhēlo *v.i.t.* 1, to pant; exhale
ănhēlus, a, um *adj*, panting
ănĭcŭla, ae *f*, little old woman
ănīlis, e *adj, adv*, ĭter, old womanish
ănĭma, ae *f*, breeze, breath, life, soul
ănĭmadversĭo, ōnis *f*, attention, reproof
ănĭmadverto, ti, sum *v.t.* 3, to pay attention to, notice, punish
ănĭmăl, ālis *n*, animal
ănĭmālis, e *adj, adv*, ĭter, of air, living
ănĭmans, ntis *adj*, living
ănĭmātus, a, um *adj*, disposed, courageous
ănĭmo *v.i.t.* 1, to have life; revive, give life to

ănĭmōsus, a, um *adj, adv,* ē, bold
ănĭmōsus, a, um *adj,* gusty, living, spirited
ănĭmus, i *m,* soul, mind, memory, opinion, anger, purpose, courage, attitude
annāles, ĭum *m.pl,* chronicles
annālis, e *adj,* annual
annĕ introduces a question
annecto, xŭi, xum *v.t.* 3, to fasten to, add
annītor, nīsus nixus *v.i.* 3, *dep,* to lean against, exert oneself
ănnivversārĭus, a, um *adj,* anniversary
anno *v.i.* 1, to swim to
annon *conj,* or not
annōna, ae *f,* annual produce, grain price
annōsus, a, um *adj,* old
annŏtātĭo, ōnis *f,* annotation, note
annŏto *v.t.* 1, to note down
annŭa, ōrum *n.pl,* annuity
annŭmĕro *v.t.* 1, to pay, include
annŭo, ŭi, ŭtum *v.i.* 3, to nod, assent
annus, i *m,* year
annŭus, a, um *adj,* annual, yearly
ănōmălĭa, ae *f,* anomaly
anquīro, sīvi, sītum *v.t.* 3, to search for
ansa, ae *f,* handle, opportunity
anser, ĕris *m,* goose
antĕ *prep. with acc,* before, in front of
antĕ (antĕā) *adv,* before
antĕcēdo, ssi, ssum *v.i.t.* 3, to distinguish oneself; precede
antĕcello *v.i.t.* 3, to be outstanding; surpass
antĕcessĭo, ōnis *f,* antecedent
antĕcursor, ōris *m,* advanced guard
antĕ-ĕo *v.i.* 4, to go before, excel
antĕfĕro, ferre, tŭli, lātum *v.t, irreg,* to carry in front, prefer
antĕgrĕdĭor, gressus *v.t.* 3, *dep,* to go in front
antĕhāc *adv,* previously
antĕlūcānus, a, um *adj,* before day-break
antĕmĕrīdĭānus, a, um *adj,* before midday

antĕmitto, mīsi, missum *v.t.* 3, to send on
antenna, ae *f,* sail-yard
antĕpōno, pŏsŭi, ĭtum *v.t.* 3, to place in front
antĕquam *conj,* before
antēris, ĭdis *f,* buttress (pl.)
antes, ĭum *m.pl.* ranks
antĕsignānus, i *m,* in front of the standard, selected soldier
antesto, ĕti *v.i.* 1, to stand before, excel
antestor *v.* 1, *dep,* to call a witness
antĕverto, ti, sum *v.t.* 3, to precede, anticipate
anthrōpŏphăgus, i *m,* cannibal
antīcus, a, um *adj,* foremost
antīcĭpo *v.t.* 1, to anticipate
antīdŏtum, i *n,* remedy
antīpŏdes, um *m.pl,* antipodes
antīquĭtas, ātis *f,* age, olden times
antīqui, ōrum *m.pl,* old writers
antīquus, a, um *adj, adv,* ē, old
antistĕs, ĭtis *m,* *f,* high priest
antistīta, ae *f,* high priestess
antlīa, ae *f,* pump
antrum, i *n,* cave
ānŭlus, i *m,* ring
ănus, ūs *f,* old woman
anxĭĕtas, ātis *f,* anxiety
anxĭus, a, um *adj, adv,* ē, troubled
ăpăgĕ! *interj,* begone
ăper, pri *m,* wild boar
ăpĕrĭo, rŭi, rtum *v.t.* 4, to open, explain
ăpertus, a, um *adj, adv,* ē, open, frank
ăpex, ĭcis *m,* summit, crown
ăpis, is *f,* bee
ăpiscor, aptus *v.t.* 3, *dep,* to reach for, acquire
ăpĭum, ii *n,* parsley
ăplustre, is *n,* stern
ăpo, (*no perf.*) aptum *v.t.* 3, to fasten
ăpŏcha, ae *f,* receipt
ăpŏthēca, ae *f,* store-place
appărātĭo, ōnis *f,* preparation
appărātus, a, um *adj, adv,* ē, ready, elaborate
appărātus, ūs *m,* preparation, apparatus, pomp

appārĕo *v.i.* 2, to appear
appărĭtĭo, ōnis *f,* service
appārĭtor, ōris *m,* public servant
appăro *v.t.* 1, to prepare
appellātĭo, ōnis *f,* calling appeal, title
appellātor, ōris *m,* appellant
appellātus, a, um *adj,* called
appello, ŭli, ulsum *v.t.* 3, to drive towards, land
appello *v.t.*1, to speak to, appeal to, name
appendix, ĭcis *f,* supplement
appendo, ndi, nsum *v.t.* 3, to weigh
appĕtens, ntis *adj, adv,* nter, eager for
appĕtentĭa, ae *f,* desire
appĕtītĭo, ōnis *f,* desire
appĕtītus, ūs *m,* attack, passion
appĕto, ii, ītum *v.i.t.* 3, to approach; strive after
applĭcātĭo, ōnis *f,* inclination
applĭco *v.t.* 1, to affix, attach, steer
appōno, pŏsŭi, sĭtum *v.t.* 3, to put near, apply, add

àprīcor *v.i.* 1, *dep,* to sun oneself
àprīcus, a, um *adj,* sunny
Ȳprīlis (mensis) April
aptātus, a, um *adj,* suitable
apto *v.t.* 1, to adjust
aptus, a, um *adj, adv,* ē, suitable
ăpŭd *with acc,* at the house of, in the works of, amongst, near
ăqua, ae *f,* water, rain; *pl,* spa
ăquaeductus, ūs *m,* aqueduct
ăquālis, is *c,* wash-basin
ăquārĭus, ii *m,* water-bearer, a sign of the zodiac
ăquātĭcus, a, um *adj,* watery
ăquātĭlis, e *adj,* aquatic
ăquātĭo, ōnis *f,* water-fetching
ăquātor, ōris *m,* water-carrier
ăquĭla, ae *f,* eagle, standard
ăquĭlĭfer, ĕri *m,* standard-bearer
ăquĭlīnus, a, um *adj,* aquiline
ăquĭlo, ōnis *m,* north wind, north
ăquĭlōnāris, e *adj,* northern
ăquor *v.i.* 1, *dep,* to fetch water
ăquōsus, a, um *adj,* moist, rainy
āra, ae *f,* altar
ărānĕa, ae *f,* spider, web
ărānĕus i *m,* spider, web

Insight

Appositions are nouns or nouns-plus-adjectives phrases that add further information about a noun already mentioned in the sentence (e.g. a 'red-brick building' house). Nouns are said to be 'in apposition' to another noun.

apporto *v.t.* 1, to conduct
appŏsĭtus *adj, adv,* ē, bordering, suitable
apprĕhendo, di, sum *v.t.*3, to seize, understand
apprīmus, a, um *adj, adv,* ē, very first
apprŏbātĭo, ōnis *f,* sanction
apprŏbo *v.t.* 1, to approve, make satisfactory
apprŏpĕro *v.i.t.* 1, to hurry; speed up
apprŏpinquātĭo, ōnis *f,* approach
apprŏpinquo *v.i.* 1, to approach
appulsus, ūs *m,* landing, approach
àprīcātĭo, ōnis *f,* sunning

ărātĭo, ōnis *f,* cultivation
ărātor, ōris *m,* ploughman
ărātrum, i *n,* plough
arbĭter, tri *m,* witness, umpire
arbĭtrātus, ūs *m,* free-will
arbĭtrĭum, ii *n,* verdict, power, inclination
arbĭtror *v.i.* 1, *dep,* to think, decide
arbor, ŏris *f,* tree
arbŏrĕus, a, um *adj,* tree-like
arbustum, i *n,* plantation
arbūtum, i *n,* wild strawberry
arbūtus, i *f,* wild strawberry tree
arca, ae *f,* box, dungeon
arcānus, a, um *adj, adv,* ō, secret
arcĕo *v.t.* 2, to confine, keep off

arcessītus, a, um *adj*, sent for, far-fetched

arcesso, sīvi, sītum *v.t.* 3, to send for

archītector *v.t.* 1, *dep*, to design

archītectūra, ae *f*, architecture

archītectus, i *m*, architect

arcītěnens, ntis *adj*, armed with bow

arctŏs, i *f*, Bear, North Pole

arctūrus, i *m*, chief star in constellation Boötes

arcŭla, ae *f*, small box

arcŭo *v.t.* 1, to bend

arcus, ūs *m*, rainbow, arch

arděa, ae *f*, heron

ardens, ntis *adj, adv*, **nter**, burning, eager

arděo, arsi, sum *v.i.* 2, to burn, be eager

ardesco, arsi *v.i* 3, to catch fire

ardor, ōris *m*, blaze, desire

ardŭus, a, um *adj*, high, difficult

ārěa, ae *f*, open space, threshing-floor

ărēna, ae *f*, sand, arena

ărēnātum, i *n*, mortar, plaster

ărēnōsus, a, um *adj*, sandy

ārens, ntis *adj*, parched

ārěo *v.i.* 2, to be dry

āresco, ŭi *v.i.* 3, to dry up

argentārĭa, ae *f*, bank, silver-mine

argentārĭus, ii *m*, banker, broker

argentātus, a, um *adj*, silver-plated

argentěus, a, um *adj*, silver

argentum, i *n*, silver, money

argilla, ae *f*, white clay

argūmentātĭo, ōnis *f*, proof

argūmentor *v.i.* 1, *dep*, to prove

argūmentum, i *n*, proof, content, artistic aim

argŭo, ŭi, ūtum *v.t.* 3, to prove, accuse, convict

argūtĭae, ārum *f.pl*, liveliness

argūtus, a, um *adj, adv*, **ē**, clear, witty, rattling

ārĭdĭtas, ātis *f*, dryness

ārĭdum, i *n*, dry land

ārĭdus, a, um *adj*, dry

ărĭēs, tis *m*, ram, battering-ram

ărista, ae *f*, ear of corn

ărĭthmētĭca, ōrum *n.pl*, arithmetic

arma, ōrum *n.pl*, armour, shield, weapons, army, equipment

armāmenta, ōrum *n.pl*, gear, tackle

armāmentārĭum, ii *n*, arsenal

armāmentum, i *n*, ship's tackle

armārĭum ii *n*, cupboard

armātura, ae *f*, equipment, (light-) armed troops

armātus, a, um *adj*, equipped

armentārĭus, ii *m*, herdsman

armentum, i *n*, plough-animal, herd

armĭfer, ěra, ěrum *adj*, warlike, armoured

armĭger, ěra, ěrum *adj*, warlike, armoured

armilla, ae *f*, bracelet

armĭpŏtens, ntis *adj*, valiant

armĭsŏnus, a, um *adj*, with clashing armour

armo *v.t.* 1, to arm, equip

armus, i *m*, shoulder, side

**ăro, ** *v.t.* 1, to plough

arquātus, a, um *adj*, bent

arrectus, a, um *adj*, steep

arrēpo, psi, ptum *v.i.* 3, to creep towards

arrha, ae *f*, money given as a pledge

arrīdĕo, si, sum *v.i.* 2, to laugh at, favour

arrĭgo, rexi, rectum *v.t.*3, to erect, excite

arrĭpĭo, ŭi, reptum *v.t.* 3, to seize, indict

arrŏgans, ntis *pres. partic, adj, adv*, **nter**, haughty

arrŏgantĭa, ae *f*, haughtiness

**arrŏgo, ** *v.t.* 1, to claim, confer

ars, tis *f*, art, skill, theory, habit, stratagem

artē *adv*, closely

arthrītĭcus, a, um *adj*, arthritic

artĭcŭlātim *adv*, piece by piece

**artĭcŭlo, ** *v.t.* 1, to articulate

artĭcŭlus, i *m*, joint, movement

artĭfex, fĭcis *m*, artist, author

artĭfĭcĭōsus, a, um *adj, adv*, **ē**, skilful

artĭfĭcĭum, ii *n*, trade, skill; *pl*, intrigue

arto *v.t.* 1, to compress

artus, ūs *m*, limb

artus, a, um *adj, adv,* **ē,** confined

ărun, ărus... see **hărun, hărus...**

arvīna, ae *f,* grease

arvum, i *n,* cultivated land

arvus, a, um *adj,* ploughed

arx, cis *f,* citadel

as, assis *m,* pound weight, coin

ascendo, ndi, nsum *v.i.t.* 3, to climb

ascensus, ūs *m,* ascent

ascĭa, ae *f,* adze

ascĭo *v.t.* 4, to receive

ascisco, īvi, ītum *v.t.* 3, to admit

ascītus, ūs *m,* reception

ascrībo, psi, ptum *v.t.* 3, to insert, enrol, attribute

ascriptīvus, a, um *adj,* supernumerary

ascriptus, a, um *adj,* appointed

ăsella, ae *f,* small ass

ăsellus, i *m,* small ass

ăsĭnus, i *m,* ass, simpleton

aspectābĭlis, e *adj,* visible

aspecto *v.t.* 1, to look at eagerly

aspectus, ūs *m,* look, sight

asper, ĕra, ĕrum *adj, adv,* **ē,** rough, bitter, austere, adverse

aspĕrītas, ātis *f,* roughness

aspĕrum, i *n,* rough ground

aspergo, si, sum *v.t.* 3, to scatter, sprinkle, defile

aspergo, ĭnis *f,* sprinkling, spray

aspĕrītas, ātis *f,* roughness

aspernātĭo, ōnis *f,* disdain

aspernor *v.t.* 1, *dep,* to despise

aspĕro *v.t.* 1, to roughen, rouse

aspersĭo, ōnis *f,* sprinkling

aspĭcĭo, exi, ectum *v.t.* 3, to look at

aspīrātĭo, ōnis *f,* exhalation

aspīro *v.i.t.* 1, to aspire to; breathe on

aspis, ĭdis *f,* adder

asporto, *v.t.* 1, to carry away

assēcla, ae *c,* attendant

assectātĭo, ōnis *f,* attendance

assectātor ōris *m,* follower

assector *v.t.* 1, *dep,* to wait upon

assensĭo, ōnis *f,* approval

assensus, ūs *m,* approval

assentātĭo, ōnis *f,* flattery

assentātor, ōris *m,* flatterer

assentĭor, sus *v.* 4, *dep, with dat,* to agree with

assentor *v.* 1, *dep, with dat,* to flatter

assĕquor, sĕcūtus *v.t.* 3, *dep,* to pursue, overtake, comprehend

asser, ĕris *m,* stake

assĕro, rŭi, sertum *v.t.* 3, to claim, set free

assertor, ōris *m,* protector

asservo *v.t.* 1, to keep, guard

assessor, ōris *m,* assessor

assĕvērātĭo, ōnis *f,* assertion

assĕvēro *v.t.* 1, to assert

assĭdĕo, sēdi, sessum *v.i.* 2, to sit by, wait upon, blockade, resemble

assĭdūĭtas, ātis *f,* constant presence

assĭdŭus, a, um *adj, adv,* **ē,** constantly present

assignātĭo, ōnis *f,* allotment

assigno *v.t.* 1, to distribute

assĭlĭo, ŭi, sultum *v.i.* 4, to spring upon

assĭmĭlis, e *adj, adv,* **īter,** like

assĭmŭlo *v.i.t.* 1, to resemble, imitate

assĭmŭlātus, a, um *adj,* similar

assisto, astĭti *v.i.* 3, to stand near, aid

assŏlĕo *v.i.* 2, to be in the habit of doing

assŭefăcĭo, fēci, factum *v.t.* 3, to make someone used to

assŭesco, ēvi, ētum *v.i.t.* 3, to become used to; familiarize

assŭētūdo, ĭnis *f,* habit

assŭētus, a, um *adj,* customary

assulto *v.t.* 1, to jump on, attack

assultus, ūs *m,* attack

assūmo, mpse, mptum *v.t.* 3, to take up, adopt

assŭo *v.t.* 3, to sew on

assurgo, surrexi, rectum *v.i.* 3, to rise, stand up

assŭla, ae *f,* splinter, chip

assus, a, um *adj,* roasted; **assa, ōrum,** *n.pl,* turkish bath

ast see **at**

astĭpŭlātor, ōris *m,* assistant

astĭpŭlor *v.* 1, *dep, with dat,* to bargain with

asto, stĭti *v.i.* 1, to stand near

astrĕpo *v.i.t.* 3, to make a noise; applaud

astringo, nxi, ctum *v.t.* 3, to bind, fasten, cool, limit
astrictus, a, um *adj, adv,* **ē,** tight, concise
astrŏlŏgĭa, ae *f,* astronomy
astrŏlŏgus, i *m,* astronomer
astrum, i *n,* star, constellation
astrŭo, xi, ctum *v.t.* 3, to build near, add
astŭpĕo *v.i.* 2, to be astonished
astus, ūs *m,* dexterity, craft
astūtĭa, ae *f,* dexterity, slyness
astūtus, a, um *adj, adv,* **ē,** shrewd, sly
ăsӯlum, i *n,* place of refuge
at *conj,* but, on the other hand
ătăvĭa, ae *f,* ancestor
ătăvus, i *m,* ancestor
āter, tra, trum *adj,* black, deadly
ăthĕŏs, i *m,* atheist
athlēta, ae *c,* wrestler, athlete
ătŏmus, i *f,* atom
atque *conj,* and, and also
atqui *conj,* but, nevertheless
ātrāmentum, i *n,* ink, varnish
ātrātus, a, um *adj,* in mourning
ātrĭensis, is *m,* house-steward
ātrĭŏlum, i *n,* ante-room
ātrĭum, ii *n,* hall, forecourt
ătrōcĭtas, ātis *f,* harshness, cruelty
ătrox, ōcis *adj, adv,* **ĭter,** horrible, fierce, stern
attactus, ūs *m,* touch
attămen *adv,* but nevertheless
attendo, di, tum *v.t.* 3, to stretch out, give attention to
attentĭo, ōnis *f,* attention
attento *v.t.* 1, to try, attack
attentus, a, um *adj, adv,* **ē,** engrossed, frugal
attĕnŭo *v.t.* 1, to impair, reduce
attĕro, trīvi, trītum *v.t.* 3, to rub away, exhaust

attĭnĕo, ŭi, tentum *v.i.t.* 2, to strech, concern; retain
attingo, tĭgi, tactum *v.t.* 3, to touch, reach, attack
attollo *v.t.* 3, to raise
attondĕo, di, sum *v.t.* 2, to shear
attŏnĭtus, a, um *adj, adv,* **ē,** astonished
attŏno, ŭi, ĭtum *v.t.* 1, to stun
attorquĕo *v.t.* 2, to hurl
attrăho, xi, ctum *v.t.* 3, to drag towards, attract
attrecto *v.t.* 1, to handle
attrĭbŭo, ŭi, ŭtum *v.t.* 3, to assign
attrĭbūtum, i *n,* predicate
attrītus, ūs *m,* rubbing against
auceps, ŭpis *c,* bird-catcher, eavesdropper
auctĭo, ōnis *f,* auction, increase
auctĭōnor *v.i.* 1, *dep,* to hold an auction
auctor, ōris *c,* creator, master, witness, supporter, author
auctōrĭtas, ātis *f,* influence, power
auctumnālis, e *adj,* autumnal
auctumnus, a, um *adj,* autumnal
auctumnus, i *m,* autumn
auctus, a, um *adj,* enlarged
auctus, ūs *m,* increase
aucŭpĭum, i *n,* bird-catching
aucŭpor, *v.i.t.* 1, *dep,* to go bird-catching; pursue, watch for
audācĭa, ae *f,* boldness, insolence
audax, ācis *adj, adv,* **cter,** bold, rash
audens, ntis *adj, adv,* **nter,** bold
audentĭa, ae *f,* boldness
audĕo, ausus *v.i.t.* 2 *semi-dep,* to dare
audĭentĭa, ae *f,* hearing, audience
audĭo, *v.t.* 4, to hear, understand, obey

Insight

There is no way of distinguishing between the first person singular, future tense, indicative of third and fourth conjugation verbs and the first person singular, present tense, subjunctive (e.g. *dicam, audiam*) except by context.

audītĭo

audītĭo, ōnis *f*, a hearing, report
audītor, ōris *m*, hearer, pupil
audītus, ūs *m*, sense of hearing
aufĕro, ferre, abstŭli, ablātum *v.t,*
  irreg, to take away, rob, obtain
aufŭgĭo, fūgi, ĭtum *v.i.* 3, to run
  away
augĕo, xi, ctum *v.i.t.* 2, to grow;
  enlarge
augesco *v.i.* 3, to grow
augur, ŭris *c*, diviner, prophet
augŭrālis, e *adj*, prophetic
augŭrātus, ūs *m*, office of augur
augŭrĭum, ii *n*, omen, augury
augŭrĭus, a, um *adj*, augural
augŭror *v.t.* 1, *dep*, to prophesy,
  suppose
augustus, a, um *adj, adv,* ē,
  venerable
aula, ae *f*, palace, court
aulaeum, i *n*, curtain
aulicus, i *m*, courtier

auspĭcātō *adv*, after taking the
  auspices
auspĭcĭum, ii *n*, divination
auspĭcor *v.i.t.* 1, *dep*, to take the
  auspices, begin
auster, tri *m*, south wind
austērus, a, um *adj, adv,* ē, harsh,
  severe
austrālis, e *adj*, southern
austrīnus, a, um *adj*, southern
ausum, i *n*, bold attempt
aut *conj*, or, **aut ... aut,** either ...
  or
autem *conj*, but
autumnālis *adj*, autumnal
autŭmo *v.i.* 1, to assert
auxĭlĭa, ōrum *n.pl*, auxiliary troops
auxĭlĭāris, e *adj*, helping
auxĭlĭāres, ĭum *m.pl*, auxiliary
  troops
auxĭlĭor *v.* 1, *dep, with dat.* to help
auxĭlĭum ii *n*, help

Insight

Auxiliary verbs, such as 'will', 'do', 'have', are used to help the main verb, defining its mood, tense and aspect. The word 'auxiliary' comes from the Latin *auxilium* (= help). Latin only uses auxiliary verbs in the perfect, pluperfect and future perfect deponent and passive.

aura, ae *f*, air, soft breeze, sky,
  publicity, gleam
aurārĭa, ae *f*, gold mine
aurātus, a, um *adj*, gilded
aurĕus, i *m*, gold piece
aurĭcŏmus, a, um *adj*, golden-
  haired
aurĭcŭla, ae *f*, ear
aurĭfer, ĕra, ĕrum *adj*, gold-
  producing
aurĭfex, fĭcis *m*, goldsmith
aurīga, ae *c*, charioteer
aurĭger, ĕra, ĕrum *adj*, bearing
  gold
auris, is *f*, ear
aurītus, a, um *adj*, long-eared
aurōra, ae *f*, dawn
aurum, i *n*, gold
ausculto *v.i.t.* 1, to listen
auspex, ĭcis *c*, diviner

ăvārĭtĭa, ae *f*, greediness
ăvārus, a, um *adj, adv,* ē, greedy
ăve! (*pl,* **ăvete**) hail! farewell!
āvĕho, vexi, ctum *v.t.* 3, to carry
  away
āvello, velli, vulsum *v.t.* 3, to tear
  away
ăvēna, ae *f*, oats, shepherd's pipe
ăvĕnācĕus, a, um *adj*, oaten
ăvĕo *v.t.* 2, to long for
ăvĕo *v.i.* 2, to be well
āversor *v.t.* 1, *dep*, to turn away
  from, avoid
āversor, ōris *m*, embezzler
āversus, a, um *adj*, backwards,
  hostile
āverto, ti, sum *v.t.* 3, to push
  aside, steal, estrange
ăvĭa, ae *f*, grandmother
ăvĭārĭum, ii *n*, bird-haunts

ăvĭdĭtas, ātis *f*, eagerness, desire
ăvĭdus, a, um *adj*, *adv*, ē, greedy
ăvis, is *f*, bird
ăvītus, a, um *adj*, ancestral
āvĭum, ii *n*, pathless place
āvĭus, a, um *adj*, pathless
āvŏcātĭo, ōnis *f*, calling away, distraction
āvŏco *v.t.* 1, to call away
āvŏlo *v.i.* 1, to fly away
ăvuncŭlus, i *m*, uncle
ăvus, i *m*, grandfather
axis, is *m*, axle, chariot, region

B

bāca, ae *f*, berry
bācātus, a, um *adj*, pearl-set
baccar, ăris *n*, fox-glove
baccha, ae *f*, bacchanal
bacchānālĭa, ĭum *n.pl*, orgies of Bacchus
bacchātĭo, ōnis *f*, orgy
bacchor, *v.i.* 1, *dep*, to rave
bācĭfer, ĕra, ĕrum *adj*, berry-bearing
băcillum, i *n*, stick
băcŭlum, i *n*, stick, sceptre
bāiŭlo, *v.t.* 1, to carry a load
bāiŭlus, i *m*, porter
bālaena, ae *f*, whale
bălănus, i *f*, acorn
bălătro, ōnis *m*, comedian
bālātus, ūs *m*, bleating
balbus, a, um *adj*, *adv*, ē, stammering
balbūtĭo *v.i.t.* 4, to stammer
ballista, ae *f*, artillery engine
balnĕae, ārum *f.pl*, baths

balsămum, i *n*, balm
baltĕus, i *m*, belt, sword-belt
bărāthrum, i *n*, abyss
barba, ae *f*, beard
barbărĭa, ae *f*, foreign country, rudeness
barbărus, i *m*, foreigner, stranger
barbărus, a, um *adj*, *adv*, ē, foreign, rude, savage
barbātus, a, um *adj*, bearded
barbĭtos *m, f*, (*pl*, a), lute, lyre
bardus, a, um *adj*, stupid
bāro, ōnis *m*, blockhead
barrus, i *m*, elephant
băsĭlĭca, ae *f*, town-hall
băsĭlĭcus, a, um *adj*, royal
bāsĭo, *v.t.* 1, to kiss
băsis, is *f*, pedestal, base
bāsĭum, ii *n*, kiss
battŭo, ŭi *v.t.* 3, to fence; beat
bĕātĭtas, ātis *f*, happiness
bĕātĭtūdo, ĭnis *f*, happiness
bĕātus, a, um *adj*, *adv*, ē, happy, fortunate
bellans   see **bello**
bellārĭa, ōrum *n.pl*, dessert
bellātor, ōris *m*, warrior
bellātrix, īcis *f*, female-warrior
bellē *adv*, prettily
bellĭcōsus, a, um *adj*, warlike
bellĭcum, i *n*, signal for march or attack
bellĭcus, a, um *adj*, military
bellĭger, ĕra, ĕrum *adj*, warlike
bellĭgĕro *v.t.* 1, to wage war
bellis, ĭdis *f*, daisy
bello, *v.i.* 1 (**bellor**, *v.i.* 1, *dep*), to make war

Insight

The stem of a noun or a verb is that part of the word to which endings are added and which does not change or decline. For example, *bell-* is the stem of *bellum* (= war); am- is the stem of *amo* (= I love).

----

balnĕātor, ōris *m*, bath-keeper
balnĕum, i *n*, bath
bālo, *v.i.* 1, to bleat

bellum, i *n*, war
bellus, a, um *adj*, pretty
bēlŭa, ae *f*, beast

běně *adv*, well, very

běnědīco, xi, ctum *v.i.t.* 3, to praise

běnědictĭo, ōnis *f*, blessing

běněfăcĭo, fēci, factum *v.t.* 3, to do well, oblige

běněfactum, i *n*, good deed

běněficentĭa, ae *f*, kind treatment

běněfĭcĭārĭi, ōrum *m.pl*, privileged soldiers (excused fatigues)

běněfĭcĭum, ii *n*, a kindness

běněfĭcus, a, um *adj*, obliging

běněvŏlentĭa, ae *f*, good will

běněvŏlus, a, um *adj, adv*, **ē**, well disposed

běnignē *adv*, thank you; no thank you; courteously

běnignus, a, um *adj*, kind, fruitful

běnignĭtas, ātis *f*, kindness

běo, *v.t.* 1, to bless, enrich

bes, bessis *m*, eight ounces

bestĭa, ae *f*, wild beast

bestĭārĭus, ii *m*, wild-beast fighter

bestĭŏla, ae *f*, small animal

bēta, ae *f*, beet

betŭla, ae *f*, birch

biblĭa, ōrum *n.pl*, the Bible

biblĭŏpōla, ae *m*, bookseller

biblĭŏthēca, ae *f*, library

biblĭŏthēcārĭus, ii *m*, librarian

bĭvo, bĭbi, ĭtum *v.t.* 3, to drink

bĭbŭlus, a, um *adj*, given to drink, porous

bĭceps, cĭpĭtis *adj*, two-headed

bĭcŏlōr, ōris *adj*, two-coloured

bĭcornis, e *adj*, two-pronged

bĭdens, ntis *m*, hoe

bĭdŭum, ii *n*, space of two days

bĭennĭum, ii *n*, space of two years

bĭfārĭam *adv*, in two ways

bĭfer, ěra, ěrum *adj*, blooming or fruiting twice a year

bĭfĭdus, a, um *adj*, cut in two

bĭfŏris, e *adj*, with double opening

bĭformis, e *adj*, two-shaped

bĭfrons, ntis *adj*, two-headed

bĭfurcus, a, um *adj*, two-pronged

bīgae, ārum *f.pl*, pair of horses, two-horsed chariot

bīgātus, a, um *adj*, stamped with a two-horsed chariot (of coins)

bĭĭŭgus, a, um *adj*, yoked two together

bīlĭbris, e *adj*, weighing two pounds

bĭlinguis, e *adj*, bilingual

bīlĭōsus, a, um *adj*, bilious

bīlis, is *f*, bile

bĭmăris, e *adj*, lying between two seas

bĭmărītus, i *m*, bigamist

bĭmembris, e *adj*, half-man, half-beast

bĭmestris, e, *adj*, two months old

bīmus, a, um *adj*, two years old

bīni, ae, a *adj*, two each, a pair

bĭpartĭo *v.t.* 4, to bisect

bĭpartīto *adv*, in two ways

bĭpědālis, e *adj*, measuring two feet

bĭpennĭfer, ěra, ěrum *adj*, carrying a double-edged axe

bĭpennis, e *adj*, double-edged

bĭpēs, ědis *adj*, two-legged

bĭrēmis, e *adj*, two-oared

bĭrēmis, is *f*, a galley with two banks of oars

bis *adv*, twice

bīsextĭlis, e *adj* (of years) leap

bīsulcus, a, um *adj*, cloven

bĭtūmen, ĭnis *n*, bitumen

bĭvĭum, ii *n*, crossroad

bĭvĭus, a, um *adj*, going in two directions

blaesus, a, um *adj*, stammering

blandīmentum, i *n*, flattery

blandĭor, *v.* 4, *dep, with dat*, to flatter

blandītĭa, ae *f*, flattery

blandus, a, um *adj, adv*, **ē**, smooth-tongued, enticing

blasphēmo, *v.t.* 1, to revile

blătěro *v.t.* 1, to babble

blătěro, ōnis *m*, gabbler

blatta, ae *f*, cockroach, moth

bŏārĭus, a, um *adj*, of cattle

bōlētus, i *m*, mushroom

bombyx, ȳcis *m*, silk, silk-worm

bŏnĭtas, ātis *f*, excellence

bŏna, ōrum *n.pl*, goods, property

bŏnum, i *n*, goodness, profit

bŏnus, a, um *adj*, good

Insight

Most adjectives add **-ior** to the stem to form the comparative and **-issimus** to form the superlative (*longus-longior-longissimus*). However, there are several irregularities, the most common of which are: *bonus-melior-optimus, malus-peior-pessimus, magnus-maior-maximus*.

---

bŏrĕas, ae *m*, north wind
bŏrēus, a, um *adj*, northern
bōs, bŏvis *c*, ox; *pl*, cattle
bŏvārĭus see **boārius**
brācae, ārum *f.pl*, trousers
brācātus, a, um *adj*, wearing trousers, foreign
bracchĭum, ii *n*, forearm, branch, dike
bractĕa, ae, *f*, thin metal plate
branchĭae, ārum *f.pl*, fish gills
brassĭca, ae *f*, cabbage
brĕvī *adv*, in a short time, in a few words
brĕvĭārĭum, ii *n*, summary
brĕvis, e *adj*, *adv*, **ĭter**, short, brief
brĕvĭtas, ātis *f*, conciseness, shortness
brūma, ae *f*, shortest day, winter
brūmālis, e *adj*, wintry
brūtus, a, um *adj*, unwieldy, dull
būbo, ōnis *m*, owl
būbulcus, i *m*, ploughman
būbŭlus, a, um *adj*, of cattle
bucca, ae *f*, the cheek
buccŭla, ae *f*, small mouth, helmet
būcĭna, ae *f*, trumpet
būcŭla, ae *f*, heifer
būfo, ōnis *m*, toad
bulbus, i *m*, bulb
bulla, ae *f*, bubble, knob, amulet
bullo, *v.i.* 1, to bubble
būmastus, i *f*, grape which grows in large bunches
būris, is *m*, plough-beam
bustum, i *n*, funeral pyre, grave
būtỹrum, i *n*, butter
buxifer, ĕra, ĕrum *adj*, growing box trees
buxum, i *n*, boxwood

buxus, i *f*, box tree
byssus, i *f*, cotton

C

căballus, i *m*, packhorse
căcăbus, i *m*, saucepan
căchinnātĭo, ōnis *f*, guffaw
căchinno, *v.i.* 1, to laugh aloud
căchinnus, i *m*, laughter, jeering
căcūmen, ĭnis *n*, extremity, peak
căcūmĭno *v.t.* 1, to make into a point
cădāver, ĕris *n*, corpse
cădo, cĕcĭdi, cāsum *v.i.* 3, to fall, wane, occur, decay
cādūcĕātor, ōris *m*, herald
cādūcĕum, i *n* (us, i *m*), herald's staff, Mercury's wand
cādūcĭfer, ĕra, ĕrum *adj*, carrying a herald's staff (Mercury)
cādūcus, a, um *adj*, falling, doomed
cădus, i *m*, large jar (for liquids)
caecĭtas, ātis *f*, blindness
caeco *v.t.* 1, to blind
caecus, a, um *adj*, blind, hidden
caedēs, is *f*, slaughter
caedo, cĕcīdi, caesum *v.t.* 3, to cut, strike, slaughter
caelātor, ōris *m*, engraver
caelātūra, ae *f*, carving
caelebs, lībis *adj*, unmarried
caelĕs, ĭtis *adj*, heavenly
caelĭtes, um *pl*, gods
caelestĭa, ĭum *n.pl*, the heavenly bodies
caelestis, e *adj*, heavenly
caelestis, is *m*, god
caelĭbātus, ūs *m*, celibacy

caelīcŏla, ae *m.* *f*, inhabitant of heaven

caelīfer, ĕra, ĕrum *adj*, supporting the heavens (Atlas)

caelo *v.t.* 1, to engrave

caelum, i *n*, heaven, climate

caelum, i *n*, chisel

caementum, i *n*, quarry stone

caenum, i *n*, dirt

caepa, ae *f* (**e, is** *n*), onion

caerĭmōnĭa, ae *f*, religious ceremony, awe

caerŭlĕus(lus), a, um *adj*, dark blue

caesărĭēs, ēi *f*, the hair

caesim *adv*, by cutting

caesĭus, a, um *adj*, green- or grey-eyed

caespĕs, ĭtis *m*, a turf

caestus, ūs *m*, boxing glove

caetra, ae *f*, native shield

călămister, tri *m*, curling-iron; *pl*, flourishes

călămītas, ātis *f*, disaster

călămītōsus, a, um *adj, adv, ē*, destructive, unhappy

călămus, i *m*, cane, reed-pen

călăthus, i *m*, basket

calcăr, āris *n*, spur, stimulus

calcĕāmentum, i *n*, shoe

calcĕo *v.t.* 1, to shoe

calcĕus, i *m*, shoe

calcītrātus, ūs *m*, kicking

calcītro *v.i.* 1, to kick, resist

calco *v.t.* 1, to tread on, oppress

calcŭlātor, ōris *m*, accountant

calcŭlus, i *m*, pebble, calculation, vote, piece (chess, draughts)

călĕfăcĭo, fēci, factum *v.t.* 3, to heat, excite

călĕo *v.i.* 2, to be warm, roused

călesco *v.i.* 3, to become warm

călīdus, a, um *adj*, warm, hot, hot-headed

călīga, ae *f*, leather boot

călīgātus, a, um *adj*, weraing soldier's boots

călīgĭnōsus, a, um *adj*, obscure

călīgo, ĭnis *f*, mist, gloom

călīgo *v.i.* 1, to steam, be dark

călix, ĭcis *m*, cup

calyx see **calix**

callĕo *v.i.t.* 2, to be callous, insensible; to know by experience

callĭdĭtas, ātis *f*, skill, cunning

callĭdus, a, um *adj, adv, ē*, skilful, sly

callis, is *m*, footpath

callum, i *n*, hard or thick skin

cālo, ōnis *m*, soldier's servant, menial

călor, ōris *m*, heat, ardour

caltha, ae *f*, marigold

călumnĭa, ae *f*, trickery, libel

călumnĭātor, ōris *m*, slanderer

călumnĭor *v.t.* 1, *dep*, to blame or accuse unjustly

calva, ae *f*, scalp

calvārĭa, ae *f*, skull

calvĭtĭum, i *n*, baldness

calvus, a, um *adj*, bald

calx, cis *f*, heel

calx, cis *f*, limestone, chalk

cămēlŏpardălis, is *f*, giraffe

cămēlus, i *m*, camel

cămēna, ae *f*, muse

cămĕra, ae *f*, vault

cămīnus, i *m*, forge, furnace

campester, tris, e *adj*, on level ground

campestre, is *n*, wrestling trunks

campus, i *m*, plain, open country, opportunity, scope

cămŭr, ŭra, ŭrum *adj*, curved inwards

cănālis, is *m*, pipe, groove

cancelli, ōrum *m.pl*, railings

cancer, cri *m*, crab

candēla, ae *f*, candle

candēlābrum, i *n*, candlestick

candens, ntis *adj*, shining white, glowing hot

candĕo *v.i.* 2, to shine, glow

candesco, ŭi *v.i.* 3, to glisten

candīdātus, i *m*, candidate

candīdus, a, um *adj, adv, ē*, dazzling white, beautiful, honest

candor, ōris *m*, whiteness, beauty, honesty

cānens, ntis *adj*, grey, white

cānĕo *v.i.* 2, to be white, grey

cānesco *v.i.* 3, to grow white

cănīcŭla, ae *f*, small dog, Dog-star

cănīnus, a, um *adj*, dog-like

cănis, is *c*, dog, Dog-star

cănistrum, i *n*, open basket

cānĭtĭes (*no genitive*) *f*, grey hair, old age

canna, ae *f*, reed, flute
cannăbis, is *f*, hemp
căno, cĕcĭni, cantum *v.i.t.* 3, to sing, play; prophesy
cănor, ōris *m*, tune
cănōrus, a, um *adj*, melodious
cantērĭus see **canthērĭus**
cantātor, ōris *m*, singer
canthăris, ĭdis *f*, beetle
canthărus, i *m*, tankard
canthērĭus, ii *m*, mule, rafter
cantĭcum, i *n*, song
cantīlēna, ae *f*, hackneyed song
canto *v.i.t.* 1, to sing, act; predict
cantor, ōris *m*, singer, actor
cantus, ūs *m*, music, prophecy, singing
cānus, a, um *adj*, white, old
căpācĭtas, ātis *f*, capacity
căpax, ācis *adj*, roomy, capable
căpella, ae *f*, she-goat
căper, pri *m*, goat
căpesso, īvi, ītum *v.t.* 3, to seize, undertake, reach for
căpillāmentum, i *n*, wig
căpillāre, is *n*, hair oil
căpillātus, a, um *adj*, hairy
căpillus, i *m*, the hair
căpĭo, cēpi, captum *v.t.* 3, to take, capture, tempt, choose, obtain, undertake, hold, grasp

capsa, ae *f*, box, satchel
captātor, ōris *m*, fortune hunter
captĭo, ōnis *f*, fraud, quibble
captīvĭtas, ātis *f*, captivity
captīvus, a, um *adj* (i *m*), prisoner
capto *v.t.* 1, to chase, entice
captus, ūs *m*, grasp, capacity
captus, a, um *adj*, taken, disabled
căpŭlus, i *m*, tomb, handle
căpŭt, ĭtis *n*, head, person, chief, origin, summit, status, paragraph, chapter
carbăsĕus, a, um *adj*, made of flax, linen
carbăsus, i *f*, flax, linen
carbo, ōnis *m*, charcoal, coal
carbuncŭlus, i *m*, ruby, carbuncle
carcer, ĕris *m*, prison, jailbird
carchēsĭum, ii *n*, goblet, masthead
cardĭăcus, a, um *adj*, dyspeptic
cardo, ĭnis *m*, hinge, crisis
cardŭus, i *m*, thistle
cărĕo *v.i.* 2, (*with abl.*) to lack
cărex, ĭcis *f*, reed-grass
cărĭes (*no genitive*) *f*, decay
cărĭca, ae *f*, dried fig
cărīna, ae *f*, hull, keel, boat
cărĭōsus, a, um *adj*, decayed
cărĭtas, ātis *f*, costliness, affection
carmen, ĭnis *n*, song, poem
carnārĭum, ii *n*, larder

Insight

In Latin verbs are conjugated. There are four conjugations and a mixed one, the third-and-fourth conjugation which takes its endings mainly from the third but also partly from the fourth conjugation. An example of a mixed conjugation verb is *capio* (= I take).

---

căpistrum, i *n*, halter
căpĭtālis, e *adj*, of life and death, criminal, dangerous
capra, ae *f*, she-goat
căprĕa, ae *f*, wild she-goat, roe
căprĕŏlus, i *m*, roebuck, prop
căprĭcornus, i *m*, capricorn
căprĭficus, i *f*, wild fig tree
căprĭgĕnus, a, um *adj*, goat-born
căprīnus, a, um *adj*, of a goat

carnĭfex, ĭcis *m*, executioner
carnĭfĭcīna, ae *f*, execution, torment
carnĭfĭco *v.t.* 1, to execute
carnĭvŏrus, a, um *adj*, carnivorous
carnōsus, a, um *adj*, fleshy
căro, carnis *f*, flesh, meat
carpentum, i *n*, chariot
carpo, psi, ptum *v.t.* 3, to pluck, graze, slander, weaken, pass over

carptim *adv*, separately
carrus, i *m*, two-wheeled cart
cartīlāgo, ĭnis *f*, cartilage
cārus, a, um *adj, adv*, **ē**, dear
cāsa, ae *f*, cottage, hut
cāsĕus, i *m*, cheese
cāsĭa, ae *f*, cinnamon (tree)
casses, ĭum *m.pl*, hunting-net, spider's web
cassis, ĭdis *f*, helmet
cassĭda, ae *f*, helmet
cassus, a, um *adj*, empty, vain
castănĕa, ae *f*, chestnut
castē *adv*, purely
castellum, i *n*, stronghold
castīgātĭo, ōnis *f*, punishment
castīgātor, ōris *m*, critic
castīgo *v.t.* 1, to correct, punish
castĭmōnĭa, ae *f*, purity
castĭtas, ātis *f*, chastity
castor, ŏris *m*, beaver
castra, ōrum *n.pl.*, camp

sly
cauda, ae *f*, tail
caudex, ĭcis *m*, tree trunk, ledger
caulae, ārum *f.pl*, hole, enclosure
caulis, is *m*, stem, cabbage
caupo, ōnis *m*, retailer, innkeeper
caupōna, ae *f*, shop, inn
caupōnor *v.t.* 1, *dep*, to trade
causa, ae *f*, reason, cause, motive; *abl.* **causā** for the sake of
causĭdĭcus, i *m*, counsel
causor *v.i.t.* 1, *dep*, to make excuses; plead
cautē *adv*, cautiously
cautēs, is *f*, crag, rock
cautĭo, ōnis *f*, precaution
cautus, a, um *adj*, safe, cautious
căvĕa, ae *f*, den, coop
căvĕo, căvi, cautum *v.i.t.* 2, to be on one's guard; stipulate
căverna, ae *f*, cave, ship's hold
căvillātĭo, ōnis *f*, jeering

Insight

Pluralia tantum are nouns that either have only the plural form or change their meaning when plural. Some examples are: *copia, -ae* = abundance/copiae, *-arum* = forces and *castrum, -i* = fort/*castra, -orum* = camp.

castrensis, e *adj*, of the camp, military
castro *v.t.* 1, to castrate
castrum, i *n*, fort
castus, a, um *adj*, pure, virtuous
cāsū *adv*, accidentally
cāsus, ūs *m*, fall, chance, mishap
cătăpulta, ae *f*, catapult
cătaracta, ae *f*, waterfall, portcullis
cătellus i *m*, (a, ae *f*), puppy
cătēna, ae *f*, chain, fetter
cătēnātus, a, um *adj*, chained
căterva, ae *f*, crowd, company
cătervātim *adv*, by companies
căthēdra, ae *f*, chair
cătillus, i *m*, dish
cătīnus, i *m*, bowl, dish
cătŭlus, i *m*, puppy, young animal
cătus, a, um *adj, adv*, **ē**, intelligent,

căvillor *v.i.t.* 1, *dep*, to jeer; taunt, quibble
căvo *v.t.* 1, to hollow out
căvum, i *n* (us, i *m*), hole
căvus, a, um *adj*, hollow
cēdo, cessi, cessum *v.i.t.* 3, to move, yield, happen; befall
cēdo *imperative*, here! say! give!
cēdrus, i *f*, cedar (wood, tree, oil)
cĕlĕbĕr, ĕbris, ĕbre *adj*, much frequented, crowded, famous
cĕlĕbrātĭo, ōnis *f*, crowd, festival
cĕlĕbrātus, a, um *adj*, popular, usual, well-known
cĕlĕbrĭtas, ātis *f*, crowd, fame
cĕlĕbro *v.t.* 1, to frequent, use, celebrate, praise, proclaim, solemnize
cĕlĕr, ĕris, ĕre *adj, adv*, **ĭter**, swift, lively, rash

cĕlĕrĭtas, ātis *f*, speed
cĕlĕro *v.i.t.* 1, to hurry; quicken
cella, ae *f*, store room
cellārĭus, i *m*, butler
cēlo *v.t.* 1, to conceal
cĕlox, ōcis *f*, yacht
celsus, a, um *adj*, high, eminent
cēna, ae *f*, dinner
cēnācŭlum, i *n*, attic, refectory
cēnātĭo, ōnis *f*, dining room
cēnātus, a, um *adj*, having dined
cēno *v.i.t.* 1, to dine; eat
censĕo, ŭi, censum *v.t.* 2, to
   assess, give an opinion
censor, ōris *m*, censor
censōrĭus, a, um *adj*, censorial
censūra, ae *f*, censorship
census, ūs *m*, census, wealth
centaurēum, i *n*, herb (centaury)
centaurus, i *m*, a Centaur
centēni, ae, a *adj* a hundred each
centēsĭmus, a, um *adj*, hundredth
centĭens (centĭes) *adv*, a hundred
   times
centĭmănus, a, um *adj*, hundred-
   handed
cento, ōnis *m*, patchwork
centum, a hundred
centumgĕmĭnus, a, um *adj*, a
   hundredfold
centumpondĭum, ii *n*, weight of a
   hundred pounds
centŭplex, plĭcis *adj* hundredfold
centŭrĭa, ae *f*, division, century
centŭrĭātim *adv*, by hundreds
centŭrĭo, ōnis *m*, centurion
centŭrĭo *v.t.* 1, to divide into
   centuries
cēnŭla, ae *f*, small dinner
cēra, ae *f*, wax, writing tablet
cĕrăsus, i *f*, cherry (tree)
cerdo, ōnis *m*, handicraftsman
cĕrĕbrōsus, a, um *adj*, hot-headed
cĕrĕbrum, i *n*, brain,
   understanding
cērēus, a, um *adj*, of wax
cērēus, i *m*, wax taper
cervisia, ae *f*, beer
cērintha, ae *f*, wax flower
cerno, crēvi, crētum *v.t.* 3, to
   perceive, decide
cernŭus, a, um *adj*, headfirst
cēro *v.t.* 1, to smear with wax

cerrītus, a, um *adj*, frantic, crazy
certāmen, ĭnis *n*, struggle
certātim *adv*, eagerly
certātĭo, ōnis *f*, contest
certē *adv*, undoubtedly
certĭōrem făcĭo to inform
certō *adv*, certainly
certo *v.i.t.* 1, to struggle; contest
certus, a, um *adj*, certain, fixed
cērussa, ae *f*, white lead
cerva, ae *f*, doe
cervĭcal, ālis *n*, pillow
cervīnus, a, um *adj*, of a deer
cervisia   see **cerevisia**
cervix, īcis *f*, neck
cervus, i *m*, deer
cessātĭo, ōnis *f*, loitering
cessātor, ōris *m*, idler
cessātrix, īcis *f*, idler
cesso *v.i.t.* 1, to loiter, cease; fail
cētārĭum, ii *n*, fishpond
cētārĭus, ii *m*, fishmonger
cētĕrōqui *adv*, in other respects
cētĕrum *adv*, otherwise, but yet
cētĕrus, a, um *adj, adv,* **um,** the
   rest, remainder
cētus, i *m*, sea monster, whale
ceu *adv*, as, just as
chălybs, ўbis *m*, steel
charta, ae *f*, writing paper
chĕlўdrus, i *m*, water snake
chĕrăgra, ae *f*, gout in the hand
chīrŏgrăphum, i *n*, handwriting
chīrurgĭa, ae *f*, surgery
chīrurgus, i *m*, surgeon
chlămys, ўdis *f*, military cloak
chorda, ae *f*, string of a musical
   instrument
chŏrēa, ae *f*, dance
chŏrus, i *m*, dance, chorus, group
Christus, i *m*, Christ
Christĭānus, a, um *adj*, Christian
cĭbārĭa, ōrum *n.pl*, food
cĭbārĭus, a, um *adj*, of food
cĭbōrĭum, ii *n*, drinking-cup
cĭbus, i *m*, food
cĭcāda, ae *f*, grasshopper
cĭcātrix, īcis *f*, scar
cĭcer, ĕris *n*, chick pea
cĭcĭnus, a, um *adj*, of the cici tree
cĭcōnĭa, ae *f*, stork
cĭcur, ŭris *adj*, tame
cĭcūta, ae *f*, hemlock

cĭĕo, cīvi, cĭtum *v.t.* 2, to rouse, move, summon

cĭlĭcĭum, ii *n*, coarse cloth

cīmex, ĭcis *m*, but

cincinnātus, a, um *adj*, with ringlets

cincinnus, i *m*, lock of hair

cinctus, ūs *m*, girdle

cĭnĕrĕus, a, um *adj*, ash-coloured

cingo, nxi, nctum *v.t.* 3, to enclose, encircle, fasten on, crown, besiege

cingŭla, ae *f*, (um, i *n*), girdle

cĭnis, ĕris *m*, ashes, death

cippus, i *m*, stake

circā *adv, and prep. with acc,* round about

circenses, ĭum *m.pl.*, The Games

circĭnus, i *m*, pair of compasses

circĭter *adv. and prep. with acc,* round about, near

circĭtor, ōris *m*, patrol

circŭĭtĭo, ōnis *f*, patrolling

circŭĭtus, ūs *m*, circuit

circŭlor *v.i.* 1, *dep*, to form a group

circŭlus, i *m*, circle, orbit

circum *adv, and prep. with acc,* around, near

circŭmăgo, ēgi, actum *v.t.* 3, to wheel, drive round, pass (time)

circumcīdo, cīdi, cīsum *v.t.* 3, to cut around, reduce

circumcīsus, a, um *adj*, cut off

circumclūdo, si, sum *v.t.* 3, to shut in, surround

circumdătus, a, um *adj*, surrounded

circumdo, dĕdi, dătum *v.t.* 1, to put around, shut in, surround

circumdūco, xi, ctum *v.t.* 3, to lead around

circŭmĕo, circŭĭtum *v.i.t.* 4, to go around; surround, canvass

circumfĕro, ferre, tŭli, lātum *v.t, irreg*, to carry or pass around

circumflecto, xi, xum *v.i.t.* 3, to bend, turn around

circumflŭo, xi, ctum *v.i.t.* 3, to flow round; overflow with

circumfŏrānĕus, a, um *adj*, movable

circumfundo, fūdi, fūsum *v.t.* 3, to pour around, envelop, hem in

circumgrĕdĭor, gressus *v.i.t.* 3, *dep*, to go around

circumĭcĭo, iēci, ctum *v.t.* 3, to throw or set round

circumiectus, a, um *adj*, surrounding

circumlīgo *v.t.* 1, to tie round

circumlĭno, (*no perf.*) ĭtum *v.t.* 3, to besmear

circummitto, mīsi, missum *v.t.* 3, to send around

circummūnĭo *v.t.* 4, to fortify round

circumplector, xus *v.t.* 3, *dep*, to embrace, surround

circumplĭco *v.t.* 1, to wind round

circumrōdo, di *v.t.* 3, to nibble round

circumscrībo, psi, ptum *v.t.* 3, to draw a line round, restrict, deceive

circumscriptĭo, ōnis *f*, circle, outline

circumsĕdĕo, sēdi, sessum *v.t.* 2, to surround, blockade

circumsisto, stĕti *v.t.* 3, to stand around; surround

circumsŏno *v.t.* 1, to resound; fill with sound

circumspecto *v.t.* 1, to look round; survey carefully

circumspectus, a, um *adj*, guarded, considered

circumspectus, ūs *m*, contemplation, spying

circumspĭcĭo, spexi, ctum *v.i.t.* 3, to look around, take care; survey, search for

circumsto stĕti *v.i.t.* 1, to stand around; surround, besiege

circumtextus, a, um *adj*, woven round

circumtŏno, ŭi, *v.t.* 1, to thunder around

circumvādo, si *v.t.* 3, to envelop

circumvallo *v.t.* 1, to surround with a wall, blockade

circumvector, *v.* 1, *dep*, to ride around

circumvĕhor, vectus *v.t.* 3, *dep*, to ride around

circumvĕnĭo, vēni, ventum *v.t.* 4, to surround

circumvŏlĭto, *v.i.t.* 1, to flit; fly around
circumvŏlo, *v.t.* 1, to fly around
circumvolvo, volvi, vŏlūtum *v.t.* 3, to roll around
circus, i *m,* circle, ring
cīris, is *f,* sea bird
cirrus, i *m,* curl
cis *prep. with acc,* on this side of, within
cĭsĭum, ii *n,* two-wheeled vehicle
cista, ae *f,* box, chest
cisterna, ae *f,* cistern
cĭtātus, a, um *adj,* urged on, quick
cĭtĕrĭor *comp. adj,* on this side
cĭthăra, ae *f,* guitar, lute
cĭthărista, ae *m,* guitar-player
cĭthăroedus, i *m,* a singing guitar player
cĭto *adv,* soon, quickly
cĭto, *v.t.* 1, to incite, call
cĭtrā *adv, and prep. with acc,* on this side (of)
cĭtrĕus, a, um *adj,* of citrus wood, of the citrus tree
cĭtrō *adv, (with* **ultro***)* to and fro, backwards and forwards
citrus, i *f,* citrus tree
cĭtus, a, um *adj,* swift, quick
cīvĭcus, a, um *adj,* of a citizen, civic, civil
cīvīlis, e *adj, adv,* **ĭter,** of a citizen, civic, civil
cīvis, is *c,* citizen
cīvĭtas, ātis *f,* citizenship, the state, the citizens
clādes, is *f,* disaster, massacre
clam *adv, and prep. with acc,* secretly; unknown to
clāmĭto *v.i.t.* 1, to call out
clāmo, *v.i.t.* 1, to shout; declare
clāmor, ōris *m,* shout, applause
clāmōsus, a, um *adj,* noisy, bawling
clandestīnus, a, um *adj, adv,* **ō,** secret, hidden, furtive
clangor, ōris *m,* noise, clash
clārĕo *v.i.* 2, to shine, be famous
clāresco, clārŭi *v.i.* 3, to become clear or famous
clārĭtas, ātis *f,* brightness, renown
clārĭtūdo, ĭnis *f,* renown
clārus, a, um *adj, adv,* **e,** clear, bright, plain, famous

classĭārĭi, ōrum *m.pl,* marines
classĭcum, i *n,* battle signal
classis, is *f,* fleet, class or muster of citizens
claudĕo *v.i.* 2, *(no perf),* to limp, be lame
claudĭco *v.i.* 1, to limp, be lame
claudĭcātĭo, ōnis *f,* limping
claudo, si, sum *v.t.* 3, to shut, cut off, enclose, blockade
claudus, a, um *adj,* lame
claustra, ōrum *n.pl,* lock, bolt, barricade
clausŭla, ae *f,* conclusion, end
clausum, i *n,* enclosed space
clāva, ae *f,* club, cudgel
clāvĭger, ĕra, ĕrum *adj,* club-armed
clāvĭger, ĕri *m,* key-bearer
clāvis, is *f,* key
clāvŭlus, i *m,* small nail
clāvus, i *m,* nail, tiller, stripe
clēmens, ntis *adj, adv,* **nter,** gentle, mild, merciful
clēmentĭa, ae *f,* mildness, mercy
clĕpo, psi, ptum *v.t.* 3, to steal
clepsȳdra, ae *f,* water-clock
clĭens, ntis *c,* retainer, follower
clĭentēla, ae *f,* patronage, train of dependants
clĭpĕus, i *m,* Roman round shield
clītellae, ārum *f.pl,* saddle bags
clīvōsus, a, um *adj,* hilly
clīvus, i, *m,* slope, hill
clŏāca, ae *f,* sewer, drain
clūnis, is *m, f,* buttock, haunch
cŏăcervo *v.t.* 1, to pile together
cŏactor, ōris *m,* money collector
cŏacum, i *n,* a thick covering
cŏactus, a, um *adj, adv,* **ē,** forced
cŏaequo *v.t.* 1, to level, equalize
cŏagmento *v.t.* 1, to join together
cŏagŭlo *v.t.* 1, to coagulate
cŏălesco, ălŭi, ălĭtum *v.i.* 3, to grow together, combine
cŏargŭo, ŭi *v.t.* 3, to convict, refute, demonstrate
cŏarto *v.t.* 1, to compress
coccĭnĕus, a, um *adj,* scarlet
coccum, i *n,* scarlet colour
cochlĕa, ae *f,* snail, spiral
cŏclĕa, ae *f,* snail, spiral
cŏclĕar, āris *n,* spoon
coctĭlis, e *adj,* baked, burned

cŏcus, i *m*, cook

cōdex, ĭcis *m*, tree trunk, ledger

cōdĭcilli, ōrum *m.pl*, notebook

cŏēmo, ēmi, emptum *v.t.* 3, to buy up

coenum, i *n*, dirt

cŏĕo *v.i.* 4, to assemble, unite, encounter, conspire

(coepĭo) coepi, coeptum *v.i.t.* 3, *defect*, to begin

coeptum, i *n*, attempt

coeptus, ūs, *m*, undertaking

cŏercĕo, *v.t.* 2, to confine, curb

cŏercĭtĭo, ōnis *f*, coercion, restraint

coetus, ūs *m*, meeting, crowd

cōgĭtātĭo, ōnis *f*, thought, reflection, purpose

cōgĭtātum, i *n*, idea, thought

cōgĭtātus, a, um *adj*, thought out

cōgĭto *v.t.* 1, to consider, think, be disposed towards, plan

cognātĭo, ōnis *f*, blood relationship, family

cognātus, a, um *adj*, related by birth; (*as a noun*) blood-relative

cognĭtĭo, ōnis *f*, study, knowledge, recognition, idea, trial

cognĭtor, ōris *m*, legal representative

cognĭtus, a, um *adj*, known, approved

cognōmen, ĭnis *n*, surname

cognōmĭnis, e *adj*, of the same name

cognosco, gnōvi, gnĭtum *v.t.* 3, to learn, understand, inquire

cōgo, cŏēgi, cŏactum *v.t.* 3, to collect, compel, restrict

cŏhaerens see cohaerĕo

cŏhaerĕo, si, sum *v.i.* 2, to cling together, agree with

cŏhēres, ēdis *c*, fellow heir

cŏhĭbĕo *v.t.* 2, to hold together, confine, restrain

cŏhŏnesto *v.t.* 1, to honour

cŏhorresco, horrŭi *v.i.* 3, to shudder

cŏhors, tis *f*, company of soldiers ('/10 of a legion); enclosure

cŏhortālis, e *adj*, of the poultry farm

cŏhortātĭo, ōnis *f*, encouragement

cŏhortor *v.t.* 1, *dep*, to encourage

cŏĭtĭo, ōnis *f*, meeting, conspiracy

cŏĭtus, ūs *m*, meeting, crowd, sexual intercourse

cŏlăphus, i *m*, blow, cuff

collăbĕfacto *v.t.* 1, to dislodge

collăbĕfĭo, fieri, factus *irreg*, to be overthrown, disabled

collābor, psus *v.i.* 3, to fall, faint, decay

collăcrĭmo *v.i.t.* 1, to weep; deplore

collactĕus, i *m*, (a, ae *f*) foster brother (sister)

collātĭo, ōnis *f*, collection, encounter, comparison

collaudo *v.t.* 1, to praise highly

collēga, ae *m*, partner, colleague

collēgĭum, ii *n*, organization, body of officials

collĭbet *v. impers*, 2, it is agreeable

collīdo, si, sum *v.t.* 3, to beat or strike together

collĭgo, lēgi, ctum *v.t.* 3, to collect, compress, consider

collĭgo *v.t.* 1, to tie together

collĭno, lēvi, lĭtum *v.t.* 3, to besmear, defile

collīnus, a, um *adj*, hilly

collis, is *m*, hill, high ground

collŏcātĭo, ōnis *f*, setting up, giving in marriage

collŏco *v.t.* 1, to arrange, give in marriage, invest, employ

collŏquĭum, ii *n*, conversation

collŏquor, cūtus *v.i.* 3, *dep*, to hold a conversation, discuss

collūcĕo *v.i*, 2, to shine

collūdo, si, sum *v.i.* 3, to play with, be in collusion with

collum, i *n*, neck, throat

columna see columna

collŭo, lŭi, lūtum *v.t.* 3, to rinse

collūsĭo, ōnis *f*, collusion

collūsor, ōris *m*, playmate

collustro *v.t.* 1, to illumine

collŭvĭo, ōnis *f*, heap of rubbish

collŭvĭes (*no genit.*) *f*, heap of rubbish

cŏlo, ŭi, cultum *v.t.* 3, to cultivate, improve, worship, study

cōlo *v.t.* 1, to filter

cŏlŏcāsĭa, ae *f*, marsh-lily

cōlon, i *n*, colon

cŏlōna, ae *f*, farmer's wife

cŏlōnĭa, ae *f,* Roman outpost, colonial settlement, farm

cŏlōnus, i *m,* farmer, colonist

cŏlor, ōris *m,* colour, dye, beauty

cŏlōrātus, a, um *adj,* coloured

cŏlōro *v.t.* 1, to colour, dye

cŏlossus, i *m,* gigantic statue

cŏlŭber, bri *m,* (bra, ae, *f)* snake

cōlum, i *n,* strainer, colander

cŏlumba, ae *f,* (us, i *m)* dove

cŏlumbārĭum, ii *n,* dovecot

cŏlumbīnus, a, um *adj,* of a dove, dove-coloured

cŏlŭmella, ae *f,* small pillar

cŏlŭmen, ĭnis *n,* summit, prop

cŏlumna, ae *f,* pillar, post

cŏlurnus, a, um *adj,* of hazel

cŏlus, ūs *f,* distaff

cŏma, ae *f,* hair, crest, foliage

cŏmans, ntis *adj,* hairy

cŏmātus, a, um *adj,* long-haired

combĭbo, bĭbi *v.t.* 3, to drink up

combūro, ussi, ustum *v.t.* 3, to burn, consume completely

cŏmĕdo, ēdi, ĕsum *v.t.* 3, to eat up, waste

cŏmes, ĭtis *c,* companion, attendant

cŏmētes, ae *m,* comet

cōmĭcus, a, um *adj, adv,* ē, comic

cōmĭcus, i *m,* comedian

cōmis, e *adj, adv,* ĭter, courteous, obliging

cōmissātĭo, ōnis *f,* drinking party

cōmissātĭo, ōris *m,* reveller

cōmissor *v.i.* 1, *dep,* to have a party

cōmĭtas, ātis *f,* affability

cŏmĭtātus, a, um *adj,* accompanied

cŏmĭtātus, ūs *m,* escort, retinue

cŏmĭtĭa, ōrum *n.pl,* Roman assembly for electing magistrates

cŏmĭtĭālis, e *adj,* of the elections; *(with* morbus) epilepsy

cŏmĭtĭum, ii *n,* assembly place for voting

cŏmĭtor *v.t.* 1, *dep,* to accompany

commăcŭlo *v.t.* 1, to stain

commĕātus, ūs *m,* expedition, leave of absence, convoy, supplies

commĕmŏrātĭo, ōnis *f,* mention

commĕmŏro *v.t.* 1, to remember, relate

commendātĭcĭus, a, um *adj,* commendatory

commendātĭo, ōnis *f,* recommendation

commendo *v.t.* 1, to entrust, recommend

commentārĭus, ii *m,* (ium, ii *n)* notebook, record

commentātĭo, ōnis *f,* careful study

commentĭcĭus, a, um *adj,* thought-out, imaginary, false

commentor *v.i.t.* 1, *dep,* to study

commentor, ōris *m,* inventor

commentum, i *n,* fabrication

commĕo, *v.i.* 1, to come and go, frequent

commercĭum, ii *n,* fabrication

commĕrĕo *v.t.* 2, to deserve fully, be guilty of

commĭgro *v.t.* 1, to migrate

commīlĭtĭum, ii *n,* comradeship

commīlĭto, ōnis *m,* comrade

commĭnātĭo, ōnis *f,* threats

commĭniscor, mentus *v.t.* 3, *dep,* to devise, invent

commĭnor *v.t.* 1, *dep,* to threaten

commĭnŭo, ŭi, ūtum *v.t.* 3, to crush, lessen, weaken

commĭnus *adv,* at close quarters

commisceo, scŭi, xtum *v.t.* 2, to mix together

commĭsĕror *v.t.* 1, *dep,* to pity

commissĭo, ōnis *f,* opening of the games, prepared speech

commissum, i *n,* offence, secret

commissūra, ae *f,* knot, joint

committo, mīsi, ssum *v.t.* 3, to connect, engage in, begin, entrust, do something wrong, bring together in combat

commŏdātum, i *n,* loan

commŏdē *adv,* appropriately, just in time

commŏdĭtas, ātis *f,* benefit

commŏdo *v.t.* 1, to adjust, lend, be kind to, oblige

commŏdum, i *n,* convenient time or opportunity, advantage

commŏdus, a, um *adj,* suitable, obliging, advantageous

commŏnĕfăcĭo, fēci, factum *v.t.* 3, to remind, impress upon

commŏnĕo *v.t.* 2, to impress upon

commonstro *v.t.* 1, to point out
commŏrātĭo, ōnis *f,* delay
commŏror *v.t.* 1, *dep,* to wait, stay
commōtĭo, ōnis *f,* commotion, excitement
commōtus, a, um *adj,* aroused
commŏvĕo, mōvi, mōtum *v.t.* 2, to shake, move, arouse, disturb
commūnĭcătĭo, ōnis *f,* communication
commūnĭco *v.t.* 1, to share with another, consult, unite, partake
commūnĭo *v.t.* 4, to fortify strongly
commūnĭo, ōnis *f,* partnership
commūnē, is *n,* community, state
commūnis, e *adj, adv,* **ĭter,** common, general
commūnĭtas, ātis *f,* fellowship
commūtābĭlis, e *adj,* changeable
commūtātĭo, ōnis *f,* change
commūto, *v.t.* 1, to change, exchange
cōmo, mpsi, mptum *v.t.* 3, to arrange, comb, braid, adorn
cōmoedĭa, ae *f,* comedy
cōmoedus, a, um *adj,* comic
cōmoedus, i *m,* comic actor
compactum, i *n,* agreement
compactus, a, um *adj,* thick set
compāges, is *f,* joint, structure
compār, ăris *adj,* equal, like
compār, ăris *m,* companion
compărātĭo, ōnis *f,* comparison, preparation
compărātīvus, a, um *adj,* comparative
compārĕo *v.t.* 2, to be evident
compăro *v.t.* 1, to pair off, compare, make ready, provide
compello, pŭli, pulsum *v.t.* 3, to collect, compel
compello *v.t.* 1, to address, rebuke
compendĭārĭus, a, um *adj,* short
compendĭum, ii *n,* gain, saving, abbreviation
compensātĭo, ōnis *f,* compensation
compenso *v.t.* 1, to make things balance, compensate
compĕrendĭno *v.t.* 1, to remand
compĕrĭo, pĕri, pertum *v.t.* 4, to ascertain
compertus, a, um *adj,* proved

compēs, ĕdis *f,* chain, shackle for the feet
compesco, scŭi *v.t.* 3, to restrain
compĕtītor, ōris *m,* rival
compĕto, īvi, ītum *v.t.* 3, to correspond, coincide
compīlo *v.t.* 1, to plunder
compingo, pēgi, pactum *v.t.* 3, to construct, fasten together
compĭtum, i *n,* crossroad
complāno *v.t.* 1, to level
complector, xus *v.t.* 3, *dep,* to embrace, value, enclose, understand
complēmentum, i *n,* complement
complĕo, ēvi, ētum *v.t.* 2, to fill up, supply
complexĭo, ōnis *f,* combination
complexus ūs *m,* embrace, love
complīco *v.t.* 1, to fold up
complōrātĭo, ōnis *f,* lamentation
complōrātus ūs *m,* lamentation
complōro *v.t.* 1, to lament
complūres, a *pl, adj,* several
compōno, pŏsŭi, pŏsĭtum *v.t.* 3, to put together, unite, build, arrange, compare, put to sleep, adjust, pretend, agree upon
comporto *v.t.* 1, to bring together
compŏs, ŏtis *adj, with genit. or abl,* having control of
compŏsĭtĭo, ōnis *f,* arranging
compŏsĭtus, a, um *adj, adv,* **ē,** well-arranged, suitable **ex compŏsĭto,** by previous agreement
comprĕhendo, di, sum *v.t.* 3, to seize, perceive, recount, understand
comprĕhensĭo, ōnis *f,* arrest
comprĭma, pressi, pressum *v.t.* 3, to press together, restrain
comprŏbo *v.t.* 1, to approve, prove
comptus, a, um *adj,* dressed-up
compulsus, a, um *adj,* collected, driven
compungo, nxi, nctum *v.t.* 3, to prick, sting
compŭto *v.t.* 1, to calculate
cōnāmen, ĭnis *n,* effort
cōnāta, ōrum *n.pl,* undertaking

cōnātum, i *n,* attempt

cōnātus, ūs *m,* effort, enterprise

concāvus, a, um *adj,* hollow, arched

concēdo, cessi, ssum *v.t.* 3, to go away, yield; permit

concĕlèbro *v.t.* 1, to frequent, celebrate, notify

concentus, ūs *m,* harmony

conceptĭo, ōnis *f,* comprehension, conception

conceptus, ūs *m,* gathering

concertātĭo, ōnis *f,* dispute

concerto *v.t.* 1, to dispute

concessĭo ōnis *f,* permission

concessu (*abl*), by permission

concessus, a, um *adj,* yielded, confirmed

concha, ae *f,* shellfish, oyster-shell, Triton's trumpet

conchŷlĭum, ii *n,* shellfish

concĭdo, cĭdĭ *v.i.* 3, to collapse

concĭdo, cĭdi, cĭsum *v.t.* 3, to cut up, kill, annihilate

concĭĕo, īvi, ĭtum *v.t.* 2, to bring together

concĭlĭābŭlum, i *n,* assembly-place

concĭlĭātĭo, ōnis *f,* union

concĭlĭātor, ōris *m,* promoter

concĭlĭo *v.t.* 1, to unite, win over, bring about

concĭlĭum, ii *n,* meeting, assembly

concinnĭtas, ātis *f,* elegance

concinnus, a, um *adj, adv,* ē, well-adjusted, graceful

concĭno, nŭi *v.t.* 3, to harmonize; celebrate

concĭpĭo, cēpi, ceptum *v.t.* 3, to take hold of, become pregnant, understand, formulate, designate

concīsus, a, um *adj, adv,* ē, cut short

concĭtātĭo, ōnis *f,* quick motion

concĭtātus, a, um *adj, adv,* ē, swift, roused

concĭto *v.t.* 1, to stir up, rouse

conclāmo *v.t.* 1, to shout out; call upon

conclāve, is *n,* room

conclūdo, si, sum *v.t.* 3, to enclose, include, conclude

concoctĭo, ōnis *f,* digestion

concŏlor, ōris *adj,* similar in colour

concŏquo, xi, ctum *v.t.* 3, to boil together, digest, put up with

concordĭa, ae *f,* agreement

concordo *v.i.* 1, to agree

concors, cordis *adj, adv,* ĭter, of the same mind

concrēdo, dĭdi, dĭtum *v.t.* 3, to entrust

concrĕmo *v.t.* 1, to burn up

concrĕpo, ŭi, ĭtum *v.i.t.* 3, to creak, crack; rattle, clash

concresco, crēvi, tum *v.i.* 3, to grow together, harden

concrētus, a, um *adj,* hardened

concŭbīna, ae *f,* concubine

concŭbĭus, a, um, *adj,* (*with* nox) at dead of night

conculco *v.t.* 1, to trample on

concŭpisco, cŭpīvi, ītum *v.t.* 3, to long for, strive after

concurro, curri, cursum *v.i.* 3, to rush together, assemble, join battle

concursātĭo, ōnis *f,* running together

concursĭo, ōnis *f,* running together

concurso *v.i.t.* 1, to run, travel about, skirmish; frequent

concursus, ūs *m,* rush, collision

concŭtĭo, cussi, ssum *v.t.* 3, to shake, disturb, terrify, examine

condemno *v.t.* 1, to convict

condenso *v.t.* 1, to condense

condensus, a, um *adj,* thick

condĭcĭo, ōnis *f,* agreement, proposition, terms, alliance, rank, situation

condīmentum, i *n,* seasoning

condĭo *v.t.* 4, to pickle

condiscĭpŭlus, i *m,* school friend

condisco, dĭdĭci *v.t.* 3, to learn carefully

condĭtor, ōris *m,* builder, author, founder

condĭtus, a, um *adj,* fashioned, composed

condītus, a, um *adj,* savoury

condo, dĭdi, dĭtum *v.t.* 3, to construct, found, store up, hide, thrust in

condŏlesco, lŭi *v.i.* 3, to suffer pain

condōno *v.t.* 1, to present, give up, surrender, pardon

condūco, xi, ctum *v.i.t.* 3, to be useful; collect, connect, hire

conductĭo, ōnis *f,* hiring

conductor, ōris *m,* tenant, contractor

conductum, i *n,* tenement

conductus, a, um *adj,* hired

cōnecto, xŭi, xum *v.t.* 3, to tie together, involve

confarrĕātĭo, ōnis *f,* marriage

confectĭo, ōnis *f,* arrangement, completion

confectus, a, um *adj,* completed, exhausted

confercĭo, *(no perf.)* **fertum** *v.t.* 4, to cram, stuff together

confĕro, ferre, tŭli, collātum *v.t, irreg,* to bring together, contribute, confer, talk about, engage, fight, compare, condense, convey, postpone; *(reflex.)* to betake oneself, go

confertus, a, um *adj, adv,* **ē,** crowded

confessĭo, ōnis *f,* confession

confessus, a, um *adj,* admitted

confestim *adv,* immediately

conficĭo, fēci, fectum *v.t.* 3, to complete, produce, exhaust, kill

confidens, ntis *adj, adv,* **nter,** bold, impudent

confidentĭa, ae *f,* boldness

confido, fisus sum *v.i.* 3, *semi-dep,* to feel confident; *with dat,* to trust

configo, xi, xum *v.t.* 3, to nail, fasten together, transfix

confingo, nxi, ctum *v.t.* 3, to fashion, invent

confinis, e, *adj,* adjoining

confinĭum, ii *n,* border

confirmātĭo, ōnis *f,* encouragement, confirming

confirmātus, a, um *adj,* resolute

confirmo, *v.t.* 1, to strengthen, encourage, prove

confisus, a, um *adj,* trusting

confĭtĕor, fessus *v.t.* 2, *dep,* to acknowledge, own

conflàgro *v.i.* 1, to burn

conflicto *v.t.* 1, to strike or dash together, ruin, harass

conflīgo, xi, ctum *v.i.t.* 3, to fight, struggle; strike or dash together

conflo *v.t.* 1, to kindle, cause

conflŭens, ntis *m,* confluence of rivers

conflŭo, xi *v.i.* 3, to flow together, unite, come in crowds

confŏdĭo, fōdi, fossum *v.t.* 3, to dig thoroughly, stab, pierce

conformātĭo, ōnis *f,* shaping

conformo *v.t.* 1, to form, fashion

confrăgōsus, a, um *adj,* broken

confringo, frēgi, fractum *v.t.* 3, to smash up

confŭgĭo, fūgi *v.i.* 3, to run away for help, take refuge

confundo, fūdi, sum *v.t.* 3, to pour together, confuse

confūsĭo, ōnis *f,* blending, disorder

confūsus, a, um *adj, adv,* **ē,** disorderly

confūto *v.t.* 1, to repress, silence

congĕlo *v.i.t.* 1, to freeze; thicken

congĕmĭno *v.t.* 1, to redouble

congĕmo, ŭi *v.i.t.* 3, to sigh; mourn

congĕrĭes, ēi *f,* heap

congĕro, ssi, stum *v.t.* 3, to bring together, accumulate

congestus, ūs *m,* heap

congĭārĭum, ii *n,* gratuity

congĭus, ii *m,* six-pint measure

conglŏbo *v.t.* 1, to gather, press into a ball

conglūtĭno *v.t.* 1, to glue or cement together, unite

congrĕdĭor, gressus *v.i.* 3, *dep,* to meet, encounter

congrĕgātĭo, ōnis *f,* assembly

congrĕgo *v.t.* 1, to collect into a flock, unite

congressus, ūs *m,* meeting, combat

congrŭens, ntis *adj, adv,* **nter,** appropriate, proper, consistent

congrŭentĭa, ae *f,* agreement

congrŭo, ŭi *v.t.* 3, to meet, coincide

cōnĭcĭo, iēci, iectum *v.t.* 3, to hurl, infer, drive

coniecto *v.t.* 1, to hurl, foretell
coniectūra, ae *f*, inference
coniectus, ūs *m*, throwing, heap
coniectus, a, um *adj*, thrown together
cōnĭfer, ĕra, ĕrum *adj*, cone-bearing
cōnītor, nīsus (nixus) *v.i.* 3, *dep*, to strive, struggle towards
cōnīvĕo, nīvi *v.i.* 2, to wink, blink
coniŭgĭum, ii *n*, union, marriage
coniunctĭo, ōnis *f*, uniting, junction
coniunctus, a, um *adj, adv*, ē, near, connected, allied
coniungo, nxi, nctum *v.t.* 3, to join together, marry
coniunx, iŭgis *m, f*, husband, wife
coniūrātĭo, ōnis *f*, conspiracy
coniūrātus, i *m*, conspirator
coniūro *v.i.* 1, to conspire, band together
conl... see coll...
connecto see cōnecto
conīvĕo see cōnīvĕo
connūbĭum, ii *n*, marriage
cōnōpèum, i *n*, gauze net
cōnor *v.t.* 1, *dep*, to try, undertake
conquĕror, questus *v.i.t.* 3, *dep*, to complain (of)
conquĭesco, quĭēvi, quĭētum *v.i.* 3, to rest, pause
conquīro, quīsīvi, sītum *v.t.* 3, to search for
conquīsītĭo, ōnis *f*, search
conquīsītus, a, um *adj*, sought after
consālūto *v.t.* 1, to greet
consānesco, ŭi *v.i.* 3, to heal
consanguĭnĕus, a, um *adj*, related by blood
consanguĭnĭtas, ātis *f*, blood relationship
conscendo, di, sum *v.i.t.* 3, to embark; mount
conscĭentĭa, ae *f*, joint knowledge, moral sense
conscindo, ĭdi, issum *v.t.* 3, to tear in pieces
conscisco, scīvi, ītum *v.t.* 3, to make a joint resolution, decree, inflict

conscĭus, a, um *adj*, sharing knowledge of, (*with* sibi) conscious of
conscĭus, i *m*, accomplice
conscrībo, psi, ptum *v.t.* 3, to enroll, enlist, compose
conscriptus, i *m*, senator
consĕco, cŭi, ctum *v.t.* 1, to cut up
consecrātĭo, ōnis *f*, consecration
consecro *v.t.* 1, to dedicate, doom
consector *v.t.* 1, *dep*, to pursue eagerly, imitate
consĕnesco, nŭi *v.i.* 3, to grow old or weak
consensĭo, ōnis *f*, agreement, plot
consensus, ūs *m*, agreement, plot
consentānĕus, a, um *adj*, suited
consentĭo, sensi, sum *v.i.t.* 4, to agree, conspire, resolve; plot
consĕquens, ntis *adj*, according to reason, fit
consĕquor, sĕcūtus *v.t.* 3, *dep*, to follow, pursue, overtake, attain, obtain
consĕro, sēvi, sĭtum (sătum) *v.t.* 3, to plant, sow
consĕro, rŭi, rtum *v.t.* 3, to fasten together
consertus, a, um *adj, adv*, ē, joined, close, serried
conservātĭo, ōnis *f*, maintenance
conservo *v.t.* 1, to maintain, keep safe
conservus, i *m*, fellow slave
consessus, ūs *m*, assembly
consīdĕrātus, a, um *adj, adv*, ē, well-considered, cautious, discreet
consīdĕrātĭo, ōnis *f*, consideration
consīdĕro *v.t.* 1, to examine, contemplate
consido, sēdi, sessum *v.i.* 3, to sit down, take up position, subside
consigno *v.t.* 1, to seal, certify
consĭlĭārĭus, ii *m*, adviser
consĭlĭor *v.i.* 1, *dep*, to consult
consĭlĭum, ii *n*, plan, deliberation, policy, advise, assembly, wisdom
consĭmĭlis, e *adj*, quite like
consisto, stĭti, stĭtum *v.i.* 3, to stand, halt, take up position, endure, settle
consōbrīnus, i *m* (a, ae, *f*), cousin
consŏcĭātus, a, um *adj*, united
consŏcĭo *v.t.* 1, to share, unite

consōlātĭo, ōnis *f*, comfort
consōlātor, ōris *m*, comforter
consōlor *v.t.* 1, *dep*, to comfort
consŏnans, ntis (*with* **littera**), consonant
consŏno, ŭi *v.i.* 1, to resound, harmonize, agree
consŏnus, a, um *adj*, *adv*, **ē**, fit, harmonious
consōpĭo *v.t.* 4, to put to sleep
consors, rtis *adj*, partner
conspectus, ūs *m*, look, sight, view, presence
conspectus, a, um *adj*, distinguished, visible
conspergo, si, sum *v.t.* 3, to sprinkle
conspĭcĭo, spexi, ctum *v.t.* 3, to look at, understand
conspĭcor *v.t.* 1, *dep*, to catch sight of
conspĭcŭus, a, um *adj*, visible, striking
conspīrātĭo, ōnis *f*, agreement, plot
conspīro *v.i.* 1, to agree, plot
consponsor, ōris *m*, joint surety
conspŭo, (*no perf.*), **ūtum** *v.t.* 3, to spit on, cover
constans, ntis *adj*, *adv* **nter**, firm, resolute, consistent
constantĭa, ae *f*, firmness, consistency
constat *v. impers*, it is agreed
consternātĭo, ōnis *f*, dismay
consterno, strāvi, strātum *v.t.* 3, to cover over
consterno *v.t.* 1, to alarm, provoke
constĭtŭo, ŭi, ūtum *v.t.* 3, to put, place, draw up, halt, establish, arrange, determine, decide
constĭtūtĭo, ōnis *f*, arrangement, establishment
constĭtūtum i *n*, agreement
constĭtūtus, a, um *adj*, arranged
consto, stĭti, stātum *v.i.* 1, to agree with, endure, be established, exist, consist of, cost
constrātus, a, um *adj*, covered
constringo, nxi, ctum *v.t.* 3, to tie up, restrain
constrūo, xi, ctum *v.t.* 3, to heap up, build

constūpro *v.t.* 1, to ravish
consŭĕfăcĭo, fēci, factum *v.t.* 3, to accustom
consŭesco, sŭēvi, sŭētum *v.i.t.* 3, to be accustomed; train
consŭētūdo, ĭnis *f*, habit, custom, intimacy
consŭētus, a, um *adj*, customary
consŭl, ŭlis *m*, consul (highest Roman magistrate)
consŭlāris, e *adj*, of a consul
consŭlātus, ūs *m*, consulship
consŭlo, ŭi, sultum *v.i.t.* 3, to consider, consult; *with dat*, promote the interests of
consulto *v.i.t.* 1, to deliberate; consult
consultor, ōris *m*, adviser, client
consultum, I *n*, decision, decree
consultus, a, um *adj*, *adv*, **ē**, **ō**, well considered
consummātĭo, ōnis *f*, summing-up, completion
consūmo, mpsi, mptum *v.t.* 3, to use, eat up, consume, waste, destroy
consumptĭo, ōnis *f*, wasting, use
consurgo, surrexi, surrectum *v.i.t.* 3, to stand up, rise
contăbŭlātĭo, ōnis *f*, flooring
contăbŭlo *v.t.* 1, to board over
contactus, ūs *m*, touch, contact, contagion
contāgĭo, ōnis *f*, touch, contact, contagion
contāmĭnātus, a, um *adj*, impure
contāmĭno *v.t.* 1, to blend, stain
contĕgo, xi, ctum *v.t.* 3, to cover up, hide
contemnendus, a, um *adj*, contemptible
contemno, mpsi, mptum *v.t.* 3, to despise
contemplātĭo, ōnis *f*, observation
contemplor *v.t.* 1, *dep*, to observe
contemptor, ōris *m*, despiser
contemptus, ūs *m*, contempt
contemptus, a, um *adj*, despicable
contendo, di, tum *v.i.t.* 3, to strive, march, fight, stretch; compare, make a bid for
contentĭo, ōnis *f*, struggle, effort, contrast, dispute

contentus, a, um *adj*, strained
contentus, a, um *adj*, satisfied
contermĭnus, a, um *adj*, bordering on
contĕro, trīvi, trītum *v.t.* 3, to grind, wear away, waste
conterrĕo *v.t.* 2, to frighten
contestor *v.t.* 1, *dep*, to call to witness
contexo, ūi, xtum *v.i.t.* 3, to weave together; build, compose
contextus, ūs *m*, connection
contĭcesco, tĭcŭi *v.i.* 3, to be silent, cease
contignātĭo, ōnis *f*, wooden floor
contĭgŭus, a, um *adj*, adjoining
contĭnens, ntis *f*, continent
contĭnens, ntis *adj, adv*, **nter**, moderate, adjacent, unbroken
continentĭa, ae *f*, self-restraint
contĭnĕo, ŭi, tentum *v.t.* 2, to keep together, contain, enclose, restrain
contingo, tĭgi, tactum *v.i.t.* 3, to happen; touch, border on, reach
contĭnŭātĭo, ōnis *f*, succession
contĭnŭō *adv*, immediately
contĭnŭo *v.t.* 1, to connect, to do one thing after another
contĭnŭus, a, um *adj*, unbroken
contĭo, ōnis *f*, meeting, speech
contĭōnātor, ōris *m*, demagogue
contĭōnor *v.* 1, *dep*, to expound
contorquĕo, torsi, tortum *v.t.* 2, to twist, brandish, hurl
contortĭo, ōnis *f*, twisting, intricacy
contortus, a, um *adj, adv*, **ē**, energetic, complicated
contrā *adv, prep. with acc*, opposite, facing, contrary to
contractĭo, ōnis *f*, contraction
contractus, a, um *adj*, compressed
contrādīco, xi, cutm *v.t.* 3, to reply
contrādictĭo, ōnis *f*, reply
contrăho, xi, ctum *v.t.* 3, to bring together, shorten, produce, check
contrārĭum, ii *n*, the contrary
contrārĭus, a, um *adj, adv*, **ē**, opposite, injurious
contrecto *v.t.* 1, to handle, feel
contrĕmisco, mŭi *v.i.t.* 3, to quake; tremble at
contrĭbŭo, ŭi, ūtum *v.t.* 3, to quake; tremble at

contrĭbŭo, ŭi, ūtum *v.t.* 3, to incorporate, unite
contristo *v.t.* 1, to sadden, cloud
contrītus, a, um *adj*, worn out
contrōversĭa, ae *f*, dispute
contrōvērsus, a, um *adj*, questionable
contrŭcīdo *v.t.* 1, to slash
contŭbernālis, is *c*, messmate
contŭbernĭum, ii *n*, companionship
contŭĕor *v.t.* 2, *dep*, to survey
contŭmācĭa, ae *f*, obstinacy
contŭmax, ācis *adj, adv*, **ĭter**, stubborn, insolent
contŭmēlĭa, ae *f*, insult
contŭmēlĭōsus, a, um *adj*, abusive
contŭmŭlo *v.t.* 1, to bury
contundo, tŭdi, tūsum *v.t.* 3, to grind, crush, subdue
conturbo *v.t.* 1, to confuse
contus, i *m*, pole
contūsum, i *n*, bruise
cōnūbĭum, ĭi, *n*, marriage
cōnus, i *m*, cone, helmet-tip
convălesco, lŭi *v.i.* 3, to regain strength or health
convallis, is *f*, valley
convecto *v.t.* 1, to collect
convĕho, xi, ctum *v.t.* 3, to bring together
convello, velli, vulsum *v.t.* 3, to tear up
convĕnĭens, ntis *adj, adv*, **nter**, consistent, appropriate
convĕnĭenta, ae *f*, consistency, symmetry
convĕnĭo, vēni, ventum *v.i.t.* 4, to assemble, agree with; meet
convĕnit *impers*, it is agreed, it is right, it suits
conventum, i *n*, agreement
conventus, ūs *m*, meeting, assizes
conversĭo, ōnis *f*, revolution
conversus, a, um *adj*, reversed, turned, transposed
converto, ti, sum *v.i.t.* 3, to turn; change, alter
convexus, a, um *adj*, arched
convīcĭum, ii *n*, outcry, squabbling, abuse
convictor, ōris *m*, close friend
convictus, ūs *m*, intimacy
convinco, vīci, victum *v.t.* 3, to conquer, prove

convīva, ae *c*, guest

convīvĭum, ii *n*, dinner party

convīvor *v.i.* 1, *dep*, to banquet

convŏco *v.t.* 1, to call together

convŏlo, *v.i.* 1, to flock together

convolvo, volvi, vŏlūtum *v.t.* 3, to roll up, interweave

convulsĭo, ōnis *f*, convulsion

convulsus, a, um *adj*, torn-up

cŏŏpĕrĭo, rŭi, rtum *v.t.* 4, to cover up, overwhelm

cŏoptātĭo, ōnis *f*, election

cŏopto *v.t.* 1, to nominate, elect

cŏŏrĭor, ortus *v.i.* 4, *dep*, to arise, break out

cŏphĭnus, i *m*, wicker basket

cōpĭa, ae *f*, abundance, power, supply, opportunity; *pl*, forces

cōpĭōsus, a, um *adj, adv,* ē, well-supplied, eloquent

cōpŭla, ae *f*, thong, grappling iron

cōpŭlo *v.t.* 1, to link, join

cŏquo, xi, ctum *v.t.* 3, to cook, burn, ripen, devise, harass

cŏquus, i *m*, cook

cŏr, cordis *n*, heart, mind

cŏrălĭum, ii *n*, coral

cōram *adv and prep. with abl*, in the presence of, openly

corbis, is *c*, basket

corbīta, ae *f*, merchant ship

cordātus, a, um *adj*, shrewd

cŏrĭārĭus ii, *m*, tanner

cŏrĭum, ii *n*, skin, hide, leather, layer, stratum

cornĕus, a, um *adj*, horny

cornĕus, a, um *adj*, of cornel wood

cornĭcen, ĭnis *m*, horn-player

cornĭcŭla, ae *f*, jackdaw

cornĭcŭlum, i *n*, little horn, feeler

cornĭger, ĕra, ĕrum *adj*, horned

cornĭpēs, ĕdis *adj*, hoofed

cornix, īcis *f*, crow

cornū, ūs *n*, horn, hoof, beak, tributary, promontory, knob, wing of army, bow, trumpet, drinking horn

cornum, i *n*, cornel-cherry

cornus, i *f*, cornel-cherry tree, cornel-wood javelin

cŏrōna, ae *f*, garland, wreath, crown, ring, circle, crowd

cŏrōno *v.t.* 1, to crown, encircle

corpŏrĕus, a, um *adj*, physical

corpŭlentus, a, um *adj*, corpulent

corpus, ŏris *n*, body

correctĭo, ōnis *f*, improvement

corrector, ōris *m*, reformer

corrēpo, psi *v.i.* 3, to creep

corrĭgĭa, ae *f*, shoe lace

corrĭgo, rexi, ctum *v.t.* 3, to put right, improve

corrĭpĭo, pŭi, pertum *v.t.* 3, to snatch, plunder, attack, shorten

corrŏbŏro *v.t.* 1, to strengthen

corrūgo *v.t.* 1, to wrinkle

corrumpo, rūpi, ptum *v.t.* 3, to destroy, corrupt, spoil

corrŭo, ŭi *v.i.t.* 3, to collapse; overthrow

corruptēla, ae *f*, corruption

corruptor, ōris *m*, corruptor, seducer

corruptus, a, um *adj, adv,* ē, spoiled, damaged, tainted

cortex, īcis *m*, bark, rind

cortīna, ae *f*, kettle, cauldron

cŏrusco *v.i.t.* 1, to glitter; shake

cŏruscus, a, um *adj*, glittering, vibrating

corvus, i *m*, raven

cŏrўlus, i *f*, hazel shrub

cŏrymbus, i *m*, cluster of fruit or flowers

cōrўtŏs, i *m*, quiver

cōs, cōtis *f*, flintstone

costa, ae *f*, rib, wall

cŏthurnus, i *m*, hunting-boot, buskin (worn by tragic actors)

cottīdĭānus, a, um *adj, adv,* ō, daily, usual

cottīdĭē/cotidie *adv*, daily

cŏturnix, īcis *f*, quail

coxendix, īcis *f*, hip

crabro, ōnis *m*, hornet

crambē, es *f*, cabbage, kale

crāpŭla, ae *f*, intoxication

crās *adv*, tomorrow

crassĭtūdo, ĭnis *f*, thickness

crassus, a, um *adj, adv,* ē, thick, fat, solid

crastīnus, a, um *adj*, of tomorrow

crātēr, ĕris *m*, mixing-bowl, basin

crātēra, ae *f*, mixing-bowl, basin

crātĭcŭla, ae *f*, gridiron

crātis, is *f*, wicker-work, hurdle

crĕātĭo, ōnis *f*, appointing

crĕātor, ōris *m*, founder, creator

crĕātrix, īcis *f*, mother

crēber, bra, brum *adj, adv*, ō, think, numerous, repeated

crēbresco, brŭi *v.i.* 3, to become frequent, gain strength

crēdens, ntis *c*, believer

crēdĭbĭlis, e *adj, adv* īter, credible, probable

crēdĭtor, ōris *m*, creditor

crēdo, dĭdi, dĭtum *v.t.* 3, to lend, entrust, trust, believe in (*with dat*); suppose

crēdŭlĭtas, ātis *f*, credulity

crēdŭlus, a, um *adj*, ready to believe

crĕmo *v.t.* 1, to burn

crĕo *v.t.* 1, to produce, appoint

crĕpĭda, ae *f*, sandal

crĕpīdo, ĭnis *f*, pedestal, dike

crĕpĭtācŭlum, i *n*, rattle

crĕpĭto *v.i.* 1, to rattle, rustle

crĕpĭtus, ūs *m*, rattling, clashing, cracking

crĕpo, ŭi, ĭtum *v.i.t.* 1, to rattle, creak, jingle; prattle about

crĕpundĭa, ōrum *n.pl*, child's rattle

crĕpuscŭlum, i *n*, twilight, dusk

cresco, crēvi, crētum *v.i.* 3, to arise, grow, appear, thrive

crēta, ae *f*, chalk

crētus, a, um *adj*, arisen, born of

crībro *v.t.* 1, to sift

crībrum, i *n*, sieve

crīmen, ĭnis *n*, accusation, offence

crīmĭnātĭo, ōnis *f*, accusation, calumny

crīmĭnor *v.t.* 1, *dep*, to accuse

crīmĭnōsus, a, um *adj, adv*, ē, slanderous, culpable

crīnālis, e *adj*, of the hair

crīnis, is *m*, the hair

crīnītus, a, um *adj*, long-haired

crispo *v.i.t.* 1, to curl; brandish

crispus, a, um *adj*, curled, quivering

crista, ae *f*, crest, plume

cristātus, a, um *adj*, crested

crītĭcus, i *m*, critic

crŏcĕus, a, um *adj*, of saffron or yellow

crōcĭo *v.i.* 4, to croak

crŏcŏdīlus, i *m*, crocodile

crŏcus, i *m* (um, i, *n*), crocus

crŭcĭātus, ūs *m*, torture, pain

crŭcĭo *v.t.* 1, to torture

crūdēlis, e *adj, adv* īter, cruel

crūdēlĭtas, ātis *f*, cruelty

crūdesco, dŭi *v.i.* 3, to get worse

crūdĭtas, ātis *f*, indigestion

crūdus, a, um *adj*, raw, fresh, unripe, cruel

crŭento *v.t.* 1, to stain with blood

crŭentus, a, um *adj*, bloodstained, bloodthirsty

crŭmēna, ae *f*, small purse

crŭor, ōris *m*, blood (from a wound), murder

crūs, ūris *n*, leg, shin

crusta, ae *f*, crust, bark, mosaic

crustŭlārĭus, ii *m*, confectioner

crustŭlum, i *n*, confectionery

crustum, i *n*, confectionery

crux, ŭcis *f*, cross

crypta, ae *f*, cloister, vault

crystallum, i *n*, crystal

cŭbĭcŭlārĭus, ii *m*, chamber-servant

cŭbĭcŭlum, i *n*, bedroom

cŭbĭcus, a, um *adj*, cubic

cŭbīle, is *n*. bed, lair

cŭbĭtăl, ālis *n*, cushion

cŭbĭtum, i *n*, elbow

cŭbĭtus, i *m*, elbow

cŭbĭtum see cŭbo

cŭbo, ŭi, ĭtum *v.i.* 1, to lie down, sleep, lie ill, slant

cŭcullus, i *m*, hood

cŭcŭlus, i *m*, cuckoo

cŭcŭmis, ĕris *m*, cucumber

cŭcurbĭta, ae *f*, cup

cūdo *v.t.* 3, to beat, strike, stamp

cūius, a, um *interr. adj*, whose?

cūius *genit.* of qui, quis

culcĭta, ae *f*, mattress, cushion

cŭlex, ĭcis *m*, gnat, mosquito

cŭlīna, ae *f*, kitchen, food

cullĕus, i *m*, leather bag

culmen, ĭnis *n*, summit, roof

culmus, i *m*, stem, stalk

culpa, ae *f*, blame, fault, weakness

culpābĭlis, e *adj*, culpable

culpandus, a, um *adj*, culpable

culpo *v.t.* 1, to blame

culter, tri *m*, knife, ploughshare

cultor, ōris *m*, cultivator, supporter, inhabitant
cultrix, īcis *f*, female inhabitant
cultūra, ae *f*, cultivation, care
cultus, a, um *adj*, cultivated, elegant
cultus, ūs, *m*, farming, education, culture-pattern, reverence, dress
cŭlullus, i, *m*, drinking-cup
cum *conj*, when, whenever, since, although **cum ... tum,** both ... and, not only ... but also
cum *prep. with abl*, together with; *it is attached to the abl. case of personal prons*, e.g. **mecum,** with me

cūpa, ae *f*, barrel, cask
cūpēdĭa, ōrum *n.pl*, delicacies
cŭpĭdē *adv*, eagerly
cŭpĭdĭtas, ātis *f*, desire, longing
cŭpīdo, ĭnis *f*, lust, greed
cŭpīdus, a, um *adj*, eager, longing for, greedy, passionate
cŭpĭens, ntis *adj, adv*, **nter**, eager or longing for
cŭpĭo, īvi, ītum *v.t.* 3, to desire
cùpressus, i *f*, cypress tree
cūr *adv*, why
cūra, ae *f*, care, attention, management, anxiety
cūrātĭo, ōnis *f*, administration, cure

Insight

Cum used as a preposition and when followed by the ablative case means 'with'; *cum* used as a conjunction means 'when', 'whenever', 'since' and 'although'. It can be followed by both the indicative and the subjunctive.

---

cumba, ae *f*, small boat
cŭmĕra, ae *f*, box, chest
cŭmīnum, i *n*, cumin (plant)
cumquĕ *adv*, however, whenever
cŭmŭlātus, a, um *adj, adv*, **ē**, full, increased
cŭmŭlo *v.t.* 1, to heap up, complete
cŭmŭlus, i *m*, heap, 'last straw'
cūnābŭla, ōrum *n.pl*, cradle
cūnae, ārum *f.pl*, cradle
cunctans, ntis *adj, adv*, **nter**, loitering, sluggish
cunctātĭo, ōnis *f*, delay, doubt
cunctātor, ōris *m*, loiterer, cautious person
cunctor *v.i.* 1, *dep*, to hesitate, delay
cunctus, a, um *adj*, all together
cŭnĕātim *adv*, wedge-shaped
cŭnĕo *v.t.* 1, to fasten with wedges
cŭnĕus, i *m*, wedge, wedge-shaped block of theatre seats or troop formation
cŭnīcŭlum, i *n*, tunnel, mine
cŭnīcŭlus, i *m*, rabbit

cūrātor, ōris *m*, manager
cūrātus, a, um *adj*, urgent
curcŭlĭo, ōnis *m*, weevil
cūrĭa, ae *f*, senate house, city ward
cūrĭālis, e *adj*, of the same ward
cūrĭōsus, a, um *adj, adv*, **ē**, careful, inquisitive
cūro *v.t.* 1, to take care of; *with acc. and gerundive*, to see to it that ..., to arrange, command
currĭcŭlum, i *n*, racecourse, chariot, racing, career
curro, cŭcurri, cursum *v.i.* 3, to run
currus, ūs *m*, chariot
cursim *adv*, swiftly
curso *v.i.* 1, to run to and fro
cursor, ōris *m*, runner, courier
cursus, ūs *m*, running, journey, speed, direction
curtus, a, um *adj*, shortened, humble
cŭrūlis, e *adj*, of a chariot; **sella cŭrūlis**, ivory chair of office used by high magistrates
curvāmen, ĭnis *n*, curve
curvo *v.t.* 1, to bend

curvus, a, um *adj*, bent, stooping
cuspis, ĭdis *f*, point, lance, spit, sting
custōdĭa, ae *f*, watch, guard, imprisonment, guard-room
custōdĭo *v.t.* 4, to guard, watch, keep, preserve
custos, ōdis *c*, guardian, gaoler
cŭtis, is *f*, skin, surface
cўăthus, i *m*, small ladle
cўcnēus, a, um *adj*, of a swan
cўcnus, i *m*, swan
cўlindrus, i *m*, roller, cylinder
cymba, ae *f*, small boat
cymbălum, i *n*, cymbal, bell
cymbĭum, ii *n*, bowl, basin
Cўnĭcus, i *m*, a Cynic philosopher
cўpărissus, i *f*, cypress tree

D

**dactўlus, i , ** *m*, dactyl (metrical foot consisting of one long and two short syllables)
daedălus, a, um *adj*, skilful
daemŏnĭum, ii *n*, demon
damma (dāma), ae *f*, deer
damnātĭo, ōnis *f*, condemnation
damnātōrĭus, a, um *adj*, condemnatory
damnātus, a, um *adj*, guilty
damno *v.t.* 1, to condemn
damnōsus, a, um *adj*, *adv* **ē**, destructive
damnum, i *n*, damage, loss, fine
daps, dăpis *f*, formal banquet
dătĭo, ōnis *f*, distribution
dător, ōris *m*, giver
dē *prep. with abl*, from, down from, about, concerning, on account of
dĕa, ae *f*, goddess
dĕalbo *v.t.* 1, to whitewash
dĕambŭlo *v.i.* 1, to take a walk
dĕarmo *v.t.* 1, to disarm
dēbacchor *v.i.* 1, *dep*, to rage
dēbellātor, ōris *m*, conqueror
dēbello *v.i.t.* 1, to finish a war; subdue
dēbĕo *v.i.t.* 2, to be indebted; owe, (one) ought
dēbĭlis, e *adj*, disabled, weak

dēbĭlĭtas, ātis *f*, weakness
dēbĭlĭtātĭo, ōnis *f*, maiming, enervating
dēbĭlĭto *v.t.* 1, to cripple, weaken
dēbĭtor, ōris *m*, debtor
dēbĭtum, i *n*, debt
dēbĭtus, a, um *adj*, owed
dēcanto *v.i.* 1, to sing repeatedly
dēcēdo, ssi, ssum *v.i.* 3, to go away, cease, yield, resign
dĕcem *indecl. adj*, ten
December (mensis) December
dĕcempĕda, ae *f*, measuring rod (ten feet long)
dĕcempĕdātor, ōris *m*, surveyor
dĕcemvĭrālis, e *adj*, of the decemviri
dĕcemvĭrātus, ūs *m*, the rank of decemvir
dĕcemvĭri, ōrum *m.pl*, commission of ten (early rulers of Rome)
dĕcens, ntis *adj*, *adv*, **nter**, proper, graceful
dĕcentĭa, ae *f*, comeliness
dēceptus, a, um *adj*, deceived
dēcerno, crēvi, crētum *v.i.t.* 3, to decide, resolve; fight
dēcerpo, psi, ptum *v.t.* 3, to pluck, gather
dēcertātĭo, ōnis *f*, struggle
dēcerto *v.i.t.* 1, to fight it out; struggle for
dēcessĭo, ōnis *f*, departure
dēcessus, ūs *m*, departure
dĕcet, cŭit *v.* 2, *impers*, it is becoming or proper
dēcĭdo, cĭdi *v.i.* 3, to fall down, die, perish
dēcĭdo, cĭdi, cīsum *v.t.* 3, to cut off, settle
dĕcĭēs, (dĕcĭens) *adv*, ten times
dĕcĭma, ae *f*, tenth part, tithe
dĕcĭmānus, a, um *adj*, of tithes, of the tenth legion; **porta dēcĭmāna**, main camp gate
dĕcĭmo *v.t.* 1, to punish every tenth man, decimate
dĕcĭmus, a, um *adj*, tenth
dēcĭpĭo, cēpi, ptum *v.t.* 3, to deceive
dēcīsĭo, ōnis *f*, decision
dēclāmātĭo ōnis *f*, practice in public speaking

dēclāmātor, ōris *m*, speech expert

dēclāmātōrĭus, a, um *adj*, rhetorical

dēclāmo *v.i.* 1, to practise speaking

dēclāro *v.t.* 1, to make clear

dēclīnātĭo, ōnis *f*, avoidance, bending

dēclīno *v.i.t.* 1, to turn aside

dēclīve, is *n*, slope

dēclīvis, e *adj*, sloping downwards

dēclīvĭtas, ātis *f*, slope

dēcoctor, ōris *m*, bankrupt

dēcoctus, a, um *adj*, boiled, refined

dēcŏlor, ōris *adj*, discoloured

dēcŏlōro *v.t.* 1, to discolour

dēcŏquo, xi, ctum *v.t.* 3, to boil down, go bankrupt

dĕcor, ōris *m*, elegance

dĕcŏro *v.t.* 1, to adorn

dĕcŏrum, I *n*, decency

dĕcŏrus, a, um *adj, adv, ē*, becoming, proper, elegant

dēcrĕpĭtus, a, um *adj*, decrepit

dēcresco, crēvi, tum *v.i.* 3, to diminish, wane

dēcrētum, i *n*, decree, decision

dĕcŭma, dĕcŭmānus see decim...

dēcumbo, cŭbŭi *v.i.* 3, to lie down, lie ill

dĕcŭrĭa, ae *f*, section of ten

dĕcŭrĭo *v.t.* 1, to divide into sections

decŭrĭo, ōnis *m*, the head of ten, superintendent

dēcurro, cŭcurri, cursum *v.i.* 3, to run down, complete a course, manoeuvre, have recourse to

dēcursus, ūs *m*, descent, course, manoeuvre, attack

dĕcus, ŏris *n*, ornament, splendour

dĕcussātĭo, ōnis *f*, intersection

dēcŭtĭo, cussi, ssum *v.t.* 3, to shake off, beat off

dēdĕcet, cŭit *v.* 2, *impers*, it is unbecoming

dēdĕcŏro *v.t.* 1, to disgrace

dēdĕcus, ŏris *n*, disgrace, shame

dēdĭcātĭo, ōnis *f*, dedication

dēdĭco *v.t.* 1, to dedicate

dēdignor *v.t.* 1, *dep*, to disdain

dēdisco, dĭdĭci *v.t.* 3, to forget

dēdĭtĭcĭus, ii *m*, prisoner-of-war

dēdĭtĭo, ōnis *f*, surrender

dēdĭtus, a, um *adj*, addicted to

dēdo, dēdĭdi, dĭtum *v.t.* 3, to give up, surrender, devote

dēdŏcĕo *v.t.* 2, to teach one not to …

dēdŏlĕo *v.i.* 2, to stop grieving

dēdūco, xi, ctum *v.t.* 3, to bring, lead down, withdraw, conduct, escort, mislead, subtract, launch

dēductĭo, ōnis *f*, diversion, transplanting, inference

dēductus, a, um *adj*, fine-spun

dēerro *v.i.* 1, to go astray

dēfătĭgātĭo, ōnis *f*, exhaustion

dēfătĭgo *v.t.* 1, to exhaust

dēfectĭo, ōnis *f*, rebellion, failure, eclipse

dēfectus, ūs *m*, rebellion, failure, eclipse

dēfectus, a, um *adj*, worn out

dēfendo, di, sum *v.t.* 3, to repel, defend, support

dēfensĭo, ōnis *f*, defence

dēfensor, ōris *m*, protector

dēfĕro, ferre, tŭli, lātum *v.t, irreg*, to bring down or away, convey, refer, announce, indict, offer

dēfervesco, fervi *v.i.* 3, to cool down

dēfessus, a, um *adj*, weary

dēfĕtiscor, fessus *v.i.* 3, *dep*, to grow tired

dēfĭcĭo, fēci, fectum *v.i.t.* 3, to fail, disappear, revolt; desert

dēfīgo, xi, xum *v.t.* 3, to fasten down, astound

dēfingo, nxi *v.t.* 3, to shape

dēfīnĭo *v.t.* 4, to mark off, restrict, define

dēfīnītĭo, ōnis *f*, definition

dēfīnītus, a, um *adj, adv, ē*, precise

dēfixus, a, um *adj*, fixed

dēflàgrātĭo, ōnis *f*, destruction by fire

dēflàgro *v.i.* 1, to burn out

dēflecto, xi, xum *v.i.t.* 3, to swerve; divert

dēflĕo, ēvi, ētum *v.t.* 2, to deplore

dēflōresco, rŭi *v.i.* 3, to wither

dēflŭo, xi, xum *v.i.* 3, to flow down, vanish

dēfŏdĭo, fōdi, ssum *v.t.* 3, to dig deep, bury

dēfŏre *fut. infinitive* (**dēsum**)

dēformis, e *adj,* deformed, ugly

dēformĭtas, ātis *f,* ugliness

dēformo *v.t.* 1, to shape

dēformo, *v.t.* 1, to disfigure

dēfossus, a, um *adj,* buried

dēfraudo *v.t.* 1, to cheat

dēfrĭco, cŭi, ctum *v.t.* 1, to rub hard

dēfringo, frēgi, fractum *v.t.* 3, to break up, break off

dēfrŭtum, i *n,* syrup

dēfŭgĭo, fūgi *v.i.t.* 3, to escape; avoid

dēfunctus, a, um *adj,* having finished, deceased

dēfundo, fūdi, fūsum *v.t.* 3, to pour out

dēfungor, functus *v.* 3, *dep, with abl,* to bring to an end

dēgĕner, ĕris *adj,* unworthy of one's birth, ignoble

dēgenĕro *v.i.t.* 1, to deteriorate; impair

dēgo, dēgi *v.i.t.* 3, to live; spend

dēgrandĭnat *v. impers,* it is hailing, ceasing to hail

dēgrăvo, *v.t.* 1, to weigh down

dēgrĕdĭor, gressus *v.i.* 3, *dep,* to step down, dismount

dēgusto *v.t.* 1, to taste, graze

dēhinc *adv,* from here, hence, next, afterwards

dēhisco, hīvi *v.i.* 3, to split open, gape

dēhŏnesto *v.t.* 1, to disgrace

dēhortor *v.t.* 1, *dep,* to dissuade

dēĭcĭo, iēci, iectum *v.t.* 3, to throw down, drive out, lower

dēiectus, a, um *adj,* downcast

dēiectus, ūs *m,* descent, felling

dēin *adv,* from there, after that, afterwards

dĕindĕ *adv,* from there, after that, afterwards

dĕinceps *adv,* in succession

dēlābor, lapsus *v.i.* 3, *dep,* to fall, sink, glide down

dēlasso *v.t.* 1, to tire out

dēlātĭo, ōnis *f,* accusation

dēlātor, ōris *m,* informer

dēlectābĭlis, e *adj,* delightful

dēlectātĭo, ōnis *f,* delight, pleasure

dēlecto *v.t.* 1, to allure, charm

dēlectus, a, um *adj,* chosen

dēlectus, ūs *m,* choice, selection, levy

dēlectum hăbēre to hold a levy

dēlēgo *v.t.* 1, to dispach, assign, attribute

dēlēnīmentum, i *n,* allurement

dēlēnĭo *v.t.* 4, to soothe, charm

dēlĕo, lēvi, lētum *v.t.* 2, to destroy, finish

dēlībĕrātĭo, ōnis *f,* careful thought

dēlībĕrātus, a, um *adj,* settled

dēlībĕro *v.t.* 1, to consider, consult, resolve

dēlībo *v.t.* 1, to taste, pluck, detract from

dēlībūtus, a, um *adj,* smeared

dēlĭcātus, a, um *adj, adv,* **e,** charming, luxurious

dēlĭcĭae, ārum *f.pl,* pleasure, luxury, sweetheart, pet

dēlictum, i *n,* crime, offence

dēlĭgo, lēgi, lectum *v.t.* 3, to pick, choose, gather

dēlĭgo *v.t.* 1, to tie down

dēlinquo, līqui, lictum *v.i.* 3, to fail, offend

dēlīrātĭo, ōnis *f,* silliness

dēlīrĭum, ii *n,* delirium

dēlīro *v.i.* 1, to be out of one's mind

dēlīrus, a, um *adj,* crazy

dēlĭtesco, tŭi *v.i.* 3, to lurk

delphīnus, i *m,* dolphin

dēlūbrum, i *n,* sanctuary

dēlūdo, si, sum *v.t.* 3, to mock

dēmando *v.t.* 1, to entrust

dēmens, ntis *adj, adv,* **nter,** out of one's mind

dēmensum, i *n,* ration

dēmentĭa, ae *f,* insanity

dēmĕrĕo *v.t.* 2, to deserve, oblige

dēmergo, si, sum *v.t.* 3, to immerse, sink

dēmētĭor, mensus *v.t.* 4, *dep,* to measure off

dēmēto, messŭi, ssum *v.t.* 3, to mow, reap, gather

dēmigro *v.i.* 1, to emigrate
dēmĭnŭo, ŭi, ūtum *v.t.* 3, to lessen, infringe
dēmĭnūtĭo, ōnis *f,* decrease
dēmīror *v.t.* 1, *dep,* to wonder
dēmissĭo, ōnis *f,* abasement
dēmissus, a, um *adj, adv,* ē, lowlying, drooping, downcast, shy
dēmitto, mīsi, ssum *v.t.* 3, to send down, lower, descend, enter upon, lose heart
dēmo, mpsi, mptum *v.t.* 3, to take away, remove
dēmōlĭor *v.t.* 4, *dep,* to pull down, destroy
dēmonstrātĭo, ōnis *f,* indication
dēmonstro *v.t.* 1, to point out
dēmŏrĭor, mortŭus *v.i.* 3, *dep,* to die
dēmŏror *v.i.t.* 1, *dep,* to loiter; restrain
dēmŏvĕo, mōvi, mōtum *v.t.* 2, to remove, put aside
dēmum *adv,* at last, not until then, only
dēmūto *v.i.t.* 1, to change
dēnārĭus, ii *m,* small Roman silver coin
dēnăto *v.i.* 1, to swim down
dēnĕgo *v.t.* 1, to deny completely
dēni, ae, a, *adj,* ten each, ten
dēnīque *adv,* and then, at last, in short
dēnōmĭno *v.t.* 1, to name
dēnormo *v.t.* 1, to disfigure
dēnŏto *v.t.* 1, to mark, point out
dens, ntis *m,* tooth, prong
denso *v.t.* 1, to thicken, close up
densus, a, um *adj,* thick, frequent
dentālĭa, ĭum *n.pl,* plough-beam
dentātus, a, um *adj,* with teeth
dentĭfrĭcĭum, ii *n,* tooth-powder
dentĭo *v.i.* 4, to teethe
dentītĭo, ōnis *f,* teething
dentiscalpĭum, ii *n,* toothpick
dēnūbo, psi, ptum *v.i.* 3, to marry
dēnūdo *v.t.* 1, to lay bare
dēnuntĭātĭo, ōnis *f,* declaration
dēnuntĭo *v.t.* 1, to announce, command, warn
dēnŭo *adv,* anew, again
dĕorsum *adv,* downwards
dēpăciscor see **dēpĕciscor**

dēpasco, pāvi, pastum *v.t.* 3, to feed on, consume
dēpĕciscor, pectus (pactus) *v.t.* 3, *dep,* to bargin for
dēpĕcŭlor *v.t.* 1, *dep,* to plunder
dēpello, pŭli, pulsum *v.t.* 3, to drive away, dissuade
dēpendĕo *v.i.* 2, to hang down, depend on
dēpendo, di, sum *v.t.* 3, to spend, pay
dēperdo, dĭdi, dĭtum *v.t.* 3, to destroy, lose
dēpĕrĕo *v.i.* 4, to perish completely, die with love for
dēpingo, pinxi, pictum *v.t.* 3, to paint, portray, sketch
dēplōro *v.i.t.* 1, to lament; deplore
dēpōno, pŏsŭi, pŏsĭtum *v.t.* 3, to put aside, entrust, bet, get rid of
dēpŏpŭlātĭo, ōnis *f,* pillaging
dēpŏpŭlor *v.t.* 1, *dep,* to plunder
dēporto *v.t.* 1, to carry down, carry away, banish, earn
dēposco, pŏposci *v.t.* 3, to demand, challenge
dēpŏsĭtum, i *n,* deposit, trust
dēprāvātĭo, ōnis *f,* corruption
dēprāvo *v.t.* 1, to pervert, corrupt
dēprĕcātĭo, ōnis *f,* pleading, intercession
dēprĕcātor, ōris *m,* pleader
dēprĕcor *v.t.* 1, *dep,* to avert by prayer, beseech, plead for
dēprĕhendo, di, sum *v.t.* 3, to catch, overtake, discover
dēpressus, a, um *adj,* low-lying
dēprĭmo, pressi, pressum *v.t.* 3, to press down, sink, suppress
dēproelĭor *v.i.* 1, *dep,* to battle fiercely
dēprōmo, mpsi, mptum *v.t.* 3, to fetch out
dēprŏpĕro *v.i.t.* 1, to hasten; prepare hastily
dēpugno *v.i.* 1, to fight it out
dēpulsĭo, ōnis *f,* warding off
dēpūto *v.t.* 1, to prune
dērēlinquo, līqui, lictum *v.t.* 3, to abandon completely
dērīdĕo, si, sum *v.t.* 2, to mock
dērĭgesco, gŭi *v.i.* 3, to stiffen
dērĭpĭo, rĭpŭi, reptum *v.t.* 3, to tear off, pull down

dērīsor, ōris *m*, scoffer
dērīvātǐo, ōnis *f*, turning off
dērīvo *v.t.* 1, to divert water
dērŏgo *v.t.* 1, to remove, restrict
dērōsus, a, um *adj*, nibbled
dēruptus, a, um *adj*, broken, steep
dēsaevǐo *v.i.* 4, to rage
dēscendo, di, sum *v.i.* 3, to go
down, come down, go into
battle, penetrate, resort to
dēscensus, ūs *m*, descent
dēscisco, īvi, ītum *v.i.* 3, to revolt,
desert, degenerate
dēscrībo, psi, ptum *v.t.* 3, to
transcribe, describe, define,
arrange
dēscrīpta, ōrum *n.pl*, records
dēscrīptǐo, ōnis *f*, sketch,
description, arrangement
dēsěco, cǔi, ctum *v.t.* 1, to cut off
dēsěro, rǔi, rtum *v.t.* 3, to
abandon
dēserta, ōrum *n.pl*, desert
dēsertor, ōris *m*, deserter
dēsertus, a, um *adj*, abandoned
dēservǐo *v.i.* 4, to serve
wholeheartedly
dēses, ǐdis *adj*, indolent
dēsǐděo, sēdi *v.i.* 2, to sit idle
dēsīděrǐum, ii *n*, longing, grief,
request
dēsīděro *v.t.* 1, to miss, crave for
dēsǐdǐa, ae *f*, idleness
dēsǐdǐōsus, a, um *adj*, lazy
dēsīdo, sēdi *v.i.* 3, to sink down
dēsignātǐo, ōnis *f*, description,
arrangement
dēsignātor, ōris *m*, master of
ceremonies, undertaker
dēsignātus, a, um *adj*, elect
dēsigno *v.t.* 1, to mark out,
indicate, appoint
dēsǐlǐo, sǐlǔi, sultum *v.i.* 4, to jump
down
dēsǐno, sǐi, ǐtum *v.i.t.* 3, to cease;
put an end to
dēsǐpǐo *v.i.* 3, to be foolish
dēsisto, stǐti, stǐtum *v.i.* 3, to leave
off, halt
dēsōlātus, a, um *adj*, forsaken
dēsōlo *v.t.* 1, to abandon
dēspecto *v.t.* 1, to look down on
dēspectus, ūs *m*, view down on

dēspectus, a, um *adj*, despicable
dēspērātǐo, ōnis *f*, hopelessness
dēspērātus, a, um *adj*, past hope
dēspēro *v.i.t.* 3, to despair; give up
as lost
dēspǐcǐo, exi, ctum *v.i.t.* 3, to look
down; despise
dēspǒlǐo *v.t.* 1, to plunder
dēsponděo, di, nsum *v.t.* 2, to
promise (in marriage)
dēspūmo *v.t.* 1, to skim off
dēspǔo *v.i.t* 3, to spit; reject
dēstillo *v.i.* 1, to trickle, drip
dēstǐnātǐo, ōnis *f*, purpose
dēstǐnātum, i *n*, aim, intention
dēstǐnātus, a, um *adj*, fixed
dēstǐno *v.t.* 1, to secure, intend
dēstǐtǔo, ǔi, ūtum *v.t.* 3, to place,
desert
dēstǐtūtus, a, um *adj*, abandoned
dēstringo, nxi, ctum *v.t.* 3, to strip
off, unsheath, graze
dēstrǔo, xi, ctum *v.t.* 3, to
demolish
dēsǔesco, sǔēvi, sǔētum *v.i.t.* 3, to
become unused; cease to use
dēsǔētus, a, um *adj*, disused
dēsultor, ōris *m*, acrobat on
horseback
dēsum, děesse, dēfǔi *v.i*, to be
lacking, fail, desert
dēsūmo, mpsi, mptum *v.t.* 3, to
select
dēsǔpěr *adv*, from above
dēsurgo *v.i.* 3, to rise from
dētěgo, xi, ctum *v.t.* 3, to expose
dētentus, a, um *adj*, kept back
dētergěo, si, sum *v.t.* 2, to wipe
clean
dētěrǐor, ǐus *adj*, lower, worse
dētěrǐus *adv*, worse, less
dētermǐno *v.t.* 1, to fix limits
dētěro, trīvi, trītum *v.t.* 3, to rub or
wear away, impair
dēterrěo *v.t.* 2, to discourage
dētestābǐlis, e *adj*, detestable
dētestātǐo, ōnis *f*, cursing
dētestor *v.t.* 1, *dep*, to curse,
loathe, ward off
dētexo, xǔi, xtum *v.t.* 3, to weave,
finish
dētǐněo, tǐnǔi, tentum *v.t.* 2, to
keep back, delay, lengthen

dētŏno, ŭi *v.i.* 1, to thunder, cease thundering
dētorquĕo, si, tum *v.t.* 2, to turn aside, distort
dētrăho, xi, ctum *v.t.* 3, to pull down, remove, deprecate
dētrecto *v.t.* 1, to reject, detract from
dētrīmentum, i *n*, loss, damage, defeat
dētrūdo, si, sum *v.t.* 3, to push down, dislodge
dētrunco *v.t.* 1, to lop off
dēturbo *v.t.* 1, to throw down
dēūro, ussi, ustum *v.t.* 3, to burn
dĕus, i *m*, god

dēvinco, vīci, ctum *v.t.* 3, to conquer completely
dēvinctus see dēvincĭo
dēvīto *v.t.* 1, to avoid
dēvĭus, a, um *adj*, out-of-the-way
dēvŏco *v.t.* 1, to call away
dēvŏlo, *v.i.*1, to fly down
dēvolvo, volvi, vŏlūtum *v.t.* 3, to roll down
dēvŏro *v.t.* 1, to gulp down
dēvōtĭo, ōnis *f*, consecration
dēvōtus, a, um *adj*, devoted
dēvŏvĕo, vōvi, vōtum *v.t.* 2, to dedicate, doom, devote
dexter, tĕra, tĕrum (tra, trum) *adj*, on the right, skilful, suitable

Insight

The following second declension nouns have minor irregularities in their declension: **deus** (= god) has nominative plural *dei* or *di*, genitive plural *deorum* or *deum*, ablative plural *deis* or *dis*; **vir** (= man) has genitive plural *virorum* or *virum*.

dēvasto *v.t.* 1, to devastate
dēvĕho, xi, ctum *v.t.* 3, to carry down, carry away
dēvĕnĭo, vēni, ventum *v.i.* 4, to come down, arrive at
dēversor *v.i.* 1, *dep,* to lodge
dēversor, ōris *m*, lodger
dēversōrĭum, ii *n*, inn
dēverto, ti, sum *v.i.t.* 3, to lodge, stay; turn aside
dēvexus, a, um *adj*, sloping down
dēvĭa, ōrum *n.pl*, lonely places
dēvincĭo, nxi, nctum *v.t.* 4, to tie up, endear

dextĕra (dextra), ae *f*, right hand
dextĕrĭtas, ātis *f*, dexterity
dextrorsum *adv*, on the right
di *pl.* of dĕus
dĭădēma, ătis *n*, crown, diadem
dĭăgōnālis, e *adj*, diagonal
dĭălectĭcus, a, um *adj*, of debate
dĭălŏgus, i *m*, conversation
dĭārĭa, ōrum *n.pl*, rations
dīca, ae *f*, lawsuit
dīcācĭtas, ātis *f*, wit
dīcax, ācis *adj*, witty
dĭcĭo, ōnis *f*, dominion, power
dīco *v.t.* 1, to dedicate, devote

Insight

The **ablative absolute** is a Latin construction where both noun and verb are in the ablative case. In addition to this, the verb is always a participle. It is independent of the structure of the rest of the sentence (*Caesar, his dictis,* ... = Caesar, after saying these things...).

dīco, xi, ctum *v.t.* 3, to say, tell, appoint

dicta see **dictum**

dictāta, ōrum *n.pl*, written exercises

dictātĭo, ōnis *f*, dictation

dictātor, ōris *m*, dictator (Roman magistrate appointed in emergencies)

dictātūra, ae *f*, dictatorship

dictĭo, ōnis *f*, speaking, style

dictĭto *v.t.* 1, to repeat, dictate, compose

dicto *v.t.* 1, to declare, dictate

dictum, i *n*, saying, proverb, order

dictus, a, um *adj*, said, told

dīdo, dīdĭdi, dīdĭtum *v.t.* 3, to distribute

dīdūco, xi, ctum *v.t.* 3, to divide, scatter

dĭēs, dĭēī *m,f*, day

diffĕro, differre, distŭli, dīlātum *v.i.t, irreg*, to differ; scatter, publish, defer

differtus, a, um *adj*, crowded

diffibŭlo *v.t.* 1, to unbuckle

difficĭlis, e *adj, adv*, **ē, ĭter**, difficult, surly

difficultas, ātis *f*, difficulty, obstinacy

diffīdens, ntis *adj*, distrustful

diffīdentĭa, ae *f*, mistrust, despair

diffīdo, fīsus sum *v.i.* 3, *semi-dep, with dative*, to mistrust, despair

diffindo, fīdi, fīsum *v.t.* 3, to split, divide

diffingo *v.t.* 3, to re-shape

diffĭtĕor *v.t.* 2, *dep*, to deny

difflŭo *v.i.* 3, to flow away

diffŭgĭo, fūgi *v.i.* 3, to disperse

diffundo, fūdi, dūsum *v.t.* 3, to pour out, scatter

diffūsus, a, um *adj, adv*, **ē**, spread out, wide

dīgĕro, gessi, gestum *v.t.* 3, to separate, arrange, interpret

dīgesta, ōrum *n.pl*, digest of writings

dīgĭtus, i *m*, finger, toe, inch

dīglădĭor *v.i.* 1, *dep*, to fight fiercely

dignātĭo, ōnis *f*, reputation

dignĭtas, ātis *f*, worthiness, rank, authority

dignor *v.t.* 1, *dep*, to consider someone worthy

dignus, a, um *adj, adv* **ē**, *with abl*, worthy, suitable

dīgrĕdĭor, gressus *v.i.* 3, *dep*, to go away

dīgressĭo, ōnis *f*, digression

dīgressus, ūs *m*, departure

dĭiūdĭco *v.t.* 1, to decide

diiun... see **disiun...**

dīlābor, lapsus *v.i.* 3, *dep*, to dissolve, scatter, perish

dīlăcĕro *v.t.* 1, to tear apart, or to pieces

dīlănĭo *v.t.* 1, to tear apart, or to pieces

dīlātĭo, ōnis *f*, delay

dīlāto *v.t.* 1, to enlarge

dīlātor, ōris *m*, delayer

dīlātus, a, um *adj*, scattered

dīlectus, a, um *adj*, beloved

dīlĭgens, ntis *adj, adv*, **nter**, scrupulous, thrifty

dīlĭgentĭa, ae *f*, care, economy

dīlĭgo, lexi, lectum *v.t.* 3, to value highly

dīlūcesco, luxi *v.i.* 3, to grow light, dawn

dīlūcĭdus, a, um *adj*, clear

dīlūcŭlum, i *n*, dawn

dīlŭo, ŭi, ūtum *v.t.* 3, to wash away, dilute, drench, weaken

dīlūtum, i *n*, solution

dīlŭvĭes, ēi *f* (...ĭum, ii, *n*), flood, destruction

dīmētĭor, mensus *v.t.* 4, *dep*, to measure out

dīmĭcātĭo, ōnis *f*, struggle

dīmĭco, *v.i.* 1, to struggle

dīmĭdĭātus, a, um *adj*, halved

dīmĭdĭum, ii *n*, a half

dīmĭdĭus, a, um *adj*, half

dīmissĭo, ōnis *f*, sending out

dīmitto, mīsi, missum *v.t.* 3, to send away, break up, disband, throw away, give up

dīmŏvĕo, mōvi, mōtum *v.t.* 2, to divide, part, remove

dīnŭmĕro *v.t.* 1, to count up

diplōma, ātis *n*, official letter of recommendation

dīra, ōrum *n.pl,* curses

dīrectus, a, um *adj, adv,* ē, straight, level

dīreptĭo, ōnis *f,* plundering

dīreptor, ōris *m,* plunderer

dīrĭgo, rexi, ctum *v.t.* 3, to put in a straight line, arrange

dīrĭmo, ēmi, emptum *v.t.* 3, to part, divide, interrupt

dīrĭpĭo, ŭi, reptum *v.t.* 3, to tear apart, plunder

dīrumpo, rŭpi, ptum *v.t.* 3, to break in pieces, sever

dīrŭo, ŭi, ŭtum *v.t.* 3, to destroy

dīrus, a, um *adj,* fearful, ill-omened

discēdo, cessi, cessum *v.i.* 3, to depart, abandon, gape, deviate

disceptātĭo, ōnis *f,* discussion

discepto *v.t.* 1, to debate

discerno, crēvi, tum *v.t.* 3, to separate, distinguish between

discerpo, psi, ptum *v.t.* 3, to tear in pieces

discessus, ūs *m,* departure

discĭdĭum, ii *n,* separation

discinctus, a, um *adj,* casually dressed, slovenly

discindo, cĭdi, cissum *v.t.* 3, to cut to pieces, divide

discingo, nxi, nctum *v.t.* 3, to take off or undo (clothing)

disciplīna, ae *f,* teaching, knowledge, system, tactics

discĭpŭlus, i *m,* pupil

disclūdo, si, sum *v.t.* 3, to keep apart, separate

disco, dĭdĭci *v.t.* 3,to learn

discŏlor, ōris *adj,* of different colours

discordĭa, ae *f,* disagreement

discordo *v.i.* 1, to differ

discors, dis *adj,* disagreeing

discrĕpantĭa, ae *f,* discrepancy

discrĕpo, ŭi *v.i.* 1, to differ

discrībo, scripsi, ptum *v.t.* 3, to distribute

discrīmen, ĭnis *n,* division, distinction, crisis, danger

discrīmĭno *v.t.* 1, to divide

discrŭcĭo *v.t.* 1, to torture

discumbo, cŭbŭi, cŭbĭtum *v.i.* 3, to recline at table

discurro, curri, cursum *v.i.* 3, to run about

discursus, ūs *m,* bustle, activity

discus, i *m,* discus, quoit

discŭtĭo, cussi, ssum *v.t.* 3, to shatter, disperse

dīsertus, a, um *adj, adv,* ē, fluent, clear

dīsĭcĭlo, īēci, ctum *v.t.* 3, to scatter, destroy

disiunctus, a, um *adj, adv,* ē, distant, abrupt

disiungo, nxi, nctum *v.t.* 3, to separate, unyoke

dispar, ăris *adj,* unlike, unequal

dispăro *v.t.* 1, to divide

dispello, pŭli, pulsum *v.t.* 3, to drive away, scatter

dispendĭum, ii *n,* expense, cost

dispenso *v.t.* 1, to pay out, distribute, manage

disperdo, dĭdi, dĭtum *v.t.* 3, to spoil, ruin

dispĕrĕo *v.i.* 4, to perish

dispergo, si, sum *v.t.* 3, to scatter about

dispertĭo *v.t.* 4, to distribute

dispĭcĭo, spexi, ctum *v.i.t.* 3, to look around; discern, reflect on

displĭcĕo *v.i.* 2, to displease

dispōno, pŏsŭi, pŏsĭtum *v.t.* 3, to arrange, dispose

dispŏsĭtus, a, um *adj,* arranged

dispungo, xi, ctum *v.t.* 3, to check

dispŭtātĭo, ōnis *f,* debate, dispute

dispŭtātor, ōris *m,* debater

dispŭto *v.i.t* 1, theorize; examine, discuss

dissēmĭno *v.t.* 1, to spread about

dissensĭo, ōnis *f,* disagreement

dissentĭo, si, sum *v.i.* 4, to disagree, differ

dissĕrēnat *v.impers.* 1, to be clear

dissĕro, rŭi, rtum *v.t.* 3, to discuss, argue

dissĭdĕo, ēdi, essum *v.i.* 2, to differ, disagree

dissĭlĭo, ŭi *v.i.* 4 to leap apart, split

dissĭmĭlis, e *adj, adv,* ĭter, unlike, different

dissĭmĭlĭtūdo, ĭnis *f,* unlikeness

dissĭmŭlātus, a, um *adj,* disguised

dissĭmŭlo *v.t.* 1, to disguise, hide

dissĭpātĭo, ōnis *f,* scattering, destruction

dissĭpo *v.t.* 1, to scatter, rout

dissŏcĭābĭlis, e *adj*, dividing

dissŏcĭo *v.t.* 1, to estrange

dissŏlūtĭo, ōnis *f*, break-up, destruction

dissŏlūtus, a, um *adj*, loose

dissolvo, solvi, sŏlūtum *v.t.* 3, to unloose, separate, pay, annul, destroy

dissŏnus, a, um *adj*, discordant

dissuādĕo, si, sum *v.t.* 2, to advise against

dissulto *v.i.* 1, to burst apart

distans, ntis *adj*, distant

distendo, di, tum *v.t.* 3, to stretch out, distend, torture

distentus, a, um *adj*, full

distentus, a, um *adj*, busy

distinctĭo, ōnis *f*, difference

distinctus, a, um *adj, adv,* ē, separate, clear, adorned

distĭnĕo, tĭnŭi, tentum *v.t.* 2, to keep apart, perplex, hinder

distinguo, nxi, nctum *v.t.* 3, to separate, discriminate, adorn

disto *v.i.*1, to be distant, differ

distorquĕo, rsi, rtum *v.t.* 2, to twist, distort, torture

distortĭo, ōnis *f*, distortion

distortus, a, um *adj*, deformed

distractĭo, ōnis *f*, division

distractus, a, um *adj*, bewildered

distrăho, xi, ctum *v.t.* 3, to pull apart, divide, distract, perplex

distrĭbŭo, ŭi, ūtum *v.t.* 3, to distribute

distrĭbūtē *adv*, methodically

distrĭbūtĭo, ōnis *f*, distribution

districtus, a, um *adj*, busy, strict

distringo, nxi, ctum *v.t.* 3, to stretch tight, distract the attention

disturbo *v.t.* 1, to disturb, demolish, frustrate

dīto *v.t.* 1, to enrich

dĭū *adj*, a long time

dĭurnus, a, um *adj*, daily

dĭurna ōrum *n.pl*, records

dĭūtĭnus, a, um *adj*, long-lasting

dĭūtĭus *comp. adv*, longer

dĭūturnĭtas, ātis *f*, long duration

dĭūturnus, a, um *adj, adv,* ē, long-lasting

dīva, ae *f*, goddess

dīvello, velli, vulsum *v.t.* 3, to tear to pieces, destroy

dīvendo, (*no perfect*), itum *v.t.* 3, to retail

dīverbĕro *v.t.* 1, to cut

dīversĭtas, ātis *f*, disagreement

dīversus, a, um *adj, adv,* ē, opposite, contrary, hostile, separate, different

dīverto, ti, sum *v.i.* 3, to diverge

dīves, ĭtis *adj*, rich

dīvĭdo, vīsi, sum *v.t.* 3, to separate, distribute, destroy

dīvĭdŭus, a, um *adj*, divisible

dīvīnĭtas, ātis *f*, divinity

dīvīnĭtus *adv*, providentially

dīvīno *v.t.* 1, to prophesy

dīvīnus, a, um *adj, adv,* ē, divine, prophetic, superhuman

dīvīnus, i *m*, prophet

dīvīsĭo, ōnis *f*, division

dīvīsor, ōris *m*, distributor of bribes to electors

dīvĭtĭae, ārum *f.pl*, wealth

dīvortĭum, ii *n*, separation

dīvulgo *v.t.* 1, to make known

dīvum, i *n*, sky

dīvus, a, um *adj*, divine

dīvus, i *m* (a, ae *f*), god, (goddess)

do, dĕdi, dătum *v.t.* 1, to give

dŏcĕo, ŭi, doctum *v.t.* 2, to teach, inform

dŏcĭlis, e *adj*, easily taught

doctor, ōris *m*, teacher

doctrīna, ae *f*, teaching, education, learning

doctus, a, um *adj, adv,* ē, learned, skilled

dŏcŭmentum, i *n*, lesson, example

dōdrans, ntis *m*, three quarters

dogma, ătis *n*, doctrine, dogma

dŏlābra, ae *f*, pickaxe

dŏlĕo *v.i.t.* 2, to suffer pain; grieve, deplore

dōlĭum, ii *n*, large jar

dŏlo *v.t.* 1, to chop, beat

dŏlor, ōris *m*, pain, sorrow

dŏlōsus, a, um *adj*, deceitful

dŏlus, i *m*, fraud, trick

dŏmābĭlis, e *adj*, tamable

dŏmestĭcus, a, um *adj*, of the home

dŏmestĭci

dŏmestĭci, ōrum *m.pl*, family, servants, escort
dŏmi *loc*, at home

dōtātus, a, um *adj*, endowed
dōto *v.t.* 1, to endow

dŏmĭcĭlĭum, ii *n*, dwelling place
dŏmĭna, ae *f*, mistress, lady
dŏmĭnans, ntis *adj*, ruling
dŏmĭnātĭo, ōnis *f*, absolute rule
dŏmĭnātus, ūs *m*, absolute rule
dŏmĭnĭum, ii *n*, banquet, property-ownership
dŏmĭnor *v.i.* 1, *dep*, to reign
dŏmĭnus, i *m*, master, owner

drachma, ae *f*, small Greek silver coin
drăco, ōnis *m*, water snake
drŏmas, ădis *m*, dromedary
drўas, ădis *f*, wood nymph
dŭbĭē *adv*, doubtfully
dŭbĭtātĭo, ōnis *f*, doubt, uncertainity
dŭbĭto *v.i.t.* 1, to hesitate; doubt

dŏmĭto *v.t.* 1, to tame
dŏmĭtor, ōris *m*, tamer
dŏmĭtus, a, um *adj*, tamed
dŏmo, ŭi, ĭtum *v.t.* 1, to tame, conquer
dŏmus, ūs *f*, house, home
dōnārĭum, ii *n*, altar, sanctuary
dōnātĭo, ōnis *f*, donation
dōnātus, a, um *adj*, presented
dōnĕc *conj*, while, until
dōno *v.t.* 1, to present, remit
dōnum, i *n*, gift, present
dorcas, ădis *m*, gazelle
dormĭo *v.i.* 4, to sleep
dormĭto *v.i.* 1, to fall asleep
dorsum, i *n*, the back, ridge, ledge
dōs, dōtis *f*, dowry
dōtālis, e *adj*, of a dowry

dŭbīum, ii *n*, doubt
dŭbĭus, a, um *adj*, doubtful, dangerous
dŭcēni, ae, a *adj*, two hundred each
dŭcenti, ae, a *adj*, two hundred
dūco, xi, ctum *v.t.* 3, to lead, marry, construct, receive, prolong, consider
ductĭlis, e *adj*, moveable, malleable
ductor, ōris *m*, leader
ductus, ūs *m*, bringing, leadership
dūdum *adv*, some time ago, formerly
dulcē *adv*, sweetly
dulcēdo, ĭnis *f*, sweetness, charm
dulcĭtūdo, ĭnis *f*, sweetness, charm

dulcis, e *adj, adv,* **ĭter,** sweet, pleasant, dear

dum *conj,* while, until, provided that

dūmētum, i *n,* thicket

dummŏdo *adv,* as long as

dūmōsus, a, um *adj,* bushy

dūmus, i *m,* bramble

dumtaxat *adv,* in so far as, merely, at least

dŭŏ, ae, ŏ *adj,* two

dŭŏdĕcĭes *adv,* twelve times

dŭŏdĕcim *adj,* twelve

dŭŏdĕcĭmus, a, um *adj,* twelfth

dŭŏdēni, ae, a *adj,* twelve each

dŭŏdēvīcensĭmus, a, um *adj,* eighteenth

dŭŏdēvīginti *adj,* eighteen

dŭŏvĭri, ōrum *m.pl,* board or commission of two men

dùplex, ĭcis *adj, adv,* **ĭter,** double, deceitful

dùplīco *v.t.* 1, to double

dùplus, a, um *adj,* double

dūra, ōrum *n.pl,* hardship

dūrābĭlis, e *adj,* durable

dūrātus, a, um *adj,* hardened

dūrē *adv,* roughly

dūresco, rŭi *v.i.* 3, to harden

dūrītĭa, ae *f,* hardness, strictness, austerity

dūro *v.i.t.* 1, to be hard, endure; harden

dūrus, a, um *adj, adv,* **ē, ĭter,** hard, rough, harsh, stern

dux, dŭcis *m,* leader, commander

dȳnastes, ae *m,* chieftain

dȳsentĕrĭa, ae *f,* dysentery

dyspnoea, ae *f,* asthma

E

ē *prep. with abl,* out of, from, since

ĕa see **is**

ĕādem see **idem**

ĕātĕnus *adv,* so far

ĕvĕnus, i *f,* ebony (tree)

ēbĭbo, bi, bĭtum *v.t.* 3, to drink up, absorb, squander

ēblandĭor *v.t.* 4, *dep,* to obtain by flattery

ēbrĭĕtas, ātis *f,* drunkenness

ēbrĭōsus, a, um *adj,* addicted to drink

ēbrĭus, a, um *adj,* drunk

ēbullĭo *v.t.* 4, to boast about

ĕbŭlum, i *n,* dwarf elder

ĕbŭr, ŏris *n,* ivory

ĕburnĕus, a, ūm *adj,* of ivory

ecce *demonstrative adv,* see!

ĕchīnus, i *m,* hedgehog, sea urchin, rinsing bowl

ēchō, ūs *f,* echo

ecquando *interr. adv,* at any time?

ecqui, ae, od *interr. pron, adj,* any? anyone?

ecquis, id *interr. pron,* anyone? anything?

ĕdācĭtas, ātis *f,* gluttony

ĕdax, ācis *adj,* greedy

ēdentŭlus, a, um *adj,* toothless

ēdīco, xi, ctum *v.t.* 3, to publish, declare

ēdictum, i *n,* proclamation

ēdisco, dĭdĭci *v.t.* 3, to learn by heart, study

ēdissĕro, rŭi, rtum *v.t.* 3, to explain in full

ēdītĭo, ōnis *f,* bringing out, publishing

ēdītus, a, um *adj,* high, raised, brought out

ĕdo, ēdi, ēsum *v.t.* 3, to eat

ēdo, dĭdi, dĭtum *v.t.* 3, to produce, bring out, declare, cause, erect

ēdŏcĕo, cŭi, ctum *v.t.* 2, to teach thoroughly

ēdŏmo, ŭi, ĭtum *v.t.* 1, to subdue

ēdŭcātĭo, ōnis *f,* bringing up, education

ēdūco, xi, ctum *v.t.* 3, to lead or bring out, summon, educate, erect

ēdŭco *v.t.* 1, to bring up (child)

ĕdūlis, e *adj,* eatable

effātus, a, um *adj,* established

effectĭo, ōnis *f,* doing, performing

effectus, a, um *adj,* completed

effectus, ūs *m,* accomplishment

effēmĭnātus, a, um *adj,* effeminate

effĕrātus, a, um *adj,* wild

effĕro, efferre, extŭli, ēlātum *v.t, irreg,* to bring out, bury, declare, raise; *in passive or with* **se,** to be haughty

effĕro *v.t.* 1, to brutalize

effĕrus, a, um *adj,* savage

effervesco, ferbŭi *v.i.* 3, to boil up, rage

effervo *v.i.* 3, to boil over
effētus, a, um *adj*, exhausted
efficax, ācis *adj*, efficient
efficiens, ntis *adj, adv,* **nter,** efficient
efficio, fēci, fectum *v.t.* 3, to bring about, complete, produce
effictus, a, um *adj*, fashioned
effiges, ēi *f*, portrait, copy
effingo, nxi, ctum *v.t.* 3, to shape, fashion, portray
efflāgito *v.t.* 1, to request urgently
efflo *v.t.* 1, to breathe out
efflōresco, rŭi *v.i.* 3, to bloom
efflŭo, xi *v.i.* 3, to flow out, vanish
effŏdĭo, fōdi, fossum *v.t.* 3, to dig out, dig up
effor *v.t.* 1, *dep*, to speak out
effrēnātus, a, um *adj*, unruly
effrēnus, a, um *adj*, unrestrained
effringo, frēgi, fractum *v.t.* 3, to break open, smash
effŭgĭo, fūgi *v.i.t.* 3, to escape; flee from, avoid
effŭgĭum, ii *n*, escape
effulgĕo, si *v.i.* 2, to gleam
effundo, fūdi, fūsum *v.t.* 3, to pour out, let loose, squander; *in passive or with reflexive,* to rush out
effūsĭo, ōnis *f*, outpouring, profusion
effūsus, a, um *adj, adv,* **ē,** poured out, spread out, wide, loosened
effūtĭo *v.t.* 4, to blurt out
ēgĕlĭdus, a, um *adj*, cool
ĕgens, ntis *adj*, in want of
ĕgēnus, a, um *adj*, in want of
ĕgĕo *v.i.* 2, *with abl*, to be in need of
ēgĕro, ssi, stum *v.t.* 3, to bring out
ĕgestas, ātis *f*, poverty
ĕgŏ *pers. pron*, I

ĕgŏmet *pron*, I myself
ēgrĕdĭor, gressus *v.i.t.* 3, *dep*, to go or come out; leave, exceed
ēgrĕgĭus, a, um *adj, adv,* **ē,** distinguished
ēgressus, ūs *m*, departure, passage
ēheu! alas!
ēiă! hey! I say!
ēiăcŭlor *v.t.* 1, *dep*, to shoot out
ēīcĭo, iēci, iectum *v.t.* 3, to drive out, expel, wreck; *with reflexive,* to rush out
ēiecto *v.t.* 1, to vomit
ēiūro *v.t.* 1, to reject on oath, abandon
ēius *genit. of* is, ea, id
ēiusmŏdi in such a manner
ēlābor, lapsus *v.i.* 3, *dep*, to slip away, escape
ēlăbōrātus, a, um *adj*, elaborate
ēlăbōro *v.i.t.* 1, to make an effort; take pains with
ēlanguesco, gŭi *v.i.* 3, to grow feeble
ēlātĭo, ōnis *f,* lifting up, passion
ēlātro *v.t.* 1, to bark loudly
ēlātus, a, um *adj*, raised, lofty
ēlectĭo, ōnis *f,* selection
ēlectrum, i *n,* amber
ēlectus, a, um *adj*, selected
ēlĕgans, ntis, *adj, adv,* **nter,** refined, tasteful
ēlĕgantĭa, ae *f,* refinement
ēlĕgi, ōrum *m.pl,* elegy
ēlĕgīa, ae *f,* elegy
ēlĕmentum, i *n,* element, first principle; *pl,* rudiments
ēlĕphantus, I *m,* elephant, ivory
ēlĕvo *v.t.* 1, to lift up, weaken, disparage
ēlĭcĭo, cŭi, cĭtum *v.t.* 3, to lure out, call out

Insight

The **dative** is the case of an indirect object. It also indicates the person to whose advantage/disadvantage something is done, the agent showing by whom something is done and possession with the verb 'to be' (*est mihi pecunia*). The main meanings are 'to', 'for', 'by' and 'from'. Several verbs are followed by the dative.

ēlīdo, si, sum *v.t.* 3, to knock or force out, shatter

ēlīgo, lēgi, ctum *v.t.* 3, to choose

ēlinguis, e *adj*, speechless

ēlixus, a, um *adj*, boiled

ellychnĭum, ii *n*, lampwick

ēlŏco *v.t.* 1, to let (a farm)

ēlŏcūtĭo, ōnis *f*, expression, elocution

ēlŏgĭum, ii *n*, saying, inscription

ēlŏquens, ntis *adj*, eloquent

ēlŏquentĭa, ae *f*, eloquence

ēlŏquor, ēlŏcūtus *v.t.* 3, *dep*, to speak out, declare

ēlūcĕo, xi *v.i.* 2, to shine out

ēluctor *v.i.t.* 1, *dep*, to struggle out; struggle out of

ēlūdo, si, sum *v.t.* 3, to evade, cheat, frustrate

ēlūgĕo, xi *v.t.* 2, to mourn for

ēlŭo, ŭi, ūtum *v.t.* 3, to wash off, clean

ēlūtus, a, um *adj*, insipid

ēlŭvĭes *(no genit)* *f*, inundation

ēlŭvĭo, ōnis *f*, inundation

ēmancĭpo *v.t.* 1, to set free, transfer, sell

ēmāno *v.i.* 1, to flow out, arise from

embŏlĭum ii *n*, interlude

ēmendātĭo, ōnis *f*, correction

ēmendātor, ōris *m*, corrector

ēmendātus, a, um *adj*, faultless

ēmendo *v.t.* 1, to correct

ēmentĭor *v.t.* 4, *dep*, to assert falsely

ēmercor *v.t.* 1, *dep*, to purchase

ēmĕrĕo *v.t.* 2, (ēmĕrĕor *v.t.* 2, *dep*), to deserve, earn, complete one's military service

ēmergo, si, sum *v.i.* 3, to come out, escape

ēmĕrĭtus, a, um *adj*, worn out

ēmētĭor, mensus *v.t.* 4, *dep*, to measure out, travel over

ēmĭco, ŭi, ātum *v.i.* 1, to spring out, appear

ēmĭgro *v.i.* 1, to depart

ēmĭnens, ntis *adj*, projecting, distinguished

ēmĭnentĭa, ae *f*, prominence

ēmĭnĕo *v.i.* 2, to stand out, excel

ēmĭnus *adv*, from or at a distance

ēmissārĭum, ii *n*, drain, vent

ēmissārĭus, ii *m*, spy

ēmissĭo, ōnis *f*, sending out, hurling (of missiles)

ēmitto, mīsi, ssum *v.t.* 3, to send out, produce, publish; with manū, to set free

ēmo, ēmi, emptum *v.t.* 3, to buy

ēmŏdŭlor *v.t.* 1, *dep*, to sing

ēmollĭo *v.t.* 4, to soften

ēmŏlŭmentum, i *n*, effort, profit

ēmŏrĭor, mortuus *v.i.* 3, *dep*, to die

ēmŏvĕo, mōvi, tum *v.t.* 2, to remove, shake

empīrĭcus, a, um *adj*, empirical

emplastrum, i *n*, plaster

empŏrĭum, ii *n*, market

emptĭo, ōnis *f*, purchase

emptor, ōris *m*, buyer

ēmunctus, a, um *adj*, clean, shrewd

ēmungo, nxi, nctum *v.t.* 3, to wipe the nose

ēmūnĭo *v.t.* 4, to fortify

ēn! see! come!

ēnarro *v.t.* 1, to expound

ēnascor, nātus *v.i.* 3, *dep*, to spring up, be born

ēnăto *v.i.* 1, to swim away

ēnectus, a, um *adj*, killed

ēnĕco, ŭi, ctum *v.t.* 1, to kill, exhaust

ēnervo *v.t.* 1, to weaken

ĕnim *conj*, for, indeed

ĕnimvēro *conj*, certainly

ēnīsus, a, um *adj*, strenuous

ēnĭtĕo *v.i.* 2, to shine out

ēnĭtesco, tŭi *v.i.* 3, to shine out

ēnītor, nīsus (nixus) *v.i.t.* 3, *dep*, to struggle upwards, climb, strive; give birth to, ascend

ēnixus, a, um *adj, adv*, ē, strenuous, earnest

ēno *v.i.* 1, to swim out or away

ēnōdātĭo, ōnis *f*, explanantion

ēnōdis, e *adj*, smooth, clear

ēnōdo *v.t.* 1, to elucidate

ēnormis, e *adj*, enormous, shapeless

ēnormĭtas, ātis *f*, shapelessness

ēnōto *v.t.* 1, to note down

ensĭger, ĕra, ĕrum *adj*, carrying a sword

ensis, is *m*, sword

ēnūclĕātus

ēnūclĕātus, a, um *adj, adv, ē,* pure, clear, simple
ēnŭmĕrātĭo, ōnis *f,* counting, recapitulation
ēnŭmĕro *v.t.* 1, to count, relate
ēnuntĭo *v.t.* 1, to disclose, declare
ĕo, īre, īvi (ii), ĭtum *v.i, irreg,* to go; *with* **pedibus,** to vote for

ĕquŭlĕus, i, *m,* colt, the rack
ĕquus, i *m,* horse
ĕra, ae *f,* lady of the house
ērādīco *v.t.* 1, to root out
ērādo, si, sum *v.t.* 3, to scrape out, abolish
ērectus, a, um *adj,* upright, noble, haughty, resolute

Insight

As well as English, Latin has some **irregular** verbs. Irregular verbs are those verbs that do not follow any of the set patterns. They are not in any of the four conjugations, and have their own individual forms. An example of irregular verb is *eo* (= I go).

ĕō *adv,* to that place, to such an extent, so long, besides
eo ... quo, *(with comparatives)* the more ... the more
ĕōdem *adv,* to the same place, to the same point or purpose
ĕōus, i *m,* **(a, um** *adj),* east
ĕphēbus, i *m,* a youth
ĕphippĭum, ii *n,* saddle
ĕphŏrus, i *m,* Spartan magistrate
ĕpĭcus, a, um *adj,* epic
ĕpiscŏpus, i *m,* bishop
ĕpĭgramma, ătis *n,* inscription
ĕpistŏla, ae *f,* letter
ĕpistŏmĭum, ii *n,* valve
ĕpĭtŏmē (ĕpĭtŏma), ēs *f,* abridgement
ĕpŏs *n,* epic poem
ĕpōto, pōtum *v.t.* 1, to drink up
ĕpŭlae, ārum *f.pl,* food, banquet
ĕpŭlor *v.i.t.* 1, *dep,* to banquet; eat
ĕqua, ae *f,* mare
ĕquārĭa, ae *f,* stud of horses
ĕques, ĭtis *m,* horseman, knight
ĕquester, tris, tre *adj,* of a horseman, of cavalry
ĕquĭdem *adv,* indeed, of course, for my part
ĕquīnus, a, um *adj,* of horses
ĕquĭtātĭo, ōnis *f,* riding on horseback
ĕquĭtātus, ūs *m,* cavalry
ĕquĭto *v.i.* 1, to ride

ērēpo, psi *v.i.t.* 3, to creep out; creep over
ergā *prep. with acc,* towards
ergastŭlum, i *n,* detention centre
ergō *adv,* therefore; *prep. following genit,* on account of
ērĭgo, rexi, rectum *v.t.* 3, to raise up, encourage
ĕrīlis, e *adj,* of the master, or mistress
ērĭpĭo, rĭpŭi, reptum *v.t.* 3, to snatch, take away; *with reflexive,* to escape
ērŏgātĭo, ōnis *f,* paying out
ērŏgo *v.t.* 1, to pay out, squander
errābundus, a, um *adj,* wandering
errātĭcus, a, um *adj,* wandering
errātĭcus, a, um *adj,* rambling
errātum, i *n,* mistake
erro *v.i.* 1, to stray, err
erro, ōnis *m,* wanderer
error, ōris *m,* straying, mistake
ĕrŭbesco, bŭi *v.i.* 1, to blush, feel ashamed
ērūca, ae *f,* caterpillar
ēructo *v.t.* 1, to belch, emit
ērŭdĭo *v.t.* 4, to polish, instruct
ērŭdītĭo, ōnis *f,* learning
ērŭdītus, a, um *adj, adv, ē,* learned, skilled
ērumpo, rūpi, ptum *v.i.t.* 1, to break out; burst
ērŭo, ŭi, ŭtum *v.t.* 3, to throw out, dig out, destroy, rescue

50

ēruptĭo, ōnis *f*, break out
ĕrus, i *m*, master of the house
ervum, i *n*, wild pea
esca, ae *f*, food, bait
ēscendo, di, sum *v.i.* 3, to climb
ēscensĭo, ōnis *f*, aascent
escŭlentus, a, um *adj*, eatable
esse see **sum**
essĕdārĭus, i *m*, chariot fighter
essĕdum, i *n*, war chariot
ēsŭrĭens, ntis *adj*, hungry
ēsŭrĭo *v.i.t.* 4, to be hungry; long for
ĕt *conj*, and, as

ēventus, ūs *m*, occurrence, result, fortune
ēverbĕro *v.t.* 1, to strike hard
ēverro, verri, versum *v.t.* 3, to sweep out
ēversĭo, ōnis *f*, destruction
ēversor, ōris *m*, destroyer
ēversus, a, um *adj*, overthrown
ēverto, ti, sum *v.t.* 3, to overthrow, ruin
ēvĭdens, ntis *adj*, apparent
ēvĭgĭlo *v.i.t.* 1, to wake up; keep awake, keep watch through
ēvincĭo, nxi, nctum *v.t.* 4, to bind round

Insight

There are several words in Latin that mean 'and': et, atque, ac, and -que joined to the second of two words; *et...et* means 'both...and'; *aut...aut* or *vel...vel* mean 'either...or'; *neque* means 'and not'; *neque...neque* or *nec...nec* mean 'neither...nor'.

ĕtĕnim *conj*, and indeed
ĕtĭam *conj*, also, even, still
ĕtĭamnum, ĕtĭamnunc *adv*, even then, till now
etsi *conj*, although, even if
eu! well done!
eurīpus, i *m*, canal
eurōus, a, um *adj*, eastern
eurus, i *m*, east wind
ēvādo, si, sum *v.i.t.* 3, to go out, escape; leave behind
ēvăgor *v.i.t.* 1, *dep*, to stray; overstep
ēvălesco, lŭi *v.i.* 3, to grow strong, to be able
ēvānesco, nŭi *v.i.* 3, to vanish
ēvānĭdus, a, um *adj*, vanishing
ēvasto *v.t.* 1, to devastate
ēvĕho, xi, ctum *v.t.* 3, to carry out; *in passive*, to ride or move out
ēvello, velli, vulsum *v.t.* 3, to tear out, eradicate
ēvĕnĭo, vēni, ventum *v.i.* 4, to come out, turn out, result
ēventum, i *n*, occurrence, result, fortune
ēventus, ūs *m*, occurrence, result, fortune

ēvinco, vīci, ctum *v.t.* 3, to conquer completely, succeed
ēviscĕro *v.t.* 1, to tear apart
ēvīto *v.t.* 1, to avoid
ēvŏcāti, ōrum *m.pl*, reservists
ēvŏco *v.t.* 1, to call out
ēvŏlo *v.i.* 1, to fly away
ēvolvo, vi, vŏlūtum *v.t.* 3, to unroll (and read a book), disclose
ēvŏmo, ŭi, ĭtum *v.t.* 3, to spit out, vomit
ēvulsĭo, ōnis *f*, pulling out
ex (ē) *prep. with abl*, out of, from, after, since, on account of, according to, made of
exăcerbo *v.t.* 1, to irritate
exactĭo, ōnis *f*, debt or tax collecting, expelling
exactor, ōris *m*, expeller, superintendent, tax collector
exactus, a, um *adj*, accurate
exăcŭo, ŭi, ūtum *v.t.* 3, to sharpen, stimulate
exadversum (...us) *adv and prep. with acc*, opposite
exaedĭfĭco *v.t.* 1, to construct
exaequo *v.t.* 1, to place equal
exaestŭo *v.i.* 1, to seethe
exaggĕro *v.i.* 1, to heap up

exăgĭto *v.t.* 1, to disturb
exalbesco, bŭi *v.i.* 3, to turn pale
exāmen, ĭnis *n*, crowd, swarm
exāmĭno *v.t.* 1, to weigh, test
exănĭmātĭo, ōnis *f*, terror
exănĭmātus, a, um *adj*, out of breath
exănĭmis, e *adj*, lifeless
exănĭmus, a, um *adj*, lifeless
exănĭmo *v.t.* 1, to deprive of breath, kill, terrify
exardesco, arsi, sum *v.i.* 3, to be inflamed
exāresco, rŭi *v.i.* 3, to dry up
exăro *v.t.* 1, to plough, write
exaspĕro *v.t.* 1, to roughen, provoke
exauctōro *v.t.* 1, to discharge honourably or dishonourably from army
exaudĭo *v.t.* 4, to hear, grant
excandesco, dŭi *v.i.* 3, to glow
excēdo, ssi, ssum *v.i.t.* 3, to depart, die; leave, exceed
excellens, ntis *adj, adv*, **nter**, distinguished, excellent
excello, cellŭi, lsum *v.i.* 3, to be eminent, excel
excelsus, a, um *adj*, distinguished
exceptĭo, ōnis *f*, restriction
excepto *v.t.* 1, to catch
excerno, crēvi, crētum *v.t.* 3, to separate
excerpo, psi, ptum *v.t.* 3, to select
excessus, ūs *m*, departure
excĭdĭum, ii *n*, destruction
excĭdo, cĭdi *v.i.* 3, to fall from, escape, disappear, slip the memory, fail in
excĭdo, cĭdi, cīsum *v.t.* 3, to cut down, destroy
excĭo *v.t.* 4, to call or bring out
excĭpĭo, cēpi, ceptum *v.t.* 3, to take out, make an exception, receive, capture, follow after, overhear, intercept

excītātus, a, um *adj*, roused, vigorous
excĭto *v.t.* 1, to rouse up, excite
exclāmātĭo, ōnis *f*, exclamation
exclāmo *v.i.t.* 1, to call out
exclūdo, si, sum *v.t.* 3, to shut out, drive out, remove, hinder, hatch
exclūsĭo, ōnis *f*, exclusion
excōgĭto *v.t.* 1, to think out
excŏlo, cŏlŭi, cultum *v.t.* 3, to cultivate, improve, refine
excŏquo, xi, ctum *v.t.* 3, to boil away, purify
excors, dis *adj*, stupid
excresco, crēvi, crētum *v.i.* 1, to grow up
excrētus, a, um *adj*, full-grown
excrētus, a, um *adj*, separated
excrŭcĭo *v.t.* 1, to torture
excŭbĭae, ārum *f.pl*, watch, guard
excŭbĭtor, ōris *m*, watchman
excŭbo, ŭi, ĭtum *v.i.* 1, to sleep out of doors, keep watch
excūdo, di, sum *v.t.* 3, to hammer out
exculco *v.t.* 1, to trample down
excurro, cŭcurri, cursum *v.i.* 3, to run out, make a sortie, extend
excursĭo, ōnis *f*, attack, invasion, sally
excursus, ūs *m*, attack, invation, sally
excūsābĭlis, e *adj*, excusable
excūsātĭo, ōnis *f*, excuse
excūso *v.t.* 1, to excuse, plead in excuse
excŭtĭo, cussi, cussum *v.t.* 3, to shake off, get rid of, hurl, examine
exĕdo, ēdi, ēsum *v.t.* 3, to eat up
exemplar, āris *n*, copy, model
exemplum, i *n*, copy, model, precedent, warning, example

Insight

Some abbreviated expressions that are commonly used in English come from Latin: For example **e.g.** stands for *exempli gratia*; **i.e.** stands for *id est*; **etc.** stands for *et cetera*; **p.s.** stands for *post scriptum*; **a.m./p.m.** stand for *ante/post meridiem*.

exemptus, a, um *adj,* removed
exĕo *v.i.t.* 4, to depart, run out (time), die; cross, avoid
exercĕo *v.t.* 2, to keep busy, train, exercise, pester
exercĭtātĭo, ōnis *f,* practice
exercĭtātus, a, um *adj,* trained
exercĭtor, ōris *m,* trainer
exercĭtus, ūs *m,* army
exercĭtus, a, um *adj,* trained, harrassed
exhālātĭo, ōnis *f,* exhalation
exhālo *v.t.* 1, to breathe out
exhaurĭo, si, stum *v.t.* 4, to draw out, exhaust, empty
exhaustus, a, um *adj,* drained, worn out
exhērēdo *v.t.* 1, to disinherit
exhĭbĕo *v.t.* 2, to present, display, procure, cause
exhĭbĭtus, a, um *adj,* produced
exhĭlăro *v.t.* 1, to delight
exhorresco, rŭi *v.i.t.* 3, to tremble; shrink from, dread
exhortor *v.t.* 1, *dep,* to encourage
exiens see **exeo**
exīgo, ēgi, actum *v.t.* 3, to drive out, enforce, demand, complete, examine, estimate, spend (time)
exĭgŭĭtas, ātis *f,* small size
exĭgŭus, a, um *adj, adv,* **ē,** small, short
exīlis, e *adj, adv,* **ĭter** small, thin, feeble, insignificant
exīlĭum, ii *n,* exile
exĭmĭus, a, um *adj, adv,* **ē,** unusual, distinguished
exĭmo, ēmis, emptum *v.t.* 3, to take away, free, waste
exĭnānĭo *v.t.* 4, to empty
exindē (exin) *adv,* from there, then, next, accordingly
existĭmātĭo, ōnis *f,* opinion, reputation, character
existĭmātor, ōris *m,* critic
existĭmo *v.t.* 1, to estimate, think
exĭtĭābĭlis, e *adj,* fatal, deadly
exĭtĭālis, e *adj,* fatal, deadly
exĭtĭōsus, a, um *adj,* destructive
exĭtĭum, ii *n,* destruction
exĭtus, ūs *m,* departure, outlet, conclusion, result, death
exŏlesco, ŏlēvi, lētum *v.i.* 3, to grow up, disappear

exŏnĕro *v.t.* 1, to unload
exoptātus, a, um *adj,* longed for
exopto *v.t.* 1, to long for
exōrābĭlis, e *adj,* easily persuaded
exordĭor, orsus *v.t.* 4, *dep,* to begin, weave
exordĭum, ii *n,* beginning, introduction
exŏrĭor, ortus *v.i.* 4, *dep,* to spring up, arise, appear
exornātĭo, ōnis *f,* decoration
exorno *v.t.* 1, to equip, adorn
exōro *v.t.* 1, to prevail upon
exorsus, a, um *adj,* begun
exortus, ūs *m,* rising
exōsus, a, um *adj,* hating, detested
expăvesco, pāvi *v.i.t.* 3, to be afraid; dread
expect... see **exspect...**
expēdĭo *v.t.* 4, to set free, prepare, arrange, explain; *impers,* it is expedient
expĕdĭo *v.t.* 4, to set free, prepare, arrange, explain; *impers,* it is expedient
expĕdītĭo, ōnis *f,* campaign
expĕdītē *adv,* promptly
expĕdītus, a, um *adj,* ready
expĕdītus, i *m,* soldier in light-marching order
expello, pŭli, pulsum *v.t.* 3, to drive away
expendo, di, sum *v.t.* 3, to pay out, consider, pay the penalty
expergēfăcĭo, fēci, factum *v.t.* 3, to arouse
expergiscor, perrectus *v.i.* 3, *dep.* to awake
expĕrĭens, ntis *adj,* enterprising
expĕrĭentĭa, ae *f,* experiment, practice
expĕrĭmentum, i *n,* proof, experience
expĕrĭor, pertus *v.t.* 4, *dep,* to prove, test, try; *perf,* know from experience
expers, rtis *adj,* devoid of
expertus, a, um *adj,* proved
expĕto, īvi (ii), ītum *v.t.* 3, to long for, aim at, reach
expĭātĭo, ōnis *f,* atonement
expīlo *v.t.* 1, to plunder
expīlātĭo, ōnis *f,* plundering

expingo, nxi, ctum *v.t.* 3, to paint
expĭo *v.t.* 1, to atone for
expiscor *v.t.* 1, *dep*, to search out
explānātĭo, ōnis *f*, explanation
explāno *v.t.* 1, to explain
explĕo, ēvi, ētum *v.t.* 2, to fill up, fulfil, finish
explētĭo, ōnis *f*, satisfying
explētus, a, um *adj*, full, complete
explĭcātĭo, ōnis *f*, unfolding, explanation
explĭcātus, a, um *adj*, spread-out, plain
explĭco *v.t.* 1, (or … ŭi … ĭtum) to unfold, spread out, deploy, arrange, explain
explōdo, si, sum *v.t.* 3, to hiss off the stage, disapprove
explōrātor, ōris *m*, spy, scout
explōrātus, a, um *adj, adv,* ē, established, certain
explōro *v.t.* 1, to search out, spy, test
expŏlĭo *v.t.* 4, to polish
expōno, pŏsŭi, pŏsĭtum *v.t.* 3, to expose, put on shore, explain
exporto *v.t.* 1, to carry away
exposco, pŏposci *v.t.* 3, to implore, require
expŏsĭtĭo, ōnis *f*, elucidation
expŏsĭtus, a, um *adj*, accessible
expostŭlātĭo, ōnis *f*, complaint
expostŭlo *v.t.* 1, to demand, upbraid, complain
expressus, a, um *adj*, clear
exprĭmo, pressi, pressum *v.t.* 3, to press out, model, extort
expròbrātĭo, ōnis *f*, reproach
exprŏbo *v.t.* 1, to reproach
exprōmo, mpsi, mptum *v.t.* 3, to fetch out, display, explain
expugnātĭo, ōnis *f*, capture by assault
expugno *v.t.* 1, to storm, capture
expurgo *v.t.* 1, to purify, justify
exquīro, sīvi, sītum *v.t.* 3, to search out
exquīsītus, a, um *adj, adv,* ē, choice, excellent
exsanguis, e *adj*, bloodless, weak
exsătĭo *v.t.* 1, to satisfy
exsătŭro *v.t.* 1, to satiate
exscensĭo, ōnis *f*, landing

exscindo, ĭdi, issum *v.t.* 3, to destroy completely
exscrībo, psi, ptum *v.t.* 3, to write out, copy
exsĕco, cŭi, ctum *v.t.* 1, to cut out, cut off
exsècrābĭlis, e *adj*, accursed
exsècrātĭo, ōnis *f*, curse
exsècrātus, a, um *adj*, accursed
exsècror *v.i.t.* 1, *dep*, to take an oath; curse
exsècūtĭo, ōnis *f*, execution
exsèquĭae, ārum *f.pl*, funeral
exsèquor, sècūtus *v.t.* 3, *dep*, to pursue, follow, carry out, describe, avenge
exsĕro, rŭi, rtum *v.t.* 3, to put out, uncover, protrude
exserto *v.t.* 1, to stretch out
exsicco *v.t.* 1, to dry up
exsĭlĭo, ĭlŭi *v.i.* 4, to leap out, jump up
exsĭlĭum, ii *n*, exile
exsisto, stĭti, stĭtum *v.i.* 3, to come out, appear, arise, exist
exsolvo, solvi, sŏlūtum *v.t.* 3, to unloose, free, discharge
exsomnis, e *adj*, sleepless
exsorbĕo *v.t.* 2, to suck up
exsors, rtis *adj*, specially chosen, deprived of
exspătĭor *v.i.* 1, *dep*, to digress, launch out
exspectātĭo, ōnis *f*, expectation
exspectātus, a, um *adj*, desired
exspecto *v.t.* 1, to look out for, wait for, hope for
exspergo (spargo) *(no perf.)*, **spersus** *v.t.* 3, to scatter
exspīrātĭo, ōnis *f*, breathing out
exspīro *v.i.t.* 1, to rush out, expire, cease; breathe out
exspŏlĭo *v.t.* 1, to plunder
exstĭmŭlo *v.t.* 1, to goad on
exstinctor, ōris *m*, destroyer
exstinctus, a, um *adj*, destroyed, extinct
exstinguo, nxi, nctum *v.t.* 3, to quench, kill, destroy
exstirpo *v.t.* 1, to uproot
exsto *v.i.* 1, to project, be conspicuous, exist
exstructĭo, ōnis *f*, structure

exstrŭo, xi, ctum *v.t.* 3, to heap up, build up

exsūdo *v.t.* 1, to toil or sweat at

exsul (exul), ŭlis *c*, an exile

exsŭlo (exulo) *v.i.* 1, to live in exile

exsultans, ntis *adj*, boastful

exsultātĭo, ōnis *f*, rapture

exsultim *adv*, friskingly

exsulto *v.i.* 1, to jump about, run riot, boast

exsŭpĕrābĭlis, e *adj*, surmountable

exsŭpĕro *v.i.t.* 1, to get the upper hand; pass over, exceed

exsurdo *v.t.* 1, to deafen, dull

exsurgo, surrexi *v.i.* 3, to rise, stand up

exsuscĭto *v.t.* 1, to awaken

exta, ōrum *n.pl*, the inwards

extemplō *adv*, immediately

extendo, di, tum *v.t.* 3, to stretch out, enlarge, prolong

extentus, a, um *adj*, extensive

extĕnŭātĭo, ōnis *f*, attenuation

extĕnŭo *v.t.* 1, to diminish, weaken

exter (extĕrus), ĕra, ĕrum *adj*, external, strange, foreign

extergĕo, si, sum *v.t.* 2, to plunder

extĕrĭor, us *comp. adj*, outer

extermĭno *v.t.* 1, to expel

externus, a, um *adj*, external, foreign

extĕro, trīvi, trītum *v.t.* 3, to rub off, wear away

exterrĕo *v.t.* 2, to frighten

extĭmesco, mŭi *v.i.t.* 2, to be afraid; to dread

extollo, sustŭli *v.t.* 3, to raise

extorquĕo, si, sum *v.t.* 2, to wrench away from, extort

extorris, e *adj*, exiled

extrā *adv and prep. with acc.* outside, beyond, except

extrăho, xi, ctum *v.t.* 3, to drag out, release, prolong

extrānĕus, i *m*, stranger

extrăordĭnārĭus, a, um *adj*, extraordinary

extrēma, ōrum *n.pl*, last resort

extrēmĭtas, ātis *f*, extremity

extrēmum, i *n*, the end

extrēmum *adv*, for the last time, finally

extrēmus, a, um *adj*, furthest, the end of, or extremity of

extrīco *v.t.* 1, to disentangle

extrinsĕcus *adv*, from, or on, the outside

extrūdo, si, sum *v.t.* 3, to push out

extundo, tŭdi, tūsum *v.t.* 3, to force out, hammer out

exturbo *v.t.* 1, to drive away

exūbĕro *v.i.* 1, to be abundant

exul see **exsul**

exulcĕro *v.t.* 1, to aggravate

exŭlŭlo *v.i.* 1, to howl

exundo *v.i.* 1, to overflow

exŭo, ŭi, ūtum *v.t.* 3, to strip, deprive of, discard

exūro, ussi, ustum *v.t.* 3, to burn up, consume

exustĭo, ōnis *f*, conflagration

exŭvĭae, ārum *f.pl*, stripped-off clothing or equipment

F

făba, ae *f*, bean

fābella, ae *f*, short story

făber, bri *m*, smith, carpenter

făbrĭca, ae *f*, workshop, a trade, a skilled work

făbricātĭo, ōnis *f*, structure

făbrĭcātor, ōris *m*, maker

făbrĭcor *v.t.* 1, *dep*, (**fabrĭco** *v.t.* 1), to construct, form

făbrīlis, e *adj*, of a craftsman

fābŭla, ae *f*, story, play

fābŭlor *v.t.* 1, *dep*, to talk, chat

fābŭlōsus, a, um *adj*, legendary

făcesso, cessi, ītum *v.i.t.* 3, to depart; perform, cause

făcētĭae, ārum *f.pl*, witticisms

făcētus, a, um *adj, adv*, **ē**, courteous, elegant, witty

făcĭes, ēi *f*, face, shape, appearance

făcĭlĭē *adv*, easily

făcĭlis, e *adj*, easy, quick, good-natured

făcĭlĭtas, ātis *f*, ease, affability

făcĭnus, ŏris *n*, deed, crime

făcĭo, fēci, factum *v.i.t.* 3, to do, act, to side with (**cum, ab**), or against (**contra**), to be useful; to make, do, produce, assert, pretend, practise (trade)

factĭo, ōnis *f,* faction, party
factĭōsus, a, um *adj,* mutinous
factĭto *v.t.* 1, to keep doing
factum, i *n,* deed
făcultas, ātis *f,* power, opportunity, supply
fācundĭa, ae *f,* eloquence
fācundus, a, um *adj, adv,* **ē,** eloquent
faecŭla, ae *f,* wine dregs
faenĕrātĭo, ōnis *f,* moneylending
faenĕrātor, ōris *m,* moneylender
faenĕrātōrĭus, a, um *adj,* usurious
faenĕror *v.t.* 1, *dep* **(faenĕro,** *v.t.* 1),** to lend on interest
faenīlĭa, ĭum *n.pl,* hayloft
faenum, i *n,* hay
faenus, ŏris *n,* interest, profit
faex, cis *f,* dregs, sediment
fāgĭnĕus (nus), a, um *adj,* of beech
fāgus, i *f,* beech tree
fălārĭca, ae *f,* burning missile
falcātus, a, um *adj,* armed with scythes, curved
falcĭfer, ĕra, ĕrum *adj,* holding a sickle
falco, ōnis *m,* falcon
fallācĭa, ae *f,* trick, deceit
fallax, ācis *adj, adv,* **ĭter,** deceitful, fallacious
fallo, fĕfelli, falsum *v.t.* 3, to deceive, betray, escape to notice of, appear
falsum, i *n,* falsehood
falsus, a, um *adj, adv,* **ē,** or **ō,** false, counterfeit, deceptive
falx, cis *f,* scythe, hook
fāma, ae *f,* rumour, public opinion, reputation, fame
fămes, is *f,* hunger, famine
fămīlĭa, ae *f,* domestic servants, family property, crowd or set
fămīlĭāris, e *adj, adv,* **ĭter,** domestic, intimate
fămīlĭāris, is *m,* friend
fămīlĭārĭtas, ātis *f,* friendship
fāmōsus, a, um *adj,* notorious
fămŭla, ae *f,* maid-servant
fămŭlātus, ūs *m,* servitude
fămŭlor *v.i.* 1, *dep,* to serve, wait on
fămŭlus, i *m,* servant
fānātĭcus, a, um *adj,* inspired, frantic

fandus, a, um *adj,* lawful
fānum, i *n,* temple, shrine
fār, farris *n,* grain, corn
farcīmen, ĭnis *n,* sausage
farcĭo, rsi, rtum *v.t.* 4, to cram
fărīna, ae *f,* flour
farrāgo, ĭnis *f,* hotchpotch
fartor, ōris *m,* poultry farmer
fartum, i *n,* stuffing
fartūra, ae *f,* cramming, padding
fās *n, (indeclinable),* divine law, right
fascēs, ĭum *m.pl,* bundle of rods and axes; symbol of magistrates' power of scourging and beheading
fascĭa, ae *f,* band, headband
fascĭcŭlus, i *m,* small bundle
fascĭnātĭo, ōnis *f,* bewiching
fascĭno *v.t.* 1, to charm, enchant
fascĭnum, i *n,* lucky charm
fascĭŏla, ae *f,* small bandage
fascis, is *m,* bundle, pack
fassus, a, um *participle,* having acknowledged
fasti, ōrum *m.pl,* working days, calendar
fastīdĭo *v.i.t.* 4, to be disgusted; to loathe
fastīdĭōsus, a, um *adj, adv,* **ē,** scornful, squeamish, disagreeable
fastīdĭum, ii *n,* loathing, scorn
fastīgātus, a, um *adj, adv,* **ē,** sloping
fastīgĭum, ii *n,* gable, top, bottom, slope
fastīgo *v.t.* 1, to make jointed
fastus, a, um (dĭes), court-day
fastus, ūs *m,* arrogance
fātālis, e *adj, adv,* **ĭter,** destined, deadly
fătĕor, fassus *v.t.* 2, *dep,* to admit, confess
fātīdĭcus, a, um *adj,* prophetic
fātĭfer, ĕra, ĕrum *adj,* deadly
fătīgātĭo, ōnis *f,* exhaustion
fătīgātus, a, um *adj,* exhausted
fătīgo *v.t.* 1, to weary, harass, torment
fātisco *v.i.* 3, to fall apart
fătŭĭtas, ātis *f,* foolishness
fātum, i *n,* destiny, calamity, prophetic saying

fătŭus, a, um *adj*, foolish

faucēs, ĭum *f.pl*, throat, narrow passage

faustus, a, um *adj, adv,* **ē,** fortunate

fautor, ōris *m*, supporter

fautrix, īcis *f*, patroness

făvĕo, făvi, fautum *v.i.* 2, *with dat;* to favour, befriend

făvilla, ae *f*, embers

făvor, ōris *m*, goodwill, applause

făvōrābĭlis, e *adj*, popular

făvus, i *m*, honeycomb

fax, făcis *f*, torch, stimulus

febrĭcŭlōsus, a, um *adj* feverish

fĕbris, is *f*, fever

Fĕbrŭārĭus (mensis) February

fĕbrŭum, i *n*, atonement

fēcundĭtas, ātis *f*, fertility

fēcundo *v.t.* 1, to fertilize

fēcundus, a, um *adj*, fertile, abundant

fel, fellis *n*, gall-bladder, poison, bitterness

fēles, is *f*, cat

fēlĭcĭtas, ātis *f*, happiness

fēlix, īcis *adj, adv,* **īter,** happy, fortunate, abundant

fēmĭna, ae *f*, woman

fēmĭnĕus, a, um *adj*, feminine

fĕmur, ŏris (ĭnis) *n*, thigh

fēn... see **faen...**

fĕnestra, ae *f*, window

fĕra, ae *f*, wild animal

fērālis, e *adj*, of the dead

fĕrax, ācis *adj*, fertile

fercŭlum, i *n*, barrow, dish

fĕrē *adv*, almost, nearly, usually

fĕrentārĭus, ii *m*, light-armed soldier

fĕrètrum, i *n*, bier

fērĭae, ārum *f.pl*, holidays

fērĭātus, a, um *adj*, on holidays

fĕrīnus, a, um *adj*, of wild animals

fĕrĭo *v.t.* 4, to strike, kill; **(**with **foedus),** to make treaty

fĕrĭtas, ātis *f*, wildness

fermē *adv*, almost, usually

fermentum, i *n*, yeast, beer

fĕro, ferre, tŭli, lātum *v.t, irreg,* to bear, bring, move, produce, plunder, offer, tolerate, show, assert; **fertur, ferunt,** it is said

fĕrōcĭa, ae *f*, high spirits, ferocity

fĕrōcĭtas, ātis *f*, high spirits, ferocity

fĕrōcĭter *adv*, bravely, fiercely

fĕrox, ōcis *adj*, brave, fierce

ferrāmentum, i *n*, iron tool

ferrātus, a, um *adj*, iron-clad

ferrĕus, a, um *adj*, made of iron

ferrūgĭnĕus, a, um *adj*, rusty, dark red

ferrūgo, ĭnis *f*, rust, dark red

ferrum, i *n*, iron, sword

ferrūmen, ĭnis *n*, cement, glue, solder

ferrūmĭno *v.t.* 1, to cement, solder

fertĭlis, e *adj*, fertile

fertĭlĭtas, ātis *f*, fertility

fĕrŭla, ae *f*, stalk, rod

fĕrus, a, um *adj*, wild, cruel

fĕrus, i *m*, wild animal

fervĕfăcĭo, fēci, factum *v.t.* 3, to heat, melt

fervens, ntis *adj, adv,* **nter,** burning, boiling hot

fervĕo, bŭi *v.i.* 2, to boil, burn, rage, swarm

fervĭdus, a, um *adj*, burning, impetuous

fervor, ōris *m*, heat, passion

fessus, a, um *adj*, tired

festīnans, ntis *adj, adv,* **nter,** in haste

festīnātĭo, ōnis *f*, haste

festīno *v.i.t.* 1, to hurry

festīnus, a, um *adj*, quick

festīvĭtas, ātis *f*, humour

festīvus, a, um *adj, adv,* **ē,** witty, lively, cheerful

festum, i *n*, holiday, banquet

festus, a, um *adj*, festive, gay

fētĕo *v.i.* 2, to stink

fētĭāles, ĭum *m.pl*, college of priests concerned with war ceremonies

fētĭdus, a, um *adj*, stinking

fētor, ōris *m*, stench

fētūra, ae *f*, bearing of young, young brood

fētus, a, um *adj*, pregnant, fruitful, newly delivered

fibra, ae *f*, fibre, nerve

fībŭla, ae *f*, brooch, pin

fībŭlo *v.t.* 1, to fasten

fictīlis, e *adj*, made of clay
fictīle, is (ia, īum) *n*, earthern pottery
fictor, ōris *m*, designer
fictus, a, um *adj*, imagined
fīcus, i or **ūs** *f*, fig tree
fīdēlis, e *adj*, *adv*, **īter**, faithful, true, sure
fīdēlītas, ātis *f*, faithfulness
fīdens, ntis *adj*, *adv*, **nter** self-confident
fīdentīa, ae *f*, confidence
fīdes, ĕi *f*, trust, faith, confidence, honesty, promise
fīdes, ĭum *f.pl*, lute, guitar
fīdīcen, īnis *m*, lute-player
fīdo, fīsus sum *v.* 3, *semi-dep. with dat;* to trust
fīdūcīa, ae *f*, confidence
fīdus, a, um *adj*, trustworthy
fīĕri see **fio**
fīgo, xi, xum *v.t.* 3, to fix, fasten, transfix
fīgŭlāris, e *adj*, of a potter
fīgŭlus, i *m*, potter
fīgūra, ae *f*, shape, phantom, atom, nature
fīgūrātus, a, um *adj*, shaped
fīgūro *v.t.* 1, to shape
fīlīa, ae *f*, daughter
fīlīŏla, ae *f*, little daughter
fīlīŏlus, i *m*, little son
fīlius, i *m*, son
fīlix, īcis *f*, hair, fern
fīlum, i *n*, thread, texture
fimbrīae, ārum *f.pl*, threads, fringe
fīmus, i *m*, manure
findo, fīdi, ssum *v.t.* 3, to split
fīnes, ĭum *m.pl*, territory
fingo, nxi, ctum *v.t.* 3, to shape, adorn, imagine, devise
fīnīo *v.t.* 4, to enclose, limit, prescribe, end, die
fīnis, is *m*, boundary, limit, end
fīnītīmus, a, um *adj*, adjoining
fīnītīmi, ōrum *m.pl*, neighbours
fīnītor, ōris *m*, surveyor
fio, fīĕri, factus sum *v*, *irreg*, to become, happen
firmāmen, īnis *n*, prop, support

firmāmentum, i *n*, prop, support
firmītsas, ātis *f*, strength, firmness
firmītūdo, īnis *f*, strength, firmness
firmo *v.t.* 1, to strengthen, encourage, promise
firmus, a, um *adj*, *adv*, **ē, īter**, strong, stable, constant, true
fiscella, ae *f*, small basket, muzzle
fiscīna, ae *f*, small basket
fiscus, i *m*, purse, imperial treasury
fissīlis, e *adj*, breakable
fissum, i *n*, cleft, chink
fissūra, ae *f*, split, chink
fistūca, ae *f*, rammer
fistŭla, ae *f*, pipe, tube
fistŭlātor, ōris *m*, piper
fīsus, a, um *adj*, trusting, relying on
flābellum, i *n*, small fan
flābra, ōrum *n.pl*, gusts
flaccĭdus, a, um *adj*, flabby
flăgello *v.t.* 1, to whip
flăgellum, i *n*, whip, thong
flāgĭtātĭo, ōnis *f*, demand
flāgĭtĭōsus, a, um *adj*, *adv*, **ē**, disgraceful
flāgĭtĭum, ii *n*, disgraceful conduct, shame
flāgĭto *v.t.* 1, to demand
flàgrans, ntis *adj*, burning
flàgro *v.i.* 1, to blaze, glow
flàgrum, i *n*, whip
flāmen, īnis *m*, priest
flāmen, īnis *n*, blast
flāmīnĭum, ii *n*, priesthood
flamma, ae *f*, flame, blaze
flammĕum, i *n*, bridal veil
flammĕus, a, um *adj*, flaming
flammĭfer, ĕra, ĕrum *adj*, flame-carrying
flammo *v.i.t.* 1, to burn
flātus, ūs *m*, blowing, bluster
flāvens, ntis *adj*, yellow
flāvĕo *v.i.* 2, to be golden, yellow
flāvesco *v.i.* 3, to turn golden
flāvus, a, um *adj*, golden, yellow
flēbĭlis, e *adj*, *adv*, **īter**, lamentable, tearful

flecto, xi, xum *v.i.t.* 3, to turn; bend, curve, wheel, persuade

flĕo, ēvi, tum *v.i.t.* 2, to weep; mourn

flētus, ūs *m*, weeping

flexĭbĭlis, e *adj*, flexible

flexĭo, ōnis *f*, curve

flexŭōsus, a, um *adj*, crooked

flexus, ūs *m*, bend, turning

flictus, ūs *m*, collision

flō *v.i.t.* 1, to blow

floccus, i *m*, lock of wool

flōrens, ntis *adj*, shining, flourishing

flōrĕo *v.i.* 2, to bloom, flourish

flōresco *v.i.* 3, to come into flower, flourish

flōrĕus, a, um *adj*, made of flowers

flōrĭdus, a, um *adj*, blooming

flōs, ōris *m*, flower, ornament

floscŭlus, i *m*, small flower

fluctŭo *v.i.* 1, to ripple, undulate, hesitate

fluctŭōsus, a, um *adj*, billowy

fluctus, ūs *m*, wave

flŭens, ntis *adj*, lax, fluent

flŭentum, i *n*, stream, flood

flŭĭdus, a, um *adj*, flowing, slack

flŭĭto *v.i.* 1, to flow, float

flūmen, ĭnis *n*, river, flood

flūmĭnĕus, a, um *adj*, of a river

flŭo, xi, xum *v.i.* 3, to flow, wave, vanish

flŭvĭālis, e *adj*, of a river

flŭvĭus, ii *m*, river

fluxĭo, ōnis *f*, flowing

fluxus, a, um *adj*, fluid, slack

fōcāle, is *n*, necktie

fŏcŭlus, i *m*, brazier

fŏcus, i *m*, fireplace, home

fŏdĭco *v.t.* 1, to dig, nudge, stab

fŏdĭo, fōdi, fossum *v.i.t.* 3, to dig; dig up, prick, stab

foedĕrātus, a, um *adj*, allied

foedĭtas, ātis *f*, filthiness

foedo *v.t.* 1, to disfigure, disgrace, stain

foedus, a, um *adj, adv*, **ē**, filthy, shameful

foedus, ĕris *n*, treaty, contract

foet... see **fet...**

fŏlĭum, ii *n*, leaf

follīcŭlus, i *m*, small bag

follis, is *m*, pair of bellows

fōmentum, *n*, poultice, comfort

fōmes, ĭtis *m*, firewood

fons, ntis *m*, fountain, origin

fontĭcŭlus, i *m*, small fountain

for *v.i.t.* 1, *dep*, to speak; say, predict

fŏrāmen, ĭnis *n*, hole

fŏrās *adv*, out-of-doors

forceps, ĭpis *m, f*, tongs, pincers

fŏrĕ = futurum esse see **esse**

fŏrem = essem see **esse**

fŏrensis, e *adj*, concerning the courts of law

fŏres, um *f.pl*, door, entrance

forfex, ĭcis *f*, scissors (*usually in pl.*)

fŏrĭca, ae *f*, public convenience

fŏrĭcŭlae, ārum *f. pl*, shutters

fŏris, is *f*, door, entrance

fŏris *adv*, outside, from outside

forma, ae *f*, form, shape, beauty

formīca, ae *f*, ant

formīdābĭlis, e *adj*, fearful

formīdo *v.i.t.* 1, to be afraid; fear

formīdo, ĭnis *f*, fear, terror

formīdŭlōsus, a, um *adj, adv*, **ē**, dreadful, fearful

formo *v.t.* 1, to shape

formōsus, a, um *adj*, beautiful

formŭla, ae *f*, rule, principle, agreement, lawsuit

fornax, ācis *f*, oven

fornix, ĭcis *m*, arch, vault

fors, rtis *f*, chance, luck

fors *adv*, perhaps

forsan *adv*, perhaps

forsĭtan *adv*, perhaps

fortassē *adv*, perhaps

fortē *adv*, by chance

fortis, e *adj, adv*, **ĭter**, strong, brave

fortĭtūdo, ĭnis *f*, bravery

fortŭĭtō(ū) *adv*, by chance

fortŭĭtus, a, um *adj*, accidental

fortūna, ae *f*, luck, fate, fortune (good or bad), circumstances, property

fortūnātus, a, um *adj, adv*, **ē**, lucky, happy

fortūno *v.t.* 1, to enrich, bless

fŏrum, i *n*, marketplace, business

Insight

The Latin term *forum* means 'marketplace' but it also relates to the legal and business centre of a town. Nowadays the term *forum* is commonly used to indicate an online space for discussion.

---

fŏrus, i *m*, gangway, passage, row of seats
fossa, ae *f*, ditch
fossĭo, ōnis *f*, excavation
fossor, ōris *m*, digger, miner
fŏvĕa, ae *f*, pit, pitfall
fŏvĕo, fōvi, fōtum *v.t.* 2, to warm, caress, love
fractūra, ae *f*, fracture
fractus, a, um *adj*, weak, feeble
frāga, ōrum *n.pl*, strawberries
frăgĭlis, e *adj*, brittle, frail
frăgĭlĭtas, ātis *f*, frailty
fragmen, ĭnis *n*, fracture, splinter
fragmentum, i *n*, fragment
frăgor, ōris *m*, crash
frăgōsus, a, um *adj*, rugged, crashing
fragro *v.i.* 1, to smell
frāgum, i *n*, strawberry plant
frango, frēgi, fractum *v.t.* 3, to break, crush, weaken
frāter, tris *m*, brother
frāternĭtas, ātis *f*, brotherhood
frāternus, a, um *adj, adv*, **ē**, brotherly
frātrĭcīda, ae *m*, a fratricide
fraudātĭo, ōnis *f*, deceit
fraudātor, ōris *m*, deceiver
fraudo *v.t.* 1, to cheat, defraud
fraudŭlentus, a, um *adj*, deceitful
fraus, dis *f*, deceit, crime, mistake, injury
fraxĭnĕus, a, um *adj*, of ash
fraxĭnus, i *f*, ash tree
frĕmĭtus, ūs *m*, murmur, roar
frĕmo, ŭi, ĭtum *v.i.t.* 3, to roar, murmur, howl; grumble at
frĕmor, ōris *m*, murmuring
frendĕo, ŭi, frēsum *v.i.* 2, to gnash the teeth, crush
frēno *v.t.* 1, to bridle, curb

frēnum, i *n*, bridle, restraint
frĕquens, ntis *adj, adv*, **nter**, usual, repeated, crowded
frĕquentātĭo, ōnis *f*, frequency
frĕquentĭa, ae *f*, crowd
frĕquento *v.t.* 1, to frequent, repeat, crowd, celebrate
frĕtum, i *n*, channel, strait
frĕtus, a, um *adj. with abl*, relying on
frĭco, cŭi, ctum *v.t.* 1, to rub
frictus, a, um *adj*, rubbed, **(frico)**; roasted **(frigo)**
frīgĕo *v.i.* 2, to be cold or languid, to be slighted
frīgesco, frixi *v.i.* 3, to grow cold, become languid
frīgĭdus, a, um *adj*, cold, stiff, feeble, spiritless
frīgĭda, ae *f*, cold water
frīgo, xi, ctum *v.t.* 3, to roast
frīgus, ŏris *n*, cold, winter
fringilla, ae *f*, small bird, robin, chaffinch
frondātor, ōris *m*, pruner
frondĕo *v.i.* 2, to be in leaf
frondesco, dŭi *v.i.* 3, to come into leaf
frondĕus, a, um *adj*, leafy
frondōsus, a, um *adj*, leafy
frons, dis *f*, foliage, leaf
frons, ntis *f*, forehead, front, appearance
fructŭōsus, a, um *adj*, fruitful, advantageous
fructus, ūs *m*, enjoyment, fruit, profit
frūgālis, e *adj, adv*, **ĭter**, thrifty, careful
frūgālĭtas, ātis *f*, thrift, worth
frūges, um *f.pl*, see **frux**
frūgi *indecl. adj*, worthy, useful

frūgĭfer, ĕra, ĕrum *adj*, fertile
frūmentārĭus, a, um *adj*, of corn
frūmentor *v.i.* 1, *dep*, to fetch corn
frūmentum, i *n*, corn
frŭor, fructus *v.* 3, *dep. with abl*, to enjoy
frustrā *adv*, in vain
frustrātĭo, ōnis *f*, deception, frustration
frustror *v.t.* 1, *dep*, to deceive
frustum, i *n*, piece
frŭtex, ĭcis *m*, bush
frŭtĭcētum, i *n*, thicket
frŭtĭcōsus, a, um *adj*, bushy
frux, frūgis *f*, fruit, crops, value, result
fūcātus, a, um *adj*, painted, counterfeit
fūco *v.t.* 1, to paint, dye
fūcōsus, a, um *adj*, coloured, spurious
fūcus, i *m*, rouge, disguise
fūcus, i *m*, drone
fŭga, ae *f*, flight, exile
fŭgax, ācis *adj*, runaway, swift
fŭgĭens, ntis *adj*, runaway, swift
fŭgĭens, ntis *adj*, fleeing
fŭgĭo, fūgi, fŭgĭtum *v.i.t.* 3, to run away; flee from, avoid
fŭgĭtĭvus, a, um *adj*, fugitive
fŭgĭtĭvus, i *m*, runaway slave, deserter
fŭgĭto *v.t.* 1, to flee, avoid
fŭgo *v.t.* 1, to rout, chase
fulcĭo, fulsi, fultum *v.t.* 4, to prop up, strenghen
fulcrum, i *n*, foot (of couch)
fulgens, ntis *adj*, shining
fulgĕo, lsi *v.i.* 2, to flash, shine
fulgĭdus, a, um *adj*, flashing, shining
fulgor, ōris *m*, lightning, gleam, splendour
fulgur, ŭris *n*, lightning
fulgŭrat *v. impers*, it lightens
fūlĭca, ae *f*, moorhen
fūlīgo, ĭnis *f*, soot
fūlīgĭnōsus, a, um *adj*, sooty
fulmen, ĭnis *n*, thunderbolt, lightning
fulmĭnĕus, a, um *adj*, of lightning, destructive, brilliant
fulmĭno *v.i.* 1, to thunder

fultūra, ae *f*, prop, tonic
fulvus, a, um *adj*, deep yellow
fūmĕus, a, um *adj*, smoky
fūmĭdus, a, um *adj*, smoky
fūmĭfer, ĕra, ĕrum *adj*, smoking, steaming
fūmĭfĭcus, a, um *adj*, smoking, steaming
fūmĭgo *v.t.* 1, to smoke out, fumigate
fūmo *v.i.* 1, to smoke
fūmōsus, a, um *adj*, smoky, smoke-dried
fūmus, i *m*, smoke
fūnāle, is *n*, cord, torch
functĭo, ōnis *f*, performing
functus, a, um *partic. adj, with abl*, having completed
funda, ae *f*, sling, missile
fundāmen, ĭnis *n*, foundation
fundāmentum, i *n*, foundation
fundĭtor, ōris *m*, slinger
fundĭtus *adv*, from the bottom, completely
fundo, fūdi, fūsum *v.t.* 3, to pour out, spread out, scatter, overthrow, produce
fundo *v.t.* 1, to found, fix
fundus, i *m*, the bottom, a farm
fundus, i *m*, guarantor
fūnèbris, e *adj*, of a funeral
fūnĕrĕus, a, um *adj*, of a funeral
fūnĕro *v.t.* 1, to bury, kill
fūnesto *v.t.* 1, to pollute
fūnestus, a, um *adj*, fatal, sad
fungor, functus *v.* 3, *dep, with abl*, to perform, complete
fungus, i *m*, mushroom, fungus
fūnis, is *m*, rope
fūnus, ĕris *n*, funeral, death, ruin
fūr, fūris *c*, thief, rogue
fūrax, ācis *adj*, light-fingered
furca, ae *f*, two-pronged fork or pole for punishment
furcĭfer, ĕri *m*, gallows-bird
furcilla, ae *f*, small fork
furcŭla, a *f*, fork-shaped prop, ravine
fŭrens, ntis *adj*, raging
furfur, ŭris *m*, bran
fŭrĭae, ārum *f.pl*, rage, frenzy, avenging Furies
fŭrĭālis, e *adj, adv*, **ĭter,** raging, wild

fŭrĭbundus, a, um *adj*, raging
fŭrĭo *v.t.* 1, to enrage
fŭrĭōsus, a, um *adj*, raging
furnus, i *m*, oven
fŭro, ŭi *v.i.* 3, to rage, be mad
fūror *v.t.* 1, *dep*, to steal
fŭror, ōris *m*, rage, fury
furtim *adv*, stealthily
furtīvus, a, um *adj*, stolen, secret
furtum, i *n*, theft, trick
furtō *adv*, secretly
fūruncŭlus, i *m*, pilferer, sore, boil
furvus, a, um *adj*, gloomy, swarthy
fuscīna, ae *f*, trident
fusco *v.t.* 1, to blacken, darken
fuscus, a, um *adj*, dark, swarthy
fūsĭlis, e *adj*, fluid, soft
fustis, is *m*, cudgel, club
fūsus, a, um *adj*, spread out, wide
fūsus, i *m*, spindle
futtĭlis (fūtĭlis), e, *adj*, worthless
futtĭlĭtas (fūtĭlĭtas), ātis *f*, worthlessness
fŭtūra, ōrum *n.pl*, the future
fŭtūrum, i *n*, the future
fŭtūrus, a, um *adj*, future

G

gaesum, i *n*, heavy Gallic javelin
galbĭnus, a, um *adj*, greenish-yellow
gălĕa, ae *f*, helmet
gălĕo *v.t.* 1, to issue with helmets
gălērum, i *n*, (us, i *m*), hat
galla, ae *f*, oak-apple
gallīna, ae *f*, hen
gallīnārĭŭm, ii *n*, hen-house

garrĭo *v.t.* 4, to chatter
garrŭlĭtas, ātis *f*, chattering
garrŭlus, a, um *adj*, talkative
gărum (garon), i *n*, fish sauce
gaudĕo, gāvīsus *v.i.t.* 2, *semi-dep*, to rejoice
gaudĭum, ii *n*, joy, delight
gausăpa, ae *f*, rough clothing
gāvĭa, ae *f*, seabird
gāza, ae *f*, treasure (of Persia)
gĕlīdus, a, um *adj, adv*, ē, ice-cold, frosty
gĕlo *v.i.t.* 1, to freeze
gĕlum, i (gĕlu, ūs) *n*, frost, cold
gĕmellus, a, um *adj*, (us, i *m*), twin
gĕmĭno *v.t.* 1, to double, pair
gĕmĭnus, a, um *adj*, twin
gĕmĭni, ōrum *m.pl*, twins
gĕmĭtus, ūs *m*, lamentation
gemma, ae *f*, bud, jewel, goblet, signet-ring
gemmārĭus, ii *m*, jeweller
gemmātus, a, um *adj*, set with jewels
gemmĕus, a, um *adj*, set with jewels
gemmo *v.i.* 1, to come into bud
gĕmo, ŭi, ĭtum *v.i.t.* 3, to groan, creak; deplore
gĕna, ae *f*, the cheek
gĕner, ĕri *m*, son-in-law
gĕnĕrālis, e *adj*, of a certain kind, general
gĕnĕrātim *adv*, in classes, in general
gĕnĕrātor, ōris *m*, breeder
gĕnĕro *v.t.* 1, to create, produce; (*passive*) be born

Insight

The **genitive** is the case that shows possession, author or source; it completes the meaning of a noun by describing the content or material of it. The dominant meaning is therefore 'of'.

---

gallus, i *m*, cock
gānĕa, ae *f*, eating-house
gānĕo, ōnis *m*, glutton
gannĭo *v.i.* 4, to bark, snarl
gannītus, ūs *m*, chattering

gĕnĕrōsus, a, um *adj, adv*, ē, of noble birth, generous
gĕnesta, ae *f*, small shrub with yellow flowers, broom

gĕnĕtīvus, a, um *adj,* inborn
gĕnĕtrix, īcis *f,* mother
gĕnĭālis, e *adj, adv,* **ĭter,** bridal, cheerful
gĕnĭtālis, e *adj,* of birth, fruitful
gĕnĭtor, ōris *m,* father
gĕnĭus, ii *m,* guardian angel
gens, ntis *f,* clan, race, descendant, nation
gentīlĭcĭus, a, um *adj,* of the same clan
gentīlis, e *adj,* of the same clan
gentīlis, is *c,* relative
gĕnu, ūs *n,* knee
gĕnŭīnus, a, um *adj,* innate
gĕnŭīnus, a, um *adj,* of the cheek or jaw
gĕnus, ĕris *n,* birth, race, kind, type, descendant
gĕōgrăphĭa, ae *f,* geography
gĕōmètres, ae *m,* mathematician
gĕōmètrĭa, ae *f,* geometry
germānĭtas, ātis *f,* brotherhood
germānus, a, um *adj,* own
germānus, i *m,* **(a, ae** *f*), brother, (sister)
germen, ĭnis *n,* bud, sprig
germĭno *v.i.* 1, to bud
gĕro, gessi, stum *v.t.* 3, to bear, wear, bring, produce, behave, display, carry on, honour

gestus, a, um *adj,* achieved, carried
gibber, ĕris *m,* hump; *as adj,* hunchbacked
gibbus, i *m,* hump; *as adj,* hunchbacked
gĭgantēus, a, um *adj,* of giants
gĭgās, ntis *m,* giant
gigno, gĕnŭi, gĕnĭtum *v.t.* 3, to give birth to; (*passive*) be born
gilvus, a, um *adj,* pale yellow
gingīva, ae *f,* gum
glăber, bra, brum *adj,* bald
glăcĭālis, e *adj,* frozen
glăcĭes, ēi *f,* ice
glăcĭo *v.t.* 1, to freeze
glădĭātor, ōris *m,* gladiator
glădĭātōrĭus, a, um *adj,* gladiatorial
glădĭus, ii *n,* sword
glaeba (glēba), ae *f,* clod
glans, ndis *f,* acorn, bullet
glārĕa, ae *f,* gravel
glaucus, a, um *adj,* blue-grey
glēba see **glaeba**
glis, glīris *m,* dormouse
glisco, m *v.i.* 3, to swell, grow
glŏbōsus, a, um *adj,* spherical
glŏbus, i *m,* ball, crowd
glŏmĕro *v.t.* 1, to gather into a heap, crowd together
glŏmus, ĕris *n,* ball of thread

Insight

The **gerund** and **gerundive** are two different things. The gerund is a 'verbal noun' and it therefore declines like a second declension noun (ars regendi = the art of ruling); the gerundive is a verbal adjective and it therefore declines like a first-and-second declension adjective (*hoc faciendum est* = this must be done).

---

gerrae, ārum *f.pl,* nonsense
gĕrŭlus, i *m,* porter
gestāmen, ĭnis *n,* load
gestātĭo, ōnis *f,* riding, driving
gestĭo *v.i.* 4, to be joyful, desire passionately
gesto *v.t.* 1, to carry, wear, have
gestus, ūs *m,* posture, gesture

glōrĭa, ae *f,* glory, boasting
glōrĭātĭo, ōnis *f,* boasting
glōrĭor *v.i.t.* 1, *dep,* to boast
glōrĭōsus, a, um *adj, adv,* **ē,** famous, conceited
glossārĭum, ii *n,* glossary
glūten, ĭnis *n,* glue
glūtĭnātor, ōris *m,* bookbinder

glūtĭno *v.t.* 1, to glue
gluttĭo *v.t.* 4, to gulp
gnārus, a, um *adj. with genit,* acquainted with, expert in
gnātus, a, um *adj,* born
gnāv... see **nāv...**
gossypĭum, ii *n,* cotton
grăcĭlis, e *adj,* slender
grăcĭlĭtas, ātis *f,* slenderness
grācŭlus, i *m,* jackdaw
grădātim, *adv,* gradually
grădātĭo, ōnis *f,* gradation, climax
grădĭor, gressus *v.i.* 3, *dep,* to walk, go, move
grădus, ūs *m,* pace, step, rank, position, station, stair, plait
graecor *v.i.* 1, *dep,* to live like the Greeks
grallae, ārum *f.pl,* stilts
grāmen, ĭnis *n,* grass
grāmĭnĕus, a, um *adj,* grassy
grammătĭca, ae *f,* grammar
grammătĭcus, i *m,* grammarian
grānārĭa, ōrum *n.pl,* granary
grānātus, a, um *adj,* with many seeds
grandaevus, a, um *adj,* old
grandĭlŏquus, a, um *adj,* boastful
grandĭnat *v.* 1, *impers,* it is hailing
grandis, e *adj,* full-grown, large, old, strong, noble
grando, ĭnis *f,* hail, hailstorm
grānum, i *n,* grain, seed
grānōsus, a, um *adj,* seedy
grassātor, ōris *m,* idler, footpad
grassor *v.i.* 1, *dep,* to hang about, attack, rage
grātē *adv,* gratefully, willingly
grātes *f.pl,* thanks
grātĭa, ae *f,* esteem, friendship, charm, beauty, kindness, favour, gratitude; *in abl,* for the sake of; **grātĭīs (grātīs),** as a favour; *pl,* thanks
grātĭfĭcātĭo, ōnis *f,* doing favours
grātĭfĭcor *v.* 1, *dep,* to do as a favour, oblige
grātĭōsus, a, um *adj,* popular
grātor *v.i.t.* 1, *dep,* to congratulate
grātūĭtus, a, um *adj,* voluntary
grātŭlātĭo, ōnis *f,* rejoicing
grātŭlor *v.i.t.* 1, *dep,* to congratulate

grātus, a, um *adj,* pleasing, grateful
grăvāte *adv,* unwillingly
grăvēdo, ĭnis *f,* cold, catarrh
grăvĕŏlens, ntis *adj,* stinking
grăvesco *v.i.* 3, to grow heavy
grăvĭdus, a, um *adj,* pregnant
grăvis, e *adj, adv,* **ĭter,** heavy, loaded, low, pregnant, severe, unpleasant, serious, urgent, important
grăvĭtas, ātis *f,* weight, heaviness, severity, dignity, urgency
grăvo *v.t.* 1, to load, oppress
grăvor *v.i.t.* 1, *dep,* to be irritated or reluctant; not to tolerate
grĕgālis, e *adj,* of the herd, gregarious
grĕgărĭus, a, um *adj,* common
grĕgātim *adv,* in herds
grĕmĭum, ii, *n,* bosom, lap
gressus, ūs *m,* step, way
grex, grĕgis *m,* flock, herd
grūmus, i *m,* hillock
grunnĭo *v.i.* 4, to grunt
grunnītus, ūs *m,* grunt
grus, grŭis *m, f,* crane
grӯllus, i *m,* grasshopper
gryps, gryphis *m,* griffin
gŭbernācŭlum, i *n,* rudder
gŭbernātĭo, ōnis *f,* management
gŭbernātor, ōris *m,* steersman
gŭberno *v.t.* 1, to steer, manage
gŭla, ae *f,* throat, appetite
gŭlōsus, a, um *adj,* gluttonous
gummi *n, (indecl.),* gum
gurges, ĭtis *m,* whirlpool, abyss
gustātĭo, ōnis *f,* taste
gustātus, ūs *m,* sense of taste
gusto *v.t.* 1, to taste
gustus, ūs *m,* tasting, snack
gutta, ae *f,* drop, spot
guttur, ŭris *n,* throat
gutus (guttus), i *m,* flask
gymnăsĭum, ii *m,* gymnasium
gymnĭcus, a, um *adj,* gymnastic
gypsātus, a, um *adj,* covered with lime
gypso *v.t.* 1, to plaster
gypsum, i *n,* white line
gӯrus, i *m,* circuit, ring

H

hăbēna, ae *f,* thong, rein

hăbĕo *v.t.* 2, to have, keep, be able, render, esteem, use, deal with , know; *with* **in animo** to intend

hăbĭlis, e *adj,* convenient, expert

hăbĭtābĭlis, e *adj,* habitable

hăbĭtātĭo, ōnis *f,* residence

hăbĭto *v.i.t.* 1, to live; inhabit

hăbĭtus, ūs *m,* condition, bearing, state, dress, shape

hāc *adv,* by this way, here

hactĕnus *adv,* up to this point

haec see **hic**

haedus, i *m,* young goat

haemorrhăgĭa, ae *f,* haemorrhage

haerĕo, si, sum *v.i.* 2, to hang, cling, hesitate

haesĭtans, ntis *adj,* hesitant

haesĭtantĭa, ae *f,* stammering

haesĭtātĭo, ōnis *f,* embarrassment

haesĭto *v.i.* 1, to hesitate

hālĭtus, ūs *m,* breath, steam

hālo *v.i.t.* 1, to breathe; exhale

hăma, ae *f,* bucket

hāmātus, a, um *adj,* hooked

hāmus, i *m,* hook, fish hook

hăra, ae *f,* coop, pen, sty

hărēna, ae *f,* sand, arena

hărēnārĭus, a, um *adj,* of sand

hărēnōsus, a, um *adj,* sandy

hărĭŏlor *v.i.* 1, *dep,* to foretell

hărĭŏlus, i *m,* prophet

harmŏnĭa, ae *f,* harmony

harpăgo, ōnis *m,* grappling-hook

hărundo, ĭnis *f,* reed, fishing rod, shaft, shepherd's pipe

hăruspex, ĭcis *m,* clairvoyant

hasta, ae *f,* spear, lance

hastāti, ōrum *m.pl,* pike-men; front line of a Roman army

hastīle, is *n,* spear shaft

haud (haut) *adv,* not at all

haudquāquam *adv,* by no means

haurĭo, si, stum *v.t.* 4, to draw up, drink in, drain, exhaust

haustus, ūs *m,* a drink, draught

hav… see **av…**

hĕbĕnus, i *f,* ebony

hĕbĕo *v.i.* 2, to be dull

hĕbes, ĕtis *adj,* blunt, dull

hĕbesco *v.i.* 3, to grow dull

hĕbĕto *v.t.* 1, to blunt

hĕdĕra, ae *f,* ivy

hei *interj,* ah! alas!

hellŭo, ōnis *m,* glutton

hellŭor *v.i.* 1, *dep, with abl,* to squander

hem! (em!) *interj,* ah! indeed!

hēmĭcyclĭum, ii *n,* semicircle

hēmisphaerĭum, ii *n,* hemisphere

hĕra, ae *f,* lady of the house

herba, ae *f,* grass, plant

herbārĭus, a, um *adj,* of plants

herbĭdus, a, um *adj,* grassy

herbōsus, a, um *adj,* grassy

hercŭle (hercle)! by Hercules!

hĕrĕ *adv,* yesterday

hērēdĭtārĭus, a, um *adj,* ïinherited

hērēdĭtas, ātis *f,* inheritance

hēres, ēdis *c,* heir, heiress

hĕri *adv,* yesterday

hĕrīlis, e *adj,* of the master or mistress

hernĭa, ae *f,* rupture

hērōĭcus, a, um *adj,* heroic

hēros, ōis *m,* demigod

hĕrus, i *m,* master of the house

hespĕris, ĭdis *adj,* western

hespĕrĭus, a, um *adj,* western

hesternus, a, um *adj,* yesterday's

heu! *interj,* oh! alas!

heus! *interj,* hallo there!

hexămĕter, tri *m,* a verse metre consisting of six feet

hĭans see **hĭo**

hĭātus, ūs *m,* aperture

hīberna, ōrum *n.pl,* winter quarters

hībernācŭla, ōrum *n.pl,* tents to spend winter in

hīberno *v.i.* 1, to spend the winter

hībernus, a, um *adj,* of winter

hibrĭda, ae *c,* cross breed

hīc, haec, hōc *pron,* this

hīc *adv,* here

hĭĕmālis, e *adj,* of winter

hĭĕmo *v.i.t.* 1, to spend the winter; freeze

hĭems (hiemps), hĭĕmis *f,* winter, stormy weather

hĭlăris, e *adj, adv, ē,* cheerful

hĭlărĭtas, ātis *f,* gaiety

hĭlăro *v.t.* 1, to cheer up

hillae, ārum *f.pl,* sausage

hinc *adv*, from here, hence
hinnĭo *v.i.* 4, to neigh
hinnītus, ūs *m*, neighing
hinnŭlĕus, i *m*, young stag
hĭo *v.i.* 1, to gape open
hippŏpŏtămus, i *m*, hippopotamus
hircīnus, a, um *adj*, of a goat
hircus, i *m*, goat
hirsūtus, a, um *adj*, shaggy
hirtus, a, um *adj*, rough, shaggy
hĭrūdo, ĭnis *f*, leech
hĭrundĭnīnus, a, um *adj*, of swallows
hĭrundo, ĭnis *f*, a swallow
hisco, — *v.i.t.* 3, to gape; whisper
hispĭdus, a, um *adj*, rough, shaggy
histŏrĭa, ae *f*, story, account
histŏrĭcus, a, um *adj*, historical
histŏrĭcus, i *m*, historian
histrĭo, ōnis *m*, actor
hĭulcus, a, um *adj*, gaping; (of speech) badly connected
hoc see **hic**
hŏdĭē *adv*, today
hŏdĭernus, a, um *adj*, of today
hŏlus, ĕris *n*, vegetables
hŏluscŭlum, i *n*, small vegetable
hŏmĭcīda, ae *c*, murderer
hŏmĭcīdĭum, ii *n*, homicide
hŏmo, ĭnis *c*, human being

hŏnor (hŏnos), ōris *m*, esteem, public office, reward, charm
hŏnōrārĭus, a, um *adj*, honorary
hŏnōrātus, a, um *adj*, respected
hŏnōrĭfĭcus, a, um *adj, adv*, ē, complimentary
hŏnōro *v.t.* 1, to honour, respect, adorn
hŏnos see **hŏnor**
hŏnus... see **ŏnus...**
hōra, ae *f*, hour, time, season
hōrārĭum, ii *n*, hourglass
hordĕŏlus, i *m*, sty (eye)
hordĕum, i *n*, barley
hŏrĭōla, ae *f*, fishing boat
hornōtĭnus, a, um *adj*, this year's
hornus, a, um *adj*, this year's
hōrŏlŏgĭum, ii *n*, clock
horrendus, a, um *adj*, terrible
horrĕo *v.i.t.* 2, to bristle, tremble; dread
horresco, horrŭi *v.i.* 3, to become ruffled or frightened
horrĕum, i *n*, barn, warehouse
horrĭbĭlis, e *adj*, terrible
horrĭdŭlus, a, um *adj*, rough
horrĭdus, a, um *adj, adv*, ē, rough, bristly, wild, uncouth
horrĭfer, ĕra, ĕrum *adj*, dreadful
horrĭfĭco *v.t.* 1, to ruffle, terrify
horrĭfĭcus, a, um *adj*, terrible

Insight

Latin has two words *homo* and *vir* that are commonly translated as 'man' but there is an important distinction between them. **Vir** is an adult male in contrast with **femina** 'woman'. The word **homo** means 'human being', the creature made of humus 'earth' and consequently subject to death, by contrast with a god, who lives forever and so is **immortalis** (lit. 'not dying', not subject to mors 'death').

hŏmullus, i *m*, puny man
hŏmuncŭlus, i *m*, puny man
hŏnestas, ātis *f*, honour, good name, integrity
hŏnesto *v.t.* 1, to honour, adorn
hŏnestum, i *n*, integrity
hŏnestus, a, um *adj, adv*, ē, respectable, esteemed, eminent

horrĭsŏnus, a, um *adj*, with fearful sounds
horror, ōris *m*, bristling, trembling, chill, terror
hortāmen, ĭnis *n*, encouragement
hortātĭo, ōnis *f*, encouragement
hortātor, ōris *m*, encourager
hortātus, ūs *m*, encouragement

hortor *v.t.* 1, *dep*, to encourage, urge, cheer on

hortŭlus, i *m*, little garden

hortus, i *m*, garden

hospĕs, ĭtis, *m*, **(hospĭta, ae** *f*), host(ess), guest, stranger

hospĭtālis, e *adj*, hospitable

hospĭtĭum, ii *n*, hospitality, friendship, lodgings

hostĭa, ae *f*, sacrificial victim

hostĭcus, a, um *adj*, of the enemy

hostīlis, e *adj, adv*, **īter**, hostile

hostis, is *c*, enemy, stranger

hūc *adv*, to this place or point

hui! *interj*, oh!

huius *genitive of* **hic**

hūiuscĕmŏdi, hūiusmŏdi *pron. adj,* (indecl.) of this sort

hūmāna, ōrum *n.pl*, human affairs

hūmānĕ *adv*, like a reasonable human being, courteously

hūmānĭtas, ātis *f*, humanity, gentleness, refinement

hūmānĭter *adv*, see **hūmānē**

hūmānus, a, um *adj*, human, mortal, humane, gentle, kind

hūmecto *v.t.* 1, to moisten

hūmĕo *v.i.* 2, to be wet

hūmĕrus, i *m*, shoulder, arm

hūmi *adv*, on or to the ground

hūmĭdus, a, um *adj*, damp, wet

hŭmĭlis, e *adj, adv*, **īter**, low, humble, abject

hŭmĭlĭtas, ātis *f*, lowness, insignificance, meanness

hūmo *v.t.* 1, to bury

hūmor, ōris *m*, liquid

hūmus, i *f*, the ground, region

hўăcinthus(os), i *m*, blue iris

hўaena, ae *f*, hyena

hўălus, i *m*, glass

hybrĭda, ae *c*, crossbreed

hўdra, ae *f*, seven-headed water snake

hydrĭa, ae *f*, jug

hydrops, ōpis *m*, dropsy

hydrus, i *m*, water snake

hўmen, mĕnis *m*, marriage

hўperbŏlē, es *f*, exaggeration, hyperbole

hystrĭx, īcis *f*, porcupine

I

īambēus, a, um *adj*, iambic

īambus, i *m*, iambic foot (two syllables, short followed by long)

īanthĭnus, a, um *adj*, violet in colour

īāpyx, iapЎgis *m*, West-North-West wind

īaspis, ĭdis *f*, jasper

ĭbì *adv*, there, then

ĭbĭdem *adv*, in that same place, at that very moment

ĭbis, ĭdis *f*, scared bird, ibis

īcĭo (īco), īci, ictum *v.t.* 3, to hit, strike (a bargain)

ictus, ūs *m*, blow, stroke, shot

id see **is**

idcirco *adv*, for that reason

īdem, ĕădem, ĭdem *pron*, the same

īdentĭdem *adv*, repeatedly

ĭdĕo *adv*, for that reason

ĭdĭōta, ae *m*, layman

ĭdōnĕus, a, um *adj*, suitable, capable, sufficient

īdus, ŭum *f.pl*, the ides, 13th or 15th day of the month

īdyllĭum, ii *n*, idyll

īgĭtur *adv*, therefore, then

ignārus, a, um *adj*, unaware

ignāvĭa, ae *f*, laziness, cowardice

ignāvus, a, um *adj, adv*, **ē**, lazy, cowardly

ignesco *v.i.* 3, to catch fire

ignĕus, a, um *adj*, burning

ignĭcŭlus, i *m*, spark

ignĭfer, ĕra, ĕrum *adj*, fiery

ignis, is *m*, fire, glow

ignōbĭlis, e *adj*, unknown, obscure

ignōbĭlĭtas, ātis *f*, obscurity

ignōmĭnĭa, ae *f*, disgrace

ignōmĭnĭōsus, a, um *adj*, shameful

ignōrans, ntis *adj*, unaware

ignōrantĭa, ae *f*, ignorance

ignōrātĭo, ōnis *f*, ignorance

ignōro *v.i.t.* 1, to be unaware (of)

ignosco, nōvi, nōtum *v.t.* 3 *(with dat. of person)*, to forgive

ignōtus, a, um *adj*, unknown, of low birth

ii see **is**

īlex, īcis *f*, evergreen, oak

īlĭa, ĭum *n.pl*, groin, flank
īlĭcet *adv*, immediately
īlĭco *adv*, immediately
īlignus, a, um *adj*, of oak
illa see **ille**
illăbĕfactus, a, um *adj*, unbroken
illābor, psus *v.i.* 3, *dep*, to slip, glide, fall
illac *adv*, on that side
illăcessītus, a, um *adj*, unprovoked
illăcrĭmābĭlis, e *adj*, unlamented
illăcrĭmo *v.i.* 1, to weep over
illaesus, a, um *adj*, unhurt
illaetābĭlis, e *adj*, gloomy
illăquĕo *v.t.* 1, to ensnare
illātus see **infero**
ille, a, ud *pron, adj*, that, he, she, it

illud see **ille**
illūdo, si, sum *v.i.t.* 3, to play; mock, ridicule
illūmĭno *v.t.* 1, to light up
illustris, e *adj*, lighted up, distinct, distinguished
illustro *v.t.* 1, to elucidate, make famous
illŭvĭes, ēi *f*, dirt
ĭmāgo, ĭnis *f*, statue, picture, copy, echo, conception
imbēcillĭtas, ātis *f*, weakness
imbēcillus, a, um *adj*, weak
imbellis, e *adj*, unwarlike
imber, bris *m*, rain, shower
imberbis, e *adj*, beardless
imbĭbo, bĭbi *v.t.* 3, to drink in
imbrex, ĭcis *f*, gutter, tile

Insight

On its own the pronoun *ille, illa, illud* means 'that man', 'that woman', 'that thing' depending on gender and context. Often, however, it is used as if it was a personal pronoun and is best translated as 'he', 'she', 'it'.

illĕcĕbra, ae *f*, charm, allurement, bait
illĕcĕbrōsus, a, um *adj*, alluring
illĕpĭdus, a, um *adj*, ill-mannered, rude
illex, ĭcis *c*, decoy
illībātus, a, um *adj*, unimpaired
illībĕrālis, e *adj*, mean
illic *adv*, there, over there
illĭcĭo, lexi, ctum *v.t.* 3, to allure, entice
illĭcĭtus, a, um *adj*, forbidden
illĭco *adv*, there, immediately
illīdo, si, sum *v.t.* 3, to strike, dash, beat
illīgo *v.t.* 1, to tie, fasten
illinc *adv*, from there
illĭno, lēvi, lĭtum *v.t.* 3, to smear, spread
illittĕrātus, a, um *adj*, illiterate
illīus *genitive of* **ille**
illō *adv*, to that place
illōtus, a, um *adj*, dirty
illūc *adv*, to that place
illūcesco, luxi *v.i.* 3, to grow light, dawn, shine

imbrĭfer, ĕra, ĕrum *adj*, rainy
imbŭo, ŭi, ūtum *v.t.* 3, to soak, infect, instil, train
ĭmĭtābĭlis, e *adj*, easily intimidated
ĭmĭtātio, ōnis *f*, imitation
ĭmĭtātor, ōris *m*, imitator
ĭmĭtātrix, ĭcis *f*, imitator
ĭmĭtor *v.t.* 1, *dep*, to imitate
immădesco, dŭi *v.i.* 3, to become wet
immānĭa, ĭum *n.pl*, horrors
immanis, e *adj, adv*, **ē, ĭter,** enormous, frightful, savage
immānĭtas, ātis *f*, enormity, barbarism, vastness
immansuētus, a, um *adj*, untamed
immātūrus, a, um *adj*, untimely, immature
immĕdĭcābĭlis, e *adj*, incurable
immĕmor, ōris *adj*, heedless
immĕmŏrātus, a, um *adj*, unmentioned
immensĭtas, ātis *f*, immensity
immensum, i *n*, immensity
immensus, a, um *adj*, measureless, endless

immĕrens, ntis *adj*, undeserving, innocent

immergo, si, sum *v.t.* 3, to dip, plunge, immerse

immĕrītus, a, um *adj*, undeserved

immētātus, a, um *adj*, unmeasured

immìgro, *v.i.* 1, to go into

immĭnĕo *v.i.* 2, to overhang, overlook, threaten, strive for

immĭnŭo, ŭi, ūtum *v.t.* 3, to reduce, weaken, destroy

immĭnūtĭo, ōnis *f*, weakening

immĭnūtus, a, um *adj*, unabated

immiscĕo, scŭi, xtum *v.t.* 2, to mix in, blend, unite

immĭsĕrābĭlis, e *adj*, unpitied

immĭsĕrĭcors, cordis *adj*, merciless

immissĭo, ōnis *f*, admission

immītis, e *adj*, harsh, rough

immitto, mīsi, ssum *v.t.* 3, to send in, let fly, incite, allow to grow wild

immo *adv*, on the contrary

immōbĭlis, e *adj*, immovable

immōbĭlĭtas, ātis *f*, immobility

immŏdĕrātus, a, um *adj, adv,* **ē,** excessive

immŏdĭcus, a, um *adj*, excessive

immŏlātĭo, ōnis *f*, sacrifice

immŏlo *v.t.* 1, to sacrifice, kill

immŏrĭor, mortŭus *v.i.* 3, *dep*, to die, die away

immortāles, ĭum *m.pl*, the gods

immortālis, e *adj*, immortal

immortālĭtas, ātis *f*, immortality

immōtus, a, um *adj*, unmoved

immūgĭo *v.i.* 4, to roar, resound

immundus, a, um *adj*, dirty

immūnis, e *adj*, exempt, idle, devoid of

immūnĭtas, ātis *f*, exemption

immūnītus, a, um *adj*, unfortified

immurmŭro *v.i.* 1, to murmur at

immūtābĭlis, e *adj*, unchangeable

immūtātĭo, ōnis *f*, interchange

immūto *v.t.* 1, to change, alter

impācātus, a, um *adj*, unsubdued

impar, ăris *adj, adv,* **ĭter,** unequal, uneven

impărātus, a, um *adj*, unprepared

impastus, a, um *adj*, hungry

impătĭens, ntis *adj*, impatient

impăvĭdus, a, um *adj*, fearless

impeccābĭlis, e *adj*, faultless

impĕdīmenta, ōrum *n.pl*, luggage

impĕdīmentum, i *n*, obstacle

impĕdĭo *v.t.* 4, to hinder, entangle, hamper

impĕdītus, a, um *adj*, difficult; (soldiers) in full marching-kit

impĕdītĭo, ōnis *f*, obstruction

impello, pŭli, pulsum *v.t.* 3, to strike upon, drive on, urge, overthrow

impendens, ntis *adj*, overhanging

impendĕo *v.i.t.* 2, to overhang; threaten

impendĭum, ii *n*, cost, expense

impendo, di, sum *v.t.* 3, to expend, devote

impĕnĕtrābĭlis, e *adj*, impenetrable

impensa, ae *f*, cost, expense

impensus, a, um *adj, adv,* **ē,** large, strong, expensive

impĕrātor, ōris *m*, general

impĕrātōrĭus, a, um *adj*, of a general

impĕrātum, i *n*, order

imperfectus, a, um *adj*, incomplete

impĕrĭōsus, a, um *adj*, powerful, mighty, tyrannical

impĕrītĭa, ae *f*, inexperience

impĕrīto *v.i.t.* 1, to command

impĕrītus, a, um *adj, with genit*, unskilled, or inexperienced in

impĕrĭum, ii *n*, power, command, control, dominion

impermissus, a, um *adj*, forbidden

impĕro *v.t.* 1, *with dat. of person,* to command, impose on, demand, requisition, rule

impertĭo *v.t.* 4, to share

impervĭus, a, um *adj*, impervious

impĕtĭbĭlis, e *adj*, intolerable

impĕtrābĭlis, e *adj*, attainable

impĕtro *v.t.* 1, to obtain, get

impĕtus, ūs *m*, attack, impetuosity, impulse

impexus, a, um *adj*, uncombed

impĭĕtas, ātis *f*, lack of respect for duty, disloyalty

impĭger, gra, grum *adj*, energetic

impingo, pēgi, pactum *v.t.* 3, to thrust, drive, strike (something) against

impĭus, a, um *adj*, undutiful, unpatriotic, disloyal, wicked
implācābĭlis, e *adj*, implacable
implācātus, a, um *adj*, unsatisfied
implăcĭdus, a, um *adj*, rough
implecto, xi, xum *v.t.* 3, to plait, interweave
implĕo, ēvi, ētum *v.t.* 2, to fill, complete, fulfil
implĭcātĭo, ōnis *f*, entwining, complication
implĭcātus, a, um *adj*, entangled, confused
implĭco *v.t.* 1, to entangle, involve, grasp, unite
implōrātĭo, ōnis *f*, entreaty
implōro *v.t.* 1, to implore, beg for
implūmis, e *adj*, unfledged, callow
implŭvĭum, ii *n*, rain-tank in floor of atrium of Roman house
impŏlītus, a, um *adj*, unpolished
impōno, pŏsŭi, pŏsĭtum *v.t.* 3, to place in or on, impose, assign
importo *v.t.* 1, to carry in, import, cause
importūnĭtas, ātis *f*, insolence
importūnus, a, um *adj, adv*, **ē**, inconvenient, unsuitable, troublesome, rude
impŏtens, ntis *adj*, powerless, weak, violent, headstrong
impŏtentĭa, ae *f*, violence
impransus, a, um *adj*, fasting
imprĕcātĭo, ōnis *f*, imprecation, curse

imprŏbĭtas, ātis *f*, wickedness
imprŏbo *v.t.* 1, to disapprove
imprŏbus, a, um *adj, adv*, **ē**, bad, wicked, violent, enormous, shameless
imprōvĭdus, a, um *adj*, not anticipating
imprōvīsus, a, um *adj, adv*, **o**, unexpected
imprūdens, ntis *adj, adv*, **nter**, unsuspecting, unaware
imprūdentĭa, ae *f*, lack of foresight
impūbes, is *adj*, youthful
impŭdens, ntis *adj*, shameless
impŭdentĭa, ae *f*, impudence
impŭdīcĭtĭa, ae *f*, shameful behaviour
impŭdīcus, a, um *adj*, shameless, lewd, disgusting
impugno *v.t.* 1, to attack
impulsor, ōris *m*, instigator
impulsus, ūs *m*, pressure, impulse, suggestion
impūnĕ *adv*, without punishment
impūnĭtas, ātis *f*, impunity
impūnītus, a, um *adj*, unpunished
impūrus, a, um *adj*, filthy
impŭto *v.t.* 1, to reckon, ascribe, impute
īmus, a, um *adj*, lowest, last
in *prep. with abl*, in, on, within; among; *with acc*, into, towards, till, against
ĭnaccessus, a, um *adj*, inaccessible

Insight

A **preposition** is a short word that stands in front of a noun or pronoun to produce an adverbial phrase. In Latin prepositions can be followed either by the accusative or the ablative. Only the preposition *in* can be followed by both cases, having in each instance a different meaning.

---

imprĕcor *v.t.* 1, *dep*, to pray for something for someone
impressĭo, ōnis *f*, imprint, onset
impressus, a, um *adj*, stamped, printed
imprīmīs *adv*, especially
imprĭmo, pressi, ssum *v.t.* 3, to stamp, imprint, engrave

ĭnaedĭfĭco *v.t.* 1, to build on
ĭnaequābĭlis, e *adj*, uneven, unlike
ĭnaequālis, e *adj*, uneven, unlike
ĭnaequālĭtas, ātis *f*, inequality
ĭnaestĭmābĭlis, e *adj*, inestimable
ĭnămābĭlis, e *adj*, hateful
ĭnămāresco *v.i.* 3, to become bitter

ĭnambŭlo *v.i.* 1, to walk up and down

ĭnāne, is *n*, emptiness

ĭnănĭmus, a, um *adj*, lifeless

ĭnānis, e *adj*, *adv*, **īter,** empty, useless, vain

ĭnānĭtas, ātis *f*, emptiness

ĭnărātus, a, um *adj*, unploughed

ĭnardesco, arsi *v.i.* 3, to catch fire, glow

ĭnassŭētus, a, um *adj*, unaccustomed

ĭnaudax, ācis *adj*, timid

ĭnaudĭo *v.t.* 4, to hear

ĭnaudītus, a, um *adj*, unheard of

ĭnaugŭro *v.i.t* 1, to divine omens; to consecrate, inaugurate

ĭnaurātus, a, um *adj*, golden

ĭnauro *v.t.* 1, to cover with gold

ĭnauspĭcātus, a, um *adj*, without good omens

ĭnausus, a, um *adj*, unattempted

incaedŭus, a, um *adj*, uncut

incălesco, călŭi *v.i.* 3, to grow hot, glow

incallĭdus, a, um *adj*, stupid

incandesco, dŭi *v.i.* 3, to grow hot, glow

incānesco, nŭi *v.i.* 3, to grow grey or white

incanto *v.t.* 1, to chant, bewitch

incānus, a, um *adj*, grey, white

incassum *adv*, in vain

incastīgātus, a, um *adj*, unpunished

incautus, a, um *adj*, *adv*, **ē,** rash, careless, unexpected

incēdo, cessi, ssum *v.i.* 3, to advance, appear, enter

incendĭārĭus, ii *m*, and incendiary

incendĭum, ii *n*, fire, heat

incendo, cendi, censum *v.t.* 3, to burn, excite, irritate

incensus, a, um *adj*, unregistered

incensus, a, um *adj*, burning, excited

inceptĭo, ōnis *f*, an attempt, undertaking

inceptum, i *n*, an attempt, undertaking

incertum, i *n*, uncertainity

incertus, a, um *adj*, uncertain, hesitating, doubtful

incesso, cessīvi *v.t.* 3, to attack, accuse

incessus, ūs *m*, walk, pace, approach

incesto *v.t.* 1, to pollute

incestum , i *n*, adultery, incest

incestus, a, um *adj*, impure

incĭdo, cĭdi, cāsum *v.i.* 3, to fall into or upon, meet, happen, occur

incīdo, cīdi, sum *v.t.* 3, to cut into, carve, interrupt

incingo, nxi, nctum *v.t.* 3, to encircle

incĭpĭo, cēpi, ceptum *v.i.t.* 3, to begin; undertake

incīsĭo, ōnis *f*, an incision

incĭtāmentum, i *n*, incentive

incĭtātĭo, ōnis *f*, instigation, energy

incīsūra, ae *f*, cutting, incision

incĭtātus, a, um *adj*, swift

incĭto *v.t.* 1, to urge on, rouse, excite, inspire

incĭtus, a, um *adj*, swift

incĭto *v.t.* 1, to urge on, rouse, excite, inspire

incĭtus, a, um *adj*, swift

inclāmo *v.i.t.* 1, to cry out; call out, to rebuke, abuse

inclēmens, ntis *adj*, *adv*, **nter,** harsh, severe

inclēmentĭa, ae *f*, harshness

inclīnātĭo, ōnis *f*, leaning, tendency

inclīno *v.i.t.* 1, to sink, yield; bend, turn, change

inclīnātus, a, um *adj*, bent, disposed

inclĭtus, a, um *adj*, famous

inclūdo, si, sum *v.t.* 3, to shut in, include, finish

inclūsĭo, ōnis *f*, confinement

inclŭtus, a, um *adj*, famous

incoctus, a, um *adj*, uncooked

incognĭtus, a, um *adj*, unknown

incŏhātus, a, um *adj*, incomplete

incŏho *v.i.t.* 1, to begin; undertake

incŏla, ae *c*, inhabitant

incŏlo, lŭi *v.i.t.* 3, to settle; inhabit

incŏlŭmis, e *adj*, safe, sound

incŏlŭmĭtas, ātis *f*, safety

incŏmĭtātus, a, um *adj*, unaccompanied

incommŏdĭtas, ātis *f*, unsuitability

incommŏdo *v.i.* 1, to be annoying

incommŏdum, i *n*, disadvantage

incommŏdus, a, um *adj, adv,* **ē**, troublesome, unsuitable

incompertus, a, um *adj*, unknown

incompŏsĭtus, a, um *adj*, badly arranged

incomptus, a, um *adj*, unadorned

inconcessus, a, um *adj*, illict

inconcinnus, a, um *adj*, awkward

incondītus, a, um *adj*, irregular, confused, rude

inconsīdĕrātus, a, um *adj, adv,* **ē**, thoughtless, inconsiderate

inconsōlābĭlis, e *adj*, inconsolable

inconstans, ntis *adj, adv,* **nter**, inconsistent, fickle

inconstantĭa, ae *f*, inconstancy

inconsultus, a, um *adj, adv,* **ē**, without advice, indiscreet

inconsumptus, a, um *adj*, unconsumed

incontāmĭnātus, a, um *adj*, uncontaminated

incontĭnens, ntis *adj, adv,* **nter**, immoderate

incŏquo, xi, ctum *v.t.* 3, to boil, dye

incorruptus, a, um *adj*, unspoiled

incrēbresco, brŭi *v.i.* 3, to increase, become prevalent

incrēdībĭlis, e *adj, adv,* **ĭter**, incredible, unbelievable

incrēdŭlus, a, um *adj*, unbelieving

incrēmentum, i *n*, increase

incrĕpo, ŭi, ĭtum *v.i.t.* 1, to rattle, clatter; blare out, rebuke, reprimand

incresco, ēvi *v.i.* 3, to grow

incrŭentus, a, um *adj*, bloodless

incrusto *v.t.* 1, to coat over

incŭbo, ŭi, ĭtum *v.i.* 1, to lie in or on, rest on, fall upon

inculco *v.t.* 1, to trample on, cram in, force on, obtude

incultus, a, um *adj, adv,* **ē**, uncultivated, unpolished

incumbo, cŭbŭi, ĭtum *v.i.* 3, to lean or lie on, overhang, fall upon, take pains over, influence

incūnābŭla, ōrum *n.pl*, cradle, birthplace, origin, swaddling clothes

incūrĭa, ae *f*, neglect

incūrĭōsus, a, um *adj, adv,* **ē**, indifferent

incurro, curri, cursum *v.i.t.* 3, to run at, happen; attack

incursĭo, ōnis *f*, raid, attack

incurso *v.i.t* 1, to run to; attack, strike

incursus, ūs *m*, attack

incurvo *v.t.* 1, to bend

invurvus, a, um *adj*, bent

incūs, ūdis *f*, anvil

incūso *v.t.* 1, to accuse, blame

incustōdītus, a, um *adj*, unguarded

incŭtĭo, cussi, cussum *v.t.* 3, to strike upon, hurl, inflict

indāgātĭo, ōnis *f*, investigation

indāgo *v.t.* 1, to track down

indāgo, ĭnis *f*, enclosing

indĕ *adv*, from there, then

indēbĭtus, a, um *adj*, not due

indĕcor, ŏris *adj*, disgraceful

indĕcŏro *v.t.* 1, to disgrace

indĕcōrus, a, um *adj, adv,* **ē**, unbecoming, unsightly, disgraceful

indēfensus, a, um *adj*, undefended

indēfessus, a, um *adj*, unwearied

indēlēbĭlis, e *adj*, indestructible

indēlībātus, a, um *adj*, untouched

indemnātus, a, um *adj*, unsentenced

indēprensus, a, um *adj*, unnoticed

index, ĭcis *m, f*, forefinger, informer, sign, list

indĭcĭum, ii *n*, information, evidence, proof, indication

indĭco *v.t.* 1, to show, indicate, give evidence

indīco, xi, ctum *v.t.* 3, to announce, appoint, impose

indictus, a, um *adj*, unsaid

indĭdem *adv*, from the same place

indĭes *adv*, from day to day

indiffĕrens, ntis *adj*, indifferent

indĭgĕna, ae *adj*, native

indĭgĕo *v.i.* 2, to need, want

indīgestus, a, um *adj*, confused

indignans, ntis *adj*, enraged

indignātĭo, ōnis *f*, indignation

indignĭtas, ātis *f*, shameful behaviour, unworthiness

indignor *v.t.* 1, *dep,* to be indignant at, scorn

indignus, a, um *adj, adv,* **ē,** unworthy, shameful, cruel

indĭgus, a, um *adj,* needing

indīlĭgens, ntis *adj, adv,* **nter,** careless

indīlĭgentĭa, ae *f,* carelessness

indiscrētus, a, um *adj,* unseparated

indīsertus, a, um *adj,* at a loss for words

indīvĭdŭus, a, um *adj,* indivisible

indo, dĭdi, dĭtum *v.t.* 3, to put or place upon or into, attach

indŏcĭlis, e *adj,* unteachable, untaught

indoctus, a, um *adj,* untaught

indŏles, is *f,* inborn abilities

indŏleso, lŭi *v.i.* 3, to be in pain, to be troubled

indŏmĭtus, a, um *adj,* untamed

indormĭo *v.i.* 4, to fall asleep over

indōtātus, a, um *adj,* without a dowry, poor

indŭbĭto *v.i.* 1, to distrust

indŭbĭus, a, um *adj,* not doubtful

indūco, xi, ctum *v.t.* 3, to lead in, conduct, exhibit, spread over, put on (clothes), induce, resolve, cancel

inductĭo, ōnis *f,* introduction, exhibition, intention

indulgens, ntis *adj, adv,* **nter,** kind, indulgent, fond

indulgentĭa, ae *f,* indulgence

indulgĕo, si, tum *v.i.t.* 2, *with dat,* to be kind to; permit, grant

indŭo, ŭi, ūtum *v.t.* 3, to put on (garment), assume

indūro *v.t.* 1, to harden

indūsĭum, ii *n,* woman's petticoat

industrĭa, ae *f,* diligence; *with* **de** *or* **ex** on purpose

industrĭus, a, um *adj,* diligent

indūtĭae, ārum *f.pl,* truce

indūtus, a, um *adj,* clothed

ĭnēdĭa, ae *f,* fasting

ĭnēlĕgans, ntis *adj, adv,* **nter,** unrefined

ĭnēluctābĭlis, e *adj,* unavoidable

ĭnemptus, a, um *adj,* unbought

ĭnēnarrābĭlis, e *adj,* indescribable

ĭnĕo *v.i.t.* 4, to begin; enter, calculate, estimate, contrive

ĭneptĭae, ārum *f.pl,* absurdities

ĭneptus, a, um *adj, adv,* **ē,** improper, inept, foolish

ĭnermis, e *adj,* unarmed

ĭners, rtis *adj,* unskilful, idle, sluggish

ĭnertĭa, ae *f,* ignorance, idleness

ĭnērŭdītus, a, um *adj,* illiterate

ĭnēvītābĭlis, e *adj,* unavoidable

ĭnexcūsābĭlis, e *adj,* inexcusable

ĭnexercĭtātus, a, um *adj,* untrained

ĭnexhaustus, a, um *adj,* inexhaustible

ĭnexōrābĭlis, e *adj,* inexorable

ĭnexpectātus, a, um *adj,* unexpected

ĭnexpertus, a, um *adj,* inexperienced, untried

ĭnexpĭābĭlis, e *adj,* irreconcilable

ĭnexplēbĭlis, e *adj,* insatiable

ĭnexplētus, a, um *adj,* unsatisfied

ĭnexplĭcābĭlis, e *adj,* inexplicable

ĭnexplōrātus, a, um *adj,* unexplored

ĭnexpugnābĭlis, e *adj,* impregnable

ĭnexstinctus, a, um *adj,* imperishable

ĭnextrĭcābĭlis, e *adj,* inextricable

infàbrē *adv,* unskilfully

infăcētus, a, um *adj,* coarse

infāmĭa, ae *f,* disgrace

infāmis, e *adj,* disreputable

infāmo *v.t.* 1, to disgrace

infandus, a, um *adj,* unutterable

infans, ntis *adj,* speechless

infans, ntis *c,* child, baby

infantĭa, ae *f,* speechlessness, infancy

infātŭo *v.t.* 1, to make a fool of

infaustus, a, um *adj,* unfortunate

infector, ōris *m,* dyer

infectus, a, um *adj,* unfinished

infēcundus, a, um *adj,* unfruitful

infēlix, īcis *adj,* unhappy, unfortunate, barren

infensus, a, um *adj,* enraged

infĕri, ōrum *m.pl,* the dead

infĕrĭae, ārum *f.pl,* sacrifices in honour of the dead

infĕrĭor, ĭus *adv,* lower, later, younger, inferior

infĕrĭus *adv,* lower

infernus, a, um *adj,* lower, underground

infĕri, ōrum *m.pl,* inhabitants of the underworld, the dead

infero, inferre, intŭli, illātum *v.t, irreg,* to bring to or against, attack, produce, inflict

infĕrus, a, um *adj,* below, lower

infervesco, ferbŭi *v.i.* 3, to boil

infesto *v.t.* 1, to attack, molest

infestus, a, um *adj, adv,* ē, dangerous, hostile, unsafe

inficĭo, fēci, fectum *v.t.* 3, to stain, dye, taint, corrupt

infidēlis, e *adj,* untrustworthy

infidēlĭtas, ātis *f,* treachery

infidus, a, um *adj,* treacherous

infigo, xi, xum *v.t.* 3, to fix into, drive in, imprint

infĭmus, a, um *adj,* lowest

infindo, fīdi, fissum *v.t.* 3, to cut into

infinĭtas, ātis *f,* endlessness

infinĭtus, a, um *adj, adv,* ē, unlimited, endless

infirmātĭo, ōnis *f,* weakening

infirmĭtas, ātis *f,* weakness

infirmo *v.t.* 1, to weaken, annul

infirmus, a, um *adj, adv,* ē, weak

infit *v, defect,* he (she, it) begins

infitĭas ĕo (ire, ii) to deny

infitĭātĭo, ōnis *f,* denial

infitĭātor, ōris *m,* bad debtor

infitĭor *v.t.* 1, *dep,* to deny

inflammātĭo, ōnis *f,* inflammation, setting on fire

inflammo *v.t.* 1, to set on fire

inflātus, ūs *m,* blast

inflātus, a, um *adj,* puffed up, haughty, inflated

inflecto, xi, xum *v.t.* 3, to bend

inflētus, a, um *adj,* unmourned

inflexĭbĭlis, e *adj,* inflexible

inflexĭo, ōnis *f,* bending

infligo, xi, ctum *v.t.* 3, to strike (something) against

inflo *v.t.* 1, to blow into

inflŭo, xi, xum *v.i.* 3, to flow into, crowd in

infŏdĭo, fōdi, fossum *v.t.* 3, to dig in, bury

informātĭo, ōnis *f,* outline

informis, e *adj,* shapeless

informo *v.t.* 1, to shape, sketch, educate

infortūnātus, a, um *adj,* unfortunate

infrā *adv, and prep. with acc,* below, under

infractĭo, ōnis *f,* breaking

infractus, a, um *adj,* broken, exhausted

infrĕmo, ŭi *v.i.* 3, to growl

infrendĕo *v.i.* 2, to gnash the teeth, threaten

infrēnis, e (us, a, um) *adj,* unbridled

infrēno *v.t.* 1, to bridle, curb

infrĕquens, ntis *adj,* rare, not well filled

infrĕquentĭa, ae *f,* scantiness

infringo, frēgi, fractum *v.t.* 3, to break off, crush, weaken

infŭla, ae *f,* headband, ribbon

infundĭbŭlum, i *n,* funnel

infundo, fūdi, fūsum *v.t.* 3, to pour out, lay before, impart

infusco *v.t.* 1, to darken, stain

infūsus, a, um *adj,* streaming or falling over

ingĕmĭno *v.i.t.* 1, to increase; repeat, redouble

ingĕmisco, mŭi *v.i.* 3, to sigh

ingĕmo, ŭi *v.i.t.* 3, to groan; lament, mourn

ingĕnĕro *v.t.* 1, to produce

ingĕnĭōsus, a, um *adj, adv,* ē, talented, adapted to

ingĕnĭum, ii *n,* natural disposition, abilities, intelligence

ingens, ntis *adj,* huge, famous

ingĕnŭĭtas, ātis *f,* good birth, gentlemanly character

ingĕnŭus, a, um *adj, adv,* ē, natural, inborn, freeborn, frank, honourable

ingĕnŭus, i *m,* (a, ae *f*), freeborn man or woman

ingĕro, gessi, gestum *v.t.* 3, to carry, throw or thrust into

ingigno, gĕnŭi, gĕnĭtum *v.t.* 3, to implant, produce

inglōrĭus, a, um *adj,* inglorious

inglŭvĭes, ēi *f,* gizzard, maw

ingrātĭis *adv,* unwillingly

ingrātus, a, um *adj, adv,* ē, unpleasant, ungrateful

ingrăvesco *v.i.* 3, to become heavy or worse

ingrăvo *v.t.* 1, to aggravate

ingrĕdĭor, gressus *v.i.t.* 3, *dep*, to advance; enter, upon

ingressĭo, ōnis *f*, entering, pace

ingressus, ūs *m*, entrance, inroad, commencement

ingrŭo, ŭi *v.i.* 3, to attack

inguen, ĭnis *n*, groin, abdomen

ingurgĭto *v.t.* 1 (*with* **se**) to gorge, addict one's self to

ĭnhăbĭlis, e *adj*, unwieldy, incapable

ĭnhăbĭtābĭlis, e *adj*, uninhabitable

ĭnhaerĕo, si, sum *v.i.* 2, to cling to, adhere to

ĭnhaeresco, haesi, haesum *v.i.* 3, to cling to, adhere to

ĭnhĭbĕo *v.t.* 2, to restrain

ĭnhĭo *v.i* 1, to gape, gaze

ĭnhŏnestus, a, um *adj*, shameful

ĭnhŏnōrātus, a, um *adj*, unhonoured

ĭnhorrĕo *v.i.* 2, to bristle, shiver

ĭnhorresco *v.i.* 3, to bristle, shiver

ĭnhospĭtālis, e *adj*, inhospitable

ĭnhospĭtus, a, um *adj*, inhospitable

ĭnhūmānĭtas, ātis *f*, barbarity, niggardliness

ĭnhūmānus, a, um *adj, adv,* ē, ĭter, savage, uncivilized, rude

ĭnhūmātus, a, um *adj*, unburied

ĭnĭbi *adv*, there

ĭnĭcĭo, iēci, iectum *v.t.* 3, to throw into, seize, inspire

ĭnĭmīcĭtĭa, ae *f*, enmity

ĭnĭmīco *v.t.* 1, to make into enemies

ĭnĭmīcus, a, um *adj, adv,* ē, unfriendly, hostile

ĭnĭmīcus, i *m*, (**a, ae** *f*), enemy

ĭnīquĭtas, ātis *f*, unevenness, difficulty, injustice

ĭnīquus, a, um *adj, adv,* ē, uneven, unfair, unfortunate, hostile, disadvantageous

inĭtĭo *v.t.* 1, to initiate

ĭnĭtĭo *adv*, in the beginning

ĭnĭtĭum, ii *n*, beginning, origin; *pl*, first principles, sacred rites

ĭnĭūcundus, a, um *adj, adv,* ē, unpleasant

iniungo, nxi, nctum *v.t.* 3, to join on to, inflict, impose

ĭnĭūrātus, a, um *adj*, without taking an oath

ĭnĭūrĭa, ae *f*, injury, wrong

ĭnĭūrĭōsus, a, um *adj*, wrongful

ĭnĭussu *adv*, without orders

ĭnĭussus, a, um *adj*, of one's accord

ĭnĭustĭtĭa, ae *f*, injustice

ĭnĭustus, a, um *adj, adv,* ē, unjust, wrongful, harsh

innascor, nātus *v.i.* 3, *dep*, to be born in, grow up in

innăto *v.t.* 1, to swim, float in

innātus, a, um *adj*, innate

innāvĭgābĭlis, e *adj*, unnavigable

innecto, xŭi, xum *v.t.* 3, to tie, fasten, attach, contrive

innītor, nixus (nīsus) *v.* 3, *dep*, *with dat. or abl*, to lean on

inno *v.i.* 1, to swim, float in

innŏcens, ntis *adj*, harmless, blameless

innŏcentĭa, ae *f*, integrity

innŏcŭus, a, um *adj*, harmless

innoxĭus, a, um *adj*, harmless, innocent, unhurt

innūbus, a, um *adj*, unmarried

innŭmĕrābĭlis, e *adj*, countless

innŭmĕrus, a, um *adj*, countless

innŭo, ŭi, ūtum *v.i* 3, to nod, hint

innuptus, a, um *adj*, unmarried

ĭnobservātus, a, um *adj*, unperceived

ĭnoffensus, a, um *adj*, untouched, uninterrupted

ĭnŏlesco, lēvi, lĭtum *v.i* 3, to grow in, take root

ĭnŏpĭa, ae *f*, lack, need

ĭnŏpīnans, ntis *adj*, unaware

ĭnŏpīnātus, a, um *adj, adv,* ē, ō, unexpected

ĭnŏpīnus, a, um *adj*, unexpected

ĭnopportūnus, a, um *adj*, unfitting, inopportune

ĭnops, ŏpis *adj*, helpless, needy

ĭnordĭnātus, a, um *adj*, in disorder

ĭnornātus, a, um *adj*, unadorned

inquam *v, irreg,* I say

inquĭes, ētis *f*, restlessness

inquĭētus, a, um *adj*, restless

inquĭlīnus, i *m*, lodger

inquĭnātus, a, um *adj,* filthy

inquĭno *v.t.* 1, to stain, corrupt

inquīro, sīvi, sītum *v.t.* 3, to search for, examine

inquīsītĭo, ōnis *f,* legal investigation

insălūbris, e *adj,* unhealthy

insălūtātus, a, um *adj,* without saying goodbye

insānābĭlis, e *adj,* incurable

insānĭa, ae *f,* madness, folly

insānĭo *v.i.* 4, to be insane, to rage

insānĭtas, ātis *f,* disease

insānus, a, um *adj, adv,* ē, insane, frantic, excessive

insătĭābĭlis, e *adj,* insatiable

inscĭens, ntis *adj,* unaware

inscĭentĭa, ae *f,* ignorance, inexperience

inscītĭa, ae *f,* ignorance, inexperience

inscītus, a, um *adj, adv,* ē, ignorant, stupid

inscĭus, a, um *adj,* unaware

inscrībo, psi, ptum *v.t.* 3, to write on, attribute

inscriptĭo, ōnis *f,* title

insculpo, psi, ptum *v.t.* 3, to engrave

insĕco, cŭi, ctum *v.t.* 1, to cut up

insectātĭo, ōnis *f,* pursuit

insectātor, ōris *m,* pursuer

insector *v.t.* 1, *dep,* to pursue, reproach

insectum, i *n,* insect

insĕnesco, nŭi *v.i.* 3, to grow old at

insĕpultus, a, um *adj,* unburied

insĕquor, sĕcūtus *v.i.t.* 3, *dep,* to follow; pursue, reproach

insĕro, sēvi, sĭtum *v.t.* 3, to implant, ingraft

insĕro, rŭi, rtum *v.t.* 3, to put in, introduce

inserto *v.t.* 1, to insert

inservĭo *v.i.* 4, to serve, be submissive to, attend to

insĭdĕo, sēdi, sessum *v.i.t.* 2, to sit upon, be fixed; occupy, inhabit

insĭdĭae, ārum *f.pl,* ambush, plot; *with* ex *or* per, craftily

insĭdĭor *v.* 1, *dep, with dat,* to lie in ambush

insĭdĭōsus, a, um *adj, adv,* ē, cunning, dangerous

insīdo, sēdi, sessum *v.i.t.* 3, to settle on or in; occupy

insigne, is *n,* mark, sign, costume, signal, ornament

insignĭo *v.t.* 4, to make distinguished

insignis, e *adj,* conspicuous, famous, distinguished

insĭlĭo, ŭi *v.i.* 4, to spring upon

insĭmŭlo *v.t.* 1, to accuse

insincērus, a, um *adj,* tainted

insĭnŭo *v.i.t.* 1, to penetrate; insinuate

insĭpĭens, ntis *adj,* foolish

insĭpĭentĭa, ae *f,* folly

insisto, stĭti *v.i.t.* 3, to step, stand, begin, halt; devote oneself to

insĭtus, a, um *adj,* inborn

insŏlens, ntis *adj, adv,* **nter,** unusual, unaccustomed, haughty

insŏlentĭa, ae *f,* strangeness, novelty, affectation, arrogance

insŏlītus, a, um *adj,* unaccustomed, unusual

insomnĭa, ae *f,* sleeplessness

insomnis, e *adj,* sleepless

insomnĭum, ii *n,* dream

insŏno, ŭi *v.i.* 1, to resound

insons, ntis *adj,* innocent, harmless

inspecto *v.t.* 1, to look at

inspērans, ntis *adj,* not hoping

inspērātus, a, um *adj,* unhoped for, unexpected

inspergo, si, sum *v.t.* 3, to sprinkle

inspĭcĭo, spexi, spectum *v.t.* 3, to examine, consider

inspīro *v.t.* 1, to breathe on, inspire

instăbĭlis, e *adj,* unsteady, changeable

instans, ntis *adj,* present

instar *n, indecl,* resemblance, appearance, value; *with genit,* as big as, like

instauro *v.t.* 1, to renew

insterno, strāvi, strātum *v.t.* 3, to spread or cover over

instīgo *v.t.* 1, to incite

instillo *v.t.* 1, to instil

instĭmŭlo *v.t.* 1, to spur on

instinctus, ūs *m*, impulse

instinctus, a, um *adj*, incited

instĭtor, ōris *m*, commercial traveller

instĭtŭo, ŭi, ūtum *v.t.* 3, to set up, appoint, undertake, resolve, arrange, train

instĭtūtĭo, ōnis *f*, arrangement, custom, education

instĭtūtum, i *n*, purpose, plan, custom

insto, stĭti, stātum *v.i.* 1, to stand over, harass, impend, urge on, pursue

instructus, a, um *adj*, arranged, provided with

instrūmentum, i *n*, tool, stores

instrŭo, xi, ctum *v.t.* 3, to erect, arrange, provide, teach

insŭāvis, e *adj*, unpleasant

insuesco, ēvi, ētum *v.i.t.* 3, to become accustomed; to accustom

insuētus, a, um *adj*, unaccustomed to, unusual

insŭla, ae *f*, island, block of flats

insŭlānus, i *m*, islander

insulsĭtas, ātis *f*, silliness

insulsus, a, um *adj, adv*, ē, tasteless, silly

insulto *v.i.t.* 1, to jump, leap; to spring at, abuse

insum, inesse, infŭi *v.i, irreg*, to be in, be contained in

insūmo, mpsi, mptum *v.t.* 3, to employ, expend

insŭo, ŭi, ūtum *v.t.* 3, to sew on

insŭper *adv, and prep. with acc*, moreover, besides; above

insŭpĕrābĭlis, e *adj*, insurmountable

insurgo, surrexi, rectum *v.i.* 3, to arise, rise to

insūsurro *v.i.t.* 1, to whisper

intābesco, bŭi *v.i.* 3, to waste away

intactus, a, um *adj*, untouched, unattempted, chaste

intāmĭnātus, a, um *adj*, pure

intectus, a, um *adj*, uncovered

intĕger, gra, grum *adj, adv*, ē, untouched, perfect, blameless, unspoiled, undecided

intĕgo, xi, ctum *v.t.* 3, to cover

intĕgrĭtas, ātis *f*, completeness, uprightness

intĕgro *v.t.* 1, to renew, refresh

intĕgŭmentum, i *n*, covering, disguise

intellĕgens, ntis *adj*, understanding

intellĕgentĭa, ae *f*, understanding

intellĕgo, xi, ctum *v.t.* 3, to understand, perceive

intĕmĕrātus, a, um *adj*, pure

intempĕrans, ntis *adj*, extravagant

intempĕrantĭa, ae *f*, extravagance

intempĕrĭes, ēi *f*, inclement weather, violence

intempestīvus, a, um *adj, adv*, ē, untimely, inconvenient

intempestus, a, um *adj*, unseasonable, unhealthy; (*with* nox) the dead of night

intendo, di, tum (sum) *v.t.* 3, to stretch or spread out, aim, direct, threaten, concentrate, intend

intentātus, a, um *adj*, untried

intentĭo, ōnis *f*, tension, effort, application

intentus, a, um *adj, adv*, ē, stretched, bent, intent

intĕpesco, pŭi *v.i.* 3, to grow warm

inter *adv, and prep. with acc*, among, between, during

intercēdo, cessi, ssum *v.i.* 3, to go between, intervene, occur

intercessĭo, ōnis *f*, veto, intervention

intercessor, ōris *m*, mediator, surety, user of the veto

intercīdo, di, sum *v.t.* 3, to cut up

intercĭdo, di *v.i.* 3, to happen, fall down, perish

intercĭpĭo, cēpi, ceptum *v.t.* 3, to intercept, seize, steal

interclūdo, si, sum *v.t.* 3, to block, cut off, hinder, separate, blockade

intercurro, curri, cursum *v.i.* 3, to run between, intercede

interdīco, dixi, dictum *v.t.* 3, to prohibit, banish

interdictum, i *n*, prohibition

interdĭu *adv*, in the daytime

interdum *adv*, sometimes

intĕrĕā *adv*, meanwhile

intĕrĕo, ĭi, ĭtum *v.i.* 4, to perish, die, become lost

intĕrest see **intersum**

interfector, ōris *m*, murderer

interfícĭo, fēci, fectum *v.t.* 3, to kill, destroy

interflŭo, xi *v.i.* 3, to flow between

interfūsus, a, um *adj*, poured between, interposed, stained

intĕrim *adv*, meanwhile

intĕrĭmo, ēmi, emptum *v.t.* 3, to take away, destroy, kill

intĕrĭor, ĭus *comp. adj*, inner

intĕrĭus *adv*, inside

intĕrĭtus, ūs *m*, annihilation

interiăcĕo *v.i.* 2, to lie between

interĭcĭo, iēci, iectum *v.t.* 3, to put or throw between

interiectus, a, um *adj*, interposed

interlābor, lapsus *v.i.* 3, *dep*, to glide or flow between

interlĕgo, lēgi, lectum *v.t.* 3, to pluck, pick

interlūcĕo, luxi *v.i.* 2, to shine out, appear

interlŭo *v.t.* 3, to flow between

intermĭnātus, a, um *adj*, endless

intermiscĕo, scŭi, xtum *v.t.* 2, to intermix

intermissĭo, ōnis *f*, interruption, cessation

intermitto, mīsi, missum *v.i.t.* 3, to cease; neglect, omit, stop, pause, interrupt

intermortŭus, a, um *adj*, lifeless

internĕcīnus, a, um *adj*, deadly, internecine

internĕcĭo, ōnis *f*, massacre

internecto *v.t.* 3, to bind up

internosco, nōvi nōtum *v.t.* 3, to distinguish between

internuntĭus, ii *m*, negotiator

internus, a, um *adj*, internal

interpellātĭo, ōnis *f*, interruption

interpello *v.t.* 1, to interrupt

interpŏlo *v.t.* 1, to furbish

interpōno, pŏsŭi, ĭtum *v.t.* 3, to put between, introduce; *with* se, to interfere; *with* fidem, to pledge

interpŏsĭtĭo, ōnis *f*, insertion

interprĕs, ĕtis *c*, negotiatior

interprĕtātĭo, ōnis *f*, explanation

interprĕtor *v.t.* 1, *dep*, to explain

interpunctĭo, ōnis *f*, punctuation

interpungo, nxi, ctum *v.t.* 3, to punctuate

interquĭesco, quĭēvi, quĭētum *v.i.* 3, to rest for a while

interregnum, i *n*, vacancy in the kingship or high office

interrex, rēgis *m*, regent

interrĭtus, a, um *adj*, fearless

interrŏgātor, ōris *m*, questioner

interrŏgātum, i *n*, question

interrŏgo *v.t.* 1, to inquire

interrumpo, rūpi, ruptum *v.t.* 3, to break up, interrupt

intersaepĭo, psi, ptum *v.t.* 4, to hedge in, cut off

interscĭndo, scĭdi, scissum *v.t.* 3, to tear down, divide

intersĕro, rŭi, rtum *v.t.* 3, to interpose

intersum, esse, fŭi *v.i, irreg*, to lie between, differ, take part in; **interest**, *v, impers*, it concerns, it is of importance

intertexo, xŭi, xtum *v.t.* 3, to intertwine

intervallum, i *n*, space, pause

intervĕnĭo, vēni, ventum *v.i.* 4, to interrupt, happen, prevent

interventus, ūs *m*, intervention

intervīso, si, sum *v.t.* 3, to inspect, visit occasionally

intestābĭlis, e *adj*, abominable

intestīna, ōrum *n.pl*, intestines

intestīnus, a, um *adj*, internal

intexo, xŭi, xtum *v.t.* 3, to interlace

intĭmus, a, um *adj*, inmost

intŏlĕrābĭlis, e *adj*, intolerable

intŏlĕrandus, a, um *adj*, intolerable

intŏlĕrans, ntis *adj, adv*, **nter,** impatient, intolerable

intŏno, ŭi *v.i.* 1, to thunder

intonsus, a, um *adj*, unshaven

intorquĕo, si, sum *v.t.* 2, to twist, sprain, hurl

intrā *adv, and prep. with acc*, on the inside, within

intractābĭlis, e *adj*, unmanageable

intractātus, a, um *adj*, untried

intrĕmo, ŭi *v.i.* 3, to tremble

intrĕpĭdus, a, um *adj*, fearless

intrō *adv*, within, inside

intro *v.i.t.* 1, to enter

intrōdūco, xi, ctum *v.t.* 3, to lead in, introduce
intrŏductĭo, ōnis *f,* introduction
intrōeo *v.i.* 4, to enter
intrōfĕro, ferre, tŭli, lātum *v.t, irreg,* to bring in
intrōgrĕdĭor, gressus *v.i.* 3, *dep,* to enter
intrŏĭtus, ūs *m,* entrance
intrōmitto, mīsi, ssum *v.t.* 3, to send in
introrsum (us) *adv,* within
intrōspĭcĭo, spexi, spectum *v.t.* 3, to look into, examine
intŭĕor *v.t.* 2, *dep,* to look at
intŭmesco, mŭi *v.i.* 3, to swell
intus *adv,* within, inside
intūtus, a, um *adj,* unguarded
ĭnultus, a, um *adj,* unavenged
ĭnumbro *v.t.* 1, to shade
ĭnundātĭo, ōnis *f,* flooding
ĭnundo *v.i.t.* 1, to overflow; flood
ĭnungo, nxi, unctum *v.t.* 3, to anoint
ĭnurbānus, a, um *adj,* rude
ĭnūro, ssi, stum *v.t.* 3, to brand
ĭnūsĭtātus, a, um *adj, adv,* ē, unusual, strange
ĭnūtĭlis, e *adj,* useless
ĭnūtĭlĭtas, ātis *f,* uselessness
invādo, si, sum *v.i.t.* 3, to enter; attack, invade, seize
invălĭdus, a, um *adj,* weak
invĕho, xi, ctum *v.t.* 3, to carry, bring to; *passive or reflex,* to ride, drive, attack (with words)
invĕnĭo, vēni, ventum *v.t.* 4, to find, meet with, devise
inventĭo, ōnis *f,* invention
inventor, ōris *m,* inventor
inventum, i *n,* invention
invĕnustus, a, um *adj,* unattractive
invĕrēcundus, a, um *adj,* immodest
invergo *v.t.* 3, to pour on
inversus, a, um *adj,* inverted, perverted
inverto, ti, sum *v.t.* 3, to turn upside down, exchange
invespĕrascit *v, impers,* evening is approaching
investĭgātĭo, ōnis *f,* investigation
investĭgo *v.t.* 1, to search for
invĕtĕrasco, rāvi *v.i.* 3, to grow old, become permanent

invĕtĕrātus, a, um *adj,* old-established
invĕtĕro *v.t.* 1, to endure
invĭcem *adv,* alternately
invictus, a, um *adj,* unconquered, invincible
invĭdĕo, vīdi, vīsum *v.t.* 2, *with dat;* to envy, grudge
invĭdĭa, ae *f,* envy, ill will
invĭdĭōsus, a, um *adj, adv,* ē, jealous, enviable
invĭdus, a, um *adj,* envious
invĭgĭlo *v.i.* 1, to be watchful
invĭŏlātus, a, um *adj,* unharmed
invīso, si, sum *v.t.* 3, to visit
invīsus, a, um *adj,* hated
invīsus, a, um *adj,* unseen
invītātĭo, ōnis *f,* challenge, invitation
invīto *v.t.* 1, to invite, challenge, tempt
invītus, a, um *adj,* unwilling
invĭus, a, um *adj,* pathless
invŏcātus, a, um *adj,* uninvited
invŏco *v.t.* 1, to appeal to
invŏlĭto *v.i.* 1, to hover
invŏlo *v.i.t.* 1, to fly at; attack
invŏlūcrum, i *n,* wrapper
invŏlūtus, a, um *adj,* intricate
involvo, volvi, vŏlūtum *v.t.* 3, to roll on, wrap up, envelop
invulnĕrābĭlis, e *adj,* invulnerable
ĭō *interj,* oh! ah! ho!
ipse, a, um (*genit,* **ipsius,** dat, **ipsi**), *emphatic pron,* himself, herself, itself, precisely, just
īra, ae *f,* anger
īrācundĭa, ae *f,* rage, temper
īrācundus, a, um *adj,* irritable
īrascor, īrātus *v.* 3, *dep, with dat,* to be angry with
īrātus, a, um *adj,* angry
ire see **ĕo**
īris, ĭdis *f,* iris
īrōnīa, ae *f,* irony
irpes, ĭcis *m,* harrow
irrĕmĕābĭlis, e *adj,* irretraceable
irrĕpĕrābĭlis, e *adj,* irrecoverable
irrĕpertus, a, um *adj,* undiscovered
irrēpo, psi, ptum *v.i.* 3, to creep in, insinuate oneself
irrĕquĭētus, a, um *adj,* restless
irrētĭo *v.t.* 4, to entangle

irrĕtortus, a, um *adj*, not turned back

irrĕvŏcābĭlis, e *adj*, irrevocable

irrīdĕo, si, sum *v.i.t.* 2, to joke, jeer; mock, ridicule

irrĭgātĭo, ōnis *f*, irrigation

irrĭgo *v.t.* 1, to water, refresh

irrĭgŭus, a, um *adj*, well-watered, moistening

irrīsĭo, ōnis *f*, mockery

irrīsus, ūs *m*, mockery

irrīsor, ōris *m*, scoffer

irrītābĭlis, e *adj*, irritable

irrītāmen, ĭnis *n*, incentive

irrītāmentum, i *n*, incentive

irrīto *v.t.* 1, to provoke

irrĭtus, a, um *adj*, invalid, unsucessful

irrŏgo *v.t.* 1, to propose (against someone), inflict

irrōro *v.t.* 1, to bedew

irrumpo, rūpi, ptum *v.i.t.* 3, to break in; attack, interrupt

irrŭo, ŭi *v.i.* 3, to rush in, seize

irruptus, a, um *adj*, unbroken

ĭs, ĕa, id *demonst. pron*, he, she, it, that

ischĭas, ădis *f*, sciatica

iste, a, ud *demonst. pron*, that

isthmus, i *m*, isthmus

istīc *adv*, there

istinc *adv*, from there

istūc *adv*, to that place

ĭtă *adv*, in such a way, so

ĭtăque *conj*, and so, therefore

ĭtem *adv*, likewise, also

ĭter, ĭtĭnĕris *n*, route, journey, march

ĭtĕrātĭo, ōnis *f*, repetition

ĭtĕro *v.t.* 1, to repeat

ĭtĕrum *adv*, again

ĭtĭdem *adv*, in the same way

ĭtĭo, ōnis *f*, travelling

J (consonantal i)

iăcĕo *v.i.* 2, to lie (recumbent), lie sick

iăcĭo, iēci, iactum *v.t.* 3, to throw, lay down

iactans, ntis *pres. part, adj*, boastful

iactantĭa, ae *f*, ostentation

iactātĭo, ōnis *f*, tossing, bragging

iactātor, ōris *m*, braggart

iacto *v.t.* 1, to throw about, boast

iactūra, ae *f*, throwing overboard, sacrifice

iactus, ūs *m*, throw, shot

iăcŭlātor, ōris *m*, thrower

iăcŭlātrix, īcis *f*, huntress

iăcŭlor *v.t.* 1, *dep*, to hurl

iăcŭlum, i *n*, javelin

iam *adv*, already, now

iamdūdum *adv*, a long time ago

iamprīdem *adv*, for a long time now

iānĭtor, ōris *m*, doorkeeper

iānŭa, ae *f*, door, entrance

Iānŭārĭus (mensis) January

iĕcur, ŏris *n*, liver

iēiūnĭtas, ātis *f*, meagreness

iēiūnĭum, ii *n*, fast, hunger

iēiūnus, a, um *adj*, hungry, barren

ientācŭlum, i *n*, breakfast

iento *v.i.* 1, to breakfast

iŏcātĭo, ōnis *f*, joke

iŏcor *v.i.t.* 1, *dep*, to joke

iŏcōsus, a, um *adj*, humorous

iŏcŭlāris, e *adj*, amusing

iŏcŭlātor, ōris *m*, joker

iŏcus, i *m*, joke

iŭba, ae *f*, mane, crest

iŭbar, ăris *n*, radiance

iŭbĕo, iussi, iussum *v.t.* 2, to order, tell

iūcundĭtas, ātis *f*, pleasantness

iūcundus, a, um *adj*, pleasant

iūdex, ĭcis *m*, judge

iudicialis, e *adj*, judicial

iudicatio, ōnis *f*, judgement

iūdĭcĭum, ii *n*, trial, verdict, court, discretion, judgement

iūdīco *v.t.* 1, to judge, decide

iŭgālis, e *adj*, yoked together

iŭgāles *m.pl*, chariot horses

iŭgĕrum, i *n*, acre (approx.)

iūgis, e *adj*, perpetual

iūglans, dis *f*, walnut

iŭgo *v.t.* 1, to marry, connect

iŭgōsus, a, um *adj*, mountainous

iŭgŭlo *v.t.* 1, to cut the throat

iŭgum, i *n*, yoke, bench, mountain-ridge

Iūlĭus (mensis), July

iūmentum, i *n*, pack animal
iuncĕus, a, um *adj*, made of rushes
iuncōsus, a, um *adj*, full of rushes
iunctĭo, ōnis *f*, junction
iunctūra, ae *f*, joint
iuncus, i *m*, bullrush
iungo, nxi, nctum *v.t.* 3, to join
iūnĭor *comp. adj*, from **iŭvĕnis,**
   younger
iūnĭpĕrus, i *f*, juniper tree
Iūnĭus (mensis) June
iūrātor, ōris *m*, commissioner of
   oaths
iūrātus, a, um *adj*, bound by oath
iurgĭum, ii *n*, quarrel
iurgo *v.i.t.* 1, to quarrel; upbraid
iūris consultus, i *m*, lawyer
iūris dictĭo, ōnis *f*, jurisdiction
iūro *v.i.t.* 1, to take an oath; to
   swear by
iūs, iūris *n*, law, legal status, right,
   authority
iūs, iūris *n*, soup
iusiūrandum, i *n*, oath
iussum, i *n*, order
iusta, ōrum *n.pl*, due ceremonies
iustē *adv*, rightly
iustĭtĭa, ae *f*, justice
iustĭtĭum *n*, holiday for lawcourts,
   public mourning
iusum, i *n*, fairness
iustus, a, um *adj*, fair, lawful
iŭvĕnālis, e *adj*, youthful
iŭvenca, ae *f*, heifer
iŭvencus, i *m*, bullock
iŭvĕnesco, nŭi *v.i.* 3, to reach
   youth
iŭvĕnīlis, e *adj*, youthful
iŭvĕnis, is *m, f*, young person;
   (*adj*) young
iŭvĕnor *v.i.* 1, *dep*, to act
   youthfully
iŭventa, ae *f*, the age of youth
iŭventas, ātis *f*, the age of youth
iŭventus, ūtis *f*, the age of youth
iŭvo, iūvi, iūtum *v.t.* 1, to help,
   gratify; **iŭvat** (*impers, with acc*),
   it pleases, it is of use
iuxtā *adv, and prep. with acc*, near
iuxtim *adv, and prep. with acc*,
   next to

K

Kalendae, ārum *f.pl*, the Kalends,
   the first day of the month

L

lăbĕfăcĭo, fēci, factum *v.t.* 3, to
   shake, loosen, overthrow
lăbĕfacto *v.t.* 1, to shake, destroy
lăbellum, i *n*, a lip
lăbellum, i *n*, tub, basin
lābes, is *f*, sinking, downfall
lābes, is *f*, spot, blemish
lăbo *v.i.* 1, to totter, waver
lābor, lapsus *v.i.* 3, *dep*, to slip,
   slide, glide, pass away, be
   mistaken
lăbor, ōris *m*, work, toil,
   workmanship, distress
lăbōrĭōsus, a, um *adj, adv*, **ē,**
   laborious, industrious
lăbōro *v.i.t.* 1, to strive, be in
   trouble or difficulty; to make,
   prepare
lăbrum, i *n*, lip
lābrum, i *n*, tub, basin
lăbў̆rinthus, i *m*, labyrinth
lac, lactis *n*, milk
lăcer, ĕra, ĕrum *adj*, mangled
lăcerna, ae *f*, cloak
lăcĕātĭo, ōnis *f*, laceration
lăcēro *v.t.* 1, to tear, rend,
   censure, destroy
lăcerta, ae *f* (us, i *m*), lizard
lăcertōsus, a, um *adj*, brawny
lăcertus, i *m*, arm, strength
lăcertus, i *m*, lizard, newt
lăcesso, īvi, ītum *v.t.* 3, to
   provoke, attack, irritate, urge
lăcĭnĭa, ae *f*, edge of garment
làcrĭma, ae *f*, tear
làcrĭmābilis, e *adj*, mournful
làcrĭmo *v,i.* 1, to weep
làcrĭmōsus, a, um *adj*, tearful
lactens, ntis *f*, very young
   (unweaned) animal
lactĕus, a, um *adj*, milky
lacto *v.i.t.* 1, to have milk; suck
lactūca, ae *f*, lettuce
lăcūna, ae *f*, ditch, pond, gap

lăcūnar, āris *n*, ceiling
lăcus, ūs *m*, lake, tank, tub
laedo, si, sum *v.t.* 3, to injure, offend
laena, ae *f*, cloak
laetābĭlis, e *adj*, joyful
laetĭfĭco *v.t.* 1, to delight
laetĭtĭa, ae *f*, joyfulness
laetor *v.i.* 1, *dep*, to rejoice
laetus, a, um *adj, adv*, **ē**, glad, cheerful, willing, pleased, prosperous, beautiful
laeva, ae *f*, the left hand
laevus, a, um *adj*, on the left side, unfortunate, foolish
lăgănum, i *n*, a cake
lăgēna, ae *f*, wine jar
lăgōis, ĭdis *f*, grous
lăgōpūs, ŏdis *f*, grouse
lăguncŭla, ae *f*, small bottle
lambo, bi, bĭtum *v.t.* 3, to lick
lāmentābĭlis, e *adj*, mournful
lāmentātĭo, ōnis *f*, mourning
lāmentor *v.i.t.* 1, *dep*, to weep; mourn
lāments, ōrum *n.pl*, moaning
lămĭa, ae *f*, witch, vampire
lāmĭna, ae *f*, thin metal plate
lampas, ădis *f*, torch
lāna, ae *f*, wool
lancĕa, ae *f*, lance, spear
lānĕus, a, um *adj*, woollen
languens, ntis *adj*, faint, weak
languĕo *v.i.* 2, to be faint or listless
languesco, gŭi *v.i.* 3, to become faint or listless
languĭdus, a, um *adj*, faint, weary, sluggish
languor, ōris *m*, weakness, weariness, sluggishness
lănĭātus, ūs *m*, laceration
lānĭcĭum, ii *n*, wool
lănĭēna, ae *f*, butcher's stall
lānĭfĭcus, a, um *adj*, weaving
lānĭger, ĕra, ĕrum *adj*, fleecy
lănĭo *v.t.* 1, to mutilate
lănista, ae *m*, fencing master
lănĭus, ii *m*, butcher
lanterna, ae *f*, lamp, torch
lānūgo, ĭnis *f*, down, hair
lanx, ncis *f*, dish, plate
lăpăthus, i *f*, sorrel

lăpĭcīda, ae *m*, quarryman
lăpĭcīdīnae, ārum *f.pl*, stone quarries
lăpĭdātĭo, ōnis *f*, stoning
lăpĭdĕus, a, um *adj*, of stone
lăpĭdōsus, a, um *adj*, stony
lăpillus, i *m*, pebble, grain
lăpis, ĭdis *m*, stone, milestone, jewel
lappa, ae *f*, burr
lapso *v.i.* 1, to slip, stumble
lapsus, a, um *adj*, fallen, sinking, ruined
lapsus, ūs *m*, fall, slip, gliding
lăquĕar, āris *n*, ceiling
lăquĕātus, a, um *adj*, panelled
lăquĕus, i *m*, noose, snare
lar, ăris *m*, guardian deity of a house, home
largĭor *v.t.* 4, *dep*, to lavish, give
largītas, ātis *f*, abundance
largītĭo, ōnis *f*, generous distribution, bribery
largītor, ōris *m*, briber, generous giver
largus, a, um *adj, adv*, **ē**, **ĭter**, abundant, lavish, large
lārĭdum (lardum), i *n*, lard
lărix, ĭcis *f*, larch
larva, ae *f*, ghost, mask
lascīvĭa, ae *f*, playfulness
lascīvĭo *v.i.* 4, to frolic
lascīvus, a, um *adj*, playful, licentious
lassĭtūdo, ĭnis *f*, weariness
lasso *v.t.* 1, to tire, fatigue
lassus, a, um *adj*, exhausted
lātē *adv*, far and wide
lătĕbra, ae *f*, hiding-place, subterfuge
lătĕbrōsus, a, um *adj*, full of hiding places, secret
lătens, ntis *adj, adv*, **nter**, hidden, secret
lătĕo *v.i.* 2, to lie hidden, keep out of sight
lăter, ĕris *m*, brick, tile, ingot
lătĕrīcĭus, a, um *adj*, made of bricks
lătex, ĭcis *m*, liquid
lătībŭlum, *n*, hiding-place
Lătīnē *adv*, in Latin
lătĭto *v.i.* 1, to lie hidden

lātĭtūdo, ĭnis *f*, breadth
lātor, ōris *m*, proposer of a law
lātrātor, ōris *m*, a barker
lātrātus, ūs *m*, barking
lātrīna, ae *f*, water-closet
lātro *v.i.t.* 1, to bark; bark at
làtro, ōnis *m*, robber
làtrōcĭnĭum, ii *n*, robbery, fraud, robber-band
làtrōcĭnor *v.i.* 1, *dep*, to practise highway robbery
làtruncŭlus, i *m*, robber
lātus, a, um *adj, adv*, ē, wide
lātus, ĕris *n*, the side, flank, lungs
laudābĭlis, e *adj*, praiseworthy
laudātĭo, ōnis *f*, praises, eulogy
laudātor, ōris *m*, praiser
laudātus, a, um *adj*, praiseworthy
laudo *v.t.* 1, to praise, name

lectĭo, ōnis *f*, selection, reading aloud
lector, ōris *m*, reader
lectŭlus, i *m*, sofa, couch
lectus, a, um *adj*, chosen, excellent
lectus, i *m*, bed, couch
lectus, ūs *m*, reading
lēgātĭo, ōnis *f*, delegation
lēgātum, i *n*, legacy
lēgātus, i *m*, ambassador, delegate, lieutenant-general
lēges see lex
lēgĭfer, ĕra, ĕrum *adj*, law-giving
lēgĭo, ōnis *f*, Roman legion (4,000–6,000 soldiers)
lēgĭōnārĭus, a, um *adj*, of a legion
lēgĭtĭmus, a, um *adj*, legal, legitimate, proper, right

Insight

Active verbs usually have four **principal parts**. Deponent verbs have three. The principal parts give the first person singular present tense, the infinitive, the first person singular perfect tense, and the supine (e.g. *laudo, laudare, laudavi, laudatum*).

laurĕa, ae *f*, laurel (tree)
laurĕātus, a, um *adj*, crowned with laurel (of victory)
laurĕus, a, um *adj*, of laurel
laurus, i *f*, laurel
laus, dis *f*, praise, merit
lautē *adv*, elegantly
lautĭtĭa, ae *f*, elegance
lautŭmĭae, ārum *f.pl*, stone quarry
lautus, a, um *adj*, elegant, splendid, noble
lăvātĭo, ōnis *f*, ablution, washing
lăvo, lāvi, lautum *v.i.t.* 1 or 3, to wash or wet
laxĭtas, ātis *f*, spaciousness
laxo *v.t.* 1, to enlarge, loosen, relax, relieve, weaken
laxus, a, um *adj*, wide, loose
lĕa, ae *f*, lioness
lĕaena, ae *f*, lioness
lĕbes, ētis *m*, copper basin
lectīca, ae *f*, sedan, litter

lēgo *v.t.* 1, to send with a commission, appoint as a deputy, leave as a legacy
lĕgo, lēgi, lectum *v.t.* 3, to read, gather, select, steal, pass through, sail by, survey
lĕgūmen, ĭnis *n*, pulse, beans
lembus, i *m*, yacht, cutter
lĕmŭres, um *m.pl*, ghosts, spirits
lēna, ae *f*, bawd
lēnīmen, ĭnis *n*, alleviation, palliative
lēnīmentum, i *n*, alleviation, palliative
lēnĭo *v.t.* 4, to soften, soothe
lēnis, e *adj, adv*, ĭter, soft, smooth, gentle, calm
lēnĭtas, ātis *f*, gentleness
lēno, ōnis *m*, pimp, seducer
lēnōcĭnĭum, ii *n*, pandering, ornamentation
lēnōcĭnor *v.* 1, *dep, with dat*, to flatter, promote

lens

lens, ntis *f*, lentil
lentesco *v.i.* 3, to become soft or sticky
lentīgo, ĭnis *f*, freckle
lentītūdo, ĭnis *f*, apathy, sluggishness
lento *v.t.* 1, to bend
lentus, a, um *adj, adv,* ē, slow, flexible, sticky, tedious, calm (of character)
lēnuncŭlus, i *m*, boat

lībāmentum, i *n*, drink offering
lībella, ae *f*, small coin
lībellus, i *m*, small book, pamphlet, diary
lībens, ntis *adj, adv,* **nter,** with pleasure, willing
līber, ĕra, ĕrum *adj, adv,* **nter,** free, frank
līber, ĕri *m*, Baccus, wine
līber, ĕri *m*, child
līber, bri *m*, book, tree bark

Insight

The word *liber* in Latin is a bit confusing: *liber, liberi* means child while *liber, libri* means book. *Liber, Liberi* (capital letter) stands for Baccus, therefore wine. Also, the first-and-second-declension adjective *liber, -a, -um* means free.

---

lĕo, ōnis *m*, lion
lĕpĭdus, a, um *adj, adv,* ē, charming, elegant, pleasant
lĕpor (lĕpos), ōris *m*, charm, pleasantness, wit
lĕŏrārĭum, ĭi *n*, warren
leprae, ārum *f.pl*, leprosy
lĕprōsus, a, um *adj*, leprous
lĕpus, ŏris *m*, a hare
lĕpuscŭlus, i *m*, leveret
lētālis, e *adj*, fatal
lēthargĭcus, a, um *adj*, lethargic
lēthargus, i *m*, stupor
lētĭfer, ĕra, ĕrum *adj*, deadly
lētum, i *n*, death
lĕvāmen, ĭnis *n*, consolation, comfort
lĕvāmentum, i *n*, consolation, comfort
lĕvātĭo, ōnis *f*, raising
lĕvis, e *adj, adv,* **ĭter,** light, mild, light-armed, agile, trivial, unreliable
lēvis, e *adj*, smooth, soft
lĕvĭtas, ātis *f*, inconstancy
lēvĭtas, ātis *f*, smoothness
lĕvo *v.t.* 1, to raise, relieve, take away, support, soothe, release
lēvo *v.t.* 1, to smooth
lex, lēgis *f*, law, condition
lībāmen, ĭnis *n*, drink offering

lībĕrālis, e *adj, adv,* **ĭter,** honourable, generous
lībĕrālĭtas, ātis *f*, generosity
lībĕrātĭo, ōnis *f*, release
lībĕrātor, ōris *m*, liberator
lībĕri, ōrum *m.pl*, children
lībĕro *v.t.* 1, to release, free from slavery, acquit
lībertas, ātis *f*, freedom
lībertīnus, i *m*, freedman
lībertīnus, a, um *adj*, of a freedman
lībertus, i *m*, a freedman
lībet, lībŭit, lībĭtum est *v.* 2, *impers*, it is agreeable
lībīdĭnōsus, a, um *adj*, lecherous
lībīdo, ĭnis *f*, desire, passion, whim
lībo *v.t.* 1, to taste, touch, pour out an offering of wine
lībra, ae *f*, Roman pound (12 oz.), pair of scales
lībrāmentum, i *n*, a weight
lībrārĭus, i *m*, secretary
lībrārĭus, a, um *adj*, of books
lībrātus, a, um *adj*, balanced
lībrīlis, e *adj*, weighing a pound
lībro *v.t.* 1, to balance, hurl
lībum, i *n*, pancake
līburna, ae *f*, fast sailing ship
līcenter *adv*, without restraint
līcentĭa, ae *f*, freedom, licence
līcĕo *v.i.* 2, to be for sale, be valued at

lĭcĕor *v.t.* 2, to be for sale, be valued at

lĭcĕor *v.t.* 2, *dep*, to bid (for)

lĭcet, cŭit, cĭtum est *v.* 2, *impers*, it is allowed, one may

lĭcet *conj*, although

lĭcĭtus, a, um *adj*, permitted

lĭcĭtātĭo, ōnis *f*, bidding

lĭcĭum, ii *n*, a thread

lictor, ōris *m*, official attendant of high magistrates

lĭēn, ēnis *m*, spleen

lĭgāmen, ĭnis *n*, bandage

lĭgāmentum, i *n*, ligament

lignārĭus, ii *m*, carpenter, joiner

lignātĭo, ōnis *f*, wood gathering

lignātor, ōris *m*, wood cutter

lignĕus, a, um *adj*, wooden

lignor *v.i.* 1, *dep*, to collect wood

lignum, i *n*, wood

lĭgo *v.t.* 1, to tie, bind

lĭgo, ōnis *m*, hoe

lĭgŭla, ae *f*, small tongue (of land); tongue of a shoe

lĭgūrĭo *v.t.* 4, to lick, desire

lĭgustrum, i *n*, a plant, privet

līlĭum, ii *n*, lily

līma, ae *f*, file

līmax, ācis *f*, slug

limbus, i *m*, border, edge

līmen, ĭnis *n*, doorstep, door, lintel

līmĕs, ĭtis *m*, boundary, track

līmo *v.t.* 1, to file, polish, finish

līmōsus, a, um *adj*, slimy, muddy

limpĭdus, a, um *adj*, clear, bright

līmus, a, um *adj*, aslant

līmus, i *m*, slime, mud

līmus, i *m*, apron

līnāmentum, i *n*, linen, lint

līnĕa, ae *f*, thread, string, line, end, goal

līnĕāmentum, i *n*, line, feature

līnĕus, a, um *adj*, linen

lingo, nxi *v.t.* 3, to lick

lingua, ae *f*, tongue, speech, language

līnĭger, ĕra, ĕrum *adj*, clothed in linen

līno, lēvi, lĭtum *v.t.* 3, to daub, smear over

linquo, līqui *v.t.* 3, to leave

lintĕo, ōnis *m*, linen weaver

linter, tris *f*, boat, tray

lintĕum, i *n*, linen

lintĕus, a, um *adj*, of linen

līnum, i *n*, flax, linen, thread, rope, net

lippĭtūdo, ĭnis *f*, inflammation of the eyes

lippus, a, um *adj*, blear-eyed

lĭquĕfăcĭo, fēci, factum *v.t.* 3, to melt, dissolve

lĭquĕfactus, a, um *adj*, molten

lĭquens, ntis *adj*, liquid

lĭquĕo, līqui *v.i.* 2, to be clear

lĭquesco, līcŭi *v.i.* 3, to melt

lĭquĭdus, a, um *adj*, liquid, flowing, clear

līquo *v.t.* 1, to melt, filter

līquor *v.i.* 3, *dep*, to melt, flow

līquor, ōris *m*, a liquid

līs, tis *f*, dispute, lawsuit

lītĭgĭōsus, a, um *adj*, quarrelsome

lītĭgo *v.i.* 1, to quarrel

līto *v.i.t.* 1, to make a sacrifice with favourable omens; appease

lītŏrĕus, a, um *adj*, of the seashore

littĕra, ae *f*, a letter of the alphabet

littĕrae, ārum *f.pl*, a letter, document, literature, learning

littĕrātus, a, um *adj*, educated

littĕrŭla, ae *f*, small letter, moderate literary knowledge

lītūra, ae *f*, smear, erasure

lītus, ōris *n*, seashore

lītŭus, i *m*, augur's staff, trumpet

līvens, ntis *adj*, bluish

līvĕo *v.i.* 2, to be black and blue

līvĭdus, a, um *adj*, bluish, black and blue, envious

līvor, ōris *m*, leaden colour, envy, malice

lixa, ae *m*, camp-follower

lŏca, ōrum *n.pl*, a region

lŏcātĭo, ōnis *f*, placing, arrangement, lease

lŏco *v.t.* 1, to place, arrange, give in marriage, lease, contract for

lŏcŭlāmentum, i *n*, box

lŏcŭlus, i *m*, satchel, purse

lŏcŭplēs, ētis *adj*, wealthy

lŏcŭplēto *v.t.* 1, to enrich

lŏcus, i *m*, place, position, topic, subject, cause, reason

lŏcusta, ae *f*, locust

lŏcūtĭo, ōnis *f*, speaking, pronunciation, phrase

lōdix, īcis *f*, blanket
lŏgĭca, ōrum *n.pl*, logic
lŏgĭcus, a, um *adj*, logical
lōlīgo, ĭnis *f*, cuttlefish
lŏlĭum, ii *n*, darnel
longaevus, a, um *adj*, ancient
longē *adv*, far off, greatly
longinquĭtas, ātis *f*, duration, distance
longinquus, a, um *adj*, distant, strange, prolonged
longĭtŭdo, ĭnis *f*, length
longŭrĭus, ii *m*, long pole
longus, a, um *adj*, long, tall, vast, distant, tedious
lŏquācĭtas, ātis *f*, talkativeness
lŏquax, ācis *adj*, *adv*, **ĭter**, talkative, babbling
lŏquēla, ae *f*, speech, discourse
lŏquor, lŏcūtus *v.i.t.* 3, *dep*, to speak; tell, mention, declare
lōrīca, ae *f*, breastplate
lōrĭpēs, pĕdis *adj*, bandy-legged
lōrum, i *n*, strap, whip
lōtos (lōtus), i *f*, lotus tree
lūbens, lŭbet see **libens, libet**
lūbrĭcus, a, um *adj*, slippery, dangerous, deceitful
lŭcellum, i *n*, slight profit
lūcĕo, xi *v.i.* 2, to shine
lūcet *v. impers*, day breaks
lŭcerna, ae *f*, lamp
lūcesco *v.i.* 3, to dawn
lūcĭdus, a, um *adj*, bright, clear
lūcĭfer, ĕra, ĕrum *adj*, light-bringing
lūcĭfer, ĕri *m*, morning star
lūcĭfŭgus, a, um *adj*, retiring
lŭcrātīvus, a, um *adj*, profitable
lŭcror *v.t.* 1, *dep*, to gain, win
lŭcrum, i *n*, profit, advantage
luctāmen, inis *n*, wrestling, struggle
luctātĭo, ōnis *f*, wrestling, struggle
luctātor, ōris *m*, wrestler
luctĭfĭcus, a, um *adj*, woeful
luctor *v.i.* 1, *dep*, to struggle
luctŭōsus, a, um *adj*, sorrowful
luctus, ūs *m*, grief, mourning (clothes)
lūcŭbrātĭo, ōnis *f*, night-work
lūcŭlentus, a, um *adj*, bright
lūcus, i *m*, wood, grove

lūdĭbrĭum, ii *n*, mockery, jest, laughing-stock
lūdĭbundus, a, um *adj*, playful
lūdĭcer, ĭcra, ĭcrum *adj*, sportive, theatrical
ludĭcrum, i *n*, public show or games, a play
lūdĭfĭcātĭo, ōnis *f*, mocking
lūdĭfĭcor *v.i.t.* 1, *dep* (**lūdĭfĭco** *v.t.* 1), to mock, deceive
lūdĭmăgister, tri *m*, schoolmaster
lūdĭus, ii *m*, pantomime-actor
lūdo, si, sum *v.i.t.* 3, to play, frolic; mock, deceive
lūdus, i *m*, a play, game, public games, school, joke
lŭes, is *f*, an epidemic
lūgĕo, xi, ctum *v.i.t.* 2, to mourn
lūgŭbris, e *adj*, lamentable, disastrous
lumbus, i *m*, loin
lūmen, ĭnis *n*, light, lamp, gleam, life, eye, glory
lūna, ae *f*, moon
lūnāris, e *adj*, lunar
lūnātus, a, um *adj*, crescent-shaped
lūno *v.t.* 1, to bend into a crescent-shape
lŭo, lŭi *v.t.* 3, to pay a debt or penalty, undergo, atone for
lŭpāta, ōrum *n.pl*, horse-bit
lŭpātus, a, um *adj*, jagged
lŭpīnus, a, um *adj*, of the wolf
lŭpīnus, i *m*, lupin (plant)
lŭpus, i *m*, wolf, pike (fish), a jagged bit, hook
lūrĭdus, a, um *adj*, lurid, sallow
luscĭnĭa, ae *f*, nightingale
lūsor, ōris *m*, player, mocker
lustrālis, e *adj*, expiatory
lustrātĭo, ōnis *f*, purification by sacrifice
lustro *v.t.* 1, to to purify by sacrifice, wander over, review
lustrum, i *n*, den, wood
lustrum, i *n*, purificatory sacrifice, period of five years
lūsus, ūs *m*, play, sport, game
lūtĕŏlus, a, um *adj*, yellow
lūtĕus, a, um *adj*, golden-yellow
lŭtĕus, a, um *adj*, muddy, worthless
lūtra, ae *f*, otter

lūtŭlentus, a, um *adj*, filthy
lūtum, i *n*, yellow
lūtum, i *n*, mud, clay
lux, lūcis *f*, light, dawn, day, life, brightness, glory
luxŭrĭa, ae *f*, luxuriance, extravagance
luxŭrĭo *v.i.* 1, **(luxŭrĭor**, *v.* 1, *dep*), to be overgrown, to have in excess, run riot
luxŭrĭōsus, a, um *adj*, luxuriant, excessive
luxus, ūs *m*, extravagance, pomp
lychnūcus, i *m*, lamp-stand
lychnus, i *m*, light, lamp
lympha, ae *f*, water
lymphātus, a, um *adj*, frenzied
lyncēus, a, um *adj*, sharp-eyed
lynx, cis *c*, lynx
lўra, ae *f*, lute, poetry, song
lўrĭcus, a, um *adj*, of the lute, lyric

M

măcellum, i *n*, food market
măcer, cra, crum *adj*, lean, thin
măcĕrĭa, ae *f*, wall
mācĕro *v.t.* 1, to soften, weaken, torment
māchĭna, ae *f*, engine, machine, battering-ram, trick, plan
māchĭnālis, e *adj*, mechanical
māchĭnātĭo, ōnis *f*, contrivance, machine, trick
māchĭnātor, ōris *m*, engineer, inventor
māchĭnor *v.t.* 1, *dep*, to design, plot
măcĭes, ēi *f*, thinness, poverty
macte or **macti** (*voc. of* **mactus**), good luck! well done!
macto *v.t.* 1, to sacrifice a victim, reward, honour, destroy
mactus, a, um *adj*, worshipped
măcŭla, ae *f*, spot, stain, fault, mesh
măcŭlo *v.t.* 1, to stain, disgrace
măcŭlōsus, a, um *adj*, spotted, dishonoured
mădĕfăcĭo, fēci, factum *v.t.* 3, to soak, drench
mădens, ntis *adj*, moist, drunk
mădĕo *v.i.* 2, to be moist, to drip, to be boiled, softened

mădesco, dŭi *v.i.* 3, to become wet
mădīdus, a, um *adj*, soaked
maena, ae *f*, small salted fish
maenĭānum, i *n*, balcony
maerens, ntis *adj*, mourning
maerĕo *v.i.t.* 2, to mourn; bewail
maeror, ōris *m*, grief, mourning
maestĭtĭa, ae *f*, sadness
maestus, a, um *adj*, sad
măga, ae *f*, witch
măgālĭa, ĭum *n.pl*, huts
măgĭcus, a, um *adj*, magic
măgis *comp. adv* **(magnus)**, more, rather
măgister, tri *m*, master, leader, director, teacher
măgistĕrĭum, ii *n*, president's position
măgistra, ae *f*, mistress
măgistrātus, ūs *m*, magistracy, magistrate
magnănĭmĭtas, ātis *f*, magnanimity
magnănĭmus, a, um *adj*, great-hearted
magnes, ētis *m*, magnet
magnētĭcus, a, um *adj*, magnet
magni see **magnus**
magnĭfĭcentĭa, ae *f*, nobleness, splendour, boasting
magnĭfĭcus, a, um *adj, adv*, **ē**, noble, distinguished, sumptuous, bragging
magnĭlŏquentĭa, ae *f*, high-sounding language
magnĭtūdo, ĭnis *f*, size
magnŏpĕrē *adv*, very much
magnus, a, um *adj*, large, great; **magni** or **magno** at a high price
măgus, i *m*, magician
Māius (mensis) May
māiestas, ātis *f*, greatness, grandeur, sovereignty, treason
māior *comp. adj*, larger, greater;
māiōres, um *m.pl*, ancestors, the Senate; **maior nātu** older
māla, ae *f*, cheekbone, jaw
mălăcĭa, ae *f*, calm at sea
mălagma, ātis *n*, poultice
mălē *adv*, badly, exceedingly; often reverses the meaning of an adj: **male sānus** deranged
mălĕdīcens, ntis *adj*, abusive

mălĕdīco, xi, ctum *v.i.* 3, to abuse, slander

mălĕdictĭo, ōnis *f,* abuse

mălĕdictum, i *n,* abusive word

mălĕdīcus, a, um *adj,* abusive

mălĕfĭcĭum, ii *n,* wrongdoing

mălĕfĭcus, a, um *adj,* evil-doing

mălĕsuādus, a, um *adj,* persuading towards wrong

mălĕvŏlens, ntis *adj,* spiteful

mălĕvŏlentĭa, ae *f,* malice

mălĕvŏlus, a, um *adj,* spiteful

mălignus, a, um *adj,* malicious

mălĭtĭa, ae *f,* malice

mălĭtĭōsus, a, um *adj,* wicked

mallĕus, i *m,* hammer

mālo, malle, mālŭi *v.t, irreg,* to prefer

mālŏbăthrum, i *n,* a costly ointment

mālum, i *n,* apple, fruit

mălum, i *n,* evil, misfortune

mălus, a, um *adj,* bad, harmful

mālus, i *m,* mast

malva, ae *f,* the mallow

mamma, ae *f,* breast, teat

manceps, cĭpis *m,* contractor

mancĭpĭum, ii *n,* legal purchase, right of ownership, slave

mancĭpo *v.t.* 1, to sell, transfer

mancus, a, um *adj,* maimed

mandātum, i *n,* order, commission

mandātus, ūs *m,* order, commission

mando *v.t.* 1, to order, commission, commit

mandūco *v.t.* 1, to chew

māne *n, indecl,* morning; *adv,* in the morning

mănĕo, nsi, nsum *v.i.t.* 2, to stay, remain, continue; await

mānes, ĭum *m.pl,* deified ghosts of the dead

mănĭcae, ārum *f.pl,* glove, gauntlet, handcuff

mănĭfestus, a, um *adj, adv,* ō, clear, apparent

mănĭpŭlāris, e *adj,* belonging to a company (a soldier)

mănĭpŭlus, i *m,* handful, bundle, company of soldiers

mannus, i *m,* coach-horse, pony

māno *v.i.t.* 1, to flow, trickle; pour out

mansĭo, ōnis *f,* a stay, inn

mansŭĕfăcĭo, fēci, factum *v.t.* 3, to tame, civilize

mansŭesco, sŭēvi, sŭētum *v.i.* 3, to grow tame or gentle

mansŭētus, a, um *adj,* gentle

mansŭētūdo, ĭnis *f,* gentleness

mansūrus, a, um *adj,* lasting

mantēle, is *n,* towel, cloth

mantĭca, ae *f,* suitcase

mănŭbĭae, ārum *f.pl,* money from the sale of booty

mănŭbrĭum, ii *n,* handle

mănūmissĭo, ōnis *f,* the freeing of a slave

mănūmitto, mīsi, missum *v.t.* 3, to set free a slave

mănus, ūs *f,* hand, bravery, combat, violence, grappling-iron, armed band

măpālĭa, ĭum *n.pl,* African huts

mappa, ae *f,* towel, napkin

marcĕo *v.i.* 2, to be weak

marcesco *v.i.* 3, to wither

marcĭdus, a, um *adj,* decayed

măre, is *n,* the sea

marga, ae *f,* marl

margărīta, ae *f,* pearl

margo, ĭnis *m, f,* edge, border

mărĭnus, a, um *adj,* of the sea

mărīta, ae *f,* wife

mărītālis, e *adj,* matrimonial

mărītĭmus, a, um *adj,* of the sea

mărītus, a, um *adj,* matrimonial

mărītus, i *m,* husband

marmor, ŏris *n,* marble, statue; *in pl,* surface of the sea

marmŏrĕus, a, um *adj,* of marble

martĭālis, e *adj,* sacred to Mars

Martĭus (mensis) March

martyr, ўris *c,* martyr

martўrĭum, ii *n,* martyrdom

mās, măris *adj,* male

mascŭlus, a, um *adj,* male, bold

massa, ae *f,* lump, mass

mătellĭo, ōnis *m,* pot

māter, tris *f,* mother

māterfămĭlĭas, mātrisfămĭlĭas *f,* mistress of the house

mātĕrĭa, ae *f,* timber, materials, topic, opportunity

matĕris, is f, Celtic javelin
māternus, a, um adj, maternal
mātertĕra, ae f, maternal aunt
măthēmătĭca, ae f, mathematics
măthēmătĭcus, a, um adj, mathematical
mātrĭcīda, ae c, murderer of his (her) mother
mātrĭmōnĭum, ii n, marriage
mātrōna, ae f, married woman
mātrōnālis, e adj, of a married woman
mātūrē adv, at the proper time, soon, quickly
mātūresco, rŭi v.i. 3, to ripen
mātūrĭtas, ātis f, ripeness
mātūro v.i.t. 1, to ripen, hurry; bring to maturity
mātūrus, a, um adj, mature, ripe, early
mātūtĭnus, a, um adj, of the morning
maxilla, ae f, jawbone, jaw
maxĭmē adv, expecially, very
maxĭmus, a, um sup. adj, very large or great
māxŏnŏmus, i m, dish
me acc. or abl. of **ĕgŏ**
mĕātus, ūs m, motion, course
mĕdĕor v. 2, dep, with dat, to heal, remedy, amend
mĕdĭastīnus, i m, drudge
mĕdĭca, ae f, a kind of clover
mĕdĭcābĭlis, e adj, curable
mĕdĭcāmen, ĭnis n, remedy, drug
mĕdĭcāmentum, i n, remedy, drug
mĕdĭcāmentārĭus, a, um adj, of drugs
mĕdĭcīna, ae f, the art of medicine, remedy
mĕdĭco v.t. 1, to heal, sprinkle, dye
mĕdĭcor v.t. 1, dep, to heal
mĕdĭcus, a, um adj, healing
mĕdĭcus, i m, doctor, surgeon
mĕdimnum, i n, bushel
mĕdĭōcris, e adj, adv, **ĭter**, ordinary, insignificant
mĕdĭòcrĭtas, ātis f, a middle state, insignificance
mĕdĭtātĭo, ōnis f, contemplation, preparation
meditātus, a, um adj, considered

mĕdĭterrānĕus, a, um adj, inland
mĕdĭtor v.i.t. 1, dep, to consider, muse; study, intend, practise
mĕdĭum, ii n, middle, the public
mĕdĭus, a, um adj, middle, neutral
mĕdĭus, i m, mediator
mĕdulla, ae f, kernel, marrow
mēio v.i. 3, to urinate
mĕl, mellis n, honey
mĕlanchŏlĭcus, a, um adj, melancholic
mēles, is f, badger
mēlĭmēla, ōrum n.pl, honey apples
mĕlĭor, us comp. adj, better
mĕlissphyllum, i n, balm
mĕlĭus comp. adv, better
mellĭfer, ĕra, ĕrum adj, honey producing
mellĭfĭco v.t. 1, to make honey
mellītus, a, um adj, of honey
mēlo, ōnis m, melon
mĕlos, i n, tune, song
membrāna, ae f, skin, parchment
membrātim adv, piece by piece
membrum, i n, limb, division
mĕmmĭni, isse v.i, defective, to remember
mĕmor, ŏris adj, remembering, mindful
mĕmŏrābĭlis, e adj, memorable
mĕmŏrandus, a, um adj, memorable
mĕmŏrātus, a, um adj, renowned
mĕmŏrĭa, ae f, memory, posterity, historical account, tradition
mĕmŏro v.t. 1, to mention
menda, ae f, defect
mendācĭum, ii n, a lie
mendax, ācis adj, lying, false
mendīcĭtas, ātis f, poverty
mendīco v.i. 1, to beg
mendĭcus, a, um adj, needy
mendĭcus, i m, beggar
mendōsus, a, um adj, adv, **ē**, faulty, false
mendum, i n, blunder, defect, mistake
mens, ntis f, mind, intellect, understanding, intention, courage
mensa, ae f, table, course;
    sĕcunda mensa dessert
mensārĭus, ii m, banker

mensis, is *m*, month

mensor, ōris *m*, valuer, surveyor

menstrŭus, a, um *adj*, monthly

mensūra, ae *f*, measurement, quantity

mensus, a, um *adj*, measured off

menta, ae *f*, mint

mentĭo, ōnis *f*, recollection, mention

mentĭor *v.i.t.* 4, *dep*, to lie, cheat; counterfeit, imitate

mentītus, a, um *adj*, counterfeit

mentum, i *n*, chin

mĕo *v.i.* 1, to go

mĕrācus, a, um *adj*, unmixed

mercātor, ōris *m*, wholesaler

mercātūra, ae *f*, trade

mercātus, ūs *m*, trade, market

mercēdŭla, ae *f*, small wages

mercēnārĭus, a, um *adj*, hired

merces, ēdis *f*, pay, wages, rent, interest, reward

merces (*pl*) see merx

mercor *v.t.* 1, *dep*, to buy

mĕrens, ntis *adj*, deserving

mĕrĕo *v.t.* (mĕrĕor *v. dep*) 2, to deserve, earn; *with* stīpendĭa, to serve as a soldier

mĕrètrīcĭus, a, um *adj*, of prostitutes

mĕrètrix, trīcis *f*, prostitute

merges, ĭtis *f*, sheaf

mergo, si, sum *v.t.* 3, to immerse

mergus, i *m*, seabird (diver)

mĕrīdĭānus, a, um *adj*, of midday

mĕrīdĭes, ēi *m*, midday, south

mĕrĭtōrĭus, a, um *adj*, bringing in money

mĕrĭtum, i *n*, reward, benefit, fault, blame

mĕrĭtus, a, um *adj, adv*, ē, deserved, deserving

mĕrops, ŏpis *m*, bee-eating bird

merso *v.t.* 1, to immerse, drown

mĕrŭla, ae *f*, blackbird

mĕrum, i *n*, pure wine

mĕrus, a, um *adj*, pure, only, genuine

merx, cis *f*, goods, commodities

messis, is *f*, harvest, crops

messor, ōris *m*, harvester

mēta, ae *f*, winning-post, end, cone

mĕtallĭcus, a, um *adj*, metallic

mĕtallĭcus, i *m*, miner

mĕtallum, i *n*, mine, metal

mētātor, ōris *m*, surveyor

mētĭor, mensus *v.t.* 4, *dep*, to measure, distribute, traverse, estimate, value

mĕto, ssŭi, ssum *v.t.* 3, to mow, gather, cut down

mētor *v.t.* 1, *dep*, to measure, mark out, traverse

mètrĭcus, a, um *adj*, metrical

mĕtŭendus, a, um *adj*, formidable

mĕtŭo, ŭi, ūtum *v.i.t.* 3, to be afraid; to fear

mĕtus, ūs *m*, fear, awe

mĕus, a, um *adj*, my, mine: mĕi, ōrum *m.pl*, my relatives

mīca, ae *f*, crumb

mĭco, ŭi *v.i.* 1, to tremble, sparkle

mìgrātĭo, ōnis *f*, migration

migro *v.i.* 1, to depart, change

mīlĕs, ĭtis *c*, soldier, army

mīlia see mille

mīlĭārĭum, ii *n*, milestone

mīlĭtāris, e *adj*, military

mīlĭtāris, is *m*, soldier

mīlĭtĭa, ae *f*, military service, warfare

mīlĭto *v.i.* 1, to serve as a soldier

mīlĭum, ii *n*, millet

mille (*pl*, mīlia, *with genit*.) a thousand; mille passus, or passuum, a mile

millēsĭmus, a, um *adj*, the thousandth

millĭes (millĭens) *adv*, a thousand times

milŭīnus, a, um *adj*, kite-like

milŭus, i *m*, kite, gurnard

mīmĭcus, a, um *adj*, farcical

mīmus, i *m*, mime, mimic actor

mīna, ae *f*, Greek silver coinage

mīnae, ārum *f.pl*, threats

mīnax, ācis *adj, adv*, ĭter, threatening, projecting

mĭnĭmē *sup. adv*, very little

mĭnĭmus, a, um *sup. adj*, very small

mĭnister, tri *m*, mĭnistra, ae *f*, servant, assistant

mĭnistĕrĭum, ii *n*, service, occupation

mĭnistrātor, ōris *m*, servant

mĭnistro *v.t.* 1, to wait upon, serve, manage

mĭnĭtor *v.i.t.* 1, *dep*, to threaten

mĭnĭum, ii red-lead

mĭnor *v.i.t.* 1, *dep*, to threaten

mĭnor, us *comp. adj*, smaller

mĭnŭo, ŭi, ūtum *v.i.t.* 3, to ebb; to reduce, weaken, chop up

mĭnus *comp. adv*, less

mĭnuscŭlus, a, um *adj*, rather small

mĭnūtal, ālis *n*, mincemeat

mĭnūtātim *adv*, little by little

mĭnūtus, a, um *adj, adv*, ē, small

mīrābĭlis, e *adj, adv*, īter, wonderful, strange

mīrācŭlum, i *n*, a wonder, marvel

mīrandus, a, um *adj*, wonderful

mīrātĭo, ōnis *f*, surprise

mīrātor, ōris *m*, admirer

mīrĭfĭcus, a, um *adj, adv*, ē, marvellous, extraordinary

mīror *v.i.t.* 1, *dep*, to be amazed; to marvel at, admire

mīrus, a, um *adj, adv*, ē, marbellous, extraordinary

miscĕo, scŭi, xtum *v.t.* 2, to mix, unite, disturb

mĭsellus, a, um *adj*, wretched

mĭser, ĕra, ĕrum *adj, adv*, ē, wretched, pitiable, worthless

mĭsĕrābĭlis, e *adj, adv*, īter, pitiable, sad

mĭsĕrandus, a, um *adj*, pitiable

mĭsĕrātĭo, ōnis *f*, pity

mĭsĕrĕor *v.* 2, *dep, with genit*, to pity

mĭsĕret (me, te, etc.) *v.* 2, *impers*, it distresses (me), I pity, am sorry for

mĭsĕresco *v.i.* 3, to feel pity

mĭsĕrĭa, ae *f*, misfortune, wretchedness

mĭsĕrĭcordĭa, ae *f*, pity

mĭsĕrĭcors, dis *adj*, merciful

mĭsĕror *v.t.* 1, *dep*, to lament, pity

missĭle, is *n*, missile, javelin

missĭlis, e *adj*, that is thrown

missĭo, ōnis *f*, throwing, discharge, release

missus, ūs *m*, dispatching, throwing, shot

mĭtella, ae *f*, turban, bandage

mītesco *v.i.* 3, to grow mild or soft or ripe

mītĭgātĭo, ōnis *f*, mitigation

mītĭgo *v.t.* 1, to make soft or ripe, to tame, soothe

mītis, e *adj*, mild, ripe, calm

mitra, ae *f*, headband

mitto, mīsi, missum *v.t.* 3, to send, announce, cease, release, throw, escort

mītŭlus, i *m*, sea mussel

mixtūta, ae *f*, mixture

mixtus, a, um *adj*, mixed

mōbĭlis, e *adj, adv*, ĭter, movable, agile, flexible, fickle

mōbĭlĭtas, ātis *f*, speed, inconstancy

mŏdĕrāmen, ĭnis *n*, rudder, management

mŏdĕrātĭo, ōnis *f*, moderation, restraint

mŏdĕrātor, ōris *m*, manager

mŏdĕrātus, a, um *adj, adv*, ē, moderate

mŏdĕror *v.t.* 1, *dep*, to restrain, govern

mŏdestĭa, ae *f*, moderation, discretion, modesty

mŏdestus, a, um *adj, adv*, ē, modest, gentle

mŏdĭcus, a, um *adj, adv*, ē, modest, ordinary

mŏdĭfĭcātus, a, um *adj*, measured

mŏdĭus, ii *m*, peck, measure

mŏdŏ *adv*, only, but, just, lately; **non mŏdŏ** not only; **mŏdŏ ... mŏdŏ** at one time ... at another time

mŏdŭlātor, ōris *m*, musician

mŏdŭlor *v.t.* 1, *dep*, to sing, play

mŏdŭlātus, a, um *adj*, sung, played

mŏdŭlus, i *m*, a small measure

mŏdus, i *m*, measure, quantity, rhythm, limit, restriction, end, method, way

moechus, i *m*, adulterer

moenĭa, ĭum *n.pl*, ramparts

mŏla, ae *f*, millstone, grain mixed with salt to be sprinkeld on sacrificial animals

mŏlāris, is *m*, millstone

mōles, is *f*, mass, bulk, dam, pier, power, difficulty

mŏlestĭa, ae *f*, trouble, affectation

mŏlestus, a, um *adj, adv,* **ē,**
  troublesome, affected
mōlīmen, ĭnis *n,* undertaking,
  attempt
mōlīmentum, i *n,* undertaking,
  attempt
mōlīor *v.i.t.* 4, to strive, depart; to
  rouse, construct, attempt
mŏlītor, ōris *m,* miller
mōlītor, ōris *m,* contriver
mollesco *v.i.* 3, to grow soft
mollīo *v.t.* 4, to soften, restrain
mollis, e *adj, adv,* **ĭter** soft, supple,
  tender, effeminate
mollĭtĭa, ae *f,* softness, weakness
mollĭtĭes, ēi *f,* softness, weakness
mollītūdo, ĭnis *f,* softness,
  weakness
mŏlo, ŭi, ĭtum *v.t.* 3, to grind
mōmentum, i *n,* movement,
  motion, moment, instant, cause,
  influence, importance
mŏnăcha, ae *f,* nun
mŏnastērĭum, ii *n,* monastery
mŏnēdŭla, ae *f,* jackdaw
mŏnĕo *v.t.* 2, to warn, advise,
  remind, instruct, tell

monstrum, i *n,* omen, monster
monstrŭōsus, a, um *adj,* strange,
  monstrous
montānus, a, um *adj,* of a
  mountain, mountainous
montĭcŏla, ae *c,* mountain-dweller
montĭvăgus, a, um *adj,* wandering
  in the mountains
montŭōsus, a, um *adj,*
  mountainous
mŏnŭmentum, i *n,* monument,
  memorial, written record
mŏra, ae *f,* delay, hindrance
mōrālis, e *adj,* moral
mōrātus, a, um *adj,* mannered;
mŏrātus *partic. from* **mŏror,**
  having delayed
morbĭdus, a, um *adj,* diseased
morbus, i *m,* illness, disease
mordax, ācis *adj,* biting, stinging
mordĕo, mŏmordi, morsum *v.t.* 2,
  to bite, clasp, sting
mordĭcus, a, um *adj,* by biting
mōres see **mos**
mŏrētum, i *n,* salad
mŏrībundus, a, um *adj,* dying
mŏrĭens, ntis *adj,* dying

Insight

The imperfect tense (e.g. *monebam*) refers to an action that
is uncompleted; the action is depicted as continuing, or being
repeated, or beginning or being attempted. The most
common translations for the imperfect are: 'I was -ing', 'I
used to –', 'I began to –', 'I tried to –'.

mŏnēta, ae *f,* the mint, coin
mŏnētālis, e *adj,* of the mint
mŏnīle, is *n,* necklace, collar
mŏnĭtĭo, ōnis *f,* warning
mŏnĭtor, ōris *m,* adviser, instructor
mŏnĭtum, i *n,* advice
mŏnĭtus, ūs *m,* warning, omen
mŏnŏcĕros, ōtis *m,* unicorn
mŏnŏpōlĭum, ii *n,* monopoly
mons, ntis *m,* mountain
monstrātĭo, ōnis *f,* showing,
  pointing out
monstrātor, ōris *m,* teacher
monstro *v.t.* 1, to show, tell

mŏrĭor, mortŭus *v.i.* 3, *dep,* to die
mŏror *v.i.t.* 1, *dep,* to delay
mōrōsĭtas, ātis *f,* fretfulness
mōrōsus, a, um *adj,* fretful,
  fastidious
mors, mortis *f,* death
morsus, ūs *m,* bite, pungency
mortālis, e *adj,* mortal, human,
  temporary
mortālis, is *c,* human being
mortālĭtas, ātis *f,* mortality
mortārĭum, ii *n,* a mortar
mortĭfer, ĕra, ĕrum *adj,* fatal
mortŭus, a, um *adj,* dead

mortŭus, i *m*, dead person
mōrum, i *n*, blackberry
mōrus, i *f*, blackberry-bush
mos, mōris *m*, custom, manner, habit, fashion; *in pl*, character
mōtăcilla, ae *f*, wagtail
mōtĭo, ōnis *f*, motion
mōto *v.t.* 1, to move about
mōtus, ūs *m*, motion, movement, impulse, emotion, rebellion
mŏvĕo, mōvi, mōtum *v.t.* 2, to move, stir, excite, cause
mox *adv*, soon, immediately
mūcĭdus, a, um *adj*, musty
mūcor, ōris *m*, mouldiness
mūcōsus, a, um *adj*, mucous
mūcro, ōnis *m*, sword's point
mūgil, is *m*, mullet
mūgĭnor *v.i.* 1, *dep*, to hesitate
mūgĭo *v.i.* 4, to low, bellow, groan, crash
mūgītus, ūs *m*, bellowing, roaring
mūla, ae *f*, she-mule
mulcĕo, si, sum *v.t.* 2, to stroke, soothe
mulco *v.t.* 1, to maltreat
mulctra, ae *f*, milk-bucket
mulctrārĭum, ii *n*, milk-bucket
mulgĕo, si, sum *v.t.* 2, to milk
mŭlĭèbris, e *adj, adv*, **ĭter**, female, effeminate
mŭlĭer, ĕris *f*, woman, wife
mŭlĭercŭla, ae *f*, girl
mūlĭo, ōnis *m*, mule-driver
mullus, i *m*, mullet
mulsum, i *n*, honey-wine
multa, ae *f*, penalty, fine
multātĭo, ōnis *f*, penalty, fine
multi see **multus**
multĭfārĭam *adv*, on many sides
multĭplex, ĭcis *adj*, with many windings, numerous, many
multĭplĭcātĭo, ōnis *f*, multiplication
multĭplĭco *v.t.* 1, to multiply
multĭtūdo, ĭnis *f*, crowd, great number
multō *adv*, a great deal
multo *v.t.* 1, to punish
multum *adv*, very much, greatly
multus, a, um *adj*, much; *pl*, many
mūlus, i *m*, mule
mundītĭa, ae *f*, cleanliness, neatness
mundītĭes, ēi *f*, cleanliness, neatness

mundo *v.t.* 1, to cleanse
mundus, a, um *adj*, clean, elegant
mundus, i *m*, world, universe, ornaments
mūnĕro *v.t.* 1 (**mūnĕror**, *v.t.* 1, *dep*.), to reward, honour
mūnĭa, ōrum *n.pl*, duties
mūnĭceps, cĭpis *c*, citizen
mūnĭcĭpālis, e, *adj*, municipal
mūnĭcĭpĭum, ii *n*, self-governing town
mūnĭficentĭa, ae *f*, generosity
mūnĭficus, a, um *adj, adv*, **ē**, generous
mūnīmen, ĭnis *n*, rampart, protection
mūnīmentum, i *n*, rampart, protection
mūnĭo *v.t.* 4, to fortify, secure, make a way
mūnītĭo, ōnis *f*, fortification
mūnītor, ōris *m*, engineer
mūnītus, a, um *adj*, fortified
mūnus, ĕris *n*, service, duty, employment, post, tax, gift, public show
mūnuscŭlum, i *n*, small present
mūrālis, e *adj*, of a wall
mūrex, ĭcis *m*, purple fish, purple dye, pointed rock
mŭrĭa, ae *f*, brine, pickle
murmur, ŭris *n*, murmur, crash
murmŭro *v.i.* 1, to murmur, roar
murra, ae *f*, myrrh (tree)
murrĕus, a, um *adj*, perfumed with myrrh
mūrus, i *m*, wall, defence
mūs, mūris *c*, mouse
mūsa, ae *f*, goddess of the arts
musca, ae *f*, a fly
muscĭpŭlum, i *n*, mousetrap
muscōsus, a, um *adj*, mossy
muscŭlus, i *m*, little mouse, mussel, muscle, military shed
muscus, i *m*, moss
mūsēum, i *n*, museum
mūsĭca, ae *f*, music
mūsĭcus, a, um *adj*, musical
mūsĭcus, i *m*, musician
musso *v.i.* 1, to mutter, be silent, be in doubt
mustēla, ae *f*, weasel
mustum, i *n*, new wine

mūtābĭlis, e *adj,* changeable
mūtābĭlĭtas, ātis *f,* changeableness
mūtātĭo, ōnis *f,* alteration
mŭtĭlo *v.t.* 1, to cut off, maim
mŭtĭlus, a, um *adj,* maimed
mūto *v.i.t.* 1, to alter, change
mūtŭlus, i *m,* bracket
mūtŭō *adv,* in turns
mūtŭor *v.t.* 1, *dep,* to borrow
mūtus, a, um *adj,* dumb, mute
mūtŭum, i *n,* loan
mūtŭus, a, um *adj,* borrowed, mutual
mўrīca, ae *f;* **mўrīce, es** *f,* a shrub, tamarisk
myrr... see **murr...**
myrtētum, i *n,* myrtle grove
myrtĕus, a, um *adj,* of myrtle
myrtum, i *n,* myrtle berry
myrtus, i *f,* myrtle tree
mysta (es), ae *f,* priest of Ceres' mysteries
mystērĭum, ii *n,* secret rites
mystĭcus, a, um *adj,* mystical

N

naevus, i *m,* wart, mole
Nāĭăs, ădis *f,* water-nymph
nam *conj,* for

nasturtĭum, ii *n,* cress
nāsus, i *m,* nose
nāsūtus, a, um *adj,* large-nosed
nāta, ae *f,* daughter
nātālĭcĭus, a, um *adj,* birthday
nātālis, e *adj,* of birth
nātālis, is *m,* birthday
nătantes, um *f.pl,* fish
nătātĭo, ōnis *f,* swimming
nătātor, ōris *m,* swimmer
nātĭo, ōnis *f,* race, nation
nātis, is, *f,* buttock
nātīvus, a, um *adj,* created, inborn, natural
năto *v.i.* 1, to swim, float, waver
nătrix, īcis *f,* water snake
nātūra, ae *f,* nature
nātūrālis, e *adj, adv,* **īter,** by birth, natural
nātus, ūs *m,* birth
nātus, i *m,* son
nātus, a, um *adj,* born, aged
nauarchus, i *m,* ship's master
naufrăgĭum, ii *n,* shipwreck
naufrăgus, a, um *adj,* shipwrecked
naumăchĭa, ae *f,* mock sea fight
nausĕa, ae *f,* seasickness
nausĕābundus, a, um *adj,* seasick
nausĕo *v.i.* 1, to be seasick
nauta, ae *m,* sailor

Insight

All nouns of the **first declension** are feminine except for a few nouns that are masculine by meaning, such as *nauta* (= sailor), *agricola* (= farmer), and *scriba* (= clerk, secretary).

namque *conj,* for indeed
nanciscor, nactus *v.t.* 3, *dep,* to obtain, meet with, find
nānus, i *m,* dwarf
nāpus, i *m,* turnip
narcissus, i *m,* narcissus
nardus, i *f,* perfumed balm
nāris, is *f,* nostril; *pl,* nose
narrātĭo, ōnis *f,* narrative
narrātor, ōris *m,* narrator
narro *v.t.* 1, to tell, relate
narthēcĭum, ii *n,* medicine chest
nascor, nātus *v.i.* 3, *dep,* to be born, rise, proceed

nautĭcus, a, um *adj,* nautical
nāvālĭa, ĭum *n.pl,* dockyard
nāvāle, is *n,* dockyard
nāvālis, e *adj,* naval
nāvĭcŭla, ae *f,* boat
nāvĭcŭlārĭus, ii *m,* shipowner
nāvĭfrăgus, a, um *adj,* ship wrecking
nāvĭgābĭlis, e *adj,* navigable
nāvĭgātĭo, ōnis *f,* sailing
nāvĭger, ĕra, ĕrum *adj,* navigable
nāvĭgĭa, ōrum *n.pl,* ships, shipping
nāvĭgĭum, ii *n,* ship, boat
nāvĭgo *v.i.t.* 1, to sail; navigate

nāvis, is *f,* ship; **nāvis longa,** warship

nāvĭta, ae *m,* **(nauta),** sailor

nāvĭter *adv,* completely

nāvo *v.t.* 1, to do vigorously

nāvus, a, um *adj,* hard-working

nē *conj,* lest; **nē ... quidem,** not even ...

-nĕ attached to the first word of a sentence to form a question

nē *interj,* indeed, truly

nĕbŭla, ae *f,* mist, fog, smoke

nĕbŭlo, ōnis *m,* rascal, wretch

nĕbŭlōsus, a, um *adj,* misty

nĕc *adv,* not; *conj,* and not; **nĕc ... nĕc,** neither ... nor

necdum *conj,* not yet

nĕcessārĭus, a, um *adj, adv,* **ō,** unavoidable, necessary, related

nĕcessārĭus, ii *m,* relative

nĕcesse *indecl. adj,* unavoidable

nĕcessĭtas, ātis *f,* necessity, compulsion, destiny

nĕcessĭtūdo, ĭnis *f,* necessity, relationship

necnĕ *adv,* or not

nec-non and also

nĕco *v.t.* 1, to kill

nĕcŏpīnans, ntis *adj,* unaware

nĕcŏpīnātus, a, um *adj, adv,* **ō,** unexpected

nĕcŏpīnus, a, um *adj,* unexpected

nectar, ăris *n,* the drink of the gods

nectărĕus, a, um *adj,* of nectar

necto, xŭi, xum *v.t.* 3, to tie, fasten together

nĕcūbi *adv,* so that nowhere

nēdum *conj,* still less

nĕfandus, a, um *adj,* abominable, heinous, wrong

nĕfārĭus, a, um *adj,* heinous, wrong

nĕfas *n, indecl,* wrong, sin

nefastus, a, um *adj, with* **dies,** a day on which neither trials nor public meetings could be held, wicked, unlucky

nĕgātĭo, ōnis *f,* denial

nĕgĭto *v.t.* 1, to persist in denying

neglectus, a, um *adj,* despised

neglĕgens (neglĭgens), ntis *adj,* careless, indifferent

neglĕgentĭa, ae *f,* carelessness

neglĕgo, xi, ctum *v.t.* 3, to neglect, slight, despise

nĕgo *v.i.t.* 1, to say no (not); refuse

nĕgōtĭātĭo, ōnis *f,* wholesale business, banking

nĕgōtĭātor, ōris *m,* wholesaler, banker

nĕgōtĭor *v.i.* 1, *dep,* to carry on business, trade or banking

nĕgōtĭōsus, a, um *adj,* busy

nĕgōtĭum, ii *n,* business, occupation, difficulty

nēmo, ĭnis *m, f,* nobody

nĕmŏrālis, e *adj,* woody

nĕmŏrōsus, a, um *adj,* woody

nempĕ *conj,* certainly

nĕmus, ŏris *n,* wood, grove

nēnĭa, ae *f,* funeral hymn, sad song, popular song

nĕo, nēvi, nētum *v.t.* 2, to spin

nĕpa, ae *f,* scorpion

nĕpos, ōtis *m, f,* grandson (...daughter), descendant, spendthrift

neptis, is *f,* granddaughter

nēquam *indecl. adj, adv* **nēquĭter,** worthless, bad

nēquăquam *adv,* not at all

nĕque *adv,* not; *conj,* and not; **nĕque ... nĕque,** neither ... nor

nĕquĕo, īvi (ĭi), ĭtum *v.i.* 4, to be unable

nēquīquam *adv,* in vain

nēquĭtĭa, ae *f,* worthlessness, idleness, extravagance

nervōsus, a, um *adj, adv,* **ē,** sinewy, energetic

nervus, i *m,* sinew, string of musical instrument or bow

nescĭo *v.t.* 4, not to know, to be unable

nescĭus, a, um *adj,* unaware

neu *adv,* and so that ... not

neuter, tra, trum *adj,* neither the one nor the other

neutĭquam *adv,* not at all

neutrō *adv,* neither way

nēve *adv,* and so that ... not

nex, nĕcis *f,* death, slaughter

nexĭlis, e *adj,* tied together

nexum, i *n,* slavery for debt, obligation

nexus, ūs *m*, tying together
nī *conj*, unless
nictātĭo, ōnis *f*, winking
nicto *v.i.* 1, to wink, blink
nīdor, ōris *m*, steam, smell
nīdŭlus, i *m*, little nest
nīdus, i *m*, nest, home; *in pl*, nestlings
nĭger, gra, grum *adj*, black, dark, ill-omened, funereal
nigrans, ntis *adj*, black
nigresco, grŭi *v.i.* 3, to grow dark
nĭhil (nīl) *n, indecl*, nothing
nĭhĭli of no value
nĭhĭlōmĭnus *adj*, nevertheless
nĭhīlum, i *n*, nothing
nīl *n, indecl*, nothing
nimbĭfer, ĕra, ĕrum *adj*, stormy, rainy
nimbōsus, a, um *adj*, stormy, rainy
nimbus, i *m*, heavy rain, rain-cloud, cloud
nīmīrum *adv*, without doubt
nĭmis *adv*, too much
nĭmĭum *adv*, too much
nĭmĭum, ii *n*, excess
nĭmĭus, a, um *adj*, excessive
ningit *v.i.* 3, *impers*, it is snowing
nĭsĭ *conj*, if not, unless
nīsus, ūs *m*, pressure, effort, labour of childbirth

nītrum, i *n*, soda
nĭvālis, e *adj*, snowy, cold
nĭvĕus, a, um *adj*, snowy, white
nĭvōsus, a, um *adj*, snowy
nix, nĭvis *f*, snow
nixor *v.i.* 1, *dep*, to strive
nixus, ūs *m*, pressure, effort, labour of childbirth
no *v.i.* 1, to swim
nōbĭlis, e *adj*, famous, noble
nōbĭlĭtas, ātis *f*, fame, noble birth
nōbĭlĭto *v.t.* 1, to make famous
nōbis *dat. or abl. of* nos
nŏcens, ntis *adj*, wicked, bad, harmful, injurious
nŏcĕo *v.i.* 2, *with dat*, to harm
nocte *adv*, at night
noctĭlūca, ae *f*, moon
noctĭvăgus, a, um *adj*, wandering at night
noctu *adv*, at night
noctŭa, ae *f*, night owl
nocturnus, a, um *adj*, nocturnal
nōdo *v.t.* 1, to tie in a knot
mōdōsus, a, um *adj*, knotty, difficult
nōdus, i *m*, knot, knob, band, obligation, difficulty
nōli, nōlīte *imper*, do not …
nōlo, nolle, nōlŭi *v, irreg*, to be unwilling

Insight

The imperative forms of *nolo*, *noli/nolite* are used for a negative command; they mean 'don't!' and are followed by the infinitive of the verb (e.g. *noli clamare* = don't shout!).

nītēdŭla, ae *f*, dormouse
nĭtens, ntis *adj*, bright, shining, sleek, beautiful
nĭtĕo *v.i.* 2, to shine, to look handsome, thrive
nĭtēsco, tŭi *v.i.* 3, to shine
nĭtĭdus, a, um *adj*, shining, sleek, handsome, refined
nītor, nīsus (nixus) *v.i.* 3, *dep*, to lean, press forward, fly, make an effort, argue
nītor, ōris *m*, brightness, splendour, beauty, elegance

nōmen, ĭnis *n*, name, debt, fame, repute, excuse, reason
nōmenclātor, ōris *m*, slave who reminded his master of the names of the people he met
nōmĭnātim *adj*, by name
nōmĭnātĭo, ōnis *f*, nomination
nōmĭnātus, a, um *adj*, renowned
nōmĭno *v.t.* 1, to name, make famous
nŏmisma, ătis *n*, a coin
nōn *adv*, not

nōnae, ārum *f.pl*, the Nones; 5th or 7th day of the month
nōnāgēni, ae *adj*, ninety each
nōnāgēsīmus, a, um *adj*, ninetieth
nōnāgĭes *adv*, ninety times
nōnāgintā *indecl. adj*, ninety
nondum *adj*, not yet
nongenti, ae, a *adj*, nine hundred
nonnē *adv*, used to introduce a question expecting the answer 'yes'
nonnēmo, ĭnis *m*, someone
nonnĭhil *n*, something
nonnĭsi *adv*, only
nonnullus, a, um *adj*, several
nonnumquam *adv*, sometimes
nōnus, a, um *adj*, ninth
norma, ae *f*, rule, pattern, standard
nōs *pron, pl.* of **ĕgŏ**, we, us

nŏvēnus, a, um *adj*, nine each
nŏverca, ae *f*, stepmother
nŏvīcĭus, a, um *adj*, new
nŏvĭens *adv*, nine times
nŏvĭes *adv*, nine times
nŏvissĭmus, a, um *adj*, last; in *m.pl, or* **nŏvissĭmum agmen** rear ranks
nŏvĭtas, ātis *f*, novelty, unusualness
nŏvo *v.t.* 1, to renew, refresh, change
nŏvus, a, um *adj*, new, recent, fresh; **nŏvus hŏmo** an upstart; **nŏvae res** revolution
nox, noctis *f*, night
noxa, ae *f*, injury, harm fault, crime

Insight

Personal pronouns **nos** (= we) and **vos** (= you plural) have two forms for the genitive plural: *nostri* and *vestri* are objective (*cupidus nostri* = desirous of us), *nostrum* and *vestrum* are partitive (*unus vestrum* = one of you).

noscīto *v.t.* 1, to know, observe
nosco, nōvi, nōtum *v.t.* 3, to get to know, know, recognize, acknowledge
noster, tra, trum *adj*, our, ours
nostras, ātis *adj*, of our country
nŏta, ae *f*, mark, sign, brand
nŏtābĭlis, e *adj*, noteworthy
nŏtātĭo, ōnis *f*, branding, observation
nŏthus, a, um *adj*, illegitimate, counterfeit
nōtĭo, ōnis *f*, investigation
nōtītĭa, ae *f*, fame, knowledge
nŏto *v.t.* 1, to mark, write, indicate, brand, reprimand
nōtus, a, um *adj*, well-known
nōtus, i *m*, the south wind
nŏvācŭla, ae *f*, razor
nŏvālis, is *f*, fallow land
nŏvellus, a, um *adj*, young, new
nŏvem *indecl. adj*, nine
Nŏvember (mensis) November
nŏvendĭālis, e *adj*, lasting nine days

noxĭa, ae *f*, injury, harm, fault, crime
noxĭus, a, um *adj*, harmful, guilty
nūbes, is *f*, cloud
nūbĭfer, ĕra, ĕrum *adj*, cloud-capped, cloud-bringing
nūbĭla, ōrum *n.pl*, the clouds
nūbĭlis, e *adj*, marriageable
nūbĭlus, a, um *adj*, overcast
nūbo, psi, ptum *v.i.t.* 3, *with dat*, to marry
nùclĕus, i *m*, nut, kernel
nŭdĭus *with a number* **(tertĭus)** (three) days ago
nūdo *v.t.* 1, to strip, expose
nūdus, a, um *adj*, naked, destitute of, poor, simple
nūgae, ārum *f.pl*, jokes, nonsense, trifles
nūgātor, ōris *m*, silly person
nūgātōrĭus, a, um *adj*, trifling
nūgor *v.i.* 1, *dep*, to play the fool
nullus, a, um *adj*, none, no
nullus, ĭus *m*, no-one

num *adv*, used to introduce a question expecting answer 'no'; whether

nūmen, ĭnis *n*, divine will, divine power, divinity

nŭmĕrābĭlis, e *adj*, able to be counted

nŭmĕrātor, ōris *m*, counter

nŭmĕrātum, i *n*, ready money

nŭmĕro *v.t.* 1, to count, pay out, number

nŭmĕrō *adv*, in number, just

nŭmĕrōsus, a, um *adj, adv*, **ē**, numerous, rhythmic

nŭmĕrus, i *m*, number, band (of soldiers), class, category, sequence, rhythm, poetic metre

nummārĭus, a, um *adj*, of money

nummātus, a, um *adj*, rich

nummus, i *m*, money, a Roman silver coin, farthing

numquam *adv*, never

numquid *interr. adv*, is there anything…?

nunc *adv*, now, at present

nuncia, nuncius … see **nunt…**

nuncŭpo *v.t.* 1, to call, name

nundĭnae, ārum *f.pl*, ninth day, market-day

nundĭnātĭo, ōnis *f*, trading

nundĭnor *v.i.t.* 1, *dep*, to trade; buy, sell

nunquam *adv*, never

nuntĭātĭo, ōnis *f*, announcement

nuntĭo *v.t.* 1, to announce, tell

nuntĭus, i *m*, messenger, message

nūper *adv*, lately, recently

nupta, ae *f*, wife, bride

nuptĭae, ārum *f.pl*, marriage

nuptĭālis, e *adj*, of marriage

nuptus, a, um *adj*, married

nŭrus, ūs *f*, daughter-in-law, young wife

nusquam *adv*, nowhere

nūto *v.i.* 1, to nod, waver

nūtrīcĭus, a, um *adj*, foster-father

nūtrīco *v.t.* 1, to nurse, rear

nūtrīcula, ae *f*, nurse

nūtrīmen, ĭnis *n*, nourishment

nūtrīmentum, i *n*, nourishment

nūtrĭo *v.t.* 4, to feed, bring up, support

nūtrix, īcis *f*, nurse

nūtus, ūs *m*, nod, command

nux, nŭcis *f*, nut

nympha, ae *f*, bride, nymph (demi-goddess inhabiting woods, trees, fountains, etc.)

O

ŏb *prep. with acc*, on account of, in front of

ŏbaerātus, a, um *adj*, involved in debt

ŏbambŭlo *v.i.* 1, to walk about

obdo, dĭdi, dĭtum *v.t.* 3, to shut, place, expose

obdormĭo *v.i.* 4, to fall asleep

obdormisco *v.i.* 3, to fall asleep

obdūco, xi, ctum *v.t.* 3, to lead forward, bring forward, cover over, swallow

obdūresco, rŭi *v.i.* 3, to become hardened

obdūro *v.i.* 1, to persist

ŏbēdĭens, ntis *adj*, obedient

ŏbēdĭentĭa, ae *f*, obedience

ŏbēdĭo *v.i.* 4, to obey, be subject to

ŏbĕliscus, i *m*, obelisk

ŏbĕo *v.i.t.* 4, to go to meet, die, set (constellations); to go to, reach, travel over, visit, undertake, perform

ŏbĕquĭto *v.i.* 1, to ride towards

ŏbēsĭtas, ātis *f*, fatness

ŏbēsus, a, um *adj*, fat, dull

ōbex, ĭcis *m, f*, bolt, barrier

obiăcĕo *v.i.* 2, to lie opposite

ōbĭcĭo, iēci, iectum *v.t.* 3, to throw forward, expose, oppose, taunt, reproach

obiectātĭo, ōnis *f*, reproach

obiecto *v.t.* 1, to place against, expose, reproach, accuse

obiectus, ūs *m*, opposing, putting in the way

obiectus, a, um *adj*, lying opposite

ōbĭtus, ūs *m*, setting, downfall

obiurgātĭo, ōnis *f*, rebuke

obiurgātor, ōris *m*, blamer

obirgātōrĭus, a, um *adj*, reproachful

obiurgo *v.t.* 1, to blame, rebuke

oblectāmen, ĭnis *n*, pleasure, delight

oblectāmentum, i *n*, pleasure, delight
oblecto *v.t.* 1, to amuse, please
oblĭgātĭo, ōnis *f*, obligation
oblĭgo *v.t.* 1, to bind, put under obligation, render liable
oblĭmo *v.t.* 1, to cover with mud, squander
oblĭno, lēvi, lĭtum *v.t.* 3, to besmear, defile
oblīquo *v.t.* 1, to bend aside
oblīquus, a, um *adj, adv*, **ē**, slanting, sideways
oblīvĭo, ōnis *f*, oblivion
oblīvĭōsus, a, um *adj*, forgetful, producing forgetfulness
oblīviscor, oblītus *v.* 3, *dep, with genit*, to forget
oblīvĭum, ii *n*, oblivion
oblŏquor, lŏcūtus *v.i.* 3, *dep*, to contradict, accompany a song
obluctor *v.i.* 1, *dep*, to struggle against
obmūtesco, tŭi *v.i.* 3, to become speechless
obnītor, xus *v.i.* 3, to become speechless
obnītor, xus *v.i.* 3, *dep*, to push or struggle against
obnixus, a, um *adj*, resolute
obnoxĭus, a, um *adj*, resolute
obnoxĭus, a, um *adj*, liable to, submissive, indebted
obnūbo, psi, ptum *v.t.* 3, to veil
obnuntĭātĭo, ōnis *f*, announcement of bad omens
obnuntĭo *v.t.* 1, to announce bad omens
ŏboedĭens, oboedĭo see **obēd...**
ŏbŏrĭor, ortus *v.i.* 4, *dep*, to arise, appear
obrēpo, psi, ptum *v.t.* 3, to creep up to, surprise
obrĭgesco, gŭi *v.i.* 3, to stiffen
obrŏgo *v.t.* 1, to invalidate
obrŭo, ŭi, ŭtum *v.t.* 3, to overwhelm, bury, hide
obsaepĭo, psi, ptum *v.t.* 4, to fence in
obscēnĭtas, ātis *f*, obscenity, foulness
obscēnus, a, um *adj*, ominous, filthy, obscene

obscūrĭtas, ātis *f*, uncertainty, lowness
obscūro *v.t.* 1, to darken, hide
obscūrus, a, um *adj, adv*, **ē**, dark, shady, indistinct, ignoble, humble, reserved
obsĕcrātĭo, ōnis *f*, appeal
obsĕcro *v.t.* 1, to implore
obsĕcundo *v.t.* 1, to humour, obey
obsēp... see **obsaep...**
obsĕquens, ntis *adj*, amenable
obsĕquĭum, ii *n*, compliance, obedience
obsĕquor, sĕcūtus *v.* 3, *dep, with dat*, to comply with, submit to, humour
obsĕro *v.t.* 1, to fasten
obsĕro, sēvi, sĭtum *v.t.* 3, to sow, plant
observans, ntis *adj*, attentive
observantĭa, ae *f*, attention, respect
observātĭo, ōnis *f*, care, observation
observo *v.t.* 1, to watch, take note of, respect, comply with
obses, ĭdis *m, f*, hostage
obsessĭo, ōnis *f*, blockade
obsessor, ōris *m*, besieger
obsĭdĕo, sēdi, sessum *v.t.* 2, to besiege, hem in, frequent
obsĭdĭo, ōnis *f*, siege
obsīdo *v.t.* 3, to besiege
obsignātor, ōris *m*, witness
obsigno *v.t.* 1, to seal up
obsisto, stĭti, stĭtum *v.i.* 3, to resist, oppose
obsĭtus, a, um *adj*, covered over
obsŏlesco, lēvi, lētum *v.i.* 3, to wear out, decay
obsŏlētus, a, um *adj*, worn out, low, mean
obsōnĭum, ii *n*, eatables
obsōnātor, ōris *m*, caterer
obsōno *v.t.* 1, (**obsōnor** *v.i.* 1, *dep*), to cater
obsorbĕo *v.t.* 2, to swallow
obstĕtrix, īcis *f*, midwife
obstĭnātĭo, ōnis *f*, firmness, obstinacy
obstĭnātus, a, um *adj, adv*, **ē**, determined, resolute, stubborn

obstŭpesco, pŭi *v.i.* 3, to be amazed

obstŭpus, a, um *adj*, bent

obsto, stĭti, ātum *v.i.* 1, *with dat*, to obstruct, withstand

obstrĕpo, ŭi, ĭtum *v.i.* 3, to roar at, resound

obstringo, nxi, ctum *v.t.* 3, to tie up, put under obligation

obstrŭo, xi, ctum *v.t.* 3, to build up, barricade, impede

obstŭpĕfăcĭo, fēci, factum *v.t.* 3, to astonish

obstŭpesco, pŭi *v.i.* 3, to be stupified, amazed

obsum, obesse, obfŭi *v.i, irreg*, to hinder, injure

obsŭo, ŭi, ūtum *v.t.* 3, to sew up

obsurdesco, dŭi *v.i.* 3, to grow deaf

obtĕgo, xi, ctum *v.t.* 3, to cover up

obtempĕro *v.t.* 1, *with dat*, to comply with

obtendo, di, tum *v.t.* 3, to spread before, hide

obtentus, ūs *m*, outspreading

obtĕro, trīvi, trītum *v.t.* 3, to crush to pieces

obtestātĭo, ōnis *f*, appeal

obtestor *v.t.* 1, *dep*, to call as a witness, implore

obtexo, xŭi *v.t.* 3, to cover up

obtĭcesco, tĭcŭi *v.i.* 3, to be struck dumb

obtĭnĕo, nŭi, tentum *v.i.t.* 2, to prevail, continue; keep, hold, gain, obtain

obtingo, tĭgi *v.i.* 3, to befall

obtorpesco, pŭi *v.i.* 3, to become stiff

obtorquĕo, si, tum *v.t.* 2, to twist, wrench

obtrectātĭo, ōnis *f*, disparagement

obtrectātor, ōris *m*, slander

obtrecto *v.i.t.* 1, to disparge

obtrunco *v.t.* 1, to trim, kill

obtundo, tŭdi, tūsum *v.t.* 3, to blunt, weaken, deafen, annoy

obtūrācŭlum, i *n*, stopper

obtūrāmentum, i *n*, stopper

obturbo *v.t.* 1, to disturb

obtūro *v.t.* 1, to close

obtūsus, a, um *adj*, blunt, dull

obtūtus, ūs *m*, gaze, stare

ŏbumbro *v.t.* 1, to overshadow

ŏbuncus, a, um *adj*, hooked

ŏbustus, a, um *adj*, hardened in fire

obvĕnĭo, vēni, ventum *v.i.* 4, to meet, befall one, happen

obversor *v.i.* 1, *dep*, to move to and fro, hover

obversus, a, um *adj*, directed towards

obverto, ti, sum *v.t.* 3, to turn downwards

obvĭam *adv, with verbs of motion*, towards, against

obvĭus, a, um *adj*, in the way, so as to meet, courteous, exposed

obvolvo, volvi, vŏlūtum *v.t.* 3, to wrap round, cover

occaeco *v.t.* 1, to blind, hide

occāsĭo, ōnis *f*, opportunity

occāsus, ūs *m*, setting (of sun, etc.) downfall, ruin

occĭdens, ntis *m*, the west

occĭdentālis, e *adj*, west

occīdĭo, ōnis *f*, massacre

occīdo, cīdi, cīsum *v.t.* 3, to strike down, crush, kill

occĭdo, cĭdi, cāsum *v.i.* 3, to fall, perish, set (of sun, etc.)

occĭdŭus, a, um *adj*, setting, western

occīsĭo, ōnis *f*, slaughter

occlūdo, si, sum *v.t.* 3, to close

occo *v.t.* 1, to harrow

occŭbo *v.i.* 1, to lie down, rest

occŭlo, lŭi, ltum *v.t.* 3, to hide

occultātĭo, ōnis *f*, concealment

occulto *v.t.* 1, to hide

occultus, a, um *adj, adv*, **ē**, hidden, secret

occumbo, cŭbŭi, cŭbĭtum *v.i.* 3, to die

occŭpātĭo, ōnis *f*, employment

occŭpātus, a, um *adj*, busy

occŭpo *v.t.* 1, to seize, occupy, attack, anticipate, fill

occurro, curri, cursum *v.i.* 3, to meet

occursātĭo, ōnis *f*, greeting

occurso *v.i.* 1, to meet, attack

occursus, ūs *m*, meeting

ōcĕănus, i *m*, ocean**

ŏcellus, i *m*, small eye, darling
ōchra, ae *f*, ochre
ōcĭor, ĭus *comp. adj*, swifter
ōcĭus *adv*, more quickly
òcrĕa, ae *f*, leg-shield, greave
octāvus, a, um *adj*, eighth
octĭens (octĭes) *adv*, eight times
octingenti, ae, a *pl. adj*, eight hundred
octŏ *indecl. adj*, eight
Octōber (mensis) October
octōgēsĭmus, a, um *adj*, eightieth
octōginta *indecl. adj*, eighty
octōgōnum, i *n*, octagon
octōni, ae, a *pl. adj*, eight each
octŏphŏron, i *m*, sedan carried by eight men
ŏcŭlārĭus, a, um *adj*, of the eyes
ŏcŭlus, i *m*, eye, bud
ōdi, ōdisse *v.t*, *defect*, to hate
ōdĭōsus, a, um *adj, adv*, ē, hateful, troublesome
ŏdĭum, ii *n*, odour, smell
ŏdor, ōris *m*, odour, smell
ŏdōrātĭo, ōnis *f*, smell
ŏdōrātus, ūs *m*, smelling
ŏdōrātus, a, um *adj*, scented
ŏdōrĭfer, ĕra, ĕrum *adj*, fragrant
ŏdōro *v.t*. 1, to perfume
ŏdōror *v.t*. 1, *dep*, to smell out, investigate
ŏdōrus, a, um *adj*, fragrant
oestrus, i *m*, gad fly
offa, ae *f*, morsel
offendo, di, sum *v.i.t*. 3, to make a mistake; strike against, meet with, find, offend
offensa, ae *f*, hatred, crime
offensĭo, ōnis *f*, stumbling, dislike, displeasure
offensus, a, um *adj*, offensive, offended
offĕro, offerre, obtŭli, oblātum *v.t*, *irreg*, to offer, show, cause, bring
officīna, ae *f*, workshop
officĭo, fēci, fectum *v.i*. 3, to obstruct, hinder
officĭōsus, a, um *adj, adv*, ē, obliging, courteous
officĭum, ii *n*, kindness, duty, employment, office
offirmātus, a, um *adj*, firm
offulgĕo, si *v.i*. 2, to shine on, appear

offundo, fūdi, fūsum *v.t*. 3, to pour out, spread over
ŏhē *interj*, ho there!
ŏlĕa, ae *f*, olive
ŏlĕācĕus, a, um *adj*, oily
ŏlĕārĭus, a, um *adj*, of oil; (…i *m*), oil-seller
ŏlĕaster, stri *m*, wild olive tree
ŏlens, ntis *adj*, fragrant, rank
ŏlĕo, ŭi *v.i.t*. 2, to smell of
ŏlĕum, i *n*, olive oil
olfācĭo, fēci, factum *v.t*. 3, to smell
ŏlīdus, a, um *adj*, stinking
ŏlim *adv*, once upon a time, once, sometime in the future
ŏlītor, ōris *m*, market gardener
ŏlīva, ae *f*, olive tree, olive branch
ŏlīvētum, i *n*, olive grove
ŏlīvĭfer, ĕra, ĕrum *adj*, olive growing
ŏlīvum, i *n*, oil
olla, ae *f*, pot, jar
ŏlor, ōris *m*, swan
ŏlōrīnus, a, um *adj*, of swans
ŏlus, ĕris *n*, vegetables
ŏmāsum, i *n*, tripe
ōmen, ĭnis *n*, omen, sign
ōmĭnor *v.t*. 1, *dep*, to forbode
ŏmitto, mīsi, missum *v.t*. 3, to put aside, give up, leave out
omnĭgĕnus, a, um *adj*, of all kinds
omnīno *adv*, altogether, entirely
omnĭpārens, ntis *adj*, all-producing
omnĭpŏtens, ntis *adj*, almighty
omnes, ĭum *c, pl*, all men
omnĭa, ĭum *n.pl*, all things
omnis, e *adj*, all, every
omnĭvăgus, a, um *adj*, wandering everywhere
ŏnăger (grus), i *m*, wild as
ŏnĕrārĭa, ae *f*, merchant ship
ŏnĕrārĭus, a, um *adj*, of, or for, freight
ŏnĕro *v.t*. 1, to load, oppress
ŏnĕrōsus, a, um *adj*, burdensome
ŏnŭs, ĕris *n*, load, burden
ŏnustus, a, um *adj*, loaded, full
ŏnyx, ychis *m, f*, yellow marble
ŏpāco *v.t*. 1, to cover, shade
ŏpācus, a, um *adj*, shady
ŏpălus, i *m*, opal
ŏpem (*no nomin.*) *f*, power, wealth, help

ŏpĕra

ŏpĕra, ae *f*, exertion, effort; *in pl*, workmen
ŏpĕram do to give careful attention to
ŏpĕrārĭus, a, um *adj*, of labour
ŏpĕrārĭus, ii *m*, labourer
ŏpercŭlum, i *n*, lid, cover
ŏpĕrĭo, ŭi, ŏpertum *v.t.* 4, to cover, hide
ŏpĕror *v.i.* 1, *dep*, to work, labour, perform a sacrifice
ŏpĕrōsus, a, um *adj, adv, ē*, painstaking, busy, troublesome
ŏpertus, a, um *adj*, hidden
ŏpes, um *f.pl*, wealth, resource
ŏpĭfer, ĕra, ĕrum *adj*, helping
ŏpĭfex, ĭcis *c*, craftsman
ŏpīmus, a, um *adj*, fat, rich, fertile;
　spŏlĭa ŏpima arms won by a general in single combat with opposing general
ŏpīnābĭlis, e *adj*, imaginary
ŏpīnātĭo, ōnis *f*, supposition
ŏpīnātus, a, um *adj*, imagined
ŏpīnĭo, ōnis *f*, supposition, belief, reputation, rumour
ŏpīnor *v.i.t.* 1, *dep*, to suppose
ŏpĭpărē *adv*, sumptuously
ŏpĭtŭlor *v.i.* 1, *dep*, to help
ŏpĭum, ii *n*, opium
ŏportet *v.* 2, *impers, with acc. of person* it is necessary
oppĕrĭor, pertus *v.i.t.* 4, *dep*, to wait; wait for
oppĕto, īvi, ītum *v.t.* 3, to encounter (especially death)
oppĭdāni, ōrum *m.pl*, townspeople
oppĭdānus, a, um *adj*, provincial
oppĭdŭlum, i *n*, small town
oppĭdum, i *n*, town
oppignĕro *v.t.* 1, to pledge
oppīlo *v.t.* 1, to shut, stop
opplĕo, ēvi, ētum *v.t.* 2, to fill up
oppōno, pŏsŭi, sĭtum *v.t.* 3, to place opposite, oppose, offer, expose, object
opportūnĭtas, ātis *f*, convenience, advantage
opportūnus, a, um *adj, adv, ē*, suitable, convenient
oppŏsĭtĭo, ōnis *f*, opposition
oppŏsĭtus, a, um *adj*, opposite
opprĭmo, pressi, ssum *v.t.* 3, to supress, close, surprise, hide

opprŏbrĭum, i *n*, scandal, taunt
oppugnātĭo, ōnis *f*, attack, siege
oppugnātor, ōris *m*, attacker
oppugno *v.t.* 1, to attack
ops, ŏpis *f*, power, aid
optābĭlis, e *adj*, desirable
optātĭo, ōnis *f*, wish
optātum, i *n*, wish
optātus, a, um *adj, adv, ō*, desired, pleasant
optĭmas, ātis *adj*, aristocratic
optĭmātes, um *c, pl*, the aristocratic party
optĭmus, a, um *adj, adv, ē*, best
optĭo, ōnis *f*, choice
optĭo, ōnis *m*, assistant
opto *v.t.* 1, to choose, desire
ŏpŭlens, ntis *adj*, rich
ŏpŭlentĭa, ae *f*, wealth
ŏpŭlentus, a, um *adj*, rich
ŏpus, ĕris *n*, work, task; **ŏpus est** there is need (a necessity)
ŏpuscŭlum, i *n*, a small work
ōra, ae *f*, border, sea coast, region
ōrācŭlum, i *n*, oracle
ōrātĭo, ōnis *f*, speech, language, eloquence
ōrātĭuncŭla, ae *f*, brief speech
ōrātor, ōris *m*, speaker, orator, ambassador
ōrātōrĭus, a, um *adj*, oratorical
orbĭcŭlātus, a, um *adj*, circular
orbis, is *m*, circle; **orbis terrarum** the world
orbĭta, ae *f*, track, rut
orbĭtas, ātis *f*, bereavement
orbo *v.t.* 1, to bereave, deprive
orbus, a, um *adj*, bereaved, destitute
orca, ae *f*, large tub
orchas, ādis *f*, olive
orchēstra, ae *f*, a place at the front of the theatre
orchis, is *f*, orchid
Orcus, i *m*, death, the Lower World
ordĭnārĭus, a, um *adj*, regular, usual, orderly
ordĭnātim *adv*, in proper order
ordĭnātus, a, um *adj*, orderly, regulated
ordĭne *adv*, in order
ordĭno *v.t.* 1, to arrange

ordĭor, orsus *v.i.t* 4, *dep*, to begin, undertake

ordo, ĭnis *m*, row, rank, band or company of soldiers, series, class of society

Òrēăs, ādis *f*, mountain-nymph

orgĭa, ōrum *n.pl*, revels in honour of Bacchus

ŏrĭchalcum, i *n*, copper ore

ŏrĭens, ntis *m*, the east

ŏrīgo, ĭnis *f*, beginning, origin, family, ancestor

ŏrĭor, ortus *v.i.* 4, *dep*, to arise, appear, originate

ŏrĭundus, a, um *adj*, descended or sprung from

ornāmentum, i *n*, equipment, decoration

ornātus, a, um *adj, adv*, **ē**, equipped, decorated

ornātus, ūs *m*, equipment, dress, ornament

orno *v.t.* 1, to equip, adorn, praise

ornus, i *f*, mountain ash

ōro *v.t.* 1, to plead, beg, pray

orsa, ōrum *n.pl*, undertaking, speech

orsus, ūs *m*, undertaking

ortus, ūs *m*, rising (of sun, etc.), beginning, source

ŏrȳsa, ae *f*, rice

ōs, ōris *n*, mouth, face, opening

ŏs, ossis *n*, bone

oscen, ĭnis *m*, singing bird from whose notes omens were taken

oscillātĭo, ōnis *f*, swinging

oscillum, i *n*, small mask

oscĭtātĭo, ōnis *f*, yawning

oscĭto *v.i.* 1, to gape, yawn

oscŭlor *v.i.t.* 1, *dep*, to kiss

oscŭlum, i *n*, mouth, kiss

ossĕus, a, um *adj*, made of bone

ossĭfrăgus, i *m*, sea eagle

ostendo, di, sum *v.t.* 3, to show, make known

ostentātĭo, ōnis *f*, display

ostento *v.t.* 1, to show, display

ostentum, i *n*, prodigy

ostĭārĭum, ii *n*, door tax

ostĭātim *adv*, from door to door

ostĭum, ii *n*, door, entrance

ostrĕa, ae *f*, oyster

ostrĕārĭum, ii *n*, oyster-bed

ostrum, i *n*, purple, purple coverings or dress

ōtĭor *v.i.* 1, *dep*, to be on holiday

ōtĭōsus, a, um *adj, adv*, **ē**, at leisure, unemployed, quiet

ōtĭum, ii *n*, leisure, peace

ŏvans, ntis *adj*, triumphant

ōvātus, a, um *adj*, oval

ŏvillus, a, um *adj*, of sheep

ŏvīlis, e *adj*, of sheep

ŏvīle, is *n*, sheepfold

ŏvis, is *f*, sheep

ŏvo *v.i.* 1, to exult

ōvum, i *n*, egg

P

păbo, ōnis *m*, wheelbarrow

pābŭlātĭo, ōnis *f*, collection of fodder

pābŭlātor, ōris *m*, forager

pābŭlor *v.i.* 1, *dep*, to look for fodder

pābŭlum, i *n*, food, fodder

pācālis, e *adj*, peaceful

pācātus, a, um *adj*, peaceful

pācĭfer, ĕra, ĕrum *adj*, peace-bringing

pācĭfĭcātĭo, ōnis *f*, pacification

pācĭfĭco *v.t.* 1, to make peace

pācĭfĭcus, a, um *adj*, peaceable

păciscor, pactus *v.i.t.* 3, *dep*, to make a bargain; barter

pāco *v.t.* 1, to subdue, pacify

pactĭo, ōnis *f*, an agreement

pactum, i *n*, an agreement

pactus, a, um *adj*, agreed

paean, ānis *m*, hymn to Apollo

paedăgōgus, i *m*, slave who took children to school, and looked after them at home

paedor, ōris *m*, filth

paelex, ĭcis *f*, concubine

paenĕ *adv*, almost, nearly

paeninsŭla, ae *f*, peninsula

paenĭtens, ntis *adj*, repentant

paenĭtentĭa, ae *f*, penitence

paenĭtet *v.* 2, *impers, with acc.* o *f person*, it grieves

paenŭla, ae *f*, cloak

paenultĭmus, a, um *adj*, penultimate

paetus, a, um *adj*, with a slight cast in the eye

pāgānus, a, um *adj,* rural

pāgānus, i *m,* country-dweller

pāgīna, ae *f,* page, leaf, book

pāgus, i *m,* village, district

pāla, ae *f,* spade

pălaestra, ae *f,* wrestling ground or school, wrestling, rhetorical exercise

pălam *adv,* openly; *prep. with abl,* in the presence of

pălētĭum, ii *n,* palace

pălātum, i *n,* palate

pălĕa, ae *f,* chaff

pălĭūrus, i *m,* Christ's thorn (plant)

palla, ae *f,* stole, robe

pallens, ntis *adj,* pale

pallĕo *v.i.* 2, to be pale

pallesco, pallŭi *v.i.* 3, to turn pale

pallĭātus, a, um *adj,* cloaked like Greeks

pallĭdus, a, um *adj,* pale

pallĭŏlum, i *n,* hood

pallĭum, ii *n,* coverlet, cloak

pallor, ōris *m,* paleness

palma, ae *f,* palm, hand, oar-blade, palm tree, broom, palm wreath, prize, glory

palmāris, e *adj,* excellent, worthy of the palm

palmātus, a, um *adj,* marked with the hand, decorated with palm

palmĕs, ĭtis *m,* wine shoot

palmētum, i *n,* palm grove

palmĭfer, ĕra, ĕrum *adj,* palm-bearing

palmōsus, a, um *adj,* with many palm trees

palmŭla, ae *f,* oar-blade

palmus, i *m,* palm of hand, span

pālor *v.i.* 1, *dep,* to wander

palpèbra, ae *f,* eyelid

palpĭtātĭo, ōnis *f,* palpitation

palpĭto *v.i.* 1, to throb, pant

palpo *v.t.* 1, to stroke, carress

pălūdāmentum, i *n,* military cloak, general's cloak

pălūdātus, a, um *adj,* dressed in general's cloak

pălūdōsus, a, um *adj,* marshy

pălumbes, is *m, f,* wood-pigeon

pālus, i *m,* stake

pălus, ūdis *f,* marsh

păluster, tris, tre *adj,* marshy

pampĭnĕus, a, um *adj,* full of vine leaves

pampĭnus, i *m, f,* vine shoot, vine leaf

pănăcēa, ae *f,* a herb which healed all diseases

panchrestus, a, um *adj,* good for anything

pando, di, nsum *v.t.* 3, to unfold, open out, spread out, publish

pandus, a, um *adj,* curved

pango, pĕpĭgi, pactum *v.t.* 3, to fasten, settle, agree upon

pānis, is *m,* bread

pannōsus, a, um *adj,* tattered

pannus, i *m,* garment, rags

panthēra, ae *f,* panther

pantŏmĭmus, i *m,* ballet dancer

păpāver, ĕris *n,* poppy

pāpĭlĭo, ōnis *m,* butterfly

păpilla, ae *f,* breast, nipple

păpŭla, ae *f,* pimple

păpÿrĭfer, ĕra, ĕrum *adj,* papyrus producing

păpÿrus, i *m, f,* paper

pār, păris *adj,* equal, suitable

pār, păris *m,* companion

părābĭlis, e *adj,* easily procured

**părăbŏla, f,* parable, comparison

părallēlus, a, um *adj,* parallel

părălÿsis, is *f,* paralysis, palsy

părăsītus, i *m,* parasite

părātus, a, um *adj,* prepared

părātus, ūs *m,* preparation

parco, pĕperci, parsum *v.i.* 3, *with dat,* to spare, desist

parcus, a, um *adj, adv,* **ē,** thrifty, sparing, scanty

părens, ntis *adj,* obedient

părens, ntis *m, f,* parent, ancestor, founder

părentālĭa, ĭum *n.pl,* festival in honour of dead relations

părentālis, e *adj,* parental

părento *v.t.* 1, to honour dead relatives, avenge a relative's death by killing

pārēo *v.i.* 2, *with dat,* to obey, to appear

părĭēs, ĕtis *m,* wall

părĭĕtĭnae, ārum *f.pl,* ruins

părĭlis, e *adj,* equal

părĭo, pĕpĕri, partum *v.t.* 3, to bring forth, produce, acquire

părĭter, *adv*, equally, at the same time

parma, ae *f*, small round shield

parmŭla, ae *f*, small round shield

păro *v.t.* 1, to prepare, intend, obtain

părŏchus, i *m*, caterer

păroecĭa, ae *f*, parish

parra, ae *f*, owl

parrĭcīda, ae *c*, murderer of a parent of relative, assassin

parrĭcīdĭum, ii *n*, murder of a parent, or relative, treason

pars, partis *f*, part, party, faction, part in a play; *in pl*, duty, office; **in utramque partem** on both sides; **pro parte** to the best of one's ability

parsĭmōnĭa, ae *f*, thrift

partĭceps, cĭpis *adj*, *with genit*, sharing; (*as noun*) sharer

partĭcĭpo *v.t.* 1, to give a share of

partĭcŭla, ae *f*, small part

partim *adv*, partly

partĭo *v.t.* 4, to share, divide

partĭor *v.t.* 4, *dep*, to share, divide

partītĭo, ōnis *f*, division

partītus, a, um *adj*, divided

partŭrĭo *v.i.t.* 4, to be pregnant of in labour; produce

pārtus, ūs *m*, birth, confinement, offspring

părum *adv*, too little

părumper *adv*, for a short time

parvĭtas, ātis *f*, smallness

parvŭlus, a, um *adj*, slight

parvus, a, um *adj*, small, petty, short; **parvi**, of little value

pasco, pāvi, pastum *v.i.t.* 3, to feed; pasture, nourish

pascor, pastus *v.i.* 3, *dep*, to graze, feast

pascŭum, i *n*, pasture

pascŭus, a, um *adj*, for grazing

passer, ĕris *m*, sparrow, turbot

passim *adv*, in all directions

passum, i *n*, raisin wine

passus, a, um *adj*, spread out, dried

passus, a, um *partic. adj*, having suffered

passus, ūs *m*, step, pace

pastillus, i *m*, lozenge to dispel bad breath

pastor, ōris *m*, shepherd

pastōrālis, e *adj*, of shepherds, pastoral

pastōrīcĭus, a, um *adj*, of shepherds, pastoral

pastōrĭus, a, um *adj*, of shepherds, pastoral

pastus, ūs *m*, pasture, food

pătĕfăcĭo, fēci, factum *v.t.* 3, to throw open, disclose

pătĕfactĭo, ōnis *f*, opening up

pătella, ae *f*, plate

pătens, ntis *adj*, open

pătĕo *v.i.* 2, to be open, to extend, to be evident

păter, tris *m*, father; *in pl*, forefathers, senators

pătĕra, ae *f*, saucer, bowl

păterfămĭlĭas, patrisfămĭlĭas *m*, master of the house

păternus, a, um *adj*, of a father

pătesco, pătŭi *v.i.* 3, to be opened, to extend, be evident

pătĭbĭlis, e *adj*, endurable

pătĭbŭlum, i *n*, fork-shaped yoke or gibbet

pătĭens, ntis *adj, adv*, nter, suffering, patient, hard

pătĭentĭa, ae *f*, endurance

pătĭna, ae *f*, pan, dish

pătĭor, passus *v.t.* 3, *dep*, to suffer, bear, allow

pătrĭa, ae *f*, fatherland

pătrĭarcha, ae *m*, patriarch

pătrĭcĭus, a, um *adj*, noble

pătrĭcĭus, i *m*, member of the Roman nobility

pătrĭmōnĭum, ii *n*, inherited estate

pătrītus, a, um *adj*, of one's father or ancestor

pătrĭus, a, um *adj*, of a father, hereditary, established, native

pătro *v.t.* 1, to perform, finish

pătrōcĭnĭum, ii *n*, defence

pătrōna, ae *f*, patroness

pătrōnus, i *m*, protector, patron, counsel

pătrŭēlis, is *c*, cousin

pătrŭus, i *m*, uncle

pătrŭus, a, um *adj*, of an uncle

pătŭlus, a, um *adj*, open wide

pauci, ae, a *pl. adj*, few

paucĭtas, ātis *f*, small number

paucŭlus, a, um *adj*, very few
paucus, a, um *adj*, few, little
paulātim *adv*, gradually
paulisper *adv*, for a short time
paulō *adv*, a little, somewhat
paulŭlum *adv*, a little, somewhat
paulum *adv*, a little, somewhat
pauper, ĕris *adj*, poor, meagre
pauper, ĕris *c*, a poor man
paupĕrĭes, ēi *f*, poverty
paupertas, ātis *f*, poverty
paupĕro *v.t.* 1, to impoverish
pausa, ae *f*, stop, end
păvĕfăcĭo, fēci, factum *v.t.* 3, to alarm
păvĕo, pāvi *v.i.t.* 2, to be afraid; dread
păvesco *v.i.* 3, to become alarmed
păvĭdus, a, um *adj*, terrified
păvīmentum, i *n*, pavement
păvĭo *v.t.* 4, to beat, strike
păvĭto *v.i.t.* 1, to tremble (at)
păvo, ōnis *m*, peacock
păvor, ōris *m*, anxiety, dread
pax, pācis *f*, peace, grace, favour, tranquillity; *in abl*, by permission
peccans, ntis *c*, offender
peccātor, ōris *m*, sinner
peccātum, i *n*, fault, mistake
pecco *v.i.t.* 1, to make a mistake; to miss
pecten, ĭnis *m*, comb, reed, rake, a plectrum to strike the strings of the lyre
pecto, pexi, xum *v.t.* 3, to comb
pectŏrālis, e *adj*, pectoral
pectus, ŏris *n*, breast, heart, soul, mind
pĕcŭārĭus, a, um *adj*, of cattle
pĕcŭārĭus, ii *m*, cattle-breeder
pĕcūlātor, ōris *m*, embezzler
pĕcūlātus, ūs *m*, embezzlement
pĕcūlĭāris, e *adj*, one's own, special
pĕcūlĭum, ii *n*, property, savings
pĕcūnĭa, ae *f*, money
pĕcūnĭārĭus, a, um *adj*, pecuniary
pĕcūnĭōsus, a, um *adj*, rich
pĕcus, ŏris *n*, cattle, herd
pĕcus, ŭdis *f*, an animal, beast
pĕdālis, e *adj*, a foot in length or thickness
pĕdes, ĭtis *m*, infantryman

pĕdes see **pes**
pĕdester, tris, tre *adj*, on foot, prosaic, plain
pĕdĕtemptim *adv*, gradually
pĕdĭca, ae *f*, shackle, snare
pĕdīcŭlōsus, a, um *adj*, lousy
pĕdīcŭlus, i *m*, louse
pĕdīsĕquus, i *m*, footman
pĕdĭtātus, ūs *m*, infantry
pĕdum, i *n*, shepherd's crook
pēiĕro *v.i.* 1, to swear falsely
pēior *comp. adj*, worse
pēius *comp. adv*, worse
pĕlăgus, i *n*, open sea
pellax, ācis *adj*, seductive
pellex, ĭcis *f*, concubine
pellĭcĭo, lexi, lectum *v.t.* 3, to allure, coax
pellĭcŭla, ae *f*, small skin
pellis, is *f*, skin, leather, tent
pellītus, a, um *adj*, clothed in skins
pello, pĕpŭli, pulsum *v.t.* 3, to strike, push, drive out, rout, affect, impress
pellūcĕo, xi *v.i.* 2, to shine through, be transparent
pellūcĭdus, a, um *adj*, transparent
pĕlōris, ĭdis *f*, mussel
pelta, ae *f*, small shield
pelvis, is *f*, basin
pēnārĭus, a, um *adj*, for provisions
pĕnātes, ĭum *m.pl*, guardian deities of the home, home
pendĕo, pĕpendi *v.i.* 2, to hang, float, loiter, depend upon, be interrupted, be in suspense
pendo, pĕpendi, pensum *v.t.* 3, to weigh or pay out, ponder
pendŭlus, a, um *adj*, hanging, uncertain
pĕnĕs *prep. with acc*, in the power of
pĕnĕtrābĭlis, e *adj*, penetrable, penetrating
pĕnĕtrālĭa, ĭum *n.pl*, inner places or rooms
pĕnĕtrālis, e *adj*, inner
pĕnĕtro *v.i.t.* 1, to enter; penetrate
pēnĭcillum, i *n*, painter's brush, pencil
pēnĭcŭlāmentum, i *n*, train of a dress
pēnĭcŭlus, i *m*, brush
pēnis, is *m*, tail, penis

pĕnĭtus *adv*, inwardly, deep within, entirely

penna, ae *f*, feather, wing

pennātus, a, um *adj*, winged

pennĭger, ĕra, ĕrum *adj*, winged

pensĭlis, e *adj*, hanging

pensĭo, ōnis *f*, payment

pensĭto *v.t.* 1, to pay, weigh, ponder

penso *v.t.* 1, to weigh out, repay, consider

pensum, i *n*, a task

pēnūrĭa, ae *f*, need, want

pĕnus, ūs (or ĭ), *m*, *f*, store of food

pĕpo, ōnis *m*, pumpkin

per *prep. with acc*, through, during, by means of, on account of

per... in compound words usually adds intensity: very ...

pĕractĭo, ōnis *f*, completion

pĕrăgo, ēgi, actum *v.t.* 3, to complete, relate, transfix

pĕràgro *v.t.* 1, to travel over

pĕrambŭlo *v.t.* 1, to go through

pĕrăro *v.t.* 1, to plough through

perbrĕvis, e *adj*, very short

perca, ae *f*, perch (fish)

percĕlĕbro *v.t.* 1, to say frequently

percello, cŭli, culsum *v.t.* 3, to upset, destroy, dishearten

percensĕo *v.t.* 2, to reckon up

perceptĭo, ōnis *f*, perception

percĭpĭo, cēpi, ceptum *v.t.* 3, to gather, perceive, understand

percontātĭo, ōnis *f*, inquiry

percontor *v.i.t.* 1, *dep*, to investigate

percŏquo, xi, ctum *v.t.* 3, to boil, cook, heat

percrēbesco, bŭi *v.i.* 3, to become prevalent

percrĕpo, ŭi, ĭtum *v.i.* 1, to resound, ring

perculsus, a, um *adj*, upset

percurro, curri, cursum *v.i.t.* 3, to run; pass over, mention

percussĭo, ōnis *f*, beating

percussor, ōris *m*, assassin

percŭtĭo, cussi, cussum *v.t.* 3, to thrust through, kill, strike, astound

perdisco, dĭdĭci *v.t.* 3, to learn thoroughly

perdĭtor, ōris *m*, destroyer

perdĭtus, a, um *adj, adv, ē*, ruined, desperate, corrupt

perdix, īcis *c*, partridge

perdo, dĭdi, dĭtum *v.t.* 3, to destroy, waste, lose

perdŏcĕo *v.t.* 2, to teach thoroughly

perdŏmo, ŭi, ĭtum *v.t.* 1, to subdue completely

perdūco, xi, ctum *v.t.* 3, to conduct, bedaub, prolong, induce

perductor, ōris *m*, pimp

perdŭellĭo, ōnis *f*, treason

perdŭellis, is *m*, public enemy

pĕrĕdo, ēdi, sum *v.t.* 3, to eat up

pĕrĕgrē *adv*, abroad

pĕrĕgrīnātĭo, ōnis *f*, travel abroad

pĕrĕgrīnātor, ōris *m*, traveller

pĕrĕgrīnor *v.i.* 1, *dep*, to live or travel abroad

pĕrĕgrīnus, a, um *adj*, foreign

pĕrĕgrīnus, i *m*, foreigner

pĕrendĭē *adv*, on the day after tomorrow

pĕrennis, e *adj*, everlasting

pĕrenno *v.i.* 1, to last, endure

pĕrĕo, ĭi, ĭtum *v.i.* 4, *irreg*, to pass away, disappear, die, to be ruined or wasted

pĕrĕquĭto *v.i.* 1, to ride about

pĕrerro *v.t.* 1, to wander through

perfectĭo, ōnis *f*, completion

perfectus, a, um *adj, adv, ē*, complete, perfect

perfĕro, ferre, tŭli, lātum *v.t*, *irreg*, to bring or bear through, convey, announce, complete, suffer

perfĭcĭo, fēci, fectum *v.t.* 3, to complete, finish

perfĭdĭa, ae *f*, treachery

perfĭdĭōsus, a, um *adj* treacherous

perfĭdus, a, um *adj*, treacherous

perflo *v.t.* 1, to blow through

perflŭo, xi *v.i.* 3, to flow through

perfŏdĭo, fōdi, fossum *v.t.* 3, to dig through

perfŏro *v.t.* 1, to bore through

perfrĭco, cŭi, cātum *v.t.* 1, to rub all over, put on a bold front

perfringo, frēgi, fractum *v.t.* 3, to shatter, infringe

perfrŭor, fructus *v.* 3, *dep, with abl*, to enjoy thoroughly

perfŭga, ae *m,* deserter
perfŭgĭo, fūgi *v.i.* 3, to flee for refuge, desert
perfŭgĭum, ii *n,* shelter
perfundo, fūdi, fūsum *v.t.* 3, to pour over, besprinkle
perfungor, functus *v.* 3, *dep, with abl,* to fulfil, discharge
perfŭro, — *v.i.* 3, to rage
pergo, perrexi, perrectum *v.i.t.* 3, to proceed, go; continue
pĕrhĭbĕo, ŭi, ĭtum *v.t.* 2, to extend, assert, name
pĕrhorresco, rŭi *v.i.t.* 3, to tremble; shudder at
pĕrīclĭtor *v.i.t.* 1, *dep,* to try, be in danger; test, endanger
pĕrīcŭlōsus, a, um *adj, adv, ē,* dangerous
pĕrīcŭlum, i *n,* danger, proof, attempt
pĕrĭmo, ēmi, emptum *v.t.* 3, to anihilate, prevent
pĕrinde *adv,* just as, equally
pĕrĭŏdus, i *f,* complete sentence
pĕrītĭa, ae *f,* experience, skill
pĕrītus, a, um *adj, adv, ē, with genit,* skilled, expert
periūrĭum, ii *n,* perjury
periūro see **pēiĕro**
periūrus, a, um *adj,* perjured, lying
perlābor, lapsus *v.i.* 3, *dep,* to glide through
perlectĭo, ōnis *f,* reading through
perlĕgo, lēgi, lectum *v.t.* 3, to survey, examine, read through
perlūcĕo, xi *v.i.* 2, to shine through, be transparent
perlŭo, ŭi, ūtum *v.t.* 3, to wash
perlūcĭdus, a, um *adj,* transparent
perlustro *v.t.* 1, to wander through
permănĕo, nsi, nsum *v.i.* 2, to flow through, penetrate
permansĭo, ōnis *f,* persisting
permĕo *v.t.* 1, to cross, penetrate
permētĭor, mensus *v.t.* 4, *dep,* to measure out, travel over
permiscĕo, scŭi, xtum *v.t.* 2, to mix together
permissĭo, ōnis *f,* permission, surrender
permissū *abl,* by permission

permitto, mīsi, missum *v.t.* 3, to let loose, commit, entrust; allow *(with dat)*
permōtĭo, ōnis *f,* excitement
permŏvĕo, mōvi, mōtum *v.t.* 2, to stir up, rouse
permulcĕo, mulsi, mulsum *v.t.* 2, to stroke, charm, flatter
permultus, a, um *adj, adv, ō,* or **um,** very much
permūtātĭo, ōnis *f,* exchange
permūto *v.t.* 1, to change
perna, ae *f,* leg of pork
pernĕgo *v.t.* 1, to deny flatly
pernĭcĭes, ēi *f,* disaster
pernĭcĭōsus, a, um *adj, adv, ē,* destructive
pernĭcĭtas, ātis *f,* agility
pernix, īcis *adj,* agile
pernocto *v.i.* 1, to stay all night
pernox, ctis *adj,* night-long
pēro, ōnis *m,* rawhide boot
pĕrōsus, a, um *adj,* detesting, detested
pĕrōro *v.t.* 1, to wind up a speech
perpendĭcŭlum, i *n,* plumb line
perpendo, pendi, pensum *v.t.* 3, to ponder, consider
perpĕram *adv,* untruly
perpĕtĭor, pessus *v.i.t.* 3, *dep,* to suffer; endure
perpĕtŭĭtas, ātis *f,* continuity
perpĕtŭus, a, um *adj, adv, ō,* perpetual, entire, continuous
perplexus, a, um *adj,* intricate
perpŏlĭo *v.t.* 4, to perfect
perprĭmo, pressi, ssum *v.t.* 3, to press hard
perpurgo *v.t.* 1, to clean up
perquam *adv,* very much
perquīro, sīvi, sītum *v.t.* 3, to make a careful search for
perrārō *adv,* very rarely
perrumpo, rūpi, ruptum *v.i.t.* 3, to break through
perscrībo, psi, ptum *v.t.* 3, to write in full
perscriptĭo, ōnis *f,* written entry or note
perscrūtor *v.t.* 1, *dep,* to examine
persĕco, cui, ctum *v.t.* 1, to cut up
persentĭo, si, sum *v.t.* 4, to perceive plainly, feel deeply

persĕquor, sĕcūtus *v.t.* 3, *dep,* to pursue, overtake, revenge

persĕvērantĭa, ae *f,* constancy

persĕvēro *v.i.t.* 1, to persevere; persist in

persīdo, sēdi, sessum *v.i.* 3, to penetrate

persisto, stĭti *v.i.* 3, to persist

persolvo, solvi, sŏlūtum *v.t.* 3, to pay out, give

persōna, ae *f,* mask, character, part, person

parsōnātus, a, um *adj,* fictitious

persŏno, ŭi, ĭtum *v.i.t.* 1, to resound; fill with sound

perspectus, a, um *adj,* well known

perspĭcācĭtas, ātis *f,* perspicacity

perspĭcax, ācis *adj,* astute

perspĭvĭo, spexi, spectum *v.t.* 3, to look at, examine, perceive

perspĭcŭĭtas, ātis *f,* clearness, perspicuity

perspĭcŭus, a, um *adj, adv, ē,* clear, evident

persto, stĭti, stātum *v.i.* 1, to endure, continue, persist

perstringo, nxi, ctum *v.t.* 3, to graze, blunt, stun, blame, allude to, slight

persuādĕo, si, sum *v.t.* 2, *with dat,* to persuade

persuāsĭo, ōnis *f,* conviction

persuāsus, a, um *adj,* settled; **persuāsum hăbēre** to be convinced

pertento *v.t.* 1, to consider

pertĕrĕbro *v.t.* 1, to bore through

perterrĕo *v.t.* 2, to frighten thoroughly

pertīca, ae *f,* pole, rod

pertĭmesco, mŭi *v.i.t.* 3, to be very afraid; to fear greatly

pertĭnācĭa, ae *f,* obstinancy

pertĭnax, ācis *adj,* firm, constant, stubborn

perttĭnĕo *v.i.* 2, to extend, pertain, concern, be applicable

pertracto *v.t.* 1, to touch

pertundo, tŭdi, tūsum *v.t.* 3, to make a hole through

perturbātĭo, ōnis *f,* confusion

perturbātus, a, um *adj,* disturbed

perturbo *v.t.* 1, to disturb

pĕrungo, nxi, nctum *v.t.* 3, to besmear

pĕrūro, ssi, stum *v.t.* 3, to burn up, rub sore, nip

pervādo, si, sum *v.i.* 3, to spread through, pervade

pervăgātus, a, um *adj,* well-known

pervăgor *v.i.t.* 1, *dep,* to wonder through; pervade

pervĕho, xi, ctum *v.t.* 3, to carry through

pervello, velli *v.t.* 3, to pull, disparage

pervĕnĭo, vēnis, ventum *v.i.* 4, to reach, arrive at

perversĭtas, ātis *f,* obstinacy

perversus, a, um *adj,* askew, perverse

perverto, ti, sum *v.t.* 3, to overturn, destroy, corrupt

pervestīgo *v.t.* 1, to investigate

pervĭcācĭa, ae *f,* obstinacy

pervĭcax, ācis *adj, adv, ĭter,* stubborn, wilful

pervĭdĕo, vīdi, vīsum *v.t.* 2, to view, survey

pervĭgĭl, is *adj,* ever-watchful

pervĭgĭlātĭo, ōnis *f,* vigil

pervĭgĭlo *v.i.* 1, to remain awake all night

pervinco, vīci, victum *v.t.* 3, to gain victory over

pervĭus, a, um *adj,* able to be crossed or passed

pervŏlīto *v.i.* 1, to flit about

pervŏlo *v.i.* 1, to fly about or through or to

pervŏlo, velle, vŏlŭi *v.i, irreg,* to wish greatly

pervulgo *v.t.* 1, to spread about

pēs, pĕdis *m,* foot; rope attached to a sail, sheet

pessĭmē *adv,* very badly

pessĭmus, a, um *adj,* very bad

pessŭlus, i *m,* latch

pessum *adv,* to the ground; **pessum ire,** to go to ruin

pestĭfer, era, ĕrum *adj,* destructive, harmful

pestĭlens, ntis *adj,* unhealthy

persĭlentĭa, ae *f, i*nfectious disease

pestis, is *f,* disease, ruin

pĕtăsātus, a, um *adj,* dressed for a journey

pĕtăsus, i *m*, travelling-hat
pĕtītĭo, ōnis *f*, blow, candidature for office
pĕtītor, ōris *m*, candidate, plaintiff
pĕto, īvi, ītum *v.t.* 3, to make for, seek, aim at, request
pĕtōrĭtum, i *n*, four-wheeled carriage
petŭlans, ntis *adj*, impudent
pĕtŭlantĭa, ae *f*, impudence
pexus, a, um *adj*, new
phălanx, ngis *f*, military formation
phălĕrae, ārum *f.pl*, military decoration
phărĕtra, ae *f*, quiver
phărĕtrātus, a, um *adj*, wearing a quiver
pharmăcŏpōla, ae *m*, quack
phărus, i *f*, lighthouse
phăsēlus, i *m, f*, kidney bean, light boat, yacht
phengītes, ae *m*, selenite, mica
phĭlŏlŏgĭa, ae *f*, love of learning
phĭlŏlŏgus, *m*, man of learning
phĭlŏmēla, ae *f*, nightingale
phĭlŏsŏphĭa, ae *f*, philosophy
phĭlŏsŏphor *v.i.* 1, *dep*, to study philosophy
phĭlŏsŏphus, i *m*, philosopher
phĭlȳra, ae *f*, bark of the linden tree
phīmus, i *m*, dice-box
phōca, ae *f*, seal, sea-dog
phoenix, ĭcis *m*, bird which was said to live 500 years
phthĭsis, is *f*, phthisis
phȳlarchus, i *m*, chief, prince
phȳsĭca, ōrum *n.pl*, physics
phȳsĭcus, i *m*, naturalist
phȳsĭŏlŏgĭa, ae *f*, physiology
pĭācŭlāris, e *adj*, expiatory
pĭācŭlum, i *n*, sacrificial offering of atonement, victim, sin, crime
pīca, ae *f*, magpie
pīcĕa, ae *f*, pitch-pine
pīcĕus, a, um *adj*, pitch-black
pictor, ōris *m*, painter
pictūra, ae *f*, painting, picture
pictūrātus, a, um *adj*, embroidered
pictus, a, um *adj*, painted, decorated
pīcus, i *m*, woodpecker

pĭĕtas, ātis *f*, sense of duty, loyalty, mercy
pĭger, gra, grum *adj*, lazy, sluggish
pĭget (me, te) *v.* 2, *impers*, *i*t annoys or displeases (me, you)
pigmentum, i *n*, paint, pigment
pignĕro *v.t.* 1, to pledge, pawn
pignĕror *v.t.* 1, *dep*, to take possession of
pignus, ŏris (ĕris) *n*, security, mortgage, pledge, bet
pĭgrĭtĭa, ae *f*, laziness, indolence
pĭgrĭtĭes, ēi *f*, laziness, indolence
pīla, ae *f*, pillar, pier
pĭla, ae *f*, ball
pīlātus, a, um *adj*, armed with javelins
pīlentum, i *n*, carriage
pĭllĕātus, a, um *adj*, wearing a felt cap, *see below*
pĭllĕus, i *m* (pĭllĕum, i, *n*), felt cap, worn by Romans at festivals, and by freed slaves
pĭlōsus, a, um *adj*, hairy
pĭlŭla, ae *f*, pill
pīlum, i *n*, the heavy javelin of the Roman infantry
pĭlus, i *m*, a hair, the hair
pīlus, i *m*, (*with* prīmus), senior centurion, senior division of trĭārĭi- men who fought in the 3rd rank
pīnētum, i *n*, a wood of pines
pīnĕus, a, um *adj*, of pinewood
pingo, nxi, ctum *v.t.* 3, to paint, decorate
pinguesco *v.i.* 3, to grow fat or fertile
pingue, is *n*, fat
pinguis, e *adj*, rich, fertile, plump, dull, stupid
pinguĭtūdo, ĭnis *f*, plumpness, richness
pīnĭfer, ĕra, ĕrum *adj*, pine-bearing
pīnĭger, ĕra, ĕrum *adj*, pine-bearing
pinna, ae *f*, feather, wing
pinnātus, a, um *adj*, winged
pinnĭger, ĕra, ĕrum *adj*, winged
pīnus, ūs (or i) *f*, pine tree
pĭo *v.t.* 1, to appease, atone for
pīpātus, ūs *m*, chirping
pĭper, ĕris *n*, pepper

pīpĭlo *v.i.* 1, to chirp
pīpĭo *v.i.* 4, to chirp
pīrāta, ae *m*, pirate
pīrātĭcus, a, um *adj*, of pirates
pĭrum, i *n*, pear
pĭrus, i *f*, pear tree
piscātor, ōris *m*, fisherman
piscātōrĭus, a, um *adj*, of fishing or fishermen
piscātus, ūs *m*, fishing
piscīna, ae *f*, fish pond
piscis, is *m*, a fish
piscor *v.i.* 1, *dep*, to fish
piscōsus, a, um *adj*, full of fish
pistor, ōris *m*, miller, baker
pistrīnum, i *n*, mill
pistris, is (pistrix, īcis) *f*, sea-monster
pĭsum, i *n*, pea
pītuīta, ae *f*, phlegm
pĭī, ōrum *m.pl*, the departed
pĭus, a, um *adj*, *adv*, ē, dutiful, loyal, kind, affectionate
pix, pĭcis *f*, pitch
plācābĭlis, e *adj*, easily pacified, mild
plācātus, a, um *adj*, *adv*, ē, calmed, still
plăcens, ntis *adj*, pleasing
plăcenta, ae *f*, cake
plăcĕo *v.i.* 2, *with dat*, to please, to be welcome
plăcĭdus, a, um *adj*, *adv*, ē, quiet, calm, peaceful
plăcĭtus, a, um *adj*, agreeable
plāco *v.t.* 1, to reconcile, soothe
plāga, ae *f*, wound, blow
plăga, ae *f*, region
plăga, ae *f*, hunting-net
plăgĭārĭus, ii *m*, oppressor
plāgōsus, a, um *adj*, fond of flogging
plăgŭla, ae *f*, curtain
planctus, ūs *m*, lamentation
plango, nxi, nctum *v.t.* 3, to beat, strike, lament
plangor, ōris *m*, lamentation
plānĭtĭes, ēi *f*, plain
planta, ae *f*, shoot, twig
plantārĭa, ĭum *n.pl*, young trees
plantārĭum, ii *n*, plantation
plānum, i *n*, plain

plānus, a, um *adj*, *adv*, ē, flat, level, clear
plānus, i *m*, imposter, cheat
plătănus, i *f*, plane tree
plătēa, ae *f*, street
plauso, si, sum *v.i.t.* 3, to applaud; strike, beat
plausĭbĭlis, e *adj*, acceptable
plaustrum, i *n*, cart, waggon
plausus, ūs *m*, applause
plēbēcŭla, ae *f*, the mob
plēbēĭus, a, um *adj*, vulgar
plēbĭcŏla, ae *c*, demagogue
plebs (plēbes), is *f*, the common people
plecto *v.t.* 3, to punish
plectrum, i *n*, quill with which to strike a stringed instrument
plēnĭtūdo, ĭnis *f*, fulness
plēnus, a, um *adj*, *adv*, ē, full, laden, complete, plentiful
plērīque, aeque, ăque *adj*, most, very many
plērumque *adv*, for the most part
plerētis, ĭdis *f*, pleurisy
plīco *v.t.* 1, to fold up
plinthus, i *m, f*, plinth
plōrātus, ūs *m*, weeping
plōro *v.i.t.* 1, to weep; bewail
plostellum, i *n*, small cart
plŭit *v. impers*, it rains
plūma, ae *f*, feather, down
plumbĕus, a, um *adj*, made of lead, heavy
plumbum, i *n*, lead, bullet
plūmeus, a, um *adj*, downy, soft
plūrālis, e *adj*, plural
plūres, es, a *comp. adj*, more
plūrĭmum *adv*, very much
plūrĭmus, a, um *adj*, very much
plūs, plūris *n*, more
plūs *adv*, more
pluscŭlum, i *n*, somewhat more
plŭtĕus, i *m*, shed, parapet, shelf
plŭvĭa, ae *f*, rain
plŭvĭālis, e *adj*, rainy
plŭvĭus, a, um *adj*, rainy
pōcŭlum, i *n*, cup, beaker
pŏdàgra, ae *f*, gout
pŏdĭa, ae *f*, sail-rope
pŏdĭum, ii *n*, height, balcony
pŏēma, ătis *n*, poem

poena, ae *f,* punishment, penalty
poenālis, e *adj,* penal
pŏēsis, is *f,* poetry
pŏēta, ae *m,* poet
pŏētĭcus, a, um *adj,* poetical
poi! *interj,* indeed!
pŏlĭo *v.t.* 4, to polish, improve
pŏlĭtĭcus, a, um *adj,* political
pŏlītus, a, um *adj, adv,* **ē,** polished, refined
pollens, ntis *adj,* powerful
pollĕo *v.i.* 2, to be powerful, to prevail
pollex, ĭcis *m,* thumb
pŏllĭcĕor *v.i.t.* 2, *dep,* to promise
pollĭcĭtātĭo, ōnis *f,* promise
pollĭcĭtum, i *n,* promise
pollinctor, ōris *m,* undertaker
pollŭo, ŭi, ūtum *v.t.* 3, to pollute, contaminate
pŏlus, i *m,* pole, north-pole
pŏlўpus, i *m,* polypus
pōmārĭum, ii *n,* orchard
pōmārĭus, ii *m,* fruiterer
pōmĕrīdĭnus, a, um *adj,* in the afternoon
pōmĭfer, ĕra, ĕrum *adj,* fruit-bearing
pōmoerĭum, ii *n,* open space inside and outside city walls
pompa, ae *f,* procession, retinue, pomp
pōmum, i *n,* fruit
pōmus, i *f,* fruit tree
pondĕro *v.t.* 1, to consider
pondĕrōsus, a, um *adj,* ponderous
pondo *adv,* by weight
pondus, ĕris *n,* weight, mass, influence, authority
pōne *adv. and prep. with acc,* behind, after
pōno, pŏsŭi, pŏsĭtum *v.t.* 3, to put, place, set, plant, wager, invest, spend, lay aside, appoint, calm, allege, propose
pons, ntis *m,* bridge
pontĭcŭlus, i *m,* drawbridge
pontĭfex, ĭcis *m,* high-priest
pontĭfĭcĭus, a, um *adj,* of a high-priest
pontus, i *m,* the sea
pŏpa, ae *m,* priest's assistant
pŏpīna, ae *f,* restaurant

poplĕs, ĭtis *m,* knee
pŏpŭlāris, e *adj, adv,* **ĭter,** of the people, popular, democratic
pŏpŭlāris *c,* fellow-countryman
pŏpŭlāres, ĭum *m.pl,* the people's party
pŏpŭlātĭo, ōnis *f,* devastation
pŏpŭlātor, ōris *m,* plunderer
pŏpŭlĕus, a, um *adj,* of poplars
pŏpŭlo *v.t.* 1, to plunder, devastate
pŏpŭlor *v.t.* 1, *dep,* to plunder, devastate
pŏpŭlus, i *m,* the people
pōpŭlus, i *f,* poplar tree
porcīna, ae *f,* pork
porcŭlus, i *m,* young pig; (*with* **mărīnus**) porpoise
porcus, i *m,* pig
porrectĭo, ōnis *f,* extension
porrectus, a, um *adj,* extended
porrĭcĭo, ēci, ctum *v.t.* 3, to offer to the gods
porrĭgo, rexi, rectum *v.t.* 3, to stretch out, offer
porrĭgo, ĭnis *f,* dandruff
porro *adv,* forwards, next, moreover
porrum, i *n,* leek
porta, ae *f,* gate, door
portendo, di, tum *v.t.* 3, to foretell
portentum, i *n,* omen, monster
portĭcus, ūs *f,* colonnade
portĭo *in phrase,* **pro prortĭōne** in proportion
portĭtor, ōris *m,* customs officer
portĭtor, ōris *m,* boatman
porto *v.t.* 1, to carry, bring
portōrĭum, ii *n,* customs duty
portŭōsus, a, um *adj,* with many harbours
portus, ūs *m,* harbour, refuge
posco, pŏposci *v.t.* 3, to demand
pŏsĭtĭo, ōnis *f,* placing, situation
pŏsĭtus, a, um *adj,* situated
pŏsĭtus, ūs *m,* arrangement, disposition
possessĭo, ōnis *f,* seizure, occupation
possessor, ōris *m,* possessor
possĭdĕo, sēdi, sessum *v.t.* 2, to be master of, possess
possīdo, sēdi, sessum *v.t.* 3, to take possession of, occupy

possum, posse, pŏtŭi *v.i. irreg*, to be able, to have power

postŭmus, a, um *adj*, last-born, posthumous

Insight

possum is a combination of the stem **pot-** meaning 'power' (e.g. *potestas, potentia, potens*) and the verb *sum* (I am). So possum means 'I am able to', 'I can'. Hence the English words 'possibility', 'possible', 'impossible', etc.

post *adv, and prep. with acc*, behind, backwards, after

pōtātĭo, ōnis *f*, drinking
pōtātor, ōris *m*, drinker

Insight

Post is a preposition, followed by a noun or a pronoun in the accusative case (post meridiem = after midday); **postea** is an adverb (= afterwards); **postquam** is a conjunction (= after…). Likewise, **ante** is a preposition that takes the accusative (before), **antea** is an adverb and **antequam** is a conjunction.

postĕā *adv*, afterwards
postĕāquam *conj*, after
postĕri, ōrum *m.pl*, posterity
postĕrĭor, ĭus *comp. adj*, next, worse
postĕrĭtas, ātis *f*, posterity
postĕrĭus *adv*, later
postĕrus, a, um *adj*, next
postgĕnĭti, ōrum *m.pl*, posterity
posthăbĕo *v.t*. 2, to postpone, neglect
posthāc *adv*, in future
postīcum, i *n*, back door
postis, is *m*, door-post
postmŏdo *adv*, afterwards
postpōno, pŏsŭi, pŏsĭtum *v.t*. 3, to postpone, neglect
postquam *conj*, after, when
postrēmo *adv*, at last
postrēmus, a, um *adj*, the last
postrīdĭē *adv*, on the next day
postŭlāta, ōrum *n.pl*, demand, request
postŭlātĭo, ōnis *f*, demands, requests
postŭlo *v.t*. 1, to demand, prosecute, accuse

pŏtens, ntis *adj*, powerful, master of (*with genit*)
pŏtentātus, ūs *m*, power, rule
pŏtentĭa, ae *f*, power, authority
pŏtestas, ātis *f*, power, dominion, control, value, force, ability, permission, opportunity
pōtĭo, ōnis *f*, a drink
pŏtĭor *v*. 4, *dep, with abl*, to obtain, hold, possess
pŏtĭor, ĭus *comp. adj*, preferable
pŏtis, e *adj*, possible
pŏtĭus *adv*, preferably
pōto *v.i.t*. 1, to drink
pōtor, ōris *m*, drinker
pōtus, a, um *adj*, intoxicated, drained
pōtus, ūs *m*, a drink
prae *adv, and prep. with abl*, before, in comparison with
prae se ferre (gĕrere) to reveal
praeăcŭo, ŭi, ūtum *v.t*. 3, to sharpen
praeăcūtus, a, um *adj*, pointed
praebĕo *v.t*. 2, to offer, give, show
praevăvĕo, cāvi, cautum *v.i.t*. 2, to be on one's guard; prevent

praecēdo, cessi, cessum *v.i.t.* 3, to lead the way; precede

praecellens, ntis *adj*, excellent

praecelsus, a, um *adj*, very high

praeceps, cĭpĭtis *adj*, headlong

praeceps, cĭpĭtis *n*, precipice, danger

praeceptor, ōris *m*, teacher

praeceptum, i *n*, rule, maxim, order, command

praecerpo, psi, ptum *v.t.* 3, to gather before time

praecīdo, cīdi, cīsum *v.t.* 3, to cut off, cut short

praecingo, nxi, nctum *v.t.* 3, to encircle, gird

praecĭno, nŭi, centum *v.i.t.* 3, to sing before; predict

praecĭpĭo, cēpi, ceptum *v.t.* 3, to receive in advance, anticipate, advise, teach

praecĭpĭto *v.i.t* 1, to rush down; throw headlong

praecĭpŭus, a, um *adj, adv,* ē, particular, especial, excellent

praeclārus, a, um *adj, adv,* ē, splendid, excellent

praeclūdo, si, sum *v.t.* 3, to close

praeco, ōnis *m*, herald

praecōnĭum, ii *n*, office of herald, proclamation

praecōnĭus, a, um *adj*, of a herald

praecordĭa, ōrum *n.pl*, midriff, heart

praecox, ŏcis *adj*, premature

praecurro, cŭcurri, cursum *v.i.t.* 3, to run in front; excel

praecursor, ōris *m*, scout, spy

praecŭtĭo, cussi, cussum *v.t.* 3, to brandish in front

praeda, ae *f*, plunder, prey

praedātor, ōris *m*, plunderer

praedātōrĭus, a, um *adj*, predatory

praedĭātor, ōris *m*, estate agent

praedĭcātĭo, ōnis *f*, proclamation, commendation

praedĭco *v.t.* 1, to proclaim, declare, praise

praedĭco, xi, ctum *v.t.* 3, to predict, advise, command

praedictĭo, ōnis *f*, prediction

praedictum, i *n*, prediction

praedisco *v.t.* 3, to learn beforehand

praedītus, a, um *adj*, provided with

praedĭum, ii *n*, farm, estate

praedīvĕs, ĭtis *adj*, very rich

praedo, ōnis *m*, robber

praedor *v.i.t.* 1, *dep*, to plunder

praedūco, xi, ctum *v.t.* 3, to make or put in front

praedulcis, e *adj*, very sweet

praedūrus, a, um *adj*, very hard

praeĕo, ĭi, ĭtum *v.i.t.* 4, to lead the way; recite, dictate

praefātĭo, ōnis *f*, preface

praefectūra, ae *f*, superintendence

praefectus, i *m*, director, commander, governor

praefĕro, ferre, tŭli, lātum *v.t, irreg,* to carry in front, offer, prefer, show

praefĭcĭo, fēci, fectum *v.t.* 3, to put in command

praefĭdens, ntis *adj*, overconfident

praefīgo, xi, xum *v.t.* 3, to fix in front

praefīnĭo *v.t.* 3, to fix, appoint

praeflŭo *v.i.* 3, to flow past

praefŏdĭo, fōdi *v.t.* 3, to dig in front

praefor, fātus *v.i.t.* 1, *dep*, to say in advance

praefringo, frēgi, fractum *v.t.* 3, to break off

praefulgĕo, si *v.i.* 2, to glitter

praegestĭo *v.i.* 4, to desire greatly

praegnans, ntis *adj*, pregnant

praegrăvis, e *adj*, very heavy

praegrĕdĭor, gressus *v.i.t.* 3, *dep*, to go in advance

praeiūdĭcātus, a, um *adj*, preconceived

praeiūdĭcĭum, ii *n*, precedent (at law)

praeiūdĭco *v.t.* 1, to pre-judge

praelābor, lapsus *v.i.t.* 3, *dep*, to glide or flow along or past

praelambo *v.t.* 3, to taste in advance

praelūcĕo, xi *v.i.* 2, to carry a light in front

praemandāta, ōrum *n.pl*, warrant of arrest

praemĕdĭtātĭo, ōnis *f*, premeditation

praemědǐtor *v.t.* 1, *dep*, to premeditate

praemitto, mīsi, missum *v.t.* 3, to send in advance

praemǐum, ii *n*, booty, reward

praemǒněo *v.t.* 2, to forewarn

praemūnǐo *v.t.* 4, to fortify

praenăto *v.i.* 1, to flow past

praenǐtěo *v.i.* 2, to outshine

praenōmen, ǐnis *n*, first (Christian) name

praenosco *v.t.* 3, to learn in advance

praenuntǐo *v.t.* 1, to predict

praenuntǐus, a, um *adj*, foreboding

praenuntǐus, i *m*, foreteller

praeoccǔpo *v.t.* 1, to seize in advance

praeopto *v.t.* 1, to prefer

praepărātǐo, ōnis *f*, preparation

praepăro *v.t.* 1, to prepare

praepědǐo *v.t.* 4, to bind, obstruct

praependěo *v.i.* 2, to hang down in front

praepes, ětis *adj*, swift

praepes, ětis *c*, bird

praepinguis, e *adj*, very fat

praepōno, pŏsǔi, pŏsǐtum *v.t.* 3, to put first, put in command, prefer

praepǒsǐtǐo, ōnis *f*, preference

praepǒsǐtus, i *m*, chief, head

praepostěrus, a, um *adj*, preposterous

praepǒtens, ntis *adj*, very powerful

praeprǒpěrus, a, um *adj*, sudden, precipitate

praerǐpǐo, rǐpǔi, reptum *v.t.* 3, to snatch away

praerōdo, rōsum *v.t.* 3, to nibble

praerǒgātīva, ae *f*, the Roman tribe to which the first vote was allotted

praerumpo, rūpi, ruptum *v.t.* 3, to break off

praeruptus, a, um *adj*, steep

praes, dis *m*, security, bail

praesaepe, is *n*, stable, pen

praesaepǐo, psi, ptum *v.t.* 4, to barricade

praesāgǐo *v.t.* 4, to have a presentiment or premonition

praesāgǐum, ii *n*, a foreboding

praesāgus, a, um *adj*, foretelling

praescisco *v.t.* 3, to learn in advance

praescǐus, a, um *adj*, knowing in advance

praescrība, psi, ptum *v.t.* 3, to order, appoint, prescribe

praescriptǐo, ōnis *f*, excuse, order, law

praescriptum, i *n*, order, law

praesens, ntis *adj*, present, prompt, powerful, resolute, helping

praesensǐo, ōnis *f*, foreboding

praesentǐa, ae *f*, presence

praesentǐa, ǐum *n.pl*, present circumstances

praesentǐo, si, sum *v.t.* 4, to have a premonition

praesēpe see **praesaepe**

praesertim *adv*, especially

pareses, ǐdis *adj*, guarding

praeses, ǐdis *c*, guardian, chief

praesǐděo, sēdi *v.i.t.* 2, to guard, direct, superintend

praesǐdǐum, ii *n*, garrison, fortification, camp

praesignis, e *adj*, excellent, distinguished

praestābǐlis, e *adj*, excellent, distinguished

praestans, ntis *adj*, excellent, distinguished

praestantǐa, ae *f*, excellence

praestat *v.* 1, *impers*, it is preferable

praestīgǐae, ārum *f.pl*, juggling tricks

praestǐtǔo, ǔi, ūtum *v.t.* 3, to appoint in advance

praesto *adv*, ready, present

praesto, stǐti, stǐtum *v.i.t.* 1, to be superior; surpass, vouch for, perform, fulfil, show, give, offer

praestringo, nxi, ctum *v.t.* 3, to tie up, graze, blunt

praestrǔo, xi, ctum *v.t.* 3, to build or block up

praesum praeesse, praefǔi *v.i*, *irreg, with dat*, to be in command of

praesūmo, mpsi, mptum *v.t.* 3, to anticipate, imagine in advance

praetento, di, tum *v.t.* 3, to hold out, pretend

praetento *v.t.* 1, to examine in advance

praeter *adv, and prep. with acc,* past, beyond, beside, except, unless

praetĕrĕā *adv,* besides, henceforth

praetĕrĕo, ĭi, ĭtum *v.i.t.* 4, to pass by; go past, omit, neglect

praeterflŭŏ, xi, ctum *v.i.* 3, to flow past

praetergrĕdĭor, gressus *v.i.t.* 3, *dep,* to pass beyond

praetĕrĭtus, a, um *adj,* past, gone

praeterlābor, lapsus *v.i.t.* 3, *dep,* to glide or flow past

praetermissĭo, ōnis *f,* omission

praetermitto, mīsi, missum *v.t.* 3, to let pass, omit, neglect

praeterquam *adv,* besides, except

praetervĕhor, vectus *v.i.t.* 3, *dep,* to sail, ride or drive past

praetervŏlo *v.i.t.* 1, to escape; fly past

praetexo, xŭi, xtum *v.t.* 3, to edge, border, pretend

praetexta, ae *f,* purple-edged toga worn by Roman magistrates and children

praetexta, ae *f,* a tragedy

praetextātus, a, um *adj,* wearing the toga praetexta

praetextus, a, um *adj,* wearing the toga praetexta

praetor, ōris *m,* chief, head, Roman magistrate concerned with administration of justice

praetōrĭum, ii *n,* general's tent, governor's residence

praetōrĭus, a, um *adj,* of the praetor or general

praetūra, ae *f,* praetorship

praeūro, ussi, ustum *v.t.* 3, to burn at the end

praeustus, a, um *adj,* burnt, frostbitten

praevălĕo *v.i.* 2, to be superior

praevălĭdus, a, um *adj,* very strong

praevĕhor, ctus *v.i.t.* 3, *dep,* to ride, fly or flow in front

praevĕnĭo, vēni, ventum *v.i.t.* 4, to come before; outstrip

praeverto, ti *v.t.* 3, to outstrip, anticipate, prevent

praevertor, sus *v.i.t.* 3, *dep,* to concentrate one's attention (on)

praevĭdĕo, vīdi, vīsum *v.t.* 2, to anticipate, see in advance

praevĭus, a, um *adj,* leading the way

prandĕo, di, sum *v.i.t.* 2, to breakfast, lunch (on)

prandĭum, ii *n,* breakfast, luncheon

pransus, a, um *adj,* having breakfasted

prātensis, e *adj,* growing in meadows

prātŭlum, i *n,* small meadow

prātum, i *n,* meadow

prāvĭtas, ātis *f,* deformity, depravity

prāvus, a, um *adj, adv,* **ē,** wrong, bad, deformed

prĕcārĭus, a, um *adj, adv,* **ō,** obtained by prayer

prĕcātĭo, ōnis *f,* prayer

prĕcīae, ārum *f.pl,* grapevine

prĕcor *v.i.t.* 1, *dep,* to pray, beg

prĕhendo, di, sum *v.t.* 3, to seize, detain, take by surprise

prĕhenso *v.t.* 1, to grasp, detain

prēlum, i *n,* wine-press

prĕmo, ssi, ssum *v.t.* 3, to press, grasp, cover, close, pursue closely, load, overwhelm, plant, prune, check, repress

prendo see **prĕhendo**

prensus, a, um *adj,* grasped

presso *v.t.* 1, to press

pressus, ūs *m,* pressure

pressus, a, um *adj,* subdued, compact

prĕtĭōsus, a, um *adj, adv,* **ē,** valuable, costly

prĕtĭum, ii *n,* price, value, money, wages, reward

prex, prĕcis *f,* prayer, request

prīdem *adv,* long ago

prīdĭē *adv,* on the day before

prīmaevus, a, um *adj,* youthful

prīmārĭus, a, um *adj,* of the first rank, chief

prīmĭgĕnus, a, um *adj,* primitive

prīmĭpīlus see **pilus**

prīmĭtĭae, ārum *f.pl,* first fruits

prīmō *adv*, at first

prīmordĭa, ōrum *n.pl*, origin

prīmōris, e *adj*, first, front end

prīmōres, um *m.pl*, nobles

prīmum *adv*, at first; **cum prīmum** as soon as; **quam prīmum** as soon as possible

prīmus, a, um *adj*, first, chief

princeps, cĭpis *adj*, first, chief

princeps, cĭpis *m*, chief, originator

princĭpālis, e *adj*, original, primitive, principal

princĭpālis, is *m*, overseer

princĭpātus, ūs *m*, the first place, command, rule

princĭpĭo *adv*, in the beginning

princĭpĭum, ii *n*, origin; *in pl*, principles, elements

prĭor, ĭus *comp. adj*, previous, former

prĭōres, um *m.pl*, ancestors

priscus, a, um *adj*, ancient

prisma, ătis *n*, prism

pristĭnus, a, um *adj*, primitive

prĭus *comp. adv*, previously

prĭusquam *conj*, before

prīvātim *adv*, privately

prīvātĭo, ōnis *f*, taking-away

prīvātus, a, um *adj*, private

prīvātus, i *m*, private citizen

prīvigna, ae *f*, step-daughter

prīvignus, i *m*, step-son

prīvīlēgĭum, ii *n*, bill or law concerned with an individual

prīvo *v.t.* 1, to deprive, release

prīvus, a, um *adj*, one's own

prō *prep. with abl*, before, in front of, on behalf of, instead of, just as, on account of, according to, in relation to

prō! (prōh!) *interj*, Ah! Alas!

prŏăvus, i *m*, great-grandfather

prŏbābĭlis, e *adj, adv*, ĭter, likely, pleasing

prŏbābĭlĭtas, ātis *f*, probability

prŏbātĭo, ōnis *f*, trial, proving

prŏbātus, a, um *adj*, tried, good

prŏbĭtae, ātis *f*, honesty

prŏbo *v.t.* 1, to try, test, approve of, recommend, prove

prŏboscis, ĭdis *f*, elephant's trunk

prŏbrōsus, a, um *adj*, shameful

prŏbrum, i *n*, disgraceful deed, lechery, disgrace, abuse

prŏbus, a, um *adj, adv*, ē, good, honest, virtuous

prŏcācĭtas, ātis *f*, impudence

prŏcax, ācis *adj*, impudent

prŏcēdo, cessi, cessum *v.i.* 3, to go forward, advance, turn out, prosper

prŏcella, ae *f*, storm, violence

prŏcellōsus, a, um *adj*, tempestuous

prŏcer, ĕris *m*, chief, prince

prŏcērĭtas, ātis *f*, height

prŏcērus, a, um *adj*, tall

prŏcessus, ūs *m*, advance

prŏcĭdo, di *v.i.* 3, to fall flat

prŏcinctus, ūs *m*, readiness for battle

prŏclāmo *v.t.* 1, to cry out

prŏclīno *v.t.* 1, to bend forwards

prŏclīve, is *n*, slope, descent

prŏclīvis, e *adj*, sloping downhill, liable, willing

prŏconsul, is *m*, provincial govenor

prŏcrastĭno *v.t.* 1, to defer

prŏcrĕātĭo, ōnis *f*, procreation

prŏcrĕātor, ōris *m*, creator

prŏcrĕo *v.t.* 1, to produce

prŏcŭbo *v.i.* 1, to lie stretched-out

prŏcūdo, di, sum *v.t.* 3, to forge

prŏcul *adv*, in the distance

prŏculo *v.t.* 1, to trample on

prŏcumbo, cŭbŭi, cŭbĭtum *v.i.* 3, to lean or fall forwards, sink

prŏcūrātĭo, ōnis *f*, administration

prŏcūrātor, ōris *m*, manager, agent

prŏcūro *v.t.* 1, to look after

prŏcurro, curri, cursum *v.i.* 3, to run forward, project

prŏcus, i *m*, suitor

prōdĕo, ĭi, ĭtum *v.i.* 3, to come forward, appear

prōdesse see prōsum

prōdĭgĭōsus, a, um *adj*, strange, marvellous

prōdĭgĭum, ii *n*, omen, monster

prōdĭgus, a, um *adj*, wasteful

prōdĭtĭo, ōnis *f*, treachery

prōdĭtor, ōris *m*, traitor

prōdo, dĭdi, dĭtum *v.t.* 3, to bring out, relate, betray, bequeath

prōdūco, xi, ctum *v.t.* 3, to lead forward, prolong, produce, promote

prōductus, a, um *adj, adv,* ē, prolonged

proelĭor *v.i.* 1, *dep,* to join battle

proelĭum, ii *n,* battle

prŏfāno *v.t.* 1, to desecrate

prŏfānus, a, um *adj,* wicked, common

prŏfectĭo, ōnis *f,* departure

prŏfectō *adv,* certainly

prŏfectus, ūs *m,* advance

prŏfectus, a, um *adj,* having advanced

prōfĕro, ferre, tŭli, lātum *v.t, irreg,* to bring out, extend, defer, reveal, mention; *with* **gradum,** to proceed; *with* **signa,** to march forward

prŏfessor ōris *m,* teacher, professor

prŏfessĭo, ōnis *f,* declaration

prŏfessus, a, um *adj,* avowed

prŏfestus, a, um *adj,* working (days)

prōfĭcĭo, fēci, fectum *v.i.t.* 3, to progress; perform, help

prŏfĭciscor, prŏfectus *v.i.* 3, *dep,* to set out, originate

prŏfĭtĕor, fessus *v.i.* 2, *dep,* to declare, acknowledge, promise

prōflīgātus, a, um *adj,* wretched, dissolute

prōflīgo *v.t.* 1, to overthrow

prōflo *v.t.* 1, to blow out

prōflŭo, xi, xum *v.i.* 3, to flow out, proceed

prōflŭens, ntis *adj,* fluent

prōflŭvĭum, ii *n,* flowing out

prŏfor *v.t.* 1, *dep,* to speak, say

prŏfŭgĭo, fūgi *v.i.t.* 3, to escape; flee from

prŏfŭgus, a, um *adj,* fugitive

prŏfŭgus, i *m,* fugitive, exile

prŏfundo, fūdi, fūsum *v.t.* 3, to pour out, utter, squander

prŏfundum, i *n,* the deep, the sea, an abyss

prŏfundus, a, um *adj,* deep

prŏfūsĭo, ōnis *f,* outpouring, prodigal use

prŏfūsus, a, um *adj,* extravagant

prōgĕnĕro *v.t.* 1, to beget

prōgĕnĭes, ēi *f,* family, offspring

prōgigno, gĕnŭi, gĕnĭtum *v.t.* 3, to produce

prōgnātus, a, um *adj,* born

prōgnātus, i *m,* descendant

prōgrĕdĭor, gressus *v.i.* 3, *dep,* to advance, proceed

prōgressĭo, ōnis *f,* growth

prōgressus, ūs *m,* advance

proh! see **prō!**

prŏhĭbĕo *v.t.* 2, to prevent, prohibit, defend

prōĭectus, a, um *adj,* projecting

prōĭcĭo, iēci, iectum *v.t.* 3, to throw forward, extend, expel, yield, disdain

prŏin or **prŏindē** *adv,* in the same way, equally, accordingly, therefore

prōlābor, lapsus *v.i.* 3, *dep,* to slip or slide forward, fall

prōlātĭo, ōnis *f,* postponement, mentioning

prōlāto *v.t.* 1, to postpone

prōles, is *f,* offspring, child

prōlētārĭus, ii *m,* citizen of lowest class

prōlixus, a, um *adj, adv,* ē, stretched out, fortunate

prōlŏgus, i *m,* prologue

prōlūdo, si, sum *v.i.* 3, to practise in advance

prōlŭo, lŭi, lūtum *v.t.* 3, to wash away, moisten

prōlūsĭo, ōnis *f,* prelude

prōlŭvĭes, ēi *f,* overflow

prōmĕrĕo *v.t.* 2, to deserve, merit

prōmĕrĕor *v.t.* 2, *dep,* to deserve, merit

prōmĭnens, ntis *adj,* prominent

prōmĭnĕo *v.i.* 2, to project

prōmiscŭus, a, um *adj,* common, indiscriminate

prōmissĭo, ōnis *f,* promise

prōmissum, i *n,* promise

prōmissus, a, um *adj,* hanging

prōmitto, mīsi, missum *v.t.* 3, to promise, assure

prōmo, mpsi, mptum *v.t.* 3, to bring out, produce, tell

prōmontŭrĭum, ii *n,* headland

prōmŏvĕo, mōvi, mōtum *v.t.* 2, to move forward, extend

promptus, a, um *adj,* ready, quick
promptus, ūs *m,* only in phrase; **in promptu,** in public; **in promptu esse,** to be at hand
prōmulgo *v.t.* 1, to publish
prōmus, i *m,* butler
prōmūtŭus, a, um *adj,* loaned
prŏnĕpos, ōtis *m,* great-grandson
prōnōmen, ĭnis *n,* pronoun
prōnŭba, ae *f,* bridesmaid
prōnuntĭātĭo, ōnis *f,* proclamation
prōnuntĭo *v.t.* 1, to announce
prōnus, a, um *adj,* leaning or bending forward, disposed; setting, sinking (of stars, etc.)
prŏoemĭum, ii *n,* preface
prŏpāgātĭo, ōnis *f,* extension
prŏpāgo *v.t.* 1, to generate, extend
prŏpāto, ĭnis *f,* shoot (of plant), offspring, child
prōpālam *adv,* openly
prōpātŭlus, a, um *adj,* uncovered
prōpe *adv, and prep. with acc,* near, nearly
prōpĕdĭem *adv,* soon
prōpello, pŭli, pulsum *v.t.* 3, to push or drive forward
prŏpĕmŏdum *adv,* almost
prŏpendĕo, di, sum *v.i.* 2, to be inclined or disposed
prōpensus, a, um *adj,* inclined, disposed
prŏpĕro *v.i.t.* 1, to hurry
prŏpĕrus, a, um *adj, adv, ē,* quick, hurrying
prōpexus, a, um *adj,* combed forward
prōpīno *v.t.* 1, to drink a toast
prŏpinquĭtas, ātis *f,* nearness, relationship
prŏpinquo *v.i.t.* 1, to approach; hasten
prŏpinquus, a, um *adj,* near
prŏpinquus, i *m,* relative
prŏpĭor, ĭus *comp. adj,* nearer
prŏpĭtĭus, a, um *adj,* kind, favourable
prŏpĭus *comp. adv,* nearer
prŏpōno, pŏsŭi, pŏsĭtum *v.t.* 3, to but forward, state, display, offer
prŏpŏsĭtĭo, ōnis *f,* representation, theme
prōpŏsĭtum, i *n,* plan, purpose

prŏprĭĕtas, ātis *f,* peculiarity
prŏprĭus, a, um *adj, adv, ē,* special, particular, its (his, her) own
propter *prep. with acc,* on account of, near; *adv,* nearby
proptĕrĕā *adv,* for that reason
prōpugnācŭlum, i *n,* rampart
prōpugnātĭo, ōnis *f,* defence
prōpugnātor, ōris *m,* defender
prōpugno *v.i.t.* 1, to make sorties; defend
prōpulso *v.t.* 1, to ward off
prōra, ae *f,* prow, ship
prōrēpo, psi, ptum *v.i.* 3, to creep out, crawl forward
prōrĭpĭo, pŭi, reptum *v.t.* 3, to drag forward; *with* se, to rush
prōrŏgātĭo, ōnis *f,* prolonging
prōrŏgo *v.t.* 1, to prolong, defer
prorsus (prorsum) *adv,* certainly, utterly
prōrumpo, rūpi, ruptum *v.i.t.* 3, to rush forward; send forward
prōrŭo, rŭi, rŭtum *v.i.t.* 3, to rush forward; overthrow
proscaenĭum ii *n,* stage
prōscindo, scĭdi, scissum *v.t.* 3, to tear up, plough
prōscrībo, psi, ptum *v.t.* 3, to publish, confiscate, outlaw
prōscriptĭo, ōnis *f,* confiscation, outlawing
prōscriptus, i *m,* outlaw
prōsēmĭno *v.t.* 1, to sow
prōsĕquor, sĕcūtus *v.t.* 3, *dep,* to accompany, follow, pursue, bestow, proceed with
prōsĭlĭo, ŭi *v.i.* 4, to leap up
prospecto *v.t.* 1, to look at, expect, await
prospectus, ūs *m,* view, sight
prospĕrus, a, um *adj, adv, ē,* favourable, fortunate
prospĕrĭtas, ātis *f,* prosperity
prospĕro *v.t.* 1, to make (something) successful
prospĭcĭo, spexi, spectum *v.i.t* 3, to look out; discern, overlook, forsee
prōsterno, strāvi, strātum *v.t.* 3, to overthrow, prostrate
prōsŭbīgo *v.t.* 3, to dig up

prōsum, prōdesse, prōfŭi *v.i, irreg, with dat,* to be useful

prōvincĭa, ae *f,* province, duty, sphere of duty

Insight

In German beer halls a common way of toasting is to raise one's stein and say, '**Prost!**' where in English we might say, 'Cheers!' The word is a contraction of the Latin prosit and a relic of student slang that has passed into general use. Prosit (from prosum *be of benefit, be useful*) is an example of an optative subjunctive with the literal meaning may it benefit (i.e. *may the drinking of this benefit us*).

prōtectum, i *n,* eaves

prōtĕgo, xi, ctum *v.t.* 3, to cover, protect

prōtēlum, i *n,* team of oxen

prōtendo, di, sum (tum) *v.t.* 3, to stretch out, extend

prōtĕro, trīvi, trītum *v.t.* 3, to trample down, crush, destroy

prōterrĕo *v.t.* 2, to terrify

prōtervĭtas, ātis *f,* impudence

prōtervus, a, um *adj, adv,* **ē,** forward, impudent, violent

prōtĭnus *adv,* straightforwards, continuously, immediately

prōtrăho, xi, ctum *v.t.* 3, to drag forward, reveal

prōtrūdo, si, sum *v.t.* 3, to push out

prōturbo *v.t.* 1, to repel

prout *adv,* just as

prōvectus, a, um *adj,* advanced (of time)

prōvĕho, xi, ctum *v.t.* 3, to carry forward, advance, promote

prōvĕnĭo, vēni, ventum *v.i.* 4, to be born, thrive, occur, turn out (well or badly)

prōventus, ūs *m,* produce, result

prōverbĭum, ii *n,* proverb

prōvĭdens, ntis *adj,* prudent

prōvĭdentĭa, ae *f,* foresight

prōvĭdĕo, vīdi, vīsum *v.i.t.* 2, to make preparations; forsee, provide for

prōvĭdus, a, um *adj,* prudent

prōvincĭālis, e *adj,* provincial

prōvŏcātĭo, ōnis *f,* appeal

prōvŏco *v.i.t.* 1, to appeal; call out, challenge, rouse

prōvŏlo *v.i.* 1, to fly out

prōvolvo, volvi, vŏlūtum *v.t.* 3, to roll forward

proxĭmē *adv,* nearest, next

proxĭmĭtas, ātis *f,* proximity

proxĭmus, a, um *adj,* nearest, next, previous

prūdens, ntis *adj, adv,* **nter,** experienced, wise, sensible

prūdentĭa, ae *f,* experience, skill, discretion

prūĭna, ae *f,* frost, snow

prūĭnōsus, a, um *adj,* frosty

prūna, ae *f,* burning coal

prūnum, i *n,* plum

prūnus, i *f,* plum tree

prūrĭo *v.i.* 4, to itch

prūrītus, ūs *m,* itching

psallo, i *v.i.* 3, to play on an instrument

psalmus, i *m,* a psalm

psittăcus, i *m,* parrot

ptĭsăna, ae *f,* pearl barley

pūbens, ntis *adj,* flourishing

pūbertas, ātis *f,* puberty, manhood

pūbes (pūber), ĕris *adj,* adult

pūbes, is *f,* young men

pūbesco, bŭi *v.i.* 3, to grow up, ripen

pūblĭcānus, i *m,* tax collector

pūblĭcātĭo, ōnis *f,* confiscation

pūblĭco *v.t.* 1, to confiscate

pūblīcum, i *n*, a public place
pūblīcus, a, um *adj, adv,* ē, of the state, public, general
pŭdendus, a, um *adj,* disgraceful
pŭdens, ntis *adj, adv,* nter, modest
pŭdet *v.* 2, *impers,* it brings shame
pŭdībundus, a, um *adj,* modest
pŭdīcītīa, ae *f,* modesty, virtue
pŭdīcus, a, um *adj,* modest, pure
pŭdor, ōris *m,* a sense of decency, shyness
pŭella, ae *f,* girl, sweetheart, young wife
pŭellāris, e *adj,* girlish
pŭer, ĕri *m,* boy

pullārĭus, ii *m,* chicken-keeper
pullŭlo *v.i.* 1, to sprout
pullus, i *m,* young animal, chicken
pullus, a, um *adj,* dark, black
pulmentārĭum, ii *n,* sauce
pulmentum, i *n,* sauce
pulmo, ōnis *m,* lung
pulpītum, i *n,* platform
puls, pultis *f,* porridge
pulsātĭo, ōnis *f,* beating
pulso *v.t.* 1, to beat, push, touch, disturb
pulsus, ūs *m,* push, blow, beating
pulvĕrĕus, a, um *adj,* dusty

....

Insight

Second declension masculine nouns usually have the nominative singular ending in *-us* except for some nouns that end in *-er*. These nouns either keep the *-e-* in the other cases (*puer, pueri* = boy) or drop it (*ager, agri* = field).

....

pŭĕrīlis, e *adj,* youthful
pŭĕrītīa (pŭertīa), ae *f,* childhood, youth
pŭgil, īlis *m,* boxer
pŭgillāres, ĭum *m.pl.* writing tablets
pŭgĭo, ōnis *m,* dagger
pugna, ae *f,* fight, battle
pugnātor, ōris *m,* fighter
pugnax, ācis *adj,* warlike, quarrelsome
pugno *v.i.* 1, to fight, disagree, struggle
pugnus, i *m,* fist
pulcher, chra, chrum *adj, adv,* ē, beautiful, handsome, glorious

pulvĕrŭlentus, a, um *adj,* dusty
pulvīnar, āris *n,* couch
pulvīnus, i *m,* cushion
pulvis, ĕris *m,* dust
pūmex, īcis *m,* pumice stone
pūmīlĭo, ōnis *m,* dwarf
punctim *adv,* with the point
punctum, i *n,* point, vote, moment
pungo, pŭpŭgi, punctum *v.t.* 3, to prick, sting, vex, annoy
pūnĭcĕus, a, um *adj,* red
pūnĭo *v.t.* (pūnĭor *v.t, dep.*) 4, to punish
pūpa, ae *f,* doll
pūpilla, ae *f,* orphan, ward
pūpillus, i *m,* orphan, ward

....

Insight

Adjectives are words which define the quality of a noun. Adjectives must agree with the nouns they are attached to in gender (feminine/masculine/neuter), case and number (singular/plural) (e.g. *pulchra puella* = beautiful girl).

....

pulchrītūdo, ĭnis *f,* beauty
pūlex, īcis *m,* flea

puppis, is *f,* ship's stern
pūpŭla, ae *f,* pupil of the eye

purgāmen, ĭnis *n*, refuse, filth

purgāmentum, i *n*, refuse, filth

purgātĭo, ōnis *f*, cleansing

purgo *v.t.* 1, to clean, purify, excuse, justify, atone for

purpŭra, ae *f*, purple, purple clothes

puprŭrĕus, a, um *adj*, purple, clothed in purple, brilliant

pūrum, i *n*, clear sky

pūrus, a, um *adj, adv*, ē, pure, clean, plain

pūs, pūris *n*, pus

pūsillus, a, um *adj*, little, petty

pūsĭo, ōnis *m*, urchin

pustŭla, ae *f*, pimple

pŭtāmen, ĭnis *f*, peel, shell

pŭtĕal, ālis *n*, fence of a well

pūtĕo *v.i.* 2, to stink

pŭter (pŭtris), tris, tre *adj*, decaying, rotten

pūtesco, pūtŭi *v.i.* 3, to rot

pŭtĕus, i *m*, well, pit

pūtĭdus, a, um *adj*, rotten, disgusting

pŭto *v.t.* 1, to think, prune

pŭtresco *v.i.* 3, to decay

pŭtrĭdus, a, um *adj*, rotten

pўra, ae *f*, funeral pyre

pўrămis, ĭdis *f*, pyramid

pўrum, i *n*, pear

pўrus, i *f*, pear tree

pўthon, ōnis *m*, python

pyxis, ĭdis *f*, box

Q

quā *adv*, where, in which direction, how; **qua ... qua**, partly...partly

quācumque *adv*, wheresoever

quàdra, ae *f*, square, dining table

quàdrāgĕni, ae, a *adj*, forty each

quàdrāgēsĭmus, a, um *adj*, fortieth

quàdrāgĭes *adv*, forty times

quàdrāginta *adv*, forty

quàdrans, ntis *m*, a quarter

quàdrātum, i *n*, square

quàdrātus, a, um *adj*, square

quàdrĭdŭum, ii *n*, period of four days

quàdrĭfārĭam *adv*, into four parts

quàdrĭfĭdus, a, um *adj*, split into four

quàdrīgae, ārum *f.pl*, four-horse team or chariot

quàdrĭiŭgis, e *adj*, yoked in a four-horse team

quàdrĭiŭgus, a, um *adj*, yoked in a four-horse team

quàdrĭlătĕrus, a, um *adj*, quadrilateral

quàdrīmus, a, um *adj*, four years old

quàdringēnārĭus, a, um *adj*, of four hundred each

quàdringenti, ae, a *adj*, four hundred

quàdringentĭes *adv*, four hundred times

quàdro *v.i.t.* 1, to be square, agree; make square, complete

quàdrum, i *n*, square

quàdrŭpēdans, ntis *adj*, galloping

quàdrŭpēs, ĕdis *adj*, galloping, going on four feet

quàdrŭplex, ĭcis *adj*, quadruple

quàdrŭplum, i *n*, fourfold amount

quaero, sīvi, sītum *v.t.* 3, to search for, acquire, inquire

quaesītĭo, ōnis *f*, investigation

quaesītor, ōris *m*, investigator

quaesītum, i *n*, question

quaesītus, a, um *adj*, far-fetched

quaeso, īvi *v.t.* 3, to beseech, seek

quaestĭo, ōnis *f*, investigation, trial, case, question, problem

quaestor, ōris *m*, Roman magistrate in charge of public revenues

quaestōrĭus, a, um *adj*, of a quaestor

quaestŭōsus, a, um *adj*, profitable

quaestūra, ae *f*, quaestorship

quaestus, ūs *m*, gain, profit, employment

quālis, e *adj*, of what kind

quāliscumque, quālĕcumque *adj*, of whatever kind

quālĭtas, ātis *f*, state, condition

quālum, i *n*, basket, hamper

quam *adv*, how; *with comparatives*, than

quamdĭu *adv*, as long as, until

quamlĭbet *adv*, as much as you wish

quămobrem *adv*, why, wherefore
quamprīmum *adv*, as soon as possible
quamquam *conj*, although
quamvīs *conj*, although; *adv*, very
quando *adv*, when?, some time; *conj*, since, because
quandōcumque *adv*, whenever
quandōque *adv*, whenever, at some time or other
quandōquĭdem *adv*, since
quanti? at what price?
quantō *adv*, by as much as
quantŏpĕrē *adv*, how much
quantŭlus, a, um *adj*, how small
quantŭluscumque *adj*, however small
quantum *adv*, as much as
quantus, a, um *adj*, how great
quantuscumque *adj*, however big
quantusvis, quantăvis, quantumvis *adj*, as big as you like
quāpropter *adv*, wherefore
quārē *adv*, wherefore, why
quartānus, a, um *adj*, occurring on the fourth day
quartum *adv*, for the fourth time
quartō *adv*, for the fourth time
quartus, a, um *adj*, fourth
quăsī *adv*, as if, just as
quăsillum, i *n*, small basket
quassātĭo, ōnis *f*, shaking
quasso *v.t.* 1, to shake, shatter
quātĕnus *adv*, to what extent, how long, since
quăter *adv*, four times
quăterni, ae, a *pl. adj*, four each
quătĭo (*no perf.*), **quassum** *v.t.* 3, to shake, shatter, excite
quattŭor *indecl. adj*, four
quattŭordĕcim *adj*, fourteen
quĕ *conj*, add
quĕmadmŏdum *adv*, how
quĕo, ĭi, ĭtum *v.i.* 4, to be able
quercētum, i *n*, oak forest
quercus, ūs *f*, oak tree
quĕrēla, ae *f*, complaint
quĕrĭbundus, a, um *adj*, complaining
quĕrĭmōnĭa, ae *f*, complaint
quernus, a, um *adj*, of oak
quĕror, questus *v.i.t.* 3, *dep*, to complain

quĕrŭlus, a, um *adj*, full of complaints, cooing, chirping
questus, ūs *m*, complaint
qui, quae, quod *rel. pron*, who, which, what
quī *adv*, how, wherewith
quĭă *conj*, because
quicquid *pron*, whatever
quīcumque, quaecumque, quodcumque *pron*, whoever, whatever
quid *interr. pron*, what? why?
quĭdam, quaedam, quoddam *pron*, a certain somebody or something
quĭdem *adv*, indeed; **ne ... quidem**, not even ...
quidni why not?
quĭes, ētis *f*, rest, quiet
quĭescens, ntis *adj*, quiescent
quĭesco, ēvi, ētum *v.i.* 3, to rest, keep quiet, sleep
quĭētus, a, um *adj*, calm
quīlĭbet, quaelĭbet, quodlĭbet *pron*, anyone or anything you like
quīn *conj*, that not, but that, indeed, why not
quīnam, quaenam, quodnam *pron*, who, what, which
quincunx, ncis *m*, five-twelfths, trees planted in oblique lines
qindĕcĭes *adv*, fifteen times
quindĕcim *indecl. adj*, fifteen
quingēni, ae, a *pl. adj*, five hundred each
quingenti, ae, a *pl. adj*, five hundred
quingentĭes *adv*, five hundred times
quīni, ae, a *pl. adj*, five each
quinquāgēni, ae, a *pl. adj*, fifty each
quinquāgēsĭmus, a, um *adj*, fiftieth
quinquāginta *indecl. adj*, fifty
quinquātrĭa, ōrum *n.pl*, festival of Minerva (19th–23rd March)
quinquĕ *indec. adj*, five
quinquennālis, e *adj*, quinquennial
quinquennis, e *adj*, every fifth year
quiquennĭum, ii *n*, period of five years
quinquĕrēmis *adj*, ship with five banks of oars

quinquĭens *adv*, five times
Quintīlis (menis) July
quintus, a, um *adj*, fifth
quippe *adv*, certainly; *conj*, in as much as
quis, quid *interr pron*, who? which? what? *indef. pron*, anyone, anything
quisnam, quaenam, quidnam *interr. pron*, who? which?
quispĭam, quaepĭam, quodpĭam *indef. pron*, anybody, anything
quisquam, quaequam, quicquam *indef. pron*, anyone, anything
quisque, quaeque, quodque *indef. pron*, each, every, everybody, everything
quisquĭlĭae, ārum *f.pl*, rubbish
quisquis, quaeque, quodquod *indef. pron*, whoever, whatever
quīvis, quaevis, quodvis *indef. pron*, anyone or anything you please
quō *adv. and conj*, wherefore, where to, whither, so that
quŏad *adv*, as long as, until, as, far as
quōcircā *conj*, wherefore
quōcumque *adv*, to whatever place
quod *conj*, because
quod *neuter* of **qui**
quōdammŏdo in a certain manner
quōmĭnus *conj*, that ... not
quōmŏdŏ *adv*, how
quondam *adv*, once, at times
quŏnĭam *adv*, since, because
quŏquam *adv*, to any place
quŏque *conj*, also, too
quŏquō *adv*, to whatever place
quorsum (quorsus) *adv*, to what place, to what purpose
quŏt *indecl. adj*, how many
quŏtannis *adv*, every year
quŏtīdĭānus, a, um *adj*, daily
quŏtīdĭe *adv*, daily
quŏtĭes (quŏtĭens) *adv*, how often
quŏtĭescumquĕ *adv*, however often

quotquŏt *adv*, however many
quŏtus, a, um *adj*, how many
quŏusquē *adv*, how long
quum see **cum**

R

răbĭdus, a, um *adj*, raving mad
răbĭes (em, e) *f*, madness, anger
răbĭōsus, a, um *adj*, raging
răbŭla, ae *f*, argumentative lawyer
răcēmĭfer, ĕra, ĕrum *adj*, clustering
răcēmux, i *m*, bunch, cluster
rādīcĭtus *adv*, by the roots
rădĭans, ntis *adj*, shining
rădĭātĭo, ōnis *f*, shining
rădĭo *v.i.* 1, to shine
rădĭus, ii *m*, rod, spoke, radius, shuttle, ray
rādix, īcis *f*, root, radish, source
rādo, si, sum *v.t.* 3, to scrape, shave
raeda, ae *f*, carriage
raedārĭus, i *m*, coachman
raia, ae *f*, ray (fish)
rāmālĭa, ĭum *n.pl*, brushwood
rāmōsus, a, um *adj*, branching
rāmus, i *m*, branch
rāna, ae *f*, frog
rancĭdus, a, um *adj*, rancid
rānuncŭlus, i *m*, tadpole
răpācĭtas, ātis *f*, rapacity
răpax, ācis *adj*, grasping
răphănus, i *m*, radish
răpĭdus, a, um *adj, adv*, **ē**, swift, violent, tearing
răpīna, ae *f*, robbery, plunder
răpĭo, ŭi, raptum *v.t.* 3, to seize, snatch, drag away
raptim *adv*, hurriedly
raptĭo, ōnis *f*, abduction
rapto *v.t.* 1, to snatch, drag away, plunder
raptor, ōris *m*, robber
raptum, i *n*, plunder
raptus, ūs *m*, robbery, rape
rāpŭlum, i *n*, turnip
rāpum, i *n*, turnip
rāresco *v.i.* 3, to grow thin, open out
rārĭtas, ātis *f*, looseness, rarity, infrequency

rārus, a, um *adj, adv,* **ē, ō,** loose, loose in texture, thin, scattered, straggling, few, remarkable, rare

rāsĭlis, e *adj,* polished

rastellus, i *m,* hoe, rake

rastrum i *n,* rake, hoe

rătĭo, ōnis *f,* account, calculation, business affairs, relationship, concern for, consideration, conduct, plan, reason, motive, reckoning, order, law, theory, system, way, manner

rătĭōcĭnor *v.i.t.* 1, *dep,* to calculate

rătĭōnālis, e *adj,* rational, theoretical

rătis, is *f,* raft

rătus, a, um *adj,* established; (*partic.*) having thought; **pro rătā,** proportionally

raucus, a, um *adj,* hoarse

rāvus, a, um *adj,* grey, tawny

rē, rēvērā *adv,* really

rēapse *adv* (**re ipsa**) in fact

rĕbellĭo, ōnis *f,* revolt

rĕbellis, e *adj,* rebellious

rĕbello *v.i.* 1, to rebel, rebuff

rĕbŏo *v.i.* 1, to re-echo

rĕcalcĭtro *v.i.* 1, to kick back

rĕcalfăcĭo, fēci *v.t.* 3, to warm

rĕcandesco, dŭi *v.i.* 3, to grow white or hot

rĕcanto (*no perf.*) *v.t.* 1, to retract

rĕcēdo, cessi, cessum *v.i.* 3, to retreat, withdraw

rĕcens, ntis *adj,* fresh, new

rĕcens *adv,* newly, recently

rĕcensĕo, ŭi, ītum *v.t.* 2, to count, rekon, survey, review

rĕcensĭo, ōnis *f,* review

rĕceptācŭlum, i *n,* shelter

rĕcepto *v.t.* 1, to recover

rĕceptor, ōris *m,* receiver

rĕceptus, ūs *m,* retreat

rĕcessus, ūs *m,* retreat, recess

rĕcĭdīvus, a, um *adj,* recurring

rĕcĭdo, cĭdi, cāsum *v.i.* 3, to fall back, recoil, return

rĕcīdo, cīdi, cīsum *v.t.* 3, to cut down, cut off, cut short

rĕcingo (*no perf.*) **cinctum** *v.t.* 3, to loosen

rĕcĭno *v.i.* 3, to re-echo

rĕcĭpĕro (rĕcŭpĕro) *v.t.* 1, to regain

rĕcĭpĭo, cēpi, ceptum *v.t.* 3, to take back, regain, receive, give an assurance; *with* **sē** to retreat, recover oneself

rĕcĭprŏco *v.i.t.* 1, to move backwards

rĕcĭprŏcus, a, um *adj,* receding

recĭtātĭo, ōnis *f,* reading aloud

rĕcĭtātor, ōris *m,* reader

rĕcĭto *v.t.* 1, to read aloud

rĕclāmătĭo, ōnis *f,* remonstrance

rĕclāmo *v.i.t.* 1, to resound; contradict loudly, remonstrate

rĕclīno *v.t.* 1, to lean back

rĕclūdo, si, sum *v.t.* 3, to reveal

rĕcognĭgĭo, ōnis *f,* review

rĕcognosco, gnōvi, gnĭtum *v.t.* 3, to recollect, investigate

rĕcŏlo, cŏlŭi, cultum *v.t.* 3, to cultivate again, renew

rĕconcĭlĭātĭo, ōnis *f,* re-establishment, reconciliation

rĕconcĭlĭo *v.t.* 1, to restore, reconcile

rĕcondĭtus, a, um *adj,* hidden

rĕcondo, dĭdi, dĭtum *v.t.* 3, to put away, hide

rĕcŏquo, xi, ctum *v.t.* 3, to cook again, forge again

rĕcordātĭo, ōnis *f,* recollection

rĕcordor *v.i.t.* 1, *dep,* to think over, remember

rĕcrĕātĭo, ōnis *f,* recovery

rĕcrĕo *v.t.* 1, to revive, reproduce

rĕcresco, crēvi, crētum *v.i.* 3, to grow again

rectā *adv,* straightforwards

rector, ōris *m,* master, leader, helmsman

rectum, i *n,* virtue

rectus, a, um *adj, adv,* **ē,** straight, upright, correct

rĕcŭbans, ntis *adj,* recumbent

rĕcŭbo *v.i.* 1, to lie back

rĕcumbo, cŭbŭi *v.i.* 3, to lie down

rĕcŭpĕrātĭo, ōnis *f,* recovery

rĕcŭpĕro *v.t.* 1, to recover, regain

rĕcurro, curri *v.i.* 3, to run back, return

rĕcurso *v.i.* 1, to return

rĕcursus, ūs *m,* return, retreat

rĕcurvo *v.t.* 1, to bend back

rĕcurvus, a, um *adj,* bent
rĕcūsātĭo, ōnis *f,* refusal
rĕcūso *v.t.* 1, to refuse
rĕcussus, a, um *adj,* roused
rĕdargŭo, ŭi *v.t.* 3, to contradict
reddo, dĭdi, dĭtum *v.t.* 3, to give back, deliver, pay, produce, render, translate, recite, repeat, resemble
rĕdemptĭo, ōnis *f,* buying back
rĕdemptor, ōris *m,* contractor
rĕdĕo, ĭi, ĭtum *v.i.* 4, to go back, return, be reduced to
rĕdĭgo, ēgi, actum *v.t.* 3, to bring back, restore, collect, reduce to
rĕdĭmīcŭlum, i *n,* necklace
rĕdmĭo *v.t.* 4, to encircle
rĕdĭmo, ēmi, emptum *v.t.* 3, to repurchase, ransom, release, hire, obtain
rĕdintĕgro *v.t.* 1, to restore
rĕdĭtus, ūs *m,* return
rĕdŏlĕo *v.i.t.* 2, to smell; smell of
rĕdōno *v.t.* 1, to restore
rĕdūco, xi, ctum *v.t.* 3, to bring back, restore
rĕductus, a, um *adj,* remote
rĕdundantĭa, ae *f,* redundancy
rĕdundo *v.i.* 1, to overflow, abound in
rĕdus, dŭcis *adj,* brought back
rĕfello, felli *v.t.* 3, to refute
rĕfercĭo, si, tum *v.t.* 4, to cram
rĕfĕro, fĕrre, rettŭli, rĕlātum *v.t, irreg,* to bring back, restore, repay, report, reply, propose, record, reckon, refer, resemble; *with* **pedem,** to retreat
rēfert *v. impers,* it is of importance, it matters
rĕfertus, a, um *adj,* filled
rĕfĭcĭo, fēci, fectum *v.t.* 3, to re-make, repair, refresh
rĕfīgo, xi, xum *v.t.* 3, to unfix
rĕfingo *v.t.* 3, to renew
rĕflecto, xi, xum *v.i.t.* 3, to turn back; bend back
rĕflo *v.i.* 1, to blow back
rĕflŭo *v.i.* 3, to flow back
rĕformīdo (*no perf.*) *v.t.* 1, to dread, avoid
rĕfrāgor *v.i.* 1, *dep,* to resist
rĕfrēno *v.t.* 1, to curb, check

rēfrīco, ŭi *v.t.* 1, to scratch open
rēfrīgĕro *v.t.* 1, to cool
rēfrīgesco, frixi *v.i.* 3, to grow cool, grow stale
rĕfringo, frēgi, fractum *v.t.* 3, to break open, break off
rĕfŭgĭo, fūgi *v.i.t.* 3, to run away, escape; flee from, avoid
rĕfulgĕo, si *v.i.* 2, to shine
rĕfundo, fūdi, fūsum *v.t.* 3, to pour out, cause to overflow
rĕfūtandus *gerundive,* see **rĕfūto**
rĕfūto *v.t.* 1, to repress, refute
rēgālis, e *adj,* royal, splendid
rēgĭa, ae *f,* palace, court
rēgĭfĭcus, a, um *adj,* royal
rēgigno *v.t.* 3, to reproduce
rēgĭmen, ĭnis *n,* guidance
rēgĭna, ae *f,* queen
rēgĭo, ōnis *f,* district, region, direction, boundary; **ē rēgĭōne** — in a straight line
rēgĭus, a, um *adj, adv,* **ē,** royal, magnificent
regnātor, ōris *m,* ruler
regno *v.i.t.* 1, to reign; rule
regnum, i *n,* kingdom, sovereignty, dominion
rĕgo, xi, ctum *v.t.* 3, to rule, guide, direct
rĕgrĕdĭor, gressus *v.i.* 3, *dep,* to return, retreat
rĕgressus, ūs *m,* return, retreat
rēgŭla, ae *f,* wooden ruler, model, pattern
rēgŭlus, i *m,* prince
rēĭcĭo, iēci, iectum *v.t.* 3, to throw back, repel, reject, postpone
rēiectĭo, ōnis *f,* rejection
rĕlābor, lapsus *v.i.* 3, *dep,* to slide or sink back
rĕlanguesco, gŭi *v.i.* 3, to grow faint, relax
rĕlātĭo, ōnis *f,* proposition
rĕlaxo *v.t.* 1, to loosen, ease
rĕlēgātĭo, ōnis *f,* banishment
rĕlēgo *v.t.* 1, to send away, banish
rĕlĕgo, lēgi, lectum *v.t.* 3, to gather together, travel over again, read over again
rĕlĕvo *v.t.* 1, to lift up, lighten, comfort, refresh

rĕlictĭo, ōnis *f*, abandonment

rĕlictus, a, um *adj*, left

rĕlĭgĭo, ōnis *f*, piety, religion, religious scruple, good faith, conscientiousness, sanctity

rĕlĭgĭōsus, a, um *adj*, devout, scrupulous, precise, sacred

rĕlĭgo *v.t.* 1, to bind, fasten

rĕlĭno, lēvi *v.t.* 3, to unseal

rĕlinquo, rĕlĭqui, lictum *v.t.* 3, to leave, leave behind, abandon, surrender

rĕlĭquĭae, ārum *f.pl*, remains

rĕlĭquum, i *n*, remainder

rĕlĭquus, a, um *adj*, remaining

rĕlūcĕo, xi *v.i.* 2, to shine

rĕluctor *v.i.* 1, *dep*, to resist

rĕmănĕo, nsi *v.i.* 2, to stay behind, endure

rĕmĕdĭum, ii *n*, cure, relief

rĕmĕo *v.i.* 1, to return

rĕmētĭor, mensus *v.t.* 4, *dep*, to remeasure

rēmex, ĭgis *m*, oarsman

rēmĭgĭum, ii *n*, rowing, oars, rowers

rēmĭgo *v.i.* 1, to row

rēmĭgro *v.i.* 1, to return

rĕmĭniscor *v.3*, *dep*, *with genit*, to remember

rĕmiscĕo (*no perf.*) **mixtum** *v.t.* 2, to mix up

rĕmissĭo, ōnis *f*, relaxation

rĕmissus, a, um *adj, adv*, **ē**, loose, gentle, cheerful

rĕmitto, mīsi, missum *v.i.t.* 3, to decrease; send back, send out, yield, loosen, slacken, grant, surrender, give up; *with infin*, to cease

rĕmollesco *v.i.* 3, to grow soft

rĕmordĕo (*no perf.*), **morsum** *v.t.* 2, to torment

rĕmŏror *v.i.t.* 1, *dep*, to loiter; obstruct

rĕmōtus, a, um *adj*, distant

rĕmŏvĕo, mōvi, mōtum *v.t.* 2, to remove, withdraw, set aside

rĕmūgĭo *v.i.* 4, to resound

rĕmulcum, i *n*, tow rope

rĕmūnĕrātĭo, ōnis *f*, reward

rĕmūnĕror *v.t.* 1, *dep*, to reward

rĕmurmŭro *v.i.t.* 1, to murmur back

rēmus, i *m*, oar

rĕnascor, nātus *v.i.* 3, *dep*, to be born again, spring up again

rēnes, um *m.pl*, kidneys

rĕnīdĕo *v.i.* 2, to glisten

rĕnŏvātĭo, ōnis *f*, revewal

rĕnŏvo *v.t.* 1, to renew, restore, refresh, repeat

rĕnuntĭātĭo, ōnis *f*, announcement

rĕnuntĭo *v.t.* 1, to report, announce, refuse, renounce

rĕnŭo, ŭi *v.i.t.* 3, to refuse

rĕor, rātus *v.t.* 2, *dep*, to suppose, think, believe

rĕpāgŭla, ōrum *n.pl*, bolts, bars

rĕpărābĭlis, e *adj*, able to be repaired

rĕpăro *v.t.* 1, to recover, repair, restore, refresh

rĕpello, pŭli, pulsum *v.t.* 3, to drive back, reject

rĕpendo, di, sum *v.t.* 3, to weigh out in return, repay

rĕpens, ntis *adj, adv*, **ē**, sudden

rĕpentīnus, a, um *adj, adv*, **ō**, sudden, unexpected

rĕpercussus, ūs *m*, reflection

rĕpercŭtĭo, cussi, cussum *v.t.* 3, to drive back, reflect

rĕpĕrĭo, repperi, rĕpertum *v.t.* 4, to find, discover

rĕpertor, ōris *m*, discoverer

rĕpĕto, īi, ītum *v.t.* 3, to attack again, re-visit, fetch back, resume, recollect, demand back

rĕpĕtundae, ārum *f.pl*, (*with* **res**), extortion

rĕplĕo, ēvi, ētum *v.t.* 2, to fill up, complete

rĕplētus, a, um *adj*, full

rēpo, psi, ptum *v.i.* 3, to creep

rĕpōno, pŏsŭi, pŏsĭtum *v.t.* 3, to replace, preserve, put away

rĕporto *v.t.* 1, to bring back, carry back, obtain

rĕposco *v.t.* 3, to demand back

rĕpraesentātĭo, ōnis *f*, representation

rĕpraesento *v.t.* 1, to display, do immediately

rĕprĕhendo, di, sum *v.t.* 3, to blame, rebuke, convict

rĕprĕhensĭo, ōnis *f*, blame

rĕprĭmo, pressi, ssum *v.t.* 3, to keep back, check, restrain

rĕpŭdĭātĭo, ōnis *f*, refusal, renunciation

rĕpŭdĭo *v.t.* 1, to divorce, reject, scorn

rĕpugnans, ntis *adj*, contradictory, irreconcilable

rĕpugnantĭa, ae *f*, opposition, inconsistency

rĕpungo *v.i.* 1, to resist, disagree with

rĕpulsa, ae *f*, refusal, rejection

rĕpurgo *v.t.* 1, to clean

rĕpŭto *v.t.* 1, to ponder, reckon

rĕquĭes, ētis *f*, rest, relaxation

rĕquĭesco, ēvi, etum *v.i.* 3, to rest

rĕquīro, sīvi, sītum *v.t.* 3, to search for, enquire, need, notice to be missing

rēs, rĕi *f*, thing, matter, affair, reality, fact, property, profit, advantage, business, affair, lawsuit; **rēs nŏvae, rērum nŏvārum** *f.pl*, revolution; **respublĭca, rĕipublĭcae** *f*, the State, statesmanship

rēscindo, scĭdi, ssum *v.t.* 3, to cut down, break down, abolish

rēscisco, īvi, ītum *v.t.* 3, to learn, ascertain

rēscrībo, psi, ptum *v.t.* 3, to write back, reply, repay

rĕsĕco, ŭi, ctum *v.t.* 1, to cut off, curtail

rĕsĕro *v.t.* 1, to unlock, open

rĕservo *v.t.* 1, to save up, keep

rĕsĕs, ĭdis *adj*, inactive

rĕsĭdĕo, sēdi *v.i.* 2, to remain, linger, sit

rĕsīdo, sēdi *v.i.* 3, to settle

rĕsĭdŭus, a, um *adj*, remaining

rĕsigno *v.t.* 1, to unseal, open

rĕsĭlĭo, ŭi *v.i.* 4, to recoil

rēsīna, ae *f*, resin

rĕsĭpĭo *v.t.* 3, to taste of

rĕsĭpisco, īvi *v.i.* 3, to revive

rĕsisto, stĭti *v.i.* 3, to stop, remain; *with dat*, to resist

rĕsolvo, solvi, sŏlūtum *v.t.* 3, to untie, release, open, relax, annul, abolish

rĕsŏno *v.i.t.* 1, to resound; re-echo with

rĕsŏnus, a, um *adj*, resounding

rĕsorbĕo *v.t.* 2, to re-swallow

respecto *v.t.* 1, to look at, respect

respectus, ūs *m*, looking back, retreat, refuge, respect

rēspergo, si, sum *v.t.* 3, to besprinkle

rēspĭcĭo, spexi, spectum *v.i.t.* 3, to look back, give attention; look at, regard, respect

rēspīrātĭo, ōnis *f*, breathing

rēspīro *v.i.t.* 1, to revive; breathe out, breathe

rēsplendĕo *v.i.* 2, to shine

rēspondĕo, di, sum *v.t.* 2, to reply, give advice, agree, correspond, answer one's hopes

rēsponso *v.t.* 1, to reply, resist

rēsponsum, i *n*, answer

respublĭca see **rēs**

rēspŭo, ŭi *v.t.* 3, to spit out, expel, reject

rēstinguo, nxi, nctum *v.t.* 3, to quench, extinguish

restis, is *f*, rope

rēstĭtŭo, ŭi, ūtum *v.t.* 3, to replace, rebuild, renew, give back, restore

rēstĭtūtĭo, ōnis *f*, restoration

rēsto, stĭti *v.i.* 1, to remain

rēstrictus, a, um *adj*, bound

rēstringo, nxi, ctum *v.t.* 3, to bind, restrain

rĕsulto (*no perf.*) *v.i.* 1, to jump back, resound

rĕsūmo, mpsi, mptum *v.t.* 3, to resume, take back, recover

rĕsŭpīnus, a, um *adj*, lying on one's back

rĕsurgo, surrexi, surrectum *v.i.* 3, to rise, reappear

rĕsurrectĭo, ōnis *f*, resurrection

rĕsuscĭto *v.t.* 1, to revive

rĕtardo *v.i.t.* 1, to delay

rēte, is *n*, net, snare

rĕtĕgo, xi, ctum *v.t.* 3, to uncover, reveal

rĕtendo, di, tum *v.t.* 3, to slacken

rĕtento *v.t.* 1, to keep back

rĕtento *v.t.* 1, to try again

rĕtexo, ŭi, xtum *v.t.* 3, to unravel, cancel

rĕtĭcĕo *v.i.t.* 2, to be silent; conceal

rētĭcŭlātus, a, um *adj*, net-like

rētĭcŭlum, i *n*, small net

rĕtĭnācŭlum, i *n*, rope, cable

rĕtĭnens, ntis *adj*, tenacious

rĕtĭnĕo, ŭi, tentum *v.t.* 2, to hold back, restrain, maintain

rĕtorquĕo, si, tum *v.t.* 2, to twist back, drive back

rĕtracto *v.t.* 1, to handle or undertake again, reconsider, refuse

rĕtrăho, xi, ctum *v.t.* 3, to draw back, call back, remove

rĕtrĭbŭo, ŭi, ūtum *v.t.* 3, to repay

rĕtrō *adv*, backwards, formerly, back, behind, on the other hand

rĕtrorsum(s) *adv*, backwards

rĕtundo, tŭdi, tūsum *v.t.* 3, to blunt, dull, weaken

rĕtūsus, a, um *adj*, blunt, dull

rĕus, i *m* (**rĕa, ae,** *f*), defendant, criminal, culprit

rĕvălesco, lŭi *v.i.* 3, to grow well again

rĕvĕho, xi, ctum *v.t.* 3, to bring back; *in passive*, to return

rĕvello, velli, vulsum *v.t.* 3, to pull out, tear away

rĕvĕnĭo, vēni, ventum *v.i.* 4, to return

rēvērā *adv*, really

rĕvĕrens, ntis *adj*, reverent

rĕvĕrentĭa, ae *f*, respect

rĕvĕrĕor *v.t.* 2, *dep*, to revere

rĕverto, ti *v.i.* 3, to return

rĕvertor, versus *v.i.* 3, *dep*, to return

rĕvincendus *gerundive*, see **revinco**

rĕvincĭo, nxi, nctum *v.t.* 4, to bind, fasten

rĕvinco, vīci, victum *v.t.* 3, to conquer, convict

rĕvīresco, rŭi *v.i.* 3, to grow green again

rĕvīso *v.i.t.* 3, to revisit

rĕvīvisco, vixi *v.i.* 3, to revive

rĕvŏcābĭlis, e *adj*, able, to be recalled

rĕvŏcāmen, ĭnis *n*, recall

rĕvŏcātĭo, ōnis *f*, recalling

rĕvŏco *v.t.* 1, to recall, restrain, refer

rĕvŏlo *v.i.* 1, to fly back

rĕvolvo, volvi, vŏlūtum *v.t.* 3, to unroll, repeat

rĕvŏmo, ŭi *v.t.* 3, to vomit up

rex, rēgis *m*, king

rhēda, ae *f*, carriage

rhētor, ŏris *m*, teacher of oratory

rhētŏrĭca, ae *f*, rhetoric

rhētŏrĭcus, a, um *adj*, rhetorical

rhīnŏcĕros, ōtis *m*, rhinoceros

rhombus, i *m*, magic circle, turbot

rhonchus, i *m*, snore, sneer

rīca, ae *f*, veil

rīcīnĭum, ii *n*, small veil

rictus, ūs *m*, gaping mouth

rīdĕo, si, sum *v.i.t.* 2, to laugh, smile; laugh at, ridicule

rīdĭcŭlum, i *n*, joke

rīdĭcŭlus, a, um *adj, adv*, ē, amusing, absurd

rĭgĕo *v.i.* 2, to be stiff

rĭgesco, gŭi *v.i.* 3, to stiffen

rĭgĭdus, a, um *adj*, stiff, stern

rĭgo *v.t.* 1, to wet, water

rĭgor, ōris *m*, stiffness, hardness, chilliness, severity

rĭgŭus, a, um *adj*, irrigating

rīma, ae *f*, crack, chink

rīmor *v.t.* 1, *dep*, to tear up, explore, examine

rīmōsus, a, um *adj*, leaky

rīpa, ae *f*, river back

rīsus, ūs *m*, laughter

rītĕ *adv*, rightly, properly

rītus, ūs *m*, religious ceremony, custom, way; **rītu** *with genit*, in the manner of

rīvālis, is *m*, rival

rīvŭlus, i *m*, brook

rīvus, i *m*, brook, stream

rixa, ae *f*, quarrel

rixor *v.i.* 1, *dep*, to quarrel

rōbīgĭnōsus, a, um *adj*, rusty

rōbīgo, ĭnis *f*, rust, mould

rōbŏro *v.t.* 1, to strengthen

rōbur, ŏris *n*, oak, strength, power, vigour, force

rōbustus, a, um *adj*, oaken, firm, strong, robust

rōdo, si, sum *v.t.* 3, to gnaw, corrode, slander

rŏgātĭo, ōnis *f*, proposed law or bill, request

rŏgātor, ōris *m,* polling-clerk
rŏgo *v.t.* 1, to ask; *with* **legem,** to propose (law), beg
rŏgus, i *m,* funeral pile
rōro *v.i.t.* 1, to drop, drip, trickle; wet, besprinkle
rōs, rōris *m,* dew, moisture
rŏsa, ae *f,* rose
rŏsārĭum, ii *n,* rose garden
roscĭdus, a, um *adj,* dewy
rŏsētum, i *n,* rosebed
rŏsĕus, a, um *adj,* of roses, rose-coloured
rostra, ōrum *n.pl,* speaker's platform
rostrātus, a, um *adj,* with beaks
rostrum, i *n,* beak, snout
rŏta, ae *f,* wheel, chariot
rŏto *v.i.t.* 1, to revolve; swing round, whirl around
rŏtundītas, ātis *f,* rotundity
rŏtundo *v.t.* 1, to round off
rŏtundus, a, um *adj,* round, polished
rŭbĕfăcĭo, fēci, factum *v.t.* 3, to redden
rŭbens, ntis *adj,* red
rŭbĕo *v.i.* 2, to be red, blush
rŭber, bra, brum *adj,* red

ructus, ūs *m,* belching
rŭdens, ntis *m,* rope, rigging
rŭdīmentum, i *n,* first try
rŭdis, e *adj,* rough, raw, wild, awkward, inexperienced
rŭdis, is *f,* stick, wooden sword
rŭdo, īvi, ītum *v.i.* 3, to bellow
rūdus, ĕris *n,* broken stones, rubbish
rūfus, a, um *adj,* red
rūga, ae *f,* wrinkle
rūgōsus, a, um *adj,* shrivelled
rŭīna, ae *f,* downfall, ruin
rŭīnōsus, a, um *adj,* in ruins
rūmĭno *v.t.* 1, to chew over
rūmor, ōris *m,* rumour, general opinion, reputation
rumpo, rūpi, ruptum *v.t.* 3, to break, burst, destroy, interrupt
runcīna, ae *f,* plane
runcīno *v.t.* 1, to plane
runco *v.t.* 1, to weed
rŭo, ŭi, ŭtum *v.i.t.* 3, to fall, rush, hurry; hurl down, throw up
rūpes, is *f,* rock
rūrĭcŏla, ae *adj,* rural
rursus (rursum) *adv,* again, on the contrary, backwards
rūs, rūris *n,* countryside

Insight

If the place is a town, city or small island, the place name is usually put into the appropriate case without the preposition. The same rule applies to three common nouns: *domus* (= house), *rus* (= country) and *humus* (= ground). Moreover, the locative case expresses 'place where' (*domi* = at home).

---

rŭbesco, bŭi *v.i.* 3, to grow red
rŭbēta, ae *f,* toad
rŭbēta, ōrum *n.pl,* brambles
rŭbĭcundus, a, um *adj,* red
rūbīgo... see **rōbīgo...**
rŭbor, ōris *m,* redness, blush, bashfulness
rùbrīca, ae *f,* red-chalk
rūbus, i *m,* bramble bush
ructo *v.i.t.* 1, to belch
ructor *v.* 1, *dep,* to belch

rustĭcānus, a, um *adj,* rustic
rustĭcītas, ātis *f,* behaviour of country-people
rustĭcor *v.i.* 1, *dep,* to live in the country
rustĭcus, a, um *adj,* rural
rustĭcus, i *m,* countryman
rūta, ae *f,* bitter herb, rue
rŭtĭlo *v.i.* 1, to be red
rŭtĭlus, a, um *adj,* red

S

sabbăta, ōrum *n.pl*, sabbath
săbīnum, i *n*, Sabine wine
săbŭlum, i *n*, gravel
săburra, ae *f*, sand, ballast
sacchăron, i *n*, sugar
saccŭlus, i *m*, small bag
saccus, i *m*, bag
săcellum, i *n*, chapel
săcer, cra, crum *adj*, sacred, venerable, accursed
săcerdos, dōtis *c*, priest
săcerdōtālis, e *adj*, priestly
săcerdōtĭum, ii *n*, priesthood
sàcra, ōrum *n.pl*, worship, religion
sàcrāmentum, i *n*, oath
sàcrārĭum, ii *n*, sanctuary
sàcrātus, a, um *adj*, sacred
sàcrĭfĭcĭum, ii *n*, sacrifice
sàcrĭfĭco *v.i.t.* 1, to sacrifice
sàcrĭfĭcus, a, um *adj*, sacrificial
sàcrĭlĕgus, a, um *adj*, temple robbing, sacrilegious
sàcro *v.t.* 1, to consecrate, condemn, doom
sàcrōsanctus, a, um *adj*, sacred, inviolable
sàcrum, i *n*, sacred thing, religious act, religion
saecŭlum, i *n*, age, generation, century
saepe *adv*, often
saepes, is *f*, hedge, fence
saepīmentum, i *n*, fencing
saepĭo, psi, ptum *v.t.* 4, to fence in, surround
saeptum i *n*, fence, pen
saeta, ae *f*, hair, bristle
saetĭger, ĕra, ĕrum *adj*, bristly
saetōsus, a, um *adj*, bristly
saevĭo *v.i.* 4, to rage
saevĭtĭa, ae *f*, savageness
saevus, a, um *adj*, savage, violent, furious, cruel
sāga, ae *f*, fortune-teller
săgācĭtas, ātis *f*, shrewdness
săgax, ācis *adj, adv*, ĭter, keen, shrewd, acute
săgīno *v.t.* 1, to fatten
săgitta, ae *f*, arrow
săgittārĭus, ii *m*, archer
săgŭlum, i *n*, military cloak

săgum, i *n*, military cloak
sal, sălis *m*, salt, sea, wit, sarcasm
sălăco, ōnis *m*, braggart
sălārĭum, ii *n*, pension, salary (salt money)
sălax, ācis *adj*, lecherous
sălèbra, ae *f*, roughness
sălĭāris, e *adj*, splendid
sălictum, i *n*, willow-grove
sălignus, a, um *adj*, of willow
Sălĭi, ōrum *m.pl*, priests of Mars
sălīnae, ārum *f.pl*, salt-works
sălīnum, i *n*, saltcellar
sălĭo, ŭi, saltum *v.i.* 4, to jump
sălīva, ae *f*, saliva
sălix, īcis *f*, willow tree
salmo, ōnis *m*, salmon
salsāmentum, i *n*, brine
salsus, a, um *adj, adv*, ē, salted, witty
saltātĭo, ōnis *f*, dancing
saltātor, ōris *m*, dancer
saltātrix, īcis *f*, dancing-girl
saltātus, ūs *m*, dancing
saltem *adv*, at least
salto *v.i.t.* 1, to dance
saltus, ūs *m*, leap, bound
saltus, ūs *m*, woodland, mountain pass
sălūbris, e *adj, adv*, ĭter, health-giving, beneficial
sălūbrĭtas, ātis *f*, wholesomeness
sălum, i *n*, sea
sălūs, ūtis *f*, welfare, safety
sălūtāris, e *adj, adv*, ĭter, beneficial, wholesome
sălūtātĭo, ōnis *f*, greeting
sălūtātor, ōris *m*, visitor
sălūtĭfer, ĕra, ĕrum *adj*, healing
sălūto *v.t.* 1, to greet
salvē, salvēte, salvēto *v. imperative*, how are you? welcome!
salvĭa, ae *f*, sage (herb)
salvus, a, um *adj*, safe, well; *with noun in abl*, e.g. **salvā lege** without violating the law
sambūcus, i *f*, elder tree
sānābĭlis, e *adj*, curable
sānātĭo, ōnis *f*, cure
sancĭo, xi, ctum *v.t.* 4, to appoint, establish, ratify
sanctĭfĭcātĭo, ōnis *f*, sanctification

sanctĭo, ōnis *f*, establishing

sanctĭtas, ātis *f*, sacredness, purity

sanctus, a, um *adj, adv*, **ē**, sacred, inviolable, good

sandix, īcis *f*, scarlet

sānē *adv*, certainly, very

sanguĭnārĭus, a, um *adj*, bloody, blood-thirsty

sanguĭnĕus, a, um *adj*, bloody

sanguĭnŏlentus, a, um *adj*, bloody

sanguis, ĭnis *m*, blood, bloodshed, race, stock

sănĭes, em, e *f*, bad blood

sānĭtas, ātis *f*, health, good sense, discretion

sannĭo, ōnis *m*, buffoon

sāno *v.t.* 1, to cure, restore

sānus, a, um *adj*, healthy, rational, discreet

sāpĭdus, a, um *adj*, tasty

săpĭens, ntis *adj, adv*, **nter**, wise, sensible

săpĭens, ntis *m*, wise man

săpĭentĭa, ae *f*, discretion, philosophy

săpĭo, īvi *v.i.t.* 3, to be wise, discreet; to taste of savour of

sāpo, ōnis *m*, soap

săpor, ōris *m*, flavour, taste

sapphīrus, i *f*, sapphire

sarcĭna, ae *f*, pack, load

sarcĭo, si, tum *v.t.* 4, to patch

sarcŏphăgus, i *m*, sarcophagus

sarcŭlum, i *n*, light hoe

sarda, ae *f*, sardine

sarīsa, ae *f*, Macedonian lance

sarmentum, i *n*, brushwood

sarrācum, i *n*, cart

sarrānus, a, um *adj*, Tyrian

sarrĭo *v.t.* 4, to hoe

sartāto, ĭnis *f*, frying pan

sartus, a, um *adj*, repaired

sāta, ōrum *n.pl*, crops

sătelles, ĭtis *c*, attendant; *in pl*, escort

sătĭas, ātis *f*, abundance, disgust

sătĭĕtas, ātis *f*, abundance, disgust

sătĭo *v.t.* 1, to satisfy, glut

sătĭo, ōnis *f*, sowing

sătĭrĭcus, a, um *adj*, satirical

sătis (săt) *adv*, or *indecl. adj*, enough

sătisdătĭo, ōnis *f*, giving bail

sătisfăcĭo, fēci, factum *v.t.* 3, to satisfy, make amends

sătisfactĭo, ōnis *f*, excuse, reparation

sătĭus *comp. adv*, better

sător, ōris *m*, sower, creator

sătrăpes, is *m*, viceroy, satrap

sătur, ŭra, ŭrum *adj*, full, fertile

sătūra, ae *f*, food made of various ingredients, satire

Sāturnālĭa, ōrum *n.pl*, festival in honour of Saturn (Dec. 17th)

sătūro *v.t.* 1, to fill, glut

sătus, ūs *m*, planting

sătus, a, um *adj*, sprung from

sătȳrus, i *m*, forest god

saucĭo *v.t.* 1, to wound

saucĭus, a, um *adj*, wounded

saxĕus, a, um *adj*, rocky

saxĭfĭcus, a, um *adj*, petrifiying

saxōsus, a, um *adj*, rocky

saxum, i *n*, rock

scăbellum, i *n*, stool

scăber, bra, brum *adj*, rough, scabby

scăbĭes, em, e *f*, roughness, scab, itch

scăbo, scăbi *v.t.* 3, to scratch

scaena, ae *f*, stage, scene

scaenĭcus, a, um *adj*, theatrical

scaenĭcus, i *m*, actor

scāla, ae *f*, ladder, stairs

scalmus, i *m*, rowlock

scalpo, psi, ptum *v.t.* 3, to carve

scalpellum, i *n*, lancet

scalprum, i *n*, chisel

scalptor, ōris *m*, engraver

scalptūra, ae *f*, engraving

scamnum, i *n*, bench

scando *v.i.t.* 3, to rise; climb

scăpha, ae *f*, small boat

scăpŭlae, ārum *f.pl*, shoulder blades

scărăbaeus, i *m*, beetle

scărus, i *m*, sea fish (scar)

scătĕbra, ae *f*, spring water

scătĕo *v.i.* 2, to bubble, swarm with

scaurus, a, um *adj*, with swollen ankles

scĕlĕrātus, a, um *adj*, wicked

scĕlĕro *v.t.* 1, to contaminate

scĕlestus, a, um *adj*, wicked

scĕlus, ĕris *n*, crime, scoundrel
scēna see **scaena**
scēnĭcus see **scaenĭcus**
sceptrum, i *n*, sceptre; *in pl*, dominion, authority
schĕda, ae *f*, sheet of paper
schŏla, ae *f*, lecture, school
scĭens, ntis *adj, adv*, **nter**, knowing (*i.e.* purposely), expert in
scĭentĭa, ae *f*, knowledge
scīlĭcet *adv*, certainly, of course, namely
scīlla, ae *f*, sea-onion, prawn
scindo, scĭdi, scissum *v.t.* 3, to split
scintilla, ae *f*, spark
scintillans, ntis *adj*, sparkling
scintillo *v.i.* 1, to sparkle
scĭo *v.t.* 4, to know, understand
scīpĭo, ōnis *m*, staff
scirpĕus, a, um *adj*, of rushes
sciscĭtor *v.t.* 1, *dep*, to enquire
scisco, scīvi, scītum *v.t.* 3, to approve, appoint, decree
scissūra, ae *f*, tearing, rending
scītor *v.t.* 1, *dep*, to enquire
scītum, i *n*, decree, statute
scītus, a, um *adj, adv*, **ē**, shrewd, sensible, witty
scĭūrus, i *m*, squirrel

draw, compose, describe, enroll
scrīnĭum, ii *n*, letter-case
scriptĭo, ōnis *f*, writing
scriptor, ōris *m*, secretary, author
scriptum, i *n*, book, writing
scriptūra, ae *f*, composition
scriptus, a, um *adj*, written
scrŏbis, is *m*, ditch
scrūpĕus, a, um *adj*, rugged
scrūpŭlus, i *m*, anxiety, embarrassment
scrūta, ōrum *n.pl*, frippery
scrūtātĭo, ōnis *f*, scrutiny
scrūtor *v.t.* 1, *dep*, to examine
sculpo, psi, ptum *v.t.* 3, to carve
sculpōnĕae, ārum *f.pl*, clogs
sculptor, ōris *m*, sculptor
sculptūra, ae *f*, sculpture
scurra, ae *m*, clown, dandy
scurrīlis, e *adj*, jeering
scūtātus, a, um *adj*, armed with oblong shields
scūtella, ae *f*, salver
scūtĭca, ae *f*, whip
scūtŭla, ae *f*, wooden roller
scūtum, i *n*, oblong shield
scȳphus, i *m*, goblet
sē *acc. or abl. of reflexive pron*, himself, herself, itself, themselves etc.

Insight

The personal pronouns 'himself', 'herself' and 'themselves' have only one form in Latin, both for the singular and plural forms, namely *se*. It declines as follows: acc. *se*, gen. *sui*, dat. *sibi*, abl. *se*. They lack the nominative and vocative forms.

scŏbīna, ae *f*, rasp, file
scŏbis, is *f*, sawdust
scomber, bri *m*, mackerel
scōpae, ārum *f.pl*, broom
scŏpŭlōsus, a, um *adj*, rocky
scŏpŭlus, i *m*, rock, cliff
scŏpus, i *m*, target
scorpĭo, ōnis *m*, scorpion, missile launcher
scortum, i *n*, prostitute
scrība, ae *m*, clerk
scrībo, psi, ptum *v.t.* 3, to write,

sēbum, i *n*, suet
sĕcāle, is *n*, rye
sēcēdo, cessi, cessum *v.i.* 3, to go away, withdraw
sēcerno, crēvi, crētum *v.t.* 3, to separate, part
sēcessĭo, ōnis *f*, withdrawal
sēcessus, ūs *m*, solitude
sēcĭus (sĕquĭus) *comp. adv*, differently
sēclūdo, si, sum *v.t.* 3, to separate, shut off

sēclūsus, a, um *adj*, remote

sĕco, ŭi, ctum *v.t.* 1, to cut, wound, separate

sēcrētum, i *n*, solitude

sēcrētus, a, um *adj, adv,* ō, separate, remote, secret

secta, ae *f*, way, method, sect

sectātor, ōris *m*, follower

sectĭo, ōnis *f*, sale by auction

sector, ōris *m*, cutthroat, bidder at an auction

sector *v.t.* 1, *dep*, to pursue

sectūra, ae *f*, mine

sēcul... see saecul

sĕcundārĭus, a, um *adj*, secondary, second-rate

sĕcundo *v.t.* 1, to favour

sĕcundum *prep. with acc,* after, behind, by, next to, according to

sĕcundus, a, um *adj*, following, second, favourable

sĕcūrĭger, ĕra, ĕrum *adj*, armed with a battle-axe

sĕcūris, is *f*, axe, hatchet

sĕcūrĭtas, ātis *f*, freedom from care

sĕcūrus, a, um *adj*, carefree, tranquil

sĕcus *adv*, differently

sĕd *conj*, but

sēdātĭo, ōnis *f*, a calming

sēdātus, a, um *adj*, calm

sēdĕcim *indecl. adj*, sixteen

sĕdentārĭus, a, um *adj*, sedentary

sĕdĕo, sēdi, sessum *v.i.* 2, to sit, remain, settle, be settled

sēdes, is *f*, seat, residence, temple, bottom, foundation

sĕdīle, is *n*, seat

sēdītĭo, ōnis *f*, mutiny

sēdītĭōsus, a, um *adj, adv,* ē, mutinous, rebellious

sēdo *v.t.* 1, to calm, check

sēdūco, xi, ctum *v.t.* 3, to lead aside, separate

sēdūlĭtas, ātis *f*, zeal

sēdūlō *adv*, diligently, on purpose

sēdūlus, a, um *adj*, industrious

sĕges, ĕtis *f*, cornfield, crop

segmenta, ōrum *n.pl*, trimmings

segmentum, i *n*, piece

segnis, e *adj, adv,* ĭter, lazy

segnĭtĭa, ae *f*, inactivity, slowness

sēgrĕgo *v.t.* 1, to separate

sēiungo, nxi, nctum *v.t.* 3, to separate, divide

sēlĭgo, lēgi, lectum *v.t.* 3, to select

sella, ae *f*, seat, chair

sĕmĕl *adv*, once

sēmen, ĭtis *n*, seed, cutting, graft, offspring, instigator

sēmentis, is *f*, sowing

sēmestris, e *adj*, half-yearly

sēmēsus, a, um *adj*, half-eaten

sēmĭănĭmĭs, e *adj*, half-dead

sēmĭdĕus, a, um *adj*, half-divine

sēmĭfer, ĕra, ĕrum *adj*, half-man, half-beast

sēmĭhŏmo, ĭnis *m*, half-human

sēmĭhōra, ae *f*, half-hour

sēmĭnārĭum, ii *n*, nursery

sēmĭnātor, ōris *m*, author

sēmĭnĕcis, is *adj*, half-dead

sēmĭno *v.t.* 1, to produce

sēmĭplēnus, a, um *adj*, half-full

sēmĭrŭtus, a, um *adj*, half-ruined

sēmis, issis *m*, (coin of very low value)

sēmĭsomnus, a, um *adj*, half-asleep

sēmĭta, ae *f*, footpath

sēmĭustus, a, um *adj*, half-burned

sēmĭvir, vĭri *m*, half-man; *as adj,* effeminate

sēmĭvīvus, a, um *adj*, half-alive

sēmōtus, a, um *adj*, remote

sēmŏvĕo, mōvi, mōtum *v.t.* 2, to remove, separate

semper *adv*, always

sempĭternus, a, um *adj*, everlasting

sēmustŭlo *v.t.* 1, to half burn

sĕnātor, ōris *m*, senator

sĕnātōrĭus, a, um *adj*, senatorial

sĕnātus, ūs *m*, the Senate

sĕnecta, ae *f*, old age

sĕnectus, ūtis *f*, old age

sĕnesco, nŭi *v.i.* 3, to grow old

sĕnex, sĕnis *m*, old man

sēni, ae, a *pl. adj*, six each

sĕnīlis, e *adj*, old (of people)

sĕnĭor, ōris *c*, elderly person

sĕnĭum, ii *n*, old age, decay, trouble

sensĭlis, e *adj*, sensitive

sensim *adv*, slowly, gently

sensus, ūs *m*, perception, disposition, good taste, sense, understanding, meaning
sententĭa, ae *f*, opinion, decision, meaning, sentence, axiom; **ex mĕā sententĭā** to my liking
sententĭōsus, a, um *adj*, sententious
sentīna, ae *f*, bilge-water, dregs, ship's hold
sentĭo, si, sum *v.t.* 4, to feel, perceive, endure, suppose
sentis, is *m*, thorn, bramble
sentus, a, um *adj*, rough
sĕorsum *adv*, separately
sēpărātim *adv*, separately
sēpărātĭo, ōnis *f*, separation
sēpărātus, a, um *adj*, separate
sēpăro *v.t.* 1, to separate
sĕpĕlĭo, līvi, pultum *v.t.* 4, to bury, overwhelm
sēpĭa, ae *f*, cuttle fish
sēpĭo see **saepĭo**
sēpōno, pŏsŭi, pŏsĭtum *v.t.* 3, to put aside, select
septem *indecl. adj*, seven
September (mensis) September
septemgĕmĭnus, a, um *adj*, seven-fold
septemplex, ĭcis *adj*, seven-fold
septendĕcim *indecl. adj*, seventeen
septēni, ae, a *pl. adj*, seven each
septentrĭōnālis, um *m.pl*, the Great Bear, the North
septĭes *adv*, seven times
septĭmus, a, um *adv*, seventh
septingenti, ae, a *pl. adj*, seven hundred
septŭāgēsĭmus, a, um *adj*, seventieth
septŭāginta *indecl. adj*, seventy
septum see **saeptum**
sĕpulcrum, i *n*, grave, tomb
sĕpultūra, ae *f*, burial
sĕquax, ācis *adj*, pursuing
sĕquens, ntis *adj*, following
sĕquester, tris *m*, agent
sĕquor, sĕcūtus *v.i.t.* 3, *dep*, to follow, attend, pursue
sĕra, ae *f*, bolt, bar
sĕrēnĭtas, ātis *f*, fair weather
sĕrēno *v.t.* 1, to brighten
sĕrēnum, i *n*, fair weather

sĕrēnus, a, um *adj*, clear, fair, cheerful, glad
sērĭa, ōrum *n.pl*, serious matters
sērĭcus, a, um *adj*, silken
sērĭes, em, e *f*, row, series
sērĭus, a, um *adj*, serious
sermo, ōnis *m*, talk, conversation, common talk
sĕro, sēvi, sătum *v.t.* 3, to sow, plant, cause
sĕro, ŭi, sertum *v.t.* 3, to plait, join, connect, compose
sērò *adv*, late
serpens, ntis *f*, snake
serpo, psi, ptum *v.i.* 3, to crawl
serpyllum, i *n*, thyme
serra, ae *f*, saw
serrŭla, ae *f*, small saw
serta, ōrum *n.pl*, garlands
sĕrum, i *n*, whey
sērus, a, um *adj*, late
serva, ae *f*, maid-servant
servātor, ōris *m*, saviour
servīlis, e *adj, adv*, **ĭter**, of a slave, servile
servĭo *v.i.* 4, to be a servant, to be of use to
servītĭum, ii *n*, slavery, slaves
servītus, ūtis *f*, slavery, slaves
servo *v.t.* 1, to save, protect, preserve, keep, keep watch
servus, a, um *adj*, servile
servus, i *m*, slave, servant
sescēni, ae, a *pl. adj*, six hundred each
sescenti, ae, a *pl. adj*, six hundred
sescentĭes *adv*, six hundred times
sesquĭpĕdālis, e *adj*, one foot and a half long
sessĭo, ōnis *f*, sitting, session
sestertĭum 1,000 sestertii
sestertĭus, ii *m*, small silver coin (worth about 1 p.)
sēt... see **saet...**
seu *conj*, whether, or
sĕvērĭtas, ātis *f*, sternness
sĕvērus, a, um *adj, adv*, **ē**, stern, serious, harsh, gloomy
sēvŏco *v.t.* 1, to call aside
sex *indecl. adj*, six
sexāgēnārĭus, i *m*, sexagenarian
sexāgēni, ae, a *pl. adj*, sixty each
sexāgēsĭmus, a, um *adj*, sixtieth

sexāgǐes *adv*, sixty times
sexāginta *indecl. adj*, sixty
sexennǐum, ii *n*, six years
sextans, ntis *m*, a sixth part
sextārǐus, ii *m*, a pint
Sextīlis (mensis) August
sextus, a, um *adj*, sixth
sexus, ūs *m*, sex
sī *conj*, if
sǐbi *dat. of reflexive pron*, to himself, herself, itself, etc.
sībǐlo *v.i.t.* 1, to hiss; hiss at
sībǐlus, i *m*, hissing
sībylla, ae *f*, prophetess
sīc *adv*, so, in this way
sīca, ae *f*, dagger
sīcārǐus, ii *m*, assassin
siccǐtas, ātis *f*, dryness, firmness
sicco *v.t.* 1, to dry up, drain
siccum, i *n*, dry land
siccus, a, um *adj*, dry, firm, tough, thirsty, sober
sīcǔbǐ *adv*, if anywhere
sīcut (sīcŭti) *adv*, just as
sīděrěus, a, um *adj*, starry
sīdo, di *v.i.* 3, to sit down, settle, sink
sīdus, ěris *n*, star, sky, constellation, season, weather
sǐgilla, ōrum *n.pl*, little figures or images
sǐgillātus, a, um *adj*, figured
signǐfer, ěri *m*, standard-bearer
signǐfǐcātǐo, ōnis *f*, sign, mark
signǐfǐco *v.t.* 1, to show, notify
signǐfǐcans, antis *adj*, significant
signo *v.t.* 1, to mark out, seal, indicate
signum, i *n*, mark, sign, military standard, watchword, statue, constellation, symptom
sǐlens, ntis *adj*, still, quiet
sǐlentǐum, ii *n*, stillness, quietness
sǐlěo *v.i.t.* 2, to be silent; to keep quiet about
sǐlesco *v.i.* 3, to grow quiet
sǐlex, ǐcis *m*, flint-stone
sǐlus, a, um *adj*, snub-nosed
silva, ae *f*, wood, forest, grove, abundance
silvestrǐa, ǐum *n.pl*, woodlands
silvestris, e *adj*, woody, rural
silvǐcǒla, ae *adj*, living in woods

sīmǐa, ae *f*, ape
sǐmǐlis, e *adj, adv*, ǐter, similar, like
sǐmǐlǐtūdo, ǐnis *f*, resemblance
sīmǐus, ii *m*, ape
simplex, ǐcis *adj, adv*, ǐter, unmixed, simple, frank
simplǐcǐtas, ātis *f*, honesty
sǐmul *adv*, at once, together, at the same time, as soon as
sǐmǔlac *conj*, as soon as
sǐmǔlatque *conj*, as soon as
sǐmǔlācrum, i *n*, portrait, statue, phantom
sǐmǔlātǐo, ōnis *f*, pretence
sǐmǔlātor, ōris *m*, pretender
sǐmǔlātus, a, um *adj*, feigned
sǐmǔlo *v.t.* 1, to imitate, pretend
sǐmultas, ātis *f*, animosity
sīmus, a, um *adj*, snub-nosed
sīn *conj*, but if
sǐnāpi, is *n*, mustard
sincērǐtas, ātis *f*, cleanness, purity, entirety, sincerity
sincērus, a, um *adj, adv*, ē, clean, pure, genuine, entire, sincere
sǐně *prep. with abl*, without
singillātim *adv*, one by one
singǔlāris, e *adj*, single, solitary, unique, remarkable
singǔlātim see **singillātim**
singǔli, ae, a *pl. adj*, one each
singultim *adv*, with sobs
singultǐo *v.i.* 4, to hiccup
singulto (no perf.) *v.i.* 1, to sob
sinultus, ūs *m*, sobbing
sǐnister, tra, trum *adj*, left, awkward, wrong, unlucky, lucky
sǐnistra, ae *f*, left hand
sǐnistrorsus *adv*, to the left
sǐno, sīvi, sǐtum *v.t.* 3, to allow
sǐnum, i *n*, drinking-cup
sǐnǔo *v.t.* 1, to bend, curve
sǐnǔōsus, a, um *adj*, curved
sǐnus, ūs *m*, curve, fold, bosom, lap, hiding-place, bay
sǐpho, ōnis *m*, siphon, syringe
sīquandō *adv*, if ever
sīquǐdem *adv*, if indeed
sīquis *pron*, if any
sīrēn, ēnis *f*, siren
sisto, stǐti, stǎtum *v.i.t* 3, to stand still, resist, hold out; put, place, bring, check, establish

sīstrum, i *n*, rattle

sĭtĭens, ntis *adj, adv*, **nter**, thirsty

sĭtĭo *v.i.t.* 4, to thirst; long for

sĭtis, is *f*, thirst, drought

sĭtŭla, ae *f*, bucket

sĭtus, a, um *adj*, situated

sĭtus, ūs *m*, position, site, rust, mould, inactivity

sīve *conj*, whether, or

smăragdus, i *c*, emerald

sŏbŏles, is *f*, sprout, twig, offspring

sōbrĭĕtas, ātis *f*, sobriety, temperance

sōbrīnus, i *m*, cousin

sōbrĭus, a, um *adj, adv*, **ē**, sober, moderate, sensible

soccus, i *m*, slipper

sŏcer, ĕri *m*, father-in-law

sŏcĭālis, e *adj*, allied

sŏcĭĕtas, ātis *f*, fellowship, partnership, alliance

sŏcĭo *v.t.* 1, to unite

sŏcĭus, ii *m*, companion, ally

sŏcĭus, a, um *adj*, allied

sōcordĭa, ae *f*, laziness, folly

sōcors, cordis *adj*, lazy, careless, stupid

socrus, ūs *f*, mother-in-law

sŏdālĭcĭum, ii *n*, secret society

sŏdālis, is *c*, companion

sŏdālĭtas, ātis *f*, friendship

sōdes if you wish

sōl, sōlis *m*, sun, sunshine

sōlācĭum, ii *n*, comfort, solace

sōlāmen, ĭnis *n*, consolation

sōlārĭum, ii *n*, sundial

sōlātĭum see **sōlācĭum**

soldūrĭi, ōrum *m.pl*, retainers of a chieftain

sŏlĕa, ae *f*, sandal, sole (fish)

sŏlĕātus, a, um *adj*, wearing sandals

sŏlĕo, sŏlĭtus *v.i.* 2, *semi-dep*, to be accustomed

sŏlĭdĭtas, ātis *f*, solidity

sŏlĭdo *v.t.* 1, to strengthen

sŏlĭdum, i *n*, a solid, solidity

sŏlĭdus, a, um *adj*, compact, complete, genuine, real

sōlĭtārĭus, a, um *adj*, alone

sōlĭtūdo, ĭnis *f*, loneliness, desert

sŏlĭtus, a, um *adj*, usual

sŏlĭum, ii *n*, seat, throne

sollemnis, e *adj*, established, appointed, usual, religious

sollemne, is *n*, religious ceremony, sacrifice

sollers, tis *adj*, skilled

sollertĭa, ae *f*, skill, ingenuity

sollĭcĭtātĭo, ōnis *f*, instigation

sollĭcĭto *v.t.* 1, to stir up, molest, instigate

sollĭcĭtūdo, ĭnis *f*, anxiety

sollĭcĭtus, a, um *adj*, troubled

sōlor *v.t.* 1, *dep*, to comfort, relieve

solstĭtĭālis, e *adj*, of summer

solstĭtĭum, ii *n*, summer time

sŏlum, i *n*, bottom, base, floor, sole, soil, ground, country, place

sōlum *adv*, only

sōlus, a, um *adj*, alone, only, lonely, deserted

sŏlūtĭo, ōnis *f*, unloosing, payment, explanation

sŏlūtus, a, um *adj, adv*, **ē**, free, loose, independent

solvendum see **solvo**

solvo, solvi, sŏlūtum *v.t.* 3, to set free, dissolve, release, open up, pay, perform, fulfil, acquit; *with* **ancŏram** to sail

somnĭcŭlūsus, a, um *adj*, drowsy

somnĭfer, ĕra, ĕrum *adj*, sleep-bringing

somnĭfĭcus, a, um *adj* sleep-bringing

somnĭo *v.t.* 1, to dream

somnĭum, ii *n*, dream

somnus, i *m*, sleep

sŏnĭpēs, pĕdis *adj*, noisy-footed

sŏnĭtus, ūs *m*, noise, sound

sŏno, ŭi, ĭtum *v.i.t.* 1, to resound; call out, utter

sŏnor, ōris *m*, noise, sound

sŏnōrus, a, um *adj*, resounding

sons, ntis *adj*, guilty

sŏnus, i *m*, noise, sound

sŏphistes, ae *m*, philosopher

sōpĭo *v.t.* 4, to lull to sleep

sŏpor, ōris *m*, sleep

sŏpōrĭfer, ĕra, ĕrum *adj*, sleep-bringing

sŏpōro *v.t.* 1, to heat, stupefy

sŏpōrus, a, um *adj*, sleep-bringing

sorběo *v.t.* 2, to suck in
sorděo *v.i.* 2, to be dirty, to be
despised
sordes, is *f*, dirt, mourning dress,
meanness
sordīdātus, a, um *adj*, shabbily
dressed (in mourning)
sordīdǐus, a, um *adj, adv,* ē, dirty,
despicable, mean
sŏror, ōris *f*, sister
sŏrōrǐus, a, um *adj*, of a sister
sors, tis *f*, chance, lot, drawing of
lots, prophesy, fortune, share,
destiny
sortǐor *v.i.t.* 4, *dep*, to draw lots;
to appoint by lot, obtain by lot,
choose
sortītǐo, ōnis *f*, drawing of lots
sortītō *adv*, by lot
sortītus, a, um *adj*, drawn by lot
sospěs, ǐtis *adj*, safe, lucky
spādix, īcis *adj*, nut-brown
spargo, si, sum *v.t.* 3, to sprinkle,
scatter, spread
spǎrus, i *m*, hunting spear
spasmus, i *m*, spasm
spătǐor *v.i.* 1, *dep*, to walk about
spătǐōsus, a, um *adj*, spacious
spătǐum, ii *n*, space, room,
distance, walk, track, interval
spěcǐes, ēi *f*, sight, view, shape,
appearance, pretence, display,
beauty
spěcǐmen, ǐnis *n*, mark, sign,
pattern
spěcǐōsus, a, um *adj*, handsome,
plausible
spectābǐlis, e *adj*, visible,
remarkable
spectācǔlum, i *n*, show, spectacle
spectātǐo, ōnis *f*, sight
spectātor, ōris *m*, onlooker
spectātus, a, um *adj*, tested,
respected
speco *v.t.* 1, to watch, face,
examine, consider, refer
spectrum, i *n*, image
spěcǔla, ae *f*, look-out point
spēcǔla, ae *f*, slight hope
spěcǔlātor, ōris *m*, spy, scout
spěcǔlor *v.t.* 1, *dep*, to watch,
observe, explore
spěcǔlum, i *n*, mirror
spěcus, ūs *m*, cave, pit
spēlunca, ae *f*, cave, den

sperno, sprēvi, sprētum *v.t.* 3, to
despise, scorn
spēro *v.t.* 1, to hope, expect
spes, spēi *f*, hope
sphaera, ae *f*, sphere
spīca, ae *f*, ear (of corn)
spīcěus, a, um *adj*, made of ears of
corn
spīcǔlum, i *n*, point, dart
spīna, ae *f*, thorn, spine,
difficulties
spīnētum, i *n*, thorn-hedge
spīnōsus, a, um *adj*, thorny
spīnus, i *f*, sloe-tree
spīra, ae *f*, coil, twist
spīrābǐlis, e *adj*, breathable
spīrācǔlum, i *n*, air-hole
spīrāmentum, i *n*, air-hole
spīrǐtus, ūs *m*, breath, breeze,
pride, arrogance, soul
spīro *v.i.t.* 1, to breathe, blow,
live; exhale
spisso *v.t.* 1, to condense
spissus, a, um *adj*, thick, dense
splenděo *v.i.* 2, to shine
splendesco *v.i.* 3, to become
bright
splendǐdus, a, um *adj, adv,* ē,
shining, magnificent, noble
splendor, ōris *m*, brilliance,
excellence
spŏlǐa see **spŏlǐum**
spŏlǐātǐo, ōnis *f*, plundering
spŏlǐo *v.t.* 1, to plunder, rob
spŏlǐum, ii *n*, skin (of an animal);
in pl, booty, spoils
sponda, ae *f*, couch, sofa
sponděo, spŏpondi, sponsum *v.t.*
2, to promise, pledge, betroth,
warrant
spongǐa, ae *f*, sponge
spongǐōsus, a, um *adj*, spongy
sponsa, ae *f*, bride
sponsālǐa, ǐum *n.pl*, betrothal
sponsǐo, ōnis *f*, promise,
guarantee, security
sponsor, ōris *m*, surety
sponsum, i *n*, covenant
sponsus, a, um *adj*, promised
sponsus, i *m*, bridegroom
spontē (*abl.*) *f*, *with* **měā, sǔā,**
etc., voluntarily
sportella, ae *f*, fruit basket
sportǔla, ae *f*, little basket
spūma, ae *f*, froth, foam

spūměus, a, um *adj*, foaming
spūmǐfer, ěra, ěrum *adj*, foaming
spūmǐger, ěra, ěrum *adj*, foaming
spūmo *v.i.*1, to foam, froth
spūmōsus, a, um *adj*, foaming
spǔo, ǔi, ūtum *v.i.t.* 3, to spit
spūtum, i *n*, spit
spurcus, a, um *adj*, dirty
squālěo *v.i.* 2, to be stiff or rough, to be neglected, filthy
squālǐdus, a, um *adj*, stiff, dirty, neglected
squālor, ōris *m*, filthiness
squāma, ae *f*, scale (of fish)
squāměus, a, um *adj*, scaly
squāmǐger, ěra, ěrum *adj*, scaly
squāmōsus, a, um *adj*, scaly
stăbǐlǐo *v.t.* 4, to fix
stăbǐlis, e *adj*, firm, steadfast
stăbǐlǐtas, ātis *f*, firmness
stăbǔlo *v.i.* (**stăbǔlor**, *v.i. dep*,) 1, to have a home, resting-place
stăbǔlum, i *n*, stable, hut
stădǐum, ii *n*, stade (distance of 200 yds./metres approx.), racecourse
stagnans, ntis *adj*, stagnant
stagno *v.i.* 1, to stagnate
stagnum, i *n*, pool, pond
stălagmǐum, i *n*, pendant
stāmen, ǐnis *n*, thread
stătārǐus, a, um *adj*, firm, calm,
stătim *adv*, immediately
stătǐo, ōnis *f*, post, station, outposts, sentries
stătīva, ōrum *n.pl*, permanent camp
stătīvus, a, um *adj*, stationary
stător, ōris *m*, messenger
stătǔa, ae *f*, statue
stătǔo, ǔi, ūtum *v.t.* 3, to set up, place, build, establish, settle, decide
stătūra, ae *f*, stature
stătus, ūs *m*, posture, position, condition, state, circumstance

stătus, a, um *adj*, fixed
stella, ae *f*, star
stellātus, a, um *adj*, starry
stellǐger, ěra, ěrum *adj*, starry
stellǐo, ōnis *n*, newt
stemma, ătis *n*, garland, pedigree
stercus, ŏris *n*, manure
stěrǐlis, e *adj*, barren
stěrǐlǐtas, ātis *f*, sterility
sternax, ācis *adj*, bucking (horse)
sterno, strāvi, strātum *v.t.* 3, to scatter, extend, smooth, arrange, cover, overthrow, pave
sternūmentum, i *n*, sneezing
sternǔo, ǔi *v.i.t.* 3, to sneeze
sterto, ǔi *v.i.* 3, to snore
stigma, ătis *n*, brand
stillǐcǐdǐum, ii *n*, dripping rain-water
stillo *v.i.t.* 1, to drip; distil
stǐlus, i *m*, pen, style
stǐmǔlo *v.t.* 1, to torment, incite
stǐmǔlus, i *m*, goad, sting, incentive
stǐpātor, ōris *m*, attendant
stǐpendǐārǐus, a, um *adj*, tribute paying
stǐpendǐum, ii *n*, tax, dues, pay, military service campaign
stǐpes, ǐtis *m*, log, post
stǐpo *v.t.* 1, to compress, surround, accompany
stips, stǐpis *f*, donation
stǐpǔla, ae *f*, stalk, stem
stǐpǔlātǐo, ōnis *f*, agreement
stǐpǔlor *v.i.t.* 1, *dep*, to bargain; demand
stīria, ae *f*, icicle
stirps, pis *f*, root, stem, plant, race, family
stīva, ae *f*, plough-handle
sto, stěti, stătum *v.i.* 1, to stand, remain, endure, persist, cost

Insight

Verbs can be transitive or intransitive. **Intransitive** verbs do not require a direct object to complete their meaning (e.g. sto = I stand). In English such intransitive verbs can be used transitively as well, when they adopt a different meaning (e.g. I cannot stand that man).

stoīcus, a, um *adj,* stoic
stŏla, ae *f,* gown, robe
stŏlĭdus, a, um *adj,* dull, stupid
stŏmăchor *v.i.* 1, *dep,* to be angry
stŏmăchōsus, a, um *adj,* irritable
stŏmăchus, i *m,* gullet, stomach, taste, distaste
stŏrĕa, ae *f,* straw mat
strābo, ōnis *m,* one who squints
strāges, is *f,* destruction, massacre, slaughter
strāgŭlum, i *n,* rug
strāgŭlus, a, um *adj,* covering
strāmen, ĭnis *n,* straw
strāmentum, i *n,* straw
strāmĭnĕus, a, um *adj,* of straw
strangŭlo *v.t.* 1, to strangle
strătēgēma, ătis *n,* stratagem
strātum, i *n,* blanket, quilt, pillow, bed
strātus, a, um *adj,* stretched out
strēnŭus, a, um *adj, adv,* **ē,** brisk, quick, vigorous
strĕpĭto *v.i.* 1, to rattle
strĕpĭtus, ūs *m,* din
strĕpo, ŭi *v.i.* 3, to rattle, rumble, roar
strictim *adv,* briefly
strictūra, ae *f,* iron bar
strictus, a, um *adj,* tight
strīdĕo, si (strīdo, di 3) *v.i.* 2, to creak, hiss, rattle
strīdor, ōris *m,* creaking, hissing
strīdŭlus, a, um *adj,* creaking, hissing
strĭgĭlis, is *f,* scraper used by bathers for cleaning the skin
stringo, nxi, ctum *v.t.* 3, to draw tight, graze, strip off, draw (sword)
stringor, ōris *m,* touch, shock
strix, strĭgis *f,* screech owl
structor, ōris *m,* builder
structūra, ae *f,* construction
strŭes, is *f,* heap, pile
strŭo, xi, ctum *v.t.* 3, to pile up, build, contrive
strūthĭŏcămēlus, i *m,* ostrich
stŭdĕo *v.i.t.* 2, *with dat,* to be eager about, strive; pursue, favour
stŭdĭōsus, a, um *adj, adv,* **ē,** eager, anxious, friendly
stŭdĭum, ii *n,* eagerness, endeavour, affection, devotion, study
stultĭtĭa, ae *f,* foolishness
stultus, a, um *adj, adv,* **ē,** foolish
stūpa, ae *f,* flax, tow
stŭpĕfăcĭo, fēci, factum *v.t.* 3, to stun, daze
stŭpĕfactus, a, um *adj,* stunned
stŭpĕo *v.i.t.* 2, to be stunned, amazed; be astonished at
stŭpĕus, a, um *adj,* made of tow
stŭpĭdus, a, um *adj,* amazed
stŭpor, ōris *m,* astonishment, stupidity
stupp... see **stūp...**
stŭpro *v.t.* 1, to ravish
stŭprum, i *n,* disgrace, lewdness
sturnus, i *m,* starling
suādĕo, si, sum *v.i.t.* 2, *with dat,* to urge, persuade, recommend
suāsĭo, ōnis *f,* recommendation
suāsor, ōris *m,* adviser
suāvĭlŏquens, ntis *adj,* pleasant speaking
suāvĭor *v.t.* 1, *dep,* to kiss
suāvis, e *adj, adv,* **ĭter,** agreeable, pleasant
suāvĭtas, ātis *f,* pleasantness
suāvĭum, ii *n,* kiss
sub *prep. with acc. and abl,* under, beneath, near, during, towards, just after
sŭbactĭo, ōnis *f,* preparation
sŭbausculto *v.t.* 1, to eavesdrop
subcentŭrĭo, ōnis *m,* subaltern
subdĭtīvus, a, um *adj,* counterfeit
subdo, dĭdi, dĭtum *v.t.* 3, to place under, subdue
subdŏlus, a, um *adj,* crafty
subdūco, xi, ctum *v.t.* 3, to pull up, haul up, remove, calculate, balance (accounts)
sŭbĕo *v.i.t.* 4, to come up to, spring up, occur; enter, submit to, suffer, incur
sūber, ĕris *n,* cork tree
subflāvus, a, um *adj,* yellowish
sūbĭcĭo, iēci, iectum *v.t.* 3, to throw or place under or near, counterfeit, subject, affix, prompt
subiectĭo, ōnis *f,* placing under, forging

subiecto *v.t.* 1, to throw up

subiectus, a, um *adj*, lying near, subject

sŭbĭgo, ēgi, actum *v.t.* 3, to bring up, plough, conquer, subdue, compel, rub down

sŭbinde *adv*, immediately, now and then

sŭbĭtō *adv*, suddenly

sŭbĭtus, a, um *adj*, sudden

subiungo, nxi, nctum *v.t.* 3, to subordinate, subdue

sublābor, lapsus *v.i.* 3, *dep*, to glide away

sublātus, a, um *adj*, proud

sublĕgo, lēgi, lectum *v.t.* 3, to gather up, kidnap

sublĕvo *v.t.* 1, to lift up, support, alleviate

sublĭca, ae *f*, stake, palisade

sublĭgo *v.t.* 1, to tie on

sublīme *adv*, aloft, on high

sublīmis, e *adj*, high, eminent

sublūcĕo *v.i.* 2, to glimmer

sublŭo (*no perf.*) **lūtum** *v.t.* 3, to flow along, wash

sublustris, e *adj*, glimmering

subm... see **summ...**

subnecto, xŭi, xum *v.t.* 3, to tie on underneath

subnixus, a, um *adj*, propped up

sŭbŏles, is *f*, offspring, race

sŭborno *v.t.* 1, to equip, fit out, instigate

subr... see **surr...**

subscrībo, psi, ptum *v.t.* 3, to write underneath, note down

subscriptĭo, ōnis *f*, anything written underneath

subsĕco, ŭi, ctum *v.t.* 1, to clip

subsellĭum, ii *n*, seat, law court

subsĕquor, sĕcūtus *v.i.t.* 3, *dep*, to follow, ensue; follow closely, imitate

subsĭcīvus, a, um *adj*, remaining

subsĭdĭārĭus, a, um *adj*, reserve

subsĭdĭum, ii *n*, reserve-ranks, assistance, aid, protection

subsīdo, sēdi, sessum *v.i.t.* 3, to settle down, lie in anbush; waylay

subsisto, stĭti *v.i.* 3, to stop, halt, remain, withstand

subsortĭor *v.t.* 4, *dep*, to choose as a substitute

substerno, strāvi, strātum *v.t.* 3, to spread underneath, cover

substĭtŭo, ŭi, ūtum *v.t.* 3, to put under, substitute

substringo, nxi, ctum *v.t.* 3, to tie; **aurem** prick up the ear

substructĭo, ōnis *f*, foundation

substrŭo, xi, ctum *v.t.* 3, to lay foundations

subsum, esse *v*, *irreg*, to be under or near, to be at hand

subtēmen, ĭnis *n*, texture, weft

subter *adv. and prep. with abl*, beneath, below

subterfŭgĭo, fūgi *v.t.* 3, to avoid

subterlābens, ntis *adj*, gliding under

subterlābor *v.i.* 3, *dep*, to glide under

subterrānĕus, a, um *adj*, underground

subtexo, ŭi, xtum *v.t.* 3, to veil

subtīlis, e *adj, adv*, **ĭter**, slender, delicate, precise

subtīlĭtas, ātis *f*, exactness, subtlety

subtrăho, xi, ctum *v.t.* 3, to remove stealthily, carry off

sŭbūcŭla, ae *f*, shirt

sŭbulcus, i *m*, pig-keeper

sŭburbānus, a, um *adj*, suburban

sŭburbĭum, ii *n*, suburb

subvectĭo, ōnis *f*, conveyance

subvecto *v.t.* 1, to convey

subvĕho, xi, ctum *v.t.* 3, to convey

subvĕnĭo, vēni, ventum *v.i.* 4, *with dat*, to help, aid, occur to the mind

subverto, ti, sum *v.t.* 3, to overthrow

subvŏlo *v.i.* 1, to fly up

subvolvo *v.t.* 3, to roll up

succēdo, cessi, cessum *v.i.t.* 3, to go under, advance, enter; ascend, follow after, succeed

succendo, di, sum *v.t.* 3, to kindle

succensĕo, ŭi, sum *v.t.* 2, to be angry

successĭo, ōnis *f*, succession

successor, ōris *m*, successor

successus, ūs *m*, advance, success

succĭdo, di *v.i.* 3, to sink

succīdo

succīdo, di, sum *v.t.* 3, to cut
down
succingo, nxi, nctum *v.t.* 3, to
surround, girdle, tuck up
succlāmo *v.t.* 1, to shout out
succumbo, cŭbŭi, cŭbĭtum *v.i.* 3,
to surrender
succurro, curri, cursum *v.i.* 3, *with
dat*, to help, aid, occur
sūcĭnum, i *n*, amber
sūcōsus, a, um *adj*, juicy
suctus, ūs *m*, sucking
sūcus, i *m*, energy, life
sūdārĭum, i *n*, handkerchief
sŭdis, is *f*, stake, pile
sūdo *v.i.t.* 1, to sweat, toil; exude
sūdor, ōris *m*, sweat, toil

suffulcĭo, fulsi, fultum *v.t.* 4, to
prop up
suffūsus, a, um *adj*, spread over
suggĕro, gessi, gestum *v.t.* 3, to
carry up, supply
suggestum, i *n*, platform
suggestus, ūs *m*, platform
sūgo, xi, ctum *v.t.* 3, to suck
sŭi *genit. of reflexive pron*, of
himself, herself, itself etc.
sulco *v.t.* 1, to plough
sulcus, i *m*, furrow, ditch
sulfur, ŭris *n*, sulphur
sulfūrāta, ōrum *n.pl*, matches
sulfūrĕus, a, um *adj*, sulphurous
sum, esse, fŭi *v, irreg*, to be,
exist, happen

Insight

The **nominative** is the case of the subject of a sentence or clause
as well as the case of the complement of a verb, especially the
verb 'to be' (e.g. the king is angry = *rex iratus est*).

---

sūdum, i *n*, clear weather
sūdus, a, um *adj*, clear, bright
sŭesco, sŭēvi, sŭētum *v.i.t.* 3, to
be accustomed
sŭētus, a, um *adj*, accustomed
suffĕro, ferre, sustŭli, sublātum *v,
irreg*, to undergo, suffer
sufficĭo, fēci, fectum *v.i.t.* 3, to be
sufficient; impregnate, supply,
substitute, elect
suffīgo, xi, xum *v.t.* 3, to fix
suffīmentum, i *n*, incense
suffīo *v.t.* 4, to perfume
sufflāmen, ĭnis *n*, drag-chain
sufflātus, a, um *adj*, puffed up
sufflo *v.t.* 1, to inflate
suffōco *v.t.* 1, to strangle
suffŏdĭo, fōdi, fossum *v.t.* 3, to
pierce underneath
suffrāgātĭo, ōnis *f*, support
suffrāgātor, ōris *m*, supporter
suffrāgĭum, ii *n*, vote, ballot
suffrāgor *v.i.* 1, *dep, with dat*, to
vote for, support
suffundo, fūdi, fūsum *v.t.* 3, to
spread over, tinge

summa, ae *f*, top, chief, point,
perfection, amount, sum
summātim *adv*, briefly
summē *adv*, extremely
summergo, si, sum *v.t.* 3, to
submerge, overwhelm
summĭnistro *v.t.* 1, to supply
summissus, a, um *adj, adv, ē*,
gentle, soft, low, mean
summitto, mīsi, missum *v.t.* 3, to
send up, produce, rear, raise,
lower, submit, supply, send
summŏvĕo, mōvi, mōtum *v.t.* 2,
to drive away, remove
summus, a, um *adj*, highest,
topmost
sūmo, mpsi, mptum *v.t.* 3, to
take hold of, assume, inflict,
choose, claim, suppose, spend,
use, buy
sumptĭo, ōnis *f*, assumption
sumptŭōsus, a, um *adj, adv, ē*,
expensive, lavish
sumptus, ūs *m*, expense
sŭo, sŭi, sūtum *v.t.* 3, to sew
sŭpellex, lectĭlis *f*, furniture

sŭper   *adv, and prep. with acc. and abl,* above, over, on, besides, concerning

sŭpĕrābĭlis, e   *adj,* able to be overcome

sŭperbĭa, ae   *f,* pride, arrogance

sŭperbĭo,   *v.i.* 4, to be proud

sŭperbus, a, um   *adj, adv,* **ē,** proud, haughty, delicate, squeamish, magnificent

sŭpercĭlĭum, ii   *n,* eyebrow, ridge, summit, arrogance

sŭpercresco, crēvi   *v.i.* 3, to grow up

sŭpĕrēmĭnĕo   *v.t.* 2, to overtop

sŭperfĭcĭes, ēi   *f,* top, surface

sŭperfundo, fūdi, fūsum   *v.t.* 3, to pour over

sŭpĕri, ōrum   *m.pl,* the gods

sŭpĕrimmĭnĕo   *v.i.* 2, to overhang

sŭpĕrimpōno (*no perf.*)   **posĭtum** *v.t.* 3, to place upon

sŭpĕrīnĭcĭo (*no perf.*), **iectum** *v.t.* 3, to throw over or upon

sŭperiăcĭo, iēci, iectum *v.t.* 3, to throw over, overflow

sŭpĕrĭor, ĭus   *comp. adj,* higher, previous, former, superior

sŭperlātĭo, ōnis   *f,* exaggeraton, hyperbole

sŭpernus, a, um   *adj, adv,* **ē,** upper, on high ground

sŭpĕro   *v.i.t.* 1, to have the upper hand, remain; ascend, outstrip, conquer

sŭpersĕdĕo, sēdi, sessum   *v.i.t.* 2, *with abl,* to refrain (from)

sŭperstĕs, ĭtis   *adj,* surviving

sŭperstĭtĭo, ōnis   *f,* excessive fear of the gods

sŭperstĭtĭōsus, a, um   *adj,* superstitious

sŭpersto   *v.i.t.* 1, to stand over

sŭpersum, esse, fŭi   *v.i, irreg,* to remain, survive

sŭpĕrus, a, um   *adj,* upper, higher

sŭpervăcānĕus, a, um   *adj,* unnecessary

sŭpervăcŭus, a, um   *adj,* unnecessary

sŭpervĕnĭo, vēni, ventum   *v.i.t.* 4, to come up, arrive; fall upon

sŭpervŏlo   *v.i.t.* 1, to fly over

sŭpīno   *v.t.* 1, to bend backwards

sŭpīnus, a, um   *adj,* lying on the back, sloping

suppĕdĭto   *v.i.t.* 1, to be enough, plenty; to supply

suppĕto, īvi, ītum   *v.i.* 3, to be at hand, to be enough

supplanto   *v.t.* 1, to trip up

supplēmentum, i   *n,* reinforcements

supplĕo, ēvi, ētum   *v.t.* 2, to complete, fill up

supplex, ĭcis   *c,* suppliant

supplex, ĭcis   *adj,* beseeching

supplĭcātĭo, ōnis   *f,* public thanksgiving

supplĭcĭum, ii   *n,* punishment

supplĭco   *v.i.* 1, to implore

supplōdo, si   *v.i.t.* 3, to stamp

suppōno, pŏsŭi, pŏsĭtum   *v.t.* 3, to put under, substitute

supporto   *v.t.* 1, to convey

supprĭmo, pressi, pressum   *v.t.* 3, to sink, suppress

suppūro   *v.i.* 1, to suppurate

sùprā   *adv, and prep. with acc,* above, over, beyond, before

sùprēmus, a, um   *adj,* highest, last

sūra, ae   *f,* calf of the leg

surcŭlus, i   *m,* shoot, twig

surdĭtas, ātis   *f,* deafness

surdus, a, um   *adj,* deaf

surgo, surrexi, rectum   *v.i.t.* 3, to rise, stand up; raise

surrēgŭlus, i   *m,* subordinate ruler

surrēmīgo   *v.i.* 1, to row along

surrēpo, psi, ptum   *v.i.t.* 3, to creep under

surrīdĕo, si, sum   *v.i.* 2, to smile

surrĭpĭo, ŭi, reptum   *v.t.* 3, to snatch away, steal

surrŏgo   *v.t.* 1, to substitute

surrŭo, ŭi, ŭtum   *v.t.* 3, to undermine, overthrow

sursum   *adv,* upwards, on high

sūs, sŭis   *c,* pig

susceptĭo, ōnis   *f,* undertaking

suscĭpĭo, cēpi, ceptum   *v.t.* 3, to undertake, acknowledge, undergo

suscĭto   *v.t.* 1, to raise, arouse

suspectus, a, um   *adj,* mistrusted

suspectus, ūs   *m,* height

suspendĭum, ii   *n,* hanging

suspendo, di, sum   *v.t.* 3, to hang up, lift up, keep in suspense, interrupt

suspensus, a, um   *adj*, raised, hesitating

suspĭcĭo, spexi, ctum   *v.i.t.* 3, to look up; admire, suspect

suspĭcĭo, ōnis   *f*, suspicion

suspĭcĭōsus, a, um   *adj, adv*, ē, suspicious

suspĭcor   *v.t.* 1, *dep*, to suspect, suppose

suspīrĭtus, ūs   *m*, sigh

suspīrĭum, ii   *n*, sigh

suspīro   *v.i.t.* 1, to sigh; long for

sustento   *v.t.* 1, to support, maintain, endure

sustĭnĕo, ŭi, tentum   *v.t.* 2, to support, restrain, withstand, maintain

sŭsurro   *v.i.t.* 1, to hum; mutter

sŭsurrus, i   *m*, humming

sŭsurrus, a, um   *adj*, whispering

sūta, ōrum   *n.pl*, joints

sūtĭlis, e   *adj*, sewed together

sūtor, ōris   *m*, cobbler

sūtōrĭus, a, um   *adj*, of a cobbler

sūtūra, ae   *f*, seam

sŭus, a, um   *adj*, his, hers, its, their

sȳcŏmŏrus, i   *f*, sycamore

sȳcŏphanta, ae   *m*, sycophant, cheat

syllăba, ae   *f*, syllable

syllăbātim   *adv*, by syllables

symphōnĭa, ae   *f*, harmony

symphōnĭăcus, i   *m*, chorister

sȳnăgōga, ae   *f*, synagogue

syngrăpha, ae   *f*, promissory note

syngrăphus, i   *m*, passport

syntaxis, is   *f*, syntax

T

tăbānus, i   *m*, gadfly

tăbella, ae   *f*, small board or table, writing-tablet, letter, ballot paper, small picture

tăbellārĭus, ii   *m*, letter-bearer

tābĕo   *v.i.* 2, to melt away

tăberna, ae   *f*, hut, shop, inn

tăbernācŭlum, i   *n*, tent

tăbernārĭus, ii   *m*, shopkeeper

tābes, is   *f*, wasting-away, disease

tābesco, bŭi   *v.i.* 3, to melt away

tābĭdus, a, um   *adj*, decaying

tābŭla, ae   *f*, plank, writing-tablet, letter, account book, picture, painting, map, table

tăbŭlārĭa, ae   *f*, record office

tăbŭlārĭum, ii   *n*, archives

tăbŭlārĭus, ii   *m*, registrar

tăbŭlātum, i   *n*, floor, storey

tābum, i   *n*, pus, matter, infectious disease

tăcĕo   *v.i.t.* 2, to be silent; to be silent about

tăcĭturnĭtas, ātis   *f*, silence

tăcĭturnus, a, um   *adj*, silent

tăcĭtus, a, um   *adj, adv*, ē, secret, silent

tactus, ūs   *m*, touch, feel, influence

taeda, ae   *f*, pine tree, torch

taedet, taedŭit   *v.* 2, *impers, with acc. of person*, it offends, disgusts, wearies

taedĭum, i   *n*, weariness, disgust

taenĭa, ae   *f*, hair ribbon

taeter, tra, trum   *adj*, hideous

taetrĭcus, a, um   *adj*, harsh

tālāris, e   *adj*, ankle-length

tālĕa, ae   *f*, stick, stake

tălentum, i   *n*, sum of money (app. £400-£500); weight ($\frac{1}{2}$ cwt.)

tālĭo, ōnis   *f*, similar punishment, reprisal

tālis, e   *adj*, of such a kind

talpa, ae   *f*, mole

tālus, i   *m*, ankle bone, heel, die (marked on four sides)

tam   *adv*, so, as, equally

tamdĭu   *adv*, so long

tămen   *adv*, nevertheless, however, still

tămetsi   *conj*, although

tamquam   *adv*, as much as, just as, as if, for example

tandem   *adv*, at length

tango, tĕtĭgi, tactum   *v.t.* 3, to touch, taste, reach, strike, affect, impress, mention

tanquam   see **tamquam**

tantisper   *adv*, so long, meanwhile

tantŏpĕre   *adv*, so greatly

tantŭlus, a, um   *adj*, so little

tantum *adv*, so much, only

tantummŏdo *adv*, only, merely

tantundem *adv*, just as much

tantus, a, um *adj*, so great; **tanti esse** to be worth so much; **tantō** by so much

tăpēte, is *n*, tapestry

tardĭtas, ātis *f*, slowness

tardo *v.i.t.* 1, to delay; hinder

tardus, a, um *adj*, *adv*, **ē**, slow

tăta, ae *m*, dad, daddy

taurĕus, a, um *adj*, of a bull

taurīnus, a, um *adj*, of a bull

taurus, i *m*, bull, ox

taxus, i *f*, yew tree

tē *acc. or abl. of* **tū**

tector, ōris *m*, plasterer

tectōrĭum, ii *n*, plaster

tectum, i *n*, roof, house

tectus, a, um *adj*, *adv*, **ō**, covered, hidden, secret

tĕges, ĕtis *f*, mat

tĕgĭmen, ĭnis *n*, cover

tĕgo, xi, ctum *v.t.* 3, to cover, hide, protect

tĕgŭla, ae *f*, tile

tĕgŭmen see **tĕgĭmen**

tĕgŭmentum, i *n*, cover

tēla, ae *f*, web, warp, loom

tellūs, ūris *f*, earth, globe, land, region

tēlum, i *n*, weapon, javelin

tĕmĕrārĭus, a, um *adj*, rash

tĕmĕrē *adv*, by chance, rashly

tĕmĕrĭtas, ātis *f*, rashness

tĕmĕro *v.t.* 1, to defile, disgrace

tēmētum, i *n*, wine

temno *v.t.* 3, to despise

tēmo, ōnis *m*, pole, beam

tempĕrans, ntis *adj*, moderate

tempĕrantĭa, ae *f*, moderation

tempĕrātĭo, ōnis *f*, symmetry, temperament

tempĕrātus, a, um *adj*, moderate

tempĕrĭes, ēi *f*, mildness

tempĕro *v.i.t.* 1, to abstain, be moderate, be indulgent; mix properly, regulate, govern

tempestas, ātis *f*, time, period, weather, storm

tempestīvus, a, um *adj*, *adv*, **ē**, suitable, timely, early

templum, i *n*, temple, open space

tempto see **tento**

tempus, ŏris *n*, time, opportunity; **tempŏra** times, temples (of the head); **ad tempus** (*adv. phr.*) at the right time, for the time being

tēmŭlentus, a, um *adj*, drunk

tĕnācĭtas, ātis *f*, tenacity

tĕnax, ācis *adj*, holding tight, firm, stingy

tendo, tĕtendi, tentum *v.i.t.* 3, to aim, go, march, stretch, strive, encamp; stretch, extend

tĕnĕbrae, ārum *f.pl*, darkness

tĕnĕbrĭcōsus, a, um *adj*, dark, gloomy

tĕnĕbrōsus, a, um *adj*, dark, gloomy

tĕnĕo, ŭi, tentum *v.i.t.* 2, to hold a position, sail, continue; hold, have, keep, restrain, uphold, maintain, control, comprehend, include

tĕner, ĕra, ĕrum *adj*, tender

tĕnor, ōris *m*, course, career

tensa, ae *f*, triumphal chariot

tentāmentum, i *n*, attempt

tentātĭo, ōnis *f*, trial, attempt

tentātor, ōris *m*, tempter

tento (tempto) *v.t.* 1, to handle, attack, attempt, tempt, excite

tentōrĭum, ii *n*, tent

tentus, a, um *adj*, extended

tĕnŭis, e *adj*, *adv*, **ĭter**, thin, fine, meagre, poor, subtle

tĕnŭĭtas, ātis *f*, slenderness, poverty

tĕnŭo *v.t.* 1, to make thin, reduce, weaken, degrade

tĕnus *prep. with abl*, as far as, according to

tĕpĕfăcĭo, fēci, factum *v.t.* 3, to warm

tĕpĕo *v.i.* 2, to be warm

tĕpesco, pŭi *v.i.* 3, to grow warm

tĕpĭdus, a, um *adj*, warmth

tĕr *adv*, three times

tĕrĕbinthus, i *f*, terebinth tree

tĕrĕbra, ae *f*, tool

tĕrĕbor *v.t.* 1, to bore through

tĕrĕs, ĕtis *adj*, rounded, smooth, polished

tergĕmĭnus, a, um *adj*, triple

tergĕo, si, sum *v.t.* 2, to clean, polish

tergĭbersātĭo, ōnis *f*, backsliding

tergĭversor *v.i.* 1, *dep*, to shuffle, refuse

tergo, si, sum see **tergĕo**

tergum, i *n*, back, rear, skin; **a tergo** (*adv. phr.*) at the rear

termĭnālĭa, ĭum *n.pl*, festival of Terminus (God of boundaries)

termĭnātĭo, ōnis *f*, fixing

termĭno *v.t.* 1, to limit, fix, define, determine, end

termĭnus, i *m*, boundary, end

terni, ae, a *pl. adj*, three each

tĕro, trīvi, trītum *v.t.* 3, to rub, grind, smooth, polish, wear out, spend or waste time

terra, ae *f*, earth, land, ground, region

terrēnus, a, um *adj*, made of earth, terrestrial

terrĕo *v.t.* 2, to frighten

terrestris, e *adj*, of earth or land

terrĕus, a, um *adj*, of earth or land

terrĭbĭlis, e *adj*, dreadful

terrĭcŭla, ōrum *n.pl*, scarecrow bugbear

terrĭfĭco *v.t.* 1, to terrify

terrĭfĭcus, a, um *adj*, frightful

terrĭgĕna, ae *c*, earthborn

terrĭto *v.t.* 1, to terrify

terror, ōris *m*, terror, dread

tertĭus, a, um *adj, adv*, **ō**, third

tĕruncĭus, ii *m*, trifling sum

tessellātus, a, um *adj*, tesselated, mosaic

tessĕra, ae *f*, stone or wooden cube, die, watchword, ticket

testa, ae *f*, jug, broken piece of pottery, shell-fish

testāmentum, i *n*, will, testament

testātor, ōris *m*, testator

testātus, a, um *adj*, manifest

testĭfĭcātĭo, ōnis *f*, evidence

testĭfĭcor *v.t.* 1, *dep*, to give evidence, demonstrate

testĭmōnĭum, ii *n*, evidence

testis, is *c*, witness

testor *v.t.* 1, *dep*, to call a witness, prove, declare

testu(m), i *n*, lid, earthen pot

testūdĭnĕus, a, um *adj*, of a tortoise

testūdo, ĭnis *f*, tortoise, lute, military shelter

tètānus, i *m*, tetanus

tēter, tra, trum *adj*, hideous

tètrarches, ae *m*, petty princeling

tètrĭcus, a, um *adj*, harsh

texo, ŭi, xtum *v.t.* 3, to weave, build, devise

textĭle, is *n*, fabric

textĭlis, e *adj*, woven

textor, ōris *m*, weaver

textum, i *n*, web, fabric

textus, ūs *m*, texture

thălămus, i *m*, apartment, bedroom, marriage

thĕātrālis, e *adj*, theatrical

thĕātrum, i *n*, theatre

thēca, ae *f*, envelope

thĕŏlŏgĭa, ae *f*, theology

thĕŏlŏgus, i *m*, theologian

thĕōrēma, ătis *n*, theorem

thermae, ārum *f.pl*, warm baths

thēsaurus, i *m*, store, hoard, treasure, treasure house

thĭăsus, i *m*, dance in honour of Bacchus

thŏlus, i *m*, dome

thōrax, ācis *m*, breastplate

thunnus, i *m*, tunny fish

thūs, thūris *n*, incense

thymbra, ae *f*, savory (plant)

thȳmum, i *n*, thyme

thyrsus, i *m*, stem of plant, staff carried by Bacchus

tīāra, ae *f*, tiara

tībĭa, ae *f*, flute

tībĭāle, is *n*, stocking

tībīcen, ĭnis *m*, flute-player

tībīcĭna, ae *f*, flute-player

tībĭcĭnĭum, ii *n*, flute-playing

tignum, i *n*, timber, log

tĭgris, is (ĭdis) *c*, tiger

tīlĭa, ae *f*, linden or lime tree

tĭmĕo *v.i.t.* 2, to fear

tĭmĭdĭtas, ātis *f*, cowardice

tĭmĭdus, a, um *adj, adv*, **ē**, afraid, cowardly

tĭmor, ōris *m*, fear, alarm, object of fear

tĭnĕa, ae *f*, moth, bookworm

tingo, nxi, nctum *v.t.* 3, to moisten, dye

tinnĭo *v.i.t.* 4, to ring; tinkle
tinnītus, ūs *m,* ringing
tinnŭlus, a, um *adj,* tinkling
tintinnābŭlum, i *n,* bell
tīro, ōnis *m,* recruit, novice
tīrōcĭnĭum, ii *n,* first campaign, inexperience
tītillātĭo, ōnis *f,* tickling
tītillo *v.t.* 1, to tickle
tītŭbo *v.i.* 1, to stagger, hesitate, be perplexed
tītŭlus, i *m,* title, placard, notice, honour, glory
tōfus, i *m,* tufa (rock)
tŏga, ae *f,* toga the long outer garment of the Romans
tŏgātus, a, um *adj,* wearing the toga
tŏlĕrābĭlis, e *adj,* endurable
tŏlĕrantĭa, ae *f,* tolerance
tŏlĕro *v.t.* 1, to bear, endure
tollēno, ōnis *m,* a swing-beam
tollo, sustŭli, sublātum *v.t.* 3, to lift, raise, remove, destroy, educate, acknowledge
tŏnans, ntis *m,* god of thunder
tondĕo, tŏtondi, tonsum *v.t.* 2, to shave, crop, prune, graze
tŏnĭtrus, ūs *m,* thunder
tŏnĭtrŭum, i *n,* thunder
tŏno, ŭi *v.i.t.* 1, to thunder; thunder out
tonsa, ae *f,* oar
tonsillae, ārum *f.pl,* tonsils
tonsor, ōris *m,* barber
tonsōrĭus, a, um *adj,* of shaving
tonsūra, ae *f,* shearing
tŏpĭārĭus, ii *m,* landscape gardener
tŏreuma, ătis *n,* embossed work
tormentum, i *n,* missile, rope, missile-launcher, instrument of torture, rack, pain
tormĭna, um *n.pl,* the gripes
torno *v.t.* 1, to round off
tornus, i *m,* lathe
tŏrōsus, a, um, *adj,* muscular
torpĕfăcĭo, fēci, factum *v.t.* 3, to numb
torpens, ntis *adj,* numb
torpĕo *v.i.* 2, to be stiff, numb, sluggish, listless
torpesco, pŭi *v.i.* 3, to become stiff or listless

torpor, ōris *m,* numbness
torquātus, a, um *adj,* wearing a collar
torquĕo, torsi, sum *v.t.* 2, to twist, bend, wield, hurl, rack, torture
torquis (torques), is *m, f,* collar, necklace, wreath
torrens, ntis *adj,* burning
torrens, ntis *m,* torrent
torrĕo, ŭi, tostum *v.t.* 2, to dry, bake, scorch, burn
torrĭdus, a, um *adj,* parched
torris, is *m,* firebrand
tortĭlis, e *adj,* twined
tortor, ōris *m,* torturer
tortŭōsus, a, um *adj,* winding, complicated
tortus, a, um *adj,* twisted
tortus, ūs *m,* twisting
tŏrus, i *m,* muscle, knot, cushion, sofa, bed
torvus, a, um *adj,* wild, grim
tŏt *indecl. adj,* so many
tŏtĭdem *indecl. adj,* just as many
tŏtĭens (tŏtĭes) *adv,* so often
tōtum, i *n,* whole
tōtus, a, um *adj,* the whole
trăbālis, e *adj,* of a beam
trăbĕa, ae *f,* robe of state
trabs, trăbis *f,* beam, timber, tree, ship
tractābĭlis, e *adj,* manageable, pliant, flexible
tractātĭo, ōnis *f,* handling, treatment
tractātus, ūs *m,* handling, treatment
tractim *adv,* little by little
tracto *v.t.* 1, to handle, manage, practise, discuss, drag
tractus, ūs *m,* dragging, track, district, course, progress
trādĭtĭo, ōnis *f,* surrender
trādo, dĭdi, dĭtum *v.t.* 3, to hand over, commit, bequeath, relate
trādūco, xi, ctum *v.t.* 3, to bring over, degrade, spend (time)
trāductĭo, ōnis *f,* transferring
trăgĭcus, a, um *adj,* tragic, fearful, grand
trăgoedĭa, ae *f,* tragedy
trăgoedus, i *m,* tragic actor

trāgŭla, ae *f,* javelin, dart

trăhĕa, ae *f,* sledge

trăho, xi, ctum *v.t.* 3, to drag, extract, inhale, quaff, drag away, plunder, spin, influence, delay, protract

trāĭcĭo, iēci, iectum *v.t.* 3, to throw across, transport, transfix

trāiectĭo, ōnis *f,* crossing over, passage

trāiectus, ūs *m,* crossing

trāmĕs, ĭtis *m,* footpath, way

trāno *v.t.* 1, to swim across

tranquillĭtas, ātis *f,* calmness

tranquillo *v.t.* 1, to calm

tranquillum, i *n,* a calm

tranquillus, a, um *adj, adv,* **ē,** calm, placid, serene

trans *prep. with acc,* across, beyond, on the further side of

transăbĕo *v.t.* 4, to transfix

transădĭgo, ēgi, actum *v.t.* 3, to thrust through

transalpīnus, a, um *adj,* beyond the Alps

transcendo, si, sum *v.i.t.* 3, to climb over, surmount; exceed

transcrībo, psi, ptum *v.t.* 3, to transcribe, forge, transfer

transcurro, curri, cursum *v.i.t.* 3, to run across; pass through

transĕo *v.i.t.* 4, to go over or across, pass by, surpass

transfĕro, ferre, tŭli, lātum *v.t, irreg,* to bring across, carry along, transfer, translate

transfīgo, xi, xum *v.t.* 3, to pierce through

transfŏdĭo, fōdi, fossum *v.t.* 3, to pierce through

transformo *v.t.* 1, to transform

transfŭga, ae *c,* deserter

transfŭgĭo, fūgi *v.t.* 3, to desert

transfundo, fūdi, fūsum *v.t.* 3, to transfer

transgrĕdĭor, gressus *v.i.t.* 3, *dep,* to pass or climb over, across

transgressĭo, ōnis *f,* passage

transĭgo, ēgi, actum *v.t.* 3, to complete, transact, settle (a difference)

transĭlĭo, ŭi *v.i.t.* 4, to leap across

transĭtĭo, ōnis *f,* going over, passage

transĭtus, ūs *m,* going over, passage

translātĭcĭus, a, um *adj,* handed down

translātĭo, ōnis *f,* transferring

translātus, a, um *adj,* transferred, copied, figurative

translūcĕo *v.i.* 2, to shine through

transmărīnus, a, um *adj,* across to sea

transmìgro *v.i.* 1, to migrate

transmissus, ūs *m,* transferring

transmitto, mīsi, missum *v.i.t.* 3, to go across; send across, transfer, hand over

transmūto *v.t.* 1, to change

transnăto *v.i.* 1, to swim over

transpădānus, a, um *adj,* beyond the river Po

transporto *v.t.* 1, to carry across

transtrum, i *n,* rowing-bench

transvĕho, xi, ctum *v.t.* 3, to carry over

transverbĕro *v.t.* 1, to transfix

transversārĭus, a, um *adj,* crosswise

transversus, a, um *adj,* crosswise

transvŏlo *v.i.t.* 1, to fly across

trĕcēni, ae, a *pl. adj,* three hundred each

trecentensīmus, a, um *adj,* three hundredth

trĕcenti, ae, a *pl, adj,* three hundred

trēdĕcim *indecl. adj,* thirteen

trĕmĕbundus, a, um *adj,* trembling

trĕmĕfăcĭo, fēci, factum *v.t.* 3, to cause to tremble

trĕmendus, a, um *adj,* dreadful

trĕmesco *v.i.t.* 3, to tremble; tremble at

trĕmo, ŭi *v.i.t.* 3, to tremble; tremble at

trĕmor, ōris *m,* shuddering

trĕmŭlus, a, um *adj,* trembling

trĕpĭdans, ntis *adj,* trembling

trĕpĭdātĭo, ōnis *f,* confusion

trĕpĭdo *v.i.t.* 1, to be alarmed; tremble at

trĕpĭdus, a, um   *adj*, alarmed
trēs, trĭa   *adj*, three

trĭfaux, cis   *adj*, with three throats
trĭdĭdus, a, um   *adj*, three-forked

Insight

The **accusative** is the usual case of a direct object. Many prepositions take the accusative; in that case the meaning of the accusative depends on the preposition. The accusative case is also used to express time throughout (tres dies = for three days) and the extent of space and its measurement (*tria milia passum* = for three miles).

trĭangŭlum, i   *n*, triangle
trĭangŭlus, a, um   *adj*, triangular
trĭārĭī, ōrum   *m.pl*, veteran soldiers who fought in the third rank
trĭbŭārĭus, a, um   *adj*, of a tribe
trĭbŭlis, e   *adj*, of the same tribe
trĭbŭlum, i   *n*, threshing-platform
trĭbŭlus, i   *m*, thistle
trĭbūnal, ālis   *n*, platform, judgement seat
trĭbūnātus, ūs   *m*, position of tribune
trĭbūnĭcĭus, a, um   *adj*, of a tribune
trĭbūnus, i   *m*, tribune; 1. army officer; 2. magistrate to defend to defend the rights of the people
trĭbŭo, ŭi, ūtum   *v.t.* 3, to allot, give, attribute
trĭbus, ūs   *f*, tribe
trĭbus   see **trēs**
trĭbūtim   *adv*, by tribes
trĭbūtum, i   *n*, tribute, tax
trīcae, ārum   *f. pl*, tricks
trīcēni, ae, a   *pl. adj*, thirty each
trĭceps, cĭpĭtis   *adj*, three-headed
trĭcēsĭmus, a, um   *adj*, thirtieth
trĭcĭes   *adv*, thirty times
trĭclīnĭum, i   *n*, dining-couch, dining-room
trĭcorpor, ŏris   *adj*, three-bodied
trĭdens, ntis   *adj*, three-pronged; as *nn*, trident
trīdŭum, i   *n*, three days
trĭennĭum, i   *n*, three years
trĭens, ntis   *m*, a third part
trĭĕtērĭca, ōrum   *n.pl*, festival of Bacchus

trĭfŏlĭum, i   *n*, shamrock
trĭformis, e   *adj*, three-fold
trĭgĕmĭnus, a, um   *adj*, triple
trĭgēsĭmus, a, um   *adj*, thirtieth
trĭginta   *indecl. adj*, thirty
trĭgōn, ōnis   *m*, ball
trĭlībris, e   *adj*, weighing three pounds
trĭlinguis, e   *adj*, three-tongued
trĭlix, īcis   *adj*, with three thongs
trĭmestris, e   *adj*, of three months
trĭmus, a, um   *adj*, three years old
trīni, ae, a   *pl. adj*, three each
trĭnōdis, e   *adj*, three-knotted
trĭones, um   *m.pl*, constellation of the Great and Lesser Bear
trĭpertītus, a, um   *adj, adv*, **ō**, threefold
trĭpēs, ĕdis   *adj*, three-footed
trĭplex, ĭcis   *adj*, triple
trĭplīco   *v.t.* 1, to treble
trĭpŭdĭum, ii   *n*, religious dance, favourable omen
trĭpūs, ŏdis   *m*, tripod
trĭquètrus, a, um   *adj*, triangular
trĭrēmis, e   *adj*, with three banks of oars
tristis, e   *adj*, sad, gloomy, harsh, disagreeable
tristītĭa, ae   *f*, sadness, gloominess, harshness
trĭsulcus, a, um   *adj*, three-forked
trĭtĭcĕus, a, um   *adj*, of wheat
trĭtĭcum, i   *n*, wheat
trītūra, ae   *f*, threshing (of grain)
trītus, a, um   *adj*, beaten, common, worn, familiar
trĭumphālis, e   *adj*, triumphal

triumpho *v.i.t.* 1, to celebrate a triumph; triumph over

triumphus, i *m*, triumphal procession after a victory

triumvirātus, ūs *m*, triumvirate

triumviri, ōrum *m.pl*, board of three men

trivium, ii *n*, crossroad

trŏchaeus, i *m*, metrical foot

trochlĕa, ae *f*, pulley

trŏchus, i *m*, hoop

trŏpaeum, i *n*, trophy, victory

trŏpĭcus, a, um *adj*, tropical

trūcīdātĭo, ōnis *f*, butchery

trūcīdo *v.t.* 1, to slaughter

trūcŭlentus, a, um *adj*, harsh

trūdis, is *f*, pole, pike

trūdo, si, sum *v.t.* 3, to push, drive, put out

trulla, ae *f*, ladle

truncātus, a, um *adj*, maimed

trunco *v.t.* 1, to maim, cut off

truncus, a, um *adj*, maimed

truncus, i *m*, trunk, stem

trŭtĭna, ae *f*, pair of scales

trux, ŭcis *adj*, harsh, stern

tū *pron*, you (singular)

tŭba, ae *f*, trumpet

tŭber, ĕris *n*, swelling, tumour

tŭbĭcen, ĭnis *m*, trumpeter

tŭbŭlātus, a, um *adj*, tubular

tŭbŭlus, i *m*, tube

tŭĕor *v.t.* 2, *dep*, to look at, gaze at, consider, guard, maintain, support

tŭgŭrĭum, i *n*, cottage

tŭli see **fero**

tum *adv, and conj*, then

tŭmĕfăcĭo, fēci, factum *v.t.* 3, to cause to swell

tŭmĕo *v.i.* 2, to swell, be puffed up

tŭmesco, mui *v.i.* 3, to become swollen, be puffed up

tŭmĭdus, a, um *adj*, swollen, excited, enraged

tŭmor, ōris *m*, swelling, commotion

tŭmŭlo *v.t.* 1, to bury

tŭmultŭārĭus, a, um *adj*, hurried, hurriedly raised (troops)

tŭmultŭor *v.i.* 1, *dep*, to be confused

tŭmultŭōsus, a, um *adj, adv, ē*, restless, confused, turbulent

tŭmultus, ūs *m*, uproar, tempest, rebellion

tŭmŭlus, i *m*, hill, mound

tunc *adv*, then

tundo, tŭtŭdi, tunsum (tusum) *v.t.* 3, to beat, strike, pound

tŭnĭca, ae *f*, tunic, husk

tŭnĭcātus, a, um *adj*, dressed in a tunic

tŭnĭcopallĭum, i *n*, short cloak

tūrārĭus, ii *m*, a dealer

turba, ae *f*, hubbub, uproar, crowd, band, quarrel, confusion

turbātor, ōris *m*, disturber

turbātus, a, um *adj*, disturbed

turbĭdus, a, um *adj, adv, ē*, confused, troubled, violent

turbo *v.t.* 1, to confuse, disturb, make thick

turbo, ĭnis *m*, hurricane, spinning top, revolution

turbŭlentus, a, um *adj, adv, nter*, restless, boisterous, troublesome

turdus, i *m*, thrush

tūrĕus, a, um *adj*, of incense

turgĕo, rsi *v.i.* 2, to swell

turgesco *v.i.* 3, to swell up

turgĭdŭlus, a, um *adj*, swollen

turgĭdus, a, um *adj*, swollen

tūrĭbŭlum, i *n*, incense-vessel

tūrĭcrĕmus, a, um *adj*, for burning incense

tūrĭfer, ĕra, ĕrum *adj*, incense-producing

turma, ae *f*, cavalry troop, crowd

turmālis, e *adj*, of a squadron

turmātim *adv*, by squadrons

turpis, e *adj, adv, ĭter*, filthy, ugly, disgraceful, scandalous

turpĭtūdo, ĭnis *f*, disgrace, baseness

turbo *v.t.* 1, to pollute, soil

turrĭger, ĕra, ĕrum *adj*, turreted

turris, is *f*, tower

turrītus, a, um *adj*, turreted

turtur, ŭris *m*, turtle-dove

tūs, tūris *n*, incense

tussĭo *v.i.* 4, to cough

tussis, is *f*, cough

tūtāmen, ĭnis *n*, defence

tūtēla, ae *f*, safeguard, defence, position of guardian, object under guardianship

tūtō   *adv*, safely
tūtor ōris   *m*, guardian
tūtor   *v.t.* 1, *dep*, to guard, watch
tūtus, a, um   *adj*, safe, prudent
tŭus, a, um   *adj*, your(s)
tympănum, i   *n*, tambourine, door panel
tӯrannĭcus, a, um   *adj*, tyrannical
tӯrannis, ĭdis   *f*, despotic rule
tӯrannus, i   *m*, sovereign, ruler, despot

U

ūber, ĕris   *n*, teat, udder, breast
ūber, ĕris   *adj*, fertile, rich
ūbertas, ātis   *f*, fertility, richness
ŭbĭ   *adv*, where, when, as soon as
ŭbĭcumque   *adv*, wherever
ŭbīque   *adv*, everywhere, anywhere
ŭbĭvīs   *adv*, everywhere, anywhere
ūdus, a, um   *adj*, moist, wet
ulcĕrātĭo, ōnis   *f*, ulceration
ulcĕro   *v.t.* 1, to make sore
ulcĕrōsus, a, um   *adj*, ulcerous
ulciscor, ultus   *v.t.* 3, *dep*, to avenge, punish, take vengeance on
ulcus, ĕris   *n*, sore, ulcer
ulex, ĭcis   *m*, furze
ūlīgĭnōsus, a, um   *adj*, moist, marshy
ūlīgo, ĭnis   *f*, moisture
ullus, a, um   *adj*, (*genit*, **ullīus**, *dat*, **ullī**), any
ulmĕus, a, um   *adj*, of elm
ulmus, i   *f*, elm tree
ulna, ae   *f*, elbow, arm, ell
ultĕrĭor, ĭus   *comp. adj*, beyond, on the farther side
ultĕrĭus   *comp. adv*, beyond, farther
ultĭmus, a, um   *sup. adj*, farthest, extreme, last
ultĭo, ōnis   *f*, revenge
ultor, ōris   *m*, avenger
ultrā   *adv, and prep. with acc*, beyond, past, farther, besides
ultrix, īcis   *adj*, avenging
ultrō   *adv*, on the other side, moreover, spontaneously

ūlŭla, ae   *f*, screech owl
ŭlŭlātus, ūs   *m*, wailing
ŭlŭlo   *v.i.t.* 1, to howl; cry out to
ulva, ae   *f*, sedge
umbella, ae   *f*, parasol
umbīlĭcus, i   *m*, navel, centre, end of rod on which Roman books were rolled
umbo, ōnis   *m*, shield, knob
umbra, ae   *f*, shadow, shade, ghost, trace, shelter
umbrācŭlum, i   *n*, shady spot, school
umbrātĭlis, e   *adj*, private, retired
umbrĭfer, ĕra, ĕrum   *adj*, shady
umbro   *v.t.* 1, to shade, cover
umbrōsus, a, um   *adj*, shady
ūmecto   *v.t.* 1, to moisten
ūmĕo   *v.i.* 2, to be damp
ūmĕrus, i   *m*, shoulder, arm
ūmesco   *v.i.* 3, to grow wet
ūmĭdus, a, um   *adj*, wet, damp
ūmor, ōris   *m*, moisture, liquid
umquam   *adv*, ever
ūnā   *adv*, at the same time, in the same place, together
ūnănĭmus, a, um   *adj*, of one mind
ūnănĭmĭtas, ātis   *f*, unanimity
uncĭa, ae   *f*, a twelfth, ounce
unctĭo, ōnis   *f*, anointing
unctus, a, um   *adj*, oiled, rich, luxurious
uncus, i   *m*, hook
uncus, a, um   *adj*, hooked
unda, ae   *f*, wave, tide
undĕ   *adv*, from where, whence
undē ...   (with number)   one from
... e.g. **undēvigint i** (one from 20) 19
undĕcĭes   *adv*, eleven times
undĕcĭm   *indecl. adj*, eleven
undĕcĭmus, a, um   *adj*, eleventh
undēni, ae, a   *pl. adj*, eleven each
undīquĕ   *adv*, from all sides, everywhere
undo   *v.i.* 1, to surge, undulate
undōsus, a, um   *adj*, billowy
ungo (unguo), unxi, unctum   *v.t.* 3, to besmear, oil
unguen, ĭnis   *n*, ointment
unguentārĭus, ii   *m*, perfume seller
unguentum, i   *n*, ointment, perfume

unguis, is *m,* finger or toe nail
ungŭla, ae *f,* hoof, claw
ungo (3) see **ungo**
ūnĭcŏlor, ōris *adj,* of one colour
ūnĭcus, a, um *adj, adv,* ē, only, single, singular, unique
ūnĭo, ōnis *m, f,* unity
ūnĭversĭtas, ātis *f,* universe
ūnĭversum, i *n,* whole world
ūnĭversus, a, um *adj, adv,* ē, entire, all together
unquam *adv,* ever
ūnus, a, um *adj,* one, one only

urna, ae *f,* water-jar, urn (for voting tablets or ashes of the dead)
ūro, ussi, ustum *v.t.* 3, to burn, destroy by fire, scorch, nip with cold
ursa, ae *f,* she-bear
ursus, i *m,* bear
urtĭcă, ae *f,* nettle
ūrus, i *m,* wild fox
ūsĭtātus, a, um *adj,* usual
uspĭam *adv,* anywhere, somewhere

Insight

Cardinal **numbers** (4 to 100) do not decline except *unus* (= one), *duo* (= two) and *tres* (= three) which have their own declensions; numbers 200 to 900 decline like first-and-second-declension plural adjectives. *Mille* (= 1,000) does not decline but *milia* is a third declension noun. Ordinals decline like first-and-second-declension adjectives.

ūnusquisque *pron.* each
ūpĭlĭo, ōnis *m,* shepherd
urbānĭtas, ātis *f,* city life, elegance, courtesy, refinement
urbānus, a, um *adj, adv,* ē, of the city, refined, elegant, courteous, humorous
urbs, urbis *f,* city
urcĕus, i *m,* water jug
urgĕo, ursi *v.t.* 2, to press, push, oppress, urge, crowd
ūrīna, ae *f,* urine
ūrīnātor, ōris *m,* diver

usquam *adv,* anywhere
usquĕ *adv,* all the way, all the time, as far as, until
ustor, ōris *m,* corpse-burner
ūsūra, ae *f,* money-lending, interest
ūsurpātĭo, ōnis *f,* using, use
ūsurpo *v.t.* 1, to use, practise, exercise, acquire
ūsus, ūs *m,* using, use, practice, custom, habit, familiarity, advantage
ut (ŭti) *conj,* as, so that, that, in order to, to; *adv,* now as, when, as soon as; where

Insight

The conjunction **ut** can be used in several senses: *ut + indicative* means 'as', 'when'; *ut + subjunctive* is used in indirect commands, as a result (e.g. so...that) or as a purpose (e.g. in order to...). *Ut* (= *as*) can also be used to qualify a noun.

V

utcumquĕ (utcunquĕ) *adv*, in whatever way, however, whenever

ūter, tris *m*, bottle, bag

ŭter, tra, trum *interr. pron*, which of the two

ŭtercumquĕ, utrăcumque, utrumcumque *pron*, whichever of the two

ŭterlībet, utrălībet, utrumlībet *pron*, which of the two you please

ŭterque, utrăque, utrumque *pron*, each of the two, both

ŭtĕrus, i *m*, womb, belly

ŭtervīs, utrăvīs, utrumvīs *pron*, which of the two you please

ŭti see **ut**

ūti see **ūtor**

ūtĭlis, e *adj, adv*, **ĭter**, useful, suitable, advantageous

ūtĭlĭtas, ātis *f*, usefulness, advantage

ŭtĭnam *adv*, if only ! would that!

ūtĭquĕ *adv*, at any rate, at least, certainly

ūtor, ūsus *v*. 3, *dep, with abl*, to use, practise, be familiar with

văcans, ntis *adj*, unoccupied

văcātĭo, ōnis *f*, exemption

vacca, ae *f*, cow

vaccīnĭum, ii *n*, whortleberry

văcillātĭo, ōnis *f*, vacillation

văcillo *v.i.* 1, to stagger, sway, hesitate

văco *v.i.* 1, to be empty, free from, have leisure (for)

văcŭēfăcĭo, fēci, factum *v.t.* 3, to empty, clear

văcŭĭtas, ātis *f*, exemption

văcŭus, a, um *adj*, empty, free, without, unoccupied, worthless

vădīmōnĭum, i *n*, bail, security

vādo *v.i.* 3, to go, walk, rush

vădor *v.t.* 1, *dep*, to bind over by bail

vădōsus, a, um *adj*, shallow

vădum, i *n*, a shallow ford (*often in pl.*)

vae *interj*, ah! alas!

văfer, fra, frum *adj*, sly

văgātĭo, ōnis *f*, wandering

vāgīna, ae *f*, sheath, scabbard

vāgĭo, *v.i.* 4, to cry, bawl

Insight

In Latin the form of a verb can be active, passive or deponent. **Deponent verbs** are those verbs which are passive in form but active in meaning (e.g. *utor* = I use).

Semi-deponent verbs take active forms in the present, future and imperfect tenses, but deponent forms in the perfect, future perfect and pluperfect.

---

utpŏtĕ *adv*, namely, as, since

ùtrimquĕ *adv*, on both sides

ùtrŏbīquĕ (ùtrŭbīquĕ) *adv*, on both sides

ùtrōquĕ *adv*, in both directions

ùtrum *adv, used to form an alternative question*, is it this ... or that?

ūva, ae *f*, grape, cluster

ūbĭdus, a, um *adj*, moist, damp

uxor, ōris *f*, wife

uxōrĭus, a, um *adj*, of a wife

vāgītus, ūs *m*, crying, bawling

văgor *v.i.* 1, *dep*, to wander, roam

văgus, a, um *adj*, wandering, roaming, uncertain, vague

valdē *adv*, energetically, very much, very

văle *imperative* (*pl*, **vălēte**), farewell!

vălens, ntis *adj*, powerful, strong, healthy

vălĕo *v.i.* 2, to be strong, vigorous or healthy, to have power or influence, to be capable or effective, be worth

vălesco *v.i.* 3, to grow strong

vălētūdĭnārĭum, ii *n*, hospital

vălētūdĭnārĭus, i *m*, invalid

vălētūdo, ĭnis *f*, health (good or bad)

vălĭdus, a, um *adj*, strong, powerful, healthy

valles (vallis), is *f*, valley

vallo *v.t.* 1, to fortify with rampart, protect

vallum, i *n*, rampart, palisade

vallus, i *m*, stake, palisade

valvae, ārum *f.pl*, folding doors

vānesco *v.i.* 3, to disappear

vānĭtas, ātis *f*, emptiness, uselessness, vanity

vannus, i *f*, fan

vānus, a, um *adj*, empty, groundless, false, deceptive

văpĭdus, a, um *adj*, spoiled, flat

văpor, ōris *m*, steam, vapour

văpōro *v.t.* 1, to fumigate, warm

vappa, ae *f*, flat wine; *m*, a good-for-nothing

văpŭlo *v.i.* 1, to be flogged

vārĭco *v.i.* 1, to straddle

vărĭcōsus, a, um *adj*, varicose

vărĭĕtas, ātis *f*, variety

vārĭo *v.i.t.* 1, to vary; diversify, change

vărĭus, a, um *adj, adv*, ē, variegated, changing, varying

vărix, ĭcis *m, f*, varicose vein

vārus, a, um *adj*, knock-kneed

văs, vădis *m*, bail, security

vās, vāsis *n*, dish, utensil, military equipment

vāsārĭum, ii *n*, expense account

vascŭlārĭus, ii *m*, metal worker

vastātĭo, ōnis *f*, devastation

vastātor, ōris *m*, destroyer

vastĭtas, ātis *f*, desert, destruction, ruin

vasto *v.t.* 1, to devastate, destroy, leave vacant

vastus, a, um *adj*, deserted, desolate, rough, devastated, enormous, vast

vātes, is *c*, forecaster, poet

vātĭcĭnātĭo, ōnis *f*, prediction

vātĭcĭnātor, ōris *m*, prophet

vātĭcĭnor *v.i.t.* 1, *dep*, to predict

vătĭus, a, um *adj*, bow-legged

vĕ *conj*, or

vēcordĭa, ae *f*, folly, madness

vēcors, dis *adj*, foolish, mad

vectīgal, ālis *n*, tax, income

vectīgālis, e *adj* tax paying

vectis, is *m*, pole, bar, lever

vecto *v.t.* 1, to convey

vector, ōris *m*, carrier, traveller, passenger

vectōrĭus, a, um *adj*, for carrying

vectūra, ae *f*, transportation, fare

vectus, a, um *adj*, conveyed, carried

vĕgĕtus, a, um *adj*, lively

vēgrandis, e *adj*, small

vĕhĕmens, ntis *adj, adv*, nter, violent, powerful, strong

vĕhĭcŭlum, i *n*, vehicle

vĕho, si, ctum *v.t.* 3, to convey; *in passive, or with reflexive pron*, to ride, sail, go

vĕl *conj*, either, or, indeed

vēlāmen, ĭnis *n*, cover, garment

vēlāmentum, i *n*, olive branch

vēles, ĭtis *m*, light-armed soldier

vēlĭfer, ĕra, ĕrum *adj*, carrying sails

vēlĭfĭcātĭo, ōnis *f*, sailing

vēlĭfĭcor *v.i.* 1, *dep*, to sail, gain, procure

vēlĭvŏlus, a, um *adj*, sail-winged; (**măre**) dotted with ships

vellĭco *v.t.* 1, to nip, taunt

vello, vulsi, vulsum *v.t.* 3, to tear out, pluck off

vellus, ĕris *n*, fleece, hide

vēlo *v.t.* 1, to cover, wrap up

vēlōcĭtas, ātis *f*, speed

vēlox, ōcis *adj, adv*, ĭter, swift, fast, fleet

vēlum, i *n*, sail, covering

vĕlut *adj*, just as, like

vēna, ae *f*, vein, disposition

vēnābŭlum, i *n*, hunting spear

vēnālĭcĭum, ii *n*, slave-dealing

vēnālĭcĭus, ii *m*, slave-dealer

vēnālis, e *adj*, for sale, able to be bribed, corrupt

vēnālis, is *m*, slave for sale

vēnātĭcus, a, um *adj*, of hunting

vēnātĭo, ōnis *f*, hunting, a, hunt, combat of wild beasts

vēnātor, ōris *m*, hunter

vēnātrix, īcis *f*, huntress

vēnātus, ūs *m*, hunting

vendĭbĭlis, e *adj*, saleable

vendĭtātĭo, ōnis *f*, boasting

vendĭtĭo, ōnis *f*, sale

vendĭto *v.t.* 1, to try to sell

vendĭtor, ōris *m*, salesman

vendo, dĭdi, dĭtum *v.t.* 3, to sell, betray, praise

vĕnēfĭca, ae *f*, witch

vĕnēfĭcĭum, ii *n*, poisoning, magic

vĕnēfĭcus, a, um *adj*, poisonous, magic

vĕnēfĭcus, i *m*, poisoner, sorcerer

vĕnēnātus, a, um *adj*, poisonous

vĕnēnĭfer, ĕra, ĕrum *adj*, poisonous

vĕnēno *v.t.* 1, to poison, dye

vĕnēnum, i *n*, poison, magic charm, drug

vēnĕo, ii, ĭtum *v.i.* 4, to be sold

vĕnĕrābĭlis, e *adj*, worthy of respect

vĕnĕrābundus, a, um *adj*, devout

vĕnĕrātĭo, ōnis *f*, great respect

vĕnĕrĕus, a, um *adj*, venereal

vĕnĕror *v.t.* 1, *dep*, to worship, revere, honour, entreat

vĕnĭa, ae *f*, indulgence, mercy, permission, pardon

vĕnĭo, vēni, ventum *v.i.* 4, to come

vēnor *v.i.t.* 1, *dep*, to hunt

venter, tris *m*, belly

ventĭlo *v.t.* 1, to wave, fan

ventĭto *v.i.* 1, to keep coming

ventōsus, a, um *adj*, windy, swift, light, changeable, vain

ventrĭcŭlus, i *m*, ventricle

ventūrus *fut. partic. from* **vĕnĭo**

ventus, i *m*, wind

vēnūcŭla (uva) a preserving grape

vēnundo, dĕdi, dătum *v.t.* 1, to sell

vēnus, ūs *m*, **(vēnum, i,** *n*) sale

vĕnustas, ātis *f*, charm, beauty

vĕnustus, a, um *adj, adv,* ē, charming, graceful, beautiful

vèprēcŭla, ae *f*, small thorn-bush

vèpres, is *m*, thorn-bush

vēr, vēris *n*, spring

vēra see **vērus**

vērācĭtas, ātis *f*, veracity

vērax, ācis *adj*, true

verbēna, ae *f*, foliage, branches

verber, ĕris *n*, lash, whip, flogging, blow

verbĕrātĭo, ōnis *f*, punishment

verbĕro *v.t.* 1, to whip, strike

verbōsus, a, um *adj*, effusive

verbum, i *n*, word, language, conversation; **verba dare** to deceive

vērē *adj*, really, truly

vĕrēcundĭa, ae *f*, shyness

vĕrēcundor *v.i.* 1, *dep*, to be shy

vĕrēcundus, a, um *adj, adv,* ē, shy, modest

vĕrendus, a, um *adj*, venerable, terrible

vĕrĕor *v.i.t.* 2, *dep*, to fear, respect

verto *v.i.* 3, to turn, bend, lie, be situated

vērĭdĭcus, a, um *adj*, truthful

vērĭsĭmĭlis, e *adj*, probable

vērĭtas, ātis *f*, truth, reality

vermĭcŭlus, i *m*, worm, grub

vermĭnōsus, a, um *adj*, worm-eaten

vermis, is *m*, worm

verna, ae *c*, slave born in his master's house

vernācŭlus, a, um *adj*, domestic

vernĭlĭter *adj*, slavishly

verno *v.i.* 1, to flourish, bloom

vernus, a, um *adj*, of spring

vērō *adj*, in fact, certainly, but indeed, however

verres, is, *m*, pig

verro, verri, versum *v.t.* 3, to sweep, brush, impel, take away

verrūca, ae *f*, wart, blemish

versātĭlis, e *adj*, movable

versĭcŏlor, ŏris *adj*, of different colours

versĭcŭlus, i *m*, single line of verse (or prose)

verso *v.t.* 1, to turn, twist, whirl, consider

versor *v.i.* 1, *dep*, to live, stay, be situated, be engaged on

versūra, ae *f,* borrowing, loan

versus *adv,* towards

versus, ūs *m,* row, line, verse

versūtus, a, um *adj, adv, ē,* clever, shrewd, cunning, sly

vertèbra, ae *f,* vertebra

vertex, ĭcis *m,* whirlpool, whirlwind, flame, crown of the head, summit, peak

vertĭcōsus, a, um *adj,* eddying

vertĭgĭnōsus, a, um *adj,* suffering from giddiness

vertīgo, ĭnis *f,* dizziness

vēro see **vērus**

verto, ti, sum *v.i.t.* 3, to turn, change; turn, change, alter overthrow, translate

vĕru, ūs *n,* roasting-spit, javelin

vĕrūcŭlum, i *n,* skewer, small javelin

vērum *adv,* but, yet, still

vērum, i *n,* truth, reality, fact

vērumtămen *conj,* nevertheless

vērus, a, um *adj, adv, ō, ē,* true, real, proper, right

vĕrūtum, i *n,* javelin

vĕrūtus, a, um *adj,* armed with a javelin

vervex, ēcis *m,* wether, sheep

vēsānĭa, ae *f,* insanity

vēsănus, a, um *adj,* mad, fierce

vescor *v.i.t.* 3, *dep. with abl,* to feed on

vescus, a, um *adj,* thin, weak

vēsīca, ae *f,* bladder

vespa, ae *f,* wasp

vesper, ĕris (ĕri) *m,* evening, the West

vespĕra, ae *f,* evening, the West

vespĕrasco, āvi *v.i.* 3, to draw towards evening

vespertĭnus, a, um *adj,* of evening, western

vespillo, ōnis *m,* undertaker

vesta, ae *f,* fire

vestālis, e *adj,* of the Vesta, the Goddess of Fire, Hearth, Home

vestālis, is *f,* priestess of Vesta

vester, tra, trum *adj,* your

vestiārĭum, i *n,* wardrobe

vestībŭlum, i *n,* entrance hall

vestīgĭum, i *n,* footstep, track, sole of foot, mark, moment, instant; **ē, vestīgĭo** instantly

vestīgo *v.t.* 1, to search out, investigate

vestīmentum, i *n,* clothing

vestĭo *v.t.* 4, to clothe, cover

vestis, is *f,* clothing, clothes, carpet, curtain

vestītus, ūs *m,* clothes, dresss

vĕtĕrānus, a, um *adj,* old, veteran

vĕtĕrānus, i *m,* veteran soldier

vĕtĕrātor, ōris *m,* crafty, wily or sly person

vĕtĕrātōrĭus, a, um *adj,* sly

vĕtĕres, um *m.pl,* ancestors

vĕtĕrīnārĭus, a, um *adj,* veterinary

vĕternus, i *m,* sluggishness

vĕtĭtum, i *n,* something forbidden, prohibition

vĕtĭtus, a, um *adj,* forbidden

vĕto, ŭi, ĭtum *v.t.* 1, to forbid

vĕtŭlus, a, um *adj,* old

vĕtus, ĕris *adj,* old, former

vĕtustas, ātis *f,* old age, antiquity, posterity

vĕtustus, a, um *adj,* old

vexātĭo, ōnis *f,* distress

vexillārĭus, i *m,* standard-bearer

vexillum, i *n,* standard, ensign

vexo *v.t.* 1, to shake, injure, molest, harrass, torment

vĭa, ae *f,* road, street, way, method

vĭātĭcum, i *n,* travelling expenses, soldier's savings

vĭātor, ōris *m,* traveller

vībex, īcis *f,* weal

vĭbro *v.i.t* 1, to quiver; brandish, shake

vĭcārĭus, i *m,* deputy

vĭcēni, ae, a *pl. adj,* twenty each

vĭcēsĭmus (vĭcensĭmus), a, um *adj,* twentieth

vĭcĭa, ae *f,* vetch

vĭcĭes (vĭcĭens) *adv,* twenty times

vĭcīnĭa, ae *f,* neighbourhood

vĭcīnus, a, um *adj,* neighbouring, similar

vĭcīnus, a, um *adj,* neighbouring, similar

vĭcīnus, i *m,* neighbour

vĭcis *(genitive),* **vĭcem, vĭce** change, alternation, recompense, lot, misfortune, position, duty; **in vĭcem, per vĭces** alternately; **vĭcem, vĭce,** instead of

vĭcĭssim *adv*, in turn

vĭcissĭtūdo, ĭnis *f*, change

victĭma, ae *f*, victim for sacrifice

victor, ōris *m*, conqueror

victōrĭa, ae *f*, victory

victrix, īcis *f*, female conqueror

vĭtrix, īcis *adj*, victorious

victus, ūs *m*, nutriment, diet

vīcus, i *m*, street, village

vīdēlĭcet *adv*, obviously

vĭdĕo, vīdi, vīsum *v.t.* 2, to see, perceive, understand, consider, take care, see to it

vĭdĕor, vēsus *v.* 2, *dep*, to seem; *impers*, it seems right or good

vĭdŭa, ae *f*, widow

vĭdŭĭtas, ātis *f*, bereavement

vĭdŭlus, i *m*, valise

vĭdŭo *v.t.* 1, to deprive

vĭdŭus, a, um *adj*, robbed, widowed

vĭētus, a, um *adj*, withered

vĭgĕo *v.i.* 2, to flourish, thrive

vĭgesco, gŭi *v.i.* 3, to flourish, thrive

vĭgil, īlis *adj*, alert, watching

vĭgil, īlis *m*, watchman

vĭgĭlans, ntis *adj, adv,* **nter,** watchful, careful

vĭgĭlantĭa, ae *f*, watchfulness

vĭgĭlĭa, ae *f*, wakefulness, vigilance, guard, watch

vĭgĭlo *v.i.t.* 1, to keep awake, be vigilant; spend (time) in watching

vĭginti *indecl. adj*, twenty

vĭgor, ōris *m*, liveliness

vīlĭco *v.i.t.* 1, to superintend

vīlĭcus (villicus), i *m*, superintendent

vīlis, e *adj*, cheap, mean

vīlĭtas, ātis *f*, cheapness

villa, ae *f*, country house

villātĭcus, a, um *adj*, of a villa

villicus see **vīlicus**

villōsus, a, um *adj*, hairy, shaggy

villŭla, ae *f*, small villa

villus, i *m*, tuft of hair

vīmen, ĭnis *n*, pliant branch

Vīmĭnālis (collis) the Viminal, one of the seven hills of Rome

vīmĭnĕus, a, um *adj*, of wickerwork

vīnārĭum, ii *n*, wine bottle

vīnārĭus, a, um *adj*, of wine

vīnārĭus, i *m*, vintner

vincĭo, nxi, nctum *v.t.* 4, to bind, tie, surround

vinco, vīci, victum *v.i.t.* 3, to prevail; conquer, overcome, prove conclusively

vincŭlum (vinclum), i *n*, cord, bond fetter; *pl*, prison

vindēmĭa, ae *f*, grape-gathering, wine

vindēmĭātor, ōris *m*, grape-gatherer

vindex, īcis *c*, claimant, defender, liberator, avenger

vindĭcĭae, ārum *f.pl*, legal claim

vindĭco *v.t.* 1, to claim, appropriate, set free, protect, avenge

vindicta, ae *f*, rod used ot set free a slave

vīnĕa, ae *f*, vineyard, protective shed for soldiers

vīnētum, i *n*, vineyard

vīnĭtor, ōris *m*, vine-pruner

vīnŏlentĭa, ae *f*, wine-drinking

vīnŏlentus, a, um *adj*, drunk

vīnōsus, a, um *adj*, drunken

vīnum, i *n*, wine

vĭŏla, ae *f*, violet

vĭŏlābĭlĭs, e *adj*, able to be injured or harmed

vĭŏlārĭum, ii *n*, bed of violets

vĭŏlātĭo, ōnis *f*, violation, profanation

vĭŏlātor, ōris *m*, injurer

vĭŏlens, ntis *adj, adv,* **nter,** impetuous, furious

vĭŏlentĭa, ae *f*, ferocity

vĭŏlentus, a, um *adj*, violent, impetuous

vĭŏlo *v.t.* 1, to injure, outrage, break

vīpĕra, ae *f*, viper

vīpĕrĕus, a, um *adj*, of a viper or snake

vīpĕrīnus, a, um *adj*, of a viper or snake

vĭr, vĭri *m*, man, husband

vĭrāgo, ĭnis *f*, female soldier, heroine

vĭrectum, i *n*, glade, turf

vĭrĕo *v.i.* 2, to be green, flourish

vīres see **vis**

vīresco   *v.i.* 3, to become green, flourish

vĭrētum, i   *n*, glade, turf

virga, ae   *f*, twig, rod

virgātus, a, um   *adj*, striped

virgĕus, a, um   *adj*, made of rods

virgĭnālis, e   *adj*, girl-like

virgĭnĕus, a, um   *adj*, of a virgin

virgĭnĭtas, ātis   *f*, virginity

virgo, ĭnis   *f*, virgin girl

virgŭla, ae   *f*, small twig

virgultum, i   *n*, shrubbery

virgultus, a, um   *adj*, bushy

vĭrĭdārĭum, ii   *n*, park

vĭrĭdis, e   *adj*, green, fresh, young, blooming

vĭrĭdĭtas, ātis   *f*, greenness, freshness

vĭrĭdo   *v.i.t.* 1, to be green; make green

vĭrīlis, e   *adj*, male, manly, full-grown, vigorous

vĭrītim   *adj*, individually

vĭrōsus, a, um   *adj*, stinking

virtūs, ūtis   *f*, courage, manhood, military skill, goodness, moral perfection

vīrus, i   *n*, slime, poison, virus

vīs   (*no genit*), vim, vi   *f*, force, power, violence, quantity, meaning; vīres, ĭum   *pl*, strength, power

viscātus, a, um   *adj*, sprinkled with lime

viscĕra, um   *n.pl*, innards, flesh, bowels

viscum, i   *n*, mistletoe, birdlime

vīsĭo, ōnis   *f*, idea, notion

vīsĭto   *v.t.* 1, to visit

vīso, si, sum   *v.t.* 3, to survey, visit

vīsum, i   *n*, appearance, sight

vīsus, ūs   *m*, look, sight, appearance

vīta, ae   *f*, life

vītābĭlis, e   *adj*, to be avoided

vītālis, e   *adj*, of life, vital

vītātĭo, ōnis   *f*, avoidance

vītellus, i   *m*, small calf, egg yolk

vītĕus, a, um   *adj*, of the vine

vĭtĭo   *v.t.* 1, to spoil, mar, infect

vĭtĭōsĭtas, ātis   *f*, vice

vĭtĭōsus, a, um   *adj, adv*, ē, faulty, defective, wicked

vītis, is   *f*, vine, vine branch

vītĭsātor, ōris   *m*, vine planter

vĭtĭum, ii   *n*, fault, defect, blemish, error, crime

vīto   *v.t.* 1, to avoid

vĭtrĕus, a, um   *adj*, made of glass, transparent, shining

vĭtrīcus, i   *m*, step-father

vĭtrum, i   *n*, glass, woad

vitta, ae   *f*, hair-ribbon

vittātus, a, um   *adj*, bound with a hair-ribbon

vĭtŭlīnus, a, um   *adj*, of a calf

vĭtŭlus, i   *m* (vĭtŭla, ae,   *f*) calf

vĭtŭpĕrātĭo, ōnis   *f*, blame, censure

vĭtŭpĕro   *v.t.* 1, to blame, censure

vīvārĭum, ii   *n*, fishpond, game reserve

vīvācĭtas, ātis   *f*, vigour or length of life

vīvax, ācis   *adj*, long-lived

vīvĭdus, a, um   *adj*, lively, animated

vīvo, xi, ctum   *v.i.* 3, to live

vīvus, a, um   *adj*, alive, fresh, natural, life-like

vix   *adv*, scarcely, barely

vixdum   *adv*, scarcely then

vŏcābŭlum, i   *n*, name

vōcālis, e   *adj*, vocal

vŏcātu   *abl*, at the bidding

vōcĭfĕrātĭo, ōnis   *f*, outcry

vōcĭfĕror   *v.i.t.* 1, *dep*, to cry out

vŏcĭto   *v.i.t.* 1, to call out; name

vŏco   *v.i.t.* 1, to call; summon, urge, challenge, arouse, name

Insight

The **vocative** is the case used to indicate the person or thing addressed or called to in a speech (e.g. *Quinte, veni huc* = Quintus, come here!). It has the same endings as the nominative except in the second declension.

vōcŭla, ae *f*, feeble voice
vŏlantes, ĭum *c*, *pl*, birds
vŏlātĭcus, a, um *adj*, flighty, fleeting
vŏlātĭlis, e *adj*, flying, swift
vŏlātus, ūs *m*, flight
vŏlens, ntis *adj*, willing, favourable
volg... see **vulg...**
vŏlĭto *v.i.* 1, to fly about, flit, flutter
vŏlo, velle, vŏlŭi *v.i.t, irreg*, to wish, mean
vŏlo *v.i.* 1, to fly

vŏrāgo, ĭnis *f*, abyss, whirlpool
vŏrax, ācis *adj*, greedy, destructive
vŏro *v.t.* 1, to devour, destroy
vortex see **vertes**
vos *pron, pl*, you (*plural*)
vōtīvis, a, um *adj*, concerning a promise or vow
vōtum, i *n*, promise, vow, offering, wish, longing
vŏvĕo, vōvi, vōtum *v.t.* 2, to promise, vow, dedicate
vox, vōcis *f*, voice, sound, speech, saying, proverb

Insight

nolo (I do not want) and *malo* (I prefer) are based on the conjugation of *volo* (I want). *nolo* is a combination of *ne* + *volo*; *malo* is a combination of *magis* (more) + *volo*. All three verbs control an infinitive, as they do in English (e.g. I want to ...).

volp... see **vulp...**
volsella, ae *f*, tweezers
volt... see **vult...**
vŏlūbĭlis, e *adj*, turning, spinning, changeable
vŏlūbĭlĭtas, ātis *f*, whirling motion, fluency
vŏlŭcer, cris, cre *adj*, flying, swift, transient
vŏlūmen, ĭnis *n*, book, roll, fold
vŏluntārĭus, a, um *adj*, voluntary; (of soldiers) volunteers
vŏluntas, ātis *f*, wish, choice, will, affection, good-will
vŏluptārĭus, a, um *adj*, sensual
vŏluptas, ātis *f*, pleasure, delight
vŏlūto *v.i.t.* 1, to roll, twist, writhe about; ponder, consider
volva (vulva), ae *f*, womb
volvo, volvi, vŏlūtum *v.t.* 3, to roll, unroll, turn, ponder, consider
vōmer, ĕris *m*, ploughshare
vŏmĭca, ae *f*, abscess, boil
vŏmĭtĭo, ōnis *f*, vomiting
vŏmo, ŭi, ĭtum *v.i.t.* 3, to vomit; throw up, pour out

vulgāris, e *adj*, general, ordinary, common
vulgātor, ōris *m*, a gossip
vulgātus, a, um *adj*, ordinary, notorious
vulgo *v.t.* 1, to divulge, spread about
vulgō *v.t.* 1, to divulge, spread about
vulgō *adv*, everywhere, openly
vulgus, i *n*, the public, crowd, rabble
vulnĕrātus, a, um *adj*, wounded
vulnĕro *v.t.* 1, to wound, hurt
vulnĭfĭcus, a, um *adj*, wounding
vulnus, ĕris *n*, wound, blow
vulpēcŭla, ae *f*, small fox
vulpes, is *f*, fox
vulsus, a, um *adj*, hairless, effeminate
vultur, ŭris *m*, vulture
vultŭrĭus, ii *m*, vulture
vultus, ūs *m*, expression, look, features, aspect, face

X

xĭphĭas, ae   *m*, swordfish
xystus, i   *m*, **(systum, i**   *n*), open
  colonnade

Z

zĕphȳrus, i   *m*, west wind
zōdĭăcus, i   *m*, zodiac
zōna, ae   *f*, belt, girdle, zone

English–Latin dictionary

A

a, an (*indefinite article*), no equivalent in Latin

abandon *v.t*, rĕlinquo (3), dēsĕro (3)

abandoned dērĕlictus, dēsertus; **(person)**, perdĭtus

abandonment rĕlictĭo, *f*

abase *v.t*, dēprĭmo (3)

abasement hŭmĭlĭtas *f*, dēmĭssĭo, *f*

abash *v.t*, confundo (3), pertubo (1)

abashed pŭdōre confūsus **(perplexed with shame)**

abate *v.t*, immĭnŭo (3), rĕmitto (3)

abatement dēcessus *m*, dēcessĭo, *f*, dēmĭnūtĭo, *f*

abbot pontĭfex *m*, **(high priest)**, săcerdos, *c*

abbreviate *v.t*, immĭnŭo (3), contrăho (3)

abbreviation compendĭum *n*, contractĭo, *f*

abdicate *v.i*, se abdĭcare (1. *reflex*)

abdication abdĭcātĭo, *f*

abdomen venter, *m*, abdōmen, *n*

abduction raptus, *m*, raptĭo, *f*

abet *v.i*, adsum (*irreg. with dat. of person*), adiŭvo (1)

abettor mĭnister *m*, adiūtor, *m*

abeyance (to be in —) *v.i*, iăcĕo (2)

abhor ăbhorrĕo (2) (*with acc. or ab and abl*), ōdi. (*v. defect*)

abhorrence ŏdĭum, *n*

abide *v.i*, mănĕo (2), hăbĭto (1)

abide *v.t*, **(wait for)**, exspecto (1)

abiding *adj*, **(lasting)**, mansūrus

ability (mental —), ingĕnĭum, *n*; **(power)**, pŏtestas, *f*

abject abiectus, hŭmĭlis

abjectness hŭmĭlĭtas, *f*

abjure *v.t*, abiūro (1), ēiūro (1)

ablaze *adj*, flăgrans

able *use* possum **(be able)**, pŏtens

able (to be —) *v.i*, possum (*irreg*)

able-bodied vălĭdus

ablution lăvātĭo, *f*, ablūtĭo, *f*

ably *adv*, ingĕnĭōsē

abnegation nĕgātĭo, *f*, mŏdĕrātĭo, *f*

abnormal abnormis, ĭnūsĭtātus

aboard in nāve; **(to go —)**, *v.i*, nāvem conscendo (3); **(to put —)**, *v.t*, in nāvem impōno (3)

abode dŏmus, *f*, dŏmĭcĭlĭum, *n*, sēdes, *f*, hăbĭtātĭo, *f*

abolish *v.t*, tollo (3), ăbŏlĕo (2), dissolvo (3)

abolition dissŏlūtĭo, *f*, ăbŏlĭtĭo, *f*

abominable infandus, dētestābĭlis

abominate *v.t*, ōdī (*defect*), ăbhorrĕo (2)

abomination (hatred) ŏdĭum, *n*; **(crime)**, flāgĭtĭum, *n*

aborigines indĭgĕnae, *m.pl*

abortion ăbortus, *m*, ăbortĭo, *f*

abortive (unsuccessful) irrĭtus

abound (in) *v.i*, ăbundo (1), sŭpĕro (1), circumflŭo (3), suppĕdĭto (1)

abounding ăbundans, afflŭens, fēcundus

about *prep*, circā, circum, ăd, sŭb (*with acc*), dē (*with abl*); **(of time)**, circĭter (*with acc*)

about *adv*, **(nearly)**, circĭter, fermē, fĕrē

above *prep*, sŭper, sŭprā (*with acc*); **(more than)**, amplĭus

above *adv*, sŭprā, insŭper; **(from above)**, dēsŭper, sŭpernē

abrasion attrītus, *m*

abreast *adv*, părĭter

abridge *v.t*, contrăho (3)

abridgement ĕpĭtŏmē, *f*, ĕpĭtŏma, *f*

abroad *adv*, **(in a foreign country)**, pĕrĕgrē

abroad (to be —) *v.i*, pĕrĕgrīnor (1. *dep*)

abrogate *v.t*, abrŏgo (1); rescindo (3)

abrogation abrŏgātĭo, *f*

abrupt (sudden) sŭbĭtus; **(steep)**, praeruptus

abruptly *adv*, sŭbĭto, praerupte

abscess vŏmĭca, *f*

abscond *v.i*, lătĕo (2)

absence absentĭa, *f*

absent absens

absent (to be—) *v.i*, absum (*irreg*)

absinth absinthĭum, *n*

absolute absŏlūtus

absolute power tўrannis, *f,*
impĕrĭum, *n,* dŏmĭnātĭo, *f*

absolutely (completely) *adv,*
prorsum, prorsus

absolve *v.t,* absolvo (3), lībĕro
(1)

absorb *v.t,* bĭbo (3), haurĭo (4),
absorbĕo (2)

absorbent *adj,* bĭbŭlus

abstain *v.i,* abstĭnĕo (2)

abstemious tempĕrātus

abstinence abstĭnentĭa, *f*

abstinent abstĭnens, mŏdĕrātus

abstract *nn,* ĕpĭtŏme, *f*

abstract *adj,* abstractus

abstract *v.t,* abstrăho (3)

abstruse rĕcondĭtus, obscūrus

absurd ĭneptus, absurdus

absurdity ĭneptĭa, *f,* insulsĭtas, *f*

absurdly *adv,* ĭneptē, absurdē

abundance cōpĭa, *f,* ăbundantĭa,
f

abundant largus, fēcundus

abuse *nn,* **(insult),** contŭmelĭa

abuse *v.t,* mălĕdĭco (3); **(misuse),**
ăbūtor (*v. dep*)

abusive contŭmēlĭōsus

abut *v.i,* adĭăcĕo (2)

abutting adĭunctus

abyss gurges, *m,* vŏrāgo, *f*

acacia ăcācĭa, *f*

academic ăcădēmĭcus

academy ăcădēmĭa, *f*

accede *v.i,* consentĭo (4)

accelerate *v.t,* accĕlĕro (1)

accent vox, *f*

accentuate *v.t,* ăcŭo (3)

accentuation accentus, *m*

accept *v.t,* accĭpĭo (3), rĕcĭpĭo (3)

acceptability suāvĭtas, *f,* făcĭlĭtas,
f

acceptable grātus

acceptance acceptĭo, *f*

access (approach) ădĭtus, *m,*
accessus, *m*

accessible făcĭlis; **(to be —),** *v.i,*
pătĕo (3)

accession **(— to the throne)**
ĭnĭtĭum (*n*) regni **(beginning of
reign);** *or use phr. with* incipio **(to
begin)** *and* regno **(to reign)**

accessory (of crime) *adj,*
conscĭus; **(helper),** auctor, *m*

accident cāsus, *m*

accidental fortŭĭtus

accidentally *adv,* cāsū, fortē

acclaim *v.t,* clāmo (1)

acclamation clāmor, *m*

acclimatized assŭētus

accommodate *v.t,* accommŏdo
(1)

accommodating obsĕquens

accommodation (lodging)
hospĭtĭum, *n;* **(loan),** commŏdum,
n

accompaniment (musical) cantus,
m

accompany *v.t,* prōsĕquor (3
dep), cŏmĭtor (1 *dep*); **(— in
singing),** oblŏquor (3 *dep*

accomplice *adj,* conscĭus,
partĭceps

accomplish *v.t,* confĭcĭo (3)

accomplished (learned) ērŭdĭtus

accomplishment (completion)
confectĭo, *f*

accord (of my (your) own —) mĕā
(tŭā) spontĕ, ultrō

accord *v.t,* concēdo (3); *v.i,*
consentĭo (4)

accordance (in — with) *prep,* ex,
dē, prō (*with abl*)

according to *as above*

accordingly *adv,* ĭtăque

accost *v.t,* compello (1);
allŏquor (3 *dep*)

account *nn,* rătĭo, *f;* **(statement),**
mĕmŏrĭa, *f*

on account of *prep,* propter, ŏb
(*with acc*)

to render account for rătĭonem
reddo (3)

accountant calcŭlātor, *m,* scrība,
m

account-book tăbŭlae, *f.pl*

accoutre *v.t,* orno (1); armo (1)

accoutrements arma, *n.pl*

accredit *v.t,* **(establish),**
confirmio (1)

accrue *v.i,* accēdo (3)

accumulate *v.t,* cŭmŭlo (1),
cŏăcervo (1); *v.i,* cresco (3)

accumulation (bringing together)
collātĭo, *f*

accuracy (exactness) subtīlĭtas, *f;*
(carefulness), cūra, *f*

accurate (exact) subtīlĭs, vērus;
(careful), dīlĭgens
accursed exsēcrābĭlĭs
accusation crīmen, *n*, accūsātĭo, *f*
accuse *v.t*, accūso (1); arcesso
(3), nōmen dēfĕro (*v. irreg*)
accused person rĕus, *m*
accuser accūsātor, *m*, dēlātor, *m*
accustom *v.t*, assŭēfăcĭo (3)
to be accustomed *v.i*, sŏlĕo (2)
to become accustomed *v.i*,
assŭesco (3)
accustomed assŭētus, sŏlĭtus
ache *v.i*, dŏlĕo (2)
ache *nn*, dŏlor, *m*
achieve *v.t*. confĭcĭo (3), perfĭcĭo
(3)
achievement res gesta, *f*, făcĭnus,
n
acid *adj*, ăcerbus, ăcĭdus
acknowledge *v.t*, **(confess)**,
confĭtĕor (2 *dep*), agnosco (3);
(accept), tollo (3)
acknowledgement confessĭo, *f*
acme summa, *f*
aconite ăcŏnītum, *n*
acorn glans, *f*
acquaint *v.t*, certĭōrem făcĭo (3)
(*with acc. of person, and* dē *with
abl*)
to become acquainted with *v.t*,
nosco (3), cognosco (3)
acquaintance (knowledge of)
scĭentĭa, *f*; **(with a person)**,
consŭētūdo, *f*; **(a person)**, nōtus,
m
acquiesce *v.i*, acquĭesco (3)
acquire *v.t*, acquīro (3)
acquirement (obtaining) ădeptĭo, *f*
acquit *v.t*, absolvo (3), lībĕro (1)
acquittal absŏlūtĭo, *f*, lībĕrātĭo, *f*
acre iūgĕrum, *n*
acrid asper, ācer
acrimonious ăcerbus, asper,
ămārus
acrimony ăcerbĭtas, *f*
across *prep*, trans (*with acc*)
act *v.i*, ăgo (3), gĕro (3)
act *v.t*, **(a part in a play)**, ăgo (3)
act *nn*,factum, *n*; **(law)** lex, *f*
action (carrying out) actĭo, *f*,
actus, *m*, **(at law)** līs, *f*, **(battle)**,
proelĭum, *n*

active impĭger, ălăcer
actively impĭgrē
activity (energy) industrĭa, *f*;
(agility, mobility) ăgĭlĭtas, *f*
actor actor, *m*
actual vērus
actually *adv*, rē vērā
actuary actŭārĭus, *m*
actuate *v.t*, mŏvĕo (2), impello
(3)
acumen ăcūmen, *n*
acute ācer, ăcūtus
acuteness ăcĭes, *f*, ăcūmen, *n*
adage dictum, *n*
adapt *v.t*, accomŏdo (1),
compōno (3)
adapted accommŏdātus, aptus
add *v.t*, addo (3), adĭcĭo (3)
adder vīpĕra, *f*
addict *v.t*, dēdo (3) (*with dat*)
addicted dedĭtus
addition (numerical) *use verb*
addo (3); **(increase)** accessĭo, *f*
additional (more, new, fresh)
nŏvus
address *v.t*, **(a letter)**, inscrībo
(3); **(person)** allŏquor (3 *dep*)
address *nn*, **(letter)**, inscriptĭo, *f*;
(speaking) allŏquĭum, *n*
adduce *v.t*, prōdūco (3), prōfĕro
(*v. irreg*)
adept prītus
adequacy *use* sătis **(enough)**
(*with nn. in genit*)
adequate sătis (*with genit*)
adhere *v.i*, **(cling)** haerĕo (2)
adherent clĭens, *m*, sectātor, *m*
adhesive tĕnax
adjacency vīcīnĭtas, *f*
adjacent fīnĭtĭmus, vīcīnus,
contermĭnus
adjoin *v.i*, adiăcĕo (2)
adjoin *v.t*, adiungo (3)
adjoining coniunctus, contĭgŭus
adjourn *v.t*, differĭo (*v. irreg*)
adjournment dīlātĭo, *f*
adjudge (adjudicate) *v.t*, adiūdĭco
adjudication addictĭo, *f*
adjure *v.t*, obtestor (1 *dep*),
obsĕcro (1)
adjust *v.t*, apto (1), compōno (3)
adjustment compŏsĭtĭo, *f*
adjutant optĭo, *m*

administer *v.t*, admĭnistro (1)
administration admĭnistrātĭo, *f*,
 prōcūrātĭo, *f*
administrator procūrātor, *m*
admirable mīrābĭlis
admirably *adv*, praeclārē
admiral praefectus (*m*) classis
admiration admīrātĭo, *f*
admire *v.t*, admīror (1 *dep*),
 mīror (1 *dep*)
admirer laudātor, *m*
admissible, (letting in) ădĭtus,
 m; **(acknowledgement)** confessĭo, *f*
admit *v.t*, **(let in)** admitto (3);
 (grant) dō (1), concēdo (3);
 (confess) confĭtĕor (2 *dep*)
admonish *v.t*, mŏnĕo (2)
admonition admŏnĭtio, *f*
adolescence ădŏlescentĭa, *f*
adolescent ădŏlescens, *c*
adopt *v.t*, **(person)**, ădopto (1);
 (custom) ascisco (3)
adoption ădoptĭo, *f*
adorable cŏlendus
adoration cultus, *m*, ădōrātĭo, *f*
adore *v.t*, cŏlo (3), ădōro (1)
adorn *v.t*, orno (1)
adorned ornātus
adornment (as an act) exornātĭo,
 f; **(a decoration)** ornāmentum, *n*
adrift *adj*, in mări iactātus **(driven
 about on the sea)**
adroit callĭdus, sollers
adroitness dextĕrĭtas, *f*
adulation ădūlātĭo, *f*
adult *adj*, ădultus
adulterate *v.t*, vĭtĭo (1)
adulteration adultĕrātĭo, *f*
adulterer(-ess) ădulter, *m*, (-era, *f*)
adultery ădultĕrĭum, *n*
advance *nn*, prōgressus, *m*
advance *v.i*, prōcēdo (3),
 prōgrĕdĭor (3 *dep*), incēdo (3),
 pĕdem infĕro (*irreg*)
advance *v.t*, infĕro (*irreg*),
 prōmŏvĕo (2)
in advance *adv*, prae,
 compounded with vb: e.g. **send
 in advance,** praemitto (3)
advance-guard prīmum agmen, *n*
advantage commŏdum, *n*
to be advantageous *v.i*, prōsum
 (*irreg*), ūsui esse (*irreg*) (*with dat*)

advantageous ūtĭlis
advantageously *adv*, ūtĭlĭter
advent adventus, *m*
adventure făcĭnus, *n*
adventurous audax
adventurously *adv*, audacter
adversary hostis, *c*
adverse adversus
adversity res adversae, *f.pl*
advert to *v.t*, attingo (3)
advertise *v.t*, prōscrībo (3),
 prōnuntĭo (1)
advertisement prōscriptĭo, *f*
advice consĭlĭum, *n*
advisable (advantageous) ūtĭlis
advise *v.t*, mŏnĕo (2), suādĕo
 (2), censĕo (2)
advisedly *adv*, consultō
adviser suāsor, *m*, auctor, *m*
advocate *nn*, patrōnus, *m*
advocate *v.t*, suādĕo (2)
adze ascĭa, *f*
aedile aedīlis, *m*
aedileship aedīlĭtas, *f*
aerial *adj*, **(of the air)**, āĕrĭus
afar *adv*, prŏcŭl
affability cōmĭtas, *f*
affable cōmis
affably *adv*, cōmĭter
affair rēs, *f*, nĕgōtĭum, *n*
affect *v.t*, affĭcĭo (3); **(the
 feelings)** mŏvĕo (2)
affectation (show) sĭmŭlātĭo, *f*
affected pūtĭdus
affection (love) ămor, *m*
affectionate ămans
affiance *v.t*, spondĕo (2)
affianced sponsus
affidavit testĭmōnĭum, *n*
affiliate *v.t*, cŏ-opto (1)
affinity cognātĭo, *f*
affirm *v.t*, affirmo (1)
affix *v.t*, affīgo (3)
afflict *v.t*, afflīcĭo (3)
afflicted (with grief) mĭser
affliction (with grief etc) mĭsĕrĭa,
 f; **(a bad thing)**, mălum, *n*
affluence dīvĭtĭae, *f.pl*
affluent dīves
afford *v.t.* **(give)**, praebĕo (2);
 otherwise use phr. with satis
 pecuniae habere ut... **(to have
 enough money to ...)**

affright *v.t,* terrĕo (2)
affront contŭmēlĭa, *f*
affront *v.t,* contŭmēlĭam facio (3) (*with dat*)
afire *adj,* flăgrans
afloat (*use phr. with* in aquā (**on the water**)
afoot *adv,* pĕdĭbus
afore *adv,* sŭprā
aformentioned sŭprā scriptus
aforesaid sŭprā scriptus
afraid tĭmĭdus
afraid (to be—) *v.i. and v.t,* tĭmĕo (2), vĕrĕor (2 *dep*), mĕtŭo (3)
afresh *adv,* rursus
aft *nn,* puppis, *f*
after *prep,* post (*with acc*)
after *conj,* postquam
after *adv,* post, postĕa
after all (nevertheless) *adv,* tămen
afternoon *adv,* post mĕrīdĭem
afternoon *adj,* pōmĕrīdĭānus
afterwards *adv,* post, postĕa
again *adv,* ĭtĕrum, rursus
again and again *adv,* ĭdentĭdem
against *prep,* contra, in (*with acc*)
agape *adj,* hĭans
age aetas, *f,* aevum, *n,* (**old—**) sĕnectus, *f*
aged (old) sĕnex
aged (three) years nātus (tres) annos
agency (doing, action) ŏpĕra, *f*
agent actor, *m*
aggrandize *v.t,* amplĭfico (1)
aggrandizement amplĭfĭcātĭo, *f*
aggravate *v.t,* grăvo (1); (**annoy**) aspĕro (1); (**increase**) augĕo (2)
aggregate *nn,* summa, *f*
aggression incursĭo, *f*
aggressive hostīlis
aggressor *use phr.* suā sponte bellum infĕrre (*irreg*), (**inflict war of one's own accord**)
aggrieve *v.t. use* affĭcĭo (3) (**affect**)
aghast stŭpĕfactus
agile ăgĭlis
agility ăgĭlĭtas, *f*
agitate *v.t,* ăgĭto (1), commŏvĕo (2)

agitated sollĭcĭtus
agitation (violent movement) ăgĭtātĭo, *f*; (**of the mind**), commōtĭo, *f*
agitator (political) turbātor, *m*
ago *adv,* ăbhinc (*with acc*) e.g. **two years—** ăbhinc duos annos
agonize *v.t,* crŭcĭo (1)
agony dŏlor, *m*
agrarian ăgrārĭus
agree with *v.i,* consentĭo (4) (*with* cum *and abl*); *v.t.* compōno (3); (**it is—by all**) constat inter omnes
agreeable grātus
agreeableness dulcēdo, *f*
agreed upon (it is—) constat, convēnit, *v. impers*
agreeing congrŭens, convĕnĭens
agreement (the—itself) pactum, *n;* (**of opinions, etc**) consensĭo, *f*
agricultural rustĭcus
agriculture agrĭcultūra, *f*
agriculturist agrĭcŏla, *m*
aground (to run—) *use phr.* in vădo haerĕo (2) (**stick fast in a shallow place**)
ague horror, *m*
ah! (alas!) eheu!
ahead *adv, use* prae, pro, *compounded with verbs,* e.g. **send ahead,** praemitto (3)
aid auxĭlĭum, *n,* subsĭdĭum, *n*
aid *v.t,* adiŭvo (1), subvĕnĭo (4) (*with dat*)
ail *v.i,* aegresco (3)
ailing aeger, aegrōtus
aim *v.t,* (**point a weapon, etc.**) dīrĭgo (3); (**to aim at**) pĕto (3)
aim *nn,* (**purpose**) finis, *m;* (**throwing**) coniectus, *m*
air āēr, *m;* (**manner**) spĕcĭes, *f*
air *v.t,* ventĭlo (1)
air-hoe spīrācŭlum, *n*
airy āĕrĭus
akin *adj,* (**similar**) fĭnĭtĭmus
alabaster ălăbastrītes ae, *m*
alacrity ălăcrĭtas, *f*
alarm (fear) păvor, *m,* trĕpĭdātĭo, *f;* (**confusion**) tŭmultus, *m*
alarm *v.t,* perturbo (1), terrĕo (2)
alarmed trĕpĭdus
alas! heu!

alcove   angŭlus, *m* **(corner)**
alder   alnus, *f*
alderman   măgistrātus, *m*
ale   cerevisia, *f*
ale-house   caupona, *f*
alert   ălăcer
alertness   ălăcrĭtas, *f*
alien   (*adj and nn*) **(foreign)**, pĕrĕgrīnus
alienate   *v.t,* ălĭēno (1)
alienation   ălĭēnātĭo, *f*
alight   *v.i,* dēsĭlĭo (4)
alike   *adj,* sĭmĭlis
alike   *adv,* sĭmĭlĭter
alive   vīvus
alive (to be —)   vivo (3)
all   *adj,* **(every)** omnis; **(the whole)** tōtus; (*with superlative,* e.g. all the best people) optĭmus quisque; (at all, in all) *adv,* omnīno
all-powerful   omnĭpŏtens
allay   *v.t,* sēdo (1)
allegation   affirmātĭo, *f*
allege   *v.t.* **(assert)** argŭo (3), affĕro (*irreg*)
allegiance   fĭdes, *f,* offĭcĭum, *n*
allegory   allēgŏrĭa, *f*
alleviate   *v.t,* lĕvo (1)
alleviation, (as an act)   lĕvātĭo, *f;* **(something which brings—)** lĕvāmen, *n*
alley   angĭportus, *m*
alliance   sŏcĭĕtas, *f,* foedus, *n;* **(to make an—)** foedus făcĭo (3)
allied (states)   foedĕrātus
allot   *v.t,* distrĭbŭo (3), assigno (1)
allotment (of land)   ăger assignātus, *m*
allow   *v.t.* **(permit)**, pătĭor (3 *dep*), sĭno (3), concēdo (3); *or use impers. vb.* lĭcet (*with dat. of person allowed*)
allowable   *use* făs, (*indecl. nn*) **(right)**
allowance (to make —)   ignosco (3), rĕmitto (3)
allude to   *v.t,* signĭfĭco (1)
allure   *v.t,* allĭcĭo (3)
allurement   blandĭtĭa, *f,* illĕcĕbra
alluring   blandus
allusion   signĭfĭcātĭo, *f*
alluvium   allŭvĭo, *f*

ally   *nn,* sŏcīus, *m*
ally   *v.t,* **(unite)**, iungo (3); **(— oneself)** se coniungere (*with dat*)
almanack   fasti, *m.pl*
almighty   omnĭpŏtens
almond   ămygdălum, *n;* **(tree)**, ămygdăla, *f*
almost   *adv,* paenĕ, prŏpĕ, fĕrē, fermē
alms   stips, *f*
aloe   ălŏē, *f*
aloft   *adv,* sublīmĕ; *adj,* sublīmis
alone   *adj,* sōlus
alone   *adv,* sōlum
along   *prep,* sĕcundum, praeter (*with acc*)
aloof   *adv,* prŏcŭl; **(to stand — from)**, discēdo (3)
aloud   *adv,* magnā vōcē
alphabet   *use* litterae *f.pl* **(letters)**
already   *adv,* iam
also   *adv,* ĕtiam, quŏque, ĭtem; **(likewise)**, necnōn
altar   āra, *f*
alter   *v.t,* mūto (1), verto (3), corrĭgo (3)
alter   *v.i,* mūtor (1 *dep*)
alteration   mūtātĭo, *f*
altercation   rixa, *f*
alternate   *v.t,* alterno (1)
alternate   *adj,* alternus
alternately   *adv,* invĭcem
alternation   vĭcissĭtūdo, *f*
alternative   *use phr. with* ălĭus mŏdus **(other way)**
although   *conj,* quamquam (*indicating fact*); quamvīs (*indicating a supposition*); etsi, tametsi
altitude   altĭtūdo, *f*
altogether   *adv,* omnīno
always   *adv,* semper
amalgamate   *v.t,* iungo (3), miscĕo (2)
amalgamation   coniunctĭo, *f*
amass   *v.t,* cŏăcervo (1), cŭmŭlo (1)
amatory   ămātōrĭus
amaze   *v.t,* obstŭpĕfăcĭo (3)
amazed   stŭpĭdus, stŭpĕfactus
amazement   stŭpor, *m*
amazing   mīrus
amazingly   *adv,* mīris mŏdis

amazon vīrāgo, *f*
ambassador lēgātus, *m*
amber sŭcĭnum, *n*
ambiguity ambāges, *f.pl*
ambiguous ambĭgŭus, anceps
ambiguously *adv*, per ambāges
ambition glōrĭa, *f*, ambĭtĭo, *f*
ambitious *use phr*. cŭpĭdus
glōrĭae **(keen on glory)**
amble *v.i*, lēnĭter ambŭlo (1)
(walk quietly)
ambrosia ambrŏsĭa, *f*
ambrosial ambrŏsĭus
ambush insĭdĭae (*f.pl*) ; **(to
ambush)** insĭdĭor (1 *dep*)
ameliorate *v.t*, mēlĭōrem făcĭo (3)
amen! fiat! **(let it be)**
amenable obēdĭens
amend *v.t*, ēmendo (1), corrĭgo
(3)
amendment (correction)
ēmendātĭo, *f*
amends *use* expĭo (1) **(to make
—s)**
amenity ămoenĭtas, *f*
amethyst ămĕthystus, *f*
amiability suāvĭtas, *f*
amiable suāvis
amiably *adv*, suāvĭter
amicable ămīcus
amid(st) *prep*, inter (*with acc*)
amiss *adv*, mălē; **(to take—)**
aegre fĕro (*irreg*)
amity ămīcĭtĭa, *f*
ammunition arma, *n.pl*
amnesty vĕnĭa, *f*
among *prep*, inter, ăpud (*with
acc*)
amorous ămans
amount summa, *f*, finis, *m*
amount to *v.t*, *use* esse **(to be)**
amphitheatre amphĭthĕātrum, *n*
ample amplus, cōpĭōsus
amplify *v.t*, amplĭfĭco (1), dīlāto
(1)
amplitude amplĭtūdo, *f*
amply *adv*, amplē
amputate *v.t*, sĕco (1), ampŭto
(1)
amputation ampŭtātĭo, *f*
amuse *v.t*, dēlecto (1)
amusement dēlectātĭo, *f*
amusing făcētus

anaesthetic *adj*, sŏpōrĭfer
analogy (comparison) compărātĭo
analyse *v.t*, discerpo (3), explĭco
(1)
analysis explĭcātĭo, *f*
anarchical turbŭlentus
anarchy lĭcentĭa, *f*
anathema exsecrātĭo, *f* **(curse)**
anatomy incīsĭo (*f*) corporis
(incision of the body)
ancestor auctor, *m*; (*in pl*),
māiōres, *m.pl*
ancestral proăvītus
ancestry (descent, origin) gĕnus, *n*
anchor ancŏra, *f*
anchor *v.i*, *use phr*. nāvem ad
ancŏras dēlĭgo (1) **(fasten a ship
to the anchors)**
anchorage stătĭo, *f*
ancient antīquus, vĕtus
and et, atque, ac; quĕ (*joined to
the second of two words*, **e.g. I
and you:** ego tuque) ; **(and ... not)**
nĕque
anecdote fābella, *f*
anew *adv*, dēnŭo, dē intĕgro
anger īra, *f*, īrācundĭa, *f*
anger *v.t*, irrīto (1), lăcesso (3)
angle angŭlus, *m*
angle *v.i* **(fish)**, piscor (1 *dep*)
angler piscātor, *m*
angrily *adv*, īrācundē, īrātē
angry īrātus; **(irascible)** īrācundus
anguish angor, *m*, dŏlor, *m*,
ăcerbĭtas, *f*
angular angŭlātus, angŭlāris
animal ănĭmal, *n*, pĕcus, *f*
animal *adj*, ănĭmālis
animate *v.t*, anĭmo, excĭto (1)
animated ănĭmans; **(lively)**
vĕgĕtus, ălăcer, vĕhĕmens
animation (liveliness) vĭgor, *m*
animosity sĭmultas, *f*
ankle tālus, *m*
annalist annālĭum scriptor, *m*
annals annāles, *m.pl*
annex *v.t*, addo (3), iungo (3)
annihilate *v.t*, dēlĕo (2)
annihilation exĭtĭum, *n*,
exstinctĭo, *f*
anniversary *adj*, anniversārĭus
anniversary *nn*, dĭes
annĭversārĭus, *m*

annotate   *v.t*, annŏto (1)
annotation   annŏtātĭo, *f*
announce   *v.t*, nuntĭo (1)
announcement   prōnuntĭātĭo, *f*
announcer   nuntĭus, *m*,
  praeco, *m*
annoy   *v.t*, irrīto (1), lăcesso (3)
annoyance   mŏlestĭa, *f*,
  vexātĭo, *f*
annual   anniversārĭus
annually   *adv*, quŏtannis
annuity   annŭa, *n.pl*
annul   *v.t*, abrŏgo (1), tollo (3)
annulment   ăbŏlĭtĭo, *f*
anoint   *v.t*, unguo (3)
anointing   *nn*, unctĭo, *f*
anomaly   ănōmălĭa, *f*
anon   *adv* **(immediately)**, stătim;
  (in a short time) brĕvi tempŏre
anonymously   **(***adv. phr***)** sĭne.
  nōmĭne
another   ălĭus; **(the other of two)**,
  alter; **(another's)**, *adj*, ălĭēnus
answer   *nn*, responsum, *n*
answer   *v.t*, respondĕo (2); **(in
  writing)** rescrībo (3); **(to — for, be
  surety for)** praesto (1)
answerable   *use phr*, rătĭōnem
  reddo (3) **(to render an account)**
ant   formīca, *f*
antagonism   ĭnĭmĭcĭtĭa, *f*
antagonist   adversārĭus, *m*
antagonistic   contrārĭus
antecedent   *adj*, antĕcēdens
antechamber   ātrĭolum, *n*
anterior   prĭor
ante-room   ātrĭŏlum, *n*
anticipate   *v.t*, occŭpo (1),
  antĕverto (3), praecĭpĭo (3);
  (expect), exspecto (1)
anticipation (expectation)
  exspectātĭo, *f*
antics   lūdi, *m.pl*
antidote   rĕmĕdĭum, *n*,
  antĭdŏtum, *n*
antipathy   rĕpugnantĭa, *f* ; **(of
  people)** ŏdĭum, *n*
antipodes   antĭpŏdes, *m.pl*
antiquarian   *adj*, antīquitatis
  stŭdĭōsus **(keen on antiquity)**
antiquated   priscus
antique   *adv*, vĕtus, antīquus
antiquity   antīquĭtas, *f*, vĕtustas, *f*

antithesis (opposite)   contrārĭum,
  n; **(in argument)**, contentĭo, *f*
antler   rāmus, *m*, cornu, *n*
anvil   incūs, *f*
anxiety   anxĭĕtas *f*, sollĭcĭtūdo, *f*,
  cūra, *f*; **(alarm)** păvor, *m*
anxious   anxĭus, sollĭcĭtus;
  (alarmed) trĕpĭdus
anxiously   *adv*, anxĭē
any   *adj*, ullus (*after negatives,
  and in questions, and
  comparisons*); quisquam (*pron.
  used like* ullus); qui, quae, quod
  (*after* si, nisi, ne, num)
anyone, anybody   *pron*, quis
  (*after* si, nisi, se, num); quisquam
  (*after a negative*)
anything   *use neuter of prons.
  given above*
anywhere   *adv*, **(in any place)**,
  usquam; **(to any place)**, quŏ,
  quŏquam; **(in any place)**, ŭbīquĕ
apace   *adv*, **(quickly)**, cĕlĕrĭtĕr
apart   *adv*, sĕorsum; (*adj*)
  dīversus
apartment   conclāve, *n*
apathetic   lentus, pĭger
apathy   ignāvĭa, *f*, lentĭtūdo, *f*
ape   sīmĭa, *f*
aperture   forāmen, *n*
apex   căcūmen, *n*, ăpex, *m*
aphorism   sententĭa, *f*
apiary   alvĕārĭum, *n*
apiece   *use distributive numeral,
  e.g.* two each, bīni
apologize   *v.i*, excūso (1), dēfendo
  (3)
apology   excūsātĭo, *f*
appal   *v.t*, perterrĕo (2)
apparatus   appărātus, *m*
apparel   vestis, *f*, vestīmentum, *n*
apparent   mănĭfestus, ăpertus
apparently   *adv*, per spĕcĭem
apparition (ghost)   spĕcĭes, *f*,
  ĭmāgo, *f*
appeal   *v.i*, appello (1), prōvŏco
  (1), **(to —to)** *v.t*, obtestor (1 *dep*)
appeal   *nn*, appellātĭo, *f*,
  obsĕcrātĭo, *f*
appear   *v.i*, appārĕo (2),
  conspĭcĭor (3 *pass*); **(to seem)**
  vĭdĕor (2 *pass*); **(to come forward)**
  prōdĕo (4)

appearance (looks) spĕcĭes, *f,*
aspectus, *m;* **(show),** spĕcĭes, *f;*
(image), sĭmŭlācrum, *n*
appeasable plācābĭlis
appease *v.t,* **(people),** plāco (1);
(feelings), sēdo (1)
appeasement plācātĭo, *f*
appellant appellātor, *m*
append *v.t,* **(attach),** addo (3)
appendage appendix, *f*
appertain *v.i,* pertĭnĕo (2)
appetite appĕtītus, *m;* **(hunger),**
fămes, *f*
applaud *v.t,* plaudo (3), laudo (1)
applause (clapping) plausus, *m;*
(cheers), clāmor, *m*
apple mālum, *n;* **(–tree),** mālus,
f
appliance (apparatus) appărātus,
m
applicable to commŏdus *(with
dat)*
applicant pĕtītor, *m*
application (asking) pĕtītĭo, *f;*
(mental), stŭdĭum, *n,* dīlĭgentĭa, *f*
apply *v.t,* adhĭbĕo (2), admŏvĕo
(2); **(to — oneself to)** se dēdĕre (3
with dat) ; *v.i,* **(refer to),** pertĭnĕo
(2); **(–for),** flāgĭto (1)
appoint *v.t,* constĭtŭo (3) **(people
to office, etc),** crĕo (1) ; **(to
appoint to a command)** praefĭcĭo
(3) *(acc. of person appointed,
dat. of person or thing
commanded)*
appointment (office) mūnus, *n;*
(creation), crĕātĭo, *f* ; **(agreed
meeting),** constĭtūtum, *n*
apportion *v.t,* dīvĭdo (3),
distrĭbŭo (3)
apposite aptus
appraise *v.t,* **(evaluate),** aestĭmo
(1)
appraisement aestĭmātĭo, *f*
appreciate *v.t,* **(value),** aestĭmo
(1) magni
appreciation aesĭmātĭo, *f*
apprehend *v.t,* **(arrest),**
comprĕhendo (3) ; **(understand),**
intellĕgo (3), percĭpĭo (3)
apprehension (fear) formīdo, *f;*
(arrest) comprĕhensĭo, *f;*
(understanding), intellĕgentĭa, *f*

apprehensive (fearful) tĭmĭdus
apprentice tīro, *m*
approach *v.i,* apprŏpinquo (1)
(with ad *and acc. or dat),* accēdo
(3)
approach *nn,* ădĭtus, *m,*
adventus, *m,* accessus, *m*
approbation apprŏbātĭo, *f,* laus, *f*
appropriate *adj,* aptus,
accommŏdātus *(with dat)*
appropriate *v.t,* sūmo (3)
appropriately *adv,* aptē
approval apprŏbātĭo, *f*
approve (of) *v.t,* apprŏbo (1)
approved spectātus, prŏbātus
approximate proxĭmus
approximate *v.i,* accēdo (3)
April Aprīlis (mensis)
apron ŏpĕrīmentum, *n*
apt aptus, ĭdōnĕus; **(inclined),**
prōnus, prōpensus
aptitude (ability) ingĕnĭum, *n*
aptly *adv,* aptē
aptness *use adj,* aptus **(suitable)**
aquatic ăquātĭlis
aqueduct ăquae ductus *m*
aquiline ăquĭlīnus, ăduncus
arable land arvum, *n*
arbiter arbĭter, *m*
arbitrarily *adv,* **(according to
whim),** ad lĭbīdĭnem
arbitrary (capricious) lĭbīdĭnōsus
arbitrate *v.t,* discepto (1)
arbitration arbĭtrĭum, *n*
arbitrator arbĭter, *m*
arbour umbrācŭlum, *n*
arc arcus, *m*
arcade portĭcus, *f*
arch fornix *m,* arcus, *m*
arch *adj,* **(playful),** lascīvus
archaeology investīgātĭo, *(f)*
rērum antīquārum **(search for
ancient things)**
archaism verbum obsŏlētum, *n*
archer săgittārĭus, *m*
archipelago *use phr,* măre, *(n)*
insŭlis consĭtum **(sea set with
islands)**
architect archĭtectus, *m,* ŏpĭfex, *c*
architecture archĭtectūra, *f*
archives tăbŭlae, *f. pl*
arctic septentrĭōnālis
ardent ardens, fervĭdus

ardently *adv*, ardenter, vĕhĕmenter

ardour ardor, *m*, călor, *m*, fervor, *m*

arduous ardŭus

area spătĭum, *n*

arena hărēna, *f*, ărēna, *f*

argue *v.i*, discepto (1), dissĕro (3)

argument (quarrel) rixa, *f*, argūmentum, *n*; **(discussion)**, dispŭtātĭo, *f*

arid ārĭdus, siccus

aridity ārĭdĭtas, *f*, siccĭtas, *f*

aright *adv*, rectē

arise *v.i*, surgo (3); **(heavenly bodies)**, ŏrĭor (4 *dep*)

aristocracy (aristocratic party) optĭmātes, *c. pl*; **(govt.)** optĭmātĭum dŏmĭnātus, *m*

aristocratic patrĭcĭus

arithmetic ărĭthmētĭca, *n.pl*

ark arca, *f*

arm (fore—) brācchĭum, *n*; **(upper—)**, lăcertus, *m*; **(weapon)**, telum, *n*

arms (weapons) arma, *n.pl*, tēla, *n.pl*; **(call to —)**, ad arma vŏco (1); **(to take —s)** arma căpĭo (3); **(to lay down —s)**, arma dēdo (3)

arm *v.t*, armo (1); **(to take —s)** arma căpĭo (3)

armament (forces) cōpĭae, *f.pl*; **(weapon)**, tēlum, *n*

armed armātus

armistice indūtĭae *f.pl*

armour arma *n.pl*

armour-bearer armĭger, *m*

armourer făber, *m*

armoury armāmentārĭum, *n*

army exercĭtus, *m*; **(marching —)**, agmen, *n*; **(drawn up for battle)**, ăcĭes, *f*

around *adv, and prep. with acc*, circā, circum

arouse *v.t*, suscĭto (1), excĭto (1)

arraign *v.t*, accūso (1)

arrange *v.t*, compōno (3), constĭtŭo (3), collŏco (1), instrŭo (3)

arrangement (as an act) collŏcātĭo, *f* **(order)**, ordo, *m*

array *nn*, **(clothing)** vestis, *f*, vestīmenta, *n.pl*; **(battle—)**, ăcĭes, *f*

array *v.t*, compōno (3)

arrears rĕlĭquae pĕcūnĭae, *f.pl* **(money remaining)**

arrest *v.t*, comprĕhendo (3)

arrest *nn*, comprĕhensĭo, *f*

arrival adventus, *m*

arrive *v.i*, advĕnĭo (4), pervĕnĭo (4)

arrogance arrŏgantĭa, *f*

arrogant arrŏgans

arrogate *v.t*, arrŏgo (1) (*with dat*)

arrow săgitta, *f*

arsenal armāmentārĭum, *n*

art ars, *f*

artery vēna, *f*

artful callĭdus, văfer

artfully *adv*, callĭde

artfulness callĭdĭtas, *f*

article (thing) rēs, *f*; **(term of a treaty, etc.)**, condĭcĭo, *f*

articulate *adj*, clārus, distinctus

articulate *v.t*, exprĭmo (3)

articulation explānātĭo, *f*

artifice ars, *f*

artificer (craftsman) artĭfex, *m*, ŏpĭfex, *c*

artificial artĭfĭcĭōsus

artificially *adv*, mănu, artĕ

artillery tormenta, *n.pl*

artisa făber, *m*, ŏpĭfex, *c*

artist artĭfex, *m*; **(painter)**, pictor, *m*

artistic artĭfĭcĭōsus

artless (person) simplex; **(work)**, incomptus

artlessness simplĭcĭtas, *f*

as *conj*, **(because)**, quod, cum, quĭa; (*in a comparative phr, e.g.* **as strong as**) tam fortis quam; **(the same as)** īdem atque; **(as ... as possible)** quam *with the superlative, e.g.* **as quickly as possible;** quam cĕlerrime; **(as if)** tamquam, quăsĭ, vĕlut

ascend *v.t*, ascendo (3)

ascendant (to be in the—) *v.i*, praesto (1)

ascendancy praestantĭa, *f*

ascent ascensus, *m*

ascertain *v.t.* **(find out)**, cognosco (3), compĕrĭo (4)

ascetic *adj*, abstĭnens

ascribe *v.t,* ascrībo (3), assigno (1), attrĭbuo (3)

ash (tree) fraxĭnus, *f, (adj),* fraxĭnĕus

ashamed (to be —) pŭdet; *impers. with acc. and genit,* (e.g. **I am ashamed of my brother**) pŭdet me frātris

ashes cĭnis *m*

ashore *adv,* **(on shore),** in lītŏre; **(to shore),** in lītus

aside *use* se, *compounded with verb,* **e.g. to put aside,** sēcerno (3)

ask *v.t,* rŏgo (1) *(with 2 accs)* **e.g. I ask you for a sword,** tē glădĭum rŏgo

askance (to look — at) līmis ŏcŭlis aspĭcĭo (3) **(look with a sidelong glance)**

aslant *adv,* oblīque

asleep (to be —) *v.i,* dormĭo (4); **(to fall—)** obdormĭo (4)

asp aspis, *f*

aspect (appearance) aspectus, *m,* făcĭes, *f*

asperity ăcerbĭtas, *f*

asperse *v.t,* aspergo (3)

aspersion călumnĭa, *f*

asphalt bĭtūmen, *n*

aspirate *nn,* aspīrātĭo, *f*

aspiration (desire) affectātĭo, *f*; **(hope)** spes, f

aspire to affecto (1)

ass ăsĭnus, *m*

assail *v.t,* appĕto (3), oppugno (1)

assailant oppugnātor, *m*

assassin percussor, *m,* sīcārĭus, *m*

assassinate *v.t,* trŭcīdo (1)

assassination caedes, *f*

assault *nn,* impĕtus, *m,* oppugnātĭo, *f*

assault *v.t,* oppugno (1), ădŏrĭor (4 *dep*)

assemble *v.i,* convĕnĭo (4); *v.t,* cōgo (3)

assembly coetus, *m,* conventus, *m*; **(— of the Roman people),** cŏmĭtĭa, *n.pl*

assent *nn,* assensĭo, *f*

assent to *v.i,* assentĭor (4 *dep*) *(with dat)*

assert *v.t,* affirmo (1), confirmo (1)

assertion affirmātĭo, *f,* dēfensĭo, *f*

assess *v.t* **(evaluate),** aestĭmo (1)

assessment (valuation) aestĭmātĭo, *f*

assessor censor, *m*

assets bŏna, *n.pl*

assiduity assidŭĭtas, *f,* sēdŭlĭtas, *f*

assiduous assĭdŭus, sēdŭlus

assiduously *adv,* assĭdŭe, sēdŭlō

assign *v.t,* assigno (1), trĭbŭo (3)

assignation constĭtūtum, *n*

assimilate *v.t,* sĭmĭlem făcĭo (3)

assist *v.t,* iŭvo (1), auxĭlĭor (1 *dep*), subvĕnĭo (4) *(with dat)*

assistance auxĭlĭum, *n,* ŏpem *(no nomin),* f

assistant adiūtor, *m*

assize (provincial law court) conventus, *m*

associate *nn,* sŏcĭus, *m*

associate *v.t* **(join),** coniungo (3); *v.i,* ūtor (3 *dep. with abl*)

association sŏcĭĕtas, *f,* consortĭo, *f*

assort *v.t.* **(arrange),** dīgĕro (*irreg*)

assortment (heap) ăcervus *m*

assuage *v.t,* lĕvo (1), mītĭgo (1)

assume *v.t,* pōno (3), sūmo (3); **(take on)** suscĭpĭo (3)

assumption (hypothesis) sumptĭo, *f*

assurance (promise) fĭdes, *f*; **(confidence)** fidūcĭa, *f*

assure *v.t,* confirmo (1)

assured (certain) explōrātus

assuredly *adv,* **(certainly)** prōfecto

astern *adv,* ā puppi

asthma dyspnoea, *f*

astonish *v.t,* obstŭpĕfăcĭo (3)

astonished stŭpĕfactus; **(to be —),** *v.i,* obstŭpesco (3)

astonishing mīrĭficus, admīrābĭlis

astonishingly *adv. phr,* mīrum in mŏdum

astonishment stŭpor *m*

astound *v.t,* obstŭpĕfăcĭo (3)

astray (to go —) *v.i,* erro (1); **(to lead —),** *v.t,* indūco (3)

astrologer măthēmătĭcus, *m*

astrology astrŏlŏgĭa, *f*
astronomy astrŏlŏgĭa, *f*
astute callĭdus
astuteness callĭdĭtas, *f*
asylum (refuge) perfŭgĭum, *n*
at (*of place*) in (*with abl*), a, ăpŭd (*with acc*); *with proper names and* dŏmus *use locative case, e.g.* **at Rome,** Rōmae, **at home,** dŏmi; (*of time*) *use abl. case, e.g.* **at the third hour,** tertĭa hōra; *or sometimes* ăd *with the acc. case*
atheist ăthĕŏs, *m*
athlete āthlēta, *c*
athletic (strong) fortis
athwart *prep,* **(across),** trans (*with acc*)
Atlantic Ocĕănus, *m*
atmosphere āēr, *m*
atom ătŏmus, *f,* sēmĭna (*n.pl*) rērum **(seeds of things)**
atone for *v.t,* expĭo (1)
atonement expĭātĭo, *f*
atrocious nĕfărĭus
atrociousness fĕrĭtas, *f*
atrocity nĕfas, *n*
atrophy tābes, *f*
atrophy *v.i,* tābesco (3)
attach *v.t,* **(fasten),** affigo (3), applĭco (1); **(connect)** adiungo (3)
attached (fastened) fixus, aptus; **(fond)** dēvinctus, ămans
attachment (affection) stŭdĭum, *n,* ămor, *m*
attack *nn,* impĕtus, *m,* oppugnātĭo, *f*
attack *v.t,* oppugno (1), aggrĕdĭor (3 *dep*), ădŏrĭor (4 *dep*), invādo (3), pĕto (3)
attacker oppugnātor, *m*
attain *v.i,* **(reach),** pervĕnĭo (4) (*with* ad *and acc*); *v.t,* **(obtain),** consĕquor (3 *dep*)
attainable impĕtrābĭlis
attainment (obtaining) ădeptĭo, *f;* **(learning)** ērŭdītĭo, *f*
attempt *nn,* inceptum, *n,* cōnātum, *n*
attempt *v.i,* cōnor (1 *dep*)
attend *v.i,* **(be present at),** intersum (*irreg. with dat*); *v.t.* **(accompany),** cŏmĭtor (1 *dep*), prōsĕquor, (3 *dep*); **(pay**

attention) ŏpĕram do (1), ănĭmadverto (3)
attendance (being present) *use vb.* adsum (*irreg*) **(to be present);** **(of crowds),** frĕquentĭa, *f;* **(service),** appārĭtĭo, *f*
attendant *nn,* **(servant)** mĭnister, *m;* **(of a nobleman)** sectātor, *m,* sătellĕs, *c*
attention (concentration) attentĭo (*f*) ănĭmi; **(to pay —);** ŏpĕram, (*f*) do (1)
attentive (alert) intentus, attentus; **(respectful),** observans
attentively *adv,* sēdŭlo
attenuate *v.t,* attĕnŭo (1)
attest *v.t,* testor (1 *dep*)
attestation testĭfĭcātĭo, *f*
attire *nn,* vestis, *f*
attire *v.t,* vestĭo (4)
attitude (of mind) ănĭmus, *m;* **(of body),** gestus *m,* hăbĭtus, *m*
attract *v.t,* attrăho (3), allĭcĭo (3)
attraction (charms) illĕcĕbrae (*f.pl*)
attractive blandus, iūcundus
attribute *v.t,* attrĭbŭo (3), assigno (1)
attune *v.t,* **(adjust)** consŏnum (aptum) reddo (3) **(make harmonious (suitable))**
auburn flāvus
auction auctĭo, *f;* **(to sell by public —),** sub hastā vendo (3) **(sell under the spear)**
auctioneer praeco, *m*
audacious audax
audacity audācĭa, *f,* confidentĭa, *f*
audibly *use phr.* quod audīri pŏtest **(that can be heard)**
audience (of people) audītōres, *m.pl* **(hearing),** ădītus, *m*
audit *v.t,* inspĭcĭo (3)
auditorium audĭtorĭum, *n*
augment *v.t,* augĕo (2)
augur *nn,* augur, *c*
augur *v.t,* vātĭcĭnor (1 *dep*)
augury augŭrĭum, *n,* auspĭcĭum, *n*
August Sextīlis or Augustus (mensis)
august *adj,* augustus
aunt (paternal) ămĭta, *f;* **(maternal),** mātertĕra, *f*

auspices

auspices auspĭcĭum, *n*
auspicious faustus, sĕcundus
auspiciously *adv*, fēlīcĭter
austere (severe) sĕvērus
austerity sĕvērĭtas, *f*
authentic vērus, certus
authentically *adv*, certō
authenticate *v.t*, rĕcognosco (3)
authenticity auctōrĭtas, *f*
author (writer) scriptor, *m*;
  (instigator), auctor, *m*
authoritative grăvis, impĕrĭosus
authority auctōrĭtas, *f*, pŏtestas, *f*,
  impĕrĭum, *n*
authorize (give permission to) *v.i*,
  pŏtestătem (auctōrĭtātem), făcĭo
  (3) (*with dat*)
autocracy tўrannis, *f*
autocrat dŏmĭnus, *m*
autograph mănus, *f*
autumn auctumnus, *m*
autumnal auctumnālis
auxiliary *adj*, auxĭlĭāris,
  auxĭlĭārĭus; *nn* adiūtor, *m*;
  (—forces) auxĭlĭa, *n.pl*
avail *v.t* **(assist)**, prōsusm (*irreg*)
  (*with dat.*); **(make use of)**, ūtor (3
  dep. with abl)
available (ready) expĕdītus,
  părātus
avarice ăvārĭtĭa, *f*
avaricious ăvārus
avenge *v.t*, ulciscor (3 *dep*)
avenger ultor, *m*
avenging *adj*, ultrix
avenue xystus, *m*
aver *v.t* **(affirm)**, affirmo (1)
average *adj*, mĕdĭus **(middle)**
averse āversus
aversion ŏdĭum, *n*
avert *v.t*, āverto (3), dēpello (3)
aviary ăvĭārĭum, *n*
avid ăvĭdus
avidity ăvĭdĭtas, *f*
avoid *v.t*, vīto (1), fŭgĭo (3)
avoidance vītātĭo, *f*, fŭga, *f*
avow *v.t*, fătĕor (2 *dep*)
avowal confessĭo, *f*
avowed prŏfessus, ăpertus
await *v.t*, exspecto (1)
awake *adj*, vĭgĭlans; **(to be —)**,
  v.i, vĭgĭlo (1); **(to awake)**, *v.t*,
  excĭto (1)

award *nn*, **(judicial decision)**;
  arbĭtrĭum, *n* **(prize)**, palma,*f*
award *v.t*, trĭbŭo (3), adiūdĭco
  (1)
aware gnārus; **(to be —)**, sentĭo
  (4); **(know)**, scĭo (4)
away *use* a, ab *compounded
  with a verb, e.g.* (ăbĕo) **go
  away** (4)
awe formīdo, *f*, mĕtus, *m*,
  rĕvĕrentĭa, *f*
awe (be in —) vĕrĕor (2 *dep*)
awful vĕrendus
awestruck păvĭdus
awhile *adv*, paulisper, părumper
awkward rŭdis, impĕrītus
awkwardness inscītĭa, *f*
awning vēlum, *n*
awry *adj*, perversus; *adj*, perversē
axe sĕcūris, *f*
axiom sententia, *f*
axis, axle axis, *m*
ay, aye *adv*, ĭta, vērō; **(forever)** in
  perpĕtŭum
azure *adj*, caerŭlĕus

B

babble *v.i*, garrĭo (4), blătĕro (1)
babbler, babbling *adj*, garrŭlus
baby infans, *c*
babyhood infantĭa, *f*
bacchanalian bacchānālis
bachelor *adj*, caelebs
back *nn*, tergum, *n*, dorsum, *n*;
  (at the —) a tergo; **(to move
  something—)**, rĕtro mŏvĕo (2),
  rēĭcĭo (3); **(to go —)** se rĕcĭpĕre
  (3 *reflex*)
backbite *v.t*, obtrecto (1)
backwards *adj*, **(dull)** pĭger
backwards *adv*, rĕtro
bacon lārĭdum, *n*
bad mălus; **(of health)**, aeger; **(of
  weather)**, ādversus
badge insigne, *n*
badger mēles, *f*
badly *adv*, mălĕ, prāvē, imprŏbē
badness (worthlessness) nēquĭtĭa, *f*
baffle *v.t*, ēlūdo (3)
bag saccus, *m*
baggage (military) impĕdīmenta,
  n.pl; **(individual packs)**, sarcĭnae,
  f.pl

bail *nn,* **(person),** văs, *m;*
(**security)** vădĭmōnĭum, *n*
bail (to give — for) *v.t,* spondĕo
(2) prō *(with abl)*
bailiff (estate manager) villĭcus,
m; (**official),** appārĭtor, *m*
bait *nn,* esca, *f*
bait *v.t,* **(tease),** lăcesso (3),
illūdo (3)
bake *v.t,* torrĕo (2), cŏquo (3)
baker pistor, *m*
bakery pistrīnum, *n*
balance *nn,* **(scales),** lībra, *f;*
(**equilibrium),** lībrāmentum, *n*
balance *v.t,* lībro (1), compenso
(1)
balcony maenĭāna, *n.pl*
bald calvus, glăber; (**unadorned),**
ārĭdus
baldness calvĭtĭum, *n*
bale out *v.t,* **(discharge),** ēgĕro
(3)
bale (bundle) fascis, *m*
baleful pernĭcĭōsus
balk (beam) trabs, *f*
balk *v.t,* frustror (1 *dep*)
ball (for play) pĭla, *f;* (**globe,**
sphere), glŏbus, *m*
ballad carmen, *n*
ballad-singer cantātor, *m*
ballast săbura, *f*
ballet *use vb.* salto (1) (**dance)**
ballista ballista, *f*
ballot suffrāgĭum, *n*
ballot-box cista, *f,* urna, *f*
balm balsāmum, *n,* unguentum, *n*
balmy (soothing) mollis, lēnis
balustrade (railings) cancelli, *m.pl*
bamboo hărundo, *f* (**reed)**
ban *v.t,* vĕto (1)
band (bond) vincŭlum, *n;* (**of**
people), mănus, *f,* grex, *m*
band together *v.i,* coniūro (1)
bandage fascĭa, *f*
bandage *v.t,* lĭgo (1)
bandit lătro, *m*
bandy (to — words) *v.i,* altercor
(1 *dep*)
bandy-legged lōrĭpes
bane (injury) pernĭcĭes, *f;* (**poison),**
vĕnēnum, *n*
baneful pernĭcĭōsus
bang crĕpĭtus, *m*

bang *v.t.* **(beat)** tundo (3)
banish *v.t, use phr.* ăquā et igni
interdīco (3) *(with dat)* (**forbid on**
the use of fire and water), expello
(3)
banishment rĕlēgātĭo, *f,* exsĭlĭum, *n*
bank *nn,* **(of earth),** tŏrus, *m;* (**of**
a river) rīpa, *f;* (**for money)**
argentārĭa tăberna (**money shop)**
banker argentārĭus, mensārĭus, *m*
bankrupt *nn,* dēcoctor, *m* (**to**
be —), *v.i,* solvendo non esse
bankruptcy (personal) rŭīna, *f*
(**downfall)**
banner vexillum, *n*
banquet convīvĭum, *n,* ĕpŭlae,
f.pl
banter *nn,* căvĭllātĭo, *f*
banter *v.i,* căvillor (1 *dep*)
bar (wooden) asser, *m;* (**lock),**
claustra, *n.pl;* (**bolt),** sĕra, *f;*
(**barrier)** rĕpāgŭla, *n.pl*
bar *v.t* (**fasten),** obsĕro (1);
(**— the way),** obsto (1) *(with dat)*
barb (hook) uncus, *m*
barbarian barbărus, *m*
barbaric (barbarous) barbărus,
crūdēlis, immānis
barbarity barbărĭa, *f*
barbarously *adv,* **(cruelly),**
crūdēlĭter
barbed hāmātus
barber tonsor, *m*
bard (poet, etc.) poēta, *m*
bare nūdus; (**to make —),** *v.t,*
ăpĕrĭo (4), nūdo (1)
barefaced (shameless) impŭdens
barefoot *adv,* nūdo pĕde
barely *adv,* vix
bargain *nn,* pactum, *n*
bargain *v.i,* (**make a — with),**
paciscor (3 *dep*) *(with cum and*
abl. of person)
barge linter, *f;* (**— man),** nauta, *m*
bark *nn,* **(of trees),** cortex, *m;* (**of**
dogs), lātrātus, *m;* (**boat),** rătis, *f*
bark *v.i,* lātro (1)
barley hordĕum, *n*
barley-water ptĭsăna, *f*
barn horrĕum, *n*
baron princeps, *m*
barque rătis, *f*

barracks castra *n.pl*
barrel dōlĭum, *n*
barren stĕrĭlis
barrenness stĕrĭlĭtas, *f*
barricade *nn,* agger, *m*
barricade *v.t,* obsaepĭo (4)
barrier impĕdĭmentum, *n,* claustra, *n.pl*
barrister pătrōnus, *m*
barrow fercŭlum, *n*
barter *v.t,* **(exchange),** mūto (1)
barter *nn,* permūtātĭo, (*f*) mercĭum **(exchange of goods)**
base *nn,* băsis, *f,* fundāmentum, *n*
base *adj,* **(worthless),** turpis; **(lowborn),** hŭmĭlis
baseless *adj,* falsus
basely *adv,* turpĭter
basement băsis, *f*
baseness turpĭtūdo, *f*
bashful vĕrēcundus
bashfulness vĕrēcundĭa, *f*
basin pelvis, *f*
basin băsis, *f,* fundāmentum, *n*
bask *v.i,* ăprĭcor (1 *dep*)
basket călăthus, *m,* corbis, *f,* quālum, *n*
bass *adj,* grăvis
bastard *adj,* nŏthus
bastion turris, *f*
bat (animal) vespertīlĭo, *m;* **(club, stick),** clāva, *f*
bath *nn,* balnĕum, *n;* **(public —)** balneae, *f.pl*
bath, bathe *v.i,* lăvor (1 *pass*); *v.t,* lăvo (1)
bathing *nn,* lăvātĭo, *f*
baton scīpĭo, *m*
battalion cŏhors, *f*
batter *v.t,* pulso (1), verbĕro (1)
battering-ram ărĭes, *m*
battery (assault) vĭs, *f;* **(cannon),** tormenta *n.pl*
battle proelĭum, *n;* **(— line),** ăcĭes, *f* **(— cry),** clāmor, *m;* **(— field),** lŏcus (*m*) pugnae
battlement pinna, *f,* mūnītĭōnes, *f.pl*
bawd lēna, *f*
bawl *v.i,* clāmĭto (1)
bawling *nn,* clāmor, *m*

bay (of the sea) sĭnus, *m;* **(tree)** laurus, *f;* **(at bay)** (*adj*) pārātus ad pugnam **(ready for a fight)**
bay *v.i,* lātro (1)
bayonet pŭgĭo, *m*
be *v.i,* sum (*irreg*)
beach lītus, *n*
beacon (fire) ignis, *m*
bead bāca, *f*
beak rōstrum, *n*
beaker pōcŭlum, *n*
beam (of timber) tignum, *n,* trabs, *f;* **(cross —),** transtrum, *n;* **(ray)** rădĭus, *m*
bean făba, *f*
bear *nn,* ursus, *m,* ursa, *f;* **(constellation),** septentrĭōnes, *m.pl;* **(The Great —),** ursa maior; **(The Little —)** septentrio minor
bear *v.t,* fĕro (*irreg*), gĕro (3); **(carry),** porto (1); **(produce),** părĭo (3); **(— away)** aufĕro (*irreg*)
bearable *adj,* tŏlĕrābĭlis
beard barba, *f;* **(bearded),** barbātus
bearer (carrier) bāiŭlus, *m,* portĭtor, *m*
bearing (posture) gestus, *m*
beast (wild) bestĭa, *f,* fĕra, *f;* **(domestic),** pĕcus, *f*
beastly (filthy) obscēnus
beat (in music, poetry) ictus, *m*
beat *v.t,* caedo (3), fĕrĭo (4), vervĕro (1); **(conquer),** sŭpĕro (1), vinco (3); **(— back),** rĕpello (3); **(— down)** sterno (3); **(be beaten),** *v.i,* vāpŭlo (1)
beating *nn,* verbĕra, *n.pl*
beautiful pulcher
beautifully *adv,* pulchrē
beautify *v.t,* orno (1)
beauty pulchrĭtūdo, *f,* forma, *f*
beaver castor, *m*
becalmed vento dēstĭtūtus **(deserted by the wind)**
because *conj,* quod, quĭa, cum; **(because of)** *prep,* propter, ŏb (*with acc*)
beckon *v.t,* innŭo (3) (*with dat*)
become *v.i,* fīo (*irreg*); *v.t* **(to suit, adorn)** dĕcet (2 *impers. with acc. of person*)
becoming *adj,* dĕcōrus

176

bed lectus, *m*; **(go to —)**, cŭbĭtum ĕo (4)
bedroom cŭbĭcŭlum, *n*
bedaub *v.t,* lĭno (3)
bedeck *v.t,* orno (1); **(bedecked)**, ornātus
bedew *v.t,* irrōro (1)
bee ăpis, *f*
bee-hive alvĕārĭum, *n*
beech (tree) fāgus, *f*
beef caro būbŭla, *f,* **(ox flesh)**
beer cervisia, *f*
beetle scărăbaeus, *m*
befall *v.i,* accĭdo (3)
befit *v.i* **(suit)**, convĕnĭo (4)
before *prep,* **(time and place)**, antĕ **(***with acc***)**; **(place)**, prae, prō **(***with abl***)**; **(in the presence of)**, cōram **(***with abl***)**
before *adv,* **(time)**, antĕ, prĭus; **(space)** prae; **before** *conj,* antĕquam, prĭusquam
befoul *v.t,* inquĭno (1)
befriend *v.t,* adiŭvo (1)
beg *v.t* **(request)**, pĕto (3), ōro (1); **(be a beggar)**, *v.i,* mendĭco (1)
beget *v.t,* gigno (3)
begetter gĕnĭtor, *m*
beggar mendīcus, *m*
begin *v.i,* incĭpĭo (3), coepi (3 *defect*)
beginner (originator) auctor, *m* **(learner)**, tīro, *m*
beginning *nn,* ĭnĭtĭum, *n,* princĭpĭum, *n,* inceptum, *n*
begone! ăpăgĕ!
begrudge *v.t* **(envy)**, invĭdĕo (2) **(***with dat***)**
beguile *v.t,* fallo (3), dēcĭpĭo (3)
behalf (on — of) **(***prep***)**, prō **(***with abl***)**
behave oneself *v. reflex,* se gĕrĕre (3)
behaviour (manners) mōres, *m.pl*
behead *v.t,* sĕcūri fĕrĭo (4) **(strike with an axe)**
behest (command) iussum, *n*
behind *prep,* post **(***with acc***)**
behind *adv,* post, ā tergo
behold *v.t,* conspĭcĭo (3)
behold! (exclamation) eccĕ!
being (human —) hŏmo, *c*
belabour *v.t,* verbĕro (1)

belated sērus
belch *v.i, and v.t,* ructo (1)
belch *nn,* ructus, *m*
beleaguer *v.t,* obsĭdĕo (2)
belfry turris, *f*
belie *v.t,* **(conceal)**, dissĭmŭlo (1)
belief fĭdes, *f*; **(impression)**, ŏpīnĭo, *f,* persuāsĭo, *f*
believe *v.t,* crēdo (3) **(***with dat. of person***)** pŭto (1), arbĭtror (1 *dep*), censĕo (2)
believer crēdens, *c*
bell tintinnābŭlum, *n*
belligerent bellans, belli cŭpĭdus **(keen on war)**
bellow *v.i,* mūgĭo (4)
bellowing *nn,* mūgītus, *m*
bellows (pair of —) follis, *m*
belly venter, *m,* abdōmen, *n*
belong to *v.i,* use esse **(***irreg***) (to be)** *with genit. of person*
beloved cārus, dīlectus
below *prep,* infrā, subter **(***with acc***)**, sub **(***with abl. or acc***)**
below *adv,* infrā, subter
belt baltĕus, *m*
bemoan *v.t,* gĕmo (3)
bench scamnum, *n*; **(for rowers)** transtrum, *n*
bend *v.t,* flecto (3), curvo (1); *v.i,* se flectĕre (3 *pass*)
bend, bending *nn,* flexus, *m*
beneath see **below**
benefactor *phr,* qui bĕnĕfĭcĭa confert **(who confers favours)**
beneficence bĕnĕfĭcentĭa, *f*
beneficent bĕnĕfĭcus
beneficial sălūtāris, ūtĭlis; **(to be —)** *v.i,* prōsum **(***irreg***) (***with dat***)**
benefit *v.i* prōsum **(***irreg***) (***with dat***)**, adiŭvo (1)
benefit *nn,* bĕnĕfĭcĭum, *n*
benevolence bĕnĕfĭcentĭa, *f,* bĕnĕvŏlentĭa, *f*
benevolent bĕnĕfĭcus, bĕnĕvŏlus
benign bĕnignus
benignity bĕnignĭtas, *f*
bent *adj,* curvus; **(—on)** attentus; **(—back)** rĕsŭpīnus; **(—forward)** prōnus
benumb *v.t, phr* torpōre affĭcĭo (3) **(affect with numbness)**

bequeath v.t, lēgo (1)
bequest lēgātum, n
bereave v.t, orbo (1)
bereaved orbus
bereavement orbĭtas, f, damnum, n
berry bāca, f
berth (for a ship) stătĭo, f
beseech ōro (1), obsĕcro (1), quaeso (3)
beseem (become) dĕcet (2 *impers. with acc. of person*)
beset v.t, obsĭdĕo (2), circumvĕnĭo (4)
beside prep, **(near)**, prŏpĕ (*with acc*); **(except)**, praeter (*with acc*)
besides adv or conj, praeterquam
besides adv, **(further)**, praetĕrĕā, insŭper
besiege v.t, obsĭdĕo (2), circum sēdĕo (2)
besieger obsessor, m
besmear v.t, illĭno (3)
bespatter v.t, aspergo (3)
bespeak v.t, **(hire)** condūco (3)
besprinkle v.t, aspergo (3)
best adj, optĭmus; **(to the best of (one's) ability)** prō (vĭrīli) parte;
best adv, optĭmē
bestial use phr, bestĭārum mōre **(after the manner of beasts)**
bestir (to — oneself) v.i, expergiscor (3 dep)
bestow v.t, do (1), trĭbŭo (3), confĕro (irreg)
bestowal largītĭo, f
bet nn, pignus, n
bet v.t, pignŏre contendo (3)
betake v.t, conferre (irreg)
betimes adv, mātūrē
betray v.t, prōdo (3)
betrayal prōdĭtĭo, f
betrayer prōdĭtor, m
betroth v.t, spondĕo (2)
betrothal sponsālĭa, n.pl
better adj, mĕlĭor; **(of health)**, sānus; **better** adv, mĕlĭus
better v.t, **(improve)**, corrĭgo (3); ēmendo (1)
between prep, inter (*with acc*)
beverage pōtĭo, f, pōtus, m
bevy căterva, f

bewail v.t, dēplōro (1), lūgeo (2)
beware v.i and v.t, căvĕo (2)
bewilder v.t, perturbo (1), distrăho (3)
bewildered turbātus, distractus
bewitch v.t, fascĭno (1); **(charm)**, căpĭo (3)
beyond prep, ultrā, trans, sŭprā, extrā (*with acc*)
beyond adv, ultrā, sŭprā
bias inclīnātĭo, f
bias v.t, inclīno (1)
Bible use phr. scripta săcra, n.pl **(sacred writings)**
bicker v.i, altercor (1 dep)
bid nn, **(of a price)** lĭcĭtātĭo, f
bid v.t **(tell, order)**, iŭbĕo (2)
bide v.i **(stay)**, mănĕo (2)
bier fĕrĕtrum, n, fercŭlum, n
big magnus, vastus, ingens
bigotry obstĭnātĭo, f
bile bīlis, f
bilge-water sentīna, f
bilious bīlĭōsus
bill (written, financial) lĭbellus, m, rătĭo, f, syngrăpha, f; **(proposal in Parliament)**, rŏgātĭo, f; **(a law)**, lex, f **(of a bird)**, rōstrum, n
billet (of wood) lignum, n; **(lodging of soldiers)**, hospĭtĭum, (n) mīlĭtum
billet v.t **(soldiers)**, per hospĭtĭa dispōno (3) **(distribute through lodgings)**
billow fluctus, m
billowy fluctŭosus
bind v.t, lĭgo (1), vincĭo (4); **(oblige)**, oblĭgo (1); **(— together)**, collĭgo (1)
biographer scriptor rērum gestārum **(writer of exploits)**
biography vīta, f
birch (tree) betŭla, f
bird ăvis, f; **(— cage)**, căvĕa, f; **(— nest)**, nīdus, m
birth ortus, m, gĕnus, n
birthday (dĭes) nātālis
birth place sŏlum, (n) nātāle
bishop pontĭfex, m
bit (bite) offa, f; **(small piece of food)**, frustum, n; **(for a horse)**, frēnum, n

bitch   cănis, *f*
bite   *nn*, morsus, *m*
bite   *v.t*, mordĕo (2)
biting   *adj*, mordax, asper
bitter   ămārus, ăcerbus, asper
bitterness   ăcerbĭtas, *f*
bitumen   bĭtūmen, *n*
bivouac   *nn*, excŭbĭae, *f.pl*
bivouac   *v.i*, excŭbo (1)
blab   *v.i*, blătĕro (1)
black   nĭger; (— art), măgĭce, *f*
blackberry   mōrum, *n*, rūbus, *m*
blackbird   mĕrŭla, *f*
blacken   *v.t*, nigrum reddo (3)
blackguard   nēbŭlo, *m*
Black Sea   Pontus Euxĭnus, *m*
blacksmith   făber, *m*
bladder   vēsīca, *f*
blade (of grass)   herba, *f*; (of sword, knife), lāmĭna, *f*
blame   *nn*, culpa, *f*
blame   *v.t*, culpo (1)
blameable   culpandus
blameless   innŏcens, intĕger
blamelessness   innocentĭa, *f*
bland   blandus
blandishment   blandĭtĭa, *f*, blandīmentum, *n*
blank   *adj*, (empty), văcŭus; (paper), pūrus
blank   *nn*, ĭnāne, *n*
blanket   lōdix, *f*
blaspheme   *v.t*, blasphēmo (1)
blast   *nn*, ĭnāne, *n*
blanket   lōdix, *f*
blaspheme   *v.t*, blasphēmo (1)
blast   *nn*, flāmen, *n*, flātus, *m*
blast   *v.t*, ūro (3)
blatant   *adj*, (manifest), ăpertus
blaze   *nn*, flamma, *f*
blaze   *v.i*, ardĕo (2), flăgro (1)
bleach   candĭdum reddo (3)
bleak   algĭdus, frĭgĭdus
blear-eyed   lippus
bleat, bleating   bālātus, *m*
bleat   *v.i*, bālo (1)
bleed   *v.i*, sanguĭnem effundo (3); *v.t*, sanguĭnem mitto (3)
bleeding   *adj*, (wound), crūdus
bleeding   *nn, use phr* effūsĭo, (*f*), sanguĭnis (shedding of blood)
blemish   *nn*, (physical), vĭtĭum, *n*, (moral), măcŭla, *f*

blemish   *v.t*, măcŭlo (1)
blend   *v.t*, miscĕo (2)
bless   *v.t*, (favour, make successful), sĕcundo (1), bĕnĕdīco (3)
blessed   beātus; (of the dead), pĭus
blessedness   bĕātĭtūdo, *f*, fēlĭcĭtas, *f*
blessing   *nn*, bĕnĕdictĭo, *f*, bŏnum, *n*
blight   *nn*, rōbīgo, *f*
blight   *v.t*, ūro (3); (—of hopes) frustror (1 *dep*)
blind   *adj*, caecus
blind   *v.t*, caeco (1)
blindly (rashly)   *adv*, tĕmĕre
blindness   caecitas, *f*
blink   *v.i*, connĭvĕo (2)
bliss   fēlĭcĭtas, *f*
blissful   *adj*, fēlix
blister   pustŭla, *f*
blithe   hĭlăris
blizzard   imber, *m*
bloated   sufflātus
block   *nn*, (of wood), stĭpes, *m*, massa, *f*
block   *v.t*, obstrŭo (3), obsaepĭo (4)
blockade   *nn*, obsĭdĭo, *f*
blockade   *v.t*, obsĭdĕo (2)
blockhead   caudex, *m*
blood   sanguis, *m*; (gore), crŭor, *m*
blood-letting   *nn*, missĭo, (*f*) sanguĭnis
bloodshed   caedes, *f*
bloodshot   crŭōre suffusus (spread over with blood)
blood-stained   crŭentus
bloodthirsty   sanguĭnārĭus
bloody   crŭentus, sanguĭnĕus
bloom   *nn*, flōs, *m*
bloom   *v.i*, flōrĕo (2)
blooming   flōrens
blossom, etc.   see bloom
blot   *v.t*, măcŭlo (1); (—out, obliterate), dēlĕo (2)
blot   *nn*, măcŭla, *f*
blow   *nn*, (stroke), plāga, *f*, ictus, *m*
blow   *v.i. and v.t*, flo (1)

blowing *nn*, flātus, *m*
bludgeon fustis, *m*
blue *adj*, caerŭlĕus
bluff *v.t*, illūdo (3)
blunder *nn*, mendum, *n*, error, *m*
blunder *v.i*, offendo (3),
  erro (1)
blunt *adj*, hĕbes; **(frank)**, līber
blunt *v.t*, hĕbēto (1), obtundo
  (3)
bluntly *adv*, lībĕrē, plāne
blush *nn*, rŭbor, *m*
blush *v.i*, ērŭbesco (3)
bluster *v.i*, dēclāmo (1)
bluster *nn*, dēclāmātĭo, *f*
blusterer iactātor, *m*
boar verres, *m*, ăper, *m*
board *nn*, tăbŭla, *f*; **(council)**,
  concĭlĭum, *n*
board *v.t* **(ship)**, conscendo (3);
  (to — up), contăbŭlo (1);
  (provide food), victum praebĕo
  (2)
boast *v.i*, glōrĭor (1 *dep*.), se
  iactare (1 *reflex*)
boasting *nn*, glōrĭātĭo, *f*, iactātĭo,
  f
boat scăpha, *f*, linter, *f*
boatsman nauta, *m*
bode *v.t* **(predict)**, praesāgĭo (4)
bodily *adj*, corpŏrĕus
bodkin ăcus, *f*
body corpus, *n*; **(— of soldiers,
  etc.)**, mănus, *f*, nŭmĕrus, *m*,
  multĭtūdo, *f*
bodyguard stĭpātōres, *m.pl*
bog pălus, *f*
boggy păluster
boil *nn*, vŏmĭca, *f*
boil *v.t*, cŏquo (3); *v.i*, fervĕo
  (2)
boiled *adj*, ēlixus
boiler caldārĭum, *n*
boisterous prŏcellōsus, turbĭdus
bold audax, ănĭmōsus, fortis
boldly *adv*, audacter, ănĭmōse,
  fortĭter
boldness audācĭa, *f*, fĭdentĭa, *f*
bolster cervīcal, *n*, pulvīnus, *m*
bolt *nn*, **(door, etc.)**, ŏbex, *m*,
  rĕpāgŭla, *n.pl*
bolt *v.t* **(door, etc.)**, obsĕro (1),
  claudo (3); **(food)**, obsorbĕo (2)

bombastic inflātus
bond vincŭlum, *n*, cătēna, *f*;
  (legal), syngrăpha, *f*
bondage servĭtus, *f*
bone ŏs, *n*
book līber, *m*, lĭbellus, *m*
bookbinder glūtĭnātor, *m*
bookcase armārĭum, *n*
book-keeper actŭārĭus, *m*
bookseller bĭblĭŏpōla, *m*
boom *v.i*, sŏno (1)
boon (good thing) bŏnum, *n*
boor hŏmo ăgrestis
boorish agrestis
boot calcĕus, *m*; **(heavy —)**,
  călĭga, *f*
bootless (unsuccessful) *adj*,
  irrĭtus
booth tăberna, *f*
booty praeda, *f*, spŏlĭa, *n.pl*
booze *v.i. and* *v.t*, pōto (1)
border margo, *m*, *f*; **(of a
  country)**, finis, *m*
border *v.i*, attingo (3)
bordering *adj*, fīnĭtĭmus
bore (person) use, *adj*,
  importūnus **(rude)**
bore *v.t*, perfŏro (1), tĕrĕbro
  (1); **(— someone)**, fătīgo (1)
boredom taedĭum, *n*
born *adj*, nātus; **(to be —)**, *v.i*,
  nascor (3 *dep*)
borough mūnĭcĭpĭum, *n*
borrow mūtŭor (1 *dep*.)
bosom sĭnus, *m*, pectus, *n*
boss (of a shield) umbo, *m*
botany ars herbārĭa, *f*
botch *v.t*, măle sarcĭo (4), **(patch
  badly)**
both ambo; **(each of two)**
  ŭterquĕ; **(both ... and)**, et ... et
bother *nn*, *use adj*, mŏlestus
  (troublesome)
bother *v.t*, lăcesso (3), vexo (1)
bottle ampulla, *f*, lăgēna, *f*
bottom fundus, *m*, *or use adj*,
  īmus *in agreement with noun*,
  e.g. **at the bottom of the tree,** ad
  īmam arbŏrem
bottomless (very deep) prŏfundus
bough rāmus, *m*
boulder saxum, *n*
bounce *v.i*, rĕsĭlĭo (4)

bound (limit) fīnis, *m*, mŏdus, *m*; **(leap)**, saltus, *m*
bound *v.i*, **(leap)**, sălĭo (4); *v.t*, **(limit)**, contĭnĕo (2)
boundary fīnis, *m*
boundless infinītus
bountiful largus, bĕnignus
bounty largītas, *f*, bĕnignĭtas, *f*
bouquet serta, *n.pl*
bout (contest) certāmen, *n*
bow (archery) arcus, *m*; **(of a ship)**, prōra, *f*; **(of salutation)**, sălūtātĭo, *f*
bow *v.t*, inclīno (1), dēmitto (3); *v.i*, se dēmittĕre (3 *reflex*)
bow-legged vătĭus
bowman săgittārĭus, *m*
bowels viscĕra, *n.pl*
bower umbrācŭlum, *n*
bowl crātĕra, *f*
box arca, *f*, cista, *f*; **(tree)**, buxus, *f*; **(slap)**, cŏlăphus, *m*
box *v.i*, pugnis certo (1), **(fight with the fists)**
boxer pŭgil, *m*
boxing *nn*, pŭgĭlātĭo, *f*
boy pŭer, *m*
boyhood pŭerĭtĭa, *f*
boyish pŭerīlis
brace (support) fascĭa, *f*; **(in architecture)**, fībŭla, *f*
brace *v.t*, līgo (1), firmo (1)
bracelet armilla, *f*
bracket mūtŭlus, *m*
brackish ămārus
brag *v.i*, glōrĭor (1 *dep.*)
braggart iactātor, *m*
braid *nn*, **(of hair)**, grădus, *m*
braid *v.t*, necto (3)
brain cĕrĕbrum, *n*
brainless (stupid) sōcors
bramble dūmus, *m*
bran furfur, *m*
branch rāmus, *m*
branch *v.i*, **(separate)**, dīvĭdor (3 *pass*)
branching *adj*, rāmōsus
brand (fire —) fax, *f*, torris, *m*; **(burn-mark)**, nŏta, *f*; **(stigma)**, stigma, *n*
brand *v.t*, ĭnūro (3), nŏto (1)
brandish *v.t*, vibro (1)
brass ŏrĭchalcum, *n*

brave fortis, ănĭmōsus, ăcer
bravely *adv*, fortĭter, ănĭmōsē
bravery fortĭtūdo, *f*
brawl *v.i*, rixor (1 *dep*)
brawl *nn*, rixa, *f*
brawny lăcertōsus
bray *v.i*, rŭdo (3)
brazen (made of brass) aēnĕus, aerĕus; **(impudent)**, impŭdens
breach rŭīna, *f, or use vb*. rumpo (3) **(to burst); (— in a treaty, etc.)** *use* vĭŏlo (1) **(to violate)**
bread pānis, *m*
breadth lātĭtūdo, *f*
break *v.t*, frango (3); **(treaty, etc.)** vĭŏlo (1); **(— promise)**, fĭdem fallo (3); **(— down)**, *v.t*, rēscindo (3); **(— in)**, *v.t*, **(horses)**, dŏmo (1); **(— into)**, *v.t*, irrumpo (3); **(— loose)** ērumpo (3)
break (of day) prīma lux, *f*, **(first light); (fracture)**, fractūra, *f*
breakfast ientācŭlum, *n*
breakfast *v.i*, iento (1)
breakwater mōles, *f*
breast pectus, *n*, mamma, *f*
breast-plate lōrīca, *f*
breath spīrĭtus, *m*, ănĭma, *f*; **(out of —)**, exănĭmātus; **(to hold one's —)**, ănĭmam comprĭmo (3)
breathe *v.i*, spīro (1); **(— out)**, exspīro (1)
breathing *nn*, aspīrātĭo, *f*
breathless exănĭmātus
breed *v.t*, gĕnĕro (1); *v.i*, nascor (3 *dep.*) **(to be born)**
breed *nn*, gĕnus, *n*
breeding *nn*, **(giving birth)** partus, *m*; **(manners)**, hūmānĭtas, *f*
breeze aura, *f*
breezy ventōsus
brevity brĕvĭtas, *f*
brew *v.t*, cŏquo (3); *v.i* **(overhang) impendĕo** (2)
bribe *nn*, praemĭum, *n*
bribe *v.t*, corrumpo (3)
bribery ambĭtus, *m*
brick lăter, *m*; **(made of —)**, *adj*, lătĕrīcĭus
bricklayer structor, *m*
bridal nuptĭālis
bride (before marriage) sponsa, *f* **(after marriage)**, nupta, *f*

bridegroom (before marriage)
sponsus, *m* **(after marriage),**
nuptus, *m*, mărītus, *m*
bridge pons, *m*
bridle frēnum, *n*
brief *adj*, brĕvis
briefly *adv*, brĕvĭter
briar dūmus, *m*
brigade lĕgĭo, *f*
bright clārus
brighten *v.t*, illustro (1); *v.i*,
clāresco (3)
brightly *adv*, clāre
brilliance splendor, *m*, nĭtor, *m*
brilliant splendĭdus; **(famous),**
praeclārus
brim margo, *m*, *f*, labrum, *n*
brimstone sulfur, *n*
brine salsāmentum, *n*
bring, *v.t*, fĕro, affĕro *(irreg)*,
addūco (3) apporto (1);
(— about), confĭcĭo (3); **(— back,**
— before), rĕfĕro *(irreg)*;
(—down), dēfĕro *(irreg)*;
(—forward), prōfĕro *(irreg)*;
(— in), infĕro *(irreg)*; **(— out),**
ēffĕro *(irreg)*; **(— over),** perdūco
(3); **(—together),** cōgo (3); **(— up)**
(children), ēduco (1)
brink (river, etc.) rīpa, *f*; **(of cliff,**
etc.) *use adj*, summus **(highest)**
brisk ălăcer
briskness ălacrĭtas, *f*
bristle saeta, *f*
bristle *v.i*, horrĕo (2)
brittle frăgĭlis
broach *v.t*, ăpĕrĭo (4), prōfĕro
(irreg)
broad lātus
broadly (widely) *adv*, lātē
broil (quarrel) rixa, *f*
broil *v.t*, torrĕo (2)
broken fractus; **(disabled),**
confectus
broker interpres, *c* **(agent)**
bronze aes, *n*; *(adj)*, aēnĕus,
aerĕus
brooch fĭbŭla, *f*
brood *v.i*, incŭbo (1)
brood (of young, etc.) fētus, *m*
brook rīvus, *m*
brook (no interference etc) pătĭor
(3 *dep*)

broom scōpae, *f.pl*
broth ius, *n*
brothel gānĕa, *f*
brother frāter, *m*
brotherhood sŏcĭĕtas, *f*
brow (forehead) frons, *f*; **(eye-**
brow), sŭpercĭlĭum, *n*; **(of hill),**
căcūmen, *n*
brown fuscus
browse *v.t* **(read),** perlĕgo (3)
bruise *nn*, contūsum, *n*
bruise *v.t*, contundo (3)
brunt (bear the — of) *use* sustĭnĕo
(2) **(to bear)**
brush *nn*, pēnĭcŭlus, *m*
brush *v.t*, dētergĕo
brushwood sarmenta, *n.pl*
brutal fĕrus, ătrox
brutality immānĭtas, *f*
brutally *adv*, immānĭter
brute bestĭa, *f*, fĕra, *f*
bubble bulla, *f*
bubble *v.i*, bullo (1)
buccaneer pīrāta, *m*
buck (male stag) cervus, *m*
bucket sĭtŭla, *f*
buckle fĭbŭla, *f*
buckle *v.t*, fĭbŭlā necto (3)
(fasten with a buckle)
buckler (shield) scūtum, *n*
bud *nn*, gemma, *f*
bud *v.i*, gemmo (1), germĭno (1)
budge *v.i*, cēdo (3); *v.t*, mŏvĕo (2)
budget rătĭo, *f* **(reckoning,**
account)
buff lŭtĕus
buffet (blow) cŏlăphus, *m*
buffoon scurra, *m*
bug cīmex, *m*
bugbear terrĭcŭla, *n.pl*
bugle būcĭna, *f*
build *v.t*, aedĭfico (1)
builder aedĭfĭcātor, *m*
building (act of —) aedĭfĭcātĭo, *f*,
(structure itself), aedĭfĭcĭum, *n*
bulb bulbus, *m*
bulk magnĭtūdo, *f*, mōles, *f*
bulky ingens, grandis
bull taurus, *m*
bullet glans, *f*
bullion aurum, *n*
bullock iŭvencus, *m*
bulrush iuncus, *m*

bulwark   mūnīmentum, *n*
bump   *nn*, tūber, *n*, tŭmor, *m*
bump   *v.i*, offendo (3)
bumpkin   rustĭcus, *m*
bunch   ūva, *f*, răcēmus, *m*
bundle   fascis, *m*
bung (stopper)   obtūrāmentum, *n*
bungle   *v.i*, inscītē, ăgo (3) **(do unskilfully)**
bungler   *adj*, impĕrītus
buoyancy   lĕvĭtas, *f*
buoyant   lĕvis
burden   ŏnus, *n*
burden   *v.t*, ŏnĕro (1)
burdensome   grăvis
bureau   scrīnĭum, *n*, armārĭum, *n*
burgess   cīvis, *c*
burglar   fūr, *m*
burglary   furtum, *n*
burgle   *v.t*, fūror (1 *dep.*) **(steal)**
burial   fūnus, *n*, sĕpultūra, *f*
burial-place   lŏcus, (*m*) sĕpultūrae
burly   lăcertōsus
burn   *v.t*, ūro (3), incendo (3); *v.i*, ardĕo (2), flagro (1)
burn   *nn*, ambustum, *n*
burning   *adj*, ardens
burnish   *v.t*, pŏlĭo (4)
burrow   cŭnīcŭlum, *n*
burst   *v.t*, rumpo (3); *v.i*, rumpor (3 *pass*)
burst out   *v.i*, ērumpo (3)
bursting out   *nn*, ēruptĭo (3)
bursting out   *nn*, ēruptĭo, *f*
bury   *v.t*, sĕpĕlĭo (4), abdo (3)
bush   dūmus
bushel   mĕdimnum, *n*
bushy   frŭtĭcōsus
busily   *adv*, sēdŭlō
business   nĕgōtĭum, *n*, res, *f*
bust (statue)   ĭmāgo, *f*
bustle   *nn*, festīnātĭo, *f*
bustle   *v.i*, festīno (1)
busy   occŭpātus
but   *conj*, sed, vērum, at (*first word in clause*) autem, vēro (*second word in clause*); **(except)**, praeter (*with acc*)
butcher   lănĭus, *m*
butcher   *v.t* **(murder)**, trŭcīdo (1)
butchery   trŭcīdātĭo, *f*
butler   prōmus, *m*
butt (laughing stock)   lūdĭbrĭum, *n*

butt   *v.t*, cornū fĕrĭo (4) **(strike with the horn)**
butter   būtȳrum, *n*
butterfly   pāpĭlĭo, *m*
buttock   clūnis, *m*,   *f*
buttress   antēris, *f*
buxom   vĕnustus
buy   *v.t*, ĕmo (3)
buyer   emptor, *m*
buying   *nn*, emptĭo, *f*
by   *prep* **(of place, near)**, ad, prŏpe (*with acc*); **(of time)** *often expressed by abl. of noun, e.g.* **by night**, nocte; **(— means of)**, per (*with acc*) **(by an agent**, *e.g.* **by a spear**, *abl. case alone*), hastā; **(—chance)**, *adv*, fortē
bygone   *adj*, praetrītus
bystander   spectātor, *m*
byway   trāmes, *m*

C

cab   raeda, *f*, cĭsĭum, *n*
cabal (faction)   factĭo, *f*
cabbage   brassĭca, *f*
cabin (hut)   căsa, *f*
cabinet (furniture)   armārĭum, *n*; **(council)** summum consĭlĭum, *n*
cable (anchor —)   ancŏrāle, *n*
cackle, cackling   *nn*, strĕpĭtus, *m*
cackle   *v.i*, strĕpo (3)
cadaverous   cădāvĕrōsus
cadence   cursus, *m*
cadet   discĭpŭlus, *m*, tīro, *m*
cage   căvĕa, *f*
cajole   *v.t*, blandĭtor (4 *dep. with dat*)
cajolery   blandĭtĭae, *f.pl*
cake   *nn*, plăcenta, *f*, lībum, *n*
calamitous   exĭtĭōsus
calamity   clādes, *f*, mălum, *n*
calculate   *v.t*, compŭto (1), aestĭmo (1)
calculation   rătĭo, *f*
calendar   fasti, *m.pl*
calf   vĭtŭlus, *m*; **(of the leg)**, sūra, *f*
call   *v.t*, **(name)**, vŏco (1), appello (1); dīco (3); **(— back)**, rĕvŏco (1); **(— to, summon)**, advŏco (1); **(— together)**, convŏco (1); **(— up or out)**, suscĭto (1)

call *nn* (cry), clāmor, *m*; (visit) sălūtātĭo, *f*
caller sălūtātor, *m*
calling *nn*, (vocation), ars, *f*, artĭfĭcĭum, *n*
calling *nn*, (vocation), ars, *f*, artĭfĭcĭum, *n*
callous callōsus
callow implūmis
calm *adj*, plăcĭdus, tranquilius
calm *nn*, tranquillĭtas, *f*, mălăcĭa
calm *v.t*, sēdo (1), plāco (1)
calmly *adv*, tranquille, plăcĭde
calumniate *v.t*, crīmĭnor (1 *dep*)
calumnious crīmĭnōsus
calumny crīmĭnātĭo, *f*
camel cămēlus, *m*
camp castra, *n.pl*; (to pitch —), castra pōno (3); (to move —), castra mŏvĕo (2); (a winter ...), hīberna, *n.pl*
campaign stīpendĭum, *n*
campaign *v.i*, stīpendĭum mĕrĕor (2 *dep*)
can *nn*, urcĕus, *m*
can *v.i*, (to be able), possum (*irreg*)
canal fossa, *f*
cancel *v.t*, dēlĕo (2), abrŏgo (1)
cancer (sign of zodiac) cancer, *m*
candid ăpertus, lĭber
candidate candĭdātus, *m*
candle candēla, *f*
candlestick candēlābrum, *n*
candour lībertas, *f*
cane hărundo, *f*, băcŭlum, *n*, virga, *f*
cane *v.t*, verbĕro (1)
canister arca, *f*, pyxis, *f*
canker rōbīgo, *f*
canker *v.t*, corrumpo (3)
cannibal anthrōpŏphăgus, *m*
cannon tormentum, *n*
canoe scăpha, *f*
canon (rule) rēgŭla, *f*
canopy vēla, *n.pl*
cant ostentātĭo, *f*
canter *v.i*, lēnĭter curro (3) (run smoothly)
canton pāgus, *m*
canvas vēla, *n.pl*, carbăsus, *f*
canvass *v.i*, ambĭo (4)
canvass *nn*, ambĭtĭo, *f*; (illegal), ambĭtus

cap pillĕus, *m*
capability făcultas, *f*
capable căpax
capacious căpax
capacity căpācĭtas, *f*; (mental —), ingĕnĭum, *n*
cape prōmontŭrĭum, *n*
caper *v.i*, exsulo (1), salĭo (4)
capital *nn*, (city), căput, *n*
capital *adj*, (crime, etc.), căpĭtālis; (chief), princeps
capitulate *v.t*, dēdo (3); *v.i*, se dēdĕre (3 *reflex*)
caprice lĭbīdo, *f*
capricious lĕvis
captain dux, *m*, princeps, *m*; (of a ship), măgister, *m*, nauarchus, *m*
captivate *v.t*, căpĭo (3), dēlēnĭo (4)
captive *adj. and nn*, captīvus, *m*.
captivity captīvĭtas, *f*
capture *nn*, (of city, camp, etc.), expugnātĭo, *f*; (of persons), *use vb*, căpĭo (3) (to capture)
capture *v.t*, căpĭo (3)
car currus, *m*, plaustrum, *n*
caravan (convoy) commĕātus, *m*, (vehicle), raeda, *f*
carbuncle fūruncŭlus, *m*
carcass cădāver, *n*, corpus, *n*
card charta, *f*
cardinal *adj*, prīmus, princeps
care cūra, *f*, sollĭcĭtūdo, *f*
care *v.t* (to — about or for) cūro (1)
career currĭcŭlum, *n*
careful dīlĭgens; (carefully prepared) accūrātus; (cautious) cautus
carefully *adv*, dīlĭgenter
careless neglĕns, indīlĭgens
carelessly *adv*, neglegenter
carelessness neglĕgentĭa, *f*
caress blandīmenta *n.pl*, complexus, *m*
caress *v.t*, blandĭor (4 *dep*.) (*with dat*.)
caressing *adj*, blandus
cargo ŏnus, *n*
caricature imāgo, *f*
caricature *v.t, use phr*. vultum dĕtorquĕo (2) (distort the features)

carnage caedes, *f*, strāges, *f*
carnal corpŏrĕus
carnival fēriae, *f.pl*
carnivorous carnĭvŏrus
carol cantus, *m*
carousal cōmissātĭo, *f*
carouse *v.i*, cōmissor (1 *dep.*)
carp at *v.t*, carpo (3), mordĕo (2)
carpenter făber, *m*
capet străgŭlum, *n*
carriage (vehicle) raeda, *f*, carpentum, *n*; **(transportation)**, vectūra, *f*; **(poise)**, incessus, *m*
carrier vector, *m*
carrion căro, *f*, cădāver, *n*
carrot pastīnăca, *f*
carry *v.t*, porto (1), fĕro (*irreg.*), vĕho (3), gĕro (3); **(— away or off)**, aufĕro (*irreg.*); **(— back)** rēfĕro (*irreg.*); **(— in)** infĕro (*irreg.*); **(— on)** gĕro (3); **(— over)** transporto (1); **(— out, perform)** exsĕquor (3 *dep*); **(— through a law, etc.)** perfĕro (*irreg.*)
cart plaustrum, *n*
cart *v.t*, vĕho (3)
cart-horse iūmentum, *n*
cartilage cartĭlāgo, *f*
carve *v.t*, caelo (1), sĕco (1), sculpo (3)
carver sculptor, *m*
carving *nn*, caelātūre, *f*
case (in law) causa, *f* **(circumstances)**, cāsus, *m* **(cover)**, thēca, *f*
casement fĕnestra, *f*
cash nummus, *m*, pĕcūnĭa nŭmĕrāta, *f*
cashier *nn*, *use phr.* qui nummos dispensat **(who dispenses the cash)**
cashier *v.t*, **(from the army)**, exauctoro (1)
cask cūpa, *f*
casket arcŭla, *f*
cast *nn*, **(throw)**, iactus, *m*
cast *v.t*, iăcĭo (3), mitto (3); **(— down)** dēĭcĭo (3); **(— off)** dēpōno (3); **(— out)** expello (3)
castaway perdĭtus, *m*
caste ordo, *m*
castigate *v.t*, castīgo (1)

castle castellum, *n*
castor oil cĭcĭnum ŏlĕum, *n*
castrate *v.t*, catro (1)
casual fortūĭtus
casually *adv*, neglĕgenter
casualty (accident) cāsus, *m*; **(killed)** *adj*, interfectus
cat fēles, *f*
catalogue index, *c*
catapault cătăpulta, *f*
cataract (waterfall) cătăracta, *f*
catarrh grăvēdo, *f*
catastrophe rŭīna, *f*
catch căpĭo (3), comprĕhendo (3); **(a disease)**, contrăho (3)
categorical (absolute) simplex, plānus
category nŭmĕrus, *m*
cater *v.t*, obsōno (1)
caterpillar ērūca, *f*
catgut chorda, *f*
cattle pĕcus, *n*
cauldron cortīna, *f*
cause *nn*, causa, *f*
cause *v.t*, făcĭo (3), effĭcĭo (3)
causeway agger, *m*
caustic *adj*, mordax **(biting)**
caution cautĭo, *f*
caution *v.t*, mŏnĕo (2)
cautious cautus
cavalry ĕquĭtātus, *m*, ĕquĭtes, *m.pl*
cave spēlunca, *f*, căverna, *f*, antrum, *n*
caw *v.i*, crōcĭo (4)
cease *v.i*, dēsĭno (3) *(with infin)*
ceaseless perpĕtŭus
cedar cefrus, *f*
ceiling tectum, *n*
celebrate *v.t*, căno (3), cĕlĕbro (1)
celebrated clārus, illustris
celebration cĕlĕbrātĭo, *f*
celebrity fāma, *f*, glōrĭa, *f*; **(person)**, vir praeclārus
celerity cĕlĕrĭtas, *f*
celestial caelstis
celibacy caelĭbātus, *m*
cell, cellar cella, *f*
cement ferrūmen, *n*
cement *v.t*, glūtĭno (1), ferrūmĭno (1)

cemetery sĕpulcrētum, *n*
censor censor, *m*
censure vĭtŭpĕrātĭo, *f*
censure *v.t,* vĭtŭpĕro (1)
reprĕhendo (3)
census census, *m*
per cent *use nn,* centēsĭma, *f* **(one hundredth part)**
centaur centaurus, *m*
central mĕdĭus
centre (of) mĕdĭus, *in agreement with noun,* e.g. **in the centre of the line,** in mĕdĭā ăcĭe
centre on *v.i* **(depend on),** pendĕo (2) (*with* ab *and* abl)
centurion centŭrĭo, *m*
century saecŭlum, *n*
ceremonial rītus, *m,* caerĭmōnĭa, *f*
ceremonious sollemnis
certain certus, explōrātus;
(a — person) *use pron,* quīdam
certainly *adv,* certo, certē, prŏfecto
certainty res certa; *or use adj,* certus **(certain)**
certificate scriptum testĭmōnĭum **(written proof)**
certify *v.i,* rĕcognosco (3), confirmo (1)
cessation intermissĭo, *f*
chafe *v.t,* fŏvĕo (2), călĕfăcĭo (3); *v.i,* stŏmăchor (1 *dep.*) **(be irritated)**
chaff pălĕa, *f*
chaffinch fringilla
chagrin stŏmăchus, *m*
chain cătēna, *f,* vincŭlum, *n*
chain *v.t,* cătēnas īnĭcĭo (3) (*with dat*)
chair sella, *f*
chairman măgister, *m*
chalk crēta, *f*
chalk out (mark out) *v.t,* dēsigno (1)
challenge *nn,* prōcŏcātĭo, *f*
challenge *v.t,* prōvŏco (1)
chamber conclāve, *n*; **(bed —),** cŭbĭcŭlum, *n*
chamberlain cŭbĭcŭlārĭus, *m*
chamois căprĕŏlus, *m*
champ *v.t,* mando (3)
champion victor *m*; **(defender),** prōpugnātor, *m*

chance *nn,* cāsus, *m,* fors, *f,* fortūna, *f*
by chance *adv,* **(happen),** forte, cāsu
chance *v.i,* accĭdo (3)
chandelier candēlābrum, *n*
change, changing *nn,* mūtātĭo, *f,* permūtātĭo, *f*
change *v.t,* mūto (1), converto (3); *v.i,* mūtor (1 *pass*)
changeable mūtābĭlis
channel cănālis, *m,* alvĕus, *m*
chant *v.i and v.t,* canto (1)
chaos pertubātĭo, *f*
chaotic perturbātus
chapel săcellum, *n*
chapter căpŭt, *n*
char *v.t,* ambūro (3)
character mōres, *m.pl,* ingĕnĭum *n*; **(reputation),** existĭmātĭo, *f,* ŏpīnĭo, *f*; **(in a play),** persōna, *f*
characteristic *adj,* prōprĭus
charcoal carbo, *m*
charge *nn,* **(attack),** impĕtus, *m*; **(accusation),** crīmen, *n*; **(price),** prĕtĭum, *n*; **(care of),** cūra, *f*
charge *v.t,* **(attack),** impĕtum făcĭo (3); signa infĕro (*irreg*); **(accuse),** accūso (1); **(of price),** vendo (3) **(sell)** (3); **(put in —)** praefĭcĭo (3) (*with dat*); **(be in —)** praesum (*irreg.*) (*with dat*)
chariot currus, *m,* essēdum, *n*
charioteer aurīga, *c*
charitable bĕnignus, mītis
charity ămor, *m,* bĕnĕfĭcentĭa, *f*
charm blandīmentum, *n,* grātĭa, *f* **(trinket),** bulla, *f*
charm *v.t,* fascĭno (1), dēlēnĭo (4), dēlecto (1)
charming vĕnustus, lĕpĭdus
chart tăbŭla, *f*
charter *v.t,* **(hire),** condūco (3)
chase *nn,* **(hunt),** vēnātĭo, *f,* vēnātus, *m*
chase *v.t,* sector (1 *dep.*), vēnor (1 *dep.*)
chasm hĭātus, *m*
chaste castus
chastise *v.t,* castīgo (1), pūnĭo (4)
chastisement castĭgātĭo, *f*
chastity castĭtas, *f*

chat *v.i*, fābŭlor (1 *dep*.)
chat *nn*, sermo, *m*
chatter *v.i*, garrĭo (4); **(of teeth)**, crĕpĭto (1)
chatter *nn*, garrŭlĭtas, *f*
chattering *adj*, garrŭlus
cheap vīlis
cheapness vīlĭtas, *f*
cheat *nn*, **(person)**, fraudātor, *m*
cheat *v.t*, fraudo (1)
cheating *nn*, fraudātĭo, *f*
check *nn*, **(hindrance)**, impedīmentum, *n*, incommŏdum, *n*; **(set back)**, incommŏdum, *n*
check *v.t*, cŏhĭbĕo (2), contĭnĕo (2), comprĭmo (3), cŏercĕo (2)
cheek gĕna, *f*
cheer *nn*, **(shout)**, clāmor, *m*
cheer *v.i*, **(applaud)**, plaudo (3), clāmo (1)
cheerful hĭlăris
cheerfulness hĭlărĭtas, *f*
cheerless tristis
cheese cāsĕus, *m*
cheque perscriptĭo, *f*, **(written entry)**
chequered vărĭus
cherish *v.t*, fŏvĕo (2), cŏlo (3)
cherry, cherry tree cĕrăsus, *f*
chess latruncŭli, *m.pl*
chest (box) amārĭum, *n*, cista, *f*; **(body)**, pectus, *n*, thorax, *m*
chestnut glands, *f*; **(— tree)**, castănĕa, *f*
chew mando (3)
chicken pullus, *m*
chide *v.t*, obiurgo (1), incrĕpĭto (1), rĕprĕhendo (3)
chiding rĕprĕhensĭo, *f*
chief *nn*, princeps, *m*, prōcer, *m*
chief *adj*, prīmus, princeps
chieftain see **chief**
child pŭer, *m*, infans, *c*; **(pl.)** lībĕri, *m.pl*
childbirth partus, *m*
childhood pŭerĭtĭa, *f*
childish pŭerīlis
childless orbus
chill, chilly *adj*, frīgĭdus
chill *v.t*, rĕfrīgĕro (1)
chime *nn*, concentus, *m*
chime *v.i*, **(sound)**, căno (3)
chimney camīnus, *m*

chin mentum, *n*
chine tergum, *n*
chink rīma, *f*
chip assŭla, *f*
chirp, chirping *nn*, pīpātus, *m*
chirp *v.i*, pīpĭo (4)
chisel scalprum, *n*
chisel *v.t*, sculpo (3)
chivalrous magnănĭmus
chivalry magnănĭmĭtas, *f*
choice *nn*, dēlectus, *m*; **(— between)**, optĭo, *f*
choice *adj*, ēlectus
choir chŏrus, *m*
choke *v.t*, suffōco (1); *v.i*, suffōcor (1 *pass*)
choose *v.t*, lĕgo (3), ēlĭgo (3)
chop *v.t*, caedo (3); **(cut off)**, abscīdo (3)
chord *use* nervus, *m*, **(string)**
chorus chŏrus, *m*
Christ Christus, *m*
Christian Christĭānus
chronic (long-lasting) dĭūturnus
chronicle annāles, *m.pl*
chuckle *v.i*, căchinno (1)
church templum, *n*
churchyard ārĕa, *f*
churl hŏmo rustĭcus
churlish rustĭcus
churn *v.t*, **(stir)**, ăgĭto (1)
cinder cĭnis, *m*, făvilla, *f*
cipher (a nonentity) nŭmĕrus, *m*; **(secret writing)**, nŏta, *f*
circle orbis, *m*
circuit circŭĭtus, *m*
circuitous (route, etc.), flexŭōsus
circular rŏtundus
circulate *v.t*, spargo (3), dīvulgo (1); *v.i*, diffundor (3 *pass*), percrēbresco (3)
circulation, (to be in —) (of books etc.) in mănĭbus esse (*irreg*)
circumcise *v.t*, circumcīdo (3)
circumference ambĭtus, *m*
circumscribe *v.t*, circumscrībo (3)
circumstance res, *f*; *or use neuter of an adj*, *e.g*. adversa **(adverse circumstances)**
circumstantial evidence coniectūra, *f*
circumvent *v.t*, circumvĕnĭo (4)
circus circus, *m*

cistern cisterna, *f*
citadel arx, *f*
cite *v.t,* **(quote),** prōfĕro (*irreg*)
citizen cīvis, *c*
citizenship cīvĭtas, *f*
city urbs, *f*
civic cīvīlis
civil (polite) urbānus; **(civic)** cīvīlis; **(— war),** bellum dŏmestĭcum
civilian (opp. military) tŏgātus, *m*
civilization cultus, *m*, hūmānĭtas, *f*
civilize *v.t,* excŏlo (3), expŏlĭo (4)
civilized hūmānus, cultus
claim *v.t,* postŭlo (1), rĕposco (3)
claim *nn,* postŭlātĭo, *f*
claimant pĕtītor, *m*
clammy lentus
clamorous clāmans
clamour *nn,* clāmor, *m*, strĕpĭtus, *m*
clamour *v.i,* vōcĭfĕror (1 *dep*)
clandestine clandestīnus
clang *nn,* clangor, *m*
clang *v.i. and v.t,* strĕpo (3)
clank crĕpĭtus, *m*
clank *v.i,* crĕpo (1)
clap *nn,* **(hands),** plausus, *m*; **(thunder),** frăgor, *m*
clap *v.i. and v.t,* plaudo (3)
clash *v.i,* concrĕpo (1), crĕpĭto (1); **(opinions)** rĕpugno (1); **(fight),** conflīgo (3)
clash *nn,* **(noise),** crĕpĭtus, *m*; **(collision),** concursus, *m*
clasp *nn,* **(embrace),** complexus, *m*; **(fastener),** fibŭla, *f*
clasp *v.t,* **(fasten),** fibŭlo (1); **(embrace),** complector (3 *dep.*)
class classis, *f*, gĕnus, *n*
classic, classical (well-established), prŏbus
classify *v.t,* dēscrībo (3) ordĭne
clatter *nn,* strĕpĭtus, *m*
clatter *v.i,* incrĕpo (1)
clause membrum, *n*, căpŭt, *n*
claw unguis, *m*
clay argilla, *f*, lŭtum, *n*
clean *adj,* mundus, pūrus
clean *v.t,* purgo (1), mundo (1)
cleanliness mundĭtĭa, *f*
cleanse *v.t,* purgo (1)
clear clārus; **(weather),** sĕrēnus; **(matter),** mănĭfestus

clear *v.t,* **(open up),** expĕdĭo (4); **(— oneself),** sē purgāre (1 *reflex*); *v.i,* **(of the weather),** dissĕrēnat (1 *impers*)
clearing *nn,* **(open space),** lŏcus ăpertus
clearly *adv,* clārē, ăpertĕ, plānē
clearness clārĭtas, *f*
cleave *v.t,* **(split),** findo (3); *v.i* **(stick to),** adhaerĕo (2)
cleft hĭātus, *m*, rīma, *f*
clemency clēmentĭa, *f*
clement clēmens, lēntis
clench (the fist) *v.t,* comprĭmo (3)
clerk scrība, *m*
clever callĭdus, astūtus
cleverness *f,* callĭdĭtas, *f*
client clĭens, *m,* consultor, *m*
cliff cautes, *f,* scŏpŭlus, *m,* rūpes
climate caelum, *n*
climax grădātĭo, *f*
climb *v.i. and v.t,* ascendo (3), scando (3)
climb *nn,* ascensus, *m*
cling to *v.i,* ădhaerĕo (2) (*with dat*)
clip *v.t,* tondĕo (2)
cloak pallĭum, *n,* lăcerna, *f*
cloak *v.t,* **(hide),** dissĭmŭlo (1)
clock hŏrŏlŏgĭum, *n*
clod glaeba, *f*
clog (hindrance) impĕdīmentum, *n*; **(shoe),** sculpōnĕa, *f*
clog *v.t,* **(impede),** impĕdĭo (4)
close *adj,* **(near),** vīcīnus; **(packed together)** confertus, densus; **(at close quarters),** commĭnus, *adv*
close *nn,* **(end),** fīnis, *m,* termĭnus, *m*
close *adv,* prŏpe, iuxta
close *v.t,* claudo (3); *v.i,* claudor (3 *pass*)
close in on *v.t,* prĕmo (3) **(press)**
closely *adv,* prŏpe; **(accurately),** exacte
closeness prŏpinquĭtas, *f*
closet cella, *f*
clot (of blood) crŭor, *m*
cloth textum, *n*
clothe *v.t,* vestĭo (4), indŭo (3)
clothes vestis, *f,* vestīmenta, *n.pl*
cloud nūbes, *f*
cloudy nūbĭlus

cloven bĭsulcus
clown scurra, *m*
club (cudgel) clāva, *f*;
 (association), sŏdālĭtas, *f*
cluck *v.i*, singultĭo (4)
clump massa, *f*
clumsy ĭnhăbĭlis, rustĭcus
cluster *nn*, răcēmus, *m*; **(people)**,
 glŏbus, *m*
clutch *v.t*, arrĭpĭo (3)
coach carpentum, *n*, raeda, *f*
coachman raedārĭus, *m*
coagulate *v.i*, concresco (3)
coal carbo, *m*
coalition coniunctĭo, *f*, conspīrātĭo,
 f
coarse crassus; **(manners)**, incultus
coarseness crassĭtūdo, *f*,
 ĭnhūmānĭtas, *f*
coast ōra, *f*, lĭtus, *n*
coast *v.i*, praetervĕhor (3 *pass*)
coat tŭnĭca, *f*, ămictus, *m*;
 (animal's), pellis, *f*
coat *v.t*, illĭno (3)
coax *v.t*, mulcĕo (2), blandĭor (4
 dep)
cobble *v.t*, sarcĭo (4)
cobbler sūtor, *m*
cock gallus, *m*
code (method, system) rătĭo, *f*
coerce *v.t*, cōgo (3), cŏercĕo (2)
coercion cŏercĭtĭo, *f*
coffin arca, *f*
cog dens, *m*
cogent vălĭdus
cogitate *v.i*, cōgĭto (1)
cognizance cognĭtĭo, *f*
cohabit *v.i*, consŭesco (3)
cohere *v.i*, cŏhaerĕo (2)
coherent cŏhaerens
cohesion cŏhaerentĭa, *f*
cohort cŏhors, *f*
coil *nn*, spīra, *f*
coil *v.t*, glŏmĕro (1)
coin *nn*, nummus, *m*
coin *v.t*, cūdo (3)
coinage nummi, *m.pl*
coincide *v.i*, compĕto (3), concurro
 (3)
coincidence consursātĭo, *f*,
 concursus, *m*
cold *adj*, frīgĭdus, gĕlĭdus
cold (to be —) *v.i*, algĕo (2)

coldness frīgus, *n*
collapse *v.i*, collābor (3 *dep*)
collar torques, *m and f*
collation (comparison) collātĭo, *f*
colleague collēga, *m*
collect *v.t*, collĭgo (3), cōgo (3)
collection (act of —) collātĭo, *f*;
 (heap, etc.), congĕrĭes, *f*
collector (of taxes, etc.) exactor, *m*
college collēgĭum, *n*
collide *v.i*, conflīgo (3), concurro
 (3)
collision concursus, *m*
colloquial (speech) *use* sermo, *m*
collusion collūsĭo, *f*
colon cōlon, *n*
colonel praefectus, *m*
colonist cŏlōnus, *m*
colony cŏlōnĭa, *f*
colonnade portĭcus, *f*
collossal igens
colour cŏlor, *m*; **(flag)**, vexillum, *n*;
 (— bearer), signĭfer, *m*
colour *v.t*, cŏlōro (1)
coloured pictus
colourful fūcātus
colt equŭlĕus, *m*
column (pillar) columna, *f*;
 (military), agmen, *n*
comb *nn*, pecten, *m*
comb *v.t*, pecto (3)
combat *nn*, proelĭum, *n*
combat *v.i*, pugno (1), luctor (1
 dep)
combat *v.t*, **(oppose)** obsto (1)
combatant pugnātor, *m*
combination coniunctĭo, *f*
combine *v.t*, coinungo (3)
come *v.i*, vĕnĭo (4); **(— about,
 happen)**, ēvĕnĭo (4); **(—
 across, find)**, *v.t*, invĕnĭo (4); **(—
 back)**, *v.i*, rĕvĕnĭo (4); **(— by,
 obtain)**, *v.t*, ădĭpiscor (3 *dep*); **(—
 in)** incēdo (3); **(— near)**
 apprŏpinquo (1);
 (— on, advance), prōgrĕdĭor (3
 dep); **(— out)** exĕo (4); **(— to)**
 advĕnĭo (4) **(regain
 consciousness)** ad se rĕdire (4);
 (— together) convĕnĭo (4);
 (—upon), *v.t*, sŭpervĕnĭo (4)
 (attack) incĭdo (3)
comedian cōmoedus, *m*

comedy cōmoedĭa, *f*
comely pulcher
comet cŏmētes, *m*
comfort sōlācĭum, *n*, consōlātĭo, *f*
comfort *v.t*, consōlor (1 *dep.*)
comfortable commŏdus
comforter consōlātor, *m*
comic, comical cōmĭcus
coming *adj*, ventūrus
coming *nn*, adventus, *m*
command *nn*, (power), impĕrĭum,
n; (an order) iussum, *n*,
mandātus, *m*; (to be in —) *v.i*,
praesum (*with dat*)
command *v.t*. impĕro (1) (*with
dat.*), iŭbĕo (2)
commander dux, *m*, impĕrātor, *m*
commemorate *v.t*, cĕlĕbro (1)
commemoration cĕlĕbrātĭo, *f*
commence *v.i*, incĭpĭo (3)
commencement ĭnĭtĭum, *n*
commend *v.t*, commendo (1);
(praise), laudo (1)
commendable laudābĭlis
comment *v.i*, dīco (3), sententĭas
dīco (3) (declare one's opinion)
comment *nn*, dicta, *n.pl*
commentary commentārĭi, *m.pl*
commerce commercĭum, *n*
commercial traveller instĭtor, *m*
commiserate *v.i. and v.t*, mĭsĕror
(1 *dep.*)
commisariat praefecti (*m.pl*) rĕi
frūmentārĭae (superintendents of
corn supply); (provisions),
commĕatus, *m*
commissary prōcūrātor, *m*,
lēgātus, *m*
commission (task) mandātum, *n*
commission *v.t*, (give a task to),
mando (1) (*dat. of person*)
commit *v.t*, (crime, etc.) admitto
(3); (entrust), committo (3),
mando (1)
committee dēlecti, *m.pl*, (selected
ones)
commodious (opportune)
commŏdus; (capacious), amplus
commodity (thing) res, *f*

common *adj*, commūnis;
(belonging to the public),
pūblĭcus; (ordinary), vulgāris;
(common land), ăger pūblĭcus, *m*
(usual), ūsĭtātus
commonplace *adj*, vulgāris, trītus
commonly *adv*, (mostly),
plērumque
commonwealth respublĭca, *f*
commotion mōtus, *m*, tŭmultus,
m, commōtĭo, *f*
communicate *v.t*, commūnĭco (1);
(report), dēfĕro (*irreg*)
communication commūnĭcātĭo, *f*;
(reporting), nuntĭus, *m*
communicative līber, lŏquax
communion sŏcĭĕtas, *f*
community cīvĭtas, *f*, sŏcĭĕtas, *f*
commute *v.t*, mūto (1)
compact *adj*, confertus, pressus
compact *nn*, pactum, *n*, foedus, *n*
companion sŏcĭus, *m*, cŏmes, *c*
companionable făcĭlis
companionship sŏdālĭtas, *f*
company coetus, *m*, sŏcĭĕtas, *f*
(military body), mănĭpŭlus, *m*
comparable confĕrendus
comparative compărātīvus
compare *v.t*, compăro (1), confĕro
(*irreg*)
comparison compărātĭo, *f*
compartment lŏcŭlus, *m*
compass (range) fīnes, *m.pl*; (pair
of compasses), circĭnus, *m*
compass *v.t*, complector (3 *dep*)
compassion mĭsĕrĭcordĭa, *f*
compassionate mĭsĕrĭcors
compatability congrŭentĭa, *f*
compatible congrŭens
compatriot cīvis, *c*
compel *v.t*, cōgo (3), compello (3)
compensate for *v.t*, compenso (1)
compensation compensātĭo, *f*
compete *v.i*, certo (1) (struggle)
competent căpax; (to be — to), *v.i*,
suffĭcĭo (3)
competition certāmen, *n*
competitor compĕtĭtor, *m*
complacent sĭbi plăcens (pleasing
to oneself)
complain *v.i*, gĕmo (3); *v.t*, quĕror
(3 *dep.*)

complaint questus, *m*, quĕrēla, *f*; **(disease)**, morbus, *m*

complement complēmentum, *n*

complete plēnus, perfectus

complete *v.t*, complĕo (2), confĭcĭo (3)

completely *adv*, omnīno

completion perfectĭo, *f*, confectĭo, *f*

complex multĭplex

complexion cŏlor, *m*

compliance obsĕquĭum, *n*

compliant obsĕquens

complicated invŏlūtus

complication implĭcātĭo, *f*

compliment *nn*, **(esteem)**, hŏnor, *m*; **(praise)** laus, *f*; **(greeting)**, sălūtātĭo, *f*

compliment *v.t*, **(praise)**, laudo (1)

complimentary hŏnōrĭfĭcus

comply with *v.i*, concēdo (3) **(with dat)**

component *nn*, **(part)**, ĕlĕmentum, *n*

compose *v.t*, compōno (3)

composed (calm) sēdātus

composer scriptor, *m*

composition (act of —) compŏsĭtĭo, *f*; **(a literary —)**, ŏpus scriptum, *n*

composure tranquillĭtas, *f*

compound *adj*, compŏsĭtus

compound *v.t*, compōno (3), miscĕo (2)

comprehend *v.t*, **(understand)** intellĕgo (3)

comprehension comprĕhensĭo, *f*

comprehensive *use phr*, ad omnĭa pertĭnens **(extending to everything)**

compress *v.t*, comprĭmo (3)

comprise *v.t*, contĭnĕo (2)

compromise *nn*, **(agreement)**, compŏsĭtĭo, *f*

compromise *v.t*, compōno (3); **(implicate)**, implĭco (1)

compulsion nĕcessĭtas, *f*

compunction paenĭtentĭa, *f*

compute *v.t*, compŭto (1)

comrade sŏcĭus, *m*, cŏmes, *c*

concave căvus

conceal *v.t*, cēlo (1), abdo (3)

concede *v.t*, cēdo (3)

conceit arrŏgantĭa, *f*

conceited arrŏgans

conceive *v.t*, concĭpĭo (3)

concentrate (mentally) *v.i*, ălĭmum intendo (3); **(bring together)**, *v.t*, contrăho (3), cōgo (3)

conception (mental) nōtĭo, *f*; **(physical)**, conceptĭo, *f*

concern *nn*, **(affair, circumstance)**, rēs, *f*; **(worry)**, sollĭcĭtūdo, *f*

concern *v.t*, pertĭnĕo (2); **(it concerns)**, rēfert **(irreg. impers)**

concerned (to be —) *v.i*, sollĭcĭtus esse

concerning *prep*, dē **(with abl. of nn. etc)**

concern *v.t*, **(plans, etc.)**, confĕro **(irreg)**, compōno (3)

concession concessĭo, *f*

conciliate *v.t*, concĭlĭo (1)

conciliation concĭlĭātĭo, *f*

conciliatory pācĭfĭcus

concise brĕvis

conciseness brĕvĭtas, *f*

conclude *v.t*, **(decide)**, stătŭo (3); **(end)**, perfĭcĭo (3)

conclusion (end) exĭtus, *m*, finis, *m* **(decision)**, decrētum, *n*

conclusive certus

concord concordĭa, *f*

concourse concursus, *m*

concubine pellex, *f*

concupiscence lībĭdo, *f*

concur *v.i*, consentĭo (4)

concurrence consensus, *m*

concurrent *use adv*, sĭmŭl **(at the same time)**

concurrently *adv*, sĭmŭl

condemn *v.t*, damno (1) **(with acc of person and genit. of crime or punishment)**

condemnation damnātĭo, *f*

condense *v.t*, denso (1), comprĭmo (3)

condensed densus

condescend *v.i*, dēscendo (3)

condescension cōmĭtas, *f*, **(friendliness)**

condition condĭcĭo, *f*, stătus, *m*

condole *v.i*, dŏlĕo (2) cum **(with abl)**

condone *v.t*, condōno (1)

conduce *v.t*, condūco (3)

conductive ūtĭlis **(advantageous)**

conduct *nn*, **(personal, etc.)**, mōres, *m.pl*; **(administration)**, admĭnistrātĭo, *f*

conduct *v.t*, **(lead)**, dūco (3); **(administer)**, admĭnistro (1); **(— oneself)**, sē gĕrĕre (3 *reflex*)

conductor dux, *m*

conduit cănālis, *m*

cone cōnus, *m*

confectionery crustum, *n*

confederacy sŏcĭĕtas, *f*

confederate foedĕrātus

confer *v.t*, confĕro (*irreg*); **(—with)**, collŏquor (3 *dep*); **(—about)**, ăgo (3) dē

conference collŏquĭum, *n*

confess *v.t*, confĭtĕor (2 *dep*)

confession confessĭo, *f*

confide *v.t*, confīdo (3), fīdo (3), **(***with dat.***)**

confidence fĭdes, *f*, fĭdūcĭa, *f*

confident fīdens

confidential (trusty) fīdus; **(one's own, special)**, prŏprĭus; **(secret)**, arcānus

confine *v.t*, inclūdo (3), contĭnĕo (2)

confinement inclūsĭo, *f*, custōdĭa, *f*; **(childbirth)**, partus, *m*; pŭerpĕrĭum, *n*

confirm *v.t*, confirmo (1)

confiscate *v.t*, pūblĭco (1), ădĭmo (3)

confiscation pūblĭcātĭo, *f*

conflagration incendĭum, *n*

conflict *nn*, certāmen, *n*

conflict *v.i*, certo (1); dissentĭo (4)

confluence conflŭens, *m*

conform to *v.i*, obtempĕro (1) (*with dat*); *v.t*, accommŏdo (1)

conformity convĕnĭentĭa, *f*

confound *v.t*, **(disturb)**, turbo (1); **(amaze)**, obstŭpĕfăcĭo (3); **(bring to nothing, thwart)**, frustror (1 *dep.*)

confront *v.i*, obvĭam ĕo (*irreg.*) (*with dat*)

confuse *v.t*, turbo (1)

confused perturbātus

confusion perturbātĭo, *f*

congeal *v.i. and v.t*, congĕlo (1)

congenial concors

congested frĕquens

congratulate *v.t*, grātŭlor (1 *dep*)

congratulation grātŭlātĭo, *f*

congregate *v.i*, sē congrĕgare (1 *reflex*)

congress concĭlĭum, *n*, conventus, *m*

congruous congrŭens

conjecture *nn*, conĭectūra, *f*

conjecture *v.i*, cōnĭcĭo (3)

conjugate *v.t*, dēclīno (1)

conjunction (grammar) conĭunctĭo, *f*

conjure *v.i*, **(perform tricks)**, praestigĭis ūtor (3 *dep.*); **(image)** cōgĭto (1)

conjurer măgus, *m*

connect *v.t*, conĭungo (3)

connected conĭunctus

connection conĭunctĭo, *f*; **(by marriage)**, affĭnĭtas, *f*

connive at *v.i*, connīvĕo (2) in (*with abl*)

connoisseur *use vb*, stŭdĕo (2) **(to be keen on)**

conquer *v.t*, vinco (3), sŭpĕro (1)

conqueror victor, *m*

conquest victōrĭa, *f*

conscience conscĭentĭa, *f*

conscientious rēlĭgĭōsus

conscientiousness fĭdes, *f*

conscious conscĭus

consciously *adv, use adj*, scĭens **(knowingly)**

consciousness conscĭentĭa, *f*, sensus, *m*

conscript (recruit) tīro, *m*

consecrate *v.t*, conscĕro (1)

consecrated săcer

consecutive contĭnŭus

consent *nn*, consensus, *m*; **(by the — of)**, consensu;

consent to *v.i*, assentĭo (4)

consequence (result) exĭtus, *m*; **(importance)**, mōmentum, *n*; **(in — of)**, *prep*, propter (*with acc*)

consequent sĕquens

consequently *adv*, ĭgĭtur, ĭtăque

conserve *v.t*, conservo (1)

consider *v.t*, cōgĭto (1), dēlībĕro (1), existĭmo (1); **(— with respect)**, respĭcĭo (3)

considerable ălĭquantus

considerate hūmānus

considerateness hūmānĭtas, *f*
consideration consīdĕrātĭo, *f*; **(regard)**, rătĭo, *f*
considering *conj*, ut
consign *v.t*, mando (1), committo (3)
consignment (of goods) merces, *f.pl*
consist of *v.i*, consisto (3) in (*with abl*)
consistency constantĭa, *f*
consistent (constant) constans; **(consistent with)**, consentānĕus
console *v.t*, consōlor (1 *dep.*)
consolidate *v.t*, firmo (1), sŏlĭdo (1)
consonant consŏnans littĕra
consort (husband) mărītus, *m*; **(wife)**, mărīta, *f*
consort with *v.i*, ūtor (3 *dep*) (*with abl*)
conspicuous mănĭfestus, insignis
conspiracy conĭūrātĭo, *f*
conspirator conĭūrātus, *m*
conspire *v.i*, conĭūro (1)
constable dĕcŭrĭo, *m*, lictor, *m*
constancy fĭdes, *f*; **(steadiness)**, constantĭa, *f*, fĭdēlĭtas, *f*
constant fĭdēlis, constans
constellation sīdus, *n*
consternation păvor, *m*
constituent parts ĕlĕmenta, *n.pl*
constitute *v.t*, constĭtŭo (3), compōno (3), crĕo (1)
constitution (of a state) respūblĭca, *f*; **(of a body)**, hăbĭtus, *m*
constitutional lēgĭtĭmus
constrain *v.t*, cōgo (3), compello (3)
construct *v.t*, făbrĭcor (1 *dep*) exstrŭo (3)
construction *v.t*, făbrĭcor (1 *dep*) exstrŭo (3)
construction (act of —) făbrĭcātĭo, *f*; **(method)** fĭgūra, *f*, structūra, *f*
construe *v.t*, interprĕtor (1 *dep*)
consul consul, *m*
consulship consŭlātus, *m*
consult *v.t*, consŭlo (3); *v.i*, dēlībĕro (1); **(— someone's interests)**, consŭlo (3) (*with dat*)

consultation collŏquĭum, *n*
consume *v.t*, consumo (3), confĭcĭo (3)
consummate *v.t*, consummo (1), perfĭcĭo (3)
consummate *adj* summus
consummation connsummātĭo, *f*
consumption consumptĭo, *f*
contact tactus, *m*
contagion contāgĭo, *f*
contain *v.t*, contĭnĕo (2)
contaminate *v.t*, contāmĭno (1)
contamination contāgĭo, *f*, măcŭla, *f*
contemplate *v.t*, contemplor (1 *dep*)
contemplation (study) mĕdĭtātĭo, *f*
contemporary aequālis
contempt contemptus, *m*
contemptible contemnendus
contend *v.i*, contendo (3), certo (1), pugno (1); **(argue)**, *v.t*, affirmo (1)
content contentus
content *v.t*, sătisfăcĭo (3) (*with dat.*); *v.i*, **(be content)** sătis hăbĕo (2)
contentment aequus ănĭmus, *m*
contest *nn*, certāmen, *n*, pugna, *f*
contest *v.t*, certo (1), contendo (3)
contestant pugnātor, *m*, pĕtītor, *m*
contiguous contĭgŭus, confinis
continent *adj*, contĭnens
continent *nn*, contĭnens, *f*
contingency cāsus, *m*
continual perpĕtuus, contĭnens
continually *adv*, perpĕtuo, contĭnenter
continuation perpĕtŭĭtas, *f*
continue *v.t*, prōdūco (3), prōrŏgo (1), *v.i*, mănĕo (2)
continuity perpĕtŭĭtas, *f*
continuous contĭnens
contort *v.t*, torquĕo (2)
contour fĭgūra, *f*
contraband *adj*, vĕtĭtus
contract *nn*, pactum, *n*
contract *v.i*, **(grow smaller)**, sē contrăhĕre (3 *reflex*); *v.t*, contrăho (3)
contraction contractĭo, *f*
contractor conductor, *m*

contradict *v.t,* contrādīco (3) (*with dat*)

contradiction contrādictĭo, *f*; **(inconsistency),** rĕpugnantĭa, *f*

contradictory rĕpugnans

contrary *adj,* adversus, contrārĭus; **(— to),** *prep,* contrā (*with acc*); **the contrary,** *nn,* contrārĭum, *n*; **(on the —),** *adv,* contrā

contrast *v.t,* confĕro (*irreg*); *v.i,* discrĕpo (1)

contravene *v.t,* vĭŏlo (1)

contribute *v.t,* confĕro (*irreg*)

contribution collātĭo, *f*, trĭbūtum, *n*

contrivance (gadget) māchĭna, *f*

contrive *v.t,* **(think out),** excōgĭto (1)

control *v.t,* mŏdĕror (1 *dep*) (*with dat*); **(guide),** rĕgo (3)

control *nn,* pŏtestas, *f*, tempĕrantĭa, *f*

controversy contrōversĭa, *f*

contumacious pertĭnax

contumacy pertĭnācĭa, *f*

contumely contŭmēlĭa, *f*

convalescent convălescens

convenience commŏdĭtas, *f*, opportūnĭtas, *f*

convenient commŏdus, opportūnus

convention (meeting) conventus, *m*; **(agreement),** conventĭo, *f*

converge *v.i,* ēŏdem vergo (3)

conversation sermo, *m*, collŏquĭum, *n*

converse *v.i,* collŏquor (3 *dep*)

conversion commūtātĭo, *f*

convert *v.t,* mūto (1), converto (3)

convex convexus

convey *v.t,* vĕho (3), porto (1)

conveyance (act of —) vectūra, *f*; **(vehicle),** vĕhĭcŭlum, *n*

convict *v.t,* damno (1)

conviction (belief) *use phr,* persuāsum est (*with dat. of person*) e.g. persuāsum est mĭhi **(it is my conviction); (convicting),** damnātĭo, *f*

convince *v.t,* persuādĕo (2) (*with dat.*)

conviviality hĭlărĭtas, *f*

convoke *v.t,* convŏco (1)

convoy *nn,* commĕātus, *m*;

(escort), praesĭdĭum, *n*

convulse *v.t,* concŭtĭo (3), ăgĭto (1)

convulsion tŭmultus, *m*, mōtus, *m*; **(medical),** convulsĭo, *f*

cook *nn,* cŏquus, *m*

cook *v.t,* cŏquo (3)

cool frīgĭdus; **(of mind),** lentus

cool *v.t,* rĕfrīgĕro (1); *v.i,* rĕfrīgĕror (1 *pass*)

cooly *adv,* frīgĭde, lentē

coolness frīgus, *n*

co-operate with *v.t,* adiŭvo (1)

co-operation auxĭlĭum, *n,* **(help)**

cope with *v.i.* congrĕdĭor (3 *dep.*)

copious largus, cōpĭōsus

copper aes, *n*

copper *adj,* aēnĕus

coppice dūmētum, *n*

copy exemplum, *n*

copy *v.t,* ĭmĭtor (1 *dep*), dēscrībo (3)

coral cŏrălĭum, *n*

cord fūnis, *m*

cordial *adj,* bĕnignus

cordiality bĕnignĭtas, *f*

cordon cŏrōna, *f*

core nuclĕus, *m*

cork *nn,* cortex, *m, f*

corn frūmentum, *n*; **(crop),** sĕges, *f*; **(on the foot),** clāvus, *m*

corner angŭlus, *m*

cornice cŏrōna, *f*

coronation *use* crĕo (1) **(elect to office)**

coroner quaesītor, *m*

corporal *adj,* corpŏrĕus

corporal *nn,* dĕcŭrĭo, *m*

corps (company) mănus, *f*

corpse cădāver, *n,* corpus, *n*

corpulence ŏbēsĭtas, *f*

corpulent ŏbēsus

correct rectus, pūrus

correct *v.t,* corrĭgo (3), ēmendo (1)

correction ēmendātĭo, *f*; **(chastisement),** castĭgātĭo, *f*

correctly *adv,* rectē

correctness vērĭtas, *f*

correspond *v.i,* **(agree with),** convĕnĭo (4) (*with dat*); **(write),** littĕras mitto (3) et accĭpĭo (3) **(send and receive letters)**

correspondence missĭo et acceptĭo ĕpistŏlārum **(sending and receiving of letters)**

corresponding par, gĕmellus

corroborate *v.t*, confirmo (1)

corrode *v.t*, rōdo (3), ĕdo (3)

corrosive mordax

corrupt *v.t*, corrumpo (3)

corrupt *adj*, corruptus

corruption dēprāvātĭo, *f*

corselet lōrīca, *f*

cost *nn*, prĕtĭum, *n*, sumptus, *m*

cost *v.i*, sto (1) *(with dat. of person and abl. or genit. of price)* e.g. **the victory cost the Carthaginians much bloodshed:** victōrĭa stĕtit Poenis multo sanguĭne

costly *adj*, prĕtĭōsus

costume hăbĭtus, *m*

cot lectŭlus, *m*

cottage căsa, *f*

cotton gossypĭum, *n*

couch lectus, *m*

couch *v.i*, subsīdo (3); *v.t*, **(—a weapon)**, intendo (3)

cough *nn*, tussis, *f*

cough *v.i*, tussĭo (4)

council concĭlĭum, *n*

counsel **(advice)** consĭlĭum, *n*; **(lawyer)**, pătrōnus, *m*

count *v.t*, nŭmĕro (1); **(— upon, trust)**, confīdo (3) *(with dat)*

countenance *nn*, vultus, *m*

countenance *v.t*, permitto (3), făvĕo (2), indulgĕo (2)

counter **(in shop)** mensa, *f*; **(for counting)** calcŭlus, *m*

counter *adv*, contra

counteract *v.t*, obsisto (3) *(with dat.)*

counterbalance *v.t*, exaequo (1)

counterfeit *adj*, ădultĕrīnus, fictus

counterfeit *v.t*, sĭmŭlo (1), fingo (3)

counterpart res gĕmella **(paired, twin thing)**

countless innŭmĕrābĭlis

country **(fatherland)** pătrĭă, *f*; **(countryside)**, rūs, *n*; **(region)**, rĕgĭo, *f*

country house villa, *f*

countryman **(of the same country)** cīvis, *c*; **(living in the countryside)**, rustĭcus, *m*

couple *nn*, **(pair)**, pār *n*

couple *v.t*, coniungo (3)

courage virtus, *f*, ănĭmus, *m*

courageous fortis, ācer, fĕrox

courier **(messenger)** nuntĭus, *m*

course **(motion)** cursus, *m*; **(route)**, vĭa, *f*, ĭter *n*; **(plan)**, rătĭo, *f*; **(race —)**, circus, *m*; **(of —)**, *adv*, nīmīrum, certē

court **(— of justice)** iūdĭcĭum, *n*; **(judges themselves)**, iūdĭces, *m.pl*; **(palace)**, aula, *f*, dŏmus, *(f)* rēgis **(the house of the king)**; **(courtyard)**, ārĕa, *f*

court *v.t*, cŏlo (3)

court martial *use phr.* in castris iudĭcare (1) **(to try in camp)**

courteous cōmis, hūmānus

courtesy cōmĭtas, *f*, hūmānĭtas, *f*

courtier aulĭcus, *m*

courtship ămor, *m*

cousin consōrbrīnus, *m* (…a), *f*

covenant pactum, *n*

cover *v.t*, tĕgo (3); **(conceal)** occulto (1)

cover, covering *nn*, tĕgŭmen, *n*; **(lid)**, ŏpĕrīmentum, *n*

coverlet strāgŭlum, *n*

covert *nn*, dūmētum, *n*

covet *v.t*, cŭpĭo (3)

covetous ăvārus, ăvĭdus, cŭpĭdus

covetousness ăvārĭtĭa, *f*, cŭpĭdĭtas, *f*

cow vacca, *f*

cow *v.t*, terrĕo (2), dŏmo (1) **(tame)**

coward ignāvus, *m*

cowardice ignāvĭa, *f*

cowardly *adj*, ignāvus

cowl cŭcullus, *m*

coy **(bashful)** vĕrēcundus

crab cancer, *m*

crabbed mōrōsus

crack *nn*, **(noise)**, crĕpĭtus, *m*; **(chink)**, rĭma, *f*

crack *v.t*, findo (3), frango (3); *v.i*, **(open up)**, dĕhisco (3); **(sound)**, crĕpo (1)

cradle cūnae, *f.pl*
craft (deceit) dŏlus, *m*; **(skill)**, artĭfĭcĭum, *n*; **(boat)**, rătis, *f*, nāvis, *f*
craftsman ŏpĭfex, *m*
crafty callĭdus
crag scŏpŭlus, *m*
cram *v.t*, confercĭo (4)
cramp *v.t*, comprĭmo (3)
crane (bird) grus, *m*, *f*; **(machine)**, tollēno, *f*
crank uncus, *m*
cranny rīma, *f*
crash *nn*, frăgor, *m*
crash *v.i*, **(noise)**, strĕpo (3); **(bring into collision)**, *v.t*, collīdo (3)
crate corbis, *m*
crater crāter, *m*
crave for *v.t*, ōro (1), appĕto (3)
craving *nn*, dēsīdĕrĭum, *n*
crawl *v.i*, rēpo (3)
crayon crēta, *f*
crazy cerrītus, dēmens
creak *v.i*, crēpo (1)
creaking *nn*, strīdor, *m*, crĕpĭtus, *m*
crease *nn*, rūga, *f*
crease *v.t*, rūgo (1)
create *v.t*, crĕo (1)
creation (act of —) crĕātĭo, *f*; **(making)**, făbrĭcātĭo, *f*; **(universe)**, mundus, *m*
creator auctor, *m*, crĕātor, *m*
creature ănĭmal, *n*
credence (belief) fĭdes, *f*
credible crēdĭbĭlis
credit (belief or commercial credit) fĭdes, *f*; **(reputation)**, existĭmātĭo, *f*
credit *v.t*, **(believe)**, crēdo (3); **(—an account, person, etc.)**, acceptum rĕfĕro (*irreg*) (*with dat. of person*)
creditable (honourable) hŏnestus
creditor crēdĭtor, *m*
credulous crēdŭlus, *m*
creek sĭnus, *m*
creep *v.i*, serpo (3), rēpo (3)
crescent lūna, *f*, **(crescent moon)**
crescent-shaped lūnatus
crest crista, *f*
crested cristātus
crestfallen dēmissus
crevice rīma, *f*

crew nautae, *m.pl*, rēmĭges, *m,pl*
crib (child's bed) lectŭlus, *m*
cricket (insect) cĭcāda, *f*
crime făcĭnus, *n*, scĕlus, *n*
criminal *nn*, hŏmo sons, hŏmo nŏcens
criminal *adj*, nĕfārĭus, scĕlestus
crimson *adj*, coccĭnĕus
cringe to *v.i*, ădūlor (1 *dep*)
cripple *nn*, hŏmo claudus
cripple *v.t*, dēbĭlĭto (1); **(— a person)**, claudum reddo (3)
crippled dēbĭlis, claudus
crisis discrīmen, *n*
crisp frăgĭlis
critic existĭmātor, *m*, censor, *m*
critical ēlĕgans; **(of a crisis, etc.)**, *use* discrīmen, *n* **(crisis)**
criticize *v.t*, **(find fault)** rĕprĕhendo (3), iūdĭco (1)
croak *v.i*, căno (3), crōcĭo (4)
crockery fictĭlĭa, *n.pl*
crocodile crŏcŏdīlus, *m*
crocus crŏcus, *m*
crook (shepherd's —) pĕdum, *n*
crooked curvus; **(bad, etc.)**, prāvus
crop (of corn) sĕges, *f*, frūges, *f.pl*; **(of a bird)**, inglŭvĭes, *f*
crop *v.t*, tondĕo (2)
cross *nn*, crux, *f*
cross *adj*, transversus; **(annoyed)**, īrātus
cross *v.i. and v.t*, transĕo (4 *irreg*)
cross-examine *v.t*, interrŏgo (1)
crossing (act of —) transĭtus, *m*; **(cross-road)**, compĭtum, *n*
crouch *v.i*, sē dēmittĕre (3 *reflex*)
crow (bird) cornix, *f*
crow *v.i*, **(of a cock)**, căno (3); **(boast)**, sē iactare (1 *reflex*)
crowd turba, *f*
crowd together *v.i*, congrĕgor (1 *dep*); *v.t*, stīpo (1), frĕquento (1)
crowded confertus, cĕlĕber
crown cŏrōna, *f*; **(royal)** dĭădēma, *n*; **(of head, etc.)** vertex, *m*
crown *v.t*, crōno (1)
crucifixion *use phr. with* crux, *f*, **(cross)**
crucify *v.t*, crŭce afficĭo (3)
crude rŭdis
cruel crūdēlis, atrox

cruelty crūdēlĭtas, *f*
cruet gutus, *m*
cruise *nn*, nāvĭgātĭo
cruise *v.i.* nāvĭgo (1)
crumb mīca, *f*
crumble *v.t*, tĕro (3); *v.i*, corrŭo (3)
crumple *v.t*, rūgo (1)
crush *v.t*, contundo (3), opprĭmo (3)
crust crusta, *f*
crutch băcŭlum, *n*
cry *nn*, clāmor, *m*, vox, *f*
cry *v.i*, clāmo (1); **(weep)**, lacrĭmo (1)
crystal *nn*, crystallum, *n*
cub cătŭlus, *m*
cube tessĕra, *f*
cubic cŭbĭcus
cuckoo cŭcūlus, *m*, coccyx, *m*
cucumber cŭcŭmis, *m*
cudgel fustis, *m*
cudgel *v.t*, verbĕro (1), mulco (1)
cue signum, *n*
cuff *nn*, **(blow)**, cŏlăphus, *m*, ălăpa
cuff *v.t*, incŭtĭo (3)
cuirass lōrīca, *f*, thōrax, *m*
culminate *use adj*, summus **(topmost)**
culpable culpandus, nŏcens
culprit hŏmo nŏcens
cultivate *v.t*, cŏlo (3)
cultivation cultus, *m*, cultūra, *f*
cultivator cultor, *m*
culture cultus, *m*, cultūra, *f*
cumbersome inhăbĭlis
cunning *adj*, callĭdus, dŏlōsus
cunning *nn*, callĭdĭtas, *f*, dŏlus, *m*
cup pōcŭlum, *n*
cupboard armārĭum, *n*
cupidity cŭpĭdĭtas, *f*
cupola thŏlus, *m*
curate săcerdos, *c*, **(priest)**
curator cūrātor, *m*
curb *v.t*, frēno (1), cŏhĭbĕo (2)
curdle *v.t*, cōgo (3), cŏăgŭlo (1); *v.i*, concresco (ī)
cure *nn*, sānātĭo, *f*
cure *v.t*, mĕdĕor (*2 dep*) (*with dat*.)
curiosity stŭdĭum, *n*
curious (inquisitive) cūrĭōsus; **(rare)**, rārus

curl *v.t*, crispo (1)
curl *nn*, cincinnus, *m*
curly cincinnātus
currant ăcĭnus, *m*
currency mŏnēta, *f*, nummi, *m.pl*
current *nn*, **(of river)**, flūmen, *n*
current *adj*, **(present)**, hic; **(general)**, ūsĭtātus
curse *nn*, imprĕcātĭo, *f*, dīrae, *f.pl*
curse *v.t*, exsĕcror (1 *dep*.)
cursed exsĕcrābĭlis
cursorily *adv*, summātim, brĕvĭter
curt brĕvis
curtail *v.t*, arto (1)
curtain aulaeum, *n*
curve *nn*, flexus, *m*
curve *v.t*, flecto (3), curvo (1)
curved curvātus
cusion pulvīnar, *n*
custodian cūrātor, *m*
custody (keeping) custōdĭa, *f*; **(imprisonment)**, vincŭla, *n.pl*
custom mos, *m*, consŭētŭdo, *f*; **(— duty)**, portŏrĭum, *n*
customary ūsĭtātus, sŏlĭtus
customer emptor, *m*
cut *nn*, **(incision)**, incīsĭo, *f*; **(blow)**, ictus, *m*, plāga, *f*
cut *v.t*, sĕco (1), caedo (3); **(—away)**, abscīdo (3); **(— down)**, succīdo (3); **(— off)**, praecīdo (3); **(— off from communications, supplies, etc.)** interclūdo (3); **(— out)**, excīdo (3); **(— short)**, praecīdo (3); **(— to pieces)** concīdo (3), trŭcīdo (1)
cutaneous *use genit. of* cŭtis **(skin)**
cutlass glădĭus, *m*
cutlery cultri *m.pl* **(knives)**
cutter (boat) phăsēlus, *m*, cĕlox, *f*
cutting *adj*, **(biting)**, mordax
cuttlefish sēpĭa, *f*
cycle (circle) orbis, *m*
cygnet pullus, *m*
cylinder cȳlindrus, *m*
cymbal cymbălum, *n*
cynic cȳnĭcus, *m*
cynical mordax, diffĭcĭlis
cynicism dūrĭtĭa, *f*
cypress cupressus, *f*

D

dab *v.t*, illīdo (3)

dabble in *v.t*, attingo (3)

daffodil narcissus, *m*

dagger pŭgĭo, *m*

daily *adj*, quŏtīdĭānus

daily *adv*, quŏtīdĭē

daintiness (of manners) fastīdĭum, *n*

dainty (things) dēlĭcātus; (people), fastīdĭōsus

daisy bellis, *f*

dale valles, *f*

dalliance lūsus, *m*

dally *v.i*, (delay) mŏror (1 *dep*.)

dam (breakwater) mōles, *f*

dam *v.t*, obstrŭo (3)

damage *nn*, dētrīmentum, *n*, damnum, *n*

damage *v.t*, laedo (3), afflīgo (3)

dame dŏmĭna, *f*, mātrōna, *f*

damn *v.t*, damno (1)

damp *adj*, hūmĭdus

damp *v.t*, hūmecto (1); (enthusiasm, etc.) immĭnŭo (3) (lessen)

damp *nn*, hūmor, *m*

dance *v.i*, salto (1)

dance *nn*, saltātus, *m*

dancer saltātor, *m* (...trix, *f*)

dandy hŏmo lĕpĭdus, ēlĕgans, bellus

danger pĕrīcŭlum, *n*

dangerous pĕrīcŭlōsus

dangle *v.i*, pendĕo (2)

dank hūmĭdus, ūvĭdus

dapper (spruce) nĭtĭdus

dappled măcŭlōsus

dare *v.i*, audĕo (2 *semi-dep*) mŏlĭor (4 *dep*)

daring *adj*, audax

daring *nn*, audācĭa, *f*

dark *adj*, obscūrus tĕnĕbrōsus; (in colour), fuscus

dark, darkness *nn*, tĕnĕbrae, *f.pl*

darken *v.t*, obscūro (1), occaeco (1)

darling *nn*, dēlĭcĭae, *f.pl*; *adj*, mellītus

darn *v.t*, sarcĭo (4)

dart *nn*, tēlum, *n*, iăcŭlum, *n*

dart *v.i*, (rush), *use compound of*

vŏlo (1) (to fly)

dash *nn*, (rush), *use vb*, vŏlo (1) (to fly)

dash *v.i*, prōvŏlo (1), rŭo (3); *v.t*, afflīgo (3), impingo (3)

dashing *adj*, ălăcer

dastardly *adj*, ignāvus

date (fruit) palmŭla, *f*; (time), dĭes, *f*

date *v.t*, (something), dĭem ascrībo (3) in (*with abl*.)

daub *v.t*, oblĭno (3)

daughter fīlĭa, *f*; (— in-law), nŭrus

daunt *v.t*, percello (3)

dauntless impăvĭdus

dawdle *v.i*, cesso (1)

dawn prīma lux, aurōra, *f*

dawn *v.i*, dīlūcesco (3)

day dĭes, *m, f*; (at — break), *adv. phr*, prīma lūce; (by —), *adv*, interdĭu; (every —), *adv*, quŏtīdĭe; (late in the —), multo dĭe; (on the — before), prīdĭe; (on the next —), postrīdĭe; (— time), tempus dĭurnum, *n*

daze *v.t*, stŭpĕfăcĭo (3)

dazzle *v.t*, perstringo (3)

dazzling splendĭdus

dead *adj*, mortŭus; (the dead or departed), mānes, *m.pl*; (a — body), corpus, *n*

deaden *v.t*, (senses, etc.), hĕbēto (1)

deadly *adj*, mortĭfer, pernĭcĭōsus, fūnestus

deaf sturdus

deafen *v.t*, exsurdo (1), obtundo (3)

deafness surdĭtas, *f*

deal (a good —) ălĭquantum, (business) nĕgōtĭum, *n*

deal *v.t*, (distribute), distrĭbŭo (3); mētĭor (4 *dep*.); *v.i*, (deal with), ăgo (3) cum (*with abl*)

dealer mercātor, *m*

dealings *nn*, ūsus, *m*, commercĭum, *n*

dear cārus; (of price), prĕtĭōsus

dearly *adv* (at a high price) magni

death mors, *f*

deathbed (on his —) *use adj*, mŏrĭens (dying)

deathless immortālis

debar *v.t,* exclūdo (3)

debase *v.t,* dēmitto (3), vĭtĭo (1)

debate contrōversĭa, *f*

debate *v.t,* dispŭto (1), discepto (1)

debater dispŭtātor, *m*

debauch *v.t,* corrumpo (3)

debauchery stŭprum, *n*

debit *nn,* expensum, *n*

debit *v.t,* expensum fĕro (*irreg*) (*with dat*)

debt aes ălĭēnum, *n*

debtor dēbĭtor, *m*

debut ĭnĭtĭum, *n*

decamp *v.i,* castra mŏvĕo (2); discēdo (3)

decant *v.t,* diffundo (3)

decanter lăgēna, *f*

decapitate *v.t,* sĕcūri fĕrĭo (4)

decay *nn,* tābes, *f,* dēmĭnūtĭo, *f*

decay *v.i,* dīlābor (3 *dep*), tābesco (3)

decease dēcessus, *m*

deceased *adj,* mortŭus

deceit fraus, *f,* dŏlus, *m*

deceitful fallax

deceive *v.t,* dēcĭpĭo (3), fallo (3)

December Dĕcember (mensis)

decency dĕcōrum, *n,* hŏnestas, *f*

decent dĕcōrus, hŏnestus

deception fraus, *f,* dŏlus, *m*

deceptive fallax

decide *v.t,* constĭtŭo (3), stătŭo (3), dēcerno (3)

decided (persons) firmus; **(things),** certus

decidedly *adv,* **(assuredly),** plānē, vēro

decimate *v.t,* dĕcĭmo (1)

decision arbĭtrĭum, *n,* dēcrētum, *n*

deck pons, *m*

deck *v.t,* orno (1)

declaim *v.t,* dēclāmo (1)

declaration prŏfessĭo, *f* **(— of war),** dēnuntĭātĭo, *f,* (belli)

declare *v.i,* prŏfĭtĕor (2 *dep*), affirmo (1); *v.t,* dēclāro (1); **(— war),** dēnuntĭo (1) (bellum)

decline *nn,* dēmĭnūtĭo, *f* **(diminution)**

decline *v.t,* **(refuse),** rĕcūso (1); *v.i,* inclīno (1), dēcresco (3)

declivity clīvus, *m*

decompose *v.t,* solvo (3); *v.i,* solvor (3 *pass*)

decomposition sŏlūtĭo, *f*

decorate *v.t,* orno (1), dĕcŏro (1)

decoration (ornament) ornāmentum, *n,* dĕcus, *n;* **(badge),** insigne, *n*

decorous dĕcōrus

decorum dĕcōrum, *n,* pŭdor, *m*

decoy illex, *m;* **(bait),** esca, *f*

decrease *nn,* dēmĭnūtĭo, *f*

decrease *v.i,* dēcresco (3); *v.t,* mĭnŭo (3)

decree *nn,* dēcrētum, *n;* **(— of the Senate),** consultum, *n*

decree *v.t,* dēcerno (3), censĕo (2)

decrepit dēcrĕpĭtus, dēbĭlis

decry *v.t,* vĭtŭpĕro (1), obtrecto (1)

dedicate *v.t,* consĕcro (1)

deduce *v.t,* conclūdo (3)

deduct *v.t,* dēdūco (3)

deduction (taking away) dēductĭo, *f*

deed factum, *n,* făcĭnus, *n;* **(legal),** tăbŭla, *f*

deem *v.t,* pŭto (1)

deep *nn,* **(the sea),** altum, *n*

deep altus **(of sound),** grăvis

deepen *v.t,* altĭōrem reddo (3)

deeply *adv,* altē, pĕnĭtus **(deep within)**

deer cervus, *m,* cerva, *f*

deface *v.t,* dēformo (1)

defame *v.t,* mălĕdīco (3) (*with dat*)

default *v.i,* dēfĭcĭo (3) **(fail to answer bail),** vădĭmōnĭum dēsĕro (3)

defeat *nn,* clādes, *f*

defeat *v.t,* vinco (3), sŭpĕro (1)

decect vĭtĭum, *n*

defective vĭtĭōsus

defence (protection) praesĭdĭum, *n;* **(legal),** dēfensĭo, *f*

defenceless ĭnermis

defend *v.t,* dēfendo (3)

defendant (in a trial) rĕus, *m*

defender dēfensor, *m;* **(in court),** pătrōnus, *m*

defer *v.t,* **(put off),** diffĕro (*irreg*); *v.i,* **(show deference to),** cēdo (3)

deference observantĭa, *f*
defiance prōvŏcātĭo, *f*
defiant fĕrox
deficiency dēfectĭo, *f*
deficient ĭnops, mancus
deficit lăcūna, *f*
defile *v.t*, contāmĭno (1)
defile *nn*, augustĭae, *f.pl*
define *v.t*, circumscrībo (3)
definite constĭtūtus, certus
definition dēfinītĭo, *f*
deflect *v.t*, dēflecto (3)
deform *v.t*, dēformo (1)
deformity dēformĭtas, *f*
defraud *v.t*, fraudo (1)
defray *v.t*, suppĕdĭto (1) **(supply)**
deft doctus **(skilled)**
defy *v.t*, obsto (1), prōvŏco (1)
degenerate *v.i*, dēgĕnĕro (1)
degenerate *adj*, dēgĕner
degradation ignōmĭnĭa, *f*
degrade *v.t*, mŏvĕo (2), dē *or* ex
   (*with abl*), **(move down from)**;
   dēhŏnesto (1)
degree (interval, stage, rank)
   grădus, *m*; **(to such a degree)**,
   adv, ădĕo; **(by degrees)**, *adv*,
   (gradually), grădātim
deify *v.t*, consĕcro (1)
deign *v.t*, dignor (1 *dep*)
deity dĕus, *m*
deject *v.t*, afflīgo (3)
dejected dēmissus, afflictus
dejection maestĭtĭa, *f*
delay *nn*, mŏra, *f*
delay *v.i*, mŏror (1 *dep*.), cunctor
   (1 *dep*.); *v.t*, mŏror (1 *dep*.),
   tardo (1)
delegate *nn*, lēgātus, *m*
delegate *v.t*, **(depute)**, lēgo (1),
   mando (1) (*with acc. of thing and
   dat. of person*)
delegation lēgātĭo, *f*
deliberate *adj*, consīdĕrātus
deliberate *v.t*, consŭlo (3), dēlībĕro
   (1)
deliberately *adv*, consultō
deliberation dēlībĕrātĭo, *f*
delicacy subtīlĭtas, *f*, suāvĭtas, *f*;
   (food), cūpēdĭa, *n.pl*
delicate subtīlis, tĕner; **(of health)**,
   infirmus

delicious suāvis
delight *nn*, **(pleasure)**, vŏluptas, *f*
delight *v.t*, dēlecto (1), *v.i*, gaudĕo
   (2)
delightful iūcundus, ămoenus
delineate *v.t*, dēscrībo (3)
delinquency dēlictum, *n*
delinquent *nn*, peccātor, *m*
delirious dēlīrus
delirium dēlīrĭum, *n*
deliver *v.t*, **(set free)**, lībĕro (1);
   (hand over), do (1), trādo (3),
   dēdo (3); **(— a speech)**, hăbĕo
   (2), ōrātĭonem
deliverance (freeing) lībĕrātĭo, *f*;
   (childbirth) partus, *m*; **(of
   a speech)**, ēlŏcūtĭo, *f*
delude *v.t*, dēcĭpĭo (3)
deluge dĭlŭvĭum, *n*, ĭnundātĭo, *f*
delusion error, *m*; **(trick)**, fallācĭa,
   f, fraus, *f*
delusive (deceitful) fallax;
   (empty), vānus
demagogue plēbĭcŏla, *c*
demand *nn*, postŭlātĭo, *f*
demand *v.t*, posco (3), postŭlo (1)
demean oneself dēmittor (3 pass),
   sē dēmĭttĕre (3 *reflex*)
demeanour mōres, *m.pl*, hăbĭtus,
   m
demented dēmens
demise *nn*, **(death)**, dēcessus, *m*,
   mors, *f*
democracy cīvĭtas pŏpŭlāris, *f*
democrat plēbĭcŏla, *c*
demolish *v.t*, dīrŭo (3), dēlĕo (2),
   dēmōlĭor (4 *dep*)
demolition ēversĭo, *f*, rŭīna, *f*
demon daemŏnĭum, *n*
demonstrate *v.t*, dēmonstro (1)
demonstration dēmonstrātĭo, *f*
demur *v.i*, haesĭto (1)
demure *adj*, vērēcundus
den lătĭbŭlum, *n*
denial nĕgātĭo, *f*
denominate *v.t*, nōmĭno (1)
denote *v.t*, indĭco (1), signĭfĭco (1),
   nŏto (1)
denounce *v.t*, (nōmen) dēfĕro
   (*irreg*)
dense densus, confertus
density crassĭtūdo, *f*
dent nŏta, *f*

dentist dentĭum mĕdĭcus, *m*

denude *v.t*, nūdo (1)

deny *v.t*, nĕgo (1), abnŭo (3)

depart *v.i*, ăbĕo (4), discēdo (3)

departed (dead) mortŭus

department (of administration, etc.) prōvincĭa, *f*; **(part)**, pars, *f*

departure discessus, *m*

depend on *v.i*, pendĕo (2) ex *or* in (*with abl*); **(rely on)**, confīdo (3 *semi-dep*) (*with dat*)

dependant *nn*, clĭens, *c*

dependence on clĭentēla, *f*; **(reliance)**, fĭdes, *f*

dependency (subject state) prōvincĭa, *f*

depict *v.t*, dēscrībo (3), effingo (3)

deplorable mĭsĕrābĭlis

deplore *v.t*, dēplōro (1)

deploy *v.t*, explĭco (1)

depopulate *v.t*, pŏpŭlor (1 *dep*); vasto (1)

deport *v.t*, dēporto (1); **(behave oneself)**, se gĕrĕre (3 *reflex*)

deportment hăbĭtus, *m*

depose *v.t*, mŏvĕo (2) (*with abl*)

deposit *v.t*, dēpōno (3)

deposit *nn*, dēpŏsĭtum, *n*

deprave *v.t*, dēprāvo (1), corrumpo (3)

depravity prāvĭtas, *f*

deprecate *v.t*, dēprĕcor (1 *dep*)

depreciate *v.t*, dētrăho (3); *v.i*, mĭnŭor (3 *pass*) **(grow less)**

depreciation (decrease) dēmĭnūtĭo, *f*; **(disparagement)** obtrectātĭo, *f*

depredation expīlatĭo, *f*, praedātĭo, *f*

depress *v.t*, dēprĭmo (3); **(spirits, etc.)**, infringo (3)

depression (sadness) tristĭtĭa, *f*

deprive *v.t*, prīvo (1) (*with acc. of person deprived, and abl. of thing*)

depth altĭtūdo, *f*

deputation lēgātĭo, *f*

depute *v.t*, lēgo (1), mando (1) (*with dat*)

deputy lēgātus, *m*

deputy-governor prōcūrātor, *m*

derange *v.t*, perturbo (1)

deride *v.t*, dērīdĕo (2)

derision irrīsĭo, *f*, rīsus, *m*

derive (from) *v.t*, **(deduce)** dūco (3), ab (*and abl*)

derogate from *v.i*, dērŏgo (1) dē (*with abl*)

derogatory (remark) noxĭus

descend *v.i*, dēscendo (3)

descendant prōgĕnĭes, *f*

descent (lineage) prōgĕnĭes, *f*; **(movement)**, dēscensus, *m*; **(slope)**, dēclīve, *n*

describe *v.t*, dēscrībo (3), expōno (3)

description dēscriptĭo, *f*, narrātĭo, *f*

descry *v.t*, conspĭcor (1 *dep*)

desecrate *v.t*, prŏfāno (1)

desert (wilderness) sōlĭtūdo, *f*

desert *v.t*, dēsĕro (3), rĕlinquo (3)

deserted dēsertus

deserter perfŭga, *m*, transfŭga, *m*

deserve *v.t*, mĕrĕor (2 *dep*); dignus esse (*irreg*) (*with abl*)

deservedly *adv*, mĕrĭto

design dēscriptĭo, *f*; **(plan)**, consĭlĭum, *n*

design *v.t*, dēscrībo (3); **(intend)**, in ănĭmo hăbĕo (2)

designate *v.t*, dēsigno (1)

designing *adj*, callĭdus, dŏlōsus

desirable optābĭlis

desire *nn*, dēsīdĕrĭum, *n*, cŭpĭditas

desire *v.t*, cŭpĭo (3), opto (1)

desirous cŭpĭdus

desist *v.i*, dēsisto (3), dēsĭno (3)

desk scrīnĭum, *n*

desolate dēsertus, sōlus

despair *nn*, dēspērātĭo, *f*

despair *v.i*, dēspēro (1)

despatch *v.t*, mitto (3); **(kill)**, interfĭcĭo (3)

despatch *nn*, **(sending)**, dīmissĭo, *f*; **(letter)**, littĕrae, *f.pl*; **(speed)**, cĕlĕrĭtas, *f*

desperate dēspērātus; **(situation)**, extrēmus

desperate desperātĭo, *f*

despicable contemptus

despise *v.t*, dēspĭcĭo (3), sperno (3)

despite *prep*, contrā (*with acc*)

despoil *v.t*, spŏlĭo (1)

despond *v.i,* ănĭmum dēmitto (3)

despondent *use adv. phr,* ănĭmo dēmisso

despot dŏmĭnus, *m*

despotic tўrannĭcus, *m*

despotism dŏmĭnātus, *m*

dessert mensa sĕcunda **(second table)**

destination *often* quo? **(whither),** *or* ĕo **(to that place)**

destine *v.t,* dēstĭno (1), dēsigno (1)

destiny fātum, *n*

destitute ĭnops

destroy *v.t,* perdo (3), dēlĕo (2), ēverto (3)

destroyer vastātor, *m*

destruction pernĭcĭes, *f,* ēversĭo, *f,* exĭtĭum, *n*

destructive pernĭcĭōsus

desultory inconstans

detach *v.t,* sēiungo (3), sēpăro (1)

detached sēpărātus

detachment (of troops, etc.) mănus

details singŭla, *n.pl*

detail *v.t,* explĭco (1)

detain *v.t,* rĕtĭnĕo (2)

detect *v.t,* dēprĕhendo (3), compĕrĭo (4)

deter *v.t,* dēterrĕo (2), dēpello (3)

deteriorate *v.i,* corrumpor (3 *pass*)

determinate *adj,* certus

determination (resolution) constantĭa, *f;* **(intention),** consĭlĭum, *n*

determine *v.i and v.t,* constĭtŭo (3)

determined (resolute) firmus; **(fixed)** certus

detest *v.t,* ōdi (*v. defect*)

detestable ŏdĭōsus

dethrone *v.t,* regno pello (3) **(expel from sovereignty)**

detour circŭĭtus, *m*

detract from *v.t,* dētrăho (3) dē (*with abl*)

detriment dētrīmentum, *n*

detrimental (to be —) *v.i,* esse (*irreg*) dētrīmento (*with dat*)

devastate *v.t,* vasto (1)

devestation vastātĭo, *f*

develop *v.t,* explĭco (1), ēdŭco (1); *v.i,* cresco (3) **(grow)**

development prōlātĭo, *f;* **(unfolding),** explĭcātĭo, *f*

deviate *v.i,* dēclīno (1), discēdo (3)

deviation dēclīnātĭo, *f*

device (contrivance) artĭfĭcium, *n;* **(emblem),** insigne, *n;* **(plan),** dŏlus, *m*

devil daemŏnĭum, *n*

devilish nĕfandus

devious dēvĭus

devise *v.t,* excōgĭto (1), fingo (3)

devoid expers, văcŭus

devolve *v.i,* obvĕnĭo (4); *v.t,* dēfĕro (*irreg*)

devote *v.t,* dēdĭco (1), dēdo (3); **(consecrate),** dēvŏvĕo (2)

devoted dēdĭtus, dēvōtus

devotion stŭdĭum, *n;* **(love),** ămor, *m*

devour *v.t,* dēvŏro (1), consūmo (3)

devouring ĕdax

devout pĭus, vĕnĕrābundus, rēlĭgĭōsus

dew rōs, *m*

dexterity sollertĭa, *f,* callĭdĭtas, *f*

dexterous sollers, callĭdus

diadem dĭădēma, *n*

diagonal *adj,* dĭăgōnālis

diagram forma, *f*

dial sōlārĭum, *n*

dialect dĭălectus, *f*

dialectics dĭălectĭca, *n.pl*

dialogue sermo, *m;* **(written),** dĭălŏgus, *m*

diameter crassĭtūdo, *f*

diamond ădămas, *m*

diaphragm praecordĭa, *n.pl*

diarrhoea prōfluvĭum, *n*

diary commentārĭi dĭurni, *m.pl*

dice tāli, *m.pl;* **(the game),** ălĕa, *f*

dictate *v.t,* dicto (1); *v.i,* impĕro (1) (*with dat*)

dictation dictātĭo, *f*

dictator dictātor, *m*

dictatorial impĕrĭōsus

dictatorship dictātūra, *f*

dictionary glossārĭum, *n*

die *v.i,* mŏrĭor (3 *dep*), cădo (3)

diet victus, *m*

differ *v.i,* discrĕpo (1), diffĕro (*irreg*)

difference discrīmen, *n,* dīversĭtas, *f;* **(— of opinion),** discrĕpantĭa, *f*

different ălĭus, dīversus

difficult diffĭcĭlis

difficulty dĭffĭcultas, *f*; **(to be in—)**, lăbōro (1); **(with —)**, *adv,* aegrē

diffidence diffĭdentĭa, *f*

diffident diffĭdens

diffuse *v.t,* diffundo (3)

dig *v.t,* fŏdĭo (3)

digest *v.t,* concŏquo (3)

digestion concoctĭo, *f*

dignified grăvis

dignify *v.t,* hŏnesto (1)

dignity (of character) grăvĭtas, *f,* dignĭtas, *f*

digress *v.i,* dīgrĕdĭor (3 *dep*)

digression dīgressĭo, *f*

dike (ditch) fossa, *f*; **(mound)** agger, *m*

dilapidated rŭīnōsus

dilate *v.i,* sē dīlātāre (1 *reflex*); *v.t,* **(— upon),** dīlāto (1)

dilatory ignāvus, lentus

dilemma (difficulty) angustĭae, *f.pl*

diligence dīlĭgentĭa, *f*

dilute *v.t,* dīlŭo (3), miscĕo (2)

dim *adj,* **(light, etc.),** obscūrus; **(dull, stupid),** hĕbes

dim *v.t,* obscūro (1)

dimension mŏdus, *m*

diminish *v.t,* mĭnŭo (3); *v.i,* mĭnŭor (3 *pass*)

diminution dēmĭnūtĭo, *f*

diminutive parvus, exĭgŭus

dimness obscūrĭtas, *f*

dimple lăcūna, *f*

din strĕpĭtus, *m*

dine *v.i,* cēno (1)

dingy sordĭdus

dining room trīclīnĭum, *n,* cēnātĭo, *f*

dinner cēna, *f*

by dint of *prep,* per (*with acc*)

dip *v.t,* mergo (3); *v.i,* mergor (3 *pass*)

diploma dĭplōma, *n*

diplomacy (by —) per lēgātos **(by means of diplomats)**

diplomat(ist) lēgātus, *m*

direct *adj,* rectus

direct *v.t,* dīrĭgo (3); **(order),** praecĭpĭo (3) (*with dat. of person*); **(show),** monstro (1)

direction (of motion) cursus, *m*; **(pointing out),** monstrātĭo, *f*; **(affairs),** admĭnĭstrātĭo, *f*; **(in different —s),** (*pl. adj*), dīversi

director cūrātor, *m*

dirt sordes, *f*

dirty sordĭdus, spurcus

dirty *v.t,* inquĭno (1), foedo (1)

disable *v.t,* dēbĭlĭto (1)

disabled inhăbĭlis, confectus

disadvantage incommŏdum, *n*

disadvantageous incommŏdus

disaffected ălĭēnātus

disaffection ănĭmus āversus, *m*

disagree *v.i,* discrēpo (1), dissentĭo (4)

disagreeable (unpleasant) iniūcundus

disagreement discrĕpantĭa, *f,* dissensĭo, *f*

disappear *v.i,* ēvānesco (3), diffŭgĭo (3)

disappearance exĭtus, *m*

disappoint *v.t,* frustror (1 *dep*)

disappointment incommŏdum, *n*

disapproval rĕprĕhensĭo, *f*

disapprove *v.t,* imprŏbo (1)

disarm *v.t,* armis exŭo (3) **(strip of arms)**

disaster clādes, *f*

disastrous pernĭcĭōsus

disavow *v.t,* diffĭtĕor (2 *dep*)

disavowal infĭtĭātĭo, *f*

disband *v.t,* dīmitto (3)

disbelieve *v.t,* non crēdo (3), diffīdo (3) (*with dat*)

disburse *v.t,* expendo (3)

disc orbis, *m*

discard *v.t.* rĕpŭdĭo (1)

discern *v.t,* cerno (3)

discerning *adj,* perspĭcax

discernment intellĕgentĭa, *f*

discharge *v.t,* **(missiles, etc.),** ēmitto (3), iăcŭlor (1 *dep*); **(soldiers, etc.),** dīmitto (3); **(duties, etc.),** fungor (3 *dep*) (*with abl*)

discharge *nn,* ēmissĭo, *f,* dīmissĭo, *f*

disciple discĭpŭlus, *m*

discipline disciplīna, *f*
discipline *v.t*, instĭtŭo (3)
disclaim *v.t*, nĕgo (1), rĕpŭdĭo (1)
disclose *v.t*, ăpĕrĭo (4)
disclosure indĭcĭum, *n*
discolour *v.t*, dēcŏlōro (1)
discomfiture clādes, *f*
discomfort incommŏdum, *n*
disconcert *v.t*, perturbo (1)
disconnect *v.t*, sēiungo (3)
disconsolate maestus
discontented mălē contentus
discontinue *v.t*, intermitto (3)
discord (strife) discordĭa, *f*,
  dissensĭo, *f*
discount *nn*, dēcessĭo, *f* **(decrease)**
discourage *v.t*, ănĭmum dēmitto
  (3)
discouragement ănĭmi infractĭo, *f*,
  or dēmissĭo, *f*
discourse *v.i*, dissĕro (3)
discourse *nn*, sermo, *m*, contĭo, *f*
discover *v.t*, invĕnĭo (4), rĕpĕrĭo
  (4), cognosco (3)
discovery inventĭo, *f*; **(thing**
  discovered), inventum, *n*
discredit *v.t*, fĭdem abrŏgo (1)
discreditable ĭnhŏnestus
discreet consīdĕrātus, prūdens
discretion prūdentĭa, *f*
discriminate *v.t*, discerno (3)
discuss *v.t*, discepto (1), dispŭto
  (1)
discussion dispŭtātĭo, *f*
disdain *v.t*, sperno (3), dēspĭcĭo (3)
disdain *nn*, fastīdĭum, *n*
disdainful fastīdĭōsus
disease morbus, *m*
diseased aeger
disembark *v.t*, expōno (3); *v.i*,
  ēgrĕdĭor (3 *dep*)
disengage *v.t*, **(release)**, solvo (3)
disengaged (at leisure) ōtĭōsus;
  (free, loose) sŏlūtus
disentangle *v.t*, explĭco (1)
disfigure *v.t*, dēformo (1)
disgrace *nn*, dēdĕcus, *n*,
  ignōmĭnĭa, *f*
disgrace *v.t*, dēdĕcoro (1)
disgraceful turpis, flāgĭtĭōsus
disguise *nn*, persōna, *f*,
  intĕgŭmentum, *n*

disguise *v.t*, vestem mūto (1)
  (change the clothes); dissĭmŭlo
  (1) **(pretend, hide)**
disgust *nn*, fastīdĭum, *n*, taedĭum,
  n
disgust *v.t*, taedĭum mŏvĕo (2)
  (*with dat*)
disgusted (to be —) *use*
  impersonal vb, pĭget (2) **(it**
  disgusts)
disgusting foedus
dish *nn*, pătĭna, *f*
dishearten *v.t*, exănĭmo (1),
  percello (3)
dishonest imprŏbus, perfĭdus
dishonesty *f*, imprŏbĭtas, *f*
dishonour *nn*, dēdĕcus, *n*
dishonour *v.t*, dēdĕcŏro (1)
dishonourable inhŏnestus
disinclination dēclīnātĭo, *f*
disinherit *v.t*, exhērēdo (1)
disintegrate *v.t*, solvo (3); *v.i*,
  solvor (3 *pass*)
disinterested neutri făvens
  (favouring neither side)
disjointed ĭnordĭnātus
disk orbis, *m*
dislike *nn*, ŏdĭum, *n*
dislike *v.t*, ăbhorrĕo (2) ab (*with*
  abl); displĭcĕo (2)
dislocate *v.t*, extorquĕo (2)
dislodge *v.t*, dēĭcĭo (3), pello (3)
disloyal infĭdēlis
dismal āter, maestus
dismantle *v.t*, dīrĭpĭo (3)
dismay *nn*, păvor, *m*
dismay *v.t*, consterno (1), pertubo
  (1)
dismiss *v.t*, dīmitto (3)
dismissal dīmissĭo, *f*
dismount *v.i*, ex ĕquo dēscendo
  (3)
disobedience *use phr. with vb*,
  pārĕo **(obey)**
disobedient mălē pārens
disobey *v.t*, mălē pārĕo (*with*
  dat)
disoblige *v.t*, offendo (3)
disorder *nn*, perturbātĭo, *f*
disorderly *adv*, turbātus; **(crowd)**,
  turbŭlentus
disown *v.t*, infĭtĭor (1 *dep*)

disparage *v.t*, dētrăho (3), obtrecto (1)

dispatch *v.t*, (see **despatch**)

dispel *v.t*, dēpello (3), discŭtĭo (3)

dispense *v.t*, dispertĭor (4 *dep*) distrĭbŭo (3); (— **with**), dīmitto (3)

dispersal dissĭpātĭo, *f*

disperse *v.t*, dispergo (3), dissĭpo (1), *v.i*, diffŭgĭo (3)

dispirited *use adv. phr*, dēmisso ănĭmo

display *nn*, ostentātĭo, *f*

display *v.t*, ostento (1)

displease *v.t*, displĭcĕo (2) (*with dat*)

displeasing ŏdĭōsus

displeasure offensĭo, *f*

disposal ēmissĭo, *f*; (**power**), arbĭtrĭum, *n*

dispose *v.t*, (**arrange**), constĭtŭo (3), dispōno (3); (**induce**), inclīno (1); (**get rid of**) ēlŭo (3)

disposed inclīnātus

disposition (**arrangement**) dispŏsĭtĭo, *f*, (**of mind, etc.**), nātūra, *f*, ingĕnĭum, *n*

dispossess *v.t*, dēturbo (1), dētrūdo (3)

disproportion dissĭmĭlĭtūdo, *f*; (**of parts, etc.**) inconcinnĭtas, *f*

disprove *v.t*, rĕfello (3), rĕfūto (1)

dispute *nn*, contrōversĭa, *f*

dispute *v.t*, dispŭto (1)

disqualify *v.t*, (**prevent**), prŏhĭbĕo (2)

disregard *nn*, neglĕgentĭa, *f*

disregard *v.t*, neglĕgo (3)

disreputable infāmis

disrespectful contŭmax, insŏlens

dissatisfaction mŏlestĭa, *f*

dissatisfied (— **to be**) *use impers. vb*, paenĭtet (*with acc. of subject and genit of object*)

dissect *v.t*, insĕco (1), persĕco (1)

dissemble *v.i*, dissĭmŭlo (1)

dissension discordĭa, *f*, dissensĭo, *f*

dissent *v.i*, dissentĭo (4)

dissimilar dissĭmĭlis

dissipate *v.t*, dissĭpo (1)

dissipated dissŏlūtus, lĭbīdĭnōsus

dissipation lĭcentĭa, *f*

dissolute dissŏlūtus, lĭbīdĭnōsus

dissolve *v.t*, solvo (3), lĭquĕfăcĭo (3), *v.i*, solvor (3 *pass*), lĭquesco (3)

dissuade *v.t*, dissuādĕo (2) (*with dat*)

distaff cŏlus, *f*

distance spătĭum, *n*; (**remoteness**), longinquĭtas, *f*; (**at a —**), *adv*, longē, prŏcul

distant rĕmōtus, distans; (**to be —**), absum (*irreg*)

distaste fastīdĭum, *n*

distasteful iniŭcundus

distemper (**malady**) morbus, *m*

distend *v.t*, tendo (3)

distil *v.t*, stillo (1)

distinct (**separate**) sēpărātus; (**clear**), clārus, mănĭfestus

distinction (**difference**) discrīmen, *n*; (**mark of honour**), hŏnor, *m*, dĕcus, *n*

distinctive prŏprĭus

distinguish *v.t*, distinguo (3); *v.i*, (— **oneself**), clāresco (3), ēmĭnĕo (2)

distinguished insignis, clārus

distort *v.t*, dētorquĕo (2)

distortion distortĭo, *f*

distract *v.t*, distrăho (3)

distracted (**mentally**) āmens, turbātus

distraction (**mental**) āmentĭa, *f*

distress mĭsĕrĭa, *f*, dŏlor, *m*

distress *v.t* sollĭcĭto (1)

distressed sollĭcĭtus

distribute *v.t*, distrĭbŭo (3), partĭor (4 *dep*)

distributioon partītĭo, *f*

district rĕgĭo, *f*

distrust *nn*, diffĭdentĭa, *f*

distrust *v.t*, diffīdo (3) (*with dat*)

distrustful diffīdens

disturb *v.t*, turbo (1)

disturbance mōtus, *m*, tŭmulus, *m*

disunion discordĭa, *f*

disunite *v.t*, sēiungo (3), dissŏcĭo (1)

disused dēsŭētus

ditch fossa, *f*

ditty carmen, *n*

divan lectŭlus, *m*

dive *v.i*, sē mergĕre (3 *reflex*)

diver

diver ūrīnător, *m*
diverge *v.i,* discēdo (3)
divergence dēclīnātĭo, *f*
diverse ălĭus, dīversus
diversion dērīvātĭo, *f*; **(of thought, etc.),** āvŏcātĭo, *f*
divert *v.t,* āverto (3), āvŏco (1); **(amuse),** oblecto (1), prōlecto (1)
divide *v.t,* dīvĭdo (3); **(share out),** partĭor (4 *dep*); *v.i,* sē dīvĭdĕre (3 *reflex*)
divine dīvīnus
divine *v.t,* dīvīno (1), augŭror (1 *dep*)
diviner augur, *m*
divinity dīvīnĭtas, *f*
divisible dīvĭdŭus
division (act of —) dīvīsĭo, *f*; **(a section),** pars, *f*; **(discord),** discĭdĭum, *n*
divorce dīvortĭum, *n*
divorce *v.i,* dīvortĭum făcĭo (3), cum (*and abl*)
divulge *v.t,* pătĕfăcĭo (3), ăpĕrĭo (4)
dizziness vertīgo, *f*
dizzy vertīgĭnōsus
do *v.t,* făcĭo (3), ăgo (3); **(to be satisfactory),** *v.i,* sătĭs esse; **(—away with)** abŏlĕo (2); **(—without),** cărĕo (2) (*with abl*)
docile făcĭlis, dŏcĭlis
dock nāvālĭa, *n.pl*
doctor mĕdĭcus, *m*
doctor *v.t,* cūro (1)
doctrine dogma, *n,* rătĭo, *f*
document tăbŭla, *f,* littĕrae, *f.pl*
dodge dŏlus, *m*
dodge *v.t,* **(elude),** ēlūdo (3)
doe cerva, *f*
dog cănis, *c*
dog *v.t,* insĕquor (3 *dep*)
dogged **(stubborn)** pertīnax, pervĭcax
dogged **(by ill-luck, etc.)** ăgĭtātus
dogma dogma, *n*
dogmatic arrŏgans
dole **(small allowance)** dĭurna, *n.pl*
dole out *v.t,* dīvĭdo (3)
doleful tristis, maestus
dolefulness tristĭtĭa, *f*
doll pūpa, *f*

dolphin delphīnus, *m*
dolt caudex, *m*
dome thŏlus, *m*
domestic dŏmestĭcus, fămĭlĭāris; **(animals)** villātĭcus
domestic *nn,* **(servant),** fămŭlus, *m*
domicile dŏmĭcĭlĭum, *n*
dominant pŏtens
dominate *v.t,* dŏmĭnor (1 *dep*)
domination dŏmĭnātus, *m*
domineering impĕrĭōsus
dominion impĕrĭum, *n,* regnum, *n*
donation dōnum, *n*
donkey ăsĭnus, *m*
doom fātum, *n*
doom *v.t,* damno (1)
door iānŭa, *f*; **(out of —s)** *adv,* fŏrīs
doorkeeper iānĭtor, *m*
doorpost postis, *f*
dormitory cŭbĭcŭlum, *n*
dormouse glīs, *m*
dot *nn,* punctum, *n*
dotage sĕnĭum, *n*
dotard sĕnex, *m*
dote upon *v.i,* dēpĕrĕo (4)
double *adj,* dŭplex, gĕmĭnus
double *v.t,* dŭplĭco (1); *v.i,* dŭplex fīo (*irreg*), ingĕmĭno (1)
double-dealing *nn,* fraus, *f*
double-faced fallax
doubt *v.i,* dŭbĭto (1)
doubt *nn,* dŭbĭum, *n,* dŭbĭtātĭo
doubtful dŭbĭus, incertus
doubtless *adv,* sĭne dŭbĭo, nīmīrum
dough fărīna, *f*
dove cŏlumba, *f*
dove-coloured cŏlumbīnus
dovecot cŏlumbārĭum, *n*
dowager vĭdŭa, *f*
down *prep,* dē (*with abl*); *adv,* use dē *in a coumpound verb, e.g.* run down dēcurro (3)
down *nn,* **(feathers, etc.)** plūma, *f*
down *v.t,* **(put down)** dēpōno (3)
downcast dēiectus, dēmissus
downfall occāsus, *m,* rŭīna, *f*
down-hearted *adv,* dēmisso ănĭmo
downpour imber, *m*
downright dīrectus; **(sheer),** mĕrus
downward *adj,* dēclīvis

downwards *adv,* dĕorsum
downy *adj,* plūmĕus
dowry dos, *f*
doze *v.i,* dormīto (1)
dozen (twelve) dŭŏdĕcim
dozing *adj,* somnĭcŭlōsus
drab cĭnĕrĕus **(ash-coloured)**
drag *v.t,* trăho (3)
dragon drăco, *m*
drain *nn,* clŏāca, *f,* fossa, *f*
drain *v.t,* **(land),** sicco (1); **(a drink),** hauriŏ (4)
dram cўăthus, *m*
drama fābŭla, *f,* scēna, *f*
dramatic (theatrical) scēnĭcus
dramatist pŏēta, *m*
drapery vēlāmen, *n*
draught (of air) spīrĭtus, *m;* **(water, etc.)** haustus, *m;* **(game of —s),** lătruncŭli, *m.pl*
draw *v.t,* **(pull)** trăho (3); **(portray),** dēscrĭbo (3); **(— a sword),** glădĭum stringo (3); **(—aside),** sēdūco (3); **(— water, etc.)** hauriŏ (4); *v.i* **(— back),** pĕdem rĕfĕro *(irreg);* **(— lots),** sortes dūco (3); **(— up troops, etc.)** *v.t,* instrŭo (3)
drawback, *nn,* incommŏdum, *n*
drawbridge pontĭcŭlus, *m*
drawing (picture) pictūra, *f*
drawl *v.i,* lentē prōnuntĭo (1) **(pronounce slowly)**
dray plaustrum, *n*
dread *nn,* formīdo *f,* păvor, *m*
dread *v.t,* tĭmĕo (2), formīdo (1)
dreadful terrĭbĭlis, ătrox
dream *nn,* somnĭum, *n*
dream *v.t,* somnĭo (1)
dreamy somnĭcŭlōsus
dreary tristis
dregs faex, *f*
drench *v.t,* mădĕfăcĭo (3)
dress *nn,* vestis, *f,* hăbĭtus, *m*
dress *v.t,* **(clothe);** vestĭo (4); **(— a wound)** cūro (1) **(care for)**
dressing *nn,* **(of wound)** fōmentum, *n*
drift *nn,* **(heap),** agger, *m;* **(tendency),** *use phr. with* quōrsus **(to what end?)**
drift *v.i,* dēfĕror *(irreg. pass)*

drill (military) exercĭtātĭo, *f;* **(tool),** tĕrĕbra, *f*
drill *v.t,* **(pierce),** tĕrĕbro (1); **(train),** exercĕo (2)
drill (military) exercĭtātĭo, *f;* **(tool),** tĕrĕbra, *f*
drill *v.t,* **(pierce),** tĕrĕbro (1); **(train),** exercĕo (2)
drink *v.t,* bĭbo (3), pōto (1)
drink *nn,* pōtĭo, *f*
drinker pōtātor, *m*
drinking pōtĭo, *f;* **(— party),** cōmissātĭo, *f*
drip *v.i,* stillo (1)
dripping *adj,* mădĭdus
drive *nn,* gestātĭo, *f*
drive *v.t,* ăgo (3); **(— away),** fŭgo (1) pello (3); **(— back),** rĕpello (3); **(— out),** expello (3)
drive *v.i,* **(on horse-back, etc.)** vĕhor (3 *pass*)
drivel ĭneptĭae, *f.pl*
drivel *v.i,* dēlīro (1)
driver aurīga, *c*
drizzle *v.i,* rōro (1)
droll rīdĭcŭlus, lĕpĭdus
drollery făcētĭae, *f.pl*
dromedary drŏmas, *m*
drone *nn,* **(bee),** fūcus, *m;* **(sound),** murmur, *n*
drone *v.i,* murmŭro (1)
droop *v.i,* pendĕo (2), languesco (3)
drooping *adj,* pendŭlus; **(of spirits, etc.),** dēmissus
drop *nn,* gutta, *f*
drop *v.t,* dēmitto (3); **(leave off),** omitto (3); *v.i,* cădo (3)
dropsy hydrops, *m*
drought siccĭtas, *f*
drove (flock) grex, *m*
drown *v.t,* submergo (3); **(of noise)** obstrĕpo (3)
drowsy somnĭcŭlōsus
drudge *nn,* servus, *m*
drudge *v.i,* servĭo (4); **(weary oneself)** *v.i,* sē fătīgāre (1 *reflex*)
drudgery lăbŏr servīlis **(servile labour)**
drug *nn,* mĕdĭcāmentum, *n*
drug *v.t,* mĕdĭco (1)
drum tympănum, *n*

drunk *adj,* ēbrĭus
drunkenness ēbrĭĕtas, *f*
dry siccus, ārĭdus; **(thirsty),** sĭtĭens
dry (up) *v.t,* sicco (1); *v.i,* āresco (3)
dryness sĭccĭtas, *f,* ārĭdĭtas, *f*
dubious dŭbĭus
duck *nn,* ănas, *f*
duck *v.t,* mergo (3)
duckling ănătĭcŭla, *f*
duct fŏrāmen, *n*
due *adj,* **(owed),** dēbĭtus; **(just),** iustus; **(suitable),** ĭdōnĕus, aptus
due *nn,* **(a right),** ius, *n*; **(taxes),** vectīgal, *n*, portōrĭum, *n*
duel certāmen, *n*
dull (person) hĕbes, obtūsus; **(colour),** obscūrus; **(blunt),** hĕbes; **(weather),** subnūbĭlus
dullness (of mind) tardĭtas, *f*
duly *adv,* **(established by precedent)** rītĕ
dumb mūtus
dumbfound *v.t,* obstŭpĕfăcĭo (3)
dump *v.t,* cŏăcervo (1)
dun fuscus
dunce hŏmo stŭpĭdus
dung stercus, *n*
dungeon carcer, *m*
dupe *nn,* hŏmo crēdŭlus
dupe *v.t,* dēcĭpĭo (3)
duplicate exemplum, *n*
duplicity fallācĭa, *f*
durability firmĭtas, *f*
durable firmus
duration spătĭum, *n*; **(long —),** dĭŭturnĭtas, *f*
during *prep,* per *(with acc)*
dusk crĕpuscŭlum, *n*
dusky fuscus, nĭger
dust *nn,* pulvis, *m*
dust *v.t,* dētergĕo (2)
duster pēnĭcŭlus, *m*
dusty pulvĕrŭlentus
dutiful pĭus
dutifulness pĭĕtas, *f*
duty (moral) offĭcĭum, *n*; **(given),** mūnus, *n*; **(tax)** vectīgal, *n*; **(it is my —)** *use vb.* dēbĕo (2) **(ought)**
dwarf pūmĭlĭo, *c*
dwarfish pŭsillus

dwell *v.i,* hăbĭto (1), incŏlo (3); **(— on a theme),** commŏror (1 *dep*), haerĕo (2) in *(with abl)*
dweller incŏla, *c*
dwelling (place) dŏmĭcĭlĭum, *n*
dwindle *v.i,* dēcresco (3)
dye *nn,* fūcus, *m*
dye *v.t,* tingo (3), infĭcĭo (3)
dyer infector, *m*
dying *adj,* mŏrĭens
dynasty dŏmus, *f*
dysentry dўsentĕrĭa, *f*
dyspeptic crūdus

E

each ūnusquisque; **(— of two),** ŭterque; **(one —),** *use distributive num,* singŭli, bīni
eager cŭpĭdus, ăvĭdus *(with genit)*
eagerness cŭpĭdĭtas, *f,* ăvĭdĭtas, *f*
eagle ăquĭla, *f*
ear auris, *f*; **(— of corn),** spīca, *f*
early *adj,* **(in the morning)** mātūtīnus; **(of time, etc.),** mātūrus
early *adv,* **(in the morning)** māne; **(in time, etc.),** mātūrē
earn *v.t,* mĕrĕo (2), mĕrĕor (2 *dep*)
earnest intentus, ācer
earnestly *adv,* intentē
earth (land) terra, *f*; **(ground),** sŏlum, *n*; **(globe),** orbis *(m)* terrārum
earthenware fictĭlĭa, *n.pl*
earthly *adj* **(terrestrial)** terrestris
earthquake terrae mōtus, *m,* **(movement of the earth)**
earthwork agger, *m*
ease quĭes, *f,* ōtĭum, *n*
ease *v.t,* **(lighten),** lĕvo (1), exŏnĕro (1)
easily *adv,* făcĭlĕ
easiness făcĭlĭtas, *f*
east *nn,* ŏrĭens, *m*
eastern *use genit.* of ŏrĭens **(east)**
eastward *adv. phr,* ăd ŏrĭentem
easy făcĭlis
eat *v.t,* ĕdo (3); **(— away),** rōdo (3)
eatable escŭlentus
eating-house pŏpīna, *f*
eaves prōtectum, *n*
eavesdropper auceps, *c*

ebb *v.i,* rĕcēdo (3)

ebb-tide rĕcessus aaestus **(receding of the tide)**

ebony ĕbĕnus, *f*

eccentric (of persons) nŏvus

echo *nn,* ĭmāgo, *f,* ēcho, *f*

echo *v.t,* rĕfĕro (*irreg*), rĕsŏno (1)

echoing *adj,* rĕsŏnus

eclipse *nn,* dēfectĭo, *f*

eclipse *v.t,* obscūro (1)

economical parcus, dīlĭgens

economy parsĭmōnĭa, *f,* **(frugality)**

ecstasy fŭror, *m*

ecstatic fŭrens

eddy vertex, *m*

edge (of knife etc.) ăcĭes, *f*; **(margin),** margo, *c,* ōra, *f*

edible escŭlentus

edict ēdictum, *n*

edifice aedĭfĭcĭum, *n*

edify *v.t,* instĭtŭo (3)

edit *v.t,* ēdo (3)

edition ēdĭtĭo, *f*

educate *v.t,* ēdŭco (1)

education ēdŭcātĭo, *f,* doctrīna, *f*

eel anguilla, *f*

efface *v.t,* dēlĕo (2)

effect *v.t,* efficĭo (3)

effect *nn,* **(influence, impression),** vīs, *f*; **(result),** effectus, *m*; **(consequence),** ēventus, *m*; **(without —),** (*adv*), nēquīquem

effective (impressive) grăvis; *or use phr. with* conficĭo (3) **(to bring to a conclusion)**

effectual efficax

effeminate effēmĭnātus

effervescence (of spirit, etc.) fervor, *m*

efficacy vīs, *f*

efficiency vīs, *f*

efficient hăbĭlis, efficĭens

effigy ĭmāgo, *f*

effort ŏpĕra, *f*

effrontery ōs, *n*

effulgent fulgens

effusion effūsĭo, *f*

egg ōvum, *n*

egg on *v.t,* incĭto (1)

egoism ămor (*m*) sŭi **(fondness of oneself)**

egoist ămātor (*m*) sŭi

egregious insignis

egress exĭtus, *m*

eight octo; **(— each),** octōni; **(—times),** *adv.* octĭens; **(— hundred)** octingenti

eighteen dŭŏdēvīginti

eighteenth dŭŏdēvīcensimus

eight octāvus

eightieth octōgēsĭmus

eighty octōginta

either *pron,* altĕrŭter; *conj,* aut

either … or aut … aut, vel … vel

ejaculate *v.t,* ēmitto (3)

ejaculation (cry) vox, *f,* clāmor, *m*

eject *v.t,* ēicĭo (3)

eke out *v.t,* parco (3) (*with dat*)

elaborate *adj,* ēlăbōrātus

elaborate *v.t,* ēlăbōro (1)

elapse *v.i,* **(of time),** intercēdo (3)

elate *v.t,* effĕro (*irreg*)

elated (joyful) laetus

elbow cŭbĭtum, *n*

elder *adj,* māior nātu **(greater by birth)**

elder tree sambūcus, *f*

elderly *adj,* prŏvectus aetāte **(advanced in age)**

elect *v.t,* crĕo (1), dēlĭgo (3)

elect *adj,* dēsignātus

election ēlectĭo, *f,* cŏmĭtĭa, *n.pl*

elector suffrāgātor, *m*

elegance ēlĕgantĭa, *f,* vĕnustas, *f*

elegant ēlĕgans, vĕnustus

elegy ĕlĕgīa, *f*

element ĕlĕmentum, *n,* prĭncĭpĭa, *n.pl*

elementary prīmus, simplex

elephant ĕlĕphantus, *m*

elevate *v.t,* tollo (3)

elevated ēdĭtus; **(mind)** ēlātus

elevation altĭtūdo, *f,* ēlātĭo, *f*

eleven undĕcim; **(— each),** undēni

eleventh undĕcĭmus

elicit *v.t,* ēlĭcĭo (3)

eligible ĭdōnĕus, opportūnus

elk alces, *f*

ell ulna, *f*

elm ulmus, *f*

elocution prōnuntĭātĭo, *f*

elope *v.i,* aufŭgĭo (3) **(run away)**

eloquence ēlŏquentĭa, *f*

eloquent ēlŏquens, dĭsertus

else *adj,* ălĭus

else *adv,* ălĭter

elsewhere *adv,* ălĭbī
elude *v.t,* ēlūdo (3)
emaciate *v.t,* attĕnŭo (1)
emaciated măcer
emaciation măcĭes, *f*
emanate *v.i,* ēmāno (1)
emancipate *v.t,* lībĕro (1), mănūmitto (3)
embalm *v.t,* condĭo (4)
embankment mōles, *f*
embark *v.t,* in nāvem impōno (3); *v.i,* nāvem conscendo (3)
embarrass *v.t,* **(entangle),** impĕdĭo (4); **(confuse),** turbo (1)
embarrassment scrūpŭlus, *m;* **(difficulty),** difficultas, *f*
embassy (delegation) lēgāti, *m.pl,* **(ambassadors)**
embedded sĭtus
embellish *v.t,* orno (1)
embellishment ornāmentum, *n*
embers cĭnis, *m*
embezzle *v.t,* āverto (3), pĕcŭlor (1 *dep*)
embezzlement pĕcūlātus, *m*
embezzler āversor (*m*) pĕcūnĭae
embitter *v.t,* exăcerbo (1)
emblem insigne, *n,* indĭcĭum, *n*
embody *v.t,* inclūdo (3)
embolden *v.t,* confirmo (1)
embrace *nn,* amplexus, *m,* complexus, *m*
embrace *v.t,* amplector (3 *dep*), complector (3 *dep*); **(— an opportunity)** arrĭpĭo (3)
embroidered (clothing, etc.) pictus
embroil *v.t,* **(entangle),** implĭco (1)
emerald smăragdus, *c*
emerge *v.i,* ēmergo (3), prōdĕo (4)
emergency discrīmen, *n,* tempus, *n*
emigrate *v.i,* mĭgro (1)
emigration mĭgrātĭo, *f*
eminence (high ground) tŭmŭlus, *m;* **(of rank, etc.)** lŏcus amplissĭmus
eminent ēgrĕgĭus, insignis
emissary lēgātus, *m*
emit *v.t,* ēmitto (3)
emolument lŭcrum, *n*
emotion mōtus (*m*) ănĭmi **(movement of the mind)**

emperor impĕrātor, *m,* princeps, *m*
emphasize *v.t,* prĕmo (3)
emphatic grăvis
empire impĕrĭum, *n*
empirical empīrĭcus
employ *v.t,* ūtor (3 *dep*) **(with abl)**
employed (of persons) occŭpātus
employer conductor, *m*
employment (occupation) quaestus, *m;* **(business),** nĕgōtĭum, *n;* **(using),** ūsurpātĭo, *f*
emporium empŏrĭum, *n*
empower (someone to do ...) *v.i,* pŏtestātem făcĭo (3) **(with dat. of person and genit. of gerund(ive))**
empty *adj,* văcŭus, ĭnānis
empty *v.t,* exĭnānĭo (4)
emulate *v.t,* aemŭlor (1 *dep*)
emulous aemŭlus
enable *v.t,* făcultātem do (1) **(with dat)**
enact *v.t,* **(law)** sancĭo (4), constĭtŭo (3)
enactment lex, *f*
enamoured (to be — of someone) *v.t,* ămo (1)
encamp *v.i,* castra pōno (3)
enchant *v.t,* fascĭno (1), dēlecto (1)
enchantment (allurement) blandīmentum, *n*
encircle *v.t,* circumdo (1)
enclose *v.t,* inclūdo (3), saepĭo (4)
enclosure saeptum, *n*
encounter *v.t,* incĭdo (3) in **(with acc);** concurro (3), obvĭam ĕo (4) **(irreg) (with dat)**
encounter *nn,* congressus, *m*
encourage *v.t,* hortor (1 *dep*)
encouragement hortātus, *m,* confirmātĭo, *f,* hortātĭo, *f*
encroach upon *v.t,* occŭpo (1)
encumber *v.t,* ŏnĕro (1), impĕdĭo (4)
encumbrance impĕdīmentum, *n*
end fĭnis, *m; or use* extrēmus, *adj, agreeing with a noun; e.g.* **at the end of the bridge,** in extrēmo ponte
end *v.t,* confĭcĭo (3), fĭnĭo (4); *v.i, use phr. with* extrēmum, *n,* **(end);** **(turn out, result)** cēdo (3), ēnĕnĭo (4)

endanger *v.t,* in pĕrīcŭlum addūco (3)
endear *v.t,* dēvincĭo (4)
endeavour *nn,* cōnātus, *m*
endeavour *v.t,* cōnor (1 *dep*)
endless infīnītus, perpĕtŭus
endorse *v.t,* confirmo (1)
endow *v.t,* dōno (1)
endowed praedĭtus
endurable tŏlĕrābĭlis
endurance pătĭentĭa, *f*
endure *v.t,* pătĭor (3 *dep*), fĕro (*irreg*); *v.i,* dūro (1)
enemy (public) hostis, *c;* **(private),** ĭnĭmīcus, *m*
energetic ācer, strēnŭus, impĭger
energy vīs, *f,* vĭgor, *m*
enervate *v.t,* ēnervo (1)
enervation dēbĭlĭtātĭo, *f*
enfeeble *v.t,* dēbĭlĭto (1)
enforce *v.t,* **(carry out)** exsĕquor (3 *dep*)
enfranchise *v.t,* **(give the right of voting)** suffrāgĭum do (1) **(with dat)**
enfranchisement cīvĭtātis dōnātĭo, *f,* **(granting of citizenship)**
engage *v.t,* **(join)** iungo (3); **(hire)** condūco (3); **(— in battle);** signa conferre (*irreg*); **(enter into),** ingrĕdĭor (3 *dep*)
engaged occŭpātus; **(betrothed),** sponsus
engagement (battle) proelĭum, *n;* **(agreement),** pactum, *n;* **(promise),** sponsĭo, *f*
engender *v.t,* gigno (3), părĭo (3)
engine māchĭna, *f;* **(military —),** tormentum, *n*
engineer făber, *m*
England Brĭtannĭa, *f*
English Brĭtannus, Brĭtannĭcus
engrave *v.t,* scalpo (3)
engraver scalptor, *m*
engraving *nn,* scalptūra, *f*
engross *v.t,* occŭpo (1)
enhance *v.t,* augĕo (2), orno (1)
enigma aenigma, *n,* ambāges, *f.pl*
enigmatic ambĭgŭus
enjoin *v.t,* iŭbĕo (2), mando (1)
enjoy *v.t,* frŭor (3 *dep*) **(with abl);** **(possess),** ūtor (3 *dep*) **(with abl)**
enjoyment (pleasure) gudĭum, *n,* lĭbīdo, *f*
enlarge *v.t,* augĕo (2), amplĭfĭco (1)
enlargement prōlātĭo, *f*
enlighten *v.t,* **(instruct),** dŏcĕo (2)
enlist *v.t,* **(troops),** conscrībo (3); **(bring over),** concĭlĭo (1); *v.i,* nōmen do (1) **(give one's name)**
enliven *v.t,* excĭto (1)
enmity ĭnĭmīcĭtĭa, *f*
ennoble *v.t,* **(make honourable),** hŏnesto (1)
enormity immānĭtas, *f;* **(crime),** scĕlus, *n*
enormous ingens
enough *nn. and adv,* sătis; *(foll. by genit),* e.g. **enough water,** sătis ăquae
enquire *v.t,* quaero (3) ab (*with abl*)
enrage *v.t,* irrīto (1), inflammo (1)
enrapture *v.t,* oblecto (1)
enrich *v.t,* lŏcŭplēto (1)
enroll *v.t,* scrībo (3)
ensign signum, *n;* **(— bearer),** signĭfer, *m*
enslave *v.t,* servĭtūtem iniungo (3) (*with dat*)
ensue *v.i,* sĕquor (3 *dep*)
entail *v.t,* affĕro (*irreg*)
entangle *v.t,* impĕdĭo (4)
enter *v.i, and v.t,* intro (1), ingrĕdĭor (3 *dep*), ĭnĕo (4 *irreg*); *v.t,* **(write in),** inscrībo (3)
enterprise (undertaking) inceptum, *n*
enterprising promptus, strēnŭus
entertain *v.t,* **(people),** excĭpĭo (3) **(receive); (amuse),** oblecto (1); **(an idea, etc.)** hăbĕo (2)
entertainment (of guests) hospĭtĭum, *n*
enthusiasm stŭdĭum, *n,* fervor, *m*
enthusiastic fānātĭcus, stŭdĭōsus
entice *v.t,* illĭcĭo (3)
entire tōtus, intĕger
entirely *adv,* omnīno

entitle *v.t,* **(give the right to)** ius do (1) *(with dat)*; **(name)**, inscrībo (3)
entitled (to be — to) *v.i,* ius hăbĕo (2)
entrails viscĕra, *n.pl*
entrance (act of —) ingressĭo, *f*; **(door, etc.)** ădĭtus, *m,* ostĭum, *n*
entreat *v.t,* obsĕcro (1), ōro (1)
entreaty obsĕcrātĭo, *f*
entrust *v.t,* crēdo (3) *(with dat)* committo (3) *(with dat)*
enumerate *v.t,* nŭmĕro (1)
envelop *v.t,* involvo (3)
envelope *nn,* invŏlūcrum, *n*
enviable fortūnātus
envious invĭdus
envoy lēgātus, *m*
envy invĭdĭa, *f*
envy *v.t,* invĭdĕo (2) *(with dat)*
ephemeral brĕvis
epic *adj,* ĕpĭcus
epidemic pestĭlentĭa, *f*
epigram ĕpĭgramma, *n*
epigrammatic ĕpĭgrammătĭcus, a, um, *adj*
epilepsy morbus cŏmĭtĭālis, *m*
episode (digression) excursus, *m*; res, *f*
epitaph ĕlŏgĭum, *n*
epoch aetas, *f*
equable aequus
equal *adj,* aequus, pār
equal *nn,* use *adj,* pār
equal *v.i and v.t,* aequo (1)
equality aequālĭtas, *f*
equanimity aequus ănĭmus, *m*
equator aequĭnoctĭālis circŭlus, *m*
equestrian ĕquester
equilibrium aequĭlībrĭum, *n*
equinox aequĭnoctĭum, *n*
equip *v.t,* orno (1), armo (1)
equipment arma, *n.pl,* armāmenta, *n.pl*
equitable aequus
equity aequĭtas, *f*; **(justice)**, iustĭtĭa, *f*
equivalent *adj,* **(equal)**, pār; **(to be —)**, *v.i,* use vălĕo (2) **(to be worth)** tanti
equivocal ambĭgŭus
era tempus, *n,* aetas, *f*

eradicate *v.t,* ēvello (3), exstirpo (1)
erase *v.t,* dēlĕo (2)
ere (before) *conj,* prĭusquam
erect *v.t,* ērĭgo (3); **(build)**, exstrŭo (3)
erect *adj,* rectus
erection (act of —) aedĭfĭcātĭo, *f*; **(a building)** aedĭfĭcĭum, *n*
err *v.i,* erro (1), pecco (1)
errand mandātum, *n*
erratic văgus
erroneous falsus
error error, *m*
erudite doctus
eruption ēruptĭo, *f*
escape *nn,* fŭga, *f*
escape *v.i, and v.t,* effŭgĭo (3), ēlābor (3 *dep*)
escarpment praeruptus lŏcus, *m*
escort *nn,* comĭtātus, *m*; **(protective)**, praesĭdĭum, *n*
escort *v.t,* cŏmĭtor (1 *dep*)
especial praecĭpŭus
especially *adv,* praecĭpŭē
espouse *v.t,* **(betroth)**, spondĕo (2); **(marry)** dūco (3), nūbo (3)
essay (attempt) cōnātus, *m*; **(composition)**, lĭbellus, *m*
essence (nature) nātūra, *f,* vīs, *f*
essential (necessary) nĕcessārĭus
establish *v.t,* constĭtŭo (3), confirmo (1)
establishment constĭtŭo, *f*
estate (property) rēs, *f,* fundus, *m*
esteem *nn,* existĭmātĭo, *f*
esteem *v.t,* **(think)** aestĭmo (1), pŭto (1); **(think highly of)** magni aestĭmo (1)
estimable laudātus
estimate *nn,* aestĭmātĭo, *f*
estimate *v.t,* aestĭmo (1)
estimation (opinion) ŏpīnĭo, *f*
estrange *v.t,* ălĭēno (1)
estrangement ălĭēnātĭo, *f*
estuary aestŭārĭum, *n*
eternal aeternus
eternally *adv. phr,* in aeternum
eternity aeternĭtas, *f*
ether aether, *m*
ethereal aethĕrĭus
ethical (moral) mōrālis
eulogy laudātĭo, *f*

evacuate *v.t*, (— **troops from a place**), dēdūco (3); *v.i*, (**depart from**), excēdo (3), ex (*with abl*)

evade *v.t*, ēlūdo (3)

evaporate *v.i*, discŭtĭor (3 *pass*)

evasion lătēbra, *f*

evasive ambĭgŭus

eve (evening) vesper, *m*

even *adv*, ĕtĭam, *often use emphatic pron*, *e.g.* **even Caesar,** Caesar ipse; (**not** —), nĕ...quĭdem

even *adj*, (**level, equable**), aequus; (— **number**), pār

even if *conj*, etsi

evening vesper, *m* (**in the** —), sub vespĕrum

event (occurrence) rēs, *f*; (**outcome**), exĭtus, *m*

eventually *adv*, ălĭquando

ever *adv*, (**at any time**) umquam; (**always**), semper; (**if** —), si quando

evergreen *adj*, semper vĭrĭdis

everlasting aeternus

every (all) omnis; (**each**), quisque; (— **day**), *adv*, cottĭdĭe; (— **one**), omnes, *m.pl*; (— **thing**), omnĭa, *n.pl*; (— **where**), *adv*, ŭbīque

evict *v.t*, expello (3)

evidence testĭmōnĭum, *n*; (**factual**), argūmentum, *n*

evident mănĭfestus, perspĭcŭus; (**it is** —), appāret (2 *impers*)

evil *adj*, mălus, prāvus

evil *nn*, mălum, *n*

evil-doer hŏmo nĕfārĭus

evoke *v.t*, ēvŏco (1)

evolve *v.t*, ēvolvo (3)

ewe ŏvis, *f*

exact *adj*, (**number, etc.**), exactus; (**persons**), dīlĭgens

exact *v.t*, exĭgo (3)

exactness subtīlĭtas, *f*

exaggerate *v.t*, augĕo (2)

exaggeration sŭperlātĭo, *f*

exalt *v.t*, tollo (3), augĕo (2)

exalted celsus

examination (test, etc.) prŏbātĭo, *f*; (**enquiry**) investĭgātĭo, *f*

examine *v.t*, investĭgo (1), interrŏgo (1); (**test**), prŏbo (1)

example exemplum *n*; (**for** —),

verbi causā

exasperate *v.t*, exăcerbo (1)

excavate *v.t*, căvo (1)

excavation (cavity) căvum, *n*

exceed *v.t*, sŭpĕro (1), excēdo (3)

exceedingly *adv*, admŏdum; *or use superlative of adj*, *e.g.* (— **large**), maxĭmus

excel *v.t*, praesto (1) (*with dat*)

excellence praestantĭa, *f*

excellent praestans, ēgrĕgĭus

except *prep*, praeter (*with acc*)

except *v.t*, excĭpĭo (3)

exception (everyone, without —) omnes ad ūnum; (**take** — **to**) aegre fĕro (*irreg*)

exceptional rārus, insignis

excess (over-indulgence) intempĕrantĭa, *f*

excessive nĭmĭus

exchange *nn*, permūtātĭo, *f*

exchange *v.t*, permūto (1)

exchequer aerārĭum, *n*

excitable fervĭdus, fĕrox

excite *v.t*, excĭto (1), incendo (3)

excited commōtus, incensus

excitement commōtĭo, *f*

exclaim *v.i*, clāmo (1), conclāmo (1)

exclamation exclāmātĭo, *f*

exclude *v.t*, exclūdo (3)

exclusion exclūsĭo, *f*

exclusive (one's own) prŏprĭus

excrescence tūber, *n*

excruciating (pain, etc.) ācer

excursion ĭter, *n*

excusable excūsābĭlis

excuse *nn*, excūsātĭo, *f*

excuse *v.t*, excūso (1); (**pardon**), ignosco (3) (*with dat*)

execrable nĕfārĭus

execrate *v.t*, dētestor (1 *dep*)

execute *v.t*, (**carry out**) exsĕquor (3 *dep*); (**inflict capital punishment**), nĕco (1)

execution (carrying out) *use vb* exsĕquor; (**capital punishment**), supplĭcĭum, *n*

executioner carnĭfex, *m*

exemplary ēgrĕgĭus

exempt *v.t*, excĭpĭo (3)

exempt *adj* immūnis

exemption immūnĭtas, *f*

exercise

exercise exercĭtātĭo, *f*; (set task),
ŏpus, *n*
exercise *v.t*, exercĕo (2)
exert *v.t*, contendo (3), ūtor (3
dep) (*with abl*); (to — oneself),
v.i, nītor (3 *dep*)
exertion contentĭo, *f*, lăbor, *m*
exhale *v.t*, exhālo (1)
exhaust *v.t*, exhaurĭo (4); (weary),
confĭcĭo (3), dēfătīgo (1)
exhausted (tired out) confectus
exhaustion vīrĭum dēfectĭo, *f*,
(failing of strength)
exhibit *v.t*, expōno (3)
exhibition (spectacle)
spectācŭlum, *n*
exhilarate *v.t*, hĭlăro (1)
exhilaration hĭlărĭtas, *f*
exhort *v.t*, hortor (1 *dep*)
exhume *v.t*, ērŭo (3)
exile *nn*, (person), exsul, *c*;
(banishment), exsĭlĭum, *n*; (to be
in —), *v.i*, exsŭlo (1)
exist *v.i*, in exsĭlĭum pello (3)
(drive into exile)
exist *v.i*, sum (*irreg*), existo (3)
existence (life) vīta, *f*
exit exĭtus, *m*
exonerate *v.t*, lībĕro (1)
exorbitant nĭmĭus
exotic externus
expand *v.t*, extendo (3); *v.i*,
extendor (3 *pass*)
expanse spătĭum, *n*
expatiate (on a theme etc.) *v.*,
permulta dissĕro (3) dē (*with
abl.*)
expatriate *v.t*, ēĭcĭo (3)
expect *v.t*, exspecto (1)
expectation exspectātĭo, *f*
expediency ūtĭlĭtas, *f*
expedient *adj*, ūtĭlis
expedient *nn*, rătĭo, *f*
expedite *v.t*, expĕdĭo (4)
expedition (military, etc.)
expĕdītĭo, *f*
expeditious cĕler
expel *v.t*, expello (3)
expend *v.t*, expendo (3)
expenditure ērŏgātĭo, *f*
expense impensa, *f*, sumptus, *m*
expensive sumptŭōsus, prĕtĭōsus

experience ūsus, *m*, pĕrītĭa, *f*
experience *v.t*, expĕrĭor (4 *dep*),
pătĭor (3 *dep*)
experienced pĕrītus
experiment expĕrīmentum, *n*
expert *adj*, scĭens
expiate *v.t*, expĭo (1)
expiation expĭātĭo, *f*
expiatory pĭācŭlāris
expiration (breathing out)
exspīrātĭo, *f*; (time), *use partic.*
confectus (completed)
expire *v.i*, (persons), exspīro (1);
(time), exĕo (4), confĭcĭo (3)
explain *v.t*, explĭco (1), expōno (3)
explanation explĭcātĭo, *f*
explicit ăpertus
explode *v.i*, dīrumpor (3 *pass*)
explore *v.t*, explōro (1)
export *v.t*, exporto (1)
exports merces, *f*, *pl*
expose *v.t*, expōno (3), dētĕgo (3),
nūdo (1); (— to danger, etc.),
offĕro (*irreg*)
exposition (statement) expŏsĭtĭo,
f
expostulate *v.i*, expostŭlo (1)
expound *v.t*, explĭco (1), expōno
(3)
express *v.t*, exprĭmo (3); (— in
writing), dēscrībo (3)
expression (verbal) vox, *f*, verba,
n.pl; (facial), vultus, *m*
expressive *use phr*, multam vim
hăbens (having much significance)
expulsion exactĭo, *f*
expunge *v.t*, dēlĕo (2)
exquisite conquīsītus
extant (to be —) *v.i*, exsto (1)
extemporary extempŏrālis
extemporize *v.i*, sŭbĭta dīco (3)
extend *v.t*, extendo (3), distendo
(3); *v.i*, pătĕo (2); (— to), pertĭnĕo
(2) ad (*with acc*)
extension (act of) porrectĭo, *f*; (of
boundaries etc.) prŏpāgātĭo, *f*
extensive amplus
extent spătĭum, *n*
extenuate *v.t*, lĕvo (1), mītĭgo (1)
exterior *adj*, externus
exterior *nn*, spĕcĭes, *f*

exterminate *v.t*, interfĭcĭo (3),
dēlĕo (2)
extermination internĕcĭo, *f*
external externus
extinct exstinctus
extinguish *v.t*, exstinguo (3)
extirpate *v.t*, exstirpo (1), excīdo
(3)
extol *v.t*, laudo (1)
extort *v.t*, **(by force)**, extorquĕo (2)
extortion res rĕpĕtundae, *f.pl*
extra *adv*, praetĕrĕā
extract *nn*, **(from a book, etc.)**,
exceptĭo, *f*
extract *v.t*, extrăho (3), ēvello (3)
extraction (pulling out) ēvulsĭo, *f*
extraordinary extraordinārĭus,
insŏlĭtus
extravagance sumptus, *m*, luxŭrĭa,
f, intempĕrantĭa, *f*
extravagant immŏdĭcus,
sumptŭōsus
extreme *adj*, extrēmus, ultĭmus
extremity extrēmum, *n*; **(top)**,
căcūmen, *n*, vertex, *m*; *or use adj*,
extrēmus **(extreme)**
extricate *v.t*, expĕdĭo (4), solvo (3)
exuberance luxŭrĭa, *f*
exuberant luxŭrĭōsus, effūsus
exude *v.i*, māno (1)
exult *v.i*, exsulto (1), laetor (1 *dep*)
exultant laetus, ēlātus
eye ŏcŭlus, *m*; **(— lash)**, palpĕbrae
pĭlus, *m*; **(— lid)**, palpĕbra, *f*; **(—
sight)**, ăcĭes, *f*;
(— witness), arbĭter, *m*

F

fable fābŭla, *f*
fabric (woven) textum, *n*;
(building), aedĭfĭcĭum, *n*
fabricate *v.t*, fabrĭcor (1 *dep*)
fabrication mendācĭum, *n*
fabulous fictus, falsus
face făcĭes, *f*, vultus, *m*, ōs, *n*
face *v.t*, **(confront)**, obvĭam ĕo (4)
(with dat); **(look towards)**, specto
(1) ad **(with acc)**
facetious făcētus
facilitate *v.t*, făcĭlĭorem reddo (3)
(make easier)

facility (possibility) făcultas, *f*;
(dexterity), făcĭlĭtas, *f*
facing *prep*, adversus **(with acc)**
fact rēs, *f*; **(in —, truly)**, *conj*, ĕnim;
adv, vēro
faction factĭo, *f*
factious factĭōsus
factory offĭcīna, *f*
faculty făcultas, *f*, vīs, *f*
fade *v.i*, pallesco (3)
faggot sarmenta *n.pl*
fail *v.i*, cădo (3), dēfĭcĭo (3), dēsum
(irreg) (with dat)
failing *nn*, **(defect)** vĭtĭum, *n*
failure (of supplies, strength, etc.),
dēfectĭo, *f*, *otherwise use* irrĭtus
(vain, unsuccessful)
faint *v.i*, collābor (3 *dep*),
languesco (3)
faint *adj*, **(exhausted)** dēfessus
faint-hearted tĭmĭdus, imbellis
faintness (of body) languor, *m*
fair *nn*, **(market)**, nundĭnae, *f.pl*
(ninth day)
fair *adj*, **(beautiful)**, pulcher; **(just)**,
aequus; **(colour)**, candĭdus;
(weather), sĕrēnus; **(wind, etc.)**,
sĕcundus; **(fairly good)**, mĕdĭocris
fairly *adv* **(justly)**, iustē;
(moderately), mĕdĭocrĭter
fairness (justice) aequĭtas, *f*; **(of
complexion, etc.)** candor, *m*
faith fĭdes, *f*; **(to keep —)**, *v.i*,
fĭdem servo (1)
faithful fĭdēlis, fĭdus
faithfulness fĭdēlĭtas, *f*
faithless infĭdus, perfĭdus
faithlessness perfĭdĭa, *f*
falcon falco, *m*
fall *nn*, cāsus, *m*, rŭīna, *f*
fall *v.i*, cădo (3); **(— back)** rēcĭdo
(3); **(retreat)**, pĕdem rĕfĕro **(irreg)**;
(— headlong), praecĭpĭto (1);
(— in love with) ădămo (1);
(— off), dēlābor (3 *dep*); **(— out,
happen)**, cădo (3); **(— upon,
attack)**, *v.t*, invādo (3)
fallacious fallax, falsus
fallacy vĭtĭum, *n*
falling off *nn*, **(revolt)**, dēfectĭo, *f*
fallow nŏvālis, ĭnărātus
false falsus; **(not genuine)**, fictus;
(person), perfĭdus

falsehood mendācĭum, *n*

falsify *v.t*, vĭtĭo (1)

falter *v.i*, haerĕo (2), haesĭto (1)

faltering *adj*, haesĭtans

fame glōrĭa, *f*, fāma, *f*

familiar nōtus, fămĭlĭāris; **(usual)**, consŭētus, *f*

familiarity fămĭlĭārĭtas, *f*

familiarize *v.t*, consŭesco (3)

family *nn*, fămĭlĭa, *f*, dŏmus, *f*, gens, *f*

family *adj*, fămĭlĭāris, gentīlis

famine fămes, *f*

famished făme confectus **(exhausted from hunger)**

famous clārus

fan flābellum, *n*

fan *v.t*, ventĭlo (1)

fanatical fănātĭcus

fanaticism sŭperstĭtĭo, *f*

fancied (imaginary) fictus

fancy *nn*, **(notion)** ŏpĭnĭo, *f*; **(liking for)**, lĭbīdo, *f*

fancy *v.t*, **(imagine)**, fingo (3); **(think)**, ŏpĭnor (1 *dep*); **(want)** cŭpĭo (3)

fang dens, *m*

far *adv*, **(of distance)** prŏcul, longē **(as — as)** *prep*, tĕnus; *with comparatives*, multō, *e.g*, **far bigger,** multō māior; **(how —)** quātĕnus; **(— and wide)**, longē lātēque

far-fetched quaesītus

farce mīmus, *m*

farcical mīmĭcus

fare (food) cĭbus, *m*; **(charge)**, vectūra, *f*

farewell!! ăvē; **(pl)** ăvete; vălē, vălete; **(to bid —)**, vălēre iŭbĕo (2)

farm *nn*, fundus, *m*

farm *v.t*, cŏlo (3)

farmer agrĭcŏla, *m*, cŏlōnus, *m*

farming agrĭcultūra, *f*

farther *adj*, ultĕrĭor

farther *adv*, longĭus

farthest *adj*, ultĭmus

farhtest *adv*, longissĭme

fascinate *v.t*, fascĭno (1)

fascination fascĭnātĭo, *f*

fashion *nn*, mōs, *m*

fashion *v.t*, fingo (3)

fashionable ēlĕgans

fast *nn*, iēiūnĭum, *n*

fast *v.i*, iēiūnus sum *(irreg)* **(be hungry)**

fast *adj*, **(quick)** cĕler; **(firm)**, firmus; **(make —)**, *v.t*, firmo (1), dēlĭgo (1)

fast *adv*, **(quickly)**, cĕlĕrĭter; **(firmly)**, firme

fasten *v.t*, fīgo (3), dēlĭgo (1); **(doors etc.)** obtūro (1)

fastening *nn*, vincŭlum, *n*

fastidious dēlĭcātus

fat *adj*, pinguis

fat *nn*, ădeps, *c*

fatal (deadly) pernĭcĭōsus

fatality cāsus, *m*

fate fātum, *n*

fated fātālis

father păter, *m*; **(-in-law)**, sŏcer, *m*

fatherland pătrĭa, *f*

fatherless orbus

fathom *nn*, ulna, *f*

fatigue *nn*, dēfătĭgātĭo, *f*

fatigue *v.t*, fătīgo (1)

fatigued fătīgātus

fatten *v.t*, săgīno (1)

fault culpa *f*, vĭtĭum, *n*

faultless intĕger, perfectus

faulty mendōsus, vĭtĭōsus

favour *nn*, grātĭa, *f*, făvour, *m*, stŭdĭum, *n*; **(a benefit)**, grātĭa, *f*, bĕnĕfĭcĭum, *n*

favour *v.t*, făvĕo (2) *(with dat)*

favourable commŏdus; **(of wind)**, sĕcundus

favourite *nn*, dēlĭcĭae, *f.pl*

favourite *adj*, grātus

fawn *nn*, hinnŭlĕus, *m*

fawn upon *v.t*, ădūlor (1 *dep*)

fear *nn*, tĭmor, *m*, mĕtus, *m*

fear *v.t*, tĭmĕo (2), mĕtŭo (3), vĕrĕor (2 *dep*)

fearful *adj*, **(afraid)**, tĭmĭdus; **(terrible)**, terrĭbĭlis

fearless intrĕpĭdus

fearlessness audācĭa, *f*

feasible *use phr. with vbs*, posse **(to be able)** *and* effĭcĕre **(to bring about)**

feast *nn*, daps, *f*, ĕpŭlae, *f.pl*; **(— day)** dĭes festus, *m*

feast *v.i*, ĕpŭlor (1 *dep*); *v.t*, pasco (3)

feat făcĭnus, *n*
feather penna, *f*, plūma, *f*
feature (of face, etc.)
līnĕāmentum, *n*; (peculiarity) *use adj*, prŏprĭus (one's own)
February Fēbrŭārĭus (mensis)
fecundity fēcundĭtas, *f*
federal foedĕrātus
fee merces, *f*, hŏnor, *m*
feeble infirmus, imbēcillus
feebleness infirmĭtas, *f*
feed *v.t*, pasco (3), ălo (3); *v.i*, vescor (3 *dep.*), pascor (3 *dep*)
feel *v.t*, sentĭo (4); (with the hands), tempto (1)
feeler cornĭcŭlum, *n*
feeling *nn*, (sensation or emotion), sensus, *m*, tactus, *m*; (spirit, etc.), ănĭmus, *m*
feign *v.t*, sĭmŭlo (1)
feigned sĭmŭlātus
feint sĭmŭlātĭo, *f*
felicitous fēlix
felicity fēlĭcĭtas, *f*
fell *v.t*, excīdo (3), sterno (3)
fellow (companion) cŏmĕs, *c*; (— citizen), cīvis, *c*; (— feeling), consensĭo, *f*; (— soldier), commīlĭto, *m*; (worthless —), nĕbŭlo, *m*
fellowship (companionship), sŏcĭĕtas, *f*
felt *nn*, cŏactum, *n*
female *nn*, fēmĭna, *f*
female *adj*, mŭlĭĕbris
fen pălus, *f*
fence *nn*, saeptum, *n*, cancelli, *m,pl*
fence *v.t*, saepĭo (4); (with swords), *v.i*, băttŭo
fencing (art of —) ars, (*f*) glădĭi
ferment *nn*, (excitement), aestus, *m*
ferment *v.i*, fervĕo (2)
fern fĭlix, *f*
ferocious saevus, fĕrus
ferocity saevĭtĭa, *f*
ferry *nn*, trāiectus, *m*; (— boat), cymba, *f*
ferry *v.t*, trāĭcĭo (3)
fertile fēcundus, fertĭlis
fertility fēcundĭtas, *f*
fervent ardens, fervĭdus

fervour ardor, *m*, fervor, *m*
festival (holidays) fērĭae, *f.pl*; (religious —, etc.) sollemne, *n*
festive (gay) hĭlăris
festivity (gaiety) hĭlărĭtas, *f*
fetch *v.t*, peto (3), affĕro (*irreg*)
fetter *nn*, vincŭlum, *n*
fetter *v.t*, vincŭla ĭnĭcĭo (3) (with *dat*)
feud (quarrel) sĭmultas, *f*
fever fĕbris, *f*
feverish fĕbrĭcŭlōsus; (excited) commōtus
few *adj*, pauci (*pl*)
fewness paucĭtas, *f*
fib mendācĭum, *n*
fibre fibra, *f*
fickle inconstans
fickleness inconstantĭa, *f*
fiction commentum, *n*, fābŭla, *f*
fictitious commentĭcĭus
fiddle (instrument) fĭdes, *f.pl*
fidelity fĭdēlĭtas, *f*
fidgety inquĭētus
field ăger *m*; (plain), campus, *m*; (— of battle), lŏcus, (*m*) pugnae; (scope), lŏcus, *m*
fiendish nĕfandus
fierce fĕrox, fĕrus
fierceness fĕrōcĭtas, *f*
fiery (of temper, etc.) ardens
fifteen quindĕcim; (— times), *adv*, quindĕcĭes
fifteenth quintus dĕcĭmus
fifth quintus
fiftieth quinquāgēsĭmus
fifty quinquāginta
fig, fig tree fĭcus, *f*
fight *nn*, pugna, *f*
fight *v.i*, pugno (1)
fighter pugnātor, *m*
figurative trānslātus
figure fĭgŭra, *f*, forma, *f*
figure *v.t*, (imagine), fingo (3)
figured sĭgillātus
filch *v.t*, surrĭpĭo (3)
file (tool) scŏbīna, *f*; (rank), ordo, *m*
file *v.t*, (wood, metal), līmo (1)
filial (dutiful, respectful) pĭus
fill *v.t*, implĕo (2), complĕo (2); (a post, etc.) fungor (3 *dep*) (with *abl*)

fillet (for the hair)   vitta, *f*
film   membrāna, *f*
filter   *v.t*, cōlo (1)
filth   caenum, *n*
filthy   sordĭdus, foedus
fin   pinna, *f*
final   ultĭmus
finally   *adv*, postrēmo, dēnĭque, tandem
finance (of the state)   aerārĭum, *n*
find   *v.t*, invĕnĭo (4), rĕpĕrĭo (4); **(— out)**; cognosco (3), compĕrĭo (4); **(— fault with)**, culpo (1); accūso (1)
fine   *v.t*, multo (1)
fine   *nn*, multa, *f*
fine   *adj*, **(of texture)**, subtīlis; **(handsome, etc.)** praeclārus; **(weather)**, sĕrēnus
finery   mundĭtĭa, *f*
finger   dĭgĭtus, *m*; **(fore —)**, index dĭgĭtus
finger   *v.t*, tango (3)
finish   *nn*, **(perfection)**, perfectĭo, *f*
finish   *v.t*, confĭcĭo (3); **(limit)**, fīnĭo (4)
finished (complete, perfect) perfectus
fir, fir tree   ăbĭes, *f*
fire   ignis, *m*; **(ardour)**, vīs, *f*, ardor, *m*; **(to be on —)**, *v.i*, ardĕo (2); **(to set on —)** *v.t*, incendo (3)
fire   *v.t*, incendo (3); **(missiles)**, cōnĭcĭo (3)
firebrand   fax, *f*
fireplace   fŏcus, *m*
firewood   lignum, *n*
firm   firmus; **(constant)**, constans; **(to make —)**, *v.t*, confirmo (1)
first   *adj*, prīmus
first   *adv*, prīmum, prīmō
fish   *nn*, piscis, *m*
fish   *v.i*, piscor (1 *dep*)
fisherman   piscātor, *m*
fishing   *nn*, piscātus, *m*
fishing boat   hŏrĭŏla, *f*
fishing net   rēte, *n*
fishmonger   cētārĭus, *m*
fishpond   piscīna, *f*
fissure   rīma, *f*
fist   pugnus, *m*
fit (violent seizure)   accessĭo, *f*, impĕtus, *m*

fit, fitted   aptus, ĭdōnĕus, accommŏdātus
fit   *v.t*, accommŏdo (1), apto (1); **(— out)**, exorno (1)
five   quinque; **(— each)**, quīni; **(— times)** *adv*, quinquĭes
five hundred   quingenti
fix   *v.t*, fīgo (3); **(determine)**, stătŭo (3), constĭtŭo (3)
fixed   certus
flabby   flaccĭdus
flag   vexillum, *n*
flag   *v.i* **(become weak)**, languesco (3)
flagrant (clear)   mănĭfestus; **(heinous)**, nĕfandus
flail   pertĭca, *f*
flame   *nn*, flamma, *f*
flame   *v.i*, flagro (1)
flame-coloured   flammĕus
flank (of army, etc.)   lătus, *n*; **(of animal)** īlĭa, *n.pl*
flap (of dress, etc.)   lăcĭnĭa, *f*
flare   *v.i*, flăgro (1)
flash   *nn*, fulgor, *m*
flash   *v.i*, fulgĕo (2)
flask   ampulla, *f*
flat   aequus, plānus
flatness   plānĭtĭes, *f*
flatter   *v.t*, ădūlor (1 *dep*)
flatterer   ădūlātor, *m*
flattering   ădūlans
flattery   ădūlātĭo, *f*
flaunt   *v.t*, iacto (1)
flavour   săpor, *m*
flaw   vĭtĭum, *n*
flawless   ēmendātus
flax   līnum, *n*
flaxen   *adj*, līnĕus
flea   pūlex, *m*
flee   *v.i* **(flee from, *v.t.*)**, fŭgĭo (3)
fleece   *nn*, vellus, *n*
fleece   *v.t*, **(rob)**, spŏlĭo (1)
fleecy   lānĭger
fleet   *nn*, classis, *f*
fleet   *adj*, cĕler
fleeting   fŭgax
flexh   căro, *f*
flesh-coloured, fleshy   carnōsus
flexibility   făcĭlĭtas, *f*
flexible   flexĭbĭlis
flicker   *v.i*, trĕpĭdo (1), cŏrusco (1)

flickering trĕpĭdans, trĕmŭlus
flight (flying) cŏlātus, *m*; **(escape)** fŭga, *f*
flighty mōbĭlis, lĕvis
fling *v.t*, cōnĭcĭo (3)
flint sĭlex, *m*
flippant făcētus
flirt *v.i*, blandĭor (4 *dep*)
flit *v.i*, vŏlĭto (1); **(— in, or upon)**, inno (1) (*with dat*)
float *v.i*, năto (1); **(in the air)**, vŏlĭto (1)
flock grex, *m*, pĕcus, *n*
flock *v.i*, conflŭo (3), concurro (3)
flog *v.t*, verbĕro (1)
flogging verbĕra, *n.pl*
flood dīlŭvĭes, *f*, *n*
flood *v.t*, ĭnundo (1)
floor sŏlum, *n*; **(upper —)** contăbŭlātĭo, *f*
florid flōrĭdus
flotilla classis, *f*
flounder *v.i*, vŏlūtor (1 *pass*)
flour fărīna, *f*
flourish *v.i*, flōrĕo (2); *v.t*, vĭbro (1)
flourishes (of style) călămistri, *m.pl*
flow *nn*, cursus, *m*, fluxĭo, *f*; **(of the tide)**, accessus, *m*
flow *v.i*, flŭo (3); **(— past)**, praeterflŭo (3); **(— together)**, conflŭo (3); **(trickle)**, māno (1)
flower *nn*, flos, *m*
flower *v.i*, flōrĕo (2)
flowing flŭens; **(hair)**, fūsus
fluctuate *v.i*, iactor (1 *pass*); aestŭo (1)
fluctuation mūtātĭo, *f*
fluency vŏlūbĭlitas, *f*
fluent vŏlūbĭlis
fluid *nn*, hūmor, *m*, lĭquor, *m*
fluid *adj*, lĭquĭdus
flurry concĭtātĭo, *f*
flush *nn*, rŭbor, *m*
flush *v.i*, ērŭbĕsco (3)
fluster *v.i*, ăgĭto (1)
flute tībĭa, *f*; **(— player)**, tībĭcen, *m*
flutter *nn*, trĕpĭdātĭo, *f*
flutter *v.i*, vŏlĭto (1), **(in fear)**, trĕpĭdo (1)
flux (flow) fluctus, *m*, fluxus, *m*
fly *nn*, musca, *f*

fly *v.i*, vŏlo (1)
flying *adj*, vŏlātĭlis, vŏlŭcer
flying *nn*, vŏlātus, *m*
foal ĕquŭlĕus, *m*, pullus, *m*
foam *nn*, spūma, *f*
foam *v.i*, spūmo (1)
foaming, foamy spūmōsus
fodder pābŭlum, *n*
foe hostis, *c*
fog cālīgo, *f*
foggy cālĭgĭnōsus
foil (sword) rŭdis, *f*; **(metal leaf)**, lāmĭna, *f*
foil *v.t*, **(parry a blow, delude)**, ēlūdo (3)
fold *nn*, **(of garment, etc.)** sĭnus, *m*
fold *v.t*, plĭco (1)
folding-doors valvae *f.pl*
foliage frons, *f*
folk (people) hŏmĭnes, *c.pl*
follow *v.i. and v.t*, sĕquor (3 *dep*); sector (1 *dep*); **(succeed)**, succēdo (3) (*with dat*)
follower (attendant) assectātor, *m*; or use *adj*, e.g. **(— of Ceasar)** Caesărĭānus
following sĕquens, proxĭmus, sĕcundus
folly stultītĭa, *f*
foment *v.t*, fŏvĕo (2); **(— trouble, etc.)** sollĭcĭto (1)
fond ămans (*with genit*)
fondle *v.t*, mulcĕo (2)
fond cĭbus, *m*; **(fodder)**, pābŭlum, *n*
fool hŏmo stultus; **(to act the —)**, *v.i*, dēsĭpĭo
fool *v.t*, lūdo (3)
foolhardy tĕmĕrārĭus
foolish stultus
foot pes, *m*; **(on —)**, *adj*, pĕdester; **(— in length)**, *adj*, pĕdālis; **(bottom of)**, use *adj*, īmus, *in agreement with noun*, e.g. īma quercus **(foot of an oak)**
footing stătus, *m*, or use *vb*, consisto (3), **(to stand)**
footman pĕdĭsĕquus, *m*
footpath sēmĭta, *f*
footprint vestīgĭum, *n*
footsoldier pĕdes, *m*

for

for *prep* **(on behalf of)**, prō (*with abl*); **(on account of)**, propter, ŏb (*with acc*); **(during a certain time)**, *use acc, e.g.* **for two hours,** dŭas hōras, *or* per (*with acc*); **(expressing purpose)**, *use* ad (*with acc*)

for *conj*, nam, namque; ĕnim (*second word in clause*); **(because)**, quippe, quod

forage *nn*, pābŭlum, *n*

forage *v.i, and v.t*, pābŭlor (1 *dep*)

forbear *v.i, and v.t*, parco (3)

forbearance contĭnentĭa, *f*

forbid *v.t*, vĕto (1)

force *nn*, vīs, *f*; **(military forces)**, cōpĭae, *f.pl*

force *v.t*, **(compel)**, cōgo (3); **(break through)**, perrumpo (3)

forced (unnatural) quaesītus; **(a — march)**, magnum ĭter, *n*

forcible, forcibly *use adv. phr*, per vim

ford *nn*, vădum, *n*

ford *v.i. and v.t*, vădo transĕo (4) **(cross by a ford)**

forearm bracchĭum, *n*

forebode *v.t*, paresāgĭo (4), portendo (3)

foreboding *nn*, praesensĭo, *f*

forecast *v.t*, praevĭdĕo (2)

forefather prŏăvus, *m*; (*pl*) māiōres *m.pl*

forehead frons, *f*

foreign externus, pĕrĕgrīnus

foreigner pĕrĕgrīnus, *m*

foreman qui (servis) praeest **(who is in charge of (slaves))**

foremost prīmus

forensic fŏrensis

forerunner praenuntĭus, *m*

foresee *v.t*, prŏvĭdĕo (2)

foresight prŏvĭdentĭa, *f*

forest silva, *f*

foretell *v.t*, praedīco (3)

forethought prŏvĭdentĭa, *f*

forewarn *v.t*, preaemŏnĕo (2)

forfeit *nn*, poena, *f*

forfeit *v.t*, āmitto (3)

forge *nn*, fornax, *f*

forge *v.t*, făbrĭcor (1 *dep*), excūdo (3); **(strike counterfeit coins)**, nummos ădultĕrīnos cūdo (3); **(documents)**, suppōno (3)

forgery *use phr*. subiectĭo falsārum littĕrāum **(substitution of counterfeit letters)**

forget *v.t*, ovlīviscor (3 *dep*) (*with genit*)

forgetful immĕmor

forgetfulness oblīvĭo, *f*

forgive *v.t*, ignosco (3) (*with dat of person*)

forgiveness vĕnĭa

fork furca, *f*

forked bĭfurcus

forlorn destĭtūtus, perdĭtus

form forma, *f*, fĭgūra, *f*

form *v.t*, **(shape)**, formo (1), fingo (3); **(— a plan)**, ĭnĕo (4), căpĭo (3); **(troops, etc.)** instrŭo (3)

formality rītus, *m*

formally *adv*, rītĕ

formation conformātĭo, *f*

former prĭor, sŭpĕrĭor; **(the — and the latter)**, ille … hic

formerly *adv*, antĕă, ōlim

formidable grăvis, mĕtŭendus

formula formŭla, *f*

forsake *v.t*, rĕlinquo (3), dēsĕro (3)

forswear *v.t*, **(renounce)**, abiūro (1); **(swear falsely)**, periūro (1)

fort castellum, *n*

forth *adv, use compound vb. with* e *or* ex, *e.g.* exĕo, **go forth; (of time)**, inde

forthwith, *adv*, stătim, extemplo

fortification mūnītĭo, *f*

fortify *v.t*, mūnĭo (4)

fortitude fortĭtūdo, *f*

fortuitous fortŭītus

fortunate fēlix, fortūnātus

fortune fortūna, *f*, **(property, etc.)**, rēs, *f*, ŏpes, *f.pl*

fortune-teller hărĭolŭs, *m*

forty quădrāginta

forum fŏrum, *n*

forward, forwards *adv*, porro, prorsum, ante; *or use compound verb with* pro *e.g.* prōdūco **(lead forward)**

forward *adj*, praecox

forward *v.t,* **(send on),** perfĕro (*irreg*)

foster *v.t,* nūtrĭo (4)

foster-brother collactĕus, *m;* (— **child**), ălumnus, *m;* (— **father**), altor, *m;* (— **mother**), nūtrix, *f;* (— **sister**), collactĕa, *f*

foul *adj,* foedus

found *v.t,* condo (3); **(metal),** fundo (3)

foundation fundāmenta, *n.pl*

founder condĭtor, *m*

founder *v.i,* submergo (3 *pass*)

fountain fons, *m*

four quattŭor; (— **times**), *adv,* quătĕr; (— **each**), quăterni

fourteen quattŭordĕcim; **(-teenth),** quartus dĕcĭmus

fourth quartus; (— **part, quarter**), quădrans, *m*

fowl ăvis, *f,* gallīna, *f*

fowler auceps, *c*

fox vulpes, *f*

fraction (part) pars, *f*

fractious difficĭlis

fracture *nn,* fractūra, *f*

fracture *v.t,* frango (3)

fragile frăgĭlis

fragment fragmentum, *n*

fragile frăgĭlis

fragment fragmentum, *n*

fragrance dulcis ŏdōr, *m,* **(pleasant smell)**

fragrant dulcis, suāvis

frail frăgĭlis, dēbĭlis

frailty frăgĭlĭtas, *f,* dēbĭlĭtas, *f*

frame forma, *f,* compāges, *f;* (— **of mind**) ănĭmus, *m,* affectĭo, *f*

frame *v.t,* **(shape),** făbrĭcor (1 *dep*), fingo (3); **(form),** compōno (3)

franchise (citizenship) cīvĭtas, *f;* **(right of voting),** suffrāgĭum, *n*

frank līber, ăpertus

frantic āmens

fraternal frāternus

fraternity (association of men) sŏdālĭtas, *f*

fratricide (the person) frātrĭcīda, *m;* **(the crime),** fraternum parrĭcīdĭum, *n*

fraud fraus, *f,* dŏlus, *m*

fraudulent fraudŭlentus, dŏlōsus

fraught opplētus **(filled)**

fray certāmen, *n,* pugna, *f*

freak (prodigy) prōdĭgĭum, *n*

freckle lentīgo, *f*

free līber; **(generous),** lībĕrālis; **(of one's will),** sŭā sponte (*abl*)

free *v.t,* lībĕro (1), solvo (3)

free-born ingĕnŭus

freedman lībertus, *m*

freedom lībertas, *f;* (— **from a burden, tax, etc.),** immūnĭtas, *f*

freehold *nn,* praedĭum lībĕrum, *n,* **(free estate)**

freely *adv,* lībĕrē; **(generously),** mūnĭfĭcē, largē; **(of one's own free will),** sŭā sponte

free-will vŏluntas, *f*

freeze *v.t,* glăcĭo (1); *v.i,* congĕlo (1)

freight *nn,* ŏnus, *n*

freight *adj,* ŏnustus

French *adj,* Gallĭcus; **(The French),** Galli, *pl*

frenzied fŭrens, āmens

frenzy fŭror, *m,* āmentĭa, *f*

frequent *adj,* crēber, frĕquens

frequent *v.t,* cĕlĕbro (1)

frequently *adv,* saepe

fresh (new) rĕcens, nŏvus; **(wind),** incrēbresco (3)

freshness vĭrĭdĭtas, *f*

fret *v.i,* dŏlĕo (2)

fretful mōrōsus

fretfulness mōrōsĭtas, *f*

friction trītus, *m*

friend ămīcus, *m*

friendless ĭnops ămīcōrum **(destitute of friends)**

friendliness cōmĭtas, *f*

friendly ămīcus, cōmis

friendship ămīcĭtĭa, *f*

fright terror *m,* păvor, *m;* **(to take —),** *v.i,* păvesco (3)

frighten *v.t,* terrĕo (2)

frightful terrĭbĭlis, horrĭbĭlis

frigid frīgĭdus

frill segmenta, *n.pl*

fringe fimbrĭae, *f.pl*

frippery nūgae, *f.pl*

frisk *v.i,* lascīvĭo (4)

fritter away *v.t,* dissĭpo (1)

frivolity lĕvĭtas, *f*

frivolous lĕvis; **(opinion, etc.)** fūtĭlis

fro (to and —) *adv, phr,* hūc et illūc

frock

frock stŏla, *f*
frog rāna, *f*
frolic *nn*, lūdus, *m*
frolic *v.i*, lūdo (3)
from ā, ab, dē, ē, ex (*all with abl*) (*with expressions of place, time and cause*)
front *nn*, frons, *f*, prĭor pars; (**in —**) ā fronte, *or use adj*, adversus; (**in — of**) *prep*, prō (*with abl*)
front *adj*, prĭor
frontage frons, *f*
frontier fĭnis, *m*
frost gĕlu, *n*; (**— bitten**), *adj*, ambustus
frosty gĕlĭdus
froth *nn*, spūma, *f*
froth *v.i*, spūmo (1)
frown *nn*, contractĭo (*f*) frontis (**contraction of the forehead**)
frown *v.i*, frontem contrăho (3)
frowsy incultus
frozen rĭgĭdus, glăcĭālis
fructify *v.t*, fēcundo (1)
frugal frūgi, *indecl*
frugality parsĭmōnĭa, *f*
fruit fructus, *m*, pōmum, *n*
fruitful fēcundĭtas, *f*
fruition fructus, *m*
fruitless (**without result**) irrĭtus
fruit tree pōmum, *n*, pōmus, *f*
frustrate *v.t*, (**an undertaking, etc.**) ad vānum rĕdĭgo (3)
frustrated (**to be —**) *v.i*, frustrā esse
frustration frustrātĭo, *f*
fry *v.t*, frīgo (3)
frying pan sartāgo, *f*
fuel ligna, *n.pl*
fugitive *nn*, prŏfŭgus, *m*, fŭgĭtīvus, *m*
fugitive *adj*, fŭgĭtīvus
fulfil *v.t*, explĕo (2), exsĕquor (3 *dep*), fungor (3 *dep*) (*with abl*)
full plēnus, replētus; (**with people**), frĕquens, crēber
full-grown ădultus
fulminate *v.i*, fulmĭno (1), intŏno (1)
fulness (**abundance**) ūbertas, *f*
fulsome pūtĭdus
fumble *v.t*, (**handle**), tento (1)
fume *nn*, hālĭtus, *m*

fume *v.i*, (**with anger etc.**), fŭro (3)
fumigate *v.t*, suffĭo (4)
fun iŏcus, *m*, lūdus, *m*
function offĭcĭum, *n*, mūnus, *n*
fund (**of knowledge, etc.**) cōpĭa, *f*, with nn. in genit.
fundamental prīmus
funeral fūnus, *n*, exsĕquĭae, *f.pl*
funeral, funereal *adj*, fūnĕbris
fungus fungus, *m*
funnel infundĭbŭlum, *n*
funny rīdĭcŭlus
fur pĭlus, *m*
furbish *v.t*, interpŏlo (1)
furious fŭrens, saevus; (**to be —**), *v.i*, saevĭo (4), fŭro (3)
furl *v.t*, contrăho (3), lĕgo (3), subdūco (3)
furlough commĕātus, *m*
furnace fornax, *f*
furnish *v.t*, suppĕdĭto (1), orno (1)
furniture sŭpellex, *f*
furrow *nn*, sulcus, *m*
furrow *v.t*, sulco (1)
further *adj*, ultĕrĭor; *adv*, ultĕrĭus
further *v.t*, (**help**), adĭŭvo (1)
furthermore *adv*, porro, praetĕrĕa
furthest *adj*, ultĭmus
furtive furtīvus
fury fŭror, *m*
fuse *v.t*, (**melt**), lĭquĕfăcĭo (3); (**— together**), miscĕo (2)
fuss *nn*, perturbātĭo, *f*
fussy nĭmis stŭdĭōsus
fusty mūcĭdus
futile vānus, fūtĭlis
futility fūtĭlĭtas, *f*
future *adj*, fŭtūrus
future *nn*, fŭtūra, *n.pl*; (**in —**), *adv*, in fēlĭquum tempus
futurity tempus fŭtūrum, *n*

G

gabble *v.i*, blătĕro (1)
gabbler blătĕro, *m*
gable fastīgĭum, *n*
gad about *v.i*, văgor (1 *dep*)
gadfly tăbānus, *m*
gag *v.t*, ōs obvolvo (3) (*with dat*) (**muffle the mouth**)
gage pignus, *n*

gaiety hĭlărĭtas, *f*
gaily *adv*, hĭlăre
gain *nn*, lŭcrum, *n*, quaestus, *m*
gain *v.t*, **(profit, etc.)** lŭcror (1 *dep*); **(obtain)**, consĕquor (3 *dep*), pŏtĭor (4 *dep*) *(with abl)*; **(— a victory)**, victōrĭam rĕporto (1) *or* părĭo (3)
gainsay *v.t*, contrā dīco (3)
gait incessus, *m*
gaiters ŏcrĕae, *f.pl*
galaxy *use* vĭa lactĕa, *f*. **(milky way)**
gale ventus, *m*, prŏcella, *f*
gall *nn*, fel, *n*
gall *v.t*, **(chafe)**, ūro (3); **(annoy)**, sollĭcĭto (1); *or* pĭget (2 *impers*) **(it irks)**
gallant fortis
gallant *nn*, **(lover)**, ămātor, *m*
gallantry virtus, *f*
gallery portĭcus, *f*
galley (ship) nāvis, *f*
galling mordax
gallon congĭus, *m*
gallop *v.i*, ĕquo cĭtāto vĕhi (3 *pass*) **(to be carried by a swift horse)**
gallows furca, *f*, crux, *f*
gamble *v.i*, ālĕa lūdo (3) **(play with dice)**
gambler ālĕātor, *m*
gambling *nn*, ālĕa, *f*
gambol *v.i*, lascīvĭo (4)
game lūdus, *m*; **(wild beasts)**, fĕrae, *f.pl*
gamester ālĕātor, *m*
gammon perna, *f*
gander anser, *m*
gang grex, *m*, căterva, *f*
gangrene gangraena, *f*
gangway fŏrus, *m*
gaol carcer, *m*
gaoler custos, *m*
gap lăcūna, *f*, hĭātus, *m*
gape *v.i*, hĭo (1)
gaping *adj*, hĭans
garb vestītus, *m*
garbage quisquĭlĭae, *f.pl*
garden hortus, *m*
gardening cūra (*f*) hortōrum **(care of gardens)**
gargle *v.i*, gargărĭzo (1)
garland serta, *n.pl*
garlic ālĭum, *n*

garment vestīmentum, *n*
garner *v.t*, **(store)**, condo (3)
garnish *v.t*, dĕcŏro (1)
garret cēnācŭlum, *n*
garrison praesĭdĭum, *n*
garrison *v.t*, praesĭdĭum collŏco (1) in *(with abl)*
garrulity lŏquācĭtas, *f*
garrulous lŏquax
gas spīrĭtus, *m*
gash *nn*, plāga, *f*
gash *v.t*, percŭtĭo (3)
gasp *nn*, ănhēlĭtus, *m*
gasp *v.i*, ănhēlo (1)
gastric *use genitive* stŏmăchi **(of the stomach)**
gate porta, *f*, iānŭa, *f*; **(— keeper)**, iānĭtor, *m*
gather *v.t*, lĕgo (3), collĭgo (3); **(pluck)**, carpo (3); *v.i*, convĕnĭo (4), congrĕgor (1 *dep*)
gathering coetus, *m*
gaudy fūcātus
gauge *v.t*, mētĭor (4 *dep*)
gauge *nn*, mŏdŭlus, *m*
gaunt măcer
gay hĭlăris
gaze at *v.t*, tŭĕor (2 *dep*)
gaze *nn*, obtūtus, *m*
gazelle dorcas, *f*
gazette acta dĭurna, *n.pl*, **(daily events)**
gear appărātus, *m*
geld *v.t*, castro (1)
gelding cantērĭus, *m*
gem gemma, *f*
gender gĕnus, *n*
geneology (lineage) ŏrīgo, *f*, gĕnus, *n*
general *adj*, **(opp. to particular)**, gĕnĕrālis; **(common, widespread)**, vulgāris, commūnis
general *nn*, dux, *m*, impĕrātor, *m*
generality (majority) plērīque
generally (for the most part) *adv*, plērumque
generalship ductus, *m*
generate *v.t*, gĕnĕro (1), gigno (3)
generation saecŭlum, *n*
generosity bĕnignĭtas, *f*
generous (with money, etc.) lībĕrālis

genial cōmis
geniality cōmĭtas, *f*
genius (ability) ingĕnĭum, *n*;
(**guardian spirit**), gĕnĭus, *m*
genteel urbānus
gentle (mild) mītis; (**of birth**),
gĕnĕrōsus
gentleman hŏmo ingĕnŭus
gentlemanly *adj*, lībĕrālis, hŏnestus
gentleness lēnĭtas, *f*
gently *adv*, lēnĭter
gentry nōbĭles, *m.pl*
genuine sincērus
geography gĕōgraphĭa, *f*
geometry gĕōmĕtrĭa, *f*
germ germen, *n*
German Germānus
germane affīnis
germinate *v.i*, germĭno (1)
gesticulate *v.i*, sē iactāre (1 *reflex*)
gesture gestus, *m*
get *v.t*, (**obtain**), ădĭpiscor (3 *dep*),
nanciscor (3 *dep*); (**a request**),
impĕtro (1); (**become**), *v.i*, fīo
(*irreg*); (**— about, or spread, etc.**),
percrēbesco (3); (**— away**),
effŭgĭo (3); (**— back**), *v.t*, rĕcĭpĭo
(3); (**— the better of**), sŭpĕro (1);
(**— down**), *v.i*, dēscendo (3); (**—
out**), exĕo (4); (**— ready**) *v.t*, păro
(1); (**— rid of**), āmŏvĕo (2) in *or*
ad (*with acc*); (**— up, rise**), surgo
(3)
ghastly exsanguis
ghost mānes, *m.pl*
giant vir ingenti stătūra (**man of
huge stature**)
gibbet crux, *f*
giddy vertĭgĭnōsus
gift dōnum, *n*
gifted (mentally, etc.) ingĕnĭōsus
gigantic ingens
giggle *v.i*, *use* rīdĕo (2), (**to laugh**)
gild *v.t*, ĭnauro (1)
gills (of fish) branchĭae, *f.pl*
gimlet tĕrĕbra, *f*
gin pĕdĭca, *f*
giraffe cămēlŏpardălis, *f*
gird *v.t*, cingo (3); (**— oneself**), sē
accingĕre (3 *reflex*)
girder trabs, *f*
girdle cingŭlum, *n*

girl pŭella, *f*, virgo, *f*
girlhood aetas, (*f*) pŭellāris
girth ambĭtus, *m*
give *v.t*, do (1), dōno (1); (**render**),
reddo (3); (**— an opportunity**),
făcultātem do (1); (**— back**),
reddo (3); (**— in**), *v.i*, cēdo (3); (**—
up, deliver**), trādo (3); (**abandon**),
dīmitto (3); (**— up hope**), *v.i*,
dēspēro (1); (**— orders**), iŭbĕo (2)
glad laetus, hĭlāris
gladden *v.t*, hĭlăro (1)
glade nĕmus, *n*, saltus, *m*
gladiator glădĭātor, *m*
gladness laetĭtĭa, *f*
glance at *v.t*, aspĭcĭo (3); (**graze**)
stringo (3)
glance *nn*, aspectus, *m*
gland glans, *f*
glare *nn*, fulgor, *m*
glare *v.i*, fulgĕo (2); (**look with
stern glance**) torvis ŏcŭlis tŭĕor
(2 *dep*)
glaring (conspicuous) mănĭfestus
glass *nn*, vĭtrum, *n*; (**drinking —**),
pōcŭlum, *n*
glass *adj*, vĭtrĕus
gleam *nn*, fulgor, *m*
gleam *v.i*, fulgĕo (2)
glean *v.t*, spīcas collĭgo (3) (**collect
ears of corn**)
glee laetĭtĭa, *f*
glen valles, *f*
glib (of tongue) vŏlūbĭlis
glide lābor (3 *dep*)
glimmer *v.i*, sublūcĕo (2)
glimmering *adj*, sublustris
glimpse (get a — of) *v.t*, dispĭcĭo
(3)
glitter *v.i*, fulgĕo (2)
glittering *adj*, fulgĭdus, cŏruscus
gloat over *v.t*, gaudens aspĭcĭo (3)
globe glŏbus, *m*; (**the earth**) orbis,
m
gloom tĕnebrae, *f.pl*, tristĭtĭa, *f*
gloomy tĕnebrōsus, tristis
glorify *v.t*, laudo (1), extollo (3)
glorious praeclārus, illustris
glory glōrĭa, *f*, dĕcus, *n*, laus, *f*
gloss *n*, nĭtor, *m*
gloss over *v.t*, praetĕrĕo (4)
glossy nĭtĭdus

gloves mănĭcae, *f.pl*
glow *nn*, ardor, *m*
glow *v.i*, ardĕo (2), candĕo (2)
glue *nn*, glūten, *n*
glut *nn*, sătĭĕtas, *f*
glut *v.t*, explĕo (2), sătĭo (1)
glutton hellŭo, *m*
gluttonous ĕdax
gluttony ĕdācĭtas, *f*
gnarled nōdōsus
gnash (the teeth) *v.t*, frendĕo (2), (dentibus)
gnat cŭlex, *m*
gnaw *v.t*, rōdo (3)
gnawing *adj*, mordax
go *v.i*, ĕo (*irreg*), vādo (3); (**depart**), ăbĕo (4), prŏfĭciscor (3 *dep*); (**— abroad**), pĕrĕgre exĕo (4 *irreg*); (**— away**), ăbĕo (4 *irreg*); (**— by, past**), praetĕrĕo (4 *irreg*); (**— down**), dēscendo (3); (**— in**) ĭnĕo (4 *irreg*); (**— over**), transĕo (4 *irreg*); (**— round**), circumĕo (4 *irreg*); (**— through**) ŏbĕo (4 *irreg*); (**— up**), ascendo (3); (**— without**) cărĕo (2) (*with abl*)
goad *v.t*, stĭmŭlo (1)
goal mēta, *f*
goat căper, *m*
go-between *nn*, interpres, *c*
goblet pōcŭlum, *n*
god dĕus, *m*
goddess dĕa, *f*
godless impĭus
godlike dīvīnus
godly *adj*, pĭus
gold aurum, *n*
golden aurĕus
goldsmith aurĭfex, *m*
good *adj*, bŏnus, prŏbus, hŏnestus, aptus, commŏdus
good *nn*, bŏnum, *n*; (**advantage**), commŏdum, *n*; (**goods, possessions**), bŏna, *n.pl*; (**— for nothing**), *adj*, nēquam; (**to do —**), prōdesse (*irreg*)(*with dat*)
goodbye! vălē! (*pl*, vălete!)
good-humour cōmĭtas, *f*
good-humoured cōmis
good-looking spĕcĭōsus
good-nature cōmĭtas, *f*
good-natured cōmis

goodness (virtue) virtus, *f*, prŏbĭtas, *f*; (**excellence**) bŏnĭtas, *f*
good-tempered mītis
goose anser, *m*
gore *nn*, crŭor, *m*
gorge (throat) guttur, *n*, fauces, *f.pl*; (**mountain pass**), angustĭae, *f.pl*
gorge oneself *v.i*, sē ingurgĭtāre (1 *reflex*)
gorgeous spĕcĭōsus, splendĭdus
gorgeousness magnĭfĭcentĭa, *f*
gory crŭentus
gossip *v.i*, garrĭo (4)
gossip *nn*, (**talk**), rūmor, *m*; (**person**), garrŭlus, *m*
gouge *v.t*, (**— out eyes**), ŏcŭlos ērŭo (3)
gourd cŭcurbĭta, *f*
gout morbus (*m*) artĭcŭlōrum (**disease of the joints**)
gouty arthrītĭcus
govern *v.t*, gŭberno (1), impĕro (1), tempĕro (1), mŏdĕror (1 *dep*)
government (**act of —**) admĭnistrātĭo, *f*, cūra, *f*; (**persons**), *use phr*, ii qui summum impĕrĭum hăbent (**those who hold supreme authority**)
governor (supreme) gŭbernātor, *m*; (**subordinate**), prōcūrātor, *m*, lēgātus, *m*
gown (woman's) stŏla, *f*; (**man's**) tŏga, *f*
grace grātĭa, *f*; (**pardon**), vĕnĭa, *f*; (**charm**), vĕnustas, *f*; (**to say —**), grātĭas ăgo (3)
grace *v.t*, (**adorn**), dĕcŏro (1)
graceful vĕnustus, lĕpĭdus
gracious prŏpĭtĭus, bĕnignus
grade grădus, *m*
gradient clīvus, *m*
gradually *adv*, paulātim
graft *v.t*, insĕro (3)
grain frumentum, *n*
grammar grammătĭca, *f*
granary horrĕum, *n*
grand magnĭfĭcus, grandis
grandchild nĕpos, *m, f*
granddaughter neptis, *f*
grandeur magnĭfĭcentĭa, *f*
grandfather ăvus, *m*

grandiloquent grandĭlŏquus
grandmother ăvĭa, *f*
grandson nĕpos, *m*
granite (hard rock) *use*, sĭlex, *m*, (flint stone)
grant, granting *nn*, concessĭo, *f*
grant *v.t*, concēdo (3), do (1)
grape ăcĭnus, *m*, ūva, *f*
graphic expressus
grapple *v.i*, luctor (1 *dep*)
grappling-iron harpăgo, *m*
grasp *nn*, mănus, *f*; (of the mind), captus, *m*
grasp *v.t*, prěhendo (3); (mentally), intellěgo (3); (snatch at, aim at), capto (1)
grass grāmen, *n*, herba, *f*
grasshopper gryllus, *m*
grassy grāmĭněus
grate crātĭcŭla, *f*
grate *v.t*, těro (3); *v.i*, strīděo (2)
grateful grātus
gratification explētĭo, *f*, vŏluptas, *f*
gratify *v.t*, grātĭfĭcor (1 *dep*) (*with dat*)
grating *nn*, (noise), strīdor, *m*
gratitude grātĭa, *f*, grātus ānĭmus, *m*
gratuitous grātuĭtus
gratuity congĭārĭum, *n*
grave *nn*, sěpulcrum, *n*
grave *adj*, grăvis
gravel glārěa, *f*
gravity grăvĭtas, *f*
gravy iūs, *n*
gray see grey
grayness see grey, greyness
graze *v.t*, (animals), pasco (3); *v.i*, pascor (3 *dep*.); (touch lightly), *v.t*, stringo (3)
grease *nn*, ădeps, *c*
grease *v.t*, ungo (3)
greasy unctus
great magnus, grandis, amplus; (distinguished), illustris
greatcoat lăcerna, *f*
great-grandfather prŏāvus, *m*
great-grandson prŏněpos, *m*
greatness magnĭtūdo, *f*
greaves ŏcrěae, *f.pl*
Greece Graecĭa, *f*
greed ăvārĭtĭa, *f*
greedy ăvārus

Greek Graecus
green *adj*, vĭrĭdis; (unripe), crūdus; (to become —), *v.i*, vĭresco (3)
greet *v.t*, sălūto (1)
greeting sălūtātĭo, *f*
gregarious grěgālis
grey caesĭus, rāvus; (of hair), cānus
greyness (of hair) cānĭtĭes, *f*
gridiron crātĭcŭla, *f*
grief dŏlor, *m*, luctus, *m*
grievance quěrĭmōnĭa, *f*
grieve *v.i, and v.t*, dŏlěo (2)
grievous grāvis, ăcerbus
grim trux
grin *v.i*, rīděo (2)
grind *v.t*, contěro (3); mŏlo (3) (— down, oppress), opprĭmo (3);
grindstone cōs, *f*
grip *nn, use* mănus, *f*, (hand)
grip *v.t*, arrĭpĭo (3)
gripes tormĭna, *n.pl*
grisly horrendus
grist fărīna, *f*
gristle cartĭlāgo, *f*
grit glārěa
groan *nn*, gěmĭtus, *m*
groan *v.i*, gěmo (3)
grocer tūrārĭus, *m*
groin inguen, *n*
groom *nn*, ăgāso, *m*
groom *v.t*, (look after), cūro (1)
groove cănālis, *m*
grope *v.i*, praetento (1)
gross *adj*, crassus; (unseemly), inděcōrus
grotto antrum, *n*
grotesque monstrŭōsus
ground (earth) hŭmus, *f*, sŏlum, *n*, terra, *f*; (cause, reason), causa, *f*; (to give —), pědem rěfěro (*irreg*)
ground *v.i*, (of ships) sīdo (3)
groundless vānus
groundwork (basis) fundāmentum, *n*
group glŏbus, *m*
group *v.t*, dispōno (3)
grouse lăgōpūs, *f*
groove lūcus, *m*
grovel *v.i*, serpo (3)
grow *v.i*, cresco (3), augesco (3); (— up), ădŏlesco (3); (become), fio (*irreg*); *v.t*, cŏlo (3)
growl *nn*, frěmĭtus, *m*

growl *v.i*, frĕmo (3)
growth incrēmentum, *n*
grub *nn*, vermĭcŭlus, *m*
grudge *nn*, sĭmultas, *f*
grudge *v.t*, invĭdĕo (2) (*with dat*)
grudgingly *adv*, *use adj*, invītus
gruel ptīsāna, *f*
gruff asper
grumble *v.i*, frĕmo (3)
grunt *nn*, grunnītus, *m*
grunt *v.i*, grunnĭo (4)
guarantee *nn*, fĭdes, *f*
guarantee *v.t*, fĭdem do (1) (*with dat*)
guarantor vas, *m*
guard (person) custos, *c*; **(defence)**, custōdĭa, *f*, praesĭdĭum, *n*; **(to keep —)** *v.i*, custōdĭam ăgo (3)
guard *v.t*, custōdĭo (4)
guarded (cautious) cautus
guardian custos, *c*; **(of child)**, tūtor, *m*
guardianship custōdĭa, *f*; **(of child)**, tūtēla, *f*
guess *nn*, coniectūra, *f*
guess *v.t*, cōnĭcĭo (3), dīvīno (1)
guest hospes, *m*, hospĭta, *f*; **(at a party, etc.)** convīva, *c*
guidance (advice) consĭlĭum, *n*
guide *nn*, dux, *c*
guide *v.t*, dūco (3)
guild collēgĭum, *n*
guile dŏlus, *m*
guileful dŏlōsus
guileless simplex
guilt culpa, *f*
guiltless innŏcens, insons
guilty sons, nŏcens
guise hăbĭtus, *m*, spĕcĭes, *f*
gulf (bay) sĭnus, *m*; **(abyss)**, gurges, *m*, vŏrāgo, *f*
gullet guttur, *n*
gullible crēdŭlus
gully (channel) cănālis, *m*, fossa, *f*
gulp *v.t*, haurĭo (4)
gum (of the mouth) gingīva, *f*; **(of plants etc.)** gummi, *n*
gurgle *v.i*, singulto (1)
gush *v.i*, prŏfundor (3 *pass*)
gust flātus, *m*
gut intestīna, *n.pl*

gutter fossa, *f*, clŏāca, *f*
gutteral grăvis
gymnasium gymnăsĭum, *n*
gymnastics pălaestra, *f*

H

haberdasher lintĕo, *m*
habit consŭētūdo, *f*, mōs, *m*
habitable hăbĭtābĭlis
habitation dŏmĭcĭlĭum, *n*
habitual ūsĭtātus
habituate *v.t*, consŭēfăcĭo (3)
hack căballus, *m*
hack *v.t*, concīdo (3)
hackneyed trītus
haft mănūbrĭum, *n*
hag ănus, *f*
haggard măcĭe corruptus **(marred by leanness)**
haggle *v.i*, dē prĕtĭo căvillor (1 *dep*) **(to quibble about price)**
hail *nn*, grando, *f*
hail *v.i*, **(weather)**, grandĭnat (*impers.*); *v.t*, **(greet)**, sălūto (1)
hair căpillus, *m*, crīnis, *m*, caesărĭes, *f*
hairdresser tonsor, *m*
hairless (bald) calvus
hairy pĭlōsus
halcyon *adj*, alcўōnēus
hale (healthy) vālĭdus
half *nn*, dīmĭdĭum, *n*; *adj*, dīmĭdĭus; *adv*, *use prefix* sēmi-, *e.g.* **half-asleep**, sēmĭsomnus; **(half-dead)**, sēmĭănĭmis, mŏrĭbundus; **(— hour)** sēmĭhōra, *f*; **(— moon)**, lūna dīmĭdĭāta, *f*; **(— yearly)**, sēmestris
hall (of house) ātrĭum, *n*; **(public)**, concĭlĭābŭlum, *n*
hallo! heus!
hallow *v.t*, consĕcro (1)
hallucination somnĭa, *n.pl*
halo cŏrōna, *f*
halt *nn*, *use vb*, consisto (3)
halt *v.i*, consisto (3)
halter (horse) căpistrum, *n*; **(noose)**, lăquĕus, *m*
halve *v.t*, ex aequo dīvĭdo (3)
ham perna, *f*

hamlet vīcus, *m*

hammer *nn*, mallĕus, *m*

hammer *v.t*, contudo (3)

hamper quălum, *n*

hamper *v.t*, impĕdĭo (4)

hamstring *v.t*, poplĭtem succīdo (3) (*with dat*)

hand mănus, *f*; **(left —)**, mănus sĭnistra; **(right —)**, dextra mănus; **(to shake — s)** detras coniungĕre (3); **(— cuffs)**, mănĭcae, *f.pl*; **(— writing)**, chīrgrăphum, *n*; **(on the one—, on the other —)** et...et, *or* quĭdem (*second word in clause*) ...autem (*second word in clause*); **(— to — fighting, etc.)** commĭnus, *adv*; **(at hand)**, praesto, *adv*

hand *v.t*, do (1), trādo (3); **(— down or over)**, trādo (3)

handful (few) *use adj*, pauci

handicraft artĭfĭcĭum, *n*

handiwork ŏpus, *n*

handkerchief sūdārĭum, *n*

handle mănūbrĭum, *n*

handle *v.t*, tracto (1)

handling (treatment) tractātĭo, *f*

handsome spĕcĭōsus, pulcher

handy (manageable) hăbĭlis

hang *v.t*, suspendo (3); **(— the head)** dēmitto (3); *v.i*, pendĕo (2); **(— back, hesitate)**, dŭbĭto (1); **(overhang)** impendĕo (2)

hanger-on assecla, *c*

hanging (death by —) suspendĭum, *n*

hangman carnĭfex, *m*

hanker after *v.t*, opto (1)

haphazard *use adv. phr.* nullo ordĭne **(in no order)**

happen *v.i*, accĭdo (3), ēvĕnĭo (4)

happiness fēlīcĭtas, *f*

happy fēlix, bĕātus

harangue *nn*, contĭo, *f*

harangue *v.t*, contĭōnor (1 *dep.*)

harass *v.t*, sollĭcĭto (1)

harbour portus, *m*; **(— dues)**, portōrĭum, *n*

harbour *v.t*, **(shelter)**, excĭpĭo (3)

hard dūrus; **(difficult)**, diffĭcĭlis

hard *adv*, **(strenuously)**, strēnŭē

harden *v.t*, dūro (1); *v.i*, dūresco (3)

hard-hearted dūrus

hardiness rōbur, *n*

hardly *adv*, vix; **(harshly)**, crūdēlĭter

hardness dūrĭtĭa, *f*

hardship lăbor, *m*

hardware ferrāmenta, *n.pl*

hardy dūrus

hare lĕpus, *m*

hark! heus!

harlot mĕrĕtrix, *f*

harm *nn*, damnum, *n*

harm *v.t*, nŏcĕo (2) (*with dat*)

harmful noxĭus

harmless innŏcŭus, innŏcens

harmonious concors

harmonize *v.i*, concĭno (3)

harmony concentus, *m*, consensus, *m*

harness *nn*, ĕquestrĭa arma, *n.pl*, **(horse equipment)**, frēnum, *n*

harness *v.t*, iungo (3)

harp fĭdes, *f.pl*; **(harpist)**, fĭdĭcen, *m*

harrow *nn*, irpex, *m*

harrow *v.t*, occo (1)

harrowing *adj*, horrendus, terrĭbĭlis

harsh asper, ăcerbus

harshness aspĕrĭtas, *f*

hart cervus, *m*

harvest messis, *f*

hasp fĭbŭla, *f*

haste *nn*, festīnātĭo, *f*

hasten *v.i*, prŏpĕro (1), festīno (1); *v.t*, mātūro (1), accĕlĕro (1)

hastily *adv*, prŏpĕrē

hastiness (of temper) īrācundĭa, *f*

hasty prŏpĕrus; **(of temper)** īrācundus

hat pĕtăsus, *m*

hatch *v.t*, **(eggs)**, exclūdo (3); **(plans etc.)** ĭnĕo (4)

hatchet sĕcūris, *f*

hate *nn*, ŏdĭum, *n*

hate *v.t*, ōdi (*v. defect*)

hateful ŏdĭōsus

haughtiness sŭperbĭa, *f*

haughty sŭperbus, arrŏgans

haul *v.t*, trăho (3)

haunt *nn*, lătĕbrae, *f.pl*

haunt *v.t*, **(visit frequently)**, cĕlĕbro (1); **(trouble)**, sollĭcĭto (1)

have *v.t*, hăběo (2); *or use* esse (*irreg*) *with dat. of possessor, e.g.* **I have a brother,** est mĭhĭ frāter

haven portus, *m*

haversack saccus, *m*

havoc strāges, *f*, vastātĭo

hawk *nn*, accĭpĭter, *m, f*

hay faenum, *n*

hazard *nn*, pĕrīcŭlum, *n*

hazardous pĕrīcŭlōsus

haze nĕbŭla, *f*

hazel *nn*, cŏrўlus, *f*

hazy nĕbŭlōsus

he *pron, if not emphatic, use 3rd pers. of verb; otherwise*, ille, hic, is

head căput, *n*, vertex, *m*; **(chief)**, princeps, *m*; **(to be at the — of)** praesum (*irreg*) (*with dat*)

heat *adj*, **(of wind)** adversus

head *v.t*, **(be in charge)**, praesum (*irreg*) (*with dat*)

headache căpĭtĭs dŏlor, *m*

headband vitta, *f*

headland promontūrĭum, *n*

headlong *adj*, praeceps

headquarters praetōrĭum, *n*

headstrong *adj*, pervĭcax

heal *v.t*, sāno (1), mĕdĕor (2 *dep*) (*with dat*); *v.i*, consānesco (3)

healing *nn*, sānātĭo, *f*

healing *adj*, sălūtāris

health vălētūdo, *f*

healthy sānus, vălĭdus; **(of place or climate)**, sălūbris

heap *nn*, ăcervus, *m*

heap *v.t*, cŭmŭlo (1), congĕro (3)

hear *v.t*, audĭo (4); **(learn)**, cognosco (3)

hearer audītor, *m*

hearing *nn*, **(sense of —)**, audītus, *m*

hearsay rūmor, *m*

heart cor, *n*; **(interior)**, *use adj*, intĭmus **(inmost)**; **(feelings, etc.)**, pectus, *n*, mens, *f*; **(courage)**, ănĭmus, *m*; **(— ache)**, sollĭcĭtūdo, *f*; **(— break)**, dŏlor, *m*; **(— broken)** *adj. phr*, ănĭmo afflictus

hearth fŏcus, *m*

heartiness stŭdĭum, *n*

heartless dūrus

heartlessness crūdēlĭtas, *f*

hearty ălăcer

heat *nn*, călor, *m*, ardor, *m*, aestus, *m*, fervor, *m*

heat *v.t*, călĕfăcĭo (3); **(excite)**, incendo (3)

heath lŏca obsĭta, *n.pl*, lŏca inculta, *n.pl*

heave *v.t*, tollo (3); *v.i*, tŭmesco (3)

heaven caelum, *n*; **(— dwelling)** *adj*, caelĭcŏla

heavenly *adj*, dīvīnus

heaviness grăvĭtas, *f*; **(— of mind)**, tristĭtĭa, *f*

heavy grăvis; **(sad)**, tristis; **(air, etc.)** crassus

hectic (agitated, confused) turbŭlentus

hedge saepes, *f*

hedge in *v.t*, saepĭo (4)

hedgehog ĕchīnus, *m*

heed *v.t*, **(obey)** pārĕo (2) (*with dat*); **(to take —)**, *v.i*, căvĕo (2)

heedless incautus

heedlessness neglĕgentĭa, *f*

heel calx, *f*; **(take to one's —s)** fŭgĭo (3)

heifer iŭvenca, *f*

height altĭtūdo, *f*; **(high ground)** sŭpĕrĭor lŏcus, *m*

heighten *v.t*, *use* augĕo (2) **(increase)**

heinous ătrox

heir, heiress hēres, *c*

hell infĕri, *m.pl*. Orcus, *m*

hellish infernus

helm gŭbernācŭlum, *n*

helmet cassis, *f*, gălĕa, *f*

helmsman gŭbernātor, *m*

help *nn*, auxĭlĭum, *n*

help *v.t*, iŭvo (1), subvĕnĭo (4) (*with dat*); **(I cannot help coming)**, non possum făcĕre quīn vĕnĭam

helper adiūtor, *m*

helpful ūtĭlis

helpless ĭnops

helplessness ĭnŏpĭa, *f*

helpmate consors *m, f*

hem *nn*, limbus, *m*

hem in *v.t*, circumsĕdĕo (2), saepĭo (4)

hemisphere hēmisphaerĭum, *n*

hemp cannăbis, *f*

hen gallīna, *f*; **(— house)**, gallīnārĭum, *n*

hence *adv*, **(place or cause)**, hinc; **(time)**, posthāc

henceforth *adv*, posthāc

her *pron*, *adj*, eius; (*if it refers to the subject of the sentence*), sŭus, a, um

herald praeco, *m*

herb herba, *f*, hŏlus, *n*

herd grex, *m*

herd together *v.i*, congrĕgor (1 *pass*)

herdsman pastor, *m*

here hīc; **(hither)**, hūc; **(to be —)**, *v.i*, adsum (*irreg*)

hereafter *adv*, posthāc

hereby *adv*, ex hōc

hereditary hērēdĭtārĭus

heredity gĕnus, *n*

heretical prāvus

hereupon *adv*, hīc

heritage hērēdĭtas, *f*

hermit hŏmo sōlĭtārĭus

hernia hernĭa, *f*

hero vir fortissĭmus

heroic (brave) fortis

heroine fēmĭna fortis, *f*

heroism virtus, *f*

heron ardĕa, *f*

hers see **her**

herself *pron. reflexive*, sē; (*pron. emphatic*) ipsa

hesitancy, hesitation haesĭtātĭo, *f*

hesitate *v.i*, dŭbĭto (1), haesĭto (1)

hew *v.t*, caedo (3)

heyday (youth) iŭventus, *f*

hibernate *v.i*, condor (3 *pass*)

hiccough singultus, *m*

hidden occultus

hide *nn*, **(skin)**, cŏrĭum, *n*, pellis, *f*

hide *v.t*, abdo (3), cēlo (1)

hideous foedus

hideousness foedĭtas, *f*

hiding-place lătĕbrae, *f.pl*

high altus, celsus; **(of rank)**, amplus; **(of price)**, magnus, magni; **(— born)**, gĕnĕrōsus; **(— handed)**, impĕrĭōsus; **(— lands)**, montes, *m.pl*; **(— landers)**, montāni, *m.pl*; **(— spirited)**, ănĭmōsus;

(— treason), măiestas, *f*; **(— way)**, vĭa, *f*; **(— wayman)** lătro, *m*

hilarity hĭlărĭtas, *f*

hill collis, *m*

hillock tŭmŭlus, *m*

hilly montŭōsus

hilt căpŭlus, *m*

himself *pron, reflexive*, sē; *pron. emphatic*, ipse

hind *adj*, postĕrĭor

hinder *v.t*, impĕdĭo (4), obsto (1) (*with dat*)

hindrance impĕdīmentum, *n*

hinge *nn*, cardo, *m*

hinge on *v.i*, vertor (3 *dep*), versor (1 *dep*) in (*with abl*)

hint *nn*, signĭfĭcātĭo, *f*

hint at *v.t*, signĭfĭco (1)

hip coxendix, *f*

hippopotamus hippŏpŏtămus, *m*

hire (wages) merces, *f*

hire *v.t*, condūco (3)

hired conductus

his *pron*, ēius, hūius, illīus; *or* sŭus (*referring to the subject of the sentence*)

hiss *nn*, sībĭlus, *m*

hiss *v.i. and v.t*, sībĭlo (1)

historian scriptor (*m*) rērum

historic(al) *use nn*, historĭa, *f*, **(history)**

history histŏrĭa, *f*, rēs gestae, *f.pl*

hit *nn*, **(blow)** plāga, *f*

hit *v.t*, **(strike)** fērĭo (4); **(— upon)**, incĭdo (3)

hitch impĕdīmentum, *n*

hitch *v.t*, necto (3)

hither *adv*, hūc; **(— and thither)**, hūc illūc

hitherto *adv*, ădhūc

hive alvĕārĭum, *n*

hoard *nn*, ăcervus, *m*

hoard *v.t*, collĭgo (3), condo (3)

hoarfrost prŭīna, *f*

hoarse raucus

hoary cānus

hoax *nn*, lūdus, *m*

hoax *v.t*, lūdĭfĭcor (1 *dep*), lūdo (3)

hobble *v.i*, claudĭco (1)

hobby stŭdĭum, *n*

hobnail clāvus, *m*

hoe *nn*, sarcŭlum, *n*

hoe *v.t*, sarrĭo (4)

hog porcus, *m*

hogshead dōlĭum, *n*

hoist *v.t*, tollo (3)

hold *nn*, **(grasp)** *use* comprĕhendo (3), *or* mănus, *f*

hold *v.t*, tĕnĕo (2), obtĭnĕo (2), hăbĕo (2); **(— an office)**, obtĭnĕo (2), fungor (3 *dep*); **(— elections, etc.)**, hăbĕo (2); **(— back)**, *v.i*, cunctor (1 *dep*), *v.t*, rĕtĭnĕo (2); **(— fast)**, rĕtĭnĕo (2); **(— out)**, *v.t*, porrĭgo (3); **(endure)**, sustĭnĕo (2), perfĕro (*irreg*); **(— up, lift)**, tollo (3)

hold-fast *nn*, fibŭla, *f*

hole fŏrāmen, *n*, căvum, *n*

holiday fērĭae, *f.pl*

holiness sanctĭtas, *f*

hollow *nn*, căvum, *n*, lăcūna, *f*; **(— of the hand)**, căva mănus, *f*

hollow *adj*, căvus; **(false)**, vānus

hollow *v.t*, căvo (1)

holm-oak īlex, *f*

holy săcer

homage (respect) observantĭa, *f*

home *adj*, dŏmestĭcus; **(homely)**, rustĭcus

home dŏmus, *f*; **(at —)**, dŏmi; **(homewards)**, dŏmum; **(from —)**, dŏmo **(— less)**, cărens tecto **(lacking shelter)**

homicide (deed) caedes, *f*; **(person)**, hŏmĭcīda, *c*

honest prŏbus

honesty prŏbĭtas, *f*, intĕgrĭtas, *f*

honey mel, *n*

honeycomb făvus, *m*

honorary hŏnōrārĭus

honour hŏnos, *m*; **(glory)**, dĕcus, *n*; **(integrity)**, hŏnestas, *f*, intĕgrĭtas, *f*; **(repute)**, fāma, *f*

honour *v.t*, cŏlo (3), hŏnesto (1)

honourable hŏnōrātus, hŏnestus

hood cŭcullus, *m*

hoof ungŭla, *f*

hook hāmus, *m*

hook *v.t*, hāmo căpĭo (3) **(catch by a hook)**

hooked hāmātus

hoop circŭlus, *m*

hoot *nn*, cantus, *m*

hoot *v.i*, căno (3); *v.t*, **(hoot at)**, explōdo (3)

hop *v.i*, sălĭo (4)

hope *nn*, spes, *f*

hope *v.i. and v.t*, spēro (1)

hopeful (promising) *use genit. phr*, bŏnae spĕi

hopefully *adj*, *phr*, multa spĕrans

hopeless (desperate) dēspērātus

hopelessness dēspērātĭo, *f*

horizon orbis (*m*) fīnĭens **(limiting circle)**

horizontal lībrātus

horn cornu, *n*; **(made of —)**, *adj*, cornĕus

hornet crābro, *m*

horrible horrĭbĭlis, horrendus, ătrox, foedus

horrid horrĭbĭlis, horrendus, ătrox, foedus

horrify *v.t*, **(dismay)**, percello (3), terrĕo (2)

horror horror, *m*

horse ĕquus, *m*

horseback (to ride on —) in ĕquo vĕhor (3 *pass*); **(to fight on —)**, ex ĕquo pugno (1)

horsefly tăbānus, *m*

horserace certāmen ĕquestre, *n*

horseshoe sŏlĕa, *f*

horsewhip flăgellum, *n*

horticulture hortōrum cultus, *m*

hospitable hospĭtālis

hospital vălētūdĭnārĭum, *n*

hospitality hospĭtĭum, *n*

host (one who entertains) hospes, *m*; **(innkeeper)**, caupo, *m*; **(large number)**, multĭtūdo, *f*

hostage obses, *c*

hostess hospĭta, *f*

hostile hostĭlis, infestus

hostility ĭnĭmīcĭtĭa, *f*; **(hostilities, war)**, bellum, *n*

hot călĭdus, fervens; **(of temper)**, ācer; **(to be —)**, *v.i*, călĕo (2), fervĕo (2); **(to become —)**, *v.i*, călesco (3); **(— headed)**, *adj*, fervĭdus, fervens; **(hotly)**, *adv*, ardenter

hotel hospĭtĭum, *n*

hound cănis, *m, f*

hound on *v.t*, **(goad on)**, instīgo (1), ăgĭto (1)

hour hŏra, *f*

hourly *adv*, in hōras
hourglass hōrārĭum, *n*
house dŏmus, *f*, aedes, *f.pl*;
  (family), gens, *f*; (— hold) dŏmus,
  f, fămĭlĭa, *f*; (— keeper), prōmus,
  m; (— maid), ancĭlla, *f*; (— wife),
  māterfămĭlĭas, *f*
house *v.t*, (store) condo (3),
  rēpōno, (3)
hovel tŭgŭrĭum, *n*, căsa, *f*
hover *v.i*, vŏlĭto (1), impendĕo (2)
how (in what way?) quōmŏdŏ?;
  with adj. or adv, quam?;
  (— many), quot?; (— often),
  quŏtĭes?; (— great or big),
  quantus?
however *conj*, tămen; *adv*,
  quamvis; (how big or great),
  quantumvis
howl *nn*, ŭlŭlātus, *m*
howl *v.i*, ŭlŭlo (1)
hubbub tŭmultus, *m*
huddle *v.i*, (— together), congrĕgor
  (1 *dep*), confĕror (*irreg. pass*)
hue (colour) cŏlor, *m*
huff (to be in a — about) *v.t*,
  aegrē fĕro (*irreg*)
hug *nn*, complexus, *m*
hug *v.t*, amplector (3 *dep*)
huge ingens, immānis
hull (of a ship) alvĕus, *m*
hum *nn*, frĕmĭtus, *m*
hum *v.i*, frĕmo (3), strĕpo (3)
human *adj*, hūmānus; (— being),
  hŏmo, *c*
humane (compassionate)
  mĭsĕrĭcors
humanity hūmānĭtas, *f*; (human
  race) hŏmĭnes, *c.pl*;
  (compassion), mĭsĕrĭcordĭa, *f*
humble hŭmĭlis, vĕrēcundus
humble *v.t*, dēprĭmo (3); (— in
  war), dēbello (1); (— oneself), sē
  summittĕre (3 *reflex*)
humdrum *adj*, mĕdĭŏcris, tardus
humid hūmĭdus
humidity hūmor, *m*
humiliate *v.t*, dēprĭmo (3)
humility mŏdestĭa, *f*
humorous rīdĭcŭlus
humour făcētĭae, *f.pl*; (disposition),
  ingĕnĭum, *n*. lĭbĭdo, *f*; (to be in
  the — to), *use* lĭbet (*v*. 2 *impers*)

(*with dat. of person*)
humour *v.t*, obsĕquor (3 *dep*)
  (*with dat. of person*)
hump gibber, *m*
humpbacked *adj*, gibber
hunch, hunchbacked see
  humpbacked
hundred *adj*, centum; (— times),
  adv, centies; (— fold), *adj*,
  centŭplex
hundredth centēsĭmus
hundredweight centumpondĭum, *n*
hunger fămes, *f*
hunger *v.i*, ēsŭrĭo (4)
hungry ēsŭrĭens, ăvĭdus (cĭbi)
hunt *v.t*, vēnor (1 *dep*)
hunt, hunting *nn*, vēnātĭo, *f*
hunter vēnātor, *m*
huntress vēnātrix, *f*
hurdle crātes, *f.pl*
hurl *v.t*, iăcŭlor (1 *dep*), cōnĭcĭo
  (3)
hurricane tempestas, *f*, prŏcella, *f*
hurried praeceps
hurriedly *adv*, raptim
hurry *v.i*, festīno (1), prŏpĕro (1);
  v.t, răpĭo (3); (an action, etc.),
  mātūro (1)
hurt *nn*, (wound) vulnus, *n*
hurt *v.t*, laedo (3), nŏcĕo (2) (*with
  dat*)
hurt *adj*, (wounded), saucĭus
hurtful nŏcens, noxĭus
husband vir, *m*, mărītus, *m*
husbandry agrĭcultūra, *f*
hush! tăcē; *pl*, tăcētĕ (*from* tăcĕo)
hush up *v.t*, (conceal), tĕgo (3),
  cēlo (1)
husk follĭcŭlus, *m*
husky fuscus, raucus
hustle *v.t*, pulso (1), trūdo (3)
hut căsa, *f*, tūgŭrĭum, *n*
hutch căvĕa, *f*
hyacinth hўăcinthus, *m*
hybrid hybrĭda, ae, *c*
hymn carmen, *n*
hyperbole hўperbŏlē, *f*
hyperchondriac mĕlanchŏlĭcus
hypocrisy sĭmŭlātĭo, *f*
hypocrite sĭmŭlātor, *m*
hypocritical sĭmŭlātus
hypothesis conĭectūra, *f*, condĭcĭo,
  f

hysteria āmentĭa, *f*, perturbātĭo, *f*

I

I *pron*, (*emphatic*), ĕgo; *otherwise use* 1*st pers. sing. of verb, e.g.* **I love,** *ămo*
iambic *adj,* ĭambĕus
ice glăcĭes, *f*
icicle stīrĭa, *f*
icy gĕlĭdus, glăcĭālis
idea nōtĭo, *f*, imāgo, *f*, sententĭa, *f*; **(to form an —)** *v.i,* cōgĭtātĭōne fingo (3)
ideal *adj,* (**perfect**) perfectus, summus, optĭmus
ideal *nn,* exemplar, *n*
identical īdem **(the same)**
identify *v.t,* agnosco (3)
identity (to find the — of) cognosco (3) quis sit …
ides īdūs, *f.pl*
idiocy fătŭĭtas, *f*
idiom prŏprĭĕtas, *f*. (linguae) **(peculiarity of language)**
idiot fătŭus, *m*
idiotic fătŭus
idle (unemployed) ōtĭōsus; **(lazy)**, ignāvus; **(useless)**, vānus; **(to be —)**, *v.i,* cesso (1)
idleness ignāvĭa, *f*, cessātĭo, *f*
idler cessātor, *m*, cessātrix, *f*
idol (statue) sĭmŭlācrum, *n*; **(something loved)** dēlĭcĭae, *f.pl*
idolatry vĕnĕrātĭo, (*f*) sĭmŭlācrōrum **(worship of images)**
idolize *v.t,* cŏlo (3)
idyl īdyllĭum, *n*
if *conj,* sī; **(— not)**, sīn; *after a vb. of asking* **(— whether)** num, ŭtrum; **(whether … or if)** sīve … sīve; **(— only)**, dummŏdo
ignite *v.i,* ardesco (3); *v.t,* accendo (3)
ignoble (of birth) ignōbĭlis; **(dishonourable)** tupis
ignominious turpis
ignominy ignōmĭnĭa, *f*, infāmĭa, *f*
ignorance inscĭentĭa, *f*
ignorant ignārus, inscĭus
ignore *v.t,* praetĕrĕo

ill *adj,* aeger; **(evil)**, mălus; **(to be —)**, *v.i,* asgrōto (1); **(to fall —)**, *v.i,* in morbum incĭdo (3)
ill *adv,* mălĕ
ill *nn,* **(evil)** mălum, *n*
ill-advised (reckless) temĕrārĭus
ill-bred inhūmānus
ill-disposed mălĕvŏlus
illegal illĭcĭtus
illegitimate non lēgĭtĭmus
ill-favoured dēformis, turpis
ill-health vălētūdo, *f*
illicit illĭcĭtus
illiterate illittĕrātus
ill-natured mălĕvŏlus
ill-omened dīrus
ill-starred infēlix
ill-temper īrācundĭa
illness morbus, *m*
illogical absurdus, rĕpugnans
illuminate *v.t,* illustro (1)
illusion error, *m*
illusive vānus
illustrate *v.t,* illustro (1)
illustration exemplum, *n*
illustrious clārus, *llustris*
image ĭmāgo, *f*, effĭgĭes, *f*
imaginable *use phr,* quod concĭpi pŏtest **(that can be imagined)**
imaginary commentīcĭus
imagination cōgĭtātĭo, *f*
imagine *v.t,* ănĭmo concĭpĭo (3) *or* fingo (3)
imbecile fătŭus
imbecility imbēcillĭtas (*f*) ănĭmi
imbibe *v.t,* bĭbo (3), haurĭo (4)
imbue *v.t,* inficĭo (3)
imitate *v.t,* ĭmĭtor (1 *dep*)
imitation ĭmĭtātĭo, *f*; **(likeness)**, effĭgĭes, *f*
imitator ĭmĭtātor, *m*
immaculate intĕger
immaterial (unimportant) *use phr,* nullo mōmento
immature immātūrus
immeasurable immensus
immediate praesens, proxĭmus
immediately *adv,* stătim, confestim
immemorial (from time —), ex hŏmĭnum mĕmōrĭa
immense immensus, ingens

immensity immensĭtas, *f*
immerse *v.t,* immergo (3)
immigrant advĕna, *m. f*
immigrate *v.i,* immĭgro (1)
imminent praesens; **(to be —)** *v.i,* immĭnĕo (2)
immobility immōbĭlĭtas, *f*
immoderate immŏdĕrātus, immŏdĭcus
immodest impŭdĭcus
immodesty impŭdīcĭtĭa, *f*
immolate *v.t,* immŏlo (1)
immoral prāvus, turpis
immorality mōres mǎli, *m.pl*
immortal immortālis, aeternus
immortality immortālĭtas, *f*
immovable immōbĭlis
immunity immūnĭtas, *f,* văcātĭo, *f*
immutable immūtābĭlis
impair *v.t,* mĭnŭo (3)
impale *v.t,* transfīgo (3)
impart *v.t,* impertĭo (4)
impartial aequus, iustus
impartiality aequĭtas, *f*
impassable insŭpĕrābĭlis
impassioned concĭtātus, fervens
impassive pătĭens
impatience (haste) impătĭentĭa, *f,* festīnātĭo, *f*
impatient ǎvĭdus
impeach *v.t,* accūso (1)
impeachment accūsātĭo, *f*
impeccable impeccābĭlis
impede *v.t,* impĕdĭo (4)
impediment impĕdīmentum, *n*; **(of speech),** haesĭtantĭa, *f*
impel *v.t,* impello (3), incĭto (1)
impend *v.i,* impendĕo (2), immĭnĕo (2)
impending fŭtūrus
impenetrable impĕnĕtrābĭlis
imperfect imperfectus
imperfection (defect) vĭtĭum, *n*
imperial (kingly) rēgĭus *or use genit. of* impĕrĭum, *n,* **(empire),** *or* impĕrātor, *m,* **(emperor)**
imperil *v.t,* in pĕrīcŭlum addūco (3)
imperious impĕrĭōsus
impermeable impervĭus

impersonate *v.t,* partes sustĭnĕo (2) **(keep up a part)**
impertinence insŏlentĭa, *f*
impertinent insŏlens
imperturbable immōtus, immōbĭlis
impetuosity vīs, *f*
impetuous vĕhĕmens
impetus vīs, *f,* impĕtus, *m*
impious impĭus
implacable implācābĭlis
implant *v.t,* insĕro (3)
implement instrūmentum, *n*
implicate *v.t,* implĭco (1)
implicit *adj,* tăcĭtus; **(absolute),** omnis, tōtus
implore *v.t,* implōro (1), ōro (1)
imply *v.t,* signĭfĭco (1); **(involve),** hăbĕo (2)
impolite ĭnurbānus
import *nn,* **(meaning),** signĭfĭcātĭo, *f*
import *v.t,* importo (1)
importance mōmentum, *n*; **(of position)** amplĭtūdo, *f*
important grăvis; **(people),** amplus
importunate mŏlestus
importune *v.t,* flāgĭto (1)
impose *v.t,* impōno (3)
imposition (fraud) fraus, *f*
impossible *use phr,* quod fĭĕri nōn pŏtest **(which cannot be done)**
imposter fraudātor, *m*
impotence imbēcillĭtas, *f*
impotent imbēcillus, infirmus
impoverish *v.t,* in paupertātem rĕdĭgo (3)
impoverishment paupertas, *f*
imprecation exsĕcrātĭo, *f*
impregnable ĭnexpugnābĭlis
impregnate *v.t,* īnĭcĭo (3)
impress *v.t,* imprĭmo (3); **(the mind),** mŏvĕo (2)
impression (mental) mōtus, (*m*) ănĭmi; **(idea, thought)** ŏpīnĭo, *f,* ŏpīnātĭo, *f*; **(mark),** vestīgĭum, *n*
impressive grăvis
imprint *nn,* signum, *n*; **(of a foot),** vestīgĭum, *n*
imprison *v.t,* in vincŭla cōnĭcĭo (3) **(throw into chains)**

imprisonment vincŭla, *n.pl*
improbable nōn vērīsĭmĭlis **(not likely)**
improper indĕcōrus
improve *v.t*, mēlĭōrem făcĭo (3) *or* reddo; *v.i*, mēlĭor fīo *(irreg)*
improvement ēmendātĭo, *f*
improvident neglĕgens, imprōvĭdus
imprudence imprūdentĭa, *f*
imprudent inconsultus, imprūdens
impudence impŭdentĭa, *f*
impudent impŭdens
impulse impĕtus, *m*, impulsus, *m*
impulsive vĕhĕmens
impunity (with —) *adv*, impūnĕ
impure impūrus, foedus
impurity impūrĭtas, *f*, incestus, *m*
impute *v.t*, attrĭbŭo (3)
in *prep*, **(place)**, in *(with abl.) or use locative case if available, e.g.* Londīnĭi, **in London; (time)**, *use abl. or* in *(with abl.)*
inability (weakness) imbēcillĭtas, *f*
inaccessible ĭnaccessus
inaccuracy (fault) error, *m*
inaccurate (things) falsus
inactive ĭners
inactivity cessātĭo, *f*, ĭnertĭa, *f*
inadequate impar
inadmissible *use phr*, quod nōn lĭcet **(which is not allowed)**
inadvertent imprūdens
inane ĭnānis
inanimate ĭnănĭmus
inappropriate nōn aptus **(not suitable)**
inasmuch as *conj*, quŏnĭam, quandōquĭdem
inattention neglĕgentĭa, *f*
inattentive neglĕgens
inaudible *use phr*, quod audīri nōn pŏtest **(which cannot be heard)**
inaugurate *v.t*, ĭnaugŭro (1)
inauguration consĕcrātĭo, *f*
inauspicious infēlix
inborn insĭtus
incalculable *use phr*, quod aestĭmāri nōn pŏtest **(which cannot be estimated)**
incapable inhăbĭlis
incarcerate *v.t*, in vincŭla cōnĭcĭo (3) **(throw into chains)**

incarnate spĕcĭe hūmānā indūtus **(clothed with human form)**
incautious incautus
incendiary incendĭārĭus, *m*
incense *nn*, tūs, *n*
incense *v.t*, ad īram mŏvĕo (2) **(arouse to anger)**
incentive stĭmŭlus, *m*
incessant perpĕtŭus, assĭdŭus
incest incestum, *n*
inch uncĭa, *f*
incident rēs, *f*
incidental (casual) fortŭĭtus
incipient *use vb*. incĭpĭo **(begin)**
incision incīsūra, *f*
incisive mordax, ācer
incite *v.t*, incĭto (1)
inclemency aspĕrĭtas, *f*, sĕvērĭtas, *f*
inclement asper, sĕvērus
inclination (desire) stŭdĭum, *n*, vŏluntas, *f*; **(leaning, bias)** inclīnātĭo, *f*
incline *v.t*, inclīno (1); *v.i*, inclīnor (1 *pass*)
incline *nn*, **(slope)** acclīvĭtas, *f*
inclined (disposed) prōpensus
include *v.t*, rĕfĕro *(irreg)*, comprĕhendo (3)
including (together with) cum *(with abl)*
incoherent *use vb. phr. with* nōn *and* cŏhaerĕo (2) **(to hold together)**
income fructus, *m*, stīpendĭum, *n*
incomparable singŭlāris
incompatibility rĕpugnantĭa, *f*
incompatible rĕpugnans
incompetent ĭnhăbĭlis
incomplete imperfectus
incomprehensible *use phr*, quod intellĕgi nōn pŏtest
inconceivable *use phr*, quod ănĭmo fingi nōn pŏtest **(that cannot be conceived)**
inconclusive (weak) infirmus
incongruous rĕpugnans
inconsiderable parvus
inconsiderate inconsīdĕrātus
inconsistency inconstantĭa, *f*
inconsistent inconstans; **(to be —)**, *v.i*, rĕpugno (1)
inconsolable inconsōlābĭlis
inconspicuous obscūrus

inconstancy inconstantĭa, *f*
inconstant inconstans
inconvenience incommŏdum, *n*
inconvenient incommŏdus
incorporate *v.t*, constĭtŭo (3),
  iungo (3)
incorrect falsus
incorrigible perdĭtus
incorruptible incorruptus
increase *nn*, incrēmentum, *n*
increase *v.t*, augĕo (2), *v.i*, cresco
  (1)
incredible incrēdĭbĭlis
incredulous incrēdŭlus
incriminate *v.t*, implĭco (1)
inculcate *v.t*, inculco (1)
incumbent upon (it is —) ŏportet
  (*v*. 2 *impers. with acc. of person*)
incur *v.t*, sŭbĕo (4)
incurable insānābĭlis
indebted obnoxĭus
indecency turpĭtūdo, *f*
indecent turpis, obscēnus
indecisive dŭbĭus, anceps
indeed *adv, emphatic,* prŏfecto;
  (yes —), vēro; *concessive;* quĭdem
indefatigible assĭdŭus
indefensible *use phr,* quod nōn
  pŏtest făcĭlĕ dēfendi **(that cannot
  be defended easily)**
indefinite incertus
indemnify *v.t*, damnum rēstĭtŭo (3)
  (restore a loss)
indentation lăcuna, *f*
independence lībertas, *f*
independent līber
indescribable ĭnēnarrābĭlis
indestructible (unfailing) pĕrennis
indeterminate incertus
index index, *m*
indicate *v.t*, indĭco (1), signĭfĭco
  (1)
indication indĭcĭum, *n*
indict *v.t*, accūso (1)
indictment accūsātĭo, *f*
indifference lentĭtūdo, *f*
indifferent neglĕgens; **(middling)**
  mĕdĭŏcris
indifferently *adv* **(moderately)**
  mĕdĭŏcrĭter
indigenous *adj*, indĭgĕna
indigestible *adv*, grăvis
indigestion crūdĭtas, *f*

indignant īrātus; **(to be —)**, *v.i,*
  indignor (1 *dep*); ĭrātus ess
indignation indignātĭo, *f*, īra, *f*
indignity contŭmēlĭa, *f*
indirect oblīquus **(path, etc.)** dēvĭus
indiscreet inconsultus
indiscriminate prōmiscŭus
indispensable nĕcessārĭus
indispose *v.t*, ălĭēno (1)
indisposed (not inclined) āversus;
  (ill), aegrōtus
indisposition (unwillingness)
  ănĭmus āversus; **(sickness)**,
  vălētūdo, *f*
indisputable certus
indistinct obscūrus
individual *nn*, hŏmo, *c*
individual *adj*, prŏprĭus
indivisible indīvĭdŭus
indolence ignāvĭa, *f*
indolent ignāvus
indomitable indŏmĭtus
indoor *adj*, umbrātĭlis **(in the
  shade)**
indoors (motion) in tectum
indubitable certus
induce *v.t*, addūco (3)
inducement praemĭum, *n*
indulge *v.i and v.t*, indulgĕo (2)
indulgence indulgentĭa, *f*
indulgent indulgens
industrious industrĭus, dīlĭgens
industry (diligence) industrĭa, *f*,
  dīlĭgentĭa, *f*
inebriated ēbrĭus
ineffective ĭnūtĭlis
inefficient *use phr,* qui rem
  cĕlĕrĭter confĭcĕre nōn pŏtest
  **(who cannot complete a matter
  quickly)**
inelegant ĭnēlĕgans
inept ĭneptus
inequality dissĭmĭlĭtūdo, *f*
inert ĭners, segnis
inertly *adv,* segnĭter
inestimable ĭnaestĭmābĭlis
inevitable nēcessārĭus
inexcusable *use phr,* quod
  praetermitti nōn pŏtest **(that
  cannot be overlooked)**
inexhaustible infīnītus, sĭne fine
inexorable ĭnexōrābĭlis

inexperience impĕrītĭa, *f*,
  inscĭentĭa, *f*
inexperienced impĕrītus
inexplicable ĭnexplĭcābĭlis
inexpressible ĭnēnarrābĭlis, *or phr*,
  quod exprĭmi nōn pŏtest **(that
  cannot be expressed)**
infallible qui falli nōn pŏtest **(who
  cannot be mistaken)**
infamous infāmis
infamy infāmĭa, *f*
infancy infantĭa, *f*
infant *adj, and nn*, infans
infantry pĕdĭtātus, *m*
infatuate *v.t*, infătŭo (1)
infatuated dēmens
infect *v.t*, infĭcĭo (3)
infection contāgĭo, *f*
infer *v.t*, collĭgo (3)
inference conĭectūra, *f*
inferior *adj*, infĕrĭor, dētĕrĭor
infernal infernus
infested infestus
infidelity perfĭdĭa, *f*
infinite infinītus
infinity infinĭtas, *f*
infirm invălĭdus, infirmus
infirmity infirmĭtas, *f*
inflame *v.t*, accendo (3)
inflammable *use phr*, quod făcĭlĕ
  incendi pŏtest **(that can be set on
  fire easily)**
inflammation inflammātĭo, *f*
inflate *v.t*, inflo (1)
inflexible rĭgĭdus
inflict *v.t*, inflīgo (3); **(war, etc.)**,
  infĕro *(irreg) (with dat of person)*
infliction mălum, *n*, **(trouble)**
influence *nn*, vīs, *f*, mōmentum, *n*;
  (authority), auctōrĭtas, *f*; **(to have
  —)** *v.i*, vălĕo (2)
influence *v.t*, mŏvĕo (2)
influential grăvis
inform *v.t*, certĭōrem făcĭo (3);
  (— against someone), nōmen
  dēfĕro *(irreg) (with genit)*
information (news) nuntĭus, *m*
informer dēlātor, *m*
infrequency rārĭtas, *f*
infrequent rārus
infringe *v.t*, vĭŏla, (1)
infringement vĭŏlātĭo, *f*
infuriate *v.t*, effĕro (1)

infuriated īrā incensus
infuse *v.t*, infudo (3), ĭnĭcĭo (3)
ingenious subtīlis
ingenuity *f*, ars, *f*, callĭdĭtas, *f*
ingenuous ingĕnŭus
inglorious inglōrĭus
ingot lăter, *m*
ingrained insĭtus
ingratiate oneself with *v.t*,
  conncĭlĭo (1), sē grātum reddere
  (with dat)
ingratitude ănĭmus ĭngrātus, *m*
ingredient pars, *f*
inhabit *v.t*, incŏlo (3), hăbĭto (1)
inhabitant incŏla, *c*
inhale *v.t*, (spīrĭtum) haurĭo (4)
inherent insĭtus
inherit *v.t, use phr. with*, hēres
  (heir), *and* accĭpĭo **(to receive)**
inheritance hērēdĭtas, *f*
inherited hērēdĭtārĭus
inhibit *v.t*, interdīco (3)
inhospitable ĭnhospĭtālis
inhuman immānis, crūdēlis
inhumanity immānĭtas, *f*,
  crūdēlĭtas, *f*
inimitable nōn ĭmĭtābĭlis
iniquitous ĭnīquus, imprŏbus
iniquity imprŏbĭtas, *f*
initial *adj*, prīmus
initiate *v.t*, ĭnĭtĭo (1)
initiative (take the —) *v.i*, occŭpo
  (1)
inject *v.t*, ĭnĭcĭo (3)
injudicious inconsultus
injure *v.t*, nŏcĕo (2) *(with dat)*
injurious noxĭus, nŏcens
injury (of the body) vulnus, *n*;
  (disadvantage), dētrīmentum, *n*,
  iniūrĭa, *f*
injustice ĭnīquĭtas, *f*, iniūrĭa, *f*
ink ātrāmentum, *n*
inland mĕdĭterrānĕus
inlay *v.t*, insĕro (3)
inlet aestŭārĭum, *n*
inn dēversōrĭum, *n*, caupōna, *f*; **(—
  keeper)** caupo, *m*
innate insĭtus, innātus
inner intĕrĭor
innocence innŏcentĭa, *f*
innocent innŏcens, insons
innocuous innŏcŭus
innovate *v.t*, nŏvo (1)

innumerable innŭmĕrābĭlis
inobservant nōn perspĭcax
inoffensive innŏcens
inopportune ĭnopportūnus
inordinate immŏdĕrātus
inquest quaestĭo, *f*
inquire *v.i,* quaero (3) ab (*with abl*) *or* dē (*with abl*)
inquiry interrŏgātĭo, *f*; **(official)**, quaestĭo, *f*
inquisitive cūrĭōsus
inquisitor quaesītor, *m*
inroad incursĭo, *f*
insane insānus, dēmens
insanity insānĭa, *f*, dēmentĭa, *f*
insatiable insătĭābĭlis
inscribe *v.t,* inscrībo (3) in (*with abl*)
inscription inscriptĭo, *f*
inscrutable obscūrus
insect bestĭŏla, *f*
insecure intūtus **(unsafe)**
insecurity *use adj,* intūtus
insensible (unfeeling) dūrus
inseparable *use phr,* quod sēpărāri nōn pŏtest **(that cannot be separated)**
insert *v.t,* insĕro (3)
inside *prep,* intrā (*with acc*)
inside *adv,* intus
inside *nn,* interĭor pars *f*
insidious insĭdĭōsus
insight (understanding) intellĕgentĭa, *f*
insignia insignĭa, *n.pl*
insignificant exĭgŭus, nullĭus mōmenti
insincere sĭmŭlātus
insincerity fallācĭa, *f*, sĭmŭlātĭo, *f*
insinuate *v.t,* insĭnŭo (1); **(hint)**, signĭfico (1)
insinuating (smooth) blandus
insipid insulsus
insist *v.i,* insto (1); *v.t,* **(— on, demand)** posco (3), flāgĭto (1)
insolence contŭmācĭa, *f*, insŏlentĭa, *f*
insolent contŭmax, insŏlens
insoluble *use phr,* quod explĭcāri non pŏtest **(that cannot be explained)**
insolvent (to be —) *v.i,* nōn esse solvendo

inspect *v.t,* inspĭcĭo (3)
inspection *use vb,* inspĭcĭo (3), *or* lustro (1)
inspector (superintendent) cūrātor, *m*
inspiration (divine, poetic, etc) instinctus, *m*, afflātus, *m*
inspire *v.t,* īnĭcĭo (3) (*with acc. of thing inspired and dat. of person*); **(rouse)**, accendo (3)
inspired (of persons) incensus
instal *v.t,* ĭnaugŭro (1)
instalment pensĭo, *f*
instance (example) exemplum, *n*; **(for—)**, verbi grātĭā
instant *adj,* praesens
instant *nn,* mōmentum, *n*
instantly (at once) *adv,* stătim
instantaneous praesens
instead *adv,* măgis **(rather)**
instead of *prep,* prō (*with abl*); *with a clause, use* tantum ăbĕrat (ăbest) ut … ut
instigate *v.t,* instīgo (1)
instill *v.t,* instillo (1), īnĭtĭo (3)
instinct nātūra, *f*
instinctive nātūrālis
institute *v.t,* instĭtŭo (3)
institute, institution collēgĭum, *n*; instĭtūtum, *n*
instruct *v.t,* dŏcĕo (2), ērŭdĭo (4); **(order)**, praecĭpĭo (3)
instruction dĭscĭplīna, *f*, institutio, *f*; **(command)**, mandātum, *n*
instructor măgister, *m*
instrument instrūmentum, *n*
instrumental (in doing something) ūtĭlis
insubordinate sēdĭtĭōsus
insufferable intŏlĕrābĭlis
insufficiency ĭnŏpĭa, *f*
insufficient haud sătis (*with genit*) **(not enough …)**
insult *nn,* contŭmēlĭa, *f*
insult *v.t,* contŭmēlĭam impōno (3) (*with dat*)
insulting contŭmēlĭōsus
insuperable *use phr,* quod sŭpĕrāri nōn pŏtest **(that cannot be overcome)**
insure against *v.t,* praecăvĕo (2)
insurgent rĕbellis, *m*
insurrection mōtus, *m*

intact intĕger
integral nĕcessārĭus **(necessary)**
integrity intĕgrĭtas, *f*
intellect mens, *f*, ingĕnĭum, *n*
intellectual ingĕnĭōsus
intelligence ingĕnĭum, *n*; **(news)**, nuntĭus, *m*
intelligent săpĭens, intellĕgens
intelligible perspĭcŭus
intemperate intempĕrans
intend *v.t*, in ănĭmo hăbĕo (2) (*with infinitive*)
intense ācer
intensify *v.t*, augĕo (2), incendo (3) **(inflame, rouse)**
intensify vīs, *f*
intent *adj*, intentus; **(to be — on)**, ănĭmum intendo (3) in (*with acc*)
intention consĭlĭum, *n*, prōpŏsĭtum, *n*
intentionally *adv*, consultō
inter *v.t*, sĕpĕlĭo (4)
intercede (on behalf of) dēprĕcor (1 *dep*) pro (*with abl*)
intercept *v.t*, **(catch)** excĭpĭo (3); **(cut off)**, interclūdo (3)
intercession dēprĕcātĭo, *f*
interchange *nn*, permūtātĭo, *f*
interchange *v.t*, permūto (1)
intercourse commercĭum, *n*, ūsus, *m*
interest *nn*, **(zeal)**, stŭdĭum, *n*; **(it is in the — of)**, intĕrest (*v.impers. with genit*); **(financial)**, fēnus, *n*, ūsūra, *f*
interest *v.t*, tĕnĕo (2), plăcĕo (2); **(— oneself in)**, stŭdĕo (2) (*with dat*)
interested attentus
interesting *use vb.* **to interest**
interfere *v.i*, sē interpōnĕre (3 *reflex*)
interim *adv*, **(in the —)** intĕrim
interior *adj*, intĕrĭor; *nn*, pars intĕrĭor, *f*
interject *v.t*, intericĭo (3)
interlude embŏlĭum, *n*
intermarriage connūbĭum, *n*
intermediate mĕdĭus
interminable infinītus
intermingle *v.t*, miscĕo (2); *v.i*, sē miscēre (2 *reflex*)
intermission intermissĭo, *f*

internal intestīnus
international *use genit*, gentĭum **(of nations)**
internecine internĕcīnus
interpose *v.t*, interpōno (3)
interpret *v.t*, interprĕtor (1 *dep*)
interpretation interprĕtātĭo, *f*
interpreter interpres, *c*
interregnum interregnum, *n*
interrogate *v.t*, interrŏgo (1)
interrupt *v.t*, interpello (1), interrumpo (3)
interruption interpellātĭo, *f*
intersect *v.t*, sĕco (1) **(cut)**
interval intervallum, *n*, spătĭum, *n*
intervene *v.i*, intercēdo (3), sē interpōnĕre (3 *reflex*) (*both with dat*)
intervention intercessĭo, *f*
interview collŏquĭum, *n*
interview *v.t*, collŏquor (3 *dep*) cum (*with abl*) **(speak with)**
interweave *v.t*, intertexo (3), implĭco (1)
intestines intestīna, *n.pl*
intimacy consŭētūdo, *f*, fămĭlĭărĭtas, *f*
intimate *adj*, fămĭlĭāris
intimate *v.t*, signĭfĭco (1)
intimidate *v.t*, dēterrĕo (2)
intimidation terror, *m*, mĭnae, *f.pl*
into *prep*, in (*with acc*)
intolerable intŏlĕrābĭlis
intolerance sŭperbĭa, *f*
intolerant sŭperbus
intone *v.t*, căno (1)
intoxicate *v.t*, ēbrĭum reddo (3) **(make drunk)**
intoxicate ēbrĭus
intoxication ēbrĭĕtas, *f*
intractable diffĭcĭlis
intrepid intrĕpĭdus
intricacy (difficulty) diffĭcultas
intricate diffĭcĭlis
intrigue dŏlus, *m*
intrigue *v.i*, dŏlīs ūtor (3 *dep*)
introduce *v.t*, intrōduco (3)
introduction intrōductĭo, *f*; **(letter of —)** littĕrae commendātĭcĭae, *f.pl*
intrude *v.i*, sē inculcāre (1 *reflex*)
intrusive *use phr*, qui interpellāre sŏlet **(who usually disturbs)**

intuition cognĭtio, *f*

inundate *v.t,* ĭnundo (1)

inundation ĭnundātĭo, *f*

inure *v.t,* assuēfăcĭo (3)

invade *v.t,* bellum infĕro (*irreg*) (*with dat*), invādo (3) in (*with acc*)

invader hostis, *c*

invalid *nn,* aeger, *m*

invalid *adj,* **(of no avail)**, irrĭtus, infirmus

invalidate *v.t,* infirmo (1)

invariable constans

invasion incursĭo, *f*

invective convīcĭum, *n*

inveigh against *v.i,* invĕhor (3 *dep*) in (*with acc.*)

inveigle *v.t,* illĭcĭo (3)

invent *v.t,* invĕnĭo (4)

invention (faculty) inventĭo, *f*; **(thing invented)**, inventum, *n*

inventor inventor, *m*

inverse inversus

invert *v.t,* inverto (3)

invest *v.t,* **(money)**, collŏco (1); **(besiege)** obsĭdĕo (2); **(— someone with an office)** măgistrātum committo (3) (*with dat*)

investigate *v.t,* exquīro (3), cognosco (3)

investigation investīgātĭo, *f*, cognĭtĭo, *f*

investiture consĕcrātĭo, *f*

inveterate invĕtĕrātus

invidious (envious, hateful) invĭdĭōsus

invigorate *v.t,* vīres rĕfĭcĭo (3)

invincible invictus

inviolability sanctĭtas, *f* **(sacredness)**

inviolable invĭŏlātus

invisible caecus

invitation invītātĭo, *f*; **(at your —)**, tŭo invītātu

invite *v.t,* invīto (1)

inviting blandus

invoke *v.t,* invŏco (1)

involuntary nōn vŏluntārĭus

involve *v.t,* involvo (3), illĭgo (1), hăbĕo (2)

invulnerable *use phr,* quod vulnĕrāri nōn pŏtest **(that cannot be wounded)**

inward *adj,* intĕrĭor

inwardly, inwards *adv,* intus

irascibility īrācundĭa, *f*

irascible īrācundus

iris īris, *f*

irk (it —s) pĭget (*v.* 2 *impers.*) (*with acc. of person*)

irksome grăvis, mŏlestus

iron *nn,* ferrum, *n*

iron *adj,* ferrĕus

ironical *use nn,* īrōnīa, *f,* **(irony)**

ironmongery ferrāmenta, *n.pl*

irony īrōnīa, *f,* dissĭmŭlātĭo, *f*

irradiate *v.t,* illustro (1)

irrational rătĭōnis expers **(devoid of reason)**

irreconcilable rĕpugnans

irrefutable firmus

irregular (out of the ordinary) ĭnūsĭtātus, extrăordĭnārĭus; **(not well regulated)** nōn ordĭnātus

irregularity vĭtĭum, *n; otherwise use adjs. above*

irrelevant ălĭēnus

irreligious ĭmpĭus

irremediable insānābĭlis

irreparable *use phr,* quod rĕfĭci nōn pŏtest **(that cannot be repaired)**

irreproachable intĕger, invictus

irresistible invicus

irresolute dubĭus

irretrievable irrĕpĕrābĭlis

irreverance impĭĕtas, *f*

irreverent impĭus

irrevocable irrĕpĕrābĭlis

irrigate *v.t,* irrĭgo (1)

irrigatin irrĭgātĭo, *f*

irritable stŏmăchōsus

irritate *v.t,* irrīto (1); **(make worse)**, pēius reddo (3)

irruption (attack) incursĭo, *f*

island insŭla, *f*

islander insŭlānus, *m*

isolate *v.t,* sēpăro (1)

isolation sōlĭtūdo, *f*

issue *nn,* **(result)**, ēventus, *m*; **(topic)**, rēs, *f*; **(offspring)**, prōgĕnĭes, *f*

issue *v.i,* **(proceed)**, ēgrĕdĭor (3 *dep*); **(turn out)**, ēvĕnĭo (4); *v.t* **(give out)**, ēdo (3); **(edicts, etc.)** ēdīco (3)

isthmus isthmus, *m*
it *pron,* id, hoc, illud; *often expressed by 3rd person sing. of verb, e.g.* **it is,** est
itch *nn,* prūrītus, *m*; **(disease),** scăbĭes, *f*
itch *v.i,* prūrĭo (4)
item rēs, *f*
itinerant circumfŏrānĕus
itinerary ĭter, *n* **(route)**
itself see **himself**
ivory *nn,* ĕbur, *n*; *adj,* ĕburnĕus
ivy hĕdĕra, *f*

J

jab *v.t,* fŏdĭo (3)
jabber *v.i,* blătĕro (1)
jackass ăsĭnus, *m*
jacket tŭnĭca, *f*
jaded dēfessus
jagged asper
jail carcer, *m*
jailer custos, *c*
janitor iānĭtor, *m*
January Iānŭārĭus (mensis)
jar olla, *f,* amphŏra, *f,* dōlĭum, *n*
jarring dissŏnus
jaunt excursĭo, *f*
javelin pīlum, *n*
jaws faucēs *f.pl*
jealous invĭdus
jealousy invĭdĭa, *f*
jeer at *v.t,* dērīdĕo (2)
jeering *nn,* irrīsĭo, *f*
jejune iēiūnus
jeopardize *v.t,* pěrīclĭtor (1 *dep*)
jeopardy pěrīcŭlum, *n*
jerk *v.t,* quătĭo (3)
jerkin tŭnĭca, *f*
jest *nn,* iŏcus, *m*
jest *v.i,* iŏcor (1 *dep*)
jester scurra, *m*
jetty mōles, *f*
Jew *nn,* Iūdaeus, *m*
jewel gemma, *f*
jeweller gemmārĭus, *m*
 jibe convīcĭum, *n*
jilt *v.t,* rěpŭdĭo (1)
jingle *nn,* tinnītus, *m*
jingle *v.i,* tinnĭo (4)
job ŏpus, *n*
jockey ăgāso, *m*

jocose iŏcōsus
jocular iŏcŭlāris
jocund hĭlāris, iūcundus
jog *v.t,* fŏdĭco (1) **(nudge)**
join *v.t,* iungo (3); *v.i,* sē coniungĕre (3 *reflex*); **(— battle)** committo (3)
joiner lignārĭus, *m*
joint commissūra, *f*
joist tignum transversum, *n*
joke *nn,* iŏcus, *m*
joke *v.i,* iŏcor (1 *dep*)
joker iŏcŭlātor, *m*
jollity hĭlārĭtas, *f*
jolly hĭlăris
jolt *v.t,* concŭtĭo (3)
jostle *v.t,* pulso (1)
jot *v.t,* adnŏto (1)
journal commentārĭi dĭurni, *m.pl*
journey *nn,* ĭter, *n*
journey *v.i,* ĭter făcĭo (3)
journey-man ŏpĭfex, *c*
jovial hĭlăris
jowl gĕnae, *f.pl*
joy (outward) laetĭtĭa, *f*; **(inner),** gaudĭum, *n*
joyful laetus
joyless tristis
jubilant gaudĭo (*or* laetĭtĭā) exsultans **(exultant with joy)**
judge *nn,* iūdex, *m*
judge *v.t,* iūdĭco (1), aestĭmo (1)
judgement iūdĭcĭum, *n*
judicature iūdĭces, *m.pl*
judicial iūdĭcĭālis
judicious săpĭens
judiciously săpĭenter
judiciousness prūdentĭa, *f*
jug urcĕus, *m*
juggling tricks praestīgĭae, *f.pl*
juice sūcus, *m*
juicy sūcōsus
July (before Caesar) Quintīlis (mensis); **(after Caesar),** Iūlĭus (mensis)
jumble *nn,* congĕrĭes, *f*
jumble *v.t,* confundo (3)
jump *nn,* saltus, *m*
jump *v.i,* sălĭo (4)
junction coniunctĭo, *f*
juncture tempus, *n*
June Iūnĭus (mensis)
junior mĭnor nātu, iūnĭor

juniper iūnĭpĕrus, *f*
jurisconsult iūrisconsultus, *m*
jurisdiction iūrisdictĭo, *f*
juror iūdex, *m*
jury iūdĭces, *m.pl*
just iustus
justice iustĭtĭa, *f*
justification sătisfactĭo, *f*
justify *v.t*, purgo (1), excūso (1)
justly *adv*, iustē
jut *v.i*, exsto (1)
juvenile iūvĕnīlis

K

keel cărīna, *f*
keen ācer; **(mentally)**, perspĭcax
keenness (eagerness) stŭdĭum,
  n; **(sagacity)**, săgācĭtas, *f*;
  (sharpness, etc.) ācerbĭtas, *f*
keep *nn*, arx, *f*
keep *v.t*, **(hold)**, tĕnĕo (2), hăbĕo
  (2); **(preserve)**, servo (1); **(store)**,
  condo (3); **(support, rear)**, ălo (3);
  (— apart), distĭnĕo (2); **(— back)**,
  rĕtĭnĕo (2), dētĭnĕo (2); **(— off)**,
  arcĕo (2); *v.i*, **(remain)**, mănĕo (2)
keeper custos, *c*
keeping (protection) tūtēla, *f*,
  custōdĭa, *f*
keg dōlĭum, *n*, amphŏra, *f*
kennel stăbŭlum, *n*
kerb (stone) crĕpīdo, *f*
kernel nŭclĕus, *m*
kettle lĕbes, *m*
key clāvis, *f*
kick *nn*, calcĭtrātus, *m*
kick *v.i*, calcĭtro (1)
kid haedus, *m*
kidnap *v.t*, surrĭpĭo (3)
kidney rēn, *m*
kidney bean phăsēlus, *m, f*
kill *v.t*, nĕco (1), interfĭcĭo (3)
kiln fornax, *f*
kind *nn*, gĕnus, *n*; **(of such a —)**,
  adj, tālis
kind *adj*, bĕnignus
kindle *v.t*, accendo (3), excĭto (1)
kindliness bĕnignĭtas, *f*
kindness bĕnĕfĭcĭum, *n*; **(of
  disposition)** bĕnignĭtas, *f*
kindred (relatives) consanguĭnĕi,
  m.pl; cognāti, *m.pl*

king rex, *m*
kingdom regnum, *n*
kingfisher alcēdo, *f*
kinsman nĕcessărĭus, *m*
kiss *nn*, oscŭlum, *n*
kiss *v.t*, oscŭlor (1 *dep*)
kitchen cŭlīna, *f*
kitten fēlis cătŭlus, *m* **(the young of
  a cat)**
knapsack sarcĭna, *f*
knave scĕlestus, *m*
knavery nēquĭtĭa, *f*, imprŏbĭtas, *f*
knavish nēquam **(***indeclinable***)**;
  imprŏbus
knead *v.t*, sŭbĭgo (3)
knee gĕnu, *n*; **(knock-kneed)**, *adj*,
  vārus
kneecap pătella, *f*
kneel gĕnu (gĕnĭbus) nītor (3 *dep*)
  (rest on the knee(s))
knife cutler, *m*
knight ĕques, *m*
knighthood dignĭtas ĕquestris, *f*
knit *v.t*, texo (3); **(— the forehead)**
  frontem contrăho (3)
knob bulla, *f*, nōdus, *m*
knock *v.t*, pulso (1); **(— against)**,
  offendo (3); **(— down)**, dēpello
  (3), dēĭcĭo (3)
knock, knocking pulsus, *m*,
  pulsātĭo, *f*
knoll tŭmŭlus, *m*
knot *nn*, nōdus, *m*
knot *v.t*, nōdo (1)
knotty nōdōsus
know *v.t*, scĭo (4); **(get to —)**,
  cognosco (3); **(person,
  acquaintance)**, nosco (3); **(not
  to —)**, nescĭo (4)
knowing *adj*, **(wise)** prūdens
knowingly *adv*, consultō
knowledge scĭentĭa, *f*
known nōtus; **(to make —)**, dēclāro
  (1)
knuckle artĭcŭlus, *m*

L

label tĭtŭlus, *m*, pittăcĭum, *n*
laborious lăbōrĭōsus
labour lăbor, *m*, ŏpus, *n*; **(to be
  in —)** *v.i*, partŭrĭo (4)

labour *v.i*, lăbōro (1), ēnītor (3 *dep*)
labourer ŏpĕrārĭus, *m*
labyrinth lăbўrinthus, *m*
lace rētĭcŭlāta texta, *n.pl* **(net-like fabric)**
lacerate *v.t*, lăcĕro (1)
laceration lăcĕrātĭo, *f*
lack *nn*, ĭnŏpĭa, *f*
lack *v.i*, ĕgĕo (2), cărĕo (*both with abl*)
lackey pĕdĭsĕquus, *m*
laconic brĕvis
lad pŭer, *m*
ladder scālae, *f.pl*
ladle trulla, *f*
lady mātrōna, *f*, dŏmĭna, *f*
ladylike lībĕrālis **(gracious)**
lag *v.i*, cesso (1)
laggard cessātor, *m*
lagoon lăcus, *m*
lair lătĭbŭlum, *n*
lake lăcus, *m*
lamb agnus, *m*; (agna, *f*)
lame claudus; **(argument, etc.)** lĕvis; **(to be —)** *v.i*, claudĭco (1)
lameness claudĭcātĭo, *f*
lament lāmentātĭo, *f*, complōrātĭo, *f*, ŭlŭlātus, *m*
lament *v.i, and v.t*, lāmentor (1 *dep*), dēplōro (1), lūgĕo (2)
lamentable lāmentābĭlis
lamented dēplōrātus, flēbĭlis
lamp lŭcerna, *f*
lampoon carmen rīdĭcŭlum et fāmōsum **(facetious defamatory verse)**
lance lancĕa, *f*, hasta, *f*
lancet scalpellum, *n*
land (earth, etc.) terra, *f*; **(region of country)**, rĕgĭo, *f*, fīnes, *m.pl*; **(native —)** pătrĭa, *f*
land *v.t*, expōno (3); *v.i*, ēgrĕdĭor (3 *dep*)
landing *nn*, ēgressus, *m*
landlord (innkeeper) caupo, *m*; **(owner)**, dŏmĭnus, *m*
landmark lăpis, *m*
landslide lapus (*m*) terrae
lane sēmĭta, *f*
language lingua, *f*; **(speech, style)**, ōrātĭo, *f*
languid languĭdus, rĕmissus

languish *v.i*, langueo (2), tabesco (3)
languor languor, *m*
lank (hair) prōmissus; **(persons)**, prōcerus
lantern lanterna, *f*
lap grĕmĭum, *n*, sĭnus, *m*
lap up *v.t*, lambo (3)
lapse *nn*, **(mistake)** peccātum, *n*; **(of time)**, fŭga, *f*
lapse *v.i*, **(err)** pecco (1); **(time)**, praetĕrĕo (4)
larceny furtum, *n*
larch lărix, *f*
lard ădeps, *c*, lārĭdum, *n*
larder *use* cella, *f*, **(store-room)**, *or* armārĭum, *n* **(food cupboard)**
large magnus
largeness magnĭtūdo, *f*
largess largītĭo, *f*
lark ălauda, *f*
larynx *use* guttur, *n* **(throat)**
lascivious libīdĭnōsus
lash (whip) lōrum, *n*, flăgellum, *n*; **(eye —)**, pilus, m
lash *v.t*, **(whip)**, verbĕro (1); **(bind)**, allĭgo (1)
lass pŭella, *f*
last *adj*, ultĭmus, postrēmus, extrēmus; **(most recent)**, nŏvissĭmus, proxĭmus; **(at —)**, *adv*, tandem
last *v.i*, dūro (1), mănĕo (2)
lasting *adj*, dĭuturnus
lastly *adv*, postrēmo, dēnĭque
latch pessŭlus, *m*
late sērus, tardus; **(dead)**, mortŭus; *adv*, sĕro; **(— at night)** (*adv. phr.*), multā nocte
lately *adv*, nūper
latent occultus
lathe tornus, *m*
Latin Lătīnus; **(— language)**, lingua Lătīna, *f*
latitude (freedom, scope) lībertas, *f*
latter (the —) hic
lattice cancelli, *m. pl*
laud *v.t*, laudo (1)
laudable laudābĭlis
laugh *nn*, rīsus, *m*; **(loud —)**, cāchinnus, *m*
laugh *v.i*, cachinno (1)

laughing-stock lŭdĭbrĭum, *n*
launch *v.t*, (a ship), dēdūco (3); *v.i*, (launch out), insĕquor (3 *dep*)
laurel laurus; *f*; *adj*, laurĕus
lava massa lĭquĕfacta, *f*, (molten mass)
lavish *adj*, prōdĭgus, prŏfūsus
lavish *v.t*, prŏfundo (3)
law (a law) lex, *f*; (the law), iūs, *n*
lawful lēgĭtĭmus
lawless nĕfārĭus
lawn prātum, *n*
lawsuit līs, *f*
lawyer iūrisconsultus, *m*
lax dissŏlūtus
laxness rĕmissĭo, *f*, neglĕntĭa, *f*
laxity rĕmissĭo, *f*, neglĕgentĭa, *f*
lay *v.t*, pōno (3); (— aside), pōno (3); (— foundations), iăcĭo (3); (— an ambush), insĭdĭs collŏco (1); (— down arms), ab armis discēdo (3); (— eggs), ōva părĭo (3)
layer cŏrĭum, *n*, tăbŭlātum, *n*
laziness ignāvĭa, *f*
lazy ignāvus, pĭger
lead *nn*, plumbum, *n*; *adj*, plumbĕus
lead *v.t*, dūco (3); (— a life, etc.), ăgo (3); (— on, persuade), addūco (3)
leader dux, *c*
leadership ductus, *m*; *or use phr. in abl*, e.g. under the — of Brutus, Brūto dŭce (with Brutus leader)
leading *adj*, princeps
leaf frons, *f*, fŏlĭum, *n*; (paper) schĕda, *f*
leafy frondōsus
league foedus, *n*, sŏcĭĕtas, *f*
league together *v.i*, coniūro (1)
leak *nn*, rīma *f*
leak (let in water) ăquam per rīmas accĭpĭo (3)
leaky rīmōsus
lean *adj*, măcer, exīlis
lean *v.i*, innītor (3 *dep*); *v.t*, inclīno (1)
leanness măcĭes, *f*
leap *nn*, saltus, *m*
leap *v.i*, sălĭo (4); (— down) dēsĭlĭo (4)
leap year bĭsextĭlis annus, *m*

learn *v.t*, disco (3); (ascertain) cognosco (3)
learned doctus
learning doctrīna, *f*, ērŭdītĭo, *f*
lease *nn*, conductĭo, *f*
lease *v.t*, condūco (3)
leash cōpŭla, *f*
least *adj*, mĭnĭmus; *adv*, mĭnĭmē; (at —), *adv*, saltem
leather cŏrĭum, *n*
leave *nn*, (permission), pŏtestas, *f*, permissĭo, *f*; (— of absence) commĕātus, *m*
leave *v.i*, discēdo (3); *v.t*, rĕlinquo (3), dēsĕro (3)
leave off *v.i. and v.t*, dēsĭno (3)
leavings *nn*, rĕlĭquĭae, *f. pl*
lecture *nn*, audītĭo, *f*, (hearing)
lecture *v.i*, schŏlas hăbĕo (2)
lecture-room schŏla, *f*
ledge *use adj*, ĕmĭnens (projecting) *in agreement with a noun*
ledger cōdex, *m*
leech hĭrūdo, *f*
leek porrum, *n*
leering *adj*, līmus
left *adj*, (opp. to right), sĭnister, laevus; (remaining), rĕlĭquus
leg crus, *n*
legacy lēgātum, *n*
legal lēgĭtĭmus
legalize *v.t*, sancĭo (4)
legate lēgātus, *m*
legation lēgātĭo, *f*
legend fābŭla, *f*
legendary fābŭlōsus
leggings ŏcrĕae, *f. pl*
legible *use phr*, făcĭlis ad lĕgendum (easy for reading)
legion lĕgĭo, *f*
legislate *v.i*, lēges făcĭo (3) (make laws)
legislator lātor, (*m*) lēgum (proposer of laws)
legitimate lēgĭtĭmus
leisure ōtĭum, *n*; (to be at —), *v.i*, ōtĭor (1 *dep*)
leisurely *adj*, lentus
lend *v.t*, mūtŭum do (1) (give a loan), commŏdo (1)
length longĭtūdo, *f*; (of time), dĭūturnĭtas, *f*; (at —), *adv*, tandem

lengthen *v.t*, prōdūco (3), longĭōrem reddo (3)
leniency clēmentĭa, *f*
lenient mītis, clēmens
lentil lens, *f*
leper hŏmo lĕprōsus, *m*
leprosy lĕprae, *f. pl*
less *adj*, mĭnor; *adv*, mĭnus
lessen *v.i. and v.t*, mĭnŭo (3)
lesson dŏcŭmentum, *n*
lest *conj*, nē
let *v.t*, sĭno (3) permitto (3) (*with dat of person*); **(lease)**, lŏco (1); **(— go)**, dīmitto (3); **(— in)**, admitto (3); **(— out)**, ēmitto (3)
lethal mortĭfer
lethargic lentus
letter (of the alphabet) littĕra, *f*; **(epistle)**, littĕrae, *f. pl*, ĕpistŏla, *f*
lettering *nn*, littĕrae, *f. pl*
letters (learning) littĕrae, *f. pl*
lettuce lactūca, *f*
level *adj*, plānus; **(— place)**, *nn*, plānĭtĭes, *f*
level *v.t*, aequo (1); **(— to the ground)**, sterno (3)
lever vectis, *m*
levity lĕvĭtas, *f*
levy *nn*, dēlectus, *m*
levy *v.t*, **(troops)**, scrībo (3); **(taxes, etc.)**, impĕro (1), ĕxĭgo (3)
lewd incestus, impŭdīcus
lewdness incestum, *n*
liable obnoxĭus
liar hŏmo mendax
libellous fāmōsus
liberal lībĕrālis, largus
liberality lībĕrālĭtas, *f*, largĭtas, *f*
liberate *v.t*, lībĕro (1)
liberation lībĕrātĭo, *f*
liberty lībertas, *f*
librarian bĭblĭŏthēcārĭus, *m*
library bĭblĭŏthēca, *f*
licence lĭcentĭa, *f*; **(permission)**, pŏtestas, *f*
licentious dissŏlūtus
lick *v.t*, lambo (3)
lid ŏpercŭlum, *n*
lie *nn*, mendācĭum, *n*
lie *v.i*, **(tell a —)**, mentĭor (4 *dep*)
lie *v.i*, iăcĕo (2); **(rest)**, cŭbo (1); **(— ill)**, iăcĕo (2); **(— in wait)**, insĭdĭor (1 *dep*)

lieutenant lēgātus, *m*
life vīta, *f*, ănĭma, *f*; **(vivacity)**, vĭgor, *m*; **(— blood)**, sanguis, *m*
lifeless exănĭmis, exanguis
lifelike *use* sĭmĭlis **(similar)**
lifetime aetas, *f*
lift *v.t*, tollo (3)
ligament lĭgāmentum, *n*
light *nn*, lux, *f*, lūmen, *n*; **(to bring to —)**, in mĕdĭum prōfĕro (*irreg*)
light *adj* **(not dark)**, illustris; **(in weight)**, lĕvis; **(— armed)**, expĕdītus; **(trivial, of opinions, etc.)**, lĕvis
light *v.t*, **(illuminate)**, illustro (1); **(kindle)**, accendo (3)
lighten *v.t*, **(burden, etc.)**, lĕvo (1); *v.i*, **(of lightning)**, fulgĕo (2)
lighthouse phărus, *f*
lightly *adv*, lĕvĭter
lightning fulmen, *n*
like *v.t*, ămo (1)
like *adj*, sĭmĭlis (*with genit. or dat*), par (*with dat*)
like *adv*, sĭmĭlĭter; **(just as)**, sīcut
likelihood sĭmĭlĭtūdo, (*f*), vĕri
likely sĭmĭlis vĕri; *often use future participle, e.g. likely to come*, venturus
liken *v.t*, compăro (1)
likeness sĭmĭlĭtūdo (1)
likewise *adv*, ĭtem
liking *nn*, ămor, *m*, lĭbīdo, *f*
lily līlĭum, *n*
limb membrum, *n*, artus, *m. pl*
lime calx, *f*; **(tree)**, tĭlĭa, *f*
limit *nn*, fīnis, *m*, termĭnus, *m*
limit *v.t*, fīnĭo (4)
limitation fīnis, *m*
limited (small) parvus
limitless infīnĭtus
limp *adj*, **(slack)**, rēmissus
limp *v.i*, claudĭco (1)
limping *adj*, claudus
limpid limpĭdus
linden tree tĭlĭa, *f*
line līnĕa, *f*; **(boundary —)**, fīnis, *m*; **(of poetry)**, versus, *m*; **(of battle)**, ăcĭes, *f*; **(front —)**, prīma ăcĭes, *f*; **(second —)**, princĭpes, *m. pl*; **(third —)**, trĭārĭi, *m. pl*; **(— of march)**, agmen, *n*

line *v.t*, **(put in —)**, instrŭo (3)
lineage stirps, *f*, gĕnus, *n*
linen *nn*, lintĕum, *n*; *adj*, lintĕus
linger *v.i*, mŏror (1 *dep*); cunctor
(1 *dep*)
lingering *nn*, mŏra, *f*
link *nn*, **(of chain)**, ānŭlus, *m*
link *v.t*, coniungo (3)
lint līnāmentum, *n*
lintel līmen sŭpĕrum, *n*
lion lĕo, *m*; **(lioness)**, lĕaena
lip lābrum, *n*
liquefy *v.t*, līquĕfăcĭo (3)
liquid *nn*, līquor, *m*
liquid *adj*, līquĭdus
liquidate *v.t*, solvo (3)
liquor līquor, *m*
lisping *adj*, blaesus
list tăbŭla, *f*
listen (to) *v.t*, audĭo (4)
listener auscultātor, *m*
listless languĭdus
listlessness languor, *m*
literal *use*, prŏprĭus **(its own)**
literally *adv. phr*, ad verbum
literary (person) littĕrātus
literature littĕrae, *f. pl*
lithe flexĭbĭlis, ăgĭlis
litigation līs, *f*
litter (of straw, etc.) strāmentum,
n; **(sedan)**, lectīca, *f*; **(of young)**,
fētus, *m*
little *adj*, parvus, exĭgŭus; **(for a
— while)**, *adv*, părumper,
paulisper
little *adv*, paulum
little *nn*, paulum, *n*, nonnīhil, *n*;
(too little), părum, *n*; *with
comparatives*, paulo; *e.g.* **a little
bigger**, paulo māior
littleness exĭgŭĭtas, *f*
live *v.i*, vīvo (3); **(— in or at)**,
hăbĭto (1), incŏlo (3); **(— on)**,
vescor (3 *dep*) *(with abl)*; **(—
one's life, etc.)**, vītam ăgo (3)
live *adj*, vīvus
livelihood victus, *m*
liveliness ălăcrītas, *f*
lively *adj*, ălăcer
liver iĕcur, *n*
livery vestītus, *m*
livid līvĭdus
living *adj*, vīvus

lizard lăcerta, *f*
load ŏnus, *n*
load *v.t*, ŏnĕro (1)
loaded ŏnustus
loaf pănis, *m*
loam lŭtum, *n*
loan mūtŭum, *n, or use adj*,
mūtuus **(borrowed, lent)**
loathe *v.t*, ōdi *(defect)*
loathing *nn*, ŏdĭum, *n*
loathesome tēter
lobby vestībŭlum, *n*
local *use genit.* of lŏcus **(place)**
locality lŏcus, *m*
lock (bolt) claustra, *n. pl*; **(hair)**,
crīnis, *m*
lock *v.t*, obsĕro (1)
locker capsa, *f*, armārĭum, *n*
locust lŏcusta, *f*
lodge *v.i*, dēversor (1 *dep*); **(stick
fast)**, adhaerĕo (2) fixus; *v.t*
(accommodate temporarily),
excĭpĭo (3)
lodger inquĭlīnus, *m*
lodgings dēversōrĭum, *n*
loft cēnācŭlum, *n*
loftiness altītūdo, *f*
lofty celsus, altus
log tignum, *n*
logic dĭălectĭca, *f*
logical dĭălectĭcus
loin lumbus, *m*
loiter *v.i*, cesso (1), cunctor (1
dep)
loiterer cessātor, *m*
loneliness sōlĭtūdo, *f*
lonely *adj*, sōlus
long *adj*, longus *(with acc. of
extent of length)*, *e.g.* **three feet
long**, longus tres pĕdes; **(a —
way)**, *adv*, prŏcul, longē; **(of time)**,
dĭūtĭnus, dĭūturnus; **(how — ?)**,
quam dĭū? **(for a — time)**, *adv*,
dĭū
long *adv*, **(time)**, dĭū
long for *v.t*, dēsīdĕro (1), cŭpĭo
(3)
longevity vīvācĭtas, *f*
longing *nn*, dēsīdĕrĭum, *n*
long-suffering *adj*, pătĭens
look at *v.t*, aspĭcĭo (3); **(— back)**,
rēspĭcĭo (3); **(— down (upon))**,
dēspĭcĭo (3); **(— for)**, quaero (3);

(— round), circumspĭcĭo (3); *v.i*
(— towards), specto (1); **(seem)**,
vĭdĕor (2 *pass*)
look   *nn*, aspectus, *m*;
(appearance), spěcĭes, *f*;
(expression), vultus, *m*
looking glass   spěcŭlum, *n*
loom   tēla, *f*
loop (winding)   flexus, *m*
loophole   fěnestra, *f*
loose   *adj*, laxus; **(at liberty)**,
sŏlūtus; **(hair)**, passus, prōmissus;
(dissolute), dissŏlūtus
loose   *v.t*, laxo (1), solvo (3)
loosely   *adv*, sŏlūtē
loot   *nn*, praeda, *f*
loot   *v.t*, praedor (1 *dep*)
lop off   *v.t*, ampŭto (1)
loquacious   lŏquax
loquacity   lŏquācĭtas, *f*
lord   dŏmĭnus, *m*
lordly   *adv*, rēgālis, sŭperbus
lordship (supreme power)
impěrĭum, *n*
lore   doctrīna, *f*
lose   *v.t*, āmitto (3), perdo (3); **(—
heart)**, ănĭmo dēfĭcĭo (3)
loss (act of losing)   āmissĭo, *f*; **(the
loss itself)**, damnum, *n*,
dētrīmentum, *n*; **(to be at a —)**,
v.i, haerĕo (2)
lost   *(adj)* āmissus, perdĭtus
lot (chance)   sors, *f*; **(to draw — s)**,
sortĭor (4 *dep*); **(much)**, multum,
n
loth (unwilling)   invītus
lottery   sortītĭo, *f*
loud   clārus, magnus
loudness   magnĭtūdo, *f*
lounge   *v.i*, **(recline)**, rěcŭbo (1)
louse   pědĭcŭlus, *m*
lousy   pědĭcŭlōsus
lout   hŏmo agrestis
love   *nn*, ămor, *m*
love   *v.t*, ămo (1), dīlĭgo (3)
loveliness   věnustas, *f*
lovely   věnustus
lover   ămātor, *m*, ămans, *c*
loving   *adj*, ămans
low   hŭmĭlis; **(sounds)**; grăvis; **(—
born)**, hŭmĭli lŏco nātus; **(price)**,
vīlis; **(conduct, etc.)**, sordĭdus; **(in
spirits)**, *adv. phr*, ănĭmo dēmisso

low   *v.i*, mūgĭo (4)
lower   *comp. adj*, infěrĭor
lower   *v.t*, dēmitto (3); **(—
oneself)**, sē ăbĭcěre (3 *reflex*)
lowering   mĭnax
lowest   infĭmus
lowing   mūgītus, *m*
lowlands   lŏca, plāna, *n. pl*
lowness, lowliness   hŭmĭlĭtas, *f*
lowly   hŭmĭlis, obscūrus
loyal   fĭdēlis
loyalty   fĭdes, *f*
lozenge   pastillus, *m*
lubricate   *v.t*, ungo (3)
lucid   lūcĭdus
lucidity   perspĭcŭĭtas, *f*
luck   fortūna, *f*, fors, *f*; **(good —)**,
fēlīcĭtas, *f*; **(bad —)**, infēlīcĭtas
luckily   *adv*, fēlīcĭter
luckless   infēlix
lucky   fēlix, fortūnātus
lucrative   quaestŭōsus
ludicrous   rīdĭcŭlus
lug   *v.t*, trăho (3)
luggage   impědīmenta, *n. pl*
lugubrious   lūgŭbris
lukewarm   těpĭdus
lull   *v.t*, sēdo (1); *v.i*, **(of wind)**,
sēdor (1 *pass*)
lull   *nn, use vb*. intermitto (3)
lumber   scrūta, *n. pl*
luminary   lūmen, *n*
luminous   illustrus, lūcĭdus
lump   massa, *f*
lunacy   insānĭa, *f*, ălĭēnātĭo, *f*
lunar   lūnāris
lunatic   hŏmo insānus
lunch   *nn*, prandĭum, *n*
lunch   *v.i*, prandĕo (2)
lung   pulmo, *m*
lurch   *v.i*, ăgĭtor (1 *pass*) **(leave in
the —)**, rělinquo (3)
lure   *nn*, illex, *c*, illěcěbrae, *f. pl*
lure   *v.t*, allĭcĭo (3)
lurid   lūrĭdus
lurk   *v.i*, lătěo (2)
lurking in wait   *use* insĭdĭor (1
dep) **(lie in ambush)**
luscious   dulcis
lust   *nn*, lĭbīdo, *f*
lust after   *v.t*, concŭpisco (3)
lustful   lĭbīdĭnōsus
lustiness   vĭgor, *m*

lustre splendor, *m*
lusty vălĭdus
lute cĭthăra, *f*
luxuriance luxŭrĭa, *f*
luxuriant luxŭrĭōsus
luxurious luxŭrĭōsus, lautus
luxury luxus, *m*, luxŭrĭa, *f*
lying *adj*, **(telling lies)**, mendax
lynx lynx, *c*
lyre cĭthăra, *f*, fĭdes, *f. pl*
lyrical lўrĭcus

M

macebearer lictor, *m*
macerate *v.t*, mācĕro (1)
machination dŏlus, *m*
machine māchĭna, *f*
machinery māchĭnātĭo, *f*
mackerel scomber, *m*
mad insānus, vēcors, fŭrĭōsus; **(to be —)**, *v.i*, fŭro (3)
madden *v.t*, mentem ălĭēno (1) *(with dat)*; **(excite)**, accendo (3)
maddening *adj*, fŭrĭōsus
madman hŏmo vēcors
madness insānĭa, *f*
magazine horrĕum, *n*; **(arsenal)**, armāmentārĭum, *n*
maggot vermĭcŭlus, *m*
magic *adj*, măgĭcus
magic *nn*, ars măgĭca, *f*
magician măgus, *m*
magistracy măgistrātus, *m*
magistrate măgistrātus, *m*
magnanimity magnănĭmĭtas, *f*
magnanimous magnănĭmus
magnet lăpis magnes, *m*
magnetic magnētĭcus
magnificence magnĭfĭcentĭa, *f*
magnificent magnĭfĭcus, splendĭdus
magnify *v.t*, amplĭfĭco (1), exaggĕro (1)
magnitude magnĭtūdo, *f*
magpie pīca, *f*
maid, maiden virgo, *f*; **(servant)**, ancilla, *f*
maiden *adj*, virgĭnālis
mail (letters) littĕrae, *f. pl*, ĕpistŏlae, *f. pl*; **(armour)**, lōrĭca, *f*
maim *v.t*, mŭtĭlo (1)
main *adj*, prīmus, praecĭpŭus

mainland contĭnens terra, *f*
maintain *v.t*, servo (1), sustĭnĕo (2); **(with food, etc.)**, ălo (3); **(by argument)**, affirmo (1)
maintenance *use vb.* servo (1) **(to maintain)**
majestic augustus
majesty māiestas, *f*
major *nn*, **(officer)**, praefectus, *m*
major *adj*, māior
majority māior pars, *f*
make *v.t*, făcĭo (3), effĭcĭo (3), fingo (3), reddo (3); **(compel)**, cōgo (3); **(appoint)**, crĕo (1); **(— for, seek)**, pĕto (3); **(— haste)**, *v.i*, festīno (1), accĕlĕro (1); **(— good)**, *v.t*, rĕpăro (1), sarcĭo (1); **(— ready)**, praepăro (1); **(— up, a total, etc.)**, explĕo (2); **(— use of)**, ūtor (3 *dep*) *(with abl)*
maker făbrĭcātor, *m*
maladministration măla admĭnistrātĭo, *f*
malady morbus, *m*
malcontent cŭpĭdus nŏvārum rērum **(eager for innovations)**
male *adj*, mascŭlus, mās
male *nn*, mās, *m*
malediction dīrae, *f. pl*, **(curses)**
malefactor hŏmo mălĕfĭcus, nŏcens
malevolence mălĕvŏlentĭa, *f*
malevolent mălĕvŏlus
malice mălĕvŏlentĭa, *f*; **(envy)**, invĭdĭa, *f*
malicious mălĕvŏlus
malignant mălĕvŏlus
maligner obtrectātor, *m*
malignity mălĕvŏlentĭa, *f*
malleable ductĭlis
mallet mallĕus, *m*
maltreat *v.t*, vĕxo (1)
maltreatment vexātĭo, *f*
man (human being) hŏmo, *c*; **(opp. to woman, child)**, vĭr, *m*; **(mankind)**, hŏmĭnes, *c. pl*; **(chess, etc.)**, latruncŭlus, *m*; **(fighting —)**, mīles, *c*
man *v.t*, **(ships, etc.)**, complĕo (2)
man-of-war (ship) nāvis longa, *f*
manacle *nn*, mănĭcae, *f. pl*, vincŭla, *n. pl*
manage *v.t*, admĭnistro (1), cūro (1), gĕro (3)

manageable   tractābĭlis, hăbĭlis
management   cŭra, *f*,
  admĭnistrātĭo, *f*
manager   prōcūrātor, *m*,
  admĭnistrātor, *m*
mandate   impěrātum, *n*,
  mandātum, *n*
mane (of horse)   iŭba, *f*
manful   vĭrīlis
manger   praesēpe; *n*
mangle   *v.t*, lăcěro (1), lănĭo (1)
mangled   truncus
mangy   scăber
manhood   pūbertas, *f*, tŏga vĭrīlis,
  f (manly dress)
mania   insānĭa, *f*
maniac   hŏmo vēcors, āmens
manifest   *v.t*, ostendo (3), ăpěrĭo
  (4)
manifest   *adj*, mănĭfestus, ăpertus
manifestation   ostentātĭo, *f, or use*
  vbs. above
manifold   multĭplex
maniple (of a legion)   mănĭpŭlus,
  m
manipulate   *v.t*, tracto (1)
mankind   hŏmĭnes, *c. pl*
manliness   virtus, *f*
manly   vĭrīlis
manner (way)   mŏdus, *m*, rătĭo, *f*;
  (custom), mos, *m*; (type), gěnus,
  n; (good manners), děcōrum, *n*
mannerism   gestus prŏprĭus
manoeuvre (military)   dēcursus, *m*;
  (trick), dŏlus, *m*
manoeuvre   *v.i*, dēcurro (3)
manor   praedĭum, *n*
manservant   servus, *m*
mansion   dŏmus magna, *f*
manslaughter   hŏmĭcĭdĭum, *n*
mantle   palla, *f*, lăcerna, *f*
manual   *adj, use* mănus (hand)
manual   *nn*, (book), lĭbellus, *m*
manufacture   *nn*, făbrica, *f*
manufacture   *v.t*, făbrĭcor (1 *dep*)
manufacturer   făbrĭcātor, *m*
manumission   mănūmissĭo, *f*
manure   stercus, *n*
manuscript   lĭber, *m*
many   *adj*, multi (*pl*); (very —),
  plūrĭmi; (a good —), plērīque,
  complūres; (as — as), tŏt ...
  quŏt; (how — ?), quŏt?; (so —),
  tŏt; (— times), *adv*, saepě

map   tăbŭla, *f*
map (to — out)   *v.t*, dēsigno (1)
maple   ăcer, *n*; *adj*, ăcernus
mar   *v.t*, dēformo (1)
marauder   praedātor, *m*
marble   marmor, *n*; *adj*,
  marmŏrěus
March   Martĭus (mensis)
march   *nn*, ĭter, *n*; (forced —),
  magnum ĭter; (on the —), *adv.*
  phr, in ĭtĭněre
march   *v.i*, ĭter făcĭo (3); (—
  quickly), contendo (3); (advance),
  prōgrědĭor (3 *dep*)
mare   ěqua, *f*
margin   margo, *m*, *f*
marine   *nn*, mīles classĭcus, *m*
marine   *adj*, mărīnus
mariner   nauta, *m*
maritime   mărĭtĭmus
mark   nŏta, *f*, signum, *n*,
  vestīgĭum, *n*; (characteristic), *use*
  genit. case of nn. with esse; *e.g.* it
  is the — of a wise man, est
  săpĭentis ...
mark   *v.t*, nŏto (1); (indicate),
  dēsigno (1); (notice, observe),
  ănĭmădverto (3)
market   fŏrum, *n*, măcellum, *n*;
  (cattle —), fŏrum bŏărĭum, *n*
market   *v.t*, nundĭnor (1 *dep*)
market-day   nundĭnae, *f. pl*, (ninth
  day)
marketing   *nn, use vb.* vendo (3)
  (sell)
marketplace   fŏrum, *n*
marriage   conĭŭgĭum, *n*; (—
  feast), nuptĭae, *f. pl*; (—
  contract), pactĭo nuptĭālis, *f*
marriageable   nūbĭlis
marrow   mědulla, *f*
marry   *v.t*, (— a woman), dūco
  (3); (— a man), nūbo (3) (*with*
  dat)
marsh   pălus, *f*
marshal   appārĭtor, *m*
marshal   *v.t*, (troops, etc.),
  dispōno (3)
marshy   păluster
martial   bellĭcōsus; (court —),
  castrense iūdĭcĭum, *n*
martyr   martyr, *c*

martyrdom martўrĭum, *n*
marvel (miracle, etc.) mīrācŭlum, *n*
marvel at *v.t* mīror (1 *dep*)
marvellous mīrus, mīrābĭlis
masculine vĭrīlis
mash *nn*, farrāgo, *f*
mash *v.t* contundo (3)
mask *nn*, persōna, *f*; **(disguise)**, intĕgūmentum, *n*
mask *v.t*, **(oneself)**, persōnam indŭo (3); **(disguise)**, dissĭmŭlo (1)
mason structor, *m*
masonry structūra, *f*
mass mōles, *f*; **(of people)**, multĭtūdo, *f*
mass *v.t*, cŭmŭlo (1), ăcervo (1)
massacre *nn*, caedes, *f*
massacre *v.t*, trŭcīdo (1), caedo (3)
massive sŏlĭdus; **(huge)**, ingens
mast mālus, *m*
master dŏmĭnus, *m*; **(— of the household)**, păterfămĭlĭas, *m*; **(school —)**, măgister, *m*; **(skilled in …)**, *use adj*, pĕrītus
master *v.t*, **(subdue)**, dŏmo (1); **(knowledge, etc.)**, bĕne scĭo (4), disco (3)
masterful impĕrĭōsus
masterly *adj*, bŏnus; **(plan, etc.)**, callĭdus
masterpiece ŏpus summā laude dignum **(work worthy of the highest praise)**
masterly (rule) dŏmĭnātus, *m*
masticate *v.t*, mandūco (1)
mastiff cănis Mŏlussus **(Molossian hound)**
mat stŏrĕa, *f*
mat *v.t*, implĭco (1)
match (contest) certāmen, *n*; **(equal)**, *adj*, pār; **(marriage —)**, nuptĭae, *f. pl*
match *v.t*, **(equal)**, aequo (1)
matchless ēgrĕgĭus
matching *adj*, **(equal)** pār
mate sŏcĭus, *m*; **(— in marriage)**, conĭunx, *m*, *f*.
mate *v.i*, conĭungor (3 *pass*)
material *nn*, mātĕrĭa, *f*
material *adj*, corpŏrĕus

materially *adv*, **(much)**, multum
maternal maternus
maternity māter, *f*, **(mother)**
mathematician măthēmătĭcus, *m*
mathematics măthēmătĭca, *f*
matter (substance) corpus, *n*, mātĕrĭa, *f*; **(affair)**, res, *f*; **(what is the — ?)**, quid est?; **(it matters, it is important)**, rēfert (*v. impers*)
mattress culcĭta, *f*
mature *adj*, mātūrus, ădultus
mature *v.t*, mātūro (1); *v.i*, mātūresco (3)
maturity mātūrĭtas, *f*
maudlin ĭneptus
maul *v.t*, mulco (1), lănĭo (1)
maw inglŭvĭes, *f*
maxim praeceptum, *n*
maximum *use adj*, maxĭmus **(biggest)**
May Māius (mensis)
may *v. auxiliary*, **(having permission to)**, lĭcet (2 *impers. with dat. of person allowed*), e.g. **you may go**, lĭcet tĭbĭ īre; **(having ability to)**, possum (*irreg*); *often expressed by subjunctive mood of verb*
maybe (perhaps) *adv*, fortassĕ
May Day Kălendae Māiae **(first day of May)**
mayor praefectus, *m*
maze *nn*, lăbўrinthus, *m*
meadow prātum, *n*
meagre măcer, iēiūnus
meagreness iēiūnĭtas, *f*
meal (flour) fărīna, *f*; **(food)**, cĭbus, *m*
mean *nn*, mŏdus, *m*
mean *adj*, **(middle, average)**, mĕdĭus; **(of low rank)**, hŭmĭlis; **(miserly)**, sordĭdus
mean *v.t*, signĭfĭco (1); **(intend)**, in ănĭmo hăbĕo (2)
meander *v.i*, **(of a river)**, sĭnŭōso cursu flŭo (3) **(flow on a winding course)**
meaning *nn*, signĭfĭcātĭo, *f*
meanness hŭmĭlĭtas, *f*; **(of disposition)**, sordes, *f. pl*
means (method) mŏdus, *m*; **(opportunity)**, făcultas, *f*; **(resources)**, ŏpes, *f. pl*; **(by no**

—), *adv*, haudquāquam, nullo mŏdo

meantime, meanwhile (in the —) *adv*, intěrěā, intěrim

measure mensūra, *f*, mŏdus, *m*; **(plan)**, consĭlĭum, *n*; **(music)**, mŏdi, *m. pl*

measure *v.t*, mētĭor (4 *dep*)

measureless immensus

meat căro, *f*

mechanic făber, *m*, ŏpĭfex, *c*

mechanical māchĭnālis

mechanism māchĭnātĭo, *f*

medal, medallion phălěrae, arum, *f. pl*

meddle *v.i*, sē interpōněre (3 *reflex*)

mediate *v.i*, sē interpōněre (3 *reflex*), intervěnĭo (4)

mediator dēprěcātor, *m*

medical mědĭcus

medicine (art of —) ars mědĭcīna, *f*; **(the remedy itself)**, mědĭcāmentum, *n*

mediocre mědĭŏcris

mediocrity mědĭŏcrĭtas, *f*

meditate *v.t*, cōgĭto (1)

Mediterranean Sea mărě nostrum, *n*, **(our sea)**

medium *use adj*, mědĭus **(middle)**; **(through the — of)** per

medley farrāgo, *f*

meek mītis

meekness ănĭmus summissus, *m*

meet *v.t*, obvĭam fĭo (*irreg*) (*with dat*); **(go to —, encounter)**, obvĭam ĕo (*irreg*) (*with dat*); *v.i*, convěnĭo (4); concurro (3)

meeting *nn*, conventus, *m*

melancholy *nn*, tristĭtĭa, *f*

melancholy *adj*, tristis

mellow mītis

mellow *v.i*, mātūresco (3)

melodious cănōrus

melody mělos, *n*

melon mēlo, *m*

melt *v.t*, lĭquěfăcĭo (3); **(people, etc.)**, mŏvěo (2); *v.i*, lĭquesco (3)

member (of a society) sŏcĭus, *m*; **(of the body)**, membrum, *n*

membrane membrāna, *f*

memoirs commentārii, *m. pl*

memorable mĕmŏrābĭlis

memorandum lĭbellus mĕmŏrĭālis

memorial mŏnŭmentum, *n*

memory mĕmŏrĭa, *f*

menace mĭnae, *f. pl*

menace *v.t*, mĭnor (1 *dep*)

menacing *adj*, mĭnax

mend *v.t*, rěfĭcĭo (3), sarcĭo (4); *v.i*, **(in health)**, mělŏr fĭo (*irreg*) **(get better)**

mendacious mendax

mendicant mendīcus, *m*

menial *adj*, servīlis

mensuration rătĭo (*f*) mētĭendi **(system of measuring)**

mental *use genitive of* mens, *or* ănĭmus **(mind)**

mention *nn*, mentĭo, *f*

mention *v.t*, mĕmŏro (1), dīco (3)

mercantile mercātōrum **(of merchants)**

mercenary *adj*, mercēnārĭus

merchandise merx, *f*

merchant mercātor, *m*

merchant-ship nāvis ŏněrĭa, *f*

merciful mĭsěrĭcors

merciless crūdēlis, inclēmens

mercury (quick silver) argentum vīvum, *n*; **(god)**, Mercŭrĭus

mercy mĭsěrĭcordĭa, *f*

mere *adj*, sōlus, *or use emphathic pron*, ipse

merely *adv*, tantummŏdo

merge *v.i*, miscěor (2 *pass*)

meridian circŭlus měrĭdĭānus, *m*

meridian *adj*, měrĭdĭānus

merit *nn*, měrĭtum, *n*

merit *v.i*, měrěor (2 *dep*)

meritorious dignus laude **(worthy of praise)**

merriment hĭlărĭtas, *f*

merry hĭlăris

mesh măcŭla, *f*

mess (confused state) turba, *f*; **(dirt)**, squālor, *m*

message nuntĭus, *m*

messenger nuntĭus, *m*

metal mětallum, *n*

metallic mětallĭcus

metamorphosis *use vb*, transformo (1) **(to change in shape)**

metaphor translātĭo, *f*

metaphorical translātus

meteor fax, *f*
method rătĭo, *f*
methodically ex ordĭne, *or use adv phr*, rătĭōne et vĭā **(by reckoning and method)**
metre nŭmĕrus, *m*
metrical mĕtrĭcus
metropolis căpŭt, *n*
mettle fĕrōcĭtas, *f*
mettlesome ănĭmōsus, fĕrox
mew *v.i*, **(cat)**, quĕror (3 *dep*)
mica phengītes, *m*
mid *adj*, mĕdĭus
midday *nn*, mĕrīdĭes, *m*
midday *adj*, mĕrīdĭānus
middle *adj*, mĕdĭus
middle *nn, use* mĕdĭus *in agreement with noun, e.g.* **the middle of the river**, mĕdĭus flŭvĭus
middling *adj*, mĕdĭŏcris
midnight mĕdĭa nox, *f*
midst *nn, use adj*, mĕdĭus
midsummer mĕdĭa aestas, *f*
midwife obstĕtrix, *f*
might (power) vīs, *f*
mighty fortis, vălĭdus, magnus
migrate *v.t*, ăbĕo (4)
migratory bird advĕna ăvis, *f*
mild mītis, clēmens, lēvis
mildew rōbīgo, *f*
mildness lēnĭtas, *f*
mile mille passus (*or* passŭum) **(a thousand paces)**
milestone mīlĭārĭium, *n*
military adj, mīlĭtāris; **(— service)**, stīpendĭa, *n. pl*
militate against *v.t*, făcĭo (3) contrā (*with acc*)
milk lac, *n*
milk *v.t*, mulgĕo (2)
milky lactĕus
mill mŏla, *f*, pistrīnum, *n*
miller mŏlĭtor, *m*
million dĕcĭes centēna mīlĭa
millstone mŏla, *f*
mimic *v.t*, ĭmĭtor (1 *dep*)
mince *v.t*, concīdo (3)
mincemeat mĭnūtal, *n*
mind ănĭmus, *m*, mens, *f*; **(intellect)**, ingĕnĭum, *n*; **(to make up one's —)** constĭtŭo (3)
mind *v.t*, **(I — my own business)**, nĕgōtĭum mĕum ăgo (3)

mindful mĕmor (*with genit*)
mine *adj*, mĕus
mine *nn*, mĕtallum, *n*, cŭnīcŭlus, *m*
mine *v.i*, fŏdĭo (3)
miner fŏdĭens, *m*
mineral *nn*, mĕtallum, *n*
mineral *adj*, mĕtallĭcus
mingle *v.i*, sē miscēre (2 *reflex*)
miniature *nn*, parva tăbella, *f*
minimum *adj*, mĭnĭmus **(smallest)**
minister mĭnister, *m*, admĭnister, *m*
ministry (office) mĭnĭstĕrĭum, *n*
minor *nn*, pūpillus, *m*
minority mĭnor pars, *f*
minstrel tībīcen văgus **(wandering —)**
mint (plant) menta, *f*; **(coinage)**, mŏnēta, *f*
mint *v.t*, cūdo (3)
minute *adj*, exĭgŭus, mĭnūtus
minute *nn*, **(of time)**, mōmentum **(n)** tempŏris
miracle mīrācŭlum, *n*
miraculous mīrus
mire lŭtum, *n*
mirror spĕcŭlum, *n*
mirth hĭlărĭtas, *f*
mirthful hĭlăris
misadventure cāsus, *m*
misanthropy *use phr.* ŏdĭum, **(n)** ergā hŏmĭnes **(hatred towards mankind)**
misapply *v.t*, ăbūtor (3 *dep with abl*)
misbehave *v.i*, mălĕ sē gĕrĕre (3 *reflex*)
miscalculate *v.i*, fallor (3 *pass*), erro (1)
miscalculation error, *m*
miscarriage (childbirth) ăbortus, *m*; **(— of justice)** error, **(m)** iūdĭcum
miscarry *v.i*, **(child)**, ăbortum făcĭo (3); **(fail)** frustrā *or* irrĭtum ēvĕnĭo (4)
miscellaneous vărĭus
mischief (injury, wrong) mălĕfĭcĭum, *n*
mischievous mălĕfĭcus; **(playful)**, lascīvus
misconduct *nn*, dēlictum, *n*
miscreant hŏmŏ scĕlestus
misdeed dēlictum, *n*

misdemeanour dēlictum, *n*, peccātaum, *n*

miser hŏmŏ ăvārus

miserable mĭser, infēlix

miserliness ăvārĭtĭa, *f*

miserly *adj*, ăvārus, sordĭdus

misery mĭsĕrĭa, *f*, angor, *m*

misfortune rēs adversae, *f. pl*

misgiving praesāgĭum, *n*

misgovern *v.t*, mălĕ rĕgo (3)

misguided (deceived) dēceptus

misinterpret *v.t*, mălĕ interprĕtor (1 *dep*)

misjudge *v.t*, mălĕ iūdĭco (1)

mislay *v.t*, ămitto (3)

mislead *v.t*, dēpĭcĭo (3)

misplace *v.t*, ălĭēno lŏco pōno (3) **(put in an unsuitable place)**

misprint *nn*, mendum, *n*

misrepresent *v.t*, verto (3); **(disparage)**, obtrecto (1)

misrule *v.t*, mălĕ rĕgo (3)

miss *v.i*, **(fail to hit or meet)**, ăberro (1), frustrā mittor (3 *pass*); *v.t*, **(want)**, dēsīdĕro (1)

misshapen dēformis

missile tēlum, *n*

mission (embassy) lēgātĭo, *f*; **(task)**, ŏpus, *n*

misspend *v.t*, perdo (3)

mist nĕbŭla, *f*

mistake error, *m*; **(make a —)**, *v.i*, erro (1)

mistake *v.t*, **(for someone else)** crēdĕre ălĭum esse

mistaken falsus; **(to be —)**, *v.i*, erro (1)

mistletoe viscum, *n*

mistress (of the house, etc.) dŏmĭna, *f*; **(sweetheart)**, pŭella, *f*, concŭbīna, *f*

mistrust *v.t*, diffīdo (3 *semi-dep. with dat*)

misty nĕbŭlōsus

misunderstand *v.t*, haud rectē, *or* mălĕ, intellĕgo (3)

misunderstanding error, *m*

misuse *v.t*, ăbūtor (3 *dep. with abl*)

mitigate *v.t*, mītĭgo (1), lēnĭo (4)

mitigation mītĭgātĭo, *f*

mittens mănĭcae, *f. pl*

mix *v.t*, miscĕo (2); **(— up together)**, confundo (3); *v.i*, miscĕor (2 *pass*)

mixed *adj*, mixtus; **(indiscriminate)**, prōmiscŭus

mixture mixtūra, *f*

moan *nn*, gĕmĭtus, *m*

moan *v.i*, gĕmo (3)

moat fossa, *f*

mob turba, *f*, vulgus, *m*

mobile mōbĭlis

mock *v.t*, illūdo (3) **(with dat)**; dērīdĕo (2)

mockery irrīsus, *m*, lūdĭbrĭum, *n*

mode mŏdus, *m*, rătĭo, *f*

model exemplum, *n*, exemplar, *n*

model *v.t*, fingo (3)

moderate mŏdĕrātus, mŏdĭcus

moderate *v.t*, tempĕro (1)

moderation mŏdus, *m*, mŏdĕrātĭo, *f*

modern rĕcens, nŏvus

modest vĕrēcundus

modesty vĕrēcundĭa, *f*, pŭdor, *m*

modify *v.t*, immūto (1)

modulate *v.t*, flecto (3)

moist hūmĭdus

moisten *v.t*, hūmecto (1)

moisture hūmor, *m*

molar dens gĕnŭīnus

mole (animal) talpa, *f*; **(dam, etc.)**, mōles, *f*; **(on the body)**, naevus, *m*

molest *v.t*, vexo (1), sollĭcĭto (1)

mollify *v.t*, mollĭo (4)

molten lĭquĕfactus

moment punctum, *(n)* tempŏris; **(in a —)**, *adv*, stătim; **(importance)**, mōmentum, *n*

momentary brĕvis

momentous magni mōmenti **(of great importance)**

momentum impĕtus, *m*

monarch rex, *m*

monarch regnum, *n*

monastery mŏnastērĭum, *n*

money pĕcūnĭa, *f*; **(coin)**, nummus, *m*; **(profit)**, quaestus, *m*

moneybag fiscus, *m*

moneyed pĕcūnĭōsus

moneylender faenĕrātor, *m*

moneymaking quaestus, *m*

mongrel *nn*, hibrĭda, *c*

monkey sīmĭa, *f*

monopolize *v.i*, use *phr. with* sōlus **(alone)**, *and* hăbĕo (2)

monopoly mŏnŏpōlĭum, *n*
monotonous *use phr. with* mŏlestus **(laboured)**, *or* sĭmĭlis **(similar)**
monster monstrum, *n*
monstrous (huge) immuanis; **(shocking)**, infandus
month mensis, *m*
monthly *adj*, menstrŭus
monument mŏnŭmentum, *n*
mood affectĭo (*f*) ănĭmi
moody mōrōsus
moon lūna, *f*
moonlight lūmen (*n*) lūnae; **(by —)**, ad lūnam
moonlit *adj*, illustris lūnā **(lighted up by the moon)**
moor lŏca dēserta, *n. pl*, **(a lonely place)**
moor *v.t*, **(ship, etc.)**, rĕlĭgo (1)
moorhen fūlĭca, *f*
moot (it is a — point) nondum convĕnit … **(it is not yet decided …)**
mop *nn*, pēnĭcŭlus, *m*
mop *v.t*, dētergĕo (2)
moral *adj*, mōrālis; **(of good character)**, hŏnestus
moral *nn*, **(of a story)**, *use phr. wih* sĭgnĭfĭco (1) **(to indicate)**, *e.g.* haec fābŭla sĭgnĭfĭcat … **(this story indicates …)**
morale ănĭmus, *m*
morals, morality mōres, *m. pl*
moralize *v.i*, dē mōrĭbus dissĕro (3) **(discuss conduct)**
morbid aeger, aegrōtus
more *nn*, plus, *n* (*with genit*), *e.g.* **more corn**, plus frūmenti; (*adv. before adjs. or advs*) *use comparative of adj. or adv, e.g.* **more quickly**, cĕlĕrĭus; *otherwise use* măgis **(to a higher degree)** *or* pŏtĭus; **(in addition)**, amplĭus
moreover *adv*, praetĕrĕā
moribund mŏrĭbundus
morning *nn*, tempus mātūtīnum, *n*; **(in the —)**, *adv*, mānĕ
morning *adj*, mātūtīnus
morose tristis
morrow (following day) postĕrus dĭes, *m*
morsel offa, *f*
mortal *adj*, mortālis; **(causing death)**, mortĭfer
mortality mortālĭtas, *f*
mortar mortārĭum, *n*
mortgage pignus, *n*
mortgage *v.t*, oblĭgo (1)
mortification offensĭo, *f*
mortify *v.t*, **(vex)** offendo (3)
mosaic *adj*, tessellātus
mosquito cūlex, *m*
moss muscus, *m*
mossy muscōsus
most *adj*, plūrĭmus *or* plūrĭmum, *n, with genit, of noun, e.g.* **most importance**, plūrĭmum grăvĭtātis; **(for the — part)**, *adv*, plērumque
most *adv, with adjs. and advs. use superlative; e.g.* **most quickly**, cĕlerrĭmē; *with vbs*, maxĭmē
mostly (usually) *adv*, plērumque
moth blatta, *f*
mother māter, *f*; **(-in-law)**, socrus, *f*
motherly *adj*, māternus
motion (movement) mōtus, *m*; **(proposal)**, rŏgātĭo, *f*
motion *v.t*, gestu indĭco (1) **(indicate by a gesture)**
motionless immōtus
motive cause, *f*
mottled măcŭlōsus
motto sententĭa, *f*
mould (soil) sŏlum, *n*; **(shape)**, forma, *f*
mould *v.t*, formo (1)
mouldiness sĭtus, *m*
mouldy mūcĭdus
moult *v.i*, plūmas exŭo (3) **(lay down feathers)**
mound tŭmŭlus, *m*
mount *v.t*, **(horse, ship, etc.)**, conscendo (3); *otherwise*, scando (3)
mounted (on horseback) *adj*, ĕquo vectus
mountain mons, *m*, iŭgum, *n*
mountaineer hŏmŏ montānus
mountainous montŭōsus
mourn *v.t. and v.i*, lūgĕo (2)
mournful luctūōsus; **(of sounds, etc.)**, lūgŭbris
mourning luctus, *m*, maeror, *n*
mouse mūs, *c*
mousetrap muscĭpŭlum, *n*
mouth ōs, *n*; **(of river)**, ostĭum, *n*

mouthful   bucca, *f*, **(filled out cheek)**
mouth-piece   interpres, *c*, ōrātor, *m*
movable   mōbĭlis
move   *v.t*, mŏvĕo (2); *v.i*, sē mŏvēre (2 *reflex*)
movement   mōtus, *m*
moving   *adj*, **(of pity, etc.),** mĭsĕrābĭlis
mow   *v.t*, sĕco (1)
much   *adj*, multus; **(too —),** nĭmĭus
much   *adv*, multum; *with comparative adj. or adv*, multo, *e.g.* **much bigger,** multo māior
muck   stercus, *n*
mucous   *adj*, mūcōsus
mud, muddiness   lŭtum, *n*
muddle   *v.t*, confundo (3)
muddle   *nn*, turba, *f*
muddy   lŭtĕus
muffle   *v.t*, obvolvo (3)
mug   pōcŭlum, *n*
muggy   ūmĭdus
mulberry (tree)   mōrus, *f*; **(fruit),** mōrum, *n*
mule   mūlus, *m*
mullet   mullus, *m*
multifarious   vărĭus
multiplication   multĭplĭcātĭo
multiply   *v.t*, multĭplĭco (1)
multitude   multĭtūdo, *f*
multitudinous   plūrĭmus, crēber
mumble   *v.i. and v.t*, murmŭro (1)
munch   *v.t*, mandūco (1)
mundane   *use genit. of* mundus **(world)**
municipal   mūnĭcĭpālis
municipality   mūnĭcĭpĭum, *n*
munificence   mūnĭfĭcentĭa, *f*
munificent   mūnĭfĭcus
munition   appārātus (*m*) belli **(war-equipment),** arma, *n. pl*
murder   *nn*, caedes, *f*
murder   *v.t*, nĕco (1), interfĭcĭo (3)
murderer   hŏmĭcīda, *c*, sīcārĭus, *m*
murky   cālīgĭnōsus
murmur   *nn*, murmur, *n*
murmur   *v.i*, murmŭro (1)
muscle   tŏrus, *m*, lăcertus, *m*
muscular   lăcertōsus
muse   *nn*, mūsa, *f*
muse   *v.i*, mĕdĭtor (1 *dep*)
museum   mūsēum, *n*
mushroom   fungus, *m*

music   mūsĭca, *f*, cantus, *m*
musical   mūsĭcus; **(person);** stŭdĭōsus mūsĭcōrum **(keen on music)**
musician   mūsĭcus, *m*
muslim   byssus, *f*
must   *v.i*, **(obligation),** *use gerundive: e.g.* **Carthage must be destroyed,** Carthāgo dēlenda est; **(duty),** ŏportet (2 *impers*) *with acc. of person and infinitive, e.g.* **we must go,** nōs ŏportet īre
mustard   sĭnāpi, *n*
muster   *nn*, dēlectus, *m*
muster   *v.t*, convŏco (1), rĕcensĕo (2); *v.i*, convĕnĭo (4)
musty   mūcĭdus
mutable   mūtābĭlis
mute   *adj*, mūtus, tăcĭtus
mutilate   *v.t*, mŭtĭlo (1), trunco (1)
mutilated   mūtĭlus, truncātus
mutiny   sēdĭtĭo, *f*
mutiny   *v.i*, sēdĭtĭōnem făcĭo (3)
mutter   *v.i. and v.t*, musso (1)
muttering   *nn*, murmur, *n*
mutton   ŏvilla căro, *f*, **(sheep's flesh)**
mutual   mūtŭus
muzzle (for the mouth)   fiscella, *f*
my   mĕus
myriad (10,000)   dĕcem mīlĭa (*with genit*)
myrrh   murra, *f*
myrtle   myrtus, *f*
myself   (*emphatic*), ipse; (*reflexive*) mē
mysterious   occultus
mystery   rēs abdĭta, *f*; **(religious, etc.),** mystērĭa, *n. pl*
mystic   mystĭcus
mystification   ambāges, *f. pl*
mystify   *use adv. phr*, per ambāges **(in an obscure way)**
myth   fābula, *f*
mythology   fābŭlae, *f. pl*

N

nab   *v.t*, **(catch),** apprĕhendo (3)
nag   *nn*, căballus, *m*
nag   *v.t*, increpĭto (1), obiurgo (1)
nail (finger, toe)   unguis, *m*; **(of metal),** clāvus, *m*

nail *v.t*, clāvīs affīgo (3) **(fix on with nails)**

naive simplex

naked nūdus

nakedness *use adj*, nūdus **(naked)**

name nōmen, *n*; **(personal —, equivalent to our Christian name)**, praenōmen, *n*; **(— of a class of things)**, vŏcābŭlum, *n*; **(reputation)**, existĭmātĭo, *f*

name *v.t*, nōmĭno (1), appello (1)

nameless nōmĭnis expers **(without a name)**

namely **(I mean to say)** dīco (3)

namesake *use phr*, cui est ĭdem nōmen **(who has the same name)**

nap *v.i*, **(sleep)**, paulisper dormĭo (4)

napkin mappa, *f*

narcissus narcissus, *m*

narcotic mĕdĭcāmentum somnĭfĕrum, *n*, **(sleep-bringing drug)**

narrate narro (1)

narrative narrātĭo, *f*; *adj, use vb*, narro (1) **(narrate)**

narrator narrātor, *m*

narrow angustus

narrow *v.t*, cŏarto (1); *v.i*, sē cŏartāre (1 *reflex*)

narrowly **(nearly, scarcely)** *adj*, vix

narrow-minded anĭmi angusti **(of narrow mind)**

narrowness angustĭae, *f. pl*

nasal nārĭum **(of the nose)**

nastiness foedĭtas, *f*

nasty foedus

natal nātālis

nation gens, *f*

national dŏmestĭcus *or use genit. of* gens

nationality pŏpŭlus, *m*, cīvĭtas, *f*

native *adj*, indĭgĕna; **(— land)**, pătrĭa, *f*

native *nn*, indĭgĕna, *c*

nativity **(birth)** gĕnus, *n*, ortus, *m*

natural nātūrālis; **(inborn)**, nātīvus, innātus; **(genuine)**, sincērus

naturalize *v.t*, cīvĭtātem do (1) **(with dat) (grant citizenship)**

naturally sĕcundum nātūram **(according to nature)**

nature nātūra, *f*; **(character of**

persons)**, ingĕnĭum, *n*

naught nĭhil, *n*

naughty imprŏbus, lascīvus

nausea nausĕa, *f*

nauseate *v.t*, fastīdĭo (4)

nautical nāvālis, nautĭcus

navel umbĭlĭcus, *m*

navigable nāvĭgābĭlis

navigate *v.i*, nāvĭgo (1)

navigation nāvĭgātĭo, *f*

navy classis, *f*

nay **(no)** nōn

neaptide mĭnĭmus aestus, *m*

near *adv*, prŏpĕ, iuxtā

near *prep, adv*, prŏpĕ

nearly *adv*, prŏpĕ, fermē

nearness prŏpinquĭtas, *f*, vīcīnĭtas, *f*

neat nĭtĭdus, mundus

neatly *adv*, mundē

neatness mundĭtĭa, *f*

nebulous nēbŭlōsus

necessarily *adv*, nĕcessārĭo

necessary nĕcessārĭus, nĕcesse

necessitate *v.t*, **(compel)**, cōgo (3)

necessity **(inevitableness)** nĕcessĭtas, *f*; **(something indispensable)**, rēs nĕcessārĭa, *f*

neck collum, *n*, cervix, *f*

necklace mŏnĭle, *n*

need *nn*, ŏpus, *n*, **(with abl. of thing needed or infinitive)**; **(lack)**, ĭnŏpĭa, *f*

need *v.t*, ĕgĕo (2) **(with abl)**

needful nĕcessārĭus, *or use nn*, ŏpus, *n*, **(necessity)**

needle ăcus, *f*

needless nōn nĕcessārĭus

needy ĕgens

nefarious nĕfārĭus

negation nĕgātĭo, *f*

negative *adj, use* nōn **(not)**, *or* nēgo (1) **(to deny)**

neglect *v.t*, neglĕgo (3), praetermitto (3)

neglect *nn*, neglĕgentĭa, *f*

negligent neglĕgens

negotiate *v.t*, ăgo (3) dē **(with abl. of thing)** cum **(with abl. of person)**

negotiation *use vb*, ăgo (3), **(to negotiate)**

negress Aethĭŏpissa, *f*

negro Aethĭops, *m*

neigh *v.i*, hinnĭo (4)

neigh, neighing hinnītus, *m*
neighbour vīcīnus, *m*; **(of nations)**, *adj*, fīnĭtĭmus
neither *pron*, neuter
neither *conj*, nĕque, nĕc; **neither ... nor**, neque ... neque, *or* nec ... nec
nephew fīlĭus, (*m*) frātris (*or* sŏrōris)
nerve nervi, *m. pl*
nervous (afraid) tĭmĭdus
nervousness tĭmĭdĭtas, *f*, formīdo, *f*
nest nīdus, *m*
nestle *v.i*, haerĕo (2), ĭacĕo (2)
nestlings nīdi, *m. pl*
net rētĕ, *n*
net *v.t*, plăgīs căpĭo (3) **(catch with a net)**
nettle urtīca, *f*
network rētĭcŭlum, *n*
neuter neuter
neutral mĕdĭus; **(to be or remain —)**, neutri parti făvĕo (2) **(to favour neither side)**
neutralize *v.t*, aequo (1), compenso (1)
never *adv*, numquam
nevertheless nĭhĭlōmĭnus, tămen
new nŏvus; **(fresh)**, rĕcens
newcomer advĕna, *c*
newly *adv*, nūper, mŏdo
newness nŏvĭtas, *f*
news nuntĭus, *m*
newspaper acta dĭurna, *n. pl*
newt lăcertus, *m*
next *adj*, proxĭmus; **(on the — day)**, *adv*, postrīdĭē
next *adv*, **(of time)**, dĕinceps, dĕinde; **(of place)**, iuxtā, proxĭmē
nibble *v.t*, rōdo (3)
nice (pleasant) dulcis; **(particular)**, fastīdĭōsus; **(precise)**, subtīlis
nicety (subtlety) subtīlĭtas, *f*
niche aedĭcŭla, *f*
in the nick of time in ipso artĭcŭlo tempŏris
nickname agnōmen, *n*, **(an additional name)**
niece fīlĭa (*f*) frātris (*or* sŏrōris)
niggardly ăvārus, parcus
night nox, *f*; **(by, at —)**, *adv*, noctu, nocte; **(at mid —)**, mĕdĭā nocte; **(at the fall of —)**, prīmis tĕnĕbris
nightingale luscĭnĭa, *f*

nimble ăgĭlis
nine nŏvem; **(— times)**, *adv*, nŏvĭens; **(— each)**, nŏvēni; **(— hundred)**, nongenti
nineteen undēvīginti
ninety nōnāginta
ninth nōnus
nip *v.t*, vellĭco (1); **(with frost)**, ūro (3)
nipple păpilla, *f*
no *adj*, nullus, nĭhil (*foll. by genit*)
no *adv*, nōn, mĭnĭmē; **(to say —)**, *v.i*, nĕgo (1)
nobility (of birth) nōbĭlĭtas, *f*; **(people of noble birth)**, nōbĭles, *m. pl*
noble (of birth) nōbĭlis; **(of birth or character)**, gĕnĕrōsus
nobody nēmo, *m*, *f*
nocturnal nocturnus
nod *v.i*, nūto (1); **(assent)**, annŭo (3)
nod *nn*, nūtus, *m*
noise strĕpĭtus, *m*, sŏnĭtus, *m*; **(of shouting)**, clāmor, *m*; **(to make a —)**, *v.i*, strĕpo (3)
noiseless tăcĭtus
noisily *adv*, cum strĕpĭtu
noisy *use a phr. with* strĕpo **(to make a noise)**
nomadic văgus
nominal *use* nōmen **(name)**
nominally *adv*, nōmĭne
nominate *v.t*, nōmĭno (1)
nomination nōmĭnātĭo, *f*
nominee *use vb.* nōmĭno, **(name)**
nonchalant aequo ănĭmo **(with unruffled mind)**
nondescript non insignis
none nullus
nonentity nĭhil, *n*
nonsense nūgae, *f. pl*, ĭneptĭae, *f. pl*
nonsensical ĭneptus, absurdus
nook angŭlus, *m*
noon mĕrīdĭes, *m*; **(at —)**, *adv*, mĕrīdĭe; *adj*. mĕrīdĭanus
noose lăquĕus, *m*
nor *conj*, nĕc, nĕque
normal (usual) ūsĭtātus
north *nn*, septentrĭōnes, *m. pl*
north, northern, northerly *adj*, septentrĭōnālis

north-east wind ăquĭlo, *m*
North Pole arctos, *f*
northwards versus ad
 septentrĭŏnes
north wind ăquĭlo, *m*
nose nāsus, *m*, nāres, *f. pl*
 (nostrils)
not nōn, haud; **(— at all)**, *adv*,
 haudquāquaml **(not even ...)**, nĕ
 ... quĭdem; **(and not)**, nĕc, nĕque;
 (in commands), e.g. do not go,
 nōli īre
notable insignis, mĕmŏrăbĭlis
notary scrība, *m*
notch *nn*, incīsŭra, *f*
notch *v.t*, incīdo (3)
note (explanatory, etc.) adnŏtātĭo,
 f; **(mark)**, nŏta, *f*; **(letter)**, littĕrae,
 f. pl
note v.t, (notice), ănĭmadverto (3);
 (down), ēnŏto (*i*)
notebook commentārĭi, *m. pl*
noted (well-known) insignis
nothing nĭhĭl, *n*; **(good for —)**,
 nēquam
nothingness nĭhĭlum, *n*
notice *v.t*, ănĭmadverto (3)
notice *nn*, (act of noticing),
 ămĭmadversĭo, f; **(written —)**,
 prōscriptĭo, *f*
noticeable insignis
notification dēnuntĭātĭo, *f*
notify *v.t*, dēnuntĭo (1)
notion nōtĭo, *f*
notoriety infamĭa, *f*
notorious nōtus, fāmōsus
notwithstanding *adv*, nĭhĭlōmĭnus,
 tămen
nought nĭhĭl
noun nōmen, *n*, **(name)**
nourish *v.t*, ălo (3)
nourishment ălĭmentum, *n*
novel *nn*, **(story)**, fābŭla, *f*
novel *adj*, **(new)**, nŏvus
novelist fābŭlārum, scriptor, *m*,
 (writer of stories)
novelty (strangeness) nŏvĭtas, *f*
November Nŏvember (mensis)
novice tīro, *m*
now (at the present time) *adv*.
 nunc; **(at the time of the action)**,
 iam; **(just —)**, mŏdŏ; **(now ...
 now)**, mŏdŏ ... mŏdŏ; **(— and**

then), ălĭquandŏ
nowadays *adv*, nunc
nowhere *adv*, nusquam
noxious nŏcens
nozzle nāsus, *m*
nude nūdus
nudge *v.t*, fŏdĭco (1)
nuisance incŏmmŏdum, *n*, or use
 adj, mŏlestus **(troublesome)**
null irrĭtus, vānus
nullify *v.t*, irrĭtum făcĭo (3)
numb torpens; **(to be —)**, *v.i*,
 torpĕo (2)
numb *v.t*, torpĕfăcĭo (3)
number *nn*, nŭmĕrus, *m*; **(what —,
 how many?)**, quot?; **(a large —)**,
 multĭtūdo, *f*
number *v.t*, nŭmĕro (1)
numbering (in number) ad *(with
 acc)*
numberless innŭmĕrābĭlis
numbness torpor, *m*
numerically *adv*, nŭmĕro
numerous plūrĭmi, crēber
nun mŏnăcha, *f*
nuptial nuptĭālis, iŭgālis
nuptials nuptĭae, *f.pl*
nurse nūtrix, *f*
nurse *v.t*, **(the sick)**, cŭro (1);
 (cherish), fŏvĕo (2)
nursery (for plants) sēmĭnārĭum, *n*
nurture ēdūcātĭo, *f*
nut, nut tree nux, *f*
nutriment ălĭmentum, *n*
nutrition ălĭmentum, *n*
nutritious vălens
nutshell pŭtāmen, *n*
nymph nympha, *f*

O

o! oh! o! oh!; **(Oh that ...)** ŭtĭnam
 ...
oak quercus, *f*; **(holm —)**, īlex, *f*;
 (oak-wood), rōbur, *n*
oak, oaken *adj*, quernus
oakum stuppa, *f*
oar rēmus, *m*
oarsmen rēmĭges, *m. pl*
oats ăvēna, *f*
oath iusiūrandum; *n*; **(to take an —
)**, *v.i*, iusiūrandum accĭpĭo (3);
 (military —), săcrāmentum, *n*

oatmeal fărīna, ăvēnācĕa, *f*

obdurate obstĭnātus, dūrus

obedience ŏbēdĭentĭa, *f*; *or use vb*, pārĕo (2) **(to obey,** *with dat*)

obeisance (to make an —) ădōro (1) **(reverence)**

obelisk ŏbĕlĭscus, *m*

obese ŏbēsus

obey *v.i. and v.t*, pārĕo (2) (*with dat*), ŏbēdĭo (4) (*with dat*)

object *nn*, **(thing)**, rēs, *f*; **(aim)**, consĭlĭum, n. fĭnis, m; **(to be an — of hatred)** ŏdĭo esse (*irreg*)

object *v.t*, rĕcūso (1), nōlo (*irreg*)

objection *use vb*, rĕcūso (1) **(object to)**

objectionable ingrātus, *m*

objective *nn*, quod petitur **(that is sought)**

obligation (moral) offĭcĭum, *n*; **(legal)**, oblĭgātĭo *f*; **(religious —, conscientiousness)**, rēlĭgĭo, *f*; **(to put someone under an —)**, *v.t*, obstringo (3); **(to be under an —)**, *v.i*, dēbĕo (2)

obligatory (it is —) ŏportet (2 *impers*) *or use gerundive of vb*

oblige *v.t*, obstringo (3); **(compel)**, cōgo (3)

obliging cōmis

oblique (slanting) oblīquus

obliterate *v.t*, dēlĕo (2)

oblivion oblīvĭo, *f*

oblivious immĕmor

oblong *adj*, oblongus

obloquy vĭtŭpĕrātĭo, *f*

obnoxious invīsus, noxĭus

obscene obscēnus

obscenity obscēnĭtas, *f*

obscure obscūrus, caecus, rĕcondĭtus; **(of birth, etc.)**, hŭmĭlis

obscure *v.t*, obscūro (1)

obscurity obscūrĭtas, *f*

obsequies exsĕquĭae, *f, pl*

obsequious obsĕquens, offĭcĭōsus

observance observantĭa, *f*, conservātĭo *f*; **(practice)**, rītus, *m*

observant attentus, dĭlĭgens

observation observātĭo, *f*; **(attention)**, ănĭmadversĭo, *f*; **(remark)**, dictum, *n*

observatory spĕcŭla, *f*

observe *v.t*, observo (1),

ănĭmadverto (3); **(remark)**, dīco (3); **(maintain)**, conservo (1)

observer spectātor, *m*

obsolete obsŏlētus; **(to become —)**, *v.i*, obsŏlesco (3), sĕnesco (3)

obstacle impĕdīmentum, *n*

obstinacy pertĭnācĭa, *f*

obstinate pertĭnax

obstreperous (noisy) vōcĭfĕrans

obstruct *v.t*, obstrŭo (3), obsto (1) (*with dat*)

obstruction impĕdīmentum, *n*

obtain *v.t*, ădĭpiscor (3 *dep*), nanciscor (3 *dep*), consĕquor (3 *dep*), **(— possession of)**, pŏtĭor (4 *dep, with abl*)

obtrude *v.t*, inculco (1)

obtrusive mŏlestus

obtuse hĕbes

obviate *v.t*, **(meet)**, obvĭam ĕo (4 *irreg*) (*with dat*)

obvious ăpertus, mănĭfestus

occasion (opportunity) occāsĭo, *f*; **(cause)**, causa, *f*; **(on that —)**, illo tempŏre

occasion *v.t*, mŏvĕo (2), fĕro (*irreg*)

occasionally *adv*, interdum, rāro

occult occultus, arcānus

occupancy possessĭo, *f*

occupant possessor, *m*

occupation (act of —) *use vb*, occŭpo (1); **(employment)**, quaestus, *m*; nĕgōtĭum, *n*

occupy *v.t*, occŭpo (1), obtĭnĕo (2); **(to be occupied with something)**, *v.b*, tĕnĕor (2 *pass*)

occur *v.i*. **(take place)**, accĭdo (3); **(come into the mind)**, in mentem vēnĭo (4), sŭbĕo (4) (*with dat*)

occurrence rēs, *f*

ocean ōcĕănus, *m*

ochre ōchra, *f*

octagon octŏgōnum, *n*

October Octōber (mensis)

oculist ŏcŭlārĭus mĕdĭcus, *m*

odd (numbers, etc.) impar; **(strange)**, nŏvus

odds (to be at — with) *v.i*, dissĭdĕo (2) ab (*with abl*)

odious ŏdĭōsus, invīsus

odium invĭdĭa, *f*, ŏdĭum, *n*

odorous ŏdōrātus

odour

odour ŏdor, *m*
of *usually the genit. of the noun,*
e.g. **the head of the boy,** căput
pŭĕri; **(made —),** ex *(with abl)*;
(about, concerning) dē *(with abl)*
off *adv, often expressed by prefix*
ab- *with vb, e.g.* **to cut off,**
abscīdo (3); **(far —),** *adv,* prŏcul;
(a little way —), *prep and adv,*
prŏpe
offal (waste) quisquĭlĭae, *f.pl*
offence offensĭo, *f*; **(crime, etc.)**
dēlictum, *n*; **(to take — at),** aegrē
fĕro *(irreg.)*
offend *v.t,* offendo (3), laedo (3);
(to be offended), aegrē fĕro *(irreg)*
(tolerate with displeasure)
offensive *adj,* ŏdĭōsus, grăvis
offensive *nn,* **(military),** *use phr,*
bellum infĕro *(irreg)* **(to inflict**
war)
offer *nn,* condĭcĭo, *f*
offer *v.t,* offĕro *(irreg)*; **(stretch**
out), porrĭgo (3); **(give),** do (1)
offering (gift) dōnum, *n*
office (political power) măgistrātus
m; **(duty),** offĭcĭum, *n*; **(place of**
business), fŏrum, *n*
officer (military) praefectus, *m*
official *nn,* măgistrātus, *m,*
mĭnister, *m*
official *adj.* **(state),** pūblĭcus
officiate *v.i,* **(perform),** fungor (3
dep)
officious mŏlestus
offing, (in the —) *use* longē **(far**
off), or prŏpe **(near)** *acc. to sense*
offshoot surcŭlus, *m*
offspring prōgĕnĭes, *f* lībĕri, *m, pl*
often *adv,* saepĕ; **(how — ?),**
quŏtĭes?; **(so —),** *adv,* tŏtĭes
ogle *v.t,* ŏcŭlis līmis intŭĕor (2
dep) **(look at with sidelong**
glances)
oil ŏlĕum, *n*
oily ŏlĕācĕus
ointment unguentum, *n*
old vĕtus; **(of persons),** sĕnex; **(so**
many years — , of persons), nātus
(with acc. of extent of time), e.g.
three years old, tres annos nātus;
(— age), sĕnectus, *f*; **(— man),**
sĕnex, *m*; **(— woman),** ănus, *f*

olden priscus
oldness vĕtustas, *f*
oligarchy dŏmĭnātĭo, *(f)* paucōrum
(rule of a few)
olive (tree) ŏlĕa, *f*
Olympic *adj,* Ōlympĭcus; **(—**
Games), Ōlympĭa, *n. pl*
omelette lăgănum, *n*
omen omen, *n*
ominous infaustus
omission praetermissĭo, *f*
omit *v.t,* ŏmitto (3), praetermitto
(3)
omnipotent omnĭpotens
on *prep,* in *(with abl)*; **(in the**
direction of, *e.g.* **on the right),** ā,
āb *(with abl)*; **(— everyside),** *adv,*
undĭque; **(of time),** *abl_case, e.g.*
on the Ides of March, Īdĭbus
Martĭis; **(about a subject)** dē
(with abl)
once *num. adv,* sĕmel; **(— upon a**
time), ōlim, ălĭquandŏ; **(at — ,**
immediately), stătim; **(at the same**
time), sĭmul
one *num. adj.* ūnus; **(in — s,**
singly), *adv,* singillātim, *adj,*
singŭli; **(at — time),** *adv,*
ălĭquandŏ; **(one ... another),** ălĭus
... ălĭus **(one ... the other),** alter
... alter; **(a certain),** quīdam;
(indefinite), *use 2nd pers sing. of*
the vb
oneself *(emphatic)* ipse; *(reflexive),*
sē
one-sided ĭnaequālis
onion caepa, *f*
onlooker circumstans, *m*
only *adj,* ūnus, sōlus, ūnĭcus
only *adv,* sōlum, tantum, mŏdŏ;
(not only ...), non mŏdŏ ...
onset impĕtus, *m*
onwards *adv,* porro, *often use*
compound vb. with pro, e.g.
prōcĕdĕre (3) **(to go onwards)**
ooze *nn,* ūlīgo, *f*
ooze *v.i,* māno (1)
oozy ūlīgĭnōsus
opal ŏpălus, *m*
opaque caecus
open *v.t,* ăpĕrĭo (4), pătĕfăcĭo (3),
pandi (3); **(inaugurate),** consĕcro

(1); *v.i*, sē ăpěrīre (*4 reflex*); **(gape open)**, hisco (3)

open *adj*, ăpertus; **(wide —)**, pătens, hĭans; **(to lie, stand or be —)** pătĕo (2); **(— handed)**, *adj*, lībĕrālis

opening (dedication) consĕcrātĭo, *f*; **(hole)**, fŏrāmen, *n*; **(opportunity)**, occāsĭo, *f*

openly *adv*, pălam

operate *v.t*, **(set in motion)**, mŏvĕo (2); *v.i*, **(in war)**, rem gĕro (3)

operation (task) ŏpus, n; **(military —)**, rēs bellĭca, *f*; **(naval —)**, rēs mărĭtĭma, *f*

operative *adj*, effĭcax

opiate mĕdĭcāmentum somnĭfĕrum, *n*, **(sleep-bringing drug)**

opinion sententĭa, *f*, ŏpīnĭo, *f*, existĭmātĭo, *f*

opium ŏpĭum, *n*

opponent adversārĭus, *m*

opportune opportūnus

opportunity occāsĭo, *f*, cŏpĭa, *f*, făcultas, *f*

oppose *v.t*, oppōno (3); **(resist)**, rĕsisto (*3 with dat*), adversor (*1 dep*)

opposite *adj*, adversus, contrārĭus, dīversus

opposite (to) *prep*, contrā (*with acc*)

opposition (from people) *use partic*, adversans *or* rĕsistens; **(from a party)**, *use* factĭo, *f*, **(party)**

oppress *v.t*, opprĭmo (3)

oppression (tyranny) iniūrĭa, *f*

oppressive grăvis, mŏlestus

oppressor tўrannus, *m*

opprobrious turpis

optical *adj*, *use genit, case of* ŏcŭlus, *m*, **(eye)**

option optĭo, *f*

opulence ŏpŭlentĭa, *f*, ŏpes, *f*, *pl*

opulent dīves, lŏcŭples

or aut, vel; **(either ... or)**, aut ... aut, vel ... vel; **(whether ... or)** (*questions*), ŭtrum ... an; **(or not)** (*direct questions*), annon, (*indirect questions*), necne

oracle ōrācŭlum, *n*

oral *use* vox **(voice)**

oration ōrātĭo, *f*

orator ōrātor, *m*

oratory ars ōrātōrĭa, *f*

orb, orbit orbis, *m*

orchard pōmārĭum, *n*

orchid orchis, *f*

ordain *v.t*, ēdīco (3), stătŭo (3)

ordeal discrīmen, *n*

order *nn*, **(arrangement)**, ordo, *m*; **(in —)**, *adv*, ordĭne; **(command, direction)**, iussum, *n*; **(class, rank)**, ordo, *m*; **(in — to)**, ut

order *v.t*, **(command)**, iŭbĕo (2); **(arrange)**, dispōno (3)

orderly *adj*, **(behaviour)**, mŏdestus; **(arrangement)**, ordĭnātus dispŏsĭtus

orderly *nn*, stător, *n*

ordinary ūsĭtātus, mĕdĭŏcris

ordnance tormenta, *n*. *pl*

ore aes, *n*

organ (of the body) membrum, *n*

organization dispŏsĭtĭo, *f*

organize *v.t*, ordĭno (1)

orgies orgĭa, *n*. *pl*; **(revelry)**, cōmissātĭo, *f*

orient ŏrĭens, *m*

oriental *use genit. of* ŏrĭens **(orient)**

orifice fŏrāmen, *n*, os, *n*

origin ŏrīgo, *f*, princĭpĭum, *n*

original princĭpālis, antīquus, (one's own), prŏprĭus

originally *adv*, princĭpĭo, ĭnĭtĭo

originate *v.i*, ŏrĭor (*4 dep*)

originator auctor, *m*

ornament *nn*, ornămentum, *n*

ornament *v.t*, orno (1)

ornate *adj*, ornātus, pictus

orphan orbus, *m*

oscillate *v.i*, quătĭor (3 pass)

oscillation *use vb*. quătĭor (*above*) (*3 pass*)

osier *nn*, vīmen, *n*

osier *adj*, vīmĭnĕus

osprey ossĭfrăgus, *m*

ostensible *use adv. below*

ostensibly *adv*, per spĕcĭem

ostentation ostentātĭo, *f*

ostentatious glōrĭōsus

ostler ăgāso, *m*

ostracize *v.t*, vīto (1) **(avoid)**

ostrich strūthĭŏcămēlus, *m*
other *adj*, ălĭus; **(the — of two)**, alter; **(the others, the rest)** cētĕri
others *adj*, **(belonging to —)**, ălĭēnus
otherwise *adv*, **(differently)**, ălĭter; **(in other respects also)**, ălĭoqui
otter lūtra, *f*
ought *v.* auxil, dēbĕo (2), ŏportet (2 *impers, with acc. of person*), e.g. **I ought**, ŏportet mē
ounce uncĭa, *f*
our, ours noster
ourselves (*in apposition to subject*), ipsi; (*reflexive*), nos
out *adv*, **(being out)**, fŏris; **(going out)**, fŏras
out of *prep*, ē, ex, dē (*with abl*); extrā (with acc); **(on account of)**, propter (*with acc*)
outbid *v.t, use phr*, plūs offĕro quam … **(offer more than …)**
outbreak use *vb.* ŏrĭor (4 *dep*) (to arise); **(beginning)**, ĭnĭtĭum, *n*
outcast prŏfŭgus, *m*
outcome (result) exĭtus, *m*
outcry clāmor, *m*
outdo *v.t*, sŭpĕro (1)
outdoors *adv*, fŏras
outer *adj*, extĕrĭor
outfit (equipment) appărātus, *m*
outflank *v.i*, circŭmĕo (4)
outgrow *v.t, use phr*, magnĭtūdĭne sūpĕro (1) **(surpass in size)**
outhouse tŭgŭrĭum, *n*
outlast *v.t*, dĭūturnĭtāte sŭpĕro **(surpass in duration)**
outlaw *nn*, prōscriptus, *m*
outlaw *v.t*, prōscrībo (3)
outlay *nn*, sumptus, *m*
outlet exĭtus, *m*
outline finis, *m*, ădumbrātĭo, *f*
outlive *v.i*, sŭperstĕs sum (*irreg*) **(to be a survivor)**
outlook (future) fūtūra, *n.pl*
outnumber *v.t*, plūres nŭmĕro esse quam … **(to be more in number than …)**
outpost stătĭo, *f*
outrage *nn*, inĭūrĭa, *f*
outrage *v.t*, vĭŏlo (1)
outrageous indignus
outright *adv*, prorsus; **(immediately)**, stătim
outset ĭnĭtĭum, *n*
outside *nn*, extĕrna pars, *f*; **(on the —)**, *adv*, extrinsĕcus; **(appearance)**, spĕcĭes, *f*, frons, *f*
outside *adj*, externus
outside *adv*, extrā
outside of *prep*, extrā (*with acc*)
outskirts *use adj*. sūburbānus **(near the city)**
outspoken (frank) līber
outstretched porrectus
outstrip *v.t*, sŭpĕro (1)
outward *adj*, externus
outwardly *adv*, extrā
outweigh *v.t*, grăvĭtāte sŭpĕro (1) **(surpass in weight)**
outwit *v.t*, dēcĭpĭo (3)
oval *adj*, ōvātus
oven furnus, *m*
over *prep*, (above, across, more than), sŭper (*with acc*)
over *adv*, **(above)**, sŭper, suprā; **(left —)**, *adj*, rĕlĭquus; **(it is — , all up with)**, actum est; **(— and — again)**, *adv*, ĭdentĭdem
overawe *v.t*, percello (3)
overbearing sŭperbus
overboard *adv*, ex nāvi
overcast (sky) nūbĭlus
overcoat lăcerna, *f*
overcome *v.t*, vinco (3), sŭpĕro (1)
overdone *use adv*, nĭmis **(too much)**
overdue *use adv*, dĭūtĭus **(too long)**, *and* diffĕro (*irreg*), **(to put off)**
overflow *v.i*, effundor (3 *pass*); v.t, ĭnundo (1)
overgrown obsĭtus
overhang *v.i*, immĭnĕo (2), impendĕo (2) (*both with dat*)
overhanging impendens
overhasty praeceps
overhaul *v.t*, **(repair)**, rĕsarcĭo (4)
overhead *adv*, insŭper
overhear *v.t*, excĭpĭo (3)
overjoyed laetĭtĭā ēlātus **(elated with joy)**
overland *adv*, terrā, per terram
overlap *v.t*, **(overtake)**, sŭpervĕnĭo (4)
overlay *v.t*, indūco (3)
overload *v.t*, grăvo (1)

overlook *v.t,* prōspĭcĭo (3); **(forgive)**; ignosco (3) *(with dat)*; **(neglect)**, praetermitto (3)

overmuch *adv,* nĭmis

overpower *v.t,* opprĭmo (3)

overrate *v.t,* plūris aestĭmo (1) **(value too highly)**

override *v.t,* praeverto (3)

overrule *v.t,* vinco (3)

overrun *v.t,* pervăgor (1 *dep*)

oversea *v.t,* cūro (1), inspĭcĭo (3)

overseer cūrātor, *m*

overshadow *v.t,* officĭo (3) *(with dat)*

oversight (omission) error, *m,* neglĕgentĭa, *f, or use vb,* praetermitto (3) **(overlook)**

overspread *v.t,* obdūco (3)

overt ăpertus, plānus

overtake *v.t,* consĕquor (3 *dep*)

over tax (strength etc.) v.t, nĭmis ūtor (3 *dep*) *(with abl)*

overthrow *nn,* rŭīna, *f*

overthrow *v.t,* ēverto (3), opprĭmo (3)

overtop *v.t,* sŭpĕro (1)

overture (to make — s) *use vb.* instĭtŭo (3) **(to begin)**

overweening sŭperbus

overwhelm *v.t,* opprĭmo (3), obrŭo (3)

overwork *v.i,* nĭmis lăbōro (1)

overwrought (exhausted) confectus

owe *v.t,* dēbĕo (2)

owing to prep, **(on account of)**, propter, ob *(both with acc)*

owl būbo, *m,* strix, *f*

own *adj,* prŏprĭus; *often expressed by possessive pron, e.g.* **my own,** mĕus

own *v.t,* **(possess)**, tĕnĕo (2), possĭdĕo (2); **(confess)**, fătĕor (2 *dep*)

owner possessor *m,* dŏmĭnus, *m*

ox bōs, *c*

oxherd armentārĭus, *m*

oyster ostrĕa, *f*

P

pace *nn,* passus, *m*

pace (step) spătĭor (1 *dep*), grădĭor (3 *dep*)

pacific pācĭfĭcus

pacification pācĭfĭcātĭo, *f*

pacify *v.t,* plāco (1), sēdo (1)

pack (bundle) sarcĭna, *f*; **(— of people)**, turma, *f*

pack *v.t,* **(gather together)**, collĭgo (3); **(— close together)**, stīpo (1)

package sarcĭna, *f*

packet fascĭcŭlus, *m*

packhorse iūmentum, *n*

pact pactum, *n,* foedus, *n*

padding *nn,* fartūra, *f*

paddle *nn* **(oar)**, rēmus, *m*

paddle *v.t,* rēmĭgo (1), **(to row)**

paddock saeptum, *n*

padlock sĕra, *f*

pagan pāgānus

page (book) pāgĭna, *f*; **(boy)**, pŭer, *m*

pageant spectācŭlum, *n,* pompa, *f*

pageantry spĕcĭes (*f*) atque pompa *f* **(display and public procession)**

pail sĭtŭla, *f*

pain dŏlor, *m*; **(to be in —)**, *v.i,* dŏlĕo (2)

pain *v.t,* dŏlōre afficĭo (3) **(inflict pain)**

painful ăcerbus

painless *use adv. phr,* sĭne dŏlōre **(without pain)**

pains (endeavour) ŏpĕra, *f*; **(to take — over)**, ŏpĕram do (1) *(with dat)*

painstaking ŏpĕrōsus

paint *v.t,* pingo (3); **(colour)**, fūco (1)

paint *nn,* pigmentum, *n*

paintbrush pēnĭcullus, *m*

painter pictor, *m*

painting pictūra, *f*

pair pār, *m*

pair *v.t,* iungo (3); *v.i,* iungor (3 *pass*)

palace rēgĭa, *f*

palatable iūcundus

palate pălātum, *n*

palatial rēgĭus
pale *adj*, pallĭdus; **(to be —)**, *v.i*, pallĕo (2); **(to become —)**, *v.i*, pallesco (3)
pale *nn*, **(stake)**, pālus, *m*
paleness pallor, *m*
palisade vallum, *n*
pall *nn*, pallĭum, *n*
pall *v.i*, **(it —s)**, taedet (2 *impers*)
pallet lectŭlus, *m*
palliate *v.t*, extĕnŭo (1)
palliation *use vb*, extĕnŭo (1) **(palliate)**
palliative lēnĭmentum, *n*
pallid *adj* pallĭdus
pallor pallor, *m*
palm (of hand, tree) palma, *f*
palm (to — off) *v.t*, suppōno (3)
palpable (obvious) mănĭfestus
palpitate *v.t*, palpĭto (1)
palpitation palpĭtatĭo, *f*
palsy părălysis, *f*
paltry vīlis
pamper *v.t*, nĭmĭum indulgĕo (2) (*with dat*) **(to be too kind to ...)**
pamphlet lĭbellus, *m*
pamphleteer scriptor (*m*) lĭbellorum
pan pătĭna, *f*; **(frying —)**, sartāgo, *f*
panacea pănăcĕa, *f*
pancake lăgănum, *n*
pander *v.i*, lēnōcĭnor (1 dep)
panegyric laudătĭo, *f*
panel (of door, etc.) tympānum, *n*
panelled lăquĕātus
pang dŏlor, *m*
panic păvor, *m*
panic-stricken păvĭdus
pannier clītellae, *f, pl*
panorama prōspectus, *m*
pant *v.i*, ănhēlo (1)
panther panthēra, *f*
panting *nn*, ănhēlĭtus, *m*
pantomime mīmus, *m*
pantry cella pĕnărĭa, *f*
pap (nipple) păpilla, *f*
paper charta, *f*; **(sheet of —)**, schĕda, *f*; **(newspaper)**, acta dīurna, *n.pl*
papyrus păpyrus, *m, f*
par (on a — with) *adj*, pār
parable părăbŏla, *f*

parade (military) dēcursus, *m*; **(show)**, appărātus, *m*, pompa, *f*
parade *v.i*, **(of troops)**, dēcurro (3); *v.t* **(display)**, ostento (1)
paradise Ēlysĭum, ĭi, *n*
paragon spĕcĭmen, *n*
paragraph căput, *n*
parallel *adj*, părallēlus; **(like)**, sĭmĭlis
paralysis părălysis, *f*, dēbĭlĭtas, *f*
paralyze *v.t*, dēbĭlĭto (1)
paralyzed dēbĭlis
paramount summus
paramour ădulter, *m*, ămātor, *m*
parapet lōrīca, *f*, mūnĭtĭo, *f*
paraphernalia appărātus, *m*
parasite assecla, *c*
parasol umbella, *f*
parcel fascĭcŭlus, *m*
parcel out *v.t*, partĭor (4 dep)
parch *v.t*, torrĕo (2)
parched (dry) ārĭdus; **(scorched)**, torrĭdus
parchment membrāna, *f*
pardon *nn*, vĕnĭa, *f*
pardon *v.t*, ignosco (3) (*with dat*)
pardonable *use phr*, cui ignoscendum est **(who should be pardoned)**
pare *v.t*, (circum)sĕco (1) **(cut around)**
parent părens, *m, f*
parentage gĕnus, *n*
parental pătrĭus, *or use genit pl*, părentum **(of parents)**
parenthesis interpŏsĭtĭo, *f*
parish păroecĭa, *f*
park horti, *m. pl*
parley collŏquĭum, *n*
parley *v.i*, collŏquor (3 dep)
parliament sĕnātus, *m*
parliamentary *use genit. case of* sĕnātus
parlour conclāve, *n*
parody versus rīdĭcŭli, *m, pl*
parole fĭdes *f* **(promise)**
paroxysm *use* accessus, *m*, **(approach)**
parricide (person) parrĭcīda, *c*; **(act)**, parrĭcīdĭum, *n*
parrot psittăcus, *m*
parry *v.t*, prōpulso (1)

parse *v.t*, *use phr*, verba
singŭlātim percĭpĭo (**understand the words one by one**)
parsimonious parcus
parsimony parsĭmōnīa, *f*
parsley ăpĭum, *n*
parson (priest) săcerdos, *c*
part pars, *f*; **(in a play)**, persōna, *f*, partes, *f*, *pl*; **(side, faction)**, partes, *f*. *pl*; **(duty)**, officĭum, *n*; **(region)**, lŏca, *n.pl*; **(from all — s)**, *adv*, undīque; **(for the most —)**, *adv*, plērumque; **(to take — in)**, intersum (*irreg*) (*with dat*)
part *v.t*, dīvĭdo (3), sēpăro (1); *v.i*, discēdo (3)
partake of *v.t*, partĭceps sum (*irreg*) (*with genit*); **(food)**, gusto (1)
partaker partĭceps, *adj*
partial (affecting only a part) *use adv. phr*, ex ălĭquā parte; **(unfair)**, ĭnīquus
partiality stŭdĭum, *n*
participate *v.i*, partĭceps sum (*irreg*) (*with genit*)
participation sŏcĭĕtas, *f*
particle partĭcŭla, *f*
particular (characteristic) prŏprĭus; **(special)**, singŭlāris; **(exacting)**, dēlĭcātus
particularly (especially) *adv*, praecĭpŭē
parting *nn*, dīgressus, *m*
partisan fautor, *m*
partition (act of —) partītĭo, *f*; **(wall)**, părĭes, *m*
partly *adv*, partim
partner sŏcĭus, *m* (sŏcĭa, *f*)
partnership sŏcĭĕtas, *f*
partridge perdix, *c*
party (political, etc.) factĭo, *f*; **(of soldiers)**, mănus, *f*; **(for pleasure)**, convīvĭum, *n*
pasha sătrăpes, *m*
pass *nn* **(mountain)**, angustĭae, *f*. *pl*
pass *v.t*. **(go beyond)**, praetergrĕdĭor (3 dep); **(surpass)**, excēdo (3); **(— on, — down)**, trādo (3); **(of time)**, ăgo (3), tĕro (3); **(— over, omit)**, praetērĕo (4); **(— a law)**, sancĭo (4); **(approve)**,

prŏbo (1); *v.i*, praetērĕo (4); **(of time)**, transĕo (4); **(give satisfaction)**, sătisfăcĭo (3); **(— over, cross over)**, transĕo (4); **(come to — , happen)**, fīo (*irreg*)
passable (road, etc.) pervĭus
passage (crossing) transĭtus, *m*, trāiectĭo, *f*; **(route, way)**, ĭter, *n*, vīa, *f*; **(in a book)**, lŏcus, *m*
passenger vector, *m*
passion mōtus (*m*) ănĭmi **(impulse of the mind)**; **(love)**, ămor, *m*
passionate fervĭdus, ardens, īrācundus
passive pătĭens
passivity pătĭentĭa
passport dīplōma, *n*
password tessĕra, *f*
past *adj*, praetĕrĭtus; **(just —)**, proxĭmus
past *nn*, praetĕrĭtum tempus, *n*
past *prep*, praeter (*with acc*); **(on the far side of)**, ultrā (*with acc*)
past *adv*, *use compound vb. with* praeter, e.g. praetĕrĕo (4) **(go past)**
paste fărīna, *f*
paste *v.t*, glūtĭno (1)
pastime oblectāmentum, *n*
pastor pastor, *m*
pastoral pastōrālis
pastry crustum, *n*
pastry-cook crustŭlārĭus, *m*
pasture pascŭum, *n*
pasture *v.t*, pasco (3)
pat *v.t*, **(caress)**, permulcĕo (2)
patch *nn*, pannus, *m*
patch *v.t*, sarcĭo (4)
patent *adj*, ăpertus
paternal păternus
path sēmĭta, *f*, vĭa, *f*
pathetic mĭsĕrandus
pathless invĭus
pathos *f*, affectĭo (*f*) ănĭmi
pathway sēmĭta, *f*
patience pătĭentĭa, *f*
patient *adj*, pătĭens
patient *nn*, *use* aeger **(ill)**
patiently *adv*, pătĭenter
patrician *nn. and adj*, pătrĭcĭus
patrimony pătrĭmōnĭum, *n*
patriot *use phr*, qui pătrĭam ămat **(who loves his country)**

patriotic ămans pătrĭae
patriotism ămor (*m*) pătrĭae
patrol *nn*, *use* custŏdes, *m. pl*, (guards)
patrol *v.t*, circŭmĕo (4)
patron pătrōnus, *m*
patronage pătrōcĭnĭum, *n*
patronzie *v.t*, făvĕo (2) (*with dat*)
patter *nn*, crĕpĭtus, *m*
patter *v.i*, crĕpo (1)
pattern exemplum, *n*, exemplar, *n*
paucity paucĭtas, *f*
pauper pauper *c*, ĕgens (needy)
pause *nn*, mŏra, *f*
pause *v.i*, intermitto (3)
pave *v.t*, sterno (3)
pavement păvīmentum, *n*
pavilion *use* praetōrĭum, *n*, (general's tent), *or* tăbernācŭlum, *n*, (tent)
paw *nn*, pes, *m*
paw *v.t*, pĕdĭbus calco (1) (tread with the feet)
pawn (chess) lătruncŭlus, *m*; (security), pignus, *n*
pawn *v.t*, pignĕro (1)
pay *nn*, stīpendĭum, *n*
pay *v.t*, solvo (3), pendo (3), nŭmĕro (1); *v.i* (— attention), ŏpĕram do (1); (— the penalty), poenas do (1)
paymaster (in army) trĭbūnus aerārĭus, *m*
payment sŏlūtĭo, *f*
pea pīsum, *n*, cĭcer, *n*
peace pax, *f*, ōtĭum, *n*
peaceable plăcĭdus
peaceful plăcĭdus, pācātus
peacefulness transquillĭtas, *f*
peace offering plăcŭlum, *n*
peacock pāvo, *m*
peak ăpex, *m*; (mountain), căcūmen, *n*
peal (thunder) frăgor, *m*; *otherwise use* sŏnus, *m*, (sound)
peal *v.i*, sŏno (1)
pear pyrum, *n*; (— tree), pyrus, *f*
pearl margărīta, *f*
peasant rustĭcus, *m*, ăgrestis, *m*
peasantry ăgrestes, *m. pl*
pebble lăpillus, *m*
peck (measure) mŏdĭus, *m*

peck *v.t*, vellĭco (1)
peculation pĕcūlātus, *m*
peculiar (to one person, etc.) prŏprĭus; (remarkable), singŭlāris
peculiarity prŏprĭetas, *f*
pecuniary pĕcūnĭārĭus
pedagogue măgister, *m*
pedant hŏmo ĭneptus
pedantic (affected — of style, etc.) pūtĭdus
peddle *v.t*, vendĭto (1)
pedestal băsis, *f*
pedestrian *nn*, pĕdes, *m*
pedestrian *adj* pĕdester
pedigree stemma, *n*
pedlar instĭtor, *m*
peel *nn*, cūtis, *f*
peel *v.i*, cŭtem rĕsĕco (1)
peep *nn*, aspectus, *m*
peep *nn*, aspectus, *m*
peep at *v.t*, inspicio (3); *v.i*, sĕ prōferre (*irreg*)
peer (equal) par, *m*
peer at *v.t*, rīmor (1 *dep*)
peerless ūnĭcus
peevish stŏmăchōsus
peevishness stŏmăchus, *m*
peg clāvus, *m*
pelt *v.t*, *use* intorquĕo (2) (hurl at); v.i, (of rain, etc.) *use* plŭit (it rains)
pen călămus, *m*; (for cattle), saeptum, *n*
pen *v.t*, (write), scrībo (3)
penal poenālis
penalty poena, *f*, damnum, *n*; (to pay the —), poenas do (1)
penance (do —) *use vb*. expĭo (1) (to make amends)
pencil pēnĭcillum, *n*
pending *prep*, inter, per (*with acc*)
pendulous pendŭlus
penetrate *v.i*, and *v.t*, pĕnĕtro (1) pervādo (3)
penetrating *adj*, ăcūtus, ācer (mentally), săgax
penetration ăcūmen, *n*
peninsula paeninsŭla, *f*
penitence paenĭtentĭa, *f*
penitent *use vb*, paenĭtet (2 *impers*) (*with acc. of person*), *e.g.*
I am penitent, mĕ paenĭtet

pennant vexillum, *n*
penny as, *m*
pension annŭa, *n.pl*
pensive multa pŭtans **(thinking many things)**
penthouse vīněa, *f*
penultimate paenultĭmus
penurious parcus
penury ĕgestas, *f*, ĭnŏpĭa, *f*
people (community) pŏpŭlus, *m*; **(persons)**, hŏmĭnes, *c. pl*; **(the common —)**, plebs, *f*, vulgus, *n*
people *v.t*, frĕquento (1); **(inhabit)**, incŏlo (3)
pepper pĭper, *n*
perambulate *v.t*, pěrambŭlo (1)
perceive *v.t*, sentĭo (4), percĭpĭo (3), ănĭmadverto (3), intellĕgo (3)
percentage pars, *f*
perception perspĭcācĭtas, *f*, *or use adj*, perspĭcax **(sharp-sighted)**
perceptive perspĭcax
perch *nn*, pertĭca, *f*; **(fish)**, perca, *f*
perch *v.i*, insīdo (3)
perchance *adv*, fortĕ
percolate *v.i*, permāno (1)
percussion ictus, *m*
perdition exĭtĭum, *n*
peremptory *use vb.* obstringo (3) **(to put under obligation)**
perennial pěrennis
perfect perfectus, absŏlūtus
perfect *v.t*, perfĭcĭo (3), absolvo (3)
perfection perfectĭo, *f*, absŏlūtĭo, *f*
perfidious perfĭdus
perfidy perfĭdĭa, *f*
perforate *v.t*, perfŏro (1)
perform *v.t*, fungor (3 *dep. with abl*); pěrăgo (3), praesto (1), exsĕquor (3 *dep*)
performance functĭo, *f*
performer actor, *m*
perfume ŏdor, *m*
perfume *v.t*, ŏdōro (1)
perfunctory neglĕgens
perhaps *adv*, fortĕ, fortassĕ, forsĭtan
peril pěrīcŭlum, *m*
perilous pěrīcŭlōsus
period spătĭum, *n*
periodical *adv*, stătus
perish *v.i*, pěrěo (4)

perishable frăgĭlis
perjure *v.t*, periūro (1)
perjured periūrus
perjury periūrĭum, *n*
permanence stăbĭlĭtas, *f*
permanent stăbĭlis
permanently *adv*, perpětŭo
permeate *v.i*, permāno (1)
permissible (it is —) lĭcet (2 *impers*)
permission (to give —) permitto (3) *(with dat)*; **(without your —)**, tē invīto
permit *v.t*, sĭno (3), permitto (3)
pernicious pernĭcĭōsus
perpendicular *adj*, dīrectus
perpetrate *v.t*, admitto (3)
perpetual sempĭternus
perpetuate *v.t*, contĭnŭo (1)
perplex *v.t*, distrăho (3), sollĭcĭto (1)
perplexed dŭbĭus
perquisite pěcŭlĭum, *n*
persecute *v.t*, insector (1 *dep*)
persecution insectātĭo, *f*
persecutor insectātor, *m*
perseverance persěvērantĭa, *f*
persevere *v.i*, persěvēro (1)
persist *v.i*, persto (1)
persistence pertĭnācĭa, *f*
person hŏmo, *c*; **(body)**, corpus, *n*; **(in person)**, *use pron*, ipse **(self)**
personal (opp. to public) prīvātus
personality ingěnĭum, *n*
perspicacious perspĭcax
perspicacity perspĭcācĭtas, *f*
perspiration sūdor, *m*
perspire *v.i*, sūdo (1)
persuade *v.t*, persuāděo (2) *(with dat of person)*
persuasion persuāsĭo, *f*
persuasive suāvĭlŏquens
pert prŏcax
pertain *v.i*, attĭněo (2)
pertainacious pertĭnax
pertinacity pertĭnācĭa, *f*
perturb *v.t*, turbo (1)
perusal perlectĭo, *f*
peruse *v.t*, perlěgo (3)
pervade *v.t*, permāno (1), perfundo (3)
perverse perversus

perversion dēprāvātĭo, *f*
pervert *v.t*, dēprāvo (1)
pervious pervĭus
pest pestis, *f*
pester *v.t*, sollĭcĭto (1)
pestilence pestĭlentĭa, *f*
pestilential pestĭlens
pestle pistillum, *n*
pet *nn*, dēlĭcĭae, *f. pl*
pet *v.t*, dēlĭcĭīs hăbĕo (2) **(regard among one's favourites)**, indulgĕo (2)
petition *use vb*. pĕto (3) **(seek)**
petition *v.t*, rŏgo (1)
petitioners pĕtentes, *c.pl*
petrify v.t, **(with fear, etc.)**, terrōrem ĭnĭcĭo (3), *(with dat)*
pettifogging vīlis
petty mĭnūtus
petulance pĕtŭlantĭa, *f*
petulant pĕtŭlans
phantom sĭmŭlācrum, *n*, ĭmāgo, *f*
phases (alternations) vĭces, *f. pl*
pheasant āles (*c*) Phāsĭdis **(bird of Phasis)**
phenomenon rēs, *f*; **(remarkable occurrence)**, rēs mīrābĭlis
phial lăguncŭla, *f*
philanthropic hūmānus
philanthropy hūmānĭtas, *f*
philologist phĭlŏlŏgus, *m*
philology phĭlŏlŏgĭa, *f*
philosopher phĭlŏsŏphus, *m*
philosophical phĭlŏsŏphus
philosophy phĭlŏsŏphĭa, *f*
philtre philtrum, *n*
phlegm pītŭīta, *f*; **(of temperament)**, aequus ănĭmus, *m*
phoenix phoenix, *m*
phrase *nn*, lŏcūtĭo, *f*
phraseology *use* verba, *n.pl*, **(words)**
phthisis phthĭsis, *f*
physic mĕdĭcāmentum, *n*
physical (relating to the body) *use nn*, corpus, *n*, **(body)**; **(natural)**, *use* nātūra, *f*, **(nature)**
physician mĕdĭcus, *m*
physics phŷsĭca, *n.pl*
physiology phŷsĭŏlŏgĭa, *f*
pick (axe) dŏlăbra, *f*; **(choice)**, *use adj*, dēlectus **(chosen)**
pick *v.t*, **(pluck)**, lĕgo (3), carpo (3); **(choose)**, ēlĭgo (3); **(— up, seize)**, răpĭo (3)
picked (chosen) dēlectus
picket stătĭo, *f*
pickle mŭrĭa, *f*
pickle *v.t*, condĭo (4)
pickpocket fūr, *c*
picnic *use phr*, fŏrīs ĕpŭlor (1 *dep*) **(to eat out of doors)**
picture tăbŭla, *f*
picture *v.t*, expingo (3)
picturesque ămoenus
pie crustum, *n*
piebald bĭcŏlor
piece (part) pars, *f*; **(of food)**, frustrum, *n*; **(to pull or tear to — s)**, discerpo (3), dīvello (3); **(to fall to — s)**, dīlābor (3 *pass*)
piecemeal *adv*, membrātim
piece together *v.t*, compōno (3)
pier mōles, *f*
pierce *v.t*, perfŏdĭo (3)
piercing *adj*, ăcūtus
piety pĭĕtas, *f*
pig porcus, *m*, sūs, *c*
pigeon cŏlumba, *f*
pigheaded obstĭnātus, diffĭcĭlis
pigsty hăra, *f*
pike hasta, *f*
pile (heap) ăcervus, *m*; **(building)**, mōles, *f*; **(supporting timber)**, sublĭca, *f*
pile *v.t*, ăcervo (1), congĕro (3)
pilfer *v.t*, surrĭpĭo (3)
pilfering *nn*, furtum, *n*
pilgrim pĕrĕgrīnātor, *m*
pilgrimage pĕrĕgrīnātĭo, *f*
pill pĭlŭla, *f*
pillage *nn*, răpīna, *f*, dīreptĭo, *f*
pillage *v.t*, praedor (1 *dep*) dīrĭpĭo (3)
pillar cŏlumna, *f*
pillory vincŭla, *n.pl*
pillow pulvīnus, *m*
pillow *v.t*, suffulcĭo (4)
pilot gŭbernātor, *m*
pilot *v.t*, gŭberno (1)
pimp lēno, *m*
pimple pustŭla, *f*
pin ăcus, *f*
pin *v.t*, ăcu fīgo (3) **(fix with a pin)**
pincers forceps, *m, f*
pinch *nn*, **(bite)**, morsus, *m*

pine *nn*, pīnus, *f*; *adj*, pīnĕus
pine *v.i*, tābesco (3); *v.t*, (**— for**), dēsīdĕro (1)
pinion (nail) clāvus, *m*; (**bond**), vincŭla, *n.pl*
pinion *v.t*, rĕvincĭo (4)
pink rŭbor, *m*
pinnace lembus, *m*
pinnacle fastīgĭum, *n*
pint sextārĭus, *m*
pioneer explōrātor, *m*
pious pĭus
pip (seed) sēmen, *n*, grānum, *n*
pipe cănālis, *m*; (**musical**), fistŭla, *f*
pipe *v.i*, căno (3)
piper tībīcen, *m*
piquant ăcerbus
pique *nn*, offensĭo, *f*
pique *v.t*, laedo (3)
piracy lătrōcĭnĭum, *n*
pirate praedo, *m*, pīrāta, *m*
pit fŏvĕa, *f*; (**arm —**), āla, *f*; (**theatre**), căvĕa, *f*
pit (**— one's wits, etc.**) *use* ūtor (3 *dep*) (**to use**)
pitch *nn*, pix, *f*; (**in music**), sŏnus, *m*
pitch *v.t*, (**camp, tent, etc.**), pōno (3); (**throw**), cōnĭcĭo (3); (**ships**), *use* ăgĭtor (1 *pass*) (**to be tossed about**)
pitcher urcĕus, *m*
pitchfork furca, *f*
piteous, pitiable mĭsĕrābĭlis
pitfall fŏvĕa, *f*
pith mĕdulla, *f*
pitiful mĭser, mĭsĕrĭcors
pitifulness mĭsĕrĭa, *f*
pitiless immĭsĕrĭcors
pittance (small pay) tips, *f*
pity *v.t*, mĭsĕret (2 *impers*) (*with acc. of subject and genit. of object, e.g.* **I pity you**); mē mĭsĕret tŭi
pity *nn*, mĭsĕrĭcordĭa, *f*
pivot cardo, *m*
placard inscriptum, *n*
placate *v.t*, plāco (1)
place lŏcus, *m*; (**in this —**), *adv*, hīc; (**in that —**), illīc, ĭbĭ; (**in what — ?**) ŭbĭ?; (**in the same —**), ĭbīdem; (**to this —**) hūc; (**to that —**), illūc; (**to the same —**), ĕōdem; (**to what — ?**), quō; (**from this —**). hinc; (**from that —**),

inde; (**from the same —**), indĭdem; (**from what — ?**), unde?
(**in the first —**), prīmum; (**to take — , happen**), *v.i*, accĭdo (3)
place *v.t*, pōno (3), lŏco (1); (**— in command**), praefĭcĭo (3); (**— upon**) impōno (3)
placid plăcĭdus, tranquillus
plague *nn*, pestĭlentĭa, *f*, pestis, *f*
plague *v.t*, (**trouble**), sollĭcĭto (1)
plain *nn*, campus, *m*, plānĭtĭes, *f*
plain *adj*, (**clear**), clārus, plānus; (**unadorned**), subtĭlis, simplex; (**frank, candid**), sincērus
plainness perspĭcŭĭtas, *f*, simplĭcĭtas, *f*, sincērĭtas, *f*
plaintiff pĕtītor, *m*
plaintive *adj*, mĭsĕrābĭlis
plait *v.t*, intexo (3)
plan *nn*, consĭlĭum, *n*; (**drawing**), dēscriptĭo, *f*; (**to make a —**), consĭlĭum căpĭo (3)
plan *v.i*, (**intend**), in ănĭmo hăbĕo (2); v.t, (**design**), dēscrībo (3)
plane *nn*, (**tool**), runcīna, *f*; (**tree**), plătănus, *f*
plane *v.t*, runcīno (1)
planet sīdus (*n*) errans (**moving constellation**)
plank tăbŭla, *f*
plant *nn*, herba, *f*
plant (seeds, etc.) sĕro (3); (**otherwise**), pōno (3), stătŭo (3)
plantation plantārĭum, *n*, arbustum, *n*
planter sător, *m*
planting *nn*, sătus, *m*
plaster *nn*, tectōrĭum, *n*; (**medical**), emplastrum
plaster *v.t*, gypso (1)
plasterer tector, *m*
plate (dish) cătillus, *m*; (**thin layer of metal**), lāmĭna, *f*; (**silver, gold**), argentum, *m*
plate *v.t*, indūco (3)
platform suggestus, *m*
Platonic Plătōnĭcus
platoon dĕcŭrĭa, *f*
plausible spĕcĭōsus
play *nn*, lūdus, *m*, lūsus, *m*; (**theatre**), fābŭla, *f*; (**scope**), camous, *m*

play *v.i*, lūdo (3) (*with abl. of game played*); **(musical)**, căno (3); **(a part in a play)**, partes ăgo (3); **(a trick)**, lūdĭfĭco (1)

player (stage) historĭo, *m*; **(flute —)**, tībīcen, m; **(strings —)**, fĭdĭcen, *m*; **(lute, guitar —)**, cĭthărista, *m*

playful (frolicsome) lascīvus

playfulness lascīvĭa, *f*

playground ārĕa, *f*

playwright fābŭlārum scriptor, *m*

plea (asking) obsĕcrātĭo, *f*; **(excuse)**, excūsātĭo, *f*

plead *v.t*, ōro (1), ăgo (3); **(as an excuse)**, excūso (1); **(beg earnestly)**, obsĕcro (1); **(law)**, dīco (3)

pleader (in law) ōrātor, *m*

pleasing, pleasant iūcundus

pleasantness iūcundĭtas, *f*

please *v.t*, plăcĕo (2) (*with dat*); **(if you —)**, si vis

pleasureable iūcundus

pleasure vŏluptas, *f*; **(will)**, arbĭtrĭum, *n*; **(— gardens)**, horti, *m. pl*

plebeian plēbēius

pledge *nn*, pignus, *n*; **(to make a —, promise)**, sē obstringĕre (3 reflex)

pledge *v.t*, oblĭgo (1), prōmitto (3)

plenipotentiary lēgātus, *m*

plenitude plēnĭtūdo, *f*

plentiful largus, cōpĭōsus

plenty cōpĭa, *f*; **(enough)**, sătis (*with genit*)

pleurisy pleurītis, *f*

pliable flexĭbĭlis, lentus

plight angustĭae, *f.pl* **(difficulties)**

plight *v.t*, spondĕō (2), oblĭgo (1)

plinth plinthus, *m, f*

plod v.i, lentē prōcēdo (3)

plot (of ground) ăgellus, *m*; **(conspiracy)**, coniūrātĭo, *f*; **(story)**, argūmentum, *n*

plot *v.i*, coniūro (1)

plough *nn*, ărātrum, *n*; **(— share)**, vōmer, *m*

plough *v.t*, ăro (1)

ploughman ărātor, *m*, būbulcus, *m*

pluck *nn*, fortĭtūdo, *f*, ănĭmus, *m*

pluck *v.t*, carpo (3); **(— up courage)**, ănĭmum rĕvŏco (1)

plug *nn*, obtūrāmentum, *n*

plum prūnum, *n*

plum tree prūnus, *f*

plumage plūmae, *f, pl*

plumb line līnĕa, *f*

plume penna, *f*

plump pinguis

plumpness nĭtor, *m*, pinguĭtūdo, *f*

plunder *nn*, praeda, *f*; **(act of plundering)**, răpīna, *f*, dīreptĭo, *f*

plunder *v.t*, praedor (1 dep), dīrĭpĭo (3)

plunderer praedātor, *m*

plunge *v.i*, sē mergĕre (3 reflex); *v.t*, mergo (3)

plural *adj*, plūrālis

plurality multĭtūdo, *f*

ply *v.t*, exercĕo (2)

poach *v.t*, use răpĭo (3), **(to seize)**; **(cook)**, cŏquo (3)

poacher fur, *c*, raptor *m*

pocket sĭnus, *m*

pocket *v.t*, **(money)**, āverto (3)

pocketbook pŭgillāres, *m, pl*

pocket money pĕcūlĭum, *n*

pod sĭlĭqua, *f*

poem pŏēma, *n*, carmen, *n*

poet pŏēta, *m*

poetical pŏētĭcus

poetry pŏēsis, *f*, carmĭna, *n. pl*

poignant ăcerbus

point ăcūmen, *n* **(of a sword)**, mūcro, *m*; **(spear)**, cuspis, *f*; **(place)**, lŏcus, *m*; **(issue)**, res, *f*; **(on the — of)**, *use fut. participle of vb*, *e.g.* **on the point of coming**; ventūrus

point *v.t* **(make pointed)**, praeăcŭo (3); **(direct)**, dīrĭgo (3)

point out *or* **at** *v.t*, monstro (1)

pointed praeăcūtus; **(witty)** salsus

pointer index, *m, f*

pointless insulsus

poison vĕnēnum, *n*, vīrus, *n*

poison *v.t*, vĕnēno nĕco (1) **(kill by poison)**

poisoning *nn*, vĕnēfĭcĭum, *n*

poisonous vĕnēnātus

poke *v.t*, fŏdĭco (1)

polar septentrĭōnālis

pole (rod, staff) contus, *m*, longŭrĭus, *m*; **(earth)**, pŏlus, *m*

polemics contrōversĭae, *f. pl*

police (men) vĭgĭles, *m, pl*
policy rătĭo, *f*
polish *nn*, **(brightness)**, nĭtor, *m*
polish *v.t*, pŏlĭo (4)
polished pŏlītus
polite cōmis, urbānus
politeness cōmĭtas, *f*, urbānĭtas, *f*
politic *adj*, prūdens
political cīvĭlis, pūblĭcus
politician qui rĕĭpūblĭcae stŭdet **(who pursues state affairs)**
politics rēs pūblĭca, *f*
poll (vote) suffrāgĭum, *n*
pollute *v.t*, inquĭno (1)
pollution collŭvĭio, *f*
polytheism *use phr*, crēdĕre multos esse dĕos **(believe that there are many gods)**
pomade căpillāre, *n*
pomegranate mālum grānātum, *n*
pommel *v.t*, verbĕro (1)
pomp appărātus, *m*
pompous magnĭfĭcus
pompousness magnĭfĭcentĭa, *f*
pond stagnum, *n*; **(fish —)**, piscīna, *f*
ponder *v.t*, rēpŭto (1)
ponderous gravis
poniard pŭgĭo, *m*
pontiff pontĭfex, *m*
pontoon pons, *m*
pony mannus, *m*
pool lăcūna, *f*
poop puppis, *f*
poor pauper, ĭnops; **(worthless)**, vīlis; **(wretched)**, mĭser
poorly *adj*, **(sick, ill)**, aeger
poorly *adv*, tĕnŭĭter, mălĕ
pop *v.i*, crĕpo (1)
pope Pontĭfex Maxĭmus, *m*
poplar pōpŭlus, *f*
poppy păpāver, *n*
populace vulgus, *n*, plebs, *f*
popular grātĭosus; **(of the people)**, pŏpŭlāris
popularity făvor (*m*) pŏpŭli **(goodwill of the people)**
population cīves, *c.pl*
populous frĕquens
porch vestĭbŭlum, *n*
porcupine hystrix, *f*
pore fŏrāmen, *n*

pore over *v.i*, ănĭmum intendo (3) **(direct the mind)**
pork porcīna, *f*
porker porcus, *m*
porous rārus
porpoise porcŭlus mărīnus, *m*
porridge puls, *f*
port portus, *m*
portable quod portāri pŏtest **(that can be carried)**
portal porta, *f*, iānŭa, *f*
portcullis cătāracta, *f*
portend *v.t*, portendo (3)
portent portentum, *n*
portentous monstrŭōsus
porter (doorkeeper) iānĭtor, *m*; **(baggage carrier)** bāiŭlus, *m*
portfolio lĭbellus, *m*
portico portĭcus, *f*
portion pars, *f*
portion out *v.t*, partĭor (4 *dep*)
portrait ĭmāgo, *f*
portray *v.t*, dēpingo (3)
pose *nn*, stătus, *m*
position lŏcus, *m*; **(site)**, sĭtus, *m*
positive certus
possess *v.t*, hăbĕo (2), possĭdĕo (2)
possession possessĭo, *f*; **(to take — of)**, pŏtĭor (4 *dep. with abl*); **(property)**, *often use possessive pron. e.g.* mĕa **(my — s)**, *or* bŏna *n.pl*
possessor possessor, *m*, dŏmĭnus, *m*
possibility *use phr. with* posse; **(to be possible)**
possible *use vb*, posse (*irreg*) **(to be possible)**; **(as ... as possible)**, *use* quam *with superlative, e.g.* **as large as possible**, quam maxĭmus; **(as soon as —)**, quam prīmum
post cippus, *m*, pālus, *m*; **(military)**, stătĭo, *f*, lŏcus, *m*; **(letter)**, tăbellārĭi pūblĭci, *m. pl* **(state couriers)**
post *v.t*, **(in position)**, lŏco (1); **(letter)**, tăbellārĭo do (1) **(give to a courier)**
posterior *nn*, nătes, *f. pl*
posterity postĕri, *m. pl*

postern postīcum, *n*

posthumous *use phr*, post mortem (*with genit*) **(after the death of ...)**

postman tăbellārĭus, *m*

postpone *v.t*, diffĕro (*irreg*)

postscript verba subiecta, *n. pl*, **(words appended)**

posture stătus, *m*

pot olla, *f*

potent pŏtens, efficax

potentate tўrannus, *m*

potion pōtĭo, *f*

potsherd testa, *f*

potter fĭgŭlus, *m*

pottery (articles) fictĭlĭa, *n. pl*

pouch saccŭlus, *m*

poultice mălagma, *n*

poultry ăves cŏhortāles, *f. pl*

pounce upon v.t, invŏlo (1)

pound *nn*, **(weight)**, lībra, *f*

pound *v.t*, tundo (3), tĕro (3)

pour *v.t*, fundo (3); *v.i*, fundor (3 *pass*)

pouring *adj*. effūsus

pout *v.i*, lăbellum extendo (3) **(stretch a lip)**

poverty paupertas, *f*, ĕgestas, *f*, ĭnŏpĭa, *f*; **(— stricken)**, *adj*, ĭnops

powder *nn*, pulvis, *m*

power vīres, *f. pl*; **(dominion)**, pŏtestas, *f*; **(authority)**, ius, *n*, impĕrĭum, *n*; **(inconstitutional —)**, pŏtentĭa, *f*

powerful pŏtens; **(of body)**, vălĭdus

powerless invălĭdus; **(to be —)**, *v.i*, mĭnĭmum posse (*irreg*)

practicable *use phr*, quod fĭĕri pŏtest **(that can be done)**

practical (person) făbrĭcae pĕrītus **(skilled in practical work)**

practically (almost) *adv*., paene

practice ūsus, *m*; **(custom)**, mos, *m*, consŭētūdo, *f*

practise *v.t*, exercĕo (2), factĭto (1)

practitioner (medical) mĕdĭcus, *m*

praetor praetor, *m*

praetorship praetūra, *f*

praise *nn*, laus, *f*

praise *v.t*, laudo (1)

praiseworthy laudābĭlis

prance *v.i*, exsulto (1)

prank *use* lūdĭfĭcor (1 dep) **(to make fun of)**

prattle *v.i*, garrĭo (4)

pray *v.i*, and *v.t*, ōro (1) prĕcor (1 *dep*)

prayer prĕces, *f. pl*

preach *v.i*, contĭōnor (1 *dep*)

preamble exordĭum, *n*

precarious incertus

precaution (to take — s (against)) *v.i*, and *v.t*, praecăvĕo (2)

precede *v.t*, antēcēdo (3), antĕĕo (4)

precedence (to give —) *use vb*, cēdo (3); **(to take —)**, prĭor esse (*irreg*)

precedent exemplum, *n*

preceding *adj*, prĭor, proxĭmus

precept praeceptum, *n*

precious (of great price) magni prĕtĭī; **(dear)**, dīlectus

precipice lŏcus praeceps, *m*

precipitate *adj*, praeceps

precipitate *v.t*, praecĭpĭto (1)

precipitous praeceps

precise subtīlis

precision subtīlĭtas, *f*

preclude *v.t*, prŏhĭbĕo (2)

precocious praecox

preconceived praeiŭdĭcātus

precursor praenuntĭus, *m*

predatory praedātōrĭus

predecessor (my —) *use phr*, qui ante me ... **(who before me ...)**

predicament angustĭae, *f. pl*

predict *v.t*, praedīco (3)

prediction praedictĭo, *f*

predilection stŭdĭum, *m*

predisposed inclīnātus

predominant pŏtens

predominate *v.i*, *use phr*, qui in pŏtentĭā sunt **(who are in authority)**

pre-eminent praestans

preface praefātĭo, *f*

preface *v.t*, praefor (1 *dep*)

prefer *v.t*, with infinitive, mālo (*irreg*); **(put one thing before another)**, antĕpōno (3); **(— a charge)**, dēfĕro (*irreg*)

preferable pŏtĭor

preference (desire) vŏluntas, *f*; **(in**

—), *adv*, pŏtĭus

preferment hŏnor, *m*

pregnant praegnans, grăvĭda

prejudge *v.t*, praeiūdĭco (1)

prejudice praeiūdĭcāta ŏpīnĭo, *f*

prejudice *v.t*, **(impair)**, immĭnŭo (3)

prejudicial noxĭus; **(to be — to)**, obsum (*irreg*) (*with dat*)

prelate săcerdos, *c*

preliminary *use compound word with prae, e.g.* **to make a — announcement**, praenuntĭo (1)

prelude prŏoemĭum, *n*

premature immātūrus

premeditate *v.t*, praemĕdĭtor (1 *dep*)

premeditation praemĕdĭtātĭo, *f*

premier princeps, *m*

premise prōpŏsĭtĭo, *f*

premises (buildings) aedĭficĭa, *n.pl*

premium praemĭum, *n*

premonition mŏnĭtĭo, *f*

preoccupy (to be — with) stŭdĕo (2) (*with dat*)

preparation compărātĭo, *f*, appārātus, *m*; **(to make — s)**, compăro (1)

prepare *v.t*, păro (1), compăro (1)

prepossess *v.t*, commendo (1)

prepossessing *adj*, suāvis, blandus

preposterous praepostĕrus

prerogative iūs, *n*

presage praesāgĭum, *n*

presage *v.t*, portendo (3)

prescribe *v.t*, praescrībo (3)

presence praesentĭa, *f*; **(in the — of)**, prep, cōram (*with abl*)

present *nn* **(gift)**, dōnum, *n*; **(time)**, praesentĭa, *n.pl*

present *adj*, praesens; **(to be —)**, *v.i*, adsum (*irreg*)

present *v.t*, offĕro (*irreg*); **(give)**, dōno (1) (*with acc. of person and abl. of gift*)

presentation dōnātĭo, *f*

presentiment augŭrĭum, *n*

presently *adv*, **(soon)**, mox

preservation conservātĭo, *f*

preserve *v.t*, servo (1)

preserver servātor, *m*

preside *v.i*, praesĭdĕo (*with dat*)

presidency praefectūra, *f*

president praefectus, *m*

press *nn*, **(machine)**, prēlum, *n*

press *v.t*, prĕmo (3); **(urge)**, urgĕo (2)

pressure nīsus, *m*

prestige fāma, *f*, ŏpīnĭo, *f*

presume *v.t*, **(assume)**, crēdo (3); **(dare)**, *v.i*, audĕo (2)

presumption (conjecture) conĭectūra, *f*; **(conceitedness)**, arrŏgantĭa, *f*

presumptuous arrŏgans

pretence sĭmŭlātĭo, *f*; **(under — of)**, per sĭmŭlātĭōnem

pretend *v.t*, sĭmŭlo (1)

pretended *adj*, sĭmŭlātus

pretender (claimant) *use vb*, pĕto (3) **(aspire to)**

pretension postŭlātĭo, *f*

pretext spĕcĭes, *f*; **(on the — of)**, *use vb*. sĭmŭlo (1) **(to pretend)**

prettily *adv*, bellē, vĕnustē

prettiness concinnĭtas, *f*, vĕnustas, *f*

pretty *adj*, pulcher

pretty *adv*, sătis **(enough)**

prevail *v.i*, obtĭnĕo (2), sŭpĕrĭor esse (*irreg*); **(to — upon)**, *v.t*, persuādĕo (2) (*with dat*)

prevalent vulgātus

prevaricate *v.t*, tergĭversor (1 *dep*)

prevent *v.t*, prŏhĭbĕo (2)

prevention *use vb*, prŏhĭbĕo **(prevent)**

previous prŏxĭmus

previously *adv*, antĕā

prey *nn*, praeda, *f*

prey *v.t*, praedor (1 *dep*)

price *nn*, prĕtĭum, *n*; **(— of corn)**, annōna, *f*

price *v.t*, prĕtĭum constĭtŭo (3) **(fix the price)**

priceless inaestĭmābĭlis

prick *nn*, punctum, *n*

prick *v.t*, pungo (3); **(spur)**, stĭmŭlo (1)

prickly *adj*, ăcŭlĕātus

pride sŭperbĭa, f; **(honourable —)**, spīrĭtus, *m*

priest săcerdos, *c*

priesthood săcerdōtĭum, *n*
prim mōrōsĭor
primarily *adv*, princĭpĭō
primary prīmus
prime *nn*, (of life, etc.), *use vb*, flōrĕo (2) (flourish); (best part), flŏs, *m*
prime *adj*, ēgrĕgĭus
primeval prīmĭgenĭus
primitive prīmĭgĕnĭus
prince (king) rēgŭlus, *m*; (king's son), filĭus (*m*) rēgis
princess (king's daughter) filĭa (*f*) rēgis
principal *adj*, princĭpālis, praecĭpŭus
principal *nn*, măgister, *m*
principality regnum, *n*
principle princĭpĭum, *n*; (element), ĕlĕmentum, *n*, prīmordĭa, *n. pl*; (rule, maxim), praeceptum, *n*
print *nn*, (mark), nŏta, *f*
print *v.t*, imprĭmo (3)
prior *adj*, prĭor
priority *use adj*, prĭor
prism prisma, *n*
prison carcer, *m*
prisoner captīvus, *m*
privacy sōlĭtūdo, *f*
private prīvātus, sēcrētus
private soldier mīles grĕgārĭus, *m*
privately *adv*, prīvātim, clam
privation ĭnŏpĭa, *f*
privet lĭgustrum, *n*
privilege ĭus, *n*
privy *adj*, (acquainted with), conscĭus; (secret), prīvātus
privy *nn*, fŏrĭca, *f*
privy-council consĭlĭum, *n*
privy-purse fiscus, *m*
prize praemĭum, *n*; (booty), praeda, *f*
prize *v.t*, (value), magni aestĭmo (1)
probability sĭmĭlĭtūdo (*f*) vēri
probable sĭmĭlis vēri
probation prŏbātĭo, *f*
probe *v.t*, tento (1)
problem quaestĭo, *f*
problematical (doubtful) dŭbĭus
procedure rătĭo, *f*
proceed *v.i*, (move on), pergo (3); (originate) prŏfĭciscor (3 dep);

(take legal action against) lītem intendo (3) (*with dat*)
proceedings (legal) actĭo, *f*; (doings), acta, *n.pl*
proceeds fructus, *m*
process rătĭo, *f*; (in the — of time), *adv, use phr*, tempŏre praetĕreunte (with time going by)
procession pompa, *f*
proclaim *v.t*, praedĭco (1), prōnuntĭo (1)
proclamation prōnuntĭātĭo, *f*, ēdictum, *n*
proconsul prōconsul, *m*
procrastinate *v.t*, diffĕro (*irreg*)
procrastination tardĭtas, *f*, mŏra, *f*
procreate *v.t*, prōcrĕo (1)
procreation prōcrĕātĭo, *f*, partus, *m*
procure *v.t*, compăro (1)
procurer lēno, *m*
prodigal *adj*, prōdĭgus
prodigality effūsĭo, *f*
prodigious immānis
prodigy prōdĭgĭum, *n*
produce *nn*, fructus, *m*
produce *v.t*, (into view) prōfĕro (*irreg*); (create), păro (3); (— an effect), mŏvĕo (2)
productive fĕrax
profanation vĭŏlātĭo, *f*
profane impĭus, prŏfānus
profane *v.t*, vĭŏlo (1)
profanity impĭĕtas, *f*
profess *v.t*, prŏfĭtĕor (2 dep)
profession (occupation) mūnus, n, officĭum, n; (avowal), prŏfessĭo, *f*
professor prŏfessor, *m*
proffer *v.t*, pollĭcĕor (2 dep)
proficient (skilled) pĕrītus
profile oblīqua făcĭes, *f*
profit *nn*, ēmŏlŭmentum, *n*, lŭcrum, *n*, quaestus, *m*
profit *v.t*, (benefit), prōsum (*irreg. with dat*)
profitable fructŭōsus
profitless īnūtĭlis
profligacy nēquĭtĭa, *f*
profligate perdĭtus
profound altus
profuse effūsus
profusion effūsĭo, *f*
progeny prōgĕnĭes, *f*

prognostic sīgnum, *n*
programme lĭbellus, *m*
progress (improvement, etc.) prōgressus, *m*; **(to make —)**, prōfĭcĭo (3), prōgrĕdĭor (3 dep)
progress *v.i*, prōgrĕdĭor (3 dep)
prohibit *v.t*, vēto (1)
prohibition interdictum, *n*
project *nn*, **(plan)**, consĭlĭum, *n*
project *v.t*, prōĭcĭo (3); *v.i*, ēmĭnĕo (2)
projectile tēlum, *n*
projecting ēmĭnens
proleteriat vulgus, *n*
prolific fēcundus
prolix verbōsus
prologue prŏlŏgus, *m*
prolong *v.t*, prōdūco (3); **(— a command)**, prōrŏgo (1)
prolongation prōpāgātĭo, *f*
promenade ambulātĭo, *f*
prominence ēmĭnentĭa, *f*
prominent ēmĭnens; **(person)**, praeclārus
promiscuous prōmiscŭus
promise *nn*, prōmissum, *n*, fĭdes, *f*
promise *v.i*, prōmitto (3), pollĭcĕor (2 dep)
promising *adj*, *use adv. phr*, bŏnā spe **(of good hope)**
promissory note chīrŏgrăphum, *n*
promontory prōmontŏrĭum, *n*
promote *v.t*, prōmŏvĕo (2); **(favour, assist)**, iŭvo (1), prōsum (*irreg*) (*with dat*)
promoter auctor, *m*
promotion (act of —) *use vb.* prōmŏvĕo (2); **(honour)**, hŏnor, *m*
prompt *adj*, promptus
prompt *v.t*, **(assist in speaking)**, sūbĭcĭo (3) (*with dat. of person*); **(incite)**, incĭto (1)
promptitude, promptness cĕlĕrĭtas, *f*
promulgate *v.t*, prōmulgo (1)
prone prōnus; **(inclined to)**, prōpensus
prong dens, *m*
pronoun prōnōmen, *n*
pronounce *v.t*, prōnuntĭo (1)
pronunciation appellātĭo, *f*

proof argūmentum, *n*, dŏcŭmentum *n*, prŏbātĭo, *f*
prop *nn*, admĭnĭcŭlim, *n*
prop *v.t*, fulcĭo (4)
propagate *v.t*, prōpāgo (1)
propel *v.t*, prōpello (3)
propensity ănĭmus inclīnātus, *m*
proper dĕcōrus, vērus, aptus
properly *adv*, **(correctly)**, rectē
property (possessions) bŏna, *n. pl*, rĕs, *f*; **(characteristic quality)**, prŏprĭĕtas, *f*
prophecy praedictĭo, *f*, praedictum, *n*
prophesy *v.t*, praedīco (3), vātĭcĭnor (1 *dep*)
prophet vātes, *c*
prophetic dīvīnus
propitiate *v.t*, plāco (1)
propitious prŏpĭtĭus, praesens
proportion portĭo, *f*; **(in —)**, prōportĭōne
proportional *use adv. phr*, prō portĭōne
proposal condĭcĭo, *f*
propose *v.t*, fĕro (*irreg*), rŏgo (1)
proposer lātor, *m*
proposition condĭcĭo, *f*
proprietor dŏmĭnus, *m*
propriety (decorum) dĕcōrum, *n*
prorogation prōrŏgātĭo, *f*
prosaic (flat) iēiūnus
proscribe *v.t*, prōscrībo (3)
proscription prōscriptĭo, *f*
prose ōrātĭo, sŏlūta, *f*
prosecute *v.t*, **(carry through)**, exsĕquor (3 *dep*); **(take legal proceedings)** lītem intendo (3)
prosecution exsĕcuutĭo, *f*; **(legal)**, accuusātĭo, *f*
prosecutor accūsātor, *m*
prospect (anticipation) spes fŭtūra, *f*; **(view)**, prospectus, *m*
prospective fŭtūrus
prosper *v.i*, flōrĕo (2)
prosperity res sĕcundae, *f. pl*
prosperous sĕcundus
prostitute *nn*, mĕrĕtrix, *f*
prostitute *v.t*, vulgo (1)
prostitution mĕrĕtricĭus quaestus, *m*

prostrate (in spirit, etc.) fractus; **(lying on the back)**, sŭpīnus; **(lying on the face)**, prōnus

prostrate *v.t*, sterno (3), dēĭcĭo (3)

protect *v.t*, tĕgo (3), tŭĕor (2 *dep*), dēfendo (3)

protection tūtēla, *f*, praesĭdĭum, *n*

protector dēfensor, *m*

protest against *v.t*, intercēdo (3)

prototype exemplar, *n*

protract *v.t*, dūco (3)

protrude *v.t*, prōtrūdo (3); *v.i*, ēmĭnĕo (2)

protuberance tūber, *n*

proud sŭperbus

prove v.t, prŏbo (1); **(to — oneself)** sē praestāre (1 *reflex*); **(test)**, pērīclĭtor (1 dep); v.i, **(turn out (of things))**, fīo (*irreg*), ēvĕnĭo (4)

proverb prōverbĭum, *n*

proverbial *use nn*, prōverbĭum, *n*, **(proverb)**

provide *v.t*, **(supply)**, păro (1), praebĕo (2); v.i, **(make provision for)**, prōvĭdĕo (2); **(— against)**, căvĕo (2) ne (*with vb. in subjunctive*)

provided that *conj*, dum, dummŏdo

providence prōvĭdentĭa, *f*

provident prŏvĭdus

province prōvincĭa, f

provincial prōvincĭālis

provision (to make —) prŏvĭdĕo (2)

provisional *use adv. phr*, ad tempus **(for the time being)**

provisions cĭbus, *m*

provocation *use vb*, irrīto (1) **(to provoke)**

provoke *v.t*, irrīto (1); **(stir up)**, incĭto (1)

prow prōra, *f*

prowess virtus, *f*

prowl *v.i*, văgor (1 *dep*)

proximity prŏpinquĭtas, *f*

proxy prōcūrātor, *m*

prudence prūdentĭa, *f*

prudent prūdens

prune *nn*, prūnum, *n*, **(plum)**

prune *v.t*, ampŭto (1)

prurient lĭbīdĭnōsus

pry *v.t*, rīmor (1 *dep*)

psalm carmen, *n*

psychological *use genit. of* mens, **(mind)**

puberty pūbertas, *f*

public *adj*, pūblĭcus; **(of the state)**, *use nn*, respublĭca, *f*, **(state)**, *or* pŏpŭlus, *m*, **(people)**

public *nn*, hŏmĭnes, *c. pl*

publican (innkeeper) caupo, *m*

publication *use* ēdo (3), **(publish)**

publicity cĕlĕbrĭtas, *f*

publicly *adv*, pălam

publish *v.t*, effĕro (*irreg*), prŏfĕro (*irreg*); **(book)**, ēdo (3)

pucker *v.t*, corrūgo (1)

puddle lăcūna, *f*

puerile (silly) īnseptus

puff *v.i*, **(pant)**, ănhēlo (1); v.t, **(inflate)** inflo (1); **(puffed up)**, inflātus

pugilist pŭgil, *m*

pull *v.t*, trăho (3); **(— down, demolish)**, dēstrŭo (3)

pulley trochlĕa, *f*

pulp căro, *f*

pulpit suggestus, *m*

pulsate *v.i*, palpĭto (1)

pulse vēnae, *f. pl.* **(veins)**

pulverize *v.t*, in pulvĕrem contĕro (3) **(pound into dust)**

pumice pūmex, *m*

pump *nn*, antlĭa, *f*

pump *v.t*, haurĭo (4)

pumpkin pĕpo, *m*

pun făcētĭae, *f. pl*

punch ictus, *m*, pugnus, *m*

punch *v.t*, percŭtĭo (3)

punctilious mōrōsus

punctual, punctuality *use adv. phr*, ad tempus **(at the right time)**

punctuate *v.t*, distinguo (3)

punctuation interpunctĭo, *f*

puncture *nn*, punctum

puncture *v.t*, pungo (3)

pungency morsus, *m*, ăcerbĭtas, *f*

pungent ācer

punish *v.t*, pūnĭo (4), ănĭmadverto (3) in (*with acc*), poenas sūmo (3); **(to be — ed)**, poenas do (1)

punishment poena, *f*, supplĭcĭum, *n*; **(to undergo —)**, poenam sŭbĕo (4)

punitive *use vb*, pūnĭo **(punish)**

puny pŭsillus
pup, puppy cătŭlus, *m*
pupil (scholar) discĭpŭlus, *m*; **(of the eye)** pūpilla, *f*
puppet pūpa, *f*
purchase *nn*, emptĭo, *f*
purchase *v.t*, ĕmo (3)
pure pūrus, mĕrus; **(morally)**, intĕger
purgative *use phr. with* mĕdĭcămentum, *n*, **(medicine)**
purge *nn, use vb*, purgo (1)
purge *v.t*, purgo (1)
purification purgātĭo, *f*
purify *v.t*, purgo (1), lustro (1)
purity castĭtas, *f*, intĕgrĭtas, *f*
purloin *v.t*, surrĭpĭo (3)
purple *nn*, purpŭra, *f*
purple *adj*, purpŭrĕus
purport *nn*, **(meaning)**, signĭfĭcātĭo, *f*
purport *v.t*, **(mean)**, signĭfĭco (1)
purpose *nn*, prōpŏsĭtum, *n*, consĭlĭum, *n*; **(for the — of doing something)**, ĕo consĭlĭo ut (*with vb in subjunctive*); **(on —)**, *adv*, consulto; **(to no —, in vain)**, *adv*, frustrā; **(for what —?)** quāre
purpose *v.t*, **(intend)**, in ănĭmo hăbĕo (2)
purr *v.i*, murmŭro (1)
purse saccŭlus, *m*
in pursuance of ex (*with abl*)
pursue *v.t*, sĕquor (3 *dep*)
pursuit (chase) *use vb*, sĕquor **(to pursue)**; **(desire for)**, stŭdĭum, *n*
purvey *v.t*, obsōno (1)
purveyor obsōnātŏr, *m*
pus pūs, *n*
push, pushing *nn*, impulsus, *m*, impĕtus, *m*
push *v.t*, pello (3), trūdo (3); **(— back)**, rĕpello (3); **(— forward)**, prōmŏvĕo (2)
pushing *adj*, mŏlestus
pusillanimity ănĭmus, hŭmĭlis, *m*
pusillanimous hŭmĭlis
pustule pustŭla, *f*
put *v.t*, **(place)**, pōno (3), do (1), impōno (3); **(— aside)**, sĕpōno (3); **(— away)**, abdo (3), condo (3); **(— back)**, rĕpōno (3); **(— down)**, dēpōno (3); **(suppress)**,

exstinguo (3); **(— forward)**, praepōno (3), prōfĕro (*irreg*); **(— in)**, immitto (3); **(— into land, port, etc.)**, *v.i*, portum căpĭo (3); **(— off)**, *v.t*, pōno (3); **(delay)**, differo (*irreg*); **(— on)**, impōno (3); **(— clothes)**, indŭo (3); **(— out)**, ēĭcĭo (3), exstinguo (3); **(— to drive to)**, impello (3); **(— together)**, collĭgo (3), confĕro (*irreg*); **(— under)**, sūbĭcĭo (3); **(— up, erect)**, stătŭo (3); **(offer)**, prōpōno (3); **(put up with, bear)**, fĕro (*irreg*); **(— upon)**, impōno (3); **(— to flight)** fŭgo (1)
putrefy *v.i*, pūtesco (3)
putrid pŭtrĭdus
putty glūten, *m or n*
puzzle *nn*, **(riddle)**, nōdus, *m*; **(difficulty)**, difficultas, *f*, angustĭae, *f, pl*
puzzling *adj*, perplexus; **(in a — way)**, *adv. phr*, per ambāges
pygmy nānus, *m*
pyramid pȳrămis, *f*
pyre rŏgus, *m*
Pyrenees Montes Pȳrēnaei, *m. pl*
python pȳthon, *m*

Q

quack *nn*, **(medicine)**, pharmăcŏpōla, *m*
quadrangle ārĕa, *f*
quadrant quădrans, *m*
quadrilateral quădrĭlătĕrus
quadruped quădrŭpes
quadruple *adj*, quădruplex
quaff *v.t*, haurĭo (4)
quagmire pălus, *f*
quail *nn*, cŏturnix, *f*
quail *v.i*, trĕpĭdo (1)
quaint nŏvus
quake *nn*, trĕmor, *m*
quake *v.i*, trĕmo (3)
qualification iūs, *n*; **(condition)**, condĭcĭo, *f*
qualified (suitable) aptus, ĭdōnĕus
quality *v.t*, **(fit someone for something)**, aptum reddo (3); **(restrict)**, circumscrībo (3), mītĭgo (1)

quality nātūra, *f*
qualm (doubt) dŭbĭtātĭo, f
quantity nŭmĕrus, *m*, magnĭtūdo, *f*; **(a certain —)**, ălĭquantum, *n* (*nn*); **(a large —)** cōpĭa, *f*, multum, *n*; **(what — ?)**, use *adj*, quantus **(how great)**
quarrel iurgĭum, *n*, rixa, *f*
quarrel *v.i*, iurgo (1), rixor (1 *dep*)
quarrelsome lītĭgĭōsus
quarry (stone) lăpĭcīdĭnae, *f. pl*; **(prey)**, praeda, *f*
quarry *v.t*, caedo (3)
quart (measure) dŭo sextărĭi, *m. pl*
quarter quarta pars, *f*, quădrans, *m*; **(district)**, rĕgĭo, f; **(surrender)**, dēdĭtĭo, *f*
quarter *v.t*, quădrĭfărĭam dīvĭdo (3), **(divide into four parts)**
quarter-deck puppis, *f*
quartermaster quaestor mīlĭtāris, *m*
quarterly *adj*. trĭmestris
quarters (lodging) hospĭtĭum, *n*; **(at close —)**, *adv*, commĭnus; **(to come to close —)**, signa confĕro (*irreg*)
quash *v.t*, opprĭmo (3); **(sentence, verdict)**, rēscindo (3)
quaver *v.i*, trĕpĭdo (1)
quay crēpīdo, *f*
queen rēgīna, *f*
queer rīdĭcŭlus
queerness insŏlentĭa, *f*
quell *v.t*, opprĭmo (3)
quench *v.t*, exstinguo (3)
quenchless ĭnexstinctus
querulous quĕrŭlus
query quaestĭo, *f*
query *v.t*, quaero (3)
quest inquīsītĭo, *f*
question *nn*, rŏgātĭo, *f*, interrŏgātum, *n*, quaestĭo, *f*; *or* use *vb*, rŏgo (1) **(to ask —s)**; **(doubt)**, dŭbĭum, *n*
question *v.t*, rŏgo (1), quaero (3); **(doubt)**, dŭbĭto (1)
questionable incertus
questioner interrŏgātor, *m*
quibble *nn*, captĭo, *f*
quibble *v.i*, căvillor (1 *dep*)
quick *adj*, cĕler; **(sprightly)**, ăgĭlis; **(— witted)**, săgax

quickly *adv*, cĕlĕrĭter, cĭto
quicken *v.t*, accĕlĕro (1), stĭmŭlo (1); *v.i*, **(move quicker)**, sē incĭtāre (1 *reflex*)
quickness vēlōcĭtas, *f*; **(— of wit)**, săgācĭtas, *f*
quicksilver argentum vīvum, *n*
quick-tempered īrācundus
quiescent quĭescens
quiet *nn*, quĭes, *f*
quiet *adj*, quĭētus, tranquillus
quiet, quieten *v.t*, sēdo (1)
quietly *adv*, quĭētē, tranquillē
quill penna, *f*; **(for writing)**, *use* stĭlus, *m*, **(pen)**
quilt *nn*, strāgŭlum, *n*
quinquennial quinquennālis
quinsy angīna, *f*
quintessence vīs, *f*, flōs, *m*
quip *nn*, rēsponsum (salsum) **((witty) reply)**
quirk căvillātĭo, *f*
quit *v.t*, rĕlinquo (3)
quite *adv*, admŏdum, prorsus; **(— enough)**, sătis
quiver *nn*, phărĕtra, *f*
quiver *v.i*, trĕmo (3)
quoit discus, *m*
quota răta pars, *f*
quotation prōlātĭo, *f*
quote *v.t*, prōfĕro (*irreg*)
quotidian cottīdĭānus

R

rabbit cŭnīculus, *m*
rabble turba, *f*
rabid răbīdus
race (family) gĕnus, *n*, prōgĕnĭes, *f*; **(running)**, cursus, *m*, certāmen, *n*
race *v.i*, cursu certo (1) **(contend by running)**
racecourse stădĭum, *n*, currĭcŭlum, *n*
racehorse ĕquus cursor, *m*
rack (for torture) ĕquŭlĕus, m
rack *v.t*, **(torture)**, torquĕo (2)
racket (bat) rētĭcŭlum, *n*; **(noise)**, strĕpĭtus, *m*
racy (smart) salsus
radiance fulgor, *m*
radiant clārus, fulgens
radiate *v.i*, fulgĕo (2)

radiation rădĭātĭo, *f*

radical (fundamental) tōtus; **(original)**, innātus; **(keen on change)**, cŭpĭdus rērum nŏvārum

radically *adv*, pĕnĭtus, fundĭtus

radish rădix

radius rădĭus, *m*

raffle ālĕa, *f*

raft rătis, *f*

rafter cantērĭus, *m*

rag pannus, *m*

rage fŭror, *m*

rage *v.i*, fŭro (3)

ragged pannōsus

raging *adj*, fŭrens

raid incursĭo, *f*; **(to make a —)**, invādo (3) in (*with acc.*)

rail longŭrĭus, *m*

rail at (abuse) mălĕdīco (3) (*with dat.*)

railing cancelli, *m.pl*

raillery căvillātĭo, *f*

raiment vestīmenta, *n.pl*

rain *nn*, plŭvĭa, *f*, imber, *m*

rain *v.i*, **(it rains)**, plŭit (3 impers.)

rainbow arcus, *m*

rainy plŭvĭus

raise v.t, **(lift)**, tollo (3); **(forces)**, compăro (1); **(rouse)**, ērĭgo (3); **(— a seige)**, obsĭdĭōnem solvo (3)

raisin ăcĭnus passus, *m*, **(dried berry)**

rake *nn*, **(tool)**, rastellus, *m*; **(person)** nĕpos, *c*

rake *v.t*, rādo (3)

rally *v.t*, **(troops)** mīlĭtes in ordĭnes rĕvŏco (1), **(call back the soldiers to their ranks)**; v.i, se collĭgĕre (3 reflex)

ram (or battering —) ărĭes m; (beak of a ship), rostrum, n

ram *v.t*, fistūco (1); **(ship)** rostro laedo (3)

ramble *v.i*, erro (1)

rambler erro, *m*

rammer fistūca, *f*

rampart agger, *m*, vallum, *n*

rancid rancĭdus

rancorous infestus

rancour ŏdĭum, *n*

random *adj*, fortŭĭtus; **(at —)**, *adv*, fortŭĭto

range ordo, *m*; **(— of mountains)**, iŭga, *n.pl*; **(of a missile)**, iactus, *m*; **(scope)**, campus, *m*

rank *nn*, ordo, *m*

rank *v.i*, sē hăbere (2 *reflex*)

rank *adj*, **(smell, etc.)**, fētĭdus

rankle *v.t*, exulcĕro (1), mordĕo (2)

ransack *v.t*, dīrĭpĭo (3)

ransom *nn*, rĕdemptĭo, *f*; **(— money)**, prĕtĭum, *n*

ransom *v.t*, rĕdĭmo (3)

rant *v.t*, dēclāmo (1)

ranting *nn*, sermo tŭmĭdus, *m*, **(bombastic speech)**

rap *nn*, pulsātĭo, *f*

rap *v.t*, pulso (1)

rapacious răpax

paracity răpācĭtas, *f*

rape *nn*, raptus, *m*

rapid răpĭdus, cĕler

rapidity cĕlĕrĭtas, *f*

rapier glădĭus, *m*

rapine răpīna, *f*

rapture laetĭtĭa, *f*

rapturous laetus

rare rārus

rarefy v.t, extĕnŭo (1)

rareness, rarity rārĭtas, *f*

rascal scĕlestus, *m*

rascality scĕlĕra, *n.pl*

rase (to the ground) *v.t*, sŏlo aequo (1)

rash *adj*, tĕmĕrārĭus

rash *nn*, ēruptĭo, *f*

rashness tĕmĕrĭtas, *f*

rasp *nn*, **(file)**, scŏbīna, *f*

rasp *v.t*, rādo (3)

rat mūs, *c*

rate (price) prĕtĭum, *n*; **(tax)** vectīgal, *n*; **(speed)**, cĕlĕrĭtas, *f*; **(at any —)**, *adv*, ŭtīque

rate *v.t*, **(value)**, aestĭmo (1); **(chide)**, incrĕpo (1); **(tax)**, censĕo (2)

rather *adv*, **(preferably)**, pŏtĭus; **(somewhat)**, ălĭquantum; **(a little)**, *with comparatives, e.g.* **rather (more quickly)**, paulo (cĕlĕrĭus)

ratification sanctĭo, *f*

ratify *v.t*, rătum făcĭo (3)

ratio portĭo, *f*

ration *nn*, dēmensum, *n*, cĭbārĭa, *n.pl*

rational (a — being), partĭceps rătĭonis **(participant in reason)**

rationally *adv*, rătĭōne

rattle *nn*, crĕpĭtus, *m*; **(toy)**, crĕpĭtācŭlum, *n*

rattle *v.i*, crĕpo (1)

ravage *v.t*, pŏpŭlor (1 dep.)

ravaging *nn*, pŏpŭlātĭo, *f*

rave *v.i*, fŭro (3)

raven corvus, *m*

ravening, ravenous răpax

ravine fauces, *f.pl*

raving *adj*, fŭrens, insānus

raving *nn*, fŭror, *m*

ravish *v.t*, răpĭo (3), stŭpro (1)

ravishing suāvis

raw crūdus; **(inexperienced, unworked)**, rŭdis

ray rădĭus, *m*

razor nŏvācŭla, *f*

reach *nn*, **(range)**, iactus, *m*; **(space)**, spătĭum, *n*

reach *v.i*, **(extend)**, pertĭnĕo (2), attingo (3); *v.t*, **(come to)**, pervēnĭo (4) ad (*with acc.*)

react v.t, **(be influenced)**, afficĭor (3 pass.)

reaction (of feeling) *use vb*, commŏvĕo (2) (to make an impression on)

read v.t, lĕgo (3); **(— aloud)**, rĕcĭto (1)

readable făcĭlis lectu

reader lector, *m*

readily *adv,* **(willingly)**, lĭbenter

readiness (preparedness) *use adj*, părātus **(ready); (willingness)**, ănĭmus lĭbens, *m*

reading *nn*, lectĭo, *f*, rĕcĭtātĭo, *f*

reading-room bĭblĭothēca, *f*

ready părātus, promptus; **(to be —)**, părātus, praesto esse (*irreg.*); **(to make, get —)**, păro (1)

real *adj*, vērus

realism vērĭtas, *f*

reality rēs, *f*

realization (getting to know) cognĭtĭo, *f*; **(completion)**, confectĭo, *f*

realize *v.t*, intellĕgo (3); **(a project)**, perfĭcĭo (3), perdūco (3)

really *adv*, rēvērā; **(is it so?)**, ĭtăne est?

realm regnum, *n*

reap *v.t*, mĕto (3); **(gain)**, compăro (1)

reaper messor, *m*

reaping-hook falx, *f*

reappear *v.i*, rĕdĕo (*irreg.*)

rear *nn*, **(of a marching column)**, agmen nŏvissĭmum, n; **(of an army)**, ăcĭes nŏvissĭma, *f*; **(in the —)** *adv*, ā tergo

rear *v.t*, **(bring up)**, ēdŭco (1), ălo (3); v.i, **(of horses)**, sē ērĭgĕre (3 *reflex.*)

reason (faculty of thinking) mens, *f*; **(cause)**, causa, *f*; **(for this —)**, *adv*, ĭdĕo, idcirco; **(for what — , why?)**, cur, quārē; **(without — , heedlessly)**, *adv*, tĕmĕre

reason *v.t*, rătĭōcĭnor (1 dep.); **(— with)**, dissĕro (3), cum (*with abl.*)

reasonable (fair) aequus, iustus; **(in size)**, mŏdĭcus

reasonable (fairness) aequĭtas, *f*

reasoning *nn*, rătĭo, *f*

reassemble *v.t*, cōgo (3), in ūnum lŏcum collĭgo (3), **(collect into one place)**; *v.i*, rĕdĕo (4)

reassert *v.t*, rēstĭtŭo (3)

reassure *v.t*, confirmo (1)

rebel *nn*, sēdĭtĭōsus, *m*

rebel rĕbello (1), dēfĭcĭo (3)

rebellion sēdĭtĭo, *f*

rebellious sēdĭtĭosus

rebound *v.i*, rĕsĭlĭo (4)

rebuff *v.t*, rĕpello (3)

rebuff *nn*, rĕpulsa, *f*

rebuke *nn*, rĕprĕhensĭo, *f*

rebuke *v.t*, rĕprĕhendo (3)

recall *nn*, rĕvŏcātĭo, *f*

recall *v.t*, rēvŏco (1); **(— to mind)**, rĕpĕto (3)

recapitulate *v.t*, ēnŭmĕro (1)

recapitulation ēnūmĕrātĭo, *f*

recapture *v.t*, rĕcĭpĭo (3)

recede *v.i*, rĕcēdo (3)

receipt (act of receiving) acceptĭo, *f*; **(document)**, ăpŏcha, *f*

receipts (proceeds) rĕdĭtus, *m*

receive *v.t*, accĭpĭo (3), excĭpĭo (3)

receiver (of stolen goods) rĕceptor, *m*
recent rĕcens
recently *adv*, nūper
receptacle rĕceptācŭlum, *n*
reception ădĭtus, *m*
receptive dŏcĭlis
recess rĕcessus, *m*; **(holidays)**, fērĭae, *f. pl*
reciprocal mūtŭus
reciprocate *v.t*, rĕfĕro (*irreg.*)
recital narrātĭo, *f*
recite v.t, rĕcĭto (1), prōnuntĭo (1)
reckless tĕmĕrārĭus
recklessness tĕmĕrĭtas, *f*
reckon *v.t*, **(count)**, nŭmĕro (1); **(— on, rely on)**, confīdo (3) (*with dat.*); **(consider)**, dūco (3)
reckoning rătĭo, *f*
reclaim *v.t*, rĕpĕto (3)
recline *v.i*, rĕcŭbo (1)
recluse hŏmo sōlĭtārĭus
recognizable *use phr*, quod agnosci pōtest **(that can be recognized)**
recognize *v.t*, agnosco (3), cognosco (3); **(acknowledge)**, confĭtĕor (2 *dep.*)
recognition cognĭtĭo, *f*
recoil *v.i*, rĕsĭlĭo (4)
recollect v.t, rĕmĭniscor (3 *dep. with genit*)
recollection mĕmŏrĭa, *f*
recommence *v.t*, rĕdintĕgro (1)
recommend *v.t*, commendo (1)
recommendation commendātĭo, *f*
recompense *v.t*, rĕmūnĕror (1 *dep*)
reconcile *v.t*, rĕconcĭlĭo (1)
reconciliation rĕconcĭlĭātĭo, *f*
reconnoitre *v.t*, explōro (1)
reconsider *v.t*, rĕpŭto (1)
record *v.t*, in tăbŭlas rĕfĕro (*irreg*)
records tăbŭlae, *f. pl*, fasti, *m. pl*
recount *v.t*, (expound), ēnarro (1)
recourse (to have — to) v.i, confŭgĭo (3) ad (*with acc*)
recover *v.t*, rĕcŭpĕro (1) rĕcĭpĭo (3); *v.i*, **(from illness, etc.)**, rĕvălesco (3), rĕfĭcĭor (3 *pass*), sē collĭgĕre (3 reflex)
recovery rĕcŭpĕrātĭo, *f*; **(from illness)**, sălus, *f*

recreate *v.t*, rĕcrĕo (1)
recreation rĕmissĭo, *f*
recruit *nn*, tīro, *m*
recruit *v.t*, **(enrol)**, conscrībo (3)
recruiting *nn*, dēlectus, *m*
rectify *v.t*, corrĭgo (3)
rectitude prŏbĭtas, *f*
recumbent rĕcŭbans
recur *v.i*, rĕdĕo (4)
red rŭber, rūfus; **(redhanded)**, *adj*, mănĭfestus
redden *v.t*, rŭbĕfăcĭo (3); *v.i*. rŭbesco (3)
redeem *v.t*, rĕdĭmo (3)
redeemer lībĕrātor, *m*
redemption rĕdemptĭo, *f*
red-lead mĭnĭum, *n*
redness rŭbor, *m*
redouble *v.t*, ingĕmĭno (1)
redound rĕdundo (1)
redress *v.t*, rēstĭtŭo (3)
reduce *v.t*, rĕdĭgo (3)
reduction dēmĭnūtĭo, *f*; **(taking by storm)**, expugnātĭo, *f*
redundancy rĕdundantĭa, *f*
redundant sŭpervăcŭus
re-echo *v.i*, rĕsŏno (1)
reed ărundo, *f*
reef saxa, *n.pl*
reek *v.i*, fūmo (1)
reel v.i, (totter), văcillo (1)
re-elect *v.t*, rĕcrĕo (1)
re-establish *v.t*, rēstĭtŭo (3)
refectory cēnācŭlum, *n*
refer *v.t*, rĕfĕro *or* dēfĕro (*irreg*) ad (*with acc*); **(to — to)**, perstringo (3), specto (1) ad (*with acc*)
referee arbĭter, *m*
reference rătĭo, *f*
refill *v.t*, rĕplĕo (2)
refine *v.t*, **(polish)**, expŏlĭo (4)
refined pŏlītus, hūmānus
refinement hūmānĭtas, *f*
refinery officīna, *f*
reflect *v.t*, rĕpercŭtĭo (3), reddo (3); *v.i*, **(ponder)**, rĕpŭto (1) (ănĭmo) **(in the mind)**
reflection (image) ĭmāgo, *f*; **(thought)**, cōgĭtātĭo, *f*
reform ēmendātĭo, *f*
reform *v.t*, rēstĭtŭo (3); **(correct)**, corrĭgo (3); *v.i*, sē corrĭgĕre (3 *reflex*)

reformer ēmendātor, *m*
refract *v.t*, infringo (3)
refractory contŭmax
refrain from *v.i*, sē contĭnēre (2 *reflex*) ad (*with abl*)
refresh *v.t*, rĕcrĕo (1), rĕfĭcĭo (3)
refreshment (food) cĭbus, *m*
refuge perfŭgĭum, *n*; **(to take —)**, *v.i*, confŭgĭo (3) ad (*with acc*)
refugee *adj*, prŏfŭgus
refulgent splendĭdus
refund *v.t*, reddo (3)
refusal rĕcūsātĭo, *f*
refuse *nn*, purgāmentum, *n*
refuse *v.t*, rĕcūso (1); **(to — to do)** nōlo (*irreg*) (*with infi*n); **(say no),** nĕgo (1)
refute *v.t*, rĕfello (3)
regain *v.t*, rĕcĭpĭo (3)
regal rēgālis
regale *v.t*, excĭpĭo (3)
regalia insignĭa, *n.pl*
regard *nn*, **(esteem),** studĭum, *n*, hŏnor, *m*; **(consideration),** rēspectus, *m*
regard v.t, **(look at),** intŭĕor (2 *dep*); **(consider),** hābĕo (2); **(esteem),** aestĭmo (1)
regardless neglĕgens
regency interregnum
regent interrex, *m*
regicide caedes (*f*) rēgis **(killing of a king)**
regiment lĕgĭo, *f*
region rēgĭo, *f*, tractus, *m*
register tăbŭlae, *f.pl*
register *v.t*, perscrĭbo (3)
registrar tăbŭlārĭus, *m*
regret *nn*, dŏlor, *m*
regret *v.t*, **(repent of)** *use* paenĭtet (2 *impers*) (*with acc. of subject*), e.g. **I repent of,** mē paenĭtet (*with genit*)
regular (correctly arranged) ordĭnātus, compŏsĭtus; (customary), sollemnis
regularity ordo, *m*
regularly *adv*, **(in order),** ordĭne; **(customarily),** sollemnĭter
regulate *v.t*, ordĭno (1)
regulation (order) iussum; *n*; **(rule),** praeceptum, *n*
rehabilitate *v.t*, rēstĭtŭo (3)

rehearsal (practice) exercĭtātĭo, *f*
rehearse *v.t*, **(premeditate),** praemĕdĭtor (1 *dep*)
reign *nn*, regnum, *n*
reign *v.i*, regno (1)
reimburse *v.t*, rĕpendo (3)
rein *nn*, hăbēna, *f*
rein *v.t*, **(curb),** frēno (1)
reinforce *v.t*, confirmo (1)
reinforcement (help) auxĭlĭum, *n*
reinstate *v.t*, rēstĭtŭo (3)
reiterate *v.t*, ĭtĕro (1)
reject *v.t*, rēĭcĭo (3)
rejection rēiectĭo, *f*
rejoice *v.i*, gaudĕo (2)
rejoicing *nn*, laetĭtĭa, *f*
rejoin *v.i*, rĕdĕo (4)
relapse *v.i*, rĕcĭdo (3)
relate *v.t*, **(tell),** narro (1), expōno (3); *v.i*, pertĭnĕo (2)
related (by birth) cognātus; **(by marriage),** affinis; **(by blood),** consanguĭnĕus; **(near),** prŏpinquus
relation (relative) cognātus, *m*, affinis *m*; **(connection),** rătĭo, *f*
relationship cognātĭo, *f*, affinĭtas, *f*
relative *nn*, cognātus, *m*, affinis, *m*
relative *adj*, compărātus **(compared)**
relax *v.t*, rĕmitto (3); *v.i*, rĕlanguesco (3)
relaxation rĕmissĭo, *f*
relay *v.t*, **(send),** mitto (3)
relays of horses ĕqui dispŏsĭti, *m.pl* **(horses methodically arranged)**
release *nn*, lībĕrātĭo, *f*
release *v.t*, exsolvo (3) lībĕro (1)
relent *v.t*, rĕmitto (3)
relentless immĭsĕrĭcors
relevant *use vb*, pertĭnĕo (2) **(to concern)**
reliance fĭdūcĭa, *f*
relic rĕlĭquĭae, *f*, *pl*
relief (alleviation) lĕvātĭo, *f*; **(help),** auxĭlĭum, *n*
relieve *v.t*, lĕvo (1), rĕmitto (3); **(help),** subvĕnĭo (4) (*with dat*); **(of command, etc.),** succĕdo (3) (*followed by in and acc. or by dat*)
religion rĕlĭgĭo, *f*, săcra, *n.pl*

religious rĕlĭgĭōsus, pĭus
relinquish *v.t*, rĕlinquo (3)
relish *nn*, stŭdĭum, *n*, săpor, *m*
relish *v.t*, frŭor (3 *dep. with abl*)
reluctance *use adj*, invītus
(unwilling)
reluctant invītus
rely on *v.t*, confīdo (3) (*with dat. of person or abl. of thing*)
relying on *adj*, frētus (*with abl*)
remain *v.i*, mănĕo (2); **(be left over)**, sūpersum (*irreg*)
remainder rĕlĭquum, *n*
remaining *adj*, rĕlĭquus
remains rĕlĭquĭae, *f, pl*
remand *v.t*, remando (1)
remark *nn*, dictum, *n*
remark *v.t*, **(say)**, dīco (3); **(observe)**, observo (1)
remarkable insignis
remedy rĕmĕdĭum, *n*, mĕdĭcāmentum, *n*
remedy *v.t*, sāno (1); **(correct)**; corrĭgo (3)
remember *v.i*, mĕmĭni (*v. defect. with genit*), rĕcordor (1 *dep. with acc*)
remembrance rĕcordātĭo, *f*, mĕmŏrĭa, *f*
remind *v.t*, mŏnĕo (2)
reminiscence rĕcordātĭo, *f*
remiss neglĕgens
remission (forgiveness) vĕnĭa, *f*; **(release)**, sŏlūtĭo, *f*
remit *v.t*, rĕmitto (3)
remittance pĕcūnĭa, *f*
remnant rĕlĭquĭae, *f. pl*
remonstrate *v.i*, rĕclāmo (1) (*with dat*)
remorse conscĭentĭa, *f*
remorseless immĭsĕrĭcors, dūrus
remote rĕmōtus
remoteness longinquĭtas, *f*
removal (driving away) āmōtĭo, *f*; **(sending away)**, rĕlēgātĭo, *f*; **(— by force)**, raptus, *m*
remove *v.t*, rĕmŏvĕo (2); **(send away)**, rĕlēgo (1); *v.i*, migro (1)
remunerate *v.t*, rĕmūnĕror (1 dep)
remuneration rĕmūnĕrātĭo, f
rend *v.t*, scindo (3)
render *v.t*, reddo (3)

rendezvous (to fix a —) lŏcum (et dĭem) constĭtŭo (3), **(place (and day))**
rending (severing) discĭdĭum, *n*
renegade (deserter) transfŭga, *c*
renew *v.t*, rĕnŏvo (1), rĕdintĕgro (1)
renewal rĕnŏvātĭo, *f*
renounce *v.t*, rĕnuntĭo (1), rĕmitto (3)
renovate *v.t*, rĕnŏvo (1)
renovation rēstĭtūtĭo, *f*
renown fāma, *f*, glōrĭa, *f*
renowned clārus
rent *nn*, scissūra, *f*; **(of houses, etc.)**, merces, *f*
rent *v.t*, **(let)**, lŏco (1); **(hire)**, condūco (3)
renunciation rĕpŭdĭātĭo, f
repair *v.t*, rĕfĭcĭo (3), sarcĭo (4)
repaired sartus
reparation sătisfactĭo, *f*
repast cĭbus, *m*
repay *v.t*, **(grātĭam)** rĕfĕro (*irreg*)
repayment sŏlūtĭo, *f*
repeal *nn*, abrŏgātĭo, *f*
repeal *v.t*, abrŏgo (1), rēscindo (3)
repeat *v.t*, ĭtĕro (1), reddo (3)
repeatedly *adv*, ĭdentĭdem
repel *v.t*, rĕpello (3)
repent *v.i*, paenĭtet (2 *impers*) (*with acc. of person and genit. of cause*), *e.g.* **I repent of this deed**, mē paenĭtet huius facti
repentance paenĭtentĭa, *f*
repentant paenĭtens
repetition ĭtērātĭo, *f*
replace *v.t*, rĕpōno (3); **(substitute)**, substĭtŭo (3)
replenish *v.t*, rĕplĕo (2)
replete rĕplētus
reply *nn*, rēsponsum, *n*
reply *v.i*, rēspondĕo (2)
report *nn*, nuntĭus, *m*; **(rumour)**, fāma, *f*; **(bang)**, crĕpĭtus, *m*
report *v.t*, rĕfĕro (*irreg*), nuntĭo (1)
repose *nn*, quĭes, *f*
repose *v.i*, **(rest)** quĭesco (3)
repository rĕceptācŭlum, *n*
reprehend *v.t*, rĕprĕhendo (3)
reprehensible culpandus

represent *v.t*, exprĭmo (3), fingo (3); **(take the place of)**, persōnam gĕro (3)
representation ĭmāgo, *f*
representative (deputy) prōcūrātor, *m*
repress *v.t*, cŏhĭbĕo (2)
reprieve *nn*, **(respite)**, mŏra, *f*
reprieve *v.t*, **(put off)**, dĭffĕro (*irreg*)
reprimand *nn*, rĕprĕhensĭo, *f*
reprimand *v.t*, rĕprĕhendo (3)
reprisal *use* poena, *f*, **(punishment)**
reproach *nn*, exprŏbrātĭo, *f*, opprŏbrĭum, *n*
reproach *v.t*, exprŏbro (1), ōbĭcĭo (3) (*both with acc. of thing and dat. of person*)
reproachful obiurgātŏrĭus
reprobate *nn*, perdĭtus, *m*, nĕbŭlo, *m*
reproduce *v.t*, rĕcrĕo (1)
reproof rĕprĕhensĭo, *f*, obiurgātĭo, *f*, vĭtŭpĕrātĭo, *f*
reprove *v.t*, rĕprĕhendo (3), obiurgo (1), vĭtŭpĕro (1)
reptile serpens, *f*
republic respublĭca, *f*
republican *adj*, pŏpŭlāris
repudiate *v.t*, rĕpŭdĭo (1)
repudiation rĕpŭdĭatĭo, *f*
repugnance ŏdĭum, *n*
repugnant āversus; **(it is — to me, I hate it)**, *use phr*, ŏdĭo esse **(to be hateful)**, *with dat. of person*
repulse *v.t*, rĕpello (3)
repulsive foedus, ŏdĭōsus
reputable hŏnestus
reputation, repute fāma, *f*; **(good —)**, existĭmātĭo, *f*; **(bad —)**, infāmĭa, *f*
request nn, rŏgātĭo, *f*
request *v.t*, rŏgo (1), prĕcor (1 dep)
require *v.t*, **(demand)**, postŭlo (1) **(need)**, ĕgĕo (2) (*with abl*)
requirement (demand) postŭlātĭo, *f*; *or use adj*, nĕcessārĭus
requisite *adj*, nĕcessārĭus
requisition postŭlātĭo, *f*
requite *v.t*, rĕpŏno (3)
rescind *v.t*, rēscindo (3)
rescue *v.t*, ērĭpĭo (3)
rescue *nn*, lībĕrātĭo, *f*

research investīgātĭo, *f*
resemblance sĭmĭlĭtūdo, *f*
resemble *v.t*, rĕfĕro (*irreg*), sĭmĭlis esse (*irreg*) (*with genit. or dat*)
resembling *adj*, sĭmĭlis
resent *v.t*, aegrē fĕro (*irreg*) **(tolerate with displeasure)**
resentful īrācundus
resentment īra, *f*
reservation (restriction) exceptĭo, *f*
reserve *nn*, **(military)**, subsĭdĭum, *n*; **(of disposition)**, grăvĭtas, *f*
reserve *v.t*, servo (1); **(put aside)**, sēpōno (3)
reserved (of disposition) grăvis
reservoir lăcus, *m*
reside *v.i*, hăbĭto (1)
residence sēdes, *f.pl*, dŏmĭcĭlĭum, *n*
resident incŏla, *c*
resign *v.i*, and *v.t*, concēdo (3); **(to — oneself to)**, sē committĕre (*3 reflex. with* in *and acc*)
resignation (of office, etc.) abdĭcātĭo, *f*; **(of mind)** aequus ănĭmus, *m*
resin rēsīna, *f*
resist *v.t*, rĕsisto (3) (*with dat*)
resistance rĕpugnantĭa, *f*, *or use vb*, rĕsisto (3) **(to resist)**
resolute firmus, fortis
resolution obstĭnātĭo, *f*, constantĭa, *f*; **(decision)**, *use vb*, plăcet **(it is resolved)**
resolve *v.t*, **(determine)**, stătŭo (3); **(solve)**, dissolvo (3)
resort to *v.t*, **(a place)**, cĕlĕbro (1); **(have recourse to)**, confŭgĭo (3) ad (*with acc*)
resort *nn*, **(plan)**, consĭlĭum, *n*; **(last —)**, extrēma, *n.pl*
resound *v.i*, rĕsŏno (1)
resource (help) auxĭlĭum, *n*; **(wealth, means)** ŏpes, *f*, *pl*
respect *nn*, **(esteem)**, observantĭa, *f*; **(in all — s)**, omnĭbus partĭbus; **(in — of)**, *use abl. case, e.g.* **stronger in respect of number**, sŭpĕrĭor nŭmĕro
respect *v.t*, **(esteem)**, observo (1); **(reverence)**, sispĭcĭo (3)
respectability hŏnestas, *f*
respectable hŏnestus

respectful observans
respecting *prep,* dē (*with abl*)
respective *use* quisque (**each**) with sŭus (**his own**)
respiration respīrātĭo, *f*
respite (delay) mŏra, *f*
resplendent splendĭdus
respond *v.i,* rēspondĕo (2)
response rēsponsum, *n*
responsibility (duty, function) officĭum, *n; or use imp. vb,* ŏportet (**it behoves**)
responsible (to be — for) praesto (1)
rest *nn,* (**repose**), quĭes, *f,* ōtĭum, *n;* (**remainder**), *use adj,* rēlĭquus, *e.g.* **the — of one's life,** rēlĭqua vīta, *f*
rest *v.i,* quĭesco (3); (**— on, depend on**), nītor (3 *dep*)
resting-place cŭbīle, *n*
restitution (to make —) *v.t,* rēstĭtŭo (3)
restive *use phr,* qui nōn făcĭle dŏmāri pŏtest (**that cannot easily be subdued**)
restless inquĭētus
restlessness ĭnquĭes, *f*
restoration rēstĭtūtĭo, *f*
restore *v.t,* rēstĭtŭo (3)
restrain *v.t,* cŏercĕo (2), rĕprĭmo (3), cŏhĭbĕo (2)
restraint mŏdĕrātĭo, *f*
restrict *v.t,* circumscrībo (3)
restriction (bound) mŏdus, *m*
result *nn,* ēventus, *m*
result *v.i,* ēvĕnĭo (4)
resume *v.t,* rĕpĕto (3)
resurrection rēsurrectĭo, *f*
resuscitate *v.t,* rēsuscĭto (1)
retail *v.t,* dīvendo (3)
retailer caupo, *m*
retain *v.t,* rĕtĭnĕo (2)
retainer sătelles, *c;* (*pl*) soldūrĭi, *m. pl*
retake *v.t,* rĕcĭpĭo (3)
retaliate *v.t,* ulciscor (3 *dep*)
retaliation ultĭo, *f*
retard *v.t,* mŏror (1 *dep*)
reticent tăcĭturnus
retinue (companions) cŏmĭtes, *c.pl*
retire *v.i,* (**go away**), rĕcēdo (3), ăbĕo (4); (**from a post, etc.**),

dēcēdo (3); (**retreat**), sē rĕcĭpĕre (3 *reflex*)
retired rĕmōtus
retirement (act of —) rĕcessus, *m;* (**leisure**), ōtĭum, *n*
retiring *adj,* vĕrēcundus
retort *v.t,* rĕfĕro (*irreg*)
retrace *v.t,* rĕpĕto (3)
retract *v.t,* rĕnuntĭo (1)
retreat *nn,* rĕceptus, *m;* (**place of refuge**), rĕfŭgĭum, *n*
retreat *v.i,* sē rĕcĭpĕre (3 *reflex*)
retrench *v.t,* mĭnŭo (3)
retribution poena, *f*
retrieve *v.t,* rĕcŭpĕro (1)
retrograde *adj, use comp. adj,* pēior (**worse**)
retrogression rĕgressus, *m*
retrospect *use vb,* rēspĭcĭo (3) (**to look back**)
return *nn,* (**coming back**), rĕdĭtus, *m;* (**giving back**), rēstĭtūtĭo, *f;* (**profit**), quaestus, *m*
return *v.t,* (**give back**), reddo (3), rĕfĕro (*irreg*), v.i, (**go back**), rĕdĕo (4)
reunite *v.t,* rĕconcĭlĭo (1)
reveal *v.t,* pătĕfăcĭo (3)
revel *nn,* cōmissātĭo, *f*
revel *v.i,* cōmissor (1 *dep*)
revelation pătĕfactĭo, *f*
revenge *nn,* ultĭo, *f*
revenge oneself on *v.t,* ulciscor (3 *dep*)
revengeful cŭpĭdus ulciscendi (**keen on revenge**)
revenue vectīgal, *n*
reverberate *v.i,* rĕsŏno (1)
revere, reverence *v.t,* vĕnĕror (1 *dep*)
reverence vĕnĕrātĭo, *f*
revered vĕnĕrābĭlis
reverend vĕnĕrābĭlis
reverent rĕvĕrens
reverse (contrary) *adj,* contrārĭus (**opposite**); (**defeat**), clādes
reverse *v.t,* inverto (3)
revert *v.i,* rĕdĕo (4)
review *nn,* rĕcognĭtĭo, *f,* rĕcensĭo, *f*
review *v.t,* rĕcensĕo (2)
revile *v.t,* mălĕdīco (3) (*with dat*)
reviling *nn,* mălĕdictĭo, *f*
revise *v.t,* ēmendo (1)

revision ēmendātĭo, *f*
revisit *v.t*, rĕvīso (3)
revival rĕnŏvātĭo, *f*
revive *v.t*, rĕcrĕo (1), excĭto (1);
v.i, rĕvīvisco (3)
revocable rĕvŏcābĭlis
revoke *v.t*, abrŏgo (1)
revolt *nn*, dēfectĭo, f, sēdĭtĭo, f
revolt *v.i*, dēfĭcĭo (3)
revolting *adj*, (disgusting), foedus
revolution (turning
round) conversĭo, *f*; (political),
nŏvae res, *f. pl*
revolutionize *v.t*, nŏvo (1)
revolutionary sēdĭtĭōsus
revolve *v.i*, sē volvĕre (3 *reflex*)
reward *nn*, praemĭum, *n*
reward *v.t*, rĕmŭnĕror (1 *dep*)
rewrite *v.t*, rēscrībo (3)
rhetoric rhētŏrĭca, *f*
rhetorical rhētŏrĭcus
Rhine Rhēnus, *m*
rhinoceros rhīnŏcĕros, *m*
rhubarb rādix Pontĭca, *f* (**Black
Sea root**)
rhyme (**verse**) versus, *m*
rhythm nŭmĕrus, *m*
rhythmical nŭmĕrōsus
rib costa, *f*
ribald obsēnus
ribbon taenĭa, *f*
rice ŏrȳza, *f*
rich dīves, lŏcŭples; (**fertile**),
pinguis
riches dīvĭtĭae, *f. pl*
richness ūbertas, *f*
rick (**heap**) ăcervus, *m*
rid *v.t*, lībĕro (1); (**to get — of**),
dēpōno (3), dēpello (3)
riddle aenigma, *n*; (**in — s**), per
ambāges
riddle *v.t*, (**sift**), cerno (3); (**— with
holes**), confŏdĭo (3)
ride *v.i*, vĕhor (3 *dep*); (**— at
anchor**), consisto (3)
ride (**horseman**) ĕquĕs, *m*
ridge (**mountain —**), iŭgum, *n*
ridicule *nn*, rīdĭcŭlum, *n*
ridicule *v.t*, irrīdĕo (2)
ridiculous rīdĭcŭlus
riding *nn*, ĕquĭtātĭo, *f*
rife frĕquens, crēber
rifle *v.t*, praedor (1 *dep.*)

rift rīma, *f*
rig *v.t*, armo (1)
rigging armāmentum, *n.pl*
right *adj*, (**direction**), dexter; (**true**),
rectus, vērus; (**correct**), rectus;
(**fit**), ĭdōnĕus; (**— hand**), dextra
(manus)
right *nn*, (**moral**), fas, *n*; (**legal**), iūs,
n
rightly adv, rectē, vērē
right *v.t*, rēstĭtŭo (3)
righteous iustus
righteousness prŏbĭtas, *f*
rightful iustus
rigid rĭgĭdus, dūrus
rigorous dūrus
rigour dūrĭtĭa, *f*
rill rīvŭlus, *m*
rim ōra, *f*, lābrum, *n*
rime prūīna, *f*
rind crusta, *f*
ring (**finger, etc.**), ānŭlus, *m*;
(**circle**), orbis, *m*
ring *v.i*, tinnĭo (4); (**surround**)
circŭmĕo (4)
ringing *nn*, tinnītus, *m*
ringing *adj*, tinnŭlus
ringleader auctor, *m*
ringlet cincinnus, *m*
rinse *v.t*, collŭo (3)
riot turba, *f*, tŭmultus, *m*; (**to make
a —**), tŭmultum făcĭo (3)
riotous turbŭlentus; (**extravagant**),
luxŭrĭōsus
rip *v.t*, scindo (3)
ripe mātūrus
ripen *v.i*, mātūresco (3); *v.t*,
mātūro (1)
ripeness mātūrĭtas, *f*
ripple *v.i*, (**tremble**), trĕpĭdo (1)
rise *nn*, (**of sun, etc.**, *or* **origin**),
ortus, *m*
rise *v.i*, surgo (3); (**of sun, etc.**),
ŏrĭor (4 *dep*); (**in rank**), cresco
(3); (**in rebellion**), consurgo (3)
rising *nn*, ortus, *m*; (**in rebellion**),
mōtus, *m*
rising (**ground**) *nn*, clīvus, *m*
risk *nn*, pĕrīcŭlum, *n*
risk *v.t*, pĕrīclĭtor (1 *dep*)
ritual rītus, *m*
rival *nn*, aemŭlus, *m*, rīvālis, *c*
ribal *v.t*, aemŭlor (1 *dep*)

rivalry aemŭlātĭo, *f*
river *nn*, flūmen, *n*, flŭvĭus, *m*
riverbank rīpa, *f*
riverbed alvĕus, *m*
rivet clāvus, *m*
rivulet rīvŭlus, *m*
road vĭa, *f*, ĭter, *n*; **(to make a —)**, vĭam mūnĭo (4)
road-making mūnītĭo, *(f)* vĭārum
roadstead (for ships) stătĭo, *f*
roam *v.i*, văgor (1 *dep*), erro (1)
roaming *adj*, văgus
road *nn*, frĕmĭtus, *m*
road *v.i*, frĕmo (3)
roast *v.t*, torrĕo (2)
roasted assus
rob *v.t*, spŏlĭo (1) *(with acc. of person robbed, abl. of thing taken)*
robber lătro, *m*
robbery lătrōcĭnĭum, *n*
robe vestis, *f*, vestīmentum, *n*; **(woman's —)**, stŏla, *f*; **(— of state)**, trăbĕa, *f*; **(— of kings)**, purpŭra, *f*
robe *v.t*, vestĭo (4), indŭo (3)
robust rōbustus
rock rūpes, *f*
rock *v.t*, ăgĭto (1)
rocky scŏpŭlōsus
rod virga, *f*; **(fishing —)**, ărundo, *f*
roe căprĕa, *f*; **(of fish)**, ōva, *n.pl* **(eggs)**
rogue scĕlestus, *m*
roguery nēquĭtĭa, *f*
roll *nn*, **(something rolled up)**, vŏlūmen, *n*; **(names)**, album, *n*
roll *v.t*, volvo (3); *v.i*, volvor (3 *pass*)
roller cўlindrus, *m*
rolling *adj*, vŏlūbĭlis
Roman Rōmānus
romance (story) fābŭla, *f*
romance *v.i*, fābŭlor (1 *dep*)
romantic (fabulous) commentĭcĭus
Rome Rōma, *f*
romp *v.i*, lūdo (3)
romp *nn*, lūsus, *m*
roof *nn*, tectum, *n*
roof *v.t*, tĕgo (3)
rook (raven) corvus, *m*

room conclāve, *n*; **(space)**, spătĭum, *n*; **(bed —)**, cŭbĭcŭlum, *n*; **(dining —)** trīclīnĭum, *n*
roomy căpax
roost *nn*, pertĭca, *f*
root rādix, *f*; **(to strike — s, become rooted)**, rādīces ăgo (3); **(— ed to the spot)**, dēfixus
rope fūnis, *m*, restis, *f*, rŭdens, *m*
rosary (garden) rŏsārĭum, *n*
rose rŏsa, *f*
rosemary ros mărīnus, *m*
rostrum rostra, *n.pl*
rosy rŏsĕus
rot *nn*, tābes, *f*
rot *v.i*, pūtesco (3)
rotate *v.i*, sē volvĕre (3 *reflex*)
rotation turbo, *m*
rotten pŭtrĭdus
rotundity rŏtundĭtas, *f*
rouge *nn*, fūcus, *m*
rouge *v.t*, fūco (1)
rough asper; **(weather)**, ătrox; **(of sea)**, turbĭdus; **(of manner)**, incultus
roughness aspĕrĭtas, *f*
round *adj*, rŏtundus
round *adv*, circum
round *prep*, circum *(with acc)*
round *v.t*, **(to make —)**, rŏtundo (1), curvo (1); **(to — off)**, conclūdo (3); *v.i*, **(to go —)**, circumăgor (3 *pass*)
roundabout *adj*, dēvĭus
rouse *v.t*, excĭto (1)
rout *nn*, **(flight, defeat)**, fŭga, *f*
rout *v.t*, fŭgo (1)
route ĭter, *n*
routine ūsus, *m*
rove *v.i*, văgor (1 *dep*)
roving *nn*, văgātĭo, *f*
row (line) ordo, *m*; **(quarrel)**, rixa, *f*; **(noise)**, strĕpĭtus, *m*
row *v.i*, rēmĭgo (1)
rowing *nn*, rēmĭgĭum, *n*
royal rēgĭus
royalty regnum, *n*
rub *v.t*, tĕro (3), frĭco (1); **(— out)**, dēlĕo (2)
rubbish quisquĭlĭae, *f. pl*
rubicund rŭbĭcundus

ruby *nn*, carbuncŭlus, *m*
ruby *adj*, purpŭrĕus
rudder gŭbernācŭlum, *n*
ruddy rŭbĭcundus
rude (person) asper, ĭnurbānus
rudeness ĭnhūmānĭtas, *f*
rudimentary incŏhātus
 (incomplete)
rudiments ĕlĕmenta, *n.pl*
rue *nn*, rūta, *f*
rueful maestus
ruff torquis, *m. or f*
ruffian perdĭtus, *m*, lătro, *m*
ruffianly *adj*, scĕlestus
ruffle *v.t*, ăgĭto (1)
rug strāgŭlum, *n*
rugged asper
ruin exĭtĭum, *n*, rŭīna, *f*; **(building)**,
 părĭĕtĭnae, *f. pl*
ruin *v.t*, perdo (3)
ruinous exĭtĭōsus, damnōsus
rule *nn*, **(law)**, lex, *f*; **(precept)**,
 praeceptum, *n*; **(pattern)**, norma,
 f; **(for measuring)**, rēgŭla, *f*;
 (government), impĕrĭum, *n*
rule *v.t*, rĕgo (3); *v.i*, regno (1)
ruler (person) dŏmĭnus, *m*;
 (measurement), rēgŭla, *f*
rumble *nn*, mumur, *n*
rumble *v.i*, murmŭro (1), mūgĭo
 (4)
ruminate *v.t*, cōgĭto (1)
rummage *v.t*, rīmor (1 *dep*)
rumour *nn*, rūmor, *m*, fāma, *f*
rump clūnes, *f. pl*
rumple *v.t*, corrūgo (1)
run *v.i*, curro (3); **(— about)**, hūc
 illūc curro (3); **(— after)**,
 persĕquor (3 *dep*); **(— away)**,
 fūgio (3); **(— aground)**, impingor
 (3 *pass*), inflīgor (3 *pass*); **(—
 back)**, rĕcurro (3); **(— down)**,
 dēcurro (3); **(— forward)**,
 prōcurro (3); **(— into)**, incurro
 (3); **(— out)**, excurro (3); **(—
 over, with vehicle, etc.)**, obtēro
 (3); **(— through)**, percurro (3)
runaway *adj*, fŭgĭtīvus
runner cursor, *m*
running *nn*, cursus, *m*
running *adj*, **(water)**, vīvus
rupture (disease) hernĭa, *f*

rupture *v.t*, rumpo (3)
rural rustĭcus
rush *nn*, **(plant)**, iuncus, *m*;
 (rushing, running), impĕtus, *m*
rush *v.i*, rŭo (3); **(— forward)**, sē
 prōrĭpĕre (3 *reflex*); **(— into)**,
 irrŭo (3); **(— out)**, sē effundĕre (3
 reflex)
rusk crustum, *n*
russet rūfus
rust *nn*, rōbīgo, *f*
rustic *adj*, rustĭcus
rusticate *v.i*, rustĭcor (1 *dep*); *v.t*,
 rĕlēgo (1)
rusticity rustĭcĭtas, *f*
rustle *v.i*, crĕpo (1)
rustle, rustling *nn*, sŭsurrus, *m*
rusty rōbīgĭnōsus
ruthless immītis, sĕvērus
rye sĕcāle, *n*

S

Sabbath sabbăta, *n.pl*
sable *adj*, **(black)**, āter
sabre glădĭus, *m*
sack (bag) saccus, *m*; **(pillage)**,
 dīreptĭo, *f*
sack *v.t*, **(pillage)**, dīrĭpĭo (3)
sackcloth saccus, *m*
sacrament săcrāmentum, *n*
sacred săcer, sanctus
sacredness sanctĭtas, *f*
sacrifice săcrĭfĭcĭum, *n*; **(the
 victim)**, hostĭa, *f*
sacrifice *v.i*, săcrĭfĭco (1); *v.t*,
 immŏlo (1)
sacrificial săcrĭfĭcus
sacrilege săcrĭlĕgĭum, *n*; *or use vb*,
 dīrĭpĭo (3) **(to plunder)**
sad tristis
sadden *v.t*, tristĭtĭā affĭcĭo (3)
 (affect with sadness)
saddle *nn*, ĕphhippĭum, *n*
saddle *v.t*, sterno (3); **(impose)**,
 impōno (3)
sadness tristĭtĭa, f
safe (free from danger) tūtus;
 (having escaped from danger),
 incŏlŭmis

safe-conduct fĭdes, *f*
safeguard (act of −) cautĭo, *f*; **(defence)**, prōpugnācŭlum, *n*
safely *adv*, tūtō
safety sălus, *f*
saffron *nn*, crŏcus, *m*
saffron *adj*, crŏcĕus
sagacious prūdens, săgax
sagacity prūdentĭa, *f*, săgācĭtas, *f*
sage (wise man) săpĭens, *m*; **(plant)**, salvĭa, *f*
sail *nn*, vēlum, *n*; **(to set −)**, vēla do (1)
sail *v.i*, nāvĭgo (1), vēhor (3 *pass*); **(to go by means of sails)**, vēla făcĭo (3)
sailing *nn*, nāvĭgātĭo, *f*
sailor nauta, *m*
saint sanctus, *m*
saintly sanctus
sake (for the − of), *prep*, causā (*with genit*); **(on behalf of)**, prō (*with abl*), ŏb, propter (*with acc*)
salad ăcētārĭa, *n.pl*
salary merces, *f*
sale vendĭtĭo, *f*; **(auction)**, hasta, *f*
salient *adj*, prīmus **(first)**
saline salsus
saliva sălīva, *f*
sallow pallĭdus
sally *nn*, ēruptĭo, *f*
sally *v.i*, ēruptĭōnem făcĭo (3)
salmon salmo, *m*
saloon ātrĭum, *n*
salt *nn*, sal, *m*
salt *adj*, salsus
salt *v.t*, săle condĭo (4) **(season with salt)**
saltcellar sălīnum, *n*
saltmines sălīnae, *f. pl*
salubrious sălūbris
salutary sălūtāris; **(useful)**, ūtĭlis
salutation sălūtātĭo, *f*
salute *v.t*, sălūto (1)
salvation sălus, *f*
salve unguentum, *n*
salver scŭtella, *f*, pătella, *f*
same *prep*, īdem; **(the same as)**, īdem qui, īdem atque; **(in the − place)**, *adv*, ĭbīdem **(at the − time)**, sĭmŭl; **(fixed, constant)**, constans

sample exemplum, *n*
sanctification sanctĭfĭcātĭo, *f*
sanctify *v.t*, consĕcro (1)
sanction auctōrĭtas, *f*; **(penalty)** poena, *f*
sanction *v.t*, fătum făcĭo (3)
sanctity sanctĭtas, *f*
sanctuary fānum, *n*, templum, *n*: **(refuge)**, rĕfŭgĭum, *n*
sand hărēna, *f*
sandal sŏlĕa, *f*
sandstone tōfus, *m*
sandy hărēnōsus
sane sānus
sanguinary crŭentus, sanguĭnārĭus
sanguine *use* spēs, *f*, **(hope)**
sanity mens sāna, *f*
sap *nn*, sūcus, *m*
sap *v.t*, subrŭo (3)
sapient *adj*, săpĭens
sapless ārĭdus
sapling arbor nŏvella
sappers (military) mūnītōres, *m. pl*
sapphire sapphīrus, *f*
sarcasm căvillātĭo, *f*, **(scoffing)**
sarcastic ăcerbus
sarcophagus sarcŏphăgus, *m*
sash cingŭlum, *n*
satanic nĕfandus
satchel lŏcŭlus, *m*
satellite (star) stella, *f*; **(attendant)**, sătelles, *c*
satiate *v.t*, sătĭo (1)
satiety sătĭĕtas, *f*
satire sătŭra, *f*
satirical (bitter) ăcerbus
satirize *v.t*, perstringo (3)
satirist scriptor sătĭrĭcus, *m*
satisfaction (inner) vŏluptas, *f*; **(compensation, punishment)**, poena,
satisfactorily *adv*, ex sententĭā
satisfactory ĭdōnĕus, *or* sătis **(enough)**
satisfied contentus
satisfy *v.t*, **(a need)**, explĕo (2), (*with dat*); **(convince)**, persuādĕo (2)
satrap sătrăpes, *m*
saturate *v.t*, sătŭro (1)

satyr sătȳrus, *m*
sauce condīmentum, *n*
saucepan cācăbus, *m*, cortīna
saucer pătella, *f*
saucy pĕtŭlans
saunter *v.i*, văgor (1 *dep*)
sausage farcīmen, *n*
savage *adj*, fĕrus, ătrox, effĕrātus
savageness, savagery fĕrĭtas, *f*, saevĭtĭa, *f*
save *v.t*, servo (1); **(defend)**, tŭĕor (2 *dep*); **(lay by)**, rĕservo (1)
save *prep*, praeter (*with acc*)
saving *nn*, conservātĭo, *f*
savings pĕcūlĭum, *n*
saviour servātor, *m*
savour *nn*, săpor, *m*
savour *v.t*, săpĭo (3)
savoury *adj*, condītus
saw serra, *f*
saw *v.t*, serrā sĕco (1) **(cut with a saw)**
sawdust scŏbis, *f*
say *v.t*, dīco (3), lŏquor (3 *dep*); **(to — that something will not ...)**, *use* nĕgo (1) **(to deny); (it is said)**, fertur
saying *nn*, dictum, *n*
scab crusta, *f*
scabbard vāgīna, *f*
scabby scăber
scaffold (frame) māchĭna, *f*; **(execution)**, supplĭcĭum, *n*
scald *nn*, ădusta, *n.pl*
scale (pair of —s) lībra, *f*; **(of fish)**, squāma, *f*; **(gradation)**, grădus, *m*
scale *v.t*, **(climb with ladders)**, scālis ascendo (3)
scaling-ladders scālae, *f. pl*
scallop pecten, *m*
scalp cŭtis, *f*, **(skin)**
scalpel scalpellum, *n*
scamp scĕlestus, *m*
scamper *v.i*, fŭgĭo (3)
scan *v.t*, contemplor (1 *dep*)
scandal opprŏbrĭum, *n*; **(disparagement)** obtrectātĭo, *f*
scandalous infāmis
scanty exĭgŭus
scantiness exĭgŭĭtas, *f*
scapegrace nēbŭlo, *m*
scar cĭcātrix, *f*

scarce rārus
scarcely *adv*, vix, aegrĕ
scarcity (of supplies, etc.) ĭnŏpĭa, *f*
scare *v.t*, terrĕo (2)
scarecrow formīdo, *f*
scarf chlămys, *f*
scarlet *nn*, coccum, *n*
scarlet *adj*, coccĭnĕus
scathing ăcerbus
scatter *v.t*, spargo (3); *v.i*, sē spargĕre (3 *reflex*)
scene (of play) scēna, *f*; **(spectacle)**, spectācŭlum, *n*
scenery (natural —) *use* rĕgĭo, *f*, **(region)**
scent (sense of smell) ŏdōrātus, *m*; **(the smell itself)**, ŏdor, *m*
scent *v.t*, **(discern by smell)**, ŏdōror (1 *dep*)
scented ŏdōrātus
sceptical dŭbĭtans
sceptre sceptrum, *n*
schedule tăbŭla, *f*
scheme *nn*, consĭlĭum, *n*
scheme *v.t*, consĭlĭum căpĭo (3) **(make a plan)**
scholar (pupil) discĭpŭlus, *m*; **(learned man)**, doctus, *m*
scholarly doctus
scholarship littĕrae, *f. pl*
school lūdus, *m*, schŏla
school *v.t*, ērŭdĭo (4)
schoolmaster măgister, *m*
schoolmistress măgistra, *f*
schooner phăsēlus, *m*
sciatica ischĭas, *f*
science scĭentĭa, *f*, discĭplĭna, *f*, rătĭo, *f*
scientific *use genit. of nouns above*
scimitar ăcīnăces, *m*
scintillate *v.i*, scintillo (1)
scion prōles, *f*
scissors forfĭces, *f. pl*
scoff at *v.t*, irrīdĕo (2)
scoffer irrīsor, *m*
scoffing *nn*, irrīsĭo, *f*
scold *v.t*, obiurgo (1), incrĕpo (1)
scoop out *v.t*, căvo (1)
scoop *nn*, trulla, *f*
scope (room) campus, *m*
scorch *v.t*, ambūro (3)

scorched torrĭdus

scorching torrĭdus

score (total) summa, *f*; (account, reckoning), rătĭo, *f*; (mark), nŏta, *f*

score *v.t*, (note, mark), nŏto (1); (— a victory), victōrĭam rĕporto (1)

scorn *nn*, contemptus, *m*

scorn *v.t*, sperno (3), contemno (3)

scornful sŭperbus

scorpion scorpĭo, *m*

scoundrel nēbŭlo, *m*

scour *v.t*, (clean), tergĕo (2); (run over) percurro (3)

scourge *nn*, (whip), flăgellum, *n*; (pest), pestis, *f*, pernĭcĭes, *f*

scourge *v.t*, verbĕro (1)

scourging *nn*, verbĕra, *n.pl*

scout explōrātor, *m*

scout *v.t*, (spy out), spĕcŭlor (1 *dep*)

scowl *nn*, frontis contractĭo, *f*

scowl *v.i*, frontem contrăho (3), (contract the brow)

scramble for *v.t, use phr*, inter sē certāre (struggle among themselves)

scrap frustrum, *n*

scrape *v.t*, rādo (3)

scraper strĭgilis, *f*

scratch *v.t*, rādo (3), scalpo (3)

scream *nn*, vōcĭfĕrātĭo, *f*

scream *v.i*, vōcĭfĕror (1 *dep*)

screech owl ŭlŭla, *f*

screen tĕgĭmen, *n*

screen *v.t*, tĕgo (3)

screw *nn*, clāvus, *m*

scribble *v.t*, scrībo (3)

scribe scrība, *m*

Scripture Scriptūra, *f*

scroll vŏlūmen, *n*

scrub *v.t*, tergĕo (2)

scruple (religious, etc.) rĕlĭgĭo, *f*

scrupulous rĕlĭgĭōsus, dīlĭgens

scrutinize *v.t*, scrūtor (1 *dep*)

scrutiny scrūtātĭo, *f*

scuffle *nn*, rixa, *f*

scull (oar) rēmus, *m*; (*v.i*, rēmĭgo (1)

sculptor sculptor, *m*

sculpture (art of —) sculptūra, *f*; (the work itself), ŏpus, *n*

scum spūma, *f*

scurf furfur, *m*

scurrility prŏcācĭtas, *f*

scurrilous scurrīlis, prŏcax

scurvy foedus

scuttle *v.t*, (a ship), *use phr*, nāvem ultro dēprĭmo (3) (sink the ship of their own accord)

scythe falx, *f*

sea măre, *n*, (to be at —), nāvĭgo (1)

sea *adj*, mărĭtĭmus, mărīnus

seacoast ōra mărĭtĭma, *f*

seafaring *adj*, mărĭtĭmus

seafight pugna nāvālis, *f*

seagull lărus, *m*

seal *nn*, (of letter), signum, *n*; (animal), phōca, *f*

seal *v.t*, (letter), signo (1); (close up), comprĭmo (3)

sealing-wax cēra, *f*

seam sūtūra, *f*

seaman nauta, *m*

sear *v.t*, ădūro (3)

search for *v.t*, quaero (3); (explore), rīmor (1 *dep*)

search *nn*, investīgātĭo, *f*

seasick *adj*, nausĕăbundus; (to be —), *v.i*, nausĕo (1)

seasickness nausĕa, *f*

season tempus, *n*, tempestas, *f*; (right time), tempus, *n*

season *v.t*, condĭo (4)

seasonable tempestīvus

seasoned (flavoured) condītus; (hardened), dūrātus

seasoning *nn*, condīmentum, *n*

seat sēdes, *f*, sĕdīle, *n*, sella, *f*; (home), dŏmĭcĭlĭum, *n*: *v.t*. collŏco (1)

seaweed alga, *f*

secede *v.i*, dēcēdo (3)

secession dēfectĭo, *f*

secluded sēcrētus

seclusion sōlĭtūdo, *f*

second *adj*, sĕcundus; (— of two), alter; (for the — time), *adv*, ĭtĕrum; (— ly), *adv*, de inde

second *nn*, (time), mōmentum, *n*

second *v.t*, adiŭvo (1)

secondary infĕrĭor

second-hand ūsu trītus (worn with usage)

secrecy sēcrētum, *n*
secret arcāna, *n.pl*
secret *adj*, occultus, arcānus;
(hidden), clandestīnus; (to keep
something —), *v.t*, cēlo (1)
secretary scrība, *m*
secrete *v.t*, cēlo (1), abdo (3)
secretly *adv*, clam
sect secta, *f*
section pars, *f*
secular (not sacred), prŏfānus
secure *v.t*, mūnĭo (4), firmo (1),
lĭgo (1) (tie up)
secure *adj*, tūtus
security sălus, *f*; (guarantee),
pignus, *n*; (to give —), căvĕo (2)
sedate grăvis
sedative mĕdĭcāmentum
sŏpōrĭfĕrum
sedentary sĕdentārĭus
sedge ulva, *f*
sediment faex, *f*
sedition sēdĭtĭo, *f*
seditious sēdĭtĭōsus
seduce *v.t*, tento (1), sollĭcĭto (1)
seducer corruptor, *m*
seduction corruptēla, *f*
sedulous assĭdŭus
see *v.t* vĭdĕo (2), cerno (3), aspĭcĭo
(3); (to — to it that ...), cūro (1)
ad (*with gerund phr*);
(understand), intellĕgo (3)
seed sēmen, *n* (literal and
metaphorical)
seedling arbor nŏvella, *f*
seedy grānōsus
seeing that *conj*, cum
seek *v.t*, quaero (3), pĕto (3),
affecto (1)
seem *v.i*, vĭdĕor (2 *pass.*)
seeming *nn*, spĕcĭes, *f*
seemly *adj*, dĕcōrus, (it is —), dĕcet
(2 *impers*)
seer vātes, *c*
seethe *v.i*, fervĕo (2)
segment segmentum, *n*
segregate *v.t*, sēcerno (3)
seize *v.t*, răpĭo (3), corrĭpĭo (3),
prendo (3), occŭpo (1); (of
illness, passion, etc.), affĭcĭo (3)
seizure comprĕhensĭo, *f*
seldom *adv*, rārō
select *v.t*, lĕgo (3)

select *adj*, lectus
selection dēlectus, *m*
self *pron, (emphatic),* ipse;
(reflexive), sē
self-confident confīdens
self-satisfied contentus
selfish, selfishness, (to be —) sē
ămāre (1 *reflex*)
sell *v.t*, vendo (3)
seller vendĭtor, *m*
semblance ĭmāgo, *f*
semicircle hēmĭcyclĭum, *n*
senate sĕnātus, *m*
senate house cūrĭa, *f*
senator sĕnātor, *m*
send *v.t*, mitto (3); (— away),
dīmitto (3); (— back), rĕmitto
(3); (— for), arcesso (3); (—
forward), praemitto (3); (— in),
immitto (3)
senile sĕnīlis
senior, (in age) nātu maior
sensation (feeling) sensus, *m*;
mōtus (*m*) ănĭmi (impulse)
sensational nŏtābĭlis
sense (feeling) sensus, *m*;
(understanding), prūdentĭa, *f*;
(meaning), sententĭa, *f*
senseless (unconscious) *use adv.*
phr, sensu ablāto (with feeling
withdrawn); (stupid), sōcors
sensible prūdens
sensitive sensĭlis
sensitiveness mollĭtĭa
sensual lībīdĭnōsus
sensuality lībīdo, *f*
sentence (criminal) iūdĭcĭum, *n*;
(writing, etc.), sententĭa, *f*
sentence *v.t*, damno (1)
sententious sententĭōsus
sentiment (feeling) sensus, *m*;
(opinion), ŏpīnĭo, *f*
sentimental mollis
sentimentality mollĭtĭa, *f*
sentinel vĭgil, *m*; (to be on — duty),
in stătĭōne esse (*irreg*)
separable dīvĭdŭus
separate *v.t*, sēpăro (), dīvĭdo (3),
sēiungo (3), sēcerno (3)
separate *adj*, sēpărātus, sēcrētus
separately *adv*, sēpărātim
separation sēpărātĭo, *f*
September September (mensis)

sepulchre sĕpulcrum, *n*
sequel (outcome) exĭtus, *m*
sequence ordo, *m*
serene tranquillus
serf servus, *m*
series sĕrĭes, *f*
serious grăvis
seriousness grăvĭtas
sermon ōrātĭo, *f*
serpent serpens, *f*
serried confertus
servant mĭnister, *m*, fămŭlus, *m*, servus, *m*
serve *v.t*, servĭo (4), (*with dat*); (at table, etc.), mĭnistro (1); (in the army), stīpendĭa mĕrĕor (2 *dep*); (to — as), esse (*irreg*) (*with prō and abl*)
service mĭnistĕrĭum, *n*, ŏpĕra, (military), mīlĭtĭa, *f*
serviceable ūtĭlis
servile servīlis
servitude servĭtus, *f*
session (assembly) conventus, *m*
set *nn*, (of people), glŏbus, *m*
set *adj*, stătus
set *v.t*, (place), stătŭo (3), pōno (3); *v.i*, (of the sun), occĭdo (3); (— about, begin), incĭpĭo (3); (— aside), *v.t*, sēpōno (3); (— down in writing), nŏto (1); (— free), lībĕro (1); (set off *or* out), *v.i*, prŏfĭciscor (3 *dep*); (— up), *v.t*, stătŭo (3)
settee lectŭlus, *m*
setting (of sun) occāsus, *m*
settle *v.t*, constĭtŭo (3); (a dispute), compōno (3); (debt), solvo (3); *v.i*, (in a home, etc.), consīdo (3)
settled certus
settlement (colony) cŏlōnĭa, *f*; (— of an affair), compŏsĭtĭo, *f*
settle cŏlōnus, *m*
seven septem; (— hundred), septingenti; (— times), *adv*, septĭes
seventeen septendĕcim
seventeenth septĭmus dĕcĭmus
seventh septĭmus
seventieth septŭāgēsĭmus
seventy septŭāginta
sever *v.t*, sēpăro (1), sēiungo (3)

several complūres, ălĭquot
severe sĕvērus, dūrus
severity sĕvērĭtas, *f*, ăcerbĭtas, *f*
sew *v.t*, sŭo (3)
sewer (drain) clŏāca, *f*
sex sexus, *m*
sexagenarian sexāgēnārĭus, *m*
sexual *use nn*, sexus, *m*, (sex)
shabbiness sordes, *f. pl*
shabby sordĭdus
shackle *v.t*, vincŭlis constringo (3) (bind with chains)
shackle(s) *nn*, vincŭla, *n.pl*
shade *nn*, umbra, *f*; (the —s of the dead), mānes, *m. pl*
shade *v.t*, ŏpāco (1)
shadow umbra, *f*
shadowy ŏpācus, ĭnānis
shady ŏpācus
shaft (of a weapon) hastīle, *n*; (an arrow), săgitta, *f*; (of a mine), pŭtĕus, *m*
shaggy hirtus, hirsūtus
shake *v.t*, quătĭo (3), ăgĭto (1) lăbĕfăcĭo (3); *v.i*, trĕmo (3), trĕpido (1); (— hands), dextras iungo (3) (join right hands)
shaking *nn*, quassātĭo, *f*
shallow *adj*, (sea), vădōsus, brĕvis
shallows *nn*, văda, *n.pl*
sham *adj*, sĭmŭlātus
sham *nn*, sĭmŭlātĭo, *f* (pretence)
sham *v.t*, sĭmŭlo (1)
shamble *use* turba, *f*
shame *nn*, (feeling), pŭdor, *m*; (disgrace), dēdĕcus, *n*
shame *v.t*, rŭbōrem incŭtĭo (3) (*with dat*)
shamefaced vĕrēcundus
shameful turpis
shamefulness turbĭtūdo, *f*
shameless impŭdens
shamelessness impŭdentĭa, *f*
shamrock trĭfŏlĭum, *n*
shank crus, *n*
shape *nn*, forma, *f*
shape *v.t*, formo (1)
shapeless informis
shapely formōsus
share (part) pars, *f*; (plough —), vōmer, *m*
share *v.t*, partĭor (4 *dep*)
sharer partĭceps, *c*

shark pistrix, *f*
sharp ăcūtus, ācer
sharp-sighted perspĭcax
sharp-witted ăcūtus
sharpen *v.t*, ăcŭo (3)
sharply *adv*, ăcūte, ācrĭter
sharpness (of tongue) aspĕrĭtas, *f*; **(mental)**, ăcūmen, *n*
shatter *v.t*, frango (3)
shave *v.t*, rādo (3)
shawl ămĭcŭlum, *n*
she *pron*, illa, ĕa, haec, ista
sheaf mănĭpŭlus, *m*
shear *v.t*, tondĕo (2)
shearing *nn*, tonsūra, *f*
shears forfex, *f*
sheath vāgīna, *f*
sheathe *v.t*, in vāgīnam rĕcondo (3) **(put back into the sheath)**
shed *nn*, tŭgŭrĭum, *n*
shed *v.t*, fundo (3)
sheen fulgor, *m*
sheep ŏvis, *f*
sheepfold saeptum, *n*
sheepskin pellis ŏvilla, *f*
sheepish sōcors, *or use adv. phr*, dēmisso vultu **(with downcast face)**
sheer (steep) abruptus; **(pure, absolute)**, mĕrus
sheet (cloth) lintĕum, *n*; **(paper)**, schĕda, *f*; **(— of a sail)**, pes, *m*
shelf plŭtĕus, *m*
shell concha, *f*, crusta, *f*
shellfish conchȳlĭum, *n*
shelter *nn*, perfŭgĭum, *n*, tectum, *n*
shelter *v.t*, tĕgo (3); *v.i, use phr*, ad perfŭgĭum sē conferre (*irreg*) **(betake oneself to shelter)**
shelving *adj*, dēclīvis
shepherd pastor, *m*
shield *nn*, scūtum, *n*
shield *v.t*, tĕgo (3), dēfendo (3)
shift (change) vīcissĭtūdo, *f*.
shift *v.t*, mūto (1); *v.i*, mūtor (1 *pass*)
shifty versūtus
shin crūs, *n*
shine *v.i*, lūcĕo (2), fulgĕo (2)
ship *nn*, nāvis, *f*; **(war —)**, nāvis longa, *f*; **(transport —)**, nāvis ŏnĕrārĭa, *f*

ship *v.t*, **(put on board)**, in nāvem impōno (3); **(transport)**, nāve transporto (1)
ship-owner nāvĭcŭlārĭus, *m*
shipping nāvĭgĭa, *n.pl*
shipwreck naufrăgĭum, *n*
shipwrecked naufrăgus
shirt sŭbūcŭla, *f*
shiver *v.i*, horrĕo (2)
shivering *nn*, horror, *m*
shoal (water) vădum, *n*; **(fish)**, exāmen, *n*
shock offensĭo, *f*, ictus, *m*; **(of battle)**, concursus, *m*
shock *v.t*, offendo (3), percŭtĭo (3)
shocking *adj*, ătrox
shoe *nn*, calcĕus, *m*
shoe *v.t*, calcĕo (1)
shoemaker sūtor, *m*
shoot *nn*, **(sprout)**, surcŭlus, *m*
shoot *v.t*, **(a missile)**, mitto (3); *v.i*, **(— along, across)**, vŏlo (1)
shooting-star fax caelestis, *f*
shop tăberna, *f*
shopkeeper tăbernārĭus, *m* (*pl. only*)
shore lītus, *n*, ōra, *f*
shore-up *v.t*, fulcĭo (4)
short brĕvis, ĕxĭgŭus; **(— cut)**, via compendĭārĭa, *f*; **(in —)**, *adv*, dēnīque
shortage ĭnŏpĭa, *f* **(lack)**
shortcoming dēlictum, *n*
shorten *v.t*, contrăho (3)
shortly *adv*, **(of time)**, brĕvi; **(briefly)**, brĕvĭter
shortness brĕvĭtas, *f*
shot (firing) ictus, *m*
shoulder hŭmĕrus, *m*; **(— blade)**, scăpŭlae, *f. pl*
shoulder *v.t*, fĕro (*irreg*) **(to bear)**
shout *nn*, clāmor, *m*
shout *v.i*, clāmo (1)
shove *v.t*, trūdo (3)
shovel pāla, *f*
show *nn*, **(appearance)**, spĕcĭes, *f*; **(spectacle)**, spectācŭlum, *n*; **(procession, etc.)**, pompa, *f*
show *v.t*, monstro (1), praebĕo (2), ostendo (3); **(— off)**, *v.t*, ostento (1); *v.i*, sē ostentāre (1 *reflex*)

shower imber, *m*
shower *v.t*, fundo (3)
showery plŭvĭus
showy spĕcĭōsus
shred pannus, *m*
shrew fēmĭna prŏcax
shrewd ăcūtus, săgax
shrewdness săgācĭtas, *f*
shriek *nn*, ŭlŭlātus, *m*
shriek *v.i* ŭlŭlo (1)
shrill ăcūtus, ācer
shrine dēlūbrum, *n*
shrink *v.t*, contrăho (3); *v.i*,
  (**— from**), ăbhorrĕo (2)
shrinking *nn*, contractĭo, *f*
shrivel *v.t*, corrūgo (1)
shrivelled rūgōsus
shroud *use* lintĕum, *n*, (**cloth**)
shroud *v.t*, involvo (3)
shrub frŭtex, *m*
shrubbery frŭtĭcētum
shudder *v.i*, horrĕo (2)
shudder *nn*, horror, *m*
shuffle *v.t*, miscĕo (2); *v.i, use phr*,
  lentē ambŭlo (1) (**walk slowly**)
shun *v.t*, fŭgĭo (3), vīto (1)
shut *v.t*, claudo (3); (**— in or up**),
  inclūdo (3); (**— out**), exclūdo (3)
shutters fŏrĭcŭlae, *f. pl*
shuttle rădĭus, *m*
shy vĕrēcundus
shy *v.i*, (**of horses**), consternor (1
  pass)
shyness vĕrēcundĭa, *f*
sick aeger; (**to be —**), *v.i*, aegrōto
  (1); (**vomit**), *v.i, and v.t*, vŏmo
  (3)
sicken *v.t*, fastīdĭum mŏvĕo (2);
  v.i, aeger fĭo (*irreg*)
sickle falx, *f*
sickly infirmus
sickness morbus, *m*
side (**of the body**) lătus, *n*; (**part,
  region**), pars, *f*; (**party, faction**),
  pars, *f*; (**from (or on) all —s**), *adv*,
  undĭque; (**on both —s**), ŭtrimque;
  (**on this —**), hinc; (**on that —**),
  illinc; (**on this — of**), *prep*, citra
  (*with acc*); (**on that — of**), ŭltra
side *adj*, (**sidelong**), oblīquus
sideboard ăbăcus, *m*
sideways *adv*, oblīquē
siege *nn*, obsĭdĭo, *f*

siege-works ŏpĕra, *n.pl*
sieve crībrum, *n*
sift *v.t*, crībro (1); (**— evidence,
  etc.**), scrūtor (1 *dep*)
sigh *nn*, suspīrĭum, *n*
sigh *v.i*, suspīro (1)
sight (**sense or act**) vīsus, *m*;
  (**view**), conspectus, *m*;
  (**spectacle**), spectācŭlum, *n*
sight *v.t*, conspĭcor (1 *dep*)
sightly formōsus, vĕnustus
sign *nn*, signum, *n*; (**mark**), nŏta, *f*;
  (**trace, footprint**), vestīgĭum, *n*;
  (**portent**), portentum, *n*
sign *v.t*, subscrībo (3); (**give a —**),
  v.i, signum do (1)
signal signum, *n*
signal *v.i*, signum do (1)
signature nōmen, *n*
signet signum, *n*
significance signĭfĭcātĭo, *f*
significant signĭfĭcans
signify *v.t*, signĭfĭco (1)
silence sĭlentĭum, *n*
silent tăcĭtus, (**to be —**), *v.i*, tăcĕo
  (2), sĭlĕo (2)
silk *nn*, bombyx, *m*
silk, silken *adj*, sērĭcus
silkworm bombyx, *m*
silky mollis
sill līmen, *n*
silliness stultĭtĭa, *f*
silly stultus
silt *nn*, līmus, *m*, sentīna, *f*
silver *nn*, argentum, *n*
silver *adj*, argentĕus
silver-mine argentārium metallum
similar sĭmĭlis (*with genit. or dat*)
similarity sĭmĭlĭtūdo, *f*
similarly *adv*, sĭmĭlĭter
simmer *v.i*, lentē fervĕo (3) (**boil
  slowly**)
simper *v.i*, subrīdĕo (2)
simple simplex; (**weak-minded**),
  ĭneptus
simpleton stultus, *m*
simplicity simplĭcĭtas, *f*
simplify *v.t*, făcĭlem reddo (3)
simulation sĭmŭlātĭo, *f*
simultaneous *use adv*, sĭmul (**at
  the same time**)
sin *nn*, peccātum, *n*

sin *v.i*, pecco (1)

since *conj*, cum (*foll. by vb. in subjunctive*); **(temporal)** postquam

since *adv*, ăbhinc

since *prep*, ē, ex, ā, ăb (*with abl*)

sincere sincērus, simplex

sincerity sincērĭtas, *f*, simplĭcĭtas, *f*

sinew nervus, *m*

sinful impĭus

sinfulness impĭĕtas, *f*

sing *v.i. and v.t*, căno (3)

singe *v.t*, ădūro (3)

singer cantātor, *m*

singing *nn*, cantus, *m*

single *adj*, **(one, sole)**, ūnus, sŏlus; **(unmarried)**, caelebs

single out *v.t*, ēlĭgo (3)

singly *adv*, singŭlātim

singular, (one) singŭlaris; **(strange)**, nŏvus

singularly *adv*, ūnĭcē

sinister sĭnister

sink *v.t*, mergo (3); *v.i*, sīdo (3), consīdo (3)

sinner peccātor, *m*

sinuous sĭnŭōsus

sip *v.t*, dēgusto (1), lībo (1)

sir (respectful address) bŏne vir

sire păter, *m*

siren sīrēn, *f*

sister sŏror, *f*

sit *v.i*, sĕdĕo (2); **(— down)**, consīdo (3); **(— up, stay awake)**, vĭgĭlo (1)

site sĭtus, *m*

sitting *nn*, sessĭo, *f*

situated sĭtus

situation sĭtus, *m*

six sex; **(— each)**, sēni; **(— times)**, *adv*, sexĭens

sixteen sēdĕcim

sixteenth sextus dĕcĭmus

sixth sextus

sixtieth sexāgēsĭmus

sixty sexāginta

size magnĭtūdo, *f*; **(of great —)**, *adj*, magnus; **(of small —)**, parvus; **(of what — ?)**, quantus?

skeleton ossa, *n.pl*, **(bones)**

sketch *nn*, ădumbrātĭo, *f*

sketch *v.t*, ădumbro (1)

skewer vĕrūcŭlum, *n*

skiff scăpha, *f*

skilful, skilled pĕrītus

skilfulness, skill pĕrītĭa, *f*

skim *v.t*, **(— off)**, dēspūmo (1); **(— over)**, percurro (3)

skin cŭtis, *f*, pellis, *f*

skin *v.t*, pellem dīrĭpĭo (3) **(tear away the skin)**

skip *v.i*, exsulto (1); **(— over)**, *v.i. and v.t*, praetērĕo (4)

skipper nauarchus, *m*

skirmish *nn*, lĕve certāmen, *n*

skirmish *v.i*, parvŭlis proelĭis contendo (3) **(fight in small engagements)**

skirmisher vēlĕs, *m*

skirt *nn*, limbus, *m*

skirt *v.t*, **(scrape past)**, rādo (3)

skittish lascīvus

skulk *v.i*, lătĕo (2)

skull calvārĭa, *f*

sky caelum, *n*

sky-blue caerŭlĕus

skylark ălauda, *f*

slab (of stone) ăbăcus, *m*

slack rĕmissus

slacken *v.t*, rĕmitto (3); *v.i*, rĕmittor (3 *pass*)

slackness rĕmissĭo, *f*; **(idleness)**, pĭgrĭtĭa, *f*

slake (thirst) *v.t*, **(sĭtim)** exstinguo (3)

slander *nn*, călumnĭa, *f*

slander *v.t*, călumnĭor (1 *dep*)

slanderer obtrectātor, *m*

slanderous fāmōsus

slanting *adj*, oblīquus

slap *nn*, ălăpa, *f*

slap *v.t*, fērĭo (4)

slash *nn*, **(blow)**, ictus, *m*

slash *v.t*, caedo (3)

slate (roofing) tēgŭlae, *f. pl*.

slate *v.t*, rĕprĕhendo (3)

slaughter *nn*, caedes, *f*, strāges, *f*

slaughter *v.t*, caedo (3)

slaughterhouse *use* lānĭēna, *f* **(butcher's stall)**

slave servus, *m*

slave-dealer vēnālĭcĭus, *m*

slavery servĭtus, *f*

slave-trade vēnālĭcĭum, *n*

slavish servīlis

slay *v.t*, interfĭcĭo (3)

slayer interfector, *m*
slaying *nn*, trŭcĭdātĭo, *f*
sledge trăhĕa, *f*
sleek nĭtĭdus
sleep *nn*, somnus, *m*
sleep *v.i*, dormĭo (4), quĭesco (3); **(to go to —)**, obdormisco (3)
sleepless insomnis
sleeplessness insomnĭa, *f*
sleepy somnĭcŭlōsus
sleeve mănĭcae, *f. pl*
sleigh trăhĕa, *f*
sleight-of-hand praestĭgĭae, *f. pl*
slender grăcĭlis
slenderness grăcĭlĭtas, *f*
slice segmentum, *n*, frustum, *n*
slice *v.t*, concīdo (3)
slide *v.i*, lābor (3 *dep*)
slight *adj*, lĕvis, exĭgŭus
slight *v.t*, neglĕgo (3)
slim grăcĭlis
slime līmus, *m*
slimy līmōsus
sling *nn*, **(for throwing)**, funda, *f*; **(bandage)**, mĭtella, *f*
sling *v.t*, mitto (3)
slinger fundĭtor, *m*
slip *v.i*, lābor (3 *dep*); **(— away)**, sē subdūcĕre (3 *reflex*); **(— out from)**, ēlābor (3 *dep*)
slip *nn*, lapsus, *m*; **(mistake)**, error, *m*
slipper sŏlĕa, *f*
slippery lūbrĭcus
slipshod neglĕgens
slit *nn*, scissūra, *f*
slit *v.t*, incīdo (3)
sloop nāvis longa, *f*
slope *nn*, clīvus, *m*
slope *v.i*, sē dēmittĕre (3 *reflex*), vergo (3)
sloping *adj*, **(down)**, dēclīvis; **(up)**, acclīvis
sloth segnĭtĭa, *f*, ignāvĭa, *f*
slothful segnis
slough (mire) pălus, *f*
slovenliness cultus neglectus **(neglected dress)**
slow tardus, lentus
slowly *adv*, tardē, lentē
slowness tardĭtas, *f*
slug līmax, *f*
sluggish pĭger, segnis

sluggishness pigrĭtĭa, *f*
sluice ductus (*m*) ăquārum **(bringing of water)**
slumber *nn*, somnus, *m*
slumber *v.i*, dormĭo (4)
slur *nn*, măcŭla, *f*
sly astūtus, callĭdus
smack *nn*, **(blow)**, ălăpa, *f*; **(taste)**, săpor, *m*
smack *v.t*, **(slap)**, verbĕro (1)
small parvus, exĭgŭus
smallness exĭgŭĭtas, *f*
smart *adj*, ācer; **(clothes, etc.)**, nĭtĭdus; **(witty)**, făcētus
smart *nn*, dŏlŏr, *m*
smart *v.i*, dŏlĕo (2), ūror (3 *pass*)
smartness (alertness) ălăcrĭtas, *f*
smash *nn*, fractūra, *f*
smash *v.t*, confringo (3)
smattering lĕvis cognĭtĭo, *f*, **(slight knowledge)**
smear *v.t*, līno (3)
smell *nn*, **(sense of —)**, ŏdōrātus, *m*; **(scent)**, ŏdor, *m*
smell *v.t*, olfăcĭo (3); *v.i*, ŏlĕo (2)
smelt *v.t*, cŏquo (3)
smile *nn*, rīsus, *m*
smile *v.i*, subrīdĕo (2)
smirk *nn*, rīsus, *m*
smite *v.t*, fĕrĭo (4)
smith făber, *m*
smithy făbrĭca, *f*
smock indūsĭum, *n*
smoke *nn*, fūmus, *m*
smoke *v.i*, fūmo (1)
smoky fūmōsus
smooth lĕvis, **(of the sea)**, plăcĭdus; **(of temper)**, aequus
smooth *v.t*, lēvo (1)
smoothness lēvĭtas, *f*, lēnĭtas, *f*
smother *v.t*, suffōco (1), opprĭmo (3)
smoulder *v.i*, fūmo (1)
smudge *nn*, lābes, *f*
smuggle *v.t*, furtim importo (1) **(bring in secretly)**
snack cēnŭla, *f*
snail cochlĕa, *f*
snake anguis, *m*, *f*
snaky vīpĕrĕus
snap *v.t*, rumpo (3); **(— the fingers)**, *v.i*, concrĕpo (1); **(— up)**, *v.t*, corrĭpĭo (3)

snare lăquĕus, *m*
snarl *nn*, gannītus, *m*
snarl *v.i*, gannĭo (4)
snatch *v.t*, răpĭo (3)
sneak *v.i*, corrēpo (3)
sneer *nn*, obtrectātĭo, *f*
sneer at *v.t*, dērīdĕo (2)
sneeze *v.i*, sternŭo (3)
sneezing sternūmentum, *n*
sniff at (smell at) *v.t*, ŏdōror (1 *dep*)
snip *v.t*, (cut off), ampŭto (1)
snob nŏvus hŏmo (upstart)
snore *v.i*, sterto (3)
snore, snoring *nn*, rhonchus, *m*
snort *v.i*, frĕmo (3)
snorting *nn*, frĕmĭtus, *m*
snout rostrum, *n*
snow *nn*, nix, *f*
snow (it —s) ningit (*v. impers*)
snowy nĭvĕus
snub *v.t*, rĕprĕhendo (3)
snub-nosed sīlus
snuff *v.t*, (extinguish), exstinguo (3)
snug commŏdus
so *adv*, (in such a way), sīc, ĭtă; (to such an extent), ădĕo; (*with adj and adv*) tam, *e.g.* so quickly, tam cĕlĕrĭter; (*with a purpose or consecutive clause*, so that ...) ut; (— big, — great), tāntus; (— many), tot; (— much), tantum; (— often), tŏtĭes
soak *v.t*, mădĕfăcĭo (3)
soaking mădens; (of rain), largus
soap *nn*, sāpo, *m*
soar *v.i*, sublīme fĕror (*irreg pass*) (be borne aloft)
sob *nn*, singultus, *m*
sob *v.i*, singulto (1)
sober sōbrĭus
sobriety sōbrĭĕtas, *f*, mŏdĕrātĭo, *f*
sociability făcĭlĭtas, *f*
sociable făcĭlis
social commūnis
society (in general) sŏcĭĕtas, *f*; (companionship), sŏdālĭtas, *f*
sock tībĭāle, *n*
sod caespes, *m*
soda nĭtrum, *n*
sodden mădĭdus
sofa lectŭlus, *m*

soft mollis
soften *v.t*, mollĭo (4); *v.i*, mollĭor (4 *pass*)
softness mollĭtĭa, *f*
soil sŏlum, *n*
soil *v.t*, inquĭno (1)
sojourn *nn*, commŏrātĭo, *f*
sojourn *v.i*, commŏror (1 *dep*)
solace *nn*, sōlātĭum, *n*
solace *v.t*, consōlor (1 *dep*)
solar *use genit. case of* sōl, *m*, (sun)
solder *nn*, ferrūmen, *n*
solder *v.t*, ferrūmĭno (1)
soldier mīles, *c*; (foot —), pĕdes, *m*; (cavalry —), ĕques, *m*; *v.i*, (serve as a —), stīpendĭa mĕrĕor (2 *dep*)
soldierly *adj*, mīlĭtāris
sole *adj*, sōlus
sole *nn*, sŏlum, *n*; (fish), sŏlĕa, *f*
solely *adv*, sōlum
solemn (serious) grăvis; (festivals, etc.), sollemnis
solemnity grăvĭtas, *f*; (religious —), sollemne, *n*
solemnize *v.t*, cĕlĕbro (1)
solicit *v.t*, pĕto (3), ŏsĕcro (1), sollĭcĭto (1)
solicitation flāgĭtātĭo, *f*
solicitor advŏcātus, *m*
solicitude anxĭĕtas, *f*
solid *adj*, sŏlĭdus
solid *nn*, sŏlĭdum, *n*
solidity sŏlĭdĭtas, *f*
soliloquize *v.i*, sēcum lŏquo (3 *dep*) (speak with oneself)
solitary sōlus, sōlĭtārĭus; (places), dēsertus
solitude sōlĭtūdo, *f*
solstice (summer —) solstĭtĭum, *n*; (winter —), brūma, *f*
solution *use vb.* solvo (3) (to solve), *or nn*, explĭcātĭo, *f*
solve *v.t*, explĭco (1)
solvent (to be —) solvendo esse (*irreg*)
sombre obscūrus
some *adj*, ălĭquis, nonnullus; (a certain), quīdam
somebody, someone *pron*, ălĭquis, nonnullus; (a certain one), quīdam; (— or other), nescĭo

quis; **(some . . . others)**, ălĭi . . . ălĭi

somehow *adv*, nescĭŏ quōmŏdŏ

something *pron*, ălĭquid

sometime *adv*, ălĭquandŏ

sometimes *adv*, ălĭquandŏ, interdum; **(occasionally)**, sŭbinde; **(sometimes ... sometimes ...)**, mŏdŏ ... mŏdŏ ...

somewhat *adv*, ălĭquantum

somewhere *adv*, ălĭcŭbi; **(to —)**, ălĭquo

somnolent sēmĭsomnus

son fīlĭus, *m*; **(— in-law)**, gĕner, *m*

song carmen, *n*

sonorous sŏnōrus

soon *adv*, mox; **(as — as)**, sĭmul ac, sĭmŭl atque, cum prīmum; **(as — as possible)**, quam prīmum

sooner (earlier) mātūrĭus; **(rather)**, pŏtĭus

soot fūlīgo, *f*

soothe *v.t*, mulcĕo (2), lēnĭo (4)

soothing *adj*, lēnis

soothsayer auspex, *c*, hăruspex, *m*

sooty fūlīgĭnōsus

sop offa, *f*

sophist sŏphistes, *m*

soporific sŏpōrĭfer

sorcerer vĕnēfĭcus, *m*

sorcery vĕnēfĭcĭa, *n.pl*

sordid sordĭdus

sore ăcerbus

sore *nn*, ulcus, *n*

sorrel lăpăthus, *f*

sorrow *nn*, dŏlor, *m*, maeror, *m*

sorrow *v.i*, dŏlĕo (2)

sorrowful maestus, tristis

sorry (to be —) mĭsĕret (2 *impers*) (*with acc. of subject and genit. of object*), e.g. **I am sorry for you**, me mĭsĕret tŭi

sort gĕnus, *n*; **(what — of?)**, quālis?

sort *v.t*, dīgĕro (3)

sot pōtātor, *m*

soul ănĭma, *f*, ănĭmus, *m*, spīrĭtus, *m*

sound *nn*, sŏnus, *m*, sŏnĭtus, *m*

sound *adj*, sānus; **(of sleep)**, artus; **(of arguments)**, firmus

sound *v.i*, sŏno (1); *v.t*, inflo (1); **(— the trumpet)**, būcĭnam inflo (1), căno (3)

soundness sānĭtas, *f*, intgĕrĭtas, *f*

soup iūs, *n*

sour ăcerbus, ācer, ămārus

source fons, *m*, căput, *n*

sourness ăcerbĭtas, *f*

south *nn*, mĕrīdĭes, *m*

south, southern *adj*, mĕrīdĭānus

southwards *adv. phr*, in mĕrīdĭem

sovereign *nn*, princeps, *m*, rex, *m*, tўrannus, *m*

sovereign (independent) *adj, use phr* sŭi iūris **(of one's own authority)**

sovereignty impĕrĭum, *n*

sow *nn*, sūs, *f*

sow *v.t*, sĕro (3)

sower sător, *m*

space spătĭum, *n*; **(— of time)**, spătĭum, (*n*) tempŏris

spacious amplus

spaciousness amplĭtūdo, *f*

spade pāla, *f*

span palmus, *m*

span *v.t*, **(river, etc.)**, *use vb*, iungo (3) **(join)**

spangled distinctus

Spanish Hispānus

spar (of timber) asser, *m*

spare *adj*, exīlis **(thin)**

spare *v.t*, parco (3) (*with dat*)

sparing *adj*, **(frugal)**, parcus

spark *nn*, scintilla, *f*

sparkle *v.i*, scintillo (1)

sparkling *adj*, scintillans

sparrow passer, *m*

sparse rārus

spasm spasmus, *m*

spatter *v.t*, aspergo (3)

spawn *nn*, ōva, *n.pl*

spawn *v.i*, ōva gigno (3) **(produce eggs)**

speak *v.t*, lŏquor (3 *dep*), dīco (3); **(— out)**, ēlŏquor (3 *dep*); **(— to)**, allŏquor (3 *dep*)

speaker ōrātor, *m*

spear hasta, *f*

special (one in particular) pĕcūlĭāris; **(one's own)**, prŏprĭus; **(outstanding)**, praecĭpŭus

speciality *use adj*, prŏprĭus **(one's own)**
specially *adv*, praecĭpŭē, praesertim
species gĕnus, *n*
specific dĭsertus; *or use emphatic pron*, ipse
specify *v.t*, ēnŭmĕro (1)
specimen exemplum, *n*
specious prŏbābĭlis
speck măcŭla, *f*
spectacle spectācŭlum, *n*
spectator spectātor, *m*
spectre ĭmāgo, *f*
spectrum spectrum, *n*
speculate *v.i*, cōgĭto (1); **(guess)**, cōnĭcĭo (3)
speculation cōgĭtātĭo, *f*; **(guess)**, coniectūra, *f*
speech ōrātĭo, *f*
speechless **(literally so)** mūtus; **(struck with fear, etc.)**, stŭpĕfactus
speed cĕlĕrĭtas, *f*
speed *v.t*, mātūro (1); *v.i*, festīno (1)
speedy cĕler, cĭtus
spell **(charm)** carmen, *n*
spell *v.t, use phr. with* littĕra, *f*, **(letter)**
spellbound obstŭpĕfactus
spend *v.t*, **(money)**, impendo (3), insūmo (3); **(time)**, ăgo (3)
spendthrift nĕpos, *m*, *f*
spew *v.t*, vŏmo (3)
sphere glŏbus, *m*; **(— of responsibility, etc.)**, prōvincĭa, *f*
spherical glŏbōsus
sphinx sphinx, *f*
spice condīmentum, *n*
spice *v.t*, condĭo (4)
spicy condītus
spider ărānĕa, *f*
spider's web ărānĕa, *f*
spike clāvus, *m*
spill *v.t*, effundo (3)
spin *v.t*, **(thread, etc.)**, nĕo (2); **(turn rapidly)**, verso (1); *v.i*, versor (1 *pass*)
spinster virgo, *f*
spiral *nn*, cochlĕa, *f*
spiral *adj*, invŏlūtus
spire turris, *f*

spirit **(breath of life)** ănĭma, *f*; **(mind, soul)**, ănĭmus, *m*; **(disposition)**, ingĕnĭum, *n*; **(character)**, mōres, *m. pl*; **(courage)**, ănĭmus, *m*; **(departed —)**, mānes, *m. pl*
spirited ănĭmōsus
spiritual **(of the mind)** *use* ănĭmus, *m*
spit *nn*, **(for roasting)**, vĕru, *n*
spit *v.t*, spŭo (3)
spite mălĕvŏlentĭa, *f*; **(in — of)**, *often use abl. phr. with* obstans **(standing in the way)**
spiteful mălignus
spittle spūtum, *n*
splash *v.t*, aspergo (3)
spleen lĭen, *n*; **(vexation)**, stŏmăchus, *m*
splendid splendĭdus
splendour splendor, *m*
splint fĕrŭlae, *f. pl*
splinter fragmentum, *n*
split *v.t*, findo (3); *v.i*, findor (3 *pass*)
split *nn*, fissūra, *f*
splutter *v.i*, balbūtĭo (4)
spoil *nn*, praeda, *f*, spŏlĭa, *n.pl*
spoil *v.t*, corrumpo (3), vĭtĭo (1)
spokesman ōrātor, *m*
sponge *nn*, spongĭa, *f*
spongy spongĭōsus
sponsor auctor, *c*
spontaneous *use adv. phr*, sŭā (mĕā), sponte **(of his (my) own accord)**
spoon coclĕar, *n*
sporadic rārus
sport *nn*, lūdus, *m*, lūsus, *m*; **(ridicule)**, lūdĭbrĭum, *n*
sport *v.i*, lūdo (3)
sportive **(playful)** lascīvus
sportsman vēnātor, *m*
spot *nn*, **(stain)**, măcŭla, *f*; **(place)**, lŏcus, *m*
spot *v.t*, **(look at)**, aspĭcĭo (3); **(stain)**, măcŭlo (1)
spotless **(of character, etc.)** intĕger, pūrus
spotted măcŭlōsus
spouse coniunx, *c*
spout *nn*, ōs, *n*
spout *v.i*, ēmĭco (1); *v.t*, **(pour out)**,

effundo (3)

sprain *v.t*, intorquĕo (2)

sprawl *v.i*, fundor (3 *pass*)

spray *nn*, aspergo, *f*

spread *v.t*, extendo (3), pando (3), diffundo (3); **(— about, publish)**, diffĕro (*irreg*) dīvulgo (1); *v.i*, diffundor (3 *pass*), incrēbresco (3)

sprightly ălăcer

spring *nn*, **(season)**, vēr, *n*; **(leap)**, saltus, *m*; **(fountain)**, fons, *m*

spring *adj*, vernus

spring *v.i*, **(leap)**, sălĭo (4); **(— from, proceed from)**, ŏrĭor (4 *dep*) **(— upon, assault)**, ădŏrĭor (4 *dep*)

sprinkle *v.t*, spargo (3)

sprout *nn*, surcŭlus, *m*

sprout *v.i*, pullŭlo (1)

spruce *adj*, nĭtĭdus

spruce *nn*, **(fir)**, pīnus, *f*

spur *nn*, calcar, *n*

spur *v.t*, concĭto (1)

spurious ădultĕrīnus

spurn *v.t*, aspernor (1 *dep*)

spurt *v.i*, ēmĭco (1)

spy *nn*, explōrātor, *m*, dēlātor, *m*

spy *v.t*, spĕcŭlor (1 *dep*)

squabble *nn*, rixa, *f*

squabble *v.i*, rixor (1 *dep*)

squadron (of cavalry) turma, *f*; **(of ships)**, classis, *f*

squalid sordĭdus

squall (storm) prōcella, *f*

squall *v.i*, **(cry)**, vāgĭo (4)

squalor sordes, *f. pl*

squandor effundo (3)

squanderer nĕpos, *m*, *f*

square *adj*, quădrātus; *nn*, quădrātum, *n*

square *v.t*, quădro (1); **(accounts, etc.)**, subdūco (3), constĭtŭo (3)

squash *v.t*, contĕro (3)

squat *v.i*, subsīdo (3)

squat *adj*, **(of figure)**, brĕvis

squeak *nn*, strīdor, *m*

squeak *v.i*, strīdĕo (2)

squeamish fastīdĭōsus

squeeze *v.t*, prĕmo (3)

squint *v.i*, strābo esse (*irreg*)

squirrel scĭūrus, *m*

squirt *v.t*, ēĭcĭo (3); *v.i*, ēmĭco (1)

stab *v.t*, fŏdĭo (3)

stab *nn*, ictus, *m*

stability stăbĭlĭtas, *f*

stable *adj*, stăbĭlis

stable *nn*, stăbŭlum, *n*

stack *nn*, ăcervus, *m*

stack *v.t*, cŏăcervo (1)

staff băcŭlum, *n*; **(advisers)**, consĭlĭārĭi, *m. pl*

stag cervus, *m*

stage (theatre) proscaenĭum, *n*; **(step)**, grădus, *m*

stagger *v.i*, văcillo (1); *v.t*, concŭtĭo (3), commŏvĕo (2)

stagnant stagnans

stagnate *v.i*, stagno (1)

staid grăvis

stain *nn*, măcŭla, *f*

stain *v.t*, măcŭlo (1)

stainless pūrus, intĕger

stairs scālae, *f. pl*

stake (post, etc.) pālus, *m*, sŭdis, *f*, stīpes, *m*; **(pledge, wager)**, pignus, *n*

stake *v.t*, **(wager)**, dēpōno (3)

stale vĕtus

stalk stirps, *f*

stalk *v.i*, incēdo (3); **(game, etc.)**, *use phr*, cautē sĕquor (3 *dep*) **(follow cautiously)**

stall (cattle) stăbŭlum, *n*; **(shop, etc.)**, tăberna, *f*

stallion admissārĭus, *m*

stalwart *adj*, fortis

stamina vīres, *f. pl*

stammer *nn*, haesĭtantĭa (*f*) linguae **(hesitation of speech)**

stammer *v.i*, balbūtĭo (4)

stamp (mark) nŏta, *f*; **(with a ring, etc.)**, signum, *n*

stamp *v.t*, **(mark)**, signo (1); **(— with the foot)**, supplōdo (3)

stand *nn*, **(halt)**, mŏra, *f*; **(to make a —)** consisto (3) rēsisto (3), **(*with dat.*)**; **(platform)**, suggestus, *m*; **(stall)**, mensa, *f*

stand *v.i*, sto (1), consisto (3); **(— back)**, rĕcēdo (3), **(— by, help)**, adsum (*irreg with dat*); **(— for, seek a position)**, *v.t*, pĕto (3); **(endure)**, pătĭor (3 *dep*); **(— out, project)** exsto (1); **(— up)**, surgo (3)

standard signum, *n*; **(of the legion)**, ăquĭla, *f*; **(measure)**, norma, *f*; **(— bearer)**, signĭfer, *m*

standing *nn*, **(position)**, stătus, *m*

staple products merces, *f, pl*

star stella, *f*, sīdus, *n*

starboard *use adj*, dexter **(right)**

starch *nn*, ămȳlum, *n*

stare *nn*, obtūtus, *m*

stare *v.t*, **(— at)**, intŭĕor (2 *dep*)

stark (stiff) rĭgĭdus; **(— naked)**, nūdus; **(— mad)**, āmens

starling sturnus, *m*

start *nn*, **(movement)**, trĕmor, *m*; **(beginning)**, ĭnĭtĭum, *n*; **(setting out)**, prŏfectĭo, *f*; **(starting point)**, carcĕres, *m. pl*

start *v.i*, **(make a sudden movement)**, trĕmo (3), horrĕo (2); **(— out)**, prŏfĭciscor (3 *dep*); *v.t*, **(establish)**, instĭtŭo (3)

startle *v.t*, terrĕo (2)

startling *adj*, terrĭbĭlis

starvation fămes, *f*

starve *f.t*, făme nĕco (1) **(kill by starvation)**; *v.i*, făme nĕcor (1 *pass*)

state (condition) stătus, *m*, condĭcĭo, *f*; **(the —)**, respublĭca, *f*, cīvĭtas, *f*

state *v.t*, prŏfĭtĕor (2 *dep*)

stately magnĭfĭcus, cĕlĕber

statement dictum, *n*

statesman *use phr. with* respublĭca **(state)**, *and* admĭnistro (1), **(to manage)**

station (standing) stătus, *m*; **(occupied place)**, stătĭo, *f*

station *v.t*, lŏco (1)

stationary *adj*, immōtus

stationer bĭblĭŏpōla, *m*

statistics census, *m*

statue stătŭa, *f*

stature stătūra, *f*

status stătus, *m*

statute lex, *f*

staunch *adj*, firmus

stave off *v.t*, arcĕo (2)

stay *nn*, **(prop)**, firmāmentum, *n*; **(rest, etc.)**, mansĭo, *f*, commŏrātĭo, *f*

stay *v.i*, mănĕo (2), mŏror (1 *dep*); *v.t*, **(obstruct, stop)**, mŏror (1 *dep*)

steadfast firmus, stăbĭlis

steady firmus, stăbĭlis

steadfastness stăbĭlĭtas, *f*

steadiness stăbĭlĭtas, *f*

steak offa, *f*

steal *v.t*, fūror (1 *dep*); *v.i*, **(— upon)**, surrēpo (3) **(with dat)**

stealing *nn*, **(theft)**, furtum, *n*

stealth (by —), **(adv)** furtim

stealth furtīvus

steam văpor, *m*

steam *v.i*, exhālo (1)

steed ĕquus, *m*

steel chălybs, *m*; **(iron, sword, etc.)**, ferrum, *n*

steel *v.t*, **(strengthen)**, confirmo (1)

steep praeruptus

steep *v.t*, **(soak)**, mădĕfăcĭo (3)

steeple turris, *f*

steer *nn*, iŭvencus, *m*

steer *v.t*, gŭberno (1)

steersman gŭbernātor, *m*

stem stirps, *f*, **(— literal and metaphorical)**

stem *v.t*, **(check)**, sisto (3), rĕsisto (3) **(with dat)**

stench fētor, *m*

step *nn*, grădus, *m*, passus, *m*; **(foot —)**, vestīgĭum, *n*; **(— by —)**, pĕdĕtentim; **(steps, stairs)**, scālae, *f.pl*

step *v.i*, grădĭor (3 *dep*); **(— forward)**, prōgrĕdĭor (3 *dep*)

step-brother (father's side) fĭlĭus vĭtrĭci; **(mother's side)**, fĭlĭus nŏvercae; **(— daughter)**, prīvigna, *f*; **(— father)** vĭtrĭcus, *m*; **(— mother)**, nŏverca, *f*; **(— sister)**, fĭlĭa vĭtrĭci *or* nŏvercae; **(— son)**, prīvignus, *m*

sterile stĕrĭlis

sterility stĕrĭlĭtas, *f*

sterling *adj*, **(genuine)**, vērus

stern *nn*, puppis, *f*

stern *adj*, dūrus

sterness sĕvērĭtas, *f*

stew *v.t*, cŏquo (3)

steward vīlĭcus, *m*

stick *nn*, băcŭlum, *n*

stick *v.t*, **(fix)**, fīgo (3); *v.i*, haerĕo (2)

sticky *adj*, tĕnax
stiff rĭgĭdus; **(to be —)**, *v.i*, rĭgĕo (2)
stiffen *v.i*, rĭgĕo (2); *v.t*, rĭgĭdum făcĭo (3)
stiffness rĭgor, *m*
stifle *v.t*, suffōco (1); **(suppress)**, opprĭmo (3)
stigma stigma, *n*
stigmatize *v.t*, nŏto (1)
still *adj*, immōtus, tranquillus
still *adv*, **(nevertheless)**, tămen; **(up to this time)**, ădhuc; **(even)**, ĕtĭam
still *v.t*, sēdo (1)
stillness quĭes, *f*
stilts grallae, *f. pl*
stimulant (incentive) stĭmŭlus, *m*
stimulus (incentive) stĭmŭlus, *m*
stimulate *v.t*, stĭmŭlo (1)
sting *nn*, ăcūlĕus, *m*
sting *v.t*, pungo (3)
stinging *adj*, mordax
stingy sordĭdus
stink *nn*, fētor, *m*
stink *v.i*, fētĕo (2)
stipend merces, *f*
stipulate *v.i*, stĭpŭlor (1 *dep*)
stir *nn*, mōtus, *m*
stir *v.t*, mŏvĕo (2); *v.i* mŏvĕor (2 *pass*)
stitch *v.t*, sŭo (3)
stock (of tree, family, etc.) stirps, *f*; **(amount)**, vīs, *f*
stock *v.t*, complĕo (2)
stockbroker argentārĭus, *m*
stocking tībĭāle, *n*
stoic *nn. and adj*, stōĭcus
stoical dūrus
stoicism rătĭo Stŏĭca, *f*
stolen furtīvus
stomach stŏmăchus, *m*
stomach *v.t*, **(put up with)**, perfĕro (*irreg*)
stone lăpis, *m*; **(precious —)**, gemma, *f*; **(fruit —)**, nūclĕus, *m*
stone *adj*, lăpĭdĕus
stone *v.t*, **(— to death)**, lăpĭdĭbus cŏŏpĕrĭo (4) **(overwhelm with stones)**
stone-quarry lăpĭcīdīnae, *f. pl*
stony lăpĭdōsus; **(of heart)**, asper
stool scăbellum, *n*

stoop *v.i*, sē dēmittĕre (3 *reflex*); **(condescend)**, dēscendo (3)
stop *nn*, intermissĭo, *f*
stop *v.t*, sisto (3); **(— up a hole, etc.)**, obtūro (1); *v.i*, **(pause)**, sisto (3); **(desist)**, dēsĭno (3); **(remain)**, mănĕo (2)
stoppage (hindrance) impĕdīmentum, *n*
stopper obtūrāmentum, *n*
store (supply) cōpĭa, *f*; **(place)**, rĕceptācŭlum, *n*
store *v.t*, condo (3)
storey tăbŭlātum, *n*
stork cĭcōnĭa, *f*
storm *nn*, tempestas, *f*
storm *v.t*, **(attack)**, expugno (1)
storming *nn*, expugnātĭo, *f*
stormy (weather) turbĭdus
story fābŭla, *f*
story-teller narrātor, *m*
stout (fat) pinguis; **(strong)**, vălĭdus; **(— hearted)**, fortis
stove fŏcus, *m*
stow *v.t*, rĕpōno (3)
straddle *v.i*, vārĭco (1)
straggle *v.i*, văgor (1 *dep*)
straight *adj*, rectus
straight *adv*, rectā
straight away *adv*, stătim
straighten *v.t*, corrĭgo (3)
straightforward simplex
strain *nn*, contentĭo, *f*
strain *v.t*, **(stretch)**, tendo (3); **(liquids, etc.)**, cōlo (3); *v.i*, **(strive)**, nītor (3 *dep*)
strait *adj*, angustus
strait *nn*, **(a narrow place or a difficulty)**, angustĭae, *f. pl* **(sea)** frētum, *n*
strand (shore) lītus, *n*
stranded rĕlictus
strange insŏlĭtus, nŏvus
strangeness insŏlentĭa, *f*
stranger hospes, *m*
strangle *v.t*, strangŭlo (1)
strap *nn*, lōrum, *n*
stratagem dŏlus, *m*
strategist *use phr. with* pĕrītus **(skilled in)**, *with phr. below*
strategy ars (*f*) bellandi **(the art of making war)**
straw strāmentum, *n*

strawberry frāgum, *n*
stray *v.i*, erro (1)
stray *adj*, errābundus
streak *nn*, līnĕa, *f*
streak *v.t*, līnĕis vărĭo (1),
 (variegate with streaks)
streaky virgātus
stream *nn*, flūmen, *n*
stream *v.i*, effundor (3 *pass*)
street vĭa, *f*
strength vīres, *f. pl*, rōbur, *n*
strengthen *v.t*, firmo (1)
strenuous impĭger
stress (importance) mōmentum,
 n
stretch *nn*, (extent), spătĭum, *n*
stretch *v.t*, tendo (3); (— out),
 extendo (3); *v.i*, sē tendĕre (3
 reflex)
stretcher lectīca, *f*
strew *v.t*, sterno (3)
strict (severe) dūrus; (careful)
 dīlĭgens
strictness sĕvērĭtas, *f*
stricture rĕprĕhensĭo, *f*
stride *nn*, passus, *m*
strife certāmen, *n*, discordĭa, *f*
strike *v.t*, fĕrĭo (4), percŭtĭo (3),
 pulso (1); (— the mind, occur to),
 subvĕnĭo (4)
striking *adj*, insignis
string līnĕa, *f*; (of bow or
 instrument), nervus, *m*
stringent sĕvērus
strip *v.t*, spŏlĭo (1), nūdo (1)
strip *nn*, (flap, edge), lăcĭnĭa, *f*
stripe līmes, *m*; (blow), verber, *n*
stripling ădŏlescentŭlus, *m*
strive *v.i*, nītor (3 *dep*), contendo
 (3)
striving *nn*, contentĭo, *f*
stroke *nn*, verber, *n*, ictus, *m*;
 (line), līnĕa, *f*
stroke *v.t*, mulcĕo (2)
stroll *nn*, ambŭlātĭo, *f*
stroll *v.i*, ambŭlo (1)
strong vălĭdus, firmus; (powerful),
 fortis; (to be —), *v.i*, vălĕo (2)
stronghold arx, *f*
structure (building) aedĭfĭcĭum, *n*
struggle *nn*, certāmen, *n*

struggle *v.i*, luctor (1 *dep*), nītor
 (3 *dep*)
strumpet mĕrĕtrix, *f*
strut *v.i*, incēdo (3)
stubble stĭpŭla, *f*
stubborn pertĭnax
stucco tectōrĭum, *n*
stud clāvus, *m*; (horses), ĕquārĭa, *f*
stud *v.i*, insēro (3)
student *use adj*, stŭdĭōsus (devoted
 to), *with a suitable noun*
studied mĕdĭtātus
studious stŭdĭōsus
study *nn*, stŭdĭum, *n*; (room,
 library), bĭblĭŏthēca, *f*
study *v.t*, stŭdĕo (2) (*with dat*)
stuff (material) mātĕrĭa, *f*;
 (woven-), textĭle, *n*
stuff *v.t*, farcĭo (4)
stuffing *nn*, fartum, *n*
stumble *nn*, (fall), lapsus, *m*
stumble *v.i*, offendo (3)
stumbling block impĕdīmentum, *n*
stump (post) stīpes, *m*
stun *v.t*, obstŭpĕfăcĭo (3)
stupefaction stŭpor, *m*
stupefy *v.t*, obstŭpĕfăcĭo (3)
stupendous mīrābĭlis
stupid stŏlĭdus, stultus
stupidity stultĭtĭa, *f*
stupor stŭpor, *m*
sturdiness firmĭtas, *f*
sturdy firmus, vălĭdus
sturgeon ăcĭpenser, *m*
stutter *v.i*, balbūtĭo (4)
sty hăra, *f*; (in the eye), hordĕŏlus,
 m
style *nn*, gĕnus, *n*
style *v.t*, (name), appello (1)
stylish spĕcĭōsus
suave suāvis
subaltern sucentŭrĭo, *m*
subdivide *v.t*, dīvĭdo (3)
subdue *v.t*, sūbĭcĭo (3)
subject *adj*, subiectus
subject *nn*, (of a state, etc.), cīvis,
 c; (matter), rēs, *f*
subject *v.t*, sūbĭcĭo (3)
subjection (slavery) servĭtus, *f*
subjoin *v.t*, subiungo (3)
subjugate *v.t*, sŭbĭgo (3)

sublime ēlātus
sublimity ēlātĭo, *f*
submerge *v.t*, submergo (3)
submission (compliance)
obsĕquĭum, *n*
submissive ŏbēdĭens
submit *v.t*, sūbĭcĭo (3); **(present)**,
rĕfĕro (*irreg*); *v.i*, **(yield)**, cēdo (3)
subordinate *adj*, subiectus
subordination (obedience)
obsĕquĭum, *n*
subscribe *v.t*, **(give money, etc.)**,
confĕro (*irreg*); **(signature)**,
subscrībo (3)
subscription (of money, etc.)
collātĭo, *f*
subsequent sĕquens
subsequently *adv*, postĕā
subservient obsĕquens
subside *v.i*, rĕsīdo (3)
subsidize *v.t*, pĕcūnĭam suppĕdĭto
(1), **(furnish with money)**
subsidy subsĭdĭum, *n*
subsist *v.i*, consto (1)
subsistence victus, *m*
substance (essence) nātūra, *f*;
(being), rēs, *f*; **(goods)**, bŏna, *n.pl*
substantial (real) vērus;
(important), grăvis
substitute *nn*, vĭcārĭus, *m*
substitute *v.t*, suppōno (3)
subterfuge lătĕbra, *f*
subterranean subterrānĕus
subtle (crafty) astūtus; **(refined)**,
subtīlis
subtlety (craftiness) astūtĭa, *f*;
(fineness), subtīlĭtas, *f*
subtract *v.t*, dēdūco (3)
subtraction detractĭo, *f*
suburb sŭburbĭum, *n*
suburban sŭburbānus
subvert *v.t*, ēverto (3)
succeed *v.t*, **(in, do well)**, bĕnĕ
effĭcĭo (3); **(of things)**, *v.i*,
prospĕrē ēvĕnĭo (4); *v.t*, **(follow)**,
sĕquor (3 *dep*); **(to an office)**,
succēdo (3)
success res sĕcundae, *f.pl*
successful (persons) fēlix;
(things), prospĕrus
succession (to an office, etc.)
successĭo, *f*; **(series)**, contĭnŭātĭo, *f*
successive contĭnŭus

successor successor, *m*
succinct brĕvis
succour *nn*, auxĭlĭum, *n*
succour *v.t*, succurro (3) **(with
dat)**
succulent sūcōsus
succumb *v.i*, cēdo (3)
such *adj*, tālis, hūius mŏdi **(of this
kind)**
suck *v.t*, sūgo (3)
sucket planta, *f*
suckle *v.t*, ūbĕra do (1) **(with dat)**
suction suctus, *m*
sudden sŭbĭtus
suddenly *adv*, sŭbĭto, rĕpentē
sue *v.t*, **(in law)**, in ius vŏco (1); **(—
for, beg for)**, rŏgo (1)
suet sēbum, *n*
suffer *v.t*, pătĭor (3 *dep*), fĕro
(*irreg*); **(permit)**, permitto (3)
(with dt); *v.i*, affĭcĭor (3 *pass*)
sufferance pătĭentĭa, *f*
sufferer (of illness) aeger, *m*
suffering *nn*, dŏlor, *m*
suffice *v.i*, sătis esse (*irreg*)
sufficiency *use adv*, sătis **(enough)**
sufficient *use* sătis, *adv*, **(with
genit. of noun)**
suffocate *v.t*, suffōco (1)
suffrage suffrāgĭum, *n*
sugar sacchăron, *n*
suggest *v.t*, sūbĭcĭo (3) **(with acc.
of thing and dat. of person)**
suggestion admŏnĭtus, *m*
suicide mors vŏluntārĭa, *f*; **(to
commit —)**, sĭbĭ mortem
conscisco (3) **(inflict death upon
oneself)**
suit (law —) līs, *f*; **(clothes)**,
vestīmenta, *n.pl*
suit *v.i*, convĕnĭo (4); *or use
impers. vb*, dĕcet **(it —s)**
suitable aptus, ĭdōnĕus
suite (retinue) cŏmĭtes, *c, pl*
suitor prŏcus, *m*
sulky mōrōsus
sullen torvus
sully *v.t*, inquĭno (1)
sulphur sulfur, *n*
sultry aestŭōsus
sum (total) summa, *f*; **(— of
money)**, pĕcūnĭa, *f*

sum up *v.t*, compŭto (1); **(speak briefly)**, summātim dīco (3)

summarily *adv*, **(immediately)**, sĭne mŏrā

summary *nn*, ĕpĭtŏme, *f*

summary *adj*, **(hasty)**, sŭbĭtus

summer *nn*, aestas, *f*; *adj*, aestīvus

summit căcūmen, *n, or use adj,* summus **(top of)**

summon *v.t*, arcesso (3)

summon up *v.t*, excĭto (1)

summons vŏcātĭo, *f*, accītu (*abl. case only*: **at the — of**)

sumptuous sumptŭōsus

sumptuousness appărātus, *m*

sun sōl, *m*

sun *v.i*, **(— oneself)**, ăprīcor (1 *dep*)

sunbeam rădĭus (*m*) sōlis

sunburnt ădustus

sundial sōlārĭum, *n*

sunny aprīcus

sunrise ortus (*m*) sōlis

sunset occāsus (*m*) sōlis

sunshine sōl, *m*

sup *v.i*, cēno (1)

superabound *v.i*, sŭpersum (*irreg*)

superb magnĭficus

supercilious sŭperbus

superficial lĕvis

superfluous sŭpervăcānĕus

superhuman dīvīnus

superintend *v.t*, prōcūro (1)

superintendent cūrātor, *m*, praefectus, *m*

superior sŭpĕrĭor; **(to be —)**, *v.i*, sŭpĕro (1)

superiority *use adj*, sŭpĕrĭor

superlative exĭmĭus

supernatural dīvīnus

supernumerary ascriptīvus

superscription tĭtŭlus, *m*

supersede *v.t*, succēdo (3) (*with dat*)

superstition sŭperstĭtĭo, *f*

superstitious sŭperstĭtĭōsus

supervise *v.t*, prōcūro (1)

supper cēna, *f*

supplant *v.t*, **(surpass)**, praeverto (3)

supple flexĭbĭlis

supplement supplēmentum, *n*

suppliant supplex, *c*

supplication obsēcrātĭo, *f*

supply *nn*, cōpĭa, *f*; **(supplies, esp. military)**, commĕātus, *m*

supply *v.t*, suppĕdĭto (1); affĕro (*irreg*)

support *nn*, **(bearing)**, firmāmentum, *n*; **(military)**, subsĭdĭa, *n.pl*; **(sustenance)**, ălĭmentum, *n*

support *v.t*, sustĭnĕo (2); **(aid)**, adĭŭvo (1); **(nourish)**, ălo (3)

supportable tŏlĕrābĭlis

supporter adĭŭtor, *m*

suppose *v.t*, pŭto (1), ŏpīnor (1 *pass*)

supposition ŏpīnĭo, *f*

suppress *v.t*, opprĭmo (3)

suppurate *v.i*, suppūro (1)

supremacy impĕrĭum, *n*

supreme sŭprēmus

sure ertus; **(reliable)**, fĭdēlis; **(I am —)**, compertum hăbĕo (2)

surely *adv*, prŏfecto; **(no doubt)**, nīmīrum; (*in questions; if an affirmative answer is expected*) nonne; (*if a negative answer*), num

surety vas, *m*, sponsor, *m*

surf fluctus, *m*

surface sŭperficĭes, *f*

surge *v.i*, surgo (3)

surgeon chīrurgus, *m*

surgery chīrurgĭa, *f*

surly mōrōsus

surmise *nn*, conĭectūra, *f*

surmise *v.t*, suspĭcor (1 *dep*)

surmount *v.t*, sŭpĕro (1)

surname cognōmen, *n*

surpass *v.t*, sŭpĕro (1)

surplus rĕlĭquum, *n*

surprise *nn*, mīrātĭo, *f*

surprise *v.t*, admīrātĭōnem mŏvĕo (2) (*with dat*); **(to attack)**, ădŏrĭor (4 *dep*)

surrender *nn*, dēdĭtĭo, *f*

surrender *v.t*, dēdo (3), trādo (3); *v.i*, sē dēdĕre (3 *reflex*)

surround *v.t*, cingo (3), circumdo (1)

survey *v.t*, contemplor (1 *dep*); **(land)**, mētĭor (4 *dep*)

surveyor fīnītor, *m*
survive *v.i*, sŭpersum (*irreg*)
survivor sŭperstes, *m*, *f*
susceptibility mollĭtĭa, *f*
susceptible mollis
suspect *v.t*, suspĭcor (1 *dep*)
suspend *v.t*, suspendo (3);
　(interrupt), intermitto (3);
　(— from office), dēmŏvĕo (2)
suspense dŭbĭtātĭo, *f*
suspension (interruption)
　intermissĭo, *f*
suspicion suspīcĭo, *f*
suspicious suspīcĭōsus
sustain *v.t*, sustĭnĕo (2)
sustenance ălĭmentum, *n*
swaddling clothes incūnābŭla, *n.pl*
swagger *v.i*, sē iactāre (1 *reflex*)
swallow *nn*, hĭrundo, *f*
swallow *v.t*, gluttĭo (4), sorbĕo (2)
swamp *nn*, pălus, *f*
swamp *v.t*, opprĭmo (3)
swampy pălūdōsus
swan cycnus, *m*
swarm (people) turba, *f*; (bees),
　exāmen, *n*
swarm *v.i*, glŏmĕror (1 *pass*)
swarthy fuscus
swathe *v.t*, collĭgo (1)
sway *nn*, impĕrĭum, *n*
sway *v.t*, (rule), rĕgo (3); *v.i*,
　(— to and fro), văcillo (1)
swear *v.i*, iūro (1); (— allegiance
　to), iūro in nōmen (*with genit. of
　person*)
sweat *nn*, sūdor, *m*
sweat *v.i*, sūdo (1)
sweep *v.t*, verro (3)
sweet dulcis
sweeten *v.t*, dulcem reddo (3)
　(make sweet)
sweetheart dēlĭcĭae, *f. pl*
sweetness dulcĭtūdo, *f*
swell *nn*, (wave), fluctus, *m*
swell *v.i*, tŭmĕo (2); *v.t*, augĕo (2)
swelling tŭmor, *m*
swerve *v.i*, dēclīno (1)
swift *adj*, cĕler
swiftness cĕlĕrĭtas, *f*
swill *v.t*, (drink), pōto (1)
swim *v.i*, năto (1)
swimmer nătātor, *m*

swimming *nn*, nătātĭo, *f*
swindle *nn*, fraus, *f*
swindle *v.t*, fraudo (1)
swindler fraudātor, *m*
swine sūs, *m*, *f*
swineherd sŭbulcus, *m*
swing *nn*, oscillātĭo, *f*
swing *v.t*, ăgĭto (1); *v.i*, pendĕo (2)
switch (cane) virga, *f*
switch *v.t*, mūto (1)
swollen tŭmĭdus
swoon *v.i*, use *phr*, ănĭmus
　rĕlinquit . . . (sensibility leaves ...)
swoop *nn*, use *vb*, advŏlo (1)
swoop on *v.i*, advŏlo (1)
sword glădĭus, *m*
sword-edge ăcĭes, *f*
swordfish xĭphĭas, *m*
sworn (treaty, etc.) confirmātus
　iūrĕiūrando (confirmed by
　swearing)
sycamore sўcămōrus, *f*
sycophant sўcŏphanta, *m*
syllable syllăba, *f*
symbol signum, *n*
symmetrical congrŭens
symmetry convĕnĭentĭa, *f*
sympathetic mĭsĕrĭcors
sympathize *v.t*, consentĭo (4)
sympathy consensus, *m*
symphony symphōnĭa, *f*
symptom signum, *n*
synagogue sўnăgōga, *f*
syndicate sŏcĭĕtas, *f*
synonym verbum ĭdem signĭfĭcans
　(word expressing the same thing)
synopsis ēpĭtŏma, *f*
syntax syntaxis, *f*
syringe sīpho, *m*
syringe *v.t*, aspergo (3) (sprinkle)
system formŭla, *f*, rătĭo, *f*
systematic ordĭnātus

T

table mensa, *f*, tăbŭla, *f*; (list),
　index, *m*
tablecloth mantēle, *n*
tablet tăbŭla, *f*
tacit tăcĭtus
taciturn tăcĭturnus
tack clāvŭlus, *m*

tack

tack *v.t*, **(fix)**, fīgo (3); *v.i*, **(ships)**, rĕcīprŏcor (1 *pass*)
tackle **(fittings)** armāmenta, *n.pl*
tact dextĕrĭtas, *f*, urbănĭtas, *f*
tactician pĕrītus (*m*) rĕi mīlĭtāris
tactics **(military)** rătĭo (*f*) bellandi **(method of making war)**
tadpole rānuncŭlus, *m*
tag *v.t*, *use* fīgo (3) **(fix)**
tail cauda, *f*
tailor vestītor, *m*
taint *nn*, contāgĭo, *f*
taint *v.t*, infĭcĭo (3)
take *v.t*, căpĭo (3); **(grasp)**, prēhendo (3); **(receive)**, accĭpĭo (3); **(seize)**, răpĭo (3); **(take possession of)**, occŭpo (1); **(— by storm)**, expugno (1); **(— away)**, aufĕro (*irreg*) ădĭmo (3); **(— in)**, excĭpĭo (3); **(— off)**, dēmo (3); **(— on)**, suscĭpĭo (3); **(— up)**, sūmo (3)
taking **(capture of a city)** expugnātĭo, *f*
tale făbŭla, *f*
talent **(ability)** ingĕnĭum, *n*; **(money)**, tălentum, *n*
talk *nn*, sermo, *m*
talk *v.i*, lŏquor (3 *dep*)
talkative lŏquax
tall prōcērus
tallness prōcērĭtas, *f*
tallow sēbum, *n*
tally *v.i*, convĕnĭo (4)
talon unguis, *m*
tamable dŏmābĭlis
tame *v.t*, dŏmo (1), mansŭēfăcĭo (3)
tame *adj*, mansŭēfactus, dŏmĭtus
tameness mansŭētūdo, *f*
tamer dŏmĭtor, *m*
tamper with *v.t*, tempto (1)
tan *v.t*, **(leather, etc.)**, confĭcĭo (3)
tangent *use* līnĕa, *f*, **(line)**
tangible tractābĭlis
tangle *nn*, implĭcātĭo, *f*
tangle *v.t*, implĭco (1)
tank lăcus, *m*
tanner cŏrĭārĭus, *m*
tantalize *v.t*, **(torment)**, fătīgo (1)
tap *nn*, **(blow)**, ictus, *m*
tap *v.t*, **(hit)**, fĕrĭo (4), pulso (1); *with* lĕvĭter **(lightly)**

tape taenĭa, *f*
taper cērĕus, *m*
taper *v.i*, fastīgor (1 *pass*)
tapestry *use* vēlum, *n*, **(curtain)**
tar pix lĭquĭda, *f*
tardiness tardĭtas, *f*
tardy tardus
tare lŏlĭum, *n*
target scŏpus, *m*
tarnish *v.i*, hĕbesco (3); *v.t*, inquĭno (1)
tarry *v.i*, mŏror (1 *dep*)
tart *nn*, crustŭlum, *n*
tart *adj*, ăcĭdus
task ŏpus, *n*
taste *nn*, **(sense of —)**, gustātus, *m*; **(flavour)**, săpor, *m*; **(judgement)**, iūdĭcĭum, *n*
taste *v.t*, gusto (1); *v.i*, **(have a flavour)**, săpĭo (3)
tasteful **(elegant)** ēlĕgans
tasteless insulsus
tasty săpĭdus
tattered pannōsus
tatters pannus, *m*
tattle *v.i*, garrĭo (4)
taunt *nn*, convīcĭum, *n*
taunt *v.t*, ōbĭcĭo (3) (*dat. of person and acc. of thing*)
taunting *adj*, contŭmēlĭōsus
tavern caupōna, *f*
tavern-keeper caupo, *m*
tawdry fūcōsus
tawny fulvus
tax *nn*, vectīgal, *n*
tax *v.t*, **(impose —)**, vectīgal impōno (3) (*with dat*)
taxable vectīgālis
tax collector exactor, *m*, pūblĭcānus, *m*
teach *v.t*, dŏcĕo (2) (*with acc. of person and acc. of thing*)
teacher doctor, *m*, măgister, *m*
teaching *nn*, doctrīna, *f*
team **(— of horses)** iŭgum, *n*
tear *nn*, lăcrĭma, *f*; **(to shed —s)**, lăcrĭmas fundo (3); **(rent)**, scissūra, *f*
tear *v.t*, scindo (3); **(— away)**, abscindo (3); **(— down, open)**, rēscindo (3); **(— up, in pieces)**, distrăho (3)
tearful flēbĭlis

tease *v.t*, obtundo (3)

teat mamma, *f*

technical *use phr*, prŏprĭus artis (particular to a skill)

tedious lentus

teem with *v.i*, scătĕo (2)

teethe *v.i*, dentĭo (4)

teething *nn*, dentītĭo, *f*

tell *v.t*, (give information), dīco (3); narro (1) (*with acc. of thing said and dat. of person told*), certĭōrem făcĭo (3) (*acc. of person told, foll. by dē with abl. of thing said*); (order), iŭbĕo (2)

teller (counter) nŭmĕrātor, *m*

temerity tĕmĕrĭtas, *f*

temper (of mind) ănĭmus, *m*; (bad —), īrācundĭa, *f*

temper *v.t*, tempĕro (1)

temperament nātūra, *f*, ingĕnĭum, *n*

temperance tempĕrantĭa, *f*

temperate tempĕrātus

temperate climate tĕmpĕrĭes, *f*

temperateness mŏdĕrātĭo, *f*

tempest tempestas, *f*

tempestuous prŏcellōsus

temple templum, *n*, aedes, *f*; (of the head), tempus, *n*

temporal hūmānus

temporary *use adv. phr*, ad tempus (for the time being)

tempt *v.t*, tento (1)

temptation (allurement) illĕcĕbra, *f*

tempter tentātor, *m*

tempting *adj*, illĕcĕbrōsus

ten dĕcem; (— each), dēni; (— time), *adv*, dĕcĭes

tenacious tĕnax

tenacity tĕnācĭtas, *f*

tenant inquĭlīnus, *m*

tend *v.t*, (care for), cŏlo (3); *v.i*, (go, direct oneself), tendo (3); (incline to), inclīno (1); (be accustomed), consŭesco (3)

tendency inclīnātĭo, *f*

tender *adj*, tĕner, mollis

tender *v.t*, (offer), dēfĕro (*irreg*)

tenderness mollĭtĭa, *f*, indulgentĭa, *f*

tenement conductum, *n*

tenor (course) tĕnor, *m*, cursus, *m*

tense *adj*, tentus, intentus

tense *nn*, tempus, *n*

tension intentĭo, *f*

tent tăbernācŭlum, *n*; (general's —), praetōrĭum, *n*

tentacle cornĭcŭlum, *n*

tenth dĕcĭmus

tepid ēgĕlĭdus, tĕpĭdus; (to be —), *v.i*, tĕpĕo (2)

term (period of time) spătĭum, *n*; (limit), finis, *m*; (word), verbum, *n*; (condition), condĭcĭo, *f*

term *v.t*, vŏco (1)

terminate *v.t*, termĭno (1)

termination finis, *m*

terrace sōlārĭum, *n*

terrestrial terrestris

terrible terrĭbĭlis

terrify *v.t*, terrĕo (2)

territory fines, *m. pl*, ăger, *m*

terror terror, *m*, păvor, *m*

terse brĕvis

terseness brĕvĭtas, *f*

test *nn*, expĕrīmentum, *n*

test *v.t*, expĕrĭor (4 *dep*)

testament testāmentum, *n*

testator testātor, *m*

testify *v.t*, testĭfĭcor (1 *dep*)

testimony testĭmōnĭum, *n*

testy stŏmăchōsus

text scriptum, *n*

textile textĭle, *n*

texture textus, *m*

than *conj*, quam

thank *v.t*, grātĭas ăgo (3) (*with dat. of person*)

thankfulness grātus ănĭmus, *m*

thankless ingrātus

thanks grātĭas, *f. pl*

thanksgiving actĭo (*f*) grātĭārum

that *demonstrative pron*, ille, is, iste

that *relative pron*, qui, quae, quod

that *conj*, (*with purpose or consecutive clauses*) ut (ne *if negative*); (*after vbs introducing statements*) no separate word, but rendered by the expression itself: *e.g.* **he said that the king was coming**, rēgem vĕnīre dixit

thatch strāmentum, *n*

thaw *v.t*, solvo (3); *v.i*, sē rĕsolvĕre (3 *reflex*)

the *no equivalent in Latin*

theatre thĕătrum, *n*

theatrical thĕātrālis

theft furtum, *n*

their *reflexive*, sŭus; *otherwise* ĕōrum, (*f*, ĕārum)

them *use appropriate case of pron*, is, ille, iste

theme prŏpŏsĭtĭo, *f*

themselves *reflexive pron*, sē; *(pron. emphatic)* ipsi, ae, a

then *adv. of* **(time)**, tum; **(therefore)**, ĭgĭtur

thence *adv*, inde, illinc

theologian thĕŏlŏgus, *m*

theology thĕŏlŏgĭa, *f*

theorem thĕōrēma, *n*

theoretical rătĭōnālis

theory rătĭo, *f*

there *(in or at that place)*, ĭbĭ; **(to that place)**, ĕō; **(— is)**, est; **(— are)**, sunt *(from* esse)

thereabouts *adv*, circā

thereafter *adv*, dĕinde

therefore *adv*, ĭgĭtur, ergo

thereupon *adv*, sŭbinde

thesis prŏpŏsĭtum, *n*

they *as subject of vb. usually not rendered; otherwise use* ĭi, illi, isti

thick crassus, densus, confertus

thicken *v.t*, denso (1); *v.i*, concresco (3)

thicket dūmētum, *n*

thick-headed crassus

thickness crassĭtūdo, *f*

thick-set (of body) compactus

thick-skinned (indifferent) neglĕgens

thief fur, *c*

thieve *v.t*, fūror (1 *dep*)

thieving *nn*, **(theft)**, furtum, *n*

thigh fĕmur, *n*

thin tĕnŭis, grăcĭlis

thin *v.t*, tĕnŭo (1)

thing rēs, *f*

think *v.t*, cōgĭto (1); **(believe, suppose)**, crēdo (3), arbĭtror (1 *dep*), pŭto (1), existĭmo (1)

thinker phĭlŏsŏphus, *m*

thinness tĕnŭĭtas, *f*

third *adj*, tertĭus; **(a — part)**, tertĭa pars, *f*; **(thirdly)**, *adv*, tertĭo

thirst *v.i*, sĭtĭo (4)

thirst *nn*, sĭtis, *f*

thirsty sĭtĭens

thirteen trēdĕcim

thirteenth tertĭus dĕcĭmus

thirtieth trīgēsĭmus

thirty trīginta

this *demonstrative pron*, hīc, haec, hōc

thiste cardŭus, *m*

thither *adv*, ĕō, illūc; **(hither and —)**, hūc atque illūc

thong lōrum, *n*

thorn sentis, *m*, spīna, *f*

thorn-bush vĕpres, *m*

thorny spīnōsus

thorough perfectus; **(exact)**, subtīlis

thoroughbred gĕnĕrōsus

thoroughfare pervĭum, *n*

those *demonstrative pron*, illi

though *conj*, etsi

thought (act or faculty of thinking) cōgĭtātĭo, *f*; **(opinion)**, cōgĭtātum, *n*; **(plan, intention)**, consĭlĭum, *n*

thoughtful (careful) prōvĭdus; **(deep in thought)**, multa pŭtans

thoughtfulness cūra, *f*, cōgĭtātĭo, *f*

thoughtless tĕmĕrārĭus, inconsultus

thoughtlessness nĕglegentĭa, *f*, tĕmĕrĭtas, *f*

thousand mille *(indeclinable adj)*; *in pl*, mīlĭa *(n.pl, nn)*

thrash *v.t*, tundo (3); **(corn)**, tĕro (3)

thrashing *nn*, trītūra, *f*; **(chastisement)**, verbĕrātĭo, *f*

thrashing-floor ārĕa, *f*

thread fĭlum, *n*

thread *v.t*, **(— one's way)**, sē insĭnŭāre (1 *reflex*)

threadbare obsŏlētus

threat mĭnae, *f. pl*

threaten *v.t*, mĭnor (1 *dep*) *(with acc. of thing and dat. of person)*; *v.i*, **(impend)**, immĭnĕo (2)

threatening *adj*, mĭnax

three tres; **(— each)**, terni; **(— times)**, *adv*, ter

threefold (triple) trĭplex

threehundred trĕcenti

threehundredth trĕcentensĭmus
thresh *v.t*, tĕro (3)
threshold līmen, *n*
thrice *adj*, ter
thrift frūgālĭtas, *f*
thrifty parcus
thrill *v.t, use* afficĭo (3) **(affect)**
thrill (of pleasure) hĭlărĭtas, *f*; **(a shock)**, stringor, *m*
thrilling *adj, use vb*, afficĭo (3) **(to affect)**
thrive *v.i*, vĭgĕo (2)
throat fauces, *f. pl*
throb *v.i*, palpĭto (1)
throbbing *nn*, palpĭtātĭo, *f*
throne sŏlĭum, *n*; **(regal, imperial power)**, regnum, *n*
throng *nn*, multĭtūdo, *f*
throng *v.t*, cĕlĕbro (1)
throttle *v.t*, strangŭlo (1)
through *prep*, per (*with acc*); **(on account of)**, propter (*with acc*)
through *adv, often expressed by a compount vb, with* per; *e.g.* perfĕro **(carry through)**
throughout *prep*, per; *adv*, pĕnĭtus **(entirely, wholly)**
throw *nn*, iactus, *m*
throw *v.t*, iăcĭo (3), cōnĭcĭo (3) **(— away)**, ăbĭcĭo (3); **(— back)**, rēĭcĭo (3); **(— down)**, dēĭcĭo (3); **(— oneself at the feet of)**, se prōĭcĕre ad pĕdes (*with genit. of person*); **(— out)**, ēĭcĭo (3)
thrush turdus, *m*
thrust *nn*, pĕtītĭo, *f*
thrust *v.t*, trūdo (3); **(— forward)**, prōtrūdo (3)
thumb pollex, *m*
thump *nn*, cŏlăphus, *m*
thump *v.t*, tundo (3)
thunder *nn*, tŏnĭtrus, *m*; **(— bolt)**, fulmen, *n*
thunder *v.i*, tŏno (1)
thunderstruck attŏnĭtus
thus *adv*, īta, sīc
thwart *nn*, **(seat)**, transtrum, *n*
thwart *v.t*, obsto (1) (*with dat. of person*), impĕdĭo (4)
tiara tĭăra, *f*
ticket tessĕra, *f*
tickle *v.t*, tĭtillo (1)
tickling *nn*, tĭtillātĭo, *f*

ticklish lūbrĭcus
tide aestus, *m*
tidiness mundĭtĭa, *f*
tidings nuntĭus, *m*
tidy mundus
tie *nn*, vincŭlum, *n*
tie *v.t*, lĭgo (1), nōdo (1)
tier ordo, *m*
tiger tigris, *c*
tight strictus
tighten *v.t*, stringo (3)
tile tēgŭla, *f*
till *prep*, usque ad (*with acc*)
till *conj*, dum, dōnĕc
till *nn*, arca, *f*
till *v.t*, cŏlo (3)
tillage, tilling *nn*, cultus, *m*
tiller (boat) clāvus, (*m*) gŭbernācŭli **(handle of the rudder)**
tilt *v.t*, **(bend)**, dēclīno (1)
timber mātĕria, *f*
time tempus, *n*; **(period, space of —)**, intervallum, *n*, spătĭum, *n*; **(generation, age)**, aetas, *f*; **(— of day)**, hōra, *f*; **(at the right —)**, *adv, phr*, ad tempus; **(at —s)**, *adv*, interdum; **(once upon a —)**, *adv*, ōlim; **(at the same —)**, *adv*, sĭmŭl; **(at that —)**, *adv*, tum
timely *adj*, opportūnus
timid tĭmĭdus
timidity tĭmĭdĭtas, *f*
tin plumbum album, *n*
tincture cŏlor, *m*
tinder fōmes, *m*
tinge *v.t*, tingo (3)
tingle *v.i*, prūrĭo (4)
tinker făber, *m*, **(artificer)**
tinkle *v.i*, tinnĭo (4)
tiny exĭgŭus, parvŭlus
tip căcūmen, *n*
tip *v.t*, **(put a point on)**, praefigo (3); **(tip over)**, verto (3)
tire *v.t*, fătīgo (1); *v.i*, dēfătīgor (1 *dep*)
tired fessus
tiresome mŏlestus
tissue textus, *m*
titbits cūpēdĭa, *n.pl*
tithe dĕcŭma, *f*
title tĭtŭlus, *m*

titled (of nobility) nōbĭlis

titter *nn*, rīsus, *m*

to *prep*, (*motion towards a place, and expressions of time*), ad (*with acc*); (*sometimes, e.g. names of towns, acc. of nn. alone*); *often dat. case can be used, e.g. indirect object after vb.* to give; (*before a clause expressing purpose*), ut; (*sometimes indicates the infinitive of a vb*), *e.g.* **to love**, ămāre

toad būfo, *m*

toast *v.t*, torrĕo (2); (**a person's health**), prŏpīno (1) (*with dat. of person*)

today *adv*, hŏdĭē

toe dĭgĭtus, *m*

together *adv*, sĭmŭl, ūnā

toil *nn*, lăbor, *m*

toil *v.i*, lăbōro (1)

toilet (care of person, etc.), cultus, *m*

token signum, *n*

tolerable tŏlĕrābĭlis

tolerance tŏlĕrantĭa, *f*

tolerate *v.t*, tŏlĕro (1)

toll *nn*, vectīgal, *n*

tomb sĕpulcrum, *n*, tŭmŭlus, *m*

tombstone lăpis, *m*

tomorrow *adv*, crās

tomorrow *nn*, crastĭnus dĭes, *m*

tone sŏnus, *m*

tongs forceps, *m*

tongue lingua, *f*

tonight *adv*, hŏdĭē nocte

tonsils tonsillae, *f. pl*

too (also) ĕtĭam; (**— little**), părum; (**— much**), nĭmis; *comparative adj. or adv. can be used, e.g.* **too far**, longĭus

tool instrŭmentum, *n*

tooth dens, *m*

toothache dŏlor (*m*) dentĭum

toothed dentātus

toothless ēdentŭlus

toothpick dentiscalpĭum, *n*

top *use adj*, summus *in agreement with nn, e.g.* **the top of the rock**, summum saxum, *n*; (**summit**), căcūmen, *n*

top *v.t*, sŭpĕro (1)

topic rĕs, *f*

topmost summus

topography *use phr*, nātūra (*f*) lŏci (**nature of the land**)

torch fax, *f*

torment *nn*, crŭcĭātus, *m*

torment *v.t*, crŭcĭo (1)

tornado turbo, *m*

torpid torpens, pĭger

torpor torpor, *m*

torrent torrens, *m*

tortoise testūdo, *f*

tortuous sĭnŭōsus

torture *nn*, crŭcĭātus, *m*

torture *v.t*, crŭcĭo (1)

torturer carnĭfex, *m*

toss *nn*, iactus, *m*

toss *v.t*, iacto (1)

total *nn*, summa, *f*

total *adj*, tōtus

totally *adv*, omnīno

totter *v.i*, lăbo (1)

touch *nn*, tactus, *m*; (**contact**), contāgĭo, *f*

touch *v.t*, tango (3), attingo (3); (**move**), mŏvĕo (2)

touchy stŏmăchōsus

tough *adj*, lentus

toughness dūrĭtĭa, *f*

tour pĕrĕgrīnātĭo, *f*, ĭter, *n*

tourist pĕrĕgrīnātor, *m*

tournament *use* certāmen, *n*, (**contest**)

tow *v.t*, trăho (3)

tow *nn*, (**hemp**), stuppa, *f*

towards *prep*, (**of direction, position**), ad (*with acc*); (**of time**), sub (*with acc*); (**emotions**), ergā, in (*with acc*); (**with names of towns**), versus (*placed after the noun*)

towel mantēle, *n*

tower *nn*, turris, *f*

tower *v.i*, exsto (1)

town urbs, *f*, oppĭdum, *n*

townsman oppĭdānus, *m*

toy (child's rattle) crĕpundĭa, *n.pl*

toy with *v.i*, illūdo (3)

trace *nn*, vestīgĭum, *n*, signum, *n*

trace *v.t*, sĕquendo invĕnĭo (4) (**find by following**)

track *nn*, (**path**), callis, *m*; (**footsteps, etc.**), vestīgĭum, *n*

track *v.t*, (**— down**), investīgo (1);

(pursue), sĕquor (3 *dep*)

trackless āvĭus

tract (region) rĕgĭo, *f*; **(booklet)**, lībellus, *m*

tractable dŏcĭlis

trade mercātūra, *f*; **(a particular —)** , ars, *f*

trade *v.i*, mercātūram făcĭo (3)

trade mercātor, *m*

tradition mĕmŏrĭa, *f*

traditional *use phr*, trādĭtus ā māiōrĭbus **(handed down from our ancestors)**

traffic (trade, etc.) commercĭum, *n*; **(streets, etc.)**, *use phr. with* frĕquento (1) **(to crowd)**

tragedy trăgoedĭa, *f*

tragic trăgĭcus; **(unhappy)**, tristis

trail (path) callis, *m*

train ordo, *m*; **(procession)**, pompa, *f. pl*; **(of a dress)**, pēnĭcŭlamentum, *n*

train *v.t*, instĭtŭo (3), exercĕo (2)

trainer exercĭtor, *m*

training *nn*, disciplīna, *f*

traitor prōdĭtor, *m*

traitorous perfĭdus

tramp *v.i*, ambŭlo (1)

trample on *v.t*, obtĕro (3)

trance (elation, exaltation) ēlātĭo, *f*

tranquil tranquillus, plăcĭdus

transact *v.t*, ăgo (3)

transaction rēs, *f*, nĕgōtĭum, *n*

transcend *v.t*, sŭpĕro (1)

transcribe *v.t*, transcrībo (3)

transfer *nn*, **(of property)**, mancĭpĭum, *n*

transfer *v.t*, transfĕro (*irreg*)

transfix *v.t*, transfigo (3)

transform *v.t*, mūto (1)

transgress *v.t*, vĭŏlo (1); *v.i*, pecco (1)

transgression (fault) dēlictum, *n*

transit transĭtus, *m*

transitory cădūcus

translate *v.t*, verto (3)

translation (a work) ŏpus translātum, *n*; **(act)**, translātĭo, *f*

translator interpres, *c*

transmigrate *v.i*, transmĭgro (1)

transmit *v.t*, transmitto (3)

transparent perlūcĭdus

transpire *v.i.* **(get about)**, vulgor (1 *pass*)

transplant *v.t*, transfĕro (*irreg*)

transport *nn*, *use vb. below*; **(joy)**, laetĭtĭa, *f*, exsultātĭo, *f*

transport *v.t*, transporto (1), trāĭcĭo (3)

trap *nn*, insĭdĭae, *f. pl*; **(for animals)**, lăquĕus, *m*

trap *v.t*, *use phr*, illĭcĭo (3) in insĭdĭas **(entice into a trap)**

trappings insignĭa, *n.pl*

trash scrūta, *n.pl*, nūgae, *f. pl*

travel *nn*, ĭter, *n*

travel *v.i*, ĭter făcĭo (3)

traveller vĭātor, *m*

traverse *v.t*, ŏbĕo (4)

travesty (mockery) lūdĭbrĭum, *n*

tray fercŭlum, *n*

treacherous perfĭdus

treachery perfĭdĭa, *f*, fraus, *f*

tread *nn*, grădus, *m*

tread *v.i*, ingrĕdĭor (3 *dep*); *v.t*, **(— on)**, calco (1)

treason māiestas, *f*

treasure ōpes *f. pl*; **(hoard, treasure-house)**, thēsaurus, *m*

treasure *v.t*, **(regard highly)**, magni aestĭmo (1); **(store up)**, rĕcondo (3)

treasurer praefectus (*m*) aerārĭi **(director of the treasury)**

treasury aerārĭum, *n*

treat *nn*, dēlectātĭo, *f*

treat *v.t*, **(deal with, behave towards)**, hăbĕo (2); **(medically)**, cūro (1); **(discuss)**, ăgo (3)

treatise līber, *m*

treatment tractātĭo, *f*; **(cure)**, cūrātĭo, *f*

treaty foedus, *n*

treble *adj*, trĭplex

treble *v.t*, trĭplĭco (1)

tree arbor, *f*

trellis cancelli, *m. pl*

tremble *v.i*, trĕmo (3)

trembling *nn*, trĕmor, *m*

tremendous ingens

tremulous trĕmŭlus

trench fossa, *f*

trepidation trĕpĭdātĭo, *f*

trespass (crime) dēlictum, *n*

trespass *v.i, use phr. with* ingrēdi
(to enter), *and* tē (mē, *etc.*),
invītō (without your (my)
permission)

tress (hair) grădus, *m*

trial (legal) iūdĭcĭum, *n*;
(experiment), expĕrĭentĭa, *f*

triangle trĭangŭlum, *n*

triangular trĭangŭlus

tribe (Roman) trĭbus, *f*; (other),
pŏpŭlus, *m*

tribunal iūdĭcĭum, *n*

tribune trĭbūnus, *m*

tributary *adj*, (paying tribute),
vectīgālis

tributary *nn*, (river), *use phr*, qui in
flūmen inflŭit (which flows into a
river)

tribute trĭbūtum, *n*, vectīgal, *n*

trick *nn*, dŏlus, *m*, fraus, *f*

trick *v.t*, dēcĭpĭo (3)

trickery dŏlus, *m*

trickle *v.i*, māno (1)

trickster hŏmo dŏlōsus, fallax

tricky (dangerous) pĕrīcŭlōsus

trident trĭdens, *m*

tried (well —) prŏbātus

trifle *nn*, rēs parva, *f*, nūgae, *f. pl*

trifle *v.i.* lūdo (3)

trifling *adj*, lĕvus

trim *adj*, nĭtĭdus

trim *v.t.* pŭto (1)

trinkets mundus, *m*

trip *nn*, (journey), ĭter, *n*

trip *v.t.* supplanto (1); *v.i.*
(stumble), offendo (3), lābor (3
dep)

tripe ŏmāsum, *n*

triple trĭplex

tripod trĭpus, *m*

trite trītus

**triumph (Roman celebration of
victory)** trĭumphus, *m*; (victory),
victōrĭa, *f*

triumph *v.i, and v.t*, trĭumpho (1)

triumphant victor

triumvirate trĭumvĭrātus, *m*

trivial lĕvis, vīlis

troop (band) mănus, *f*; (— of
cavalry), turma, *f*; (—s), cōpĭae, *f,
pl*

troop *v.i*, conflŭo (3)

trooper ĕquĕs, *m*

trophy trŏpaeum, *n*

trot *nn*, lentus cursus, *m*

trot *v.i*, lento cursu ĕo (4);
(proceed on a slow course)

trouble *nn*, (disadvantage),
incommŏdum, *n*; (exertion),
ŏpĕra, *f*; (commotion), tŭmultus,
m; (annoyance), mŏlestĭa, *f*

trouble *v.t*, (disturb), sollĭcĭto (1);
(harass), vexo (1); (— oneself
about), cŭro (1)

troublesome mŏlestus

trough alvĕus, *m*

trousers brăcae, *f. pl*

trowel trulla, *f*

truant *nn*, *use phr*, qui consultō
ăbest (who is absent deliberately)

truce indūtĭae, *f. pl*

truck plaustrum, *n*

truculent (grim) trux

trudge *v.i*, *use phr*, aegrē ambŭlo
(1) (walk with difficulty)

true vērus; (faithful), fĭdus

truffle tūber, *n*

truly *adv*, vērē, prŏfectō

trumpery scrūta, *n.pl*

trumpet *nn*, tŭba, *f*, būcĭna, *f*

trumpeter tŭbĭcen, *m*

truncheon fustis, *m*

trundle *v.t*, volvo (3)

trunk truncus, *m*; (of elephant)
prŏboscis, *f*; (box), arca, *f*

truss fascĭa, *f*

trust *nn*, fĭdes, *f*

trust *v.t*, confido (3 *semi-dep*)
(*with dat. of person*), crēdo (3);
commit to), committo (3)

trustworthy, trusty certus, fĭdus

truth vērĭtas, *f*; (true things), vēra,
n.pl; (in —), *adv*, vēro

truthful vērax

truthfulness vērĭtas, *f*

try *v.i*, (attempt), cōnor (1 *dep*);
v.t, (put to the test), tento (1);
(— in court), iūdĭco (1)

trying *adj*, mŏlestus

tub lābrum, *n*

tube tŭbŭlus, *m*

tuber tŭber, *n*

tubular tŭbŭlātus

tuck up *v.t*, succingo (3)

tuft crīnis, *m*

tug *v.t*, trăho (3)

tuition instĭtuutĭo, *f*
tumble *nn*, cāsus, *m*
tumbler (beaker) pōcŭlum, *n*
tumour tŭmor, *m*
tumult tŭmultus, *m*
tumultuous tŭmultŭōsus
tun (cask) dōlĭum, *n*
tune (melody) cantus, *m*; **(out of —·),**
  adj, absŏnus
tune *v.t*, **(stringed instrument),**
  tendo (3)
tuneful cănōrus
tunic tŭnĭca, *f*
tunnel cănālis, *m*, cŭnīcŭlus, *m*
tunny fish thunnus, *m*
turban mĭtra, *f*
turbid turbĭdus
turbot rhombus, *m*
turbulence tŭmultus, *m*
turbulent turbŭlentus
turf caespes, *m*
turgid turgĭdus
turmoil turba, *f*, tŭmultus, *m*
turn (movement) conversĭo, *f*;
  (bending); flexus, *m*; **(change),**
  commūtātĭo, *f*; **(by — s, in —),**
  adv, invĭcem, per vĭces; **(a
  good —),** offĭcĭum, *n*
turn *v.t*, verto (3); **(bend),** flecto
  (3); **(— aside),** dēflecto (3); *v.i*, sē
  dēclīnāre (1 *reflex*); **(— away),**
  āverto (3); **(— the back),** *v.i*,
  tergum verto (3); **(change),** *v.i*,
  mūtor (1 *pass*); **(— back),** *v.i*,
  rĕvertor (3 *pass*); **(— out),** *v.t*
  ēĭcĭo (3); *v.i*, ēvĕnĭo (4);
  (— round), *v.t*, circumăgo (3); *v.i*,
  circumăgor (3 *pass*)
turning *nn*, flexus, *m*
turnip rāpum, *n*
turpitude turpĭtūdo, *f*
turret turris, *f*
turtledove turtur, *m*
tusk dens, *m*
tutelage tūtēla, *f*
tutor māgister, *m*
twang *nn*, sŏnĭtus, *m*
twang *v.i*, sŏno (1)
tweak *v.t*, vellĭco (1)
tweezers volsella, *f*
twelfth dŭŏdĕcĭmus
twelve dŭŏdĕcim; **(— each),**
  duodēni

twentieth vīcēsĭmus
twenty vīginti
twice *adj*, bis
twig rāmŭlus, *m*
twilight crĕpuscŭlum, *n*
twin *nn and adj*, gĕmĭnus
twine *nn*, līnum, *n*
twine *v.t*, circumplĭco (1); *v.i*,
  circumplector (3 *dep*)
twinge *nn*, dŏlor, *m*
twinkle *v.i*, mĭco (1)
twirl *v.t* verso (1)
twist *v.t*, torquĕo (2); *v.i*, sē
  torquēre (2 *reflex*)
twit *v.t*, ōbĭcĭo (3) (*acc. of thing
  and dat, of person*)
twitch *v.t*, vellĭco (1)
twitter *v.i*, **(chirp),** pīpĭlo (1)
two dŭŏ; **(— each),** bīni
two-fold dŭplex
two-footed bīpes
two hundred dŭcenti
type (class, sort) gĕnus, *n*;
  (example), exemplar, *n*
typical *use adj,* ūsĭtātus **(familiar)**
tyrannical tўrannĭcus, sŭperbus
tyrannize *v.i*, dŏmĭnor (1 *dep*)
tyranny dŏmĭnātĭo, *f*
tyrant tўrannus, *m*

U

ubiquitous praesens **(present)**
udder ūber, *n*
ugliness dēformĭtas, *f*
ugly dēformis
ulcer vŏmĭca, *f*
ulcerate *v.i*, suppūro (1)
ulceration ulcĕrātĭo, *f*
ulcerous ulcĕrōsus
ulterior ultĕrĭor
ultimate ultĭmus
ultimatum (to present —) ultĭmam
  condĭcĭōnem ferre (*irreg*)
umbrage (to take — at) *v.t*, aegrē
  fĕro (*irreg*)
umbrella umbella, *f*
umpire arbĭter, *m*
un- *prefix, often* nōn, haud, *can
  be used*
unabashed intrĕpĭdus; **(brazen),**
  impŭdens
unabated immĭnūtus

unable *use vb. phr. with* non
 posse **(to be unable)**
unacceptable ingrātus
unaccompanied incŏmĭtātus
unaccomplished infectus
unaccountable inexplĭcābĭlis
unaccustomed insŏlĭtus
unacquainted ignārus
unadorned ĭnornātus
unadulterated sincērus
unadvisable (foolhardy) audax
unadvised inconsĭdĕrātus
unaffected (natural) simplex;
 (untouched), intĕger
unaided *use adv. phr,* sĭne
 auxĭlĭo **(without help)**
unalloyed pūrus
unalterable immūtābĭlis
unambitious hŭmĭlis
unanimity ūnănĭmĭtas, *f*
unanimous ūnĭversus **(all
 together)**
unanimously *adv,* ūnā vōce
unanswerable non rĕvincendus
unanswered *use vb.* rēspondĕo
 (2) **(to answer)**
unappeased implācātus
unapproachable nōn ădĕundus
unarmed ĭnermis
unassailable ĭnexpugnābĭlis
unassailed intactus
unassuming mŏdestus
unattainable *use phr. with vb.*
 attīngo (3) **(to reach)**
unattempted ĭnexpertus
unauthorized illĭcĭtus
unavailing fūtĭlis
unavoidable ĭnēvītābĭlis
unaware inscĭus
unawares *adv,* dē imprōvīso
unbar *v.t,* rĕsĕro (1)
unbearable intŏlĕrābĭlis
unbecoming indĕcōrus
unbelieving incrēdŭlus
unbend *v.t,* rĕmitto (3)
unbending rĭgĭdus
unbiassed intĕger
unbidden iniussus
unbind *v.t,* solvo (3)
unblemished pūrus
unbound sŏlūtus
unbounded infīnītus
unbreakable *use phr,* quod frangi

non pŏtest **(that cannot be
 broken)**
unbridled effrēnātus
unbroken intĕger, perpĕtŭus
unbuckle *v.t,* diffĭbŭlo (1)
unburden *v.t,* exŏnĕro (1)
unburied ĭnhŭmātus
uncared for neglectus
unceasing perpĕtŭus
uncertain incertus, dŭbĭus; **(to
 be —),** *v.i,* dŭbĭto (1)
uncertainty dŭbĭtātĭo, *f*
unchangeable immūtābĭlis
unchanged constans; **(to
 remain —),** *v.i,* permānĕo (2)
uncharitable inhūmānus
uncivil ĭnurbānus
uncivilized incultus
uncle (father's side) pătrŭus, *m;*
 (mother's side), ăvuncŭlus, *m*
unclean inquĭnātus
unclouded sĕrēnus
uncoil *v.t,* ēvolvo (3); *v.i,* se
 ēvolvĕre (3 *reflex*)
uncombed incomptus
uncomfortable mŏlestus
uncommon rārus, insŏlĭtus
uncompleted imperfectus
unconcerned sēcūrus
unconditional simplex; **(to
 surrender —ly),** mănus do (1)
uncongenial ingrātus
unconnected disiunctus
unconquerable invictus
unconquered invictus
unconscious (unaware) inscĭus;
 (insensible); *use phr,* sensu ablāto
 (with feeling withdrawn)
unconstitutional non lēgĭtĭmus
uncontaminated incontāmĭnātus
uncontested *use phr,* quod in
 contentĭōnem non vēnit **(that has
 not come into dispute)**
uncontrollable impŏtens
uncontrolled līber
uncooked incoctus
uncouth incultus
uncover *v.t,* dētĕgo (3)
unction unctĭo, *f*
uncultivated incultus; **(person),**
 ăgrestis
uncut (hair) intonsus, prōmissus
undamaged intĕger

undaunted fortis
undeceive *v.t*, errōrem ērĭpĭo (3)
undecided incertus; **(of a battle)**, anceps
undefended nūdus, indēfensus
undeniable certus
under *prep*, sub *(with abl. to denote rest, and acc. to denote motion)*; infra *(with acc)*; **(— the leadership of)**, *use abl. phr, e.g.* tĕ dŭce **(— your leadership)**
underclothes sŭbūcŭla, *f*
undercurrent flŭentum subterlăbens, *n*
underestimate *v.t*, mĭnōris aestĭmo (1)
undergo *v.t*, sŭbĕo (3), fĕro *(irreg)*
underground *adj*, subterrānĕus
undergrowth virgulta, *n.pl*
underhand *adj*, clandestīnus
underlying (lying hidden) lătens
undermine *v.t*, subrŭo (3)
undermost *adj*, infĭmus
underneath *adv*, infrā
underrate *v.t*, mĭnōris aestĭmo (1)
understand *v.t*, intellĕgo (3), comprĕhendo (3)
understanding *nn*, mens, *f*; **(agreement)**, conventum, *n*
undertake *v.t*, suscĭpĭo (3); **(put in hand)**, incĭpĭo (3)
undertaker vespillo, *m*
undertaking, *nn*, inceptum, *n*
undervalue *v.t*, mĭnōris aestĭmo (1)
undeserved immĕrĭtus
undeserving indignus
undesirable *use phr. with* nōn *and* cŭpĭo (3) *or* expĕto (3) **(to desire)**
undetected tectus
undeveloped immātūrus
undigested crūdus
undiminished immĭnūtus
undisciplined ĭnexercĭtātus
undisguised non dissĭmŭlātus
undistinguished ignōbĭlis
undisturbed stăbĭlis, immōtus
undo *v.t*, solvo (3); **(render ineffectual)**, irrĭtum făcĭo (3)
undone infectus
undoubted certus

undoubtedly *adv*, sĭne dŭbĭo
undress *v.t*, vestem dētrăho (3) *(with dat. of person)*
undressed *adj*, nūdus
undue nĭmĭus
undulate *v.i*, fluctŭo (1)
unduly *adv*, **(excessively)**, nĭmĭum
undying immortālis
unearth *v.t*, dētĕgo (3)
unearthly *adv, use* terrĭbĭlis **(frightful)**
uneasiness anxĭĕtas, *f*
uneasy anxĭus
uneducated indoctus
unemployed ōtĭōsus
unending aeternus, infīnītus
unenterprising ĭners, ĭnaudax
unequal impar, ĭnīquus
unequalled singŭlāris
unequivocal non dŭbĭus
unerring certus
uneven ĭnaequālis; **(of ground)**, ĭnīquus
unevenness ĭnīquĭtas, *f*
unexampled ĭnaudītus, ūnĭcus
unexpected ĭnŏpīnātus
unexpectedly *adv*, ex *(or* dē*)* imprōvīso
unexplored ĭnexplōrātus
unfailing pĕrennis
unfair ĭnīquus, iniustus
unfairness ĭnīquĭtas, *f*
unfaithful infĭdēlis, perfĭdus
unfaithfulness infĭdēlĭtas
unfamiliar insŭētus
unfashionable *use phr. with* extrā consŭētūdĭnem **(outside of custom)**
unfasten *v.t*, solvo (3), rĕfĭgo (3)
unfathomable infīnītus
unfavourable ĭnīquus; **(omen)**, sĭnister, infēlix
unfeeling dūrus
unfeigned sincērus, simplex
unfinished imperfectus; **(task)** infectus
unfit incommŏdus
unfitness ĭnŭtĭlĭtas, *f*
unfitting indĕcōrus
unfix *v.t*, rĕfĭgo (3)
unfold *v.t*, explĭco (1)
unforeseen imprōvīsus

unforgiving implācābǐlis
unforgotten *use phr. with*
  mĕmor, *adj*, **(remembering)**
unfortified immūnītus
unfortunate infēlix
unfounded (groundless) vānus
unfriendliness ǐnǐmīcǐtǐa
unfriendly ǐnǐmīcus
unfulfilled irrǐtus, ǐnānis
unfurl *v.t*, pando (3)
unfurnished nūdus
ungainly rǔdis
ungentlemanly illībĕrālis
ungodly incestus
ungovernable impŏtens,
  indŏmǐtus
ungraceful ǐnēlĕgans
ungrateful ingrātus
unguarded incustōdītus; **(speech
  or action)**, incautus
unhappiness mǐsĕrǐa, *f*
unhappy mǐser, infēlix
unharmed incŏlǔmis
unhealthiness vălētūdo, *f*; **(of
  place, etc.)**, grǎvǐtas, *f*
unheard (of) ǐnaudītus
unheeded neglectus
unhesitating cofidens
unhindered expĕdītus
unhoped for inspērātus
unhorse *v.t*, ĕquo dēǐcǐo (3)
  (throw down from a horse)
unicorn mŏnŏcĕros, *m*
uniform *nn*, **(military —)**, hăbǐtus
  mīlǐtāris, *m*
uniform *adj*, aequābǐlis
unimaginable *use phr*, quod
  mente concǐpi non pŏtest **(that
  cannot be conceived in the mind)**
unimpaired intĕger
unimportant lĕvis
uninhabitable ǐnhăbǐtābǐlis
uninhabited dēsertus
uninitiated prŏfānus
uninjured incŏlǔmis
unintelligible obscūrus
unintentional non praemĕdǐtātus
uninteresting (flat, insipid) frīgǐdus
uninterruped contǐnǔus
uninvited invŏcātus
union (act of joining) iunctǐo, *f*;
  (— of states), cīvǐtātes foedĕrātae,
  f.pl; **(agreement)**, consensus, *m*

unique ūnǐcus
unit (one) ūnus
unite *v.t*, coniungo (3), consŏcǐo
  (1); *v.i*, sē consŏcǐāre (1 *reflex*), sē
  coniungĕre (3 *reflex*)
united consŏcǐātus
unity (one) ūnus; **(agreement)**,
  concordǐa, *f*
universal ūnǐversus
universe mundus, *m*
university ăcădēmǐa, *f*
unjust ǐniustus
unjustifiable *use phr*, quod
  excūsāri non pōtest **(that cannot
  be excused)**
unkind ǐnhūmānus
unkindness ǐnhūmānǐtas, *f*
unknowingly *adj*. imprūdens
unknown ignōtus, incognǐtus
unlawful (forbidden) vĕtǐtus
unlearned indoctus
unless *conj*, nǐsi
unletered indoctus, illittĕrātus
unlike dissǐmǐlis *(foll. by dat. or
  genit)*
unlikely non vēri sǐmǐlis **(not like
  the truth)**
unlimited infinītus
unload *v.t*, exŏnĕro (1); **(goods,
  etc.)**, expōno (3)
unlock *v.t*, rĕsĕro (1)
unlooked for ǐnexpectātus
unloose *v.t*, solvo (3)
unlucky infēlix
unmanageable impŏtens;
  (things), ǐnhābǐlis
unmanly mollis
unmarried caelebs
unmask *v.t*, **(plans, etc.)**, ăpĕrǐo
  (4)
unmerciful immǐsĕrǐcors
ummindful immĕmor
unmistakable certus
umitigated mĕrus
unmolested intĕger
unmoved immōtus
unnatural monstrŭōsus;
  (far-fetched), arcessītus
unnavigable innāvǐgābǐlis
unnecessary non nĕcessārǐus,
  sǔpervăcānĕus
unnoticed *use vb*, lătĕo (2) **(to lie
  hidden)**

unnumbered innŭmĕrābĭlis
unoccupied (at leisure) ōtĭōsus;
  (of land), ăpertus
unoffending innŏcens
unopposed (militarily) *use phr*,
  nullo hoste prŏhĭbente **(with no**
  enemy impending)
unpack *v.t*, exŏnĕro (1)
unpaid *use* rĕlĭquus **(remaining)**
unparalleled ūnĭcus
unpitied immĭsĕrābĭlis
unpleasant iniūcundus
unpleasantness (trouble)
  mŏlestĭa, *f*
unpolished impŏlītus
unpolluted intactus
unpopular invĭdĭōsus
unpopularity invĭdĭa, *f*
unprecedented nŏvus
unprejudiced intĕger
unpremeditated sŭbĭtus
unprepared impărātus
unpretentious hŭmĭlis
unprincipled (good for nothing)
  nēquam (*indeclinable*)
unproductive infēcundus
unprofitable non quaestŭōsus
unprotected indēfensus
unprovoked illăcessītus
unpunished impūnītus
unqualified nōn aptus;
  (unlimited), infīnītus
unquestionable certus
unravel *v.t*, rĕtexo (3); **(a problem,**
  etc.), explĭco (1)
unreasonable inīquus
unrelenting ĭnexōrābĭlis
unremitting assĭdŭus
unreserved līber
unrestrained effrēnātus
unrewarded ĭnhŏnōrātus
unrighteous iniustus
unripe immātūrus
unrivalled praestantissĭmus
unroll *v.t*, ēvolvo (3)
unruffled immōtus
unruly effrēnātus, impŏtens
unsafe intūtus
unsatisfactory nōn aptus
unscrupulous (wicked) mălus
unseal *v.t*, rĕsigno (1)
unseasonable intempestīvus
unseemly indĕcōrus

unseen invīsus
unselfish (persons) innŏcens;
  (actions), grātŭitus
unselfishness innŏcentĭa, *f*
unserviceable ĭnūtĭlis
unsettle *v.t*, turbo (1)
unsettled incertus, dŭbĭus
unshaken immōtus
unshaved intonsus
unsheath *v.t*, stringo (3)
unship *v.t*, expōno (3)
unsightly foedus
unskilful impĕrītus
unskilfulness impĕrītĭa, *f*
unslaked (thirst) nōn explētus
unsociable diffĭcĭlis
unsophisticated simplex
unsound (of health or opinions)
  infirmus; **(of mind)**, insānus
unsoundness infirmĭtas, *f*,
  insānĭtas, *f*
unsparing (severe) sĕvērus;
  (lavish), prōdĭgus; **(effort, etc.)**,
  non rĕmissus
unspeakable infandus
unspoiled intĕger
unstained pūrus
unsteadiness mōbĭlĭtas, *f*
unsteady instābĭlis, vărĭus
unstring rĕtendo (3)
unsuccessful irrĭtus; **(person)**,
  infaustus
unsuitable incommŏdus
unsuitableness incommŏdĭtas, *f*
unsuspected non suspectus
unsuspecting incautus
untameable impŏtens
untamed indŏmĭtus
untaught indoctus
unteachable indŏcĭlis
untenable (position) *use phr*, quod
  tĕnēri non pŏtest **(that cannot be**
  held)
unthankful ingrātus
unthinking (inconsiderate)
  inconsīdĕrātus
untie *v.t*, solvo (3)
until *conj*, dum, dōnec
until *prep*, ad, (*with acc*)
untilled incultus
untimely *adj*, immātūrus
untiring assĭdŭus
untold (numbers) innŭmĕrābĭlis

untouched intĕger
untried ĭnexpertus
untroubled sēcūrus
untrue falsus
untruth mendācĭum, *n*
unused (of persons) insŏlĭtus; **(things)** intĕger
unusual insŏlĭtus, ĭnūsĭtātus
unutterable infandus
unveil *v.t*, dētĕgo (3)
unwarily *adv*, incautē
unwarlike imbellis
unwarrantable ĭnīquus
unwary incautus
unwavering constans
unwearied indēfessus
unwelcome ingrātus
unwell aeger
unwholesome grăvis
unwieldy ĭnhăbĭlis
unwilling invītus; **(to be —)**, *v.i*, nolle *(irreg)*
unwillingly, unwillingness *use adj*, invītus **(unwilling)**
unwind *v.t*, rĕtexo (3), rĕvolvo (3)
unwise stultus, imprūdens
unworthiness indignĭtas, *f*
unworthy indignus, immĕrĭtus
unwrap *v.t*, explĭco (1)
unyielding firmus, inflexĭbĭlis
unyoke *v.t*, disiungo (3)
up *prep*, **(— stream or hill)**, adversus *(in agreement with noun)*; **(— to)**, tĕnus *(with abl)*
up *adv*, sursum; **(— and down)**, sursum dĕorsum
upbraid *v.t*, obiugo (1)
upbraiding *nn*, exprŏbrātĭo, *f*
uphill *adv. phr*, adverso colle
uphold *v.t*, sustĭnĕo (2)
uplift *v.t*, tollo (3)
upon *prep*, sŭper *(with acc)*; **(on)**, in *(with abl)*
upper *adj*, sŭpĕrĭor; **(to get the — hand)**, sŭpĕrĭor esse *(irreg)*
uppermost *adj*, summus
upright rectus; **(of morals)**, prŏbus
uprightness prŏbĭtas, *f*
uproar clāmor, *m*
uproarious tŭmultŭōsus
uproot ēvello (3)

upset *v.t*, ēverto (3)
upset *adj*, mōtus; **(troubled)**, anxĭus
upshot exĭtus, *m*
upside down, (to turn —) *use vb*. verto (3) **(to overturn)** *or* miscĕo (2) **(throw into confusion)**
upstart nŏvus hŏmo
upwards *adv*, sursum; **(of number, — of)**, amplĭus quam
urbane urbānus
urbanity urbānĭtas, *f*
urchin pūsĭo, *m*
urge *v.t*, urgĕo (2); **(persuade)**, suādĕo (2) *(with dat. of person)*
urgency grăvĭtas, *f*
urgent grăvis
urine ūrīna, *f*
urn urna, *f*
us *obj. pron*, nos
usage mos, *m*
use ūsus, m; **(advantage)**, commŏdum, *n*
use *v.t*, ūtor (3 *dep. with abl*)
useful ūtĭlis
usefulness ūtĭlĭtas, *f*
useless ĭnūtĭlis
uselessness ĭnūtĭlĭtas, *f*
usher in *v.t*, intrōdūco (3)
usual ūsĭtātus, sŏlĭtus
usually *adv*, plērumque, fĕrē
usurer fēnĕrātor, *m*
usurious fēnĕrātōrĭus
usurp *v.t*, occŭpo (1); **(seize)**, răpĭo (3)
usury fēnĕrātĭo, *f*, ūsūra, *f*
utensils vāsa, *n.pl*
utility ūtĭlĭtas, *f*
utilize *v.t*, ūtor (3 *dep. with abl*)
utmost extrēmus, summus
utter *adj*, tōtus
utter *v.t*, dīco (3)
utterance dictum, *n*
utterly *adv*, omnīno

V

vacancy (empty post) lŏcus văcŭus, *m*
vacant *adj*, văcŭus, ĭnānis
vacate *v.t*, rĕlinquo (3) **(a post)**, ējūro (1)
vacation fērĭae, *f.pl*

vacillate *v.i*, văcillo (1)
vacillation văcillătĭo, *f*
vacuum ĭnāne, *n*
vagabond erro, *m*
vagabond *adj*, văgus
vagary lĭbīdo, *f*
vagrant *adj*, văgus
vague incertus
vagueness obscūrĭtas, *f*
vain vānus; **(boastful, etc.),** glŏrĭōsus; **(in —),** *adv*, frustrā
vainglorious glŏrĭōsus
vainglory glōrĭa, *f*
vale valles, *f*
valet cŭbĭcŭlārĭus, *m*
valetudinarian vălētūdĭnārĭus, *m*
valiant fortis
valid firmus, vălĭdus
validity grăvĭtas, *f*
valise capsa, *f*
valley valles, *f*
valorous fortis
valour virtus, *f*
valuable prĕtĭōsus
valuation aestĭmātĭo, *f*
value *nn*, prĕtĭum, *n*
value *v.t*, aestĭmo (1); **(— highly),** magni dūco (3) **(— little),** parvi dūco
valueless vīlis
valve ĕpistŏmĭum, *n*
van (vanguard) prīmum agmen, *n*
vanish *v.i*, vānesco (3), dīlābor (3 *dep*)
vanity vānĭtas, *f*, iactātĭo, *f*
vanquish *v.t*, vinco (3)
vanquisher victor, *m*
vantage-point lŏcus sŭpĕrĭor, *m*
vapid văpĭdus
vapour văpor, *m*
variability mūtābĭlĭtas, *f*
variable vărĭus, mūtābĭlis
variance dissensĭo, *f*; **(to be at — with),** dissĭdĕo (2) ab (*with abl*)
variation vărĭĕtas, *f*
varicose vărĭcōsus; **(a — vein),** vărix, *c*
variegated vărĭus
variety vărĭĕtas, *f*, dīversĭtas, *f*
various vărĭus, dīversus
varnish *nn*, ātrāmentum, *n*
vary *v.i and v.t*, vărĭo (1)
vase vās, *n*

vassal clĭens, *m, f*
vast vastus, ingens
vastness immensĭtas, *f*
vat cūpa, *f*
vault fornix, *m*
vault *v.i*, sălĭo (4)
vaunt *v.t*, iacto (1); *v.i*, glŏrĭor (1 *dep*)
vaunting *nn*, iactātĭo, *f*
veal vĭtŭlīna căro, *f*, **(calf's flesh)**
veer *v.i*, sē vertĕre (3 *reflex*)
vegetable hŏlus, *n*
vehemence vīs, *f*
vehement vĕhĕmens, ācer
vehicle vĕhĭcŭlum, *n*
veil *v.t*, vēlo (1), tĕgo (3)
veil *nn*, rīca, *f*; **(bridal —),** flammĕum, *n*; **(disguise),** intĕgŭmentum, *n*
vein vēna, *f*
velocity vēlōcĭtas, *f*
venal vēnālis
venality vēnālĭtas, *f*
vendor vendĭtor, *m*
veneer *nn, use* cortex, *m*, **(bark, shell)**
venerable vĕnĕrābĭlis
venerate *v.t*, cŏlo (3), vĕnĕror (1 *dep*)
veneration cultus, *m*
venereal vĕnĕrĕus
vengeance ultĭo, *f*; **(to take —),** ulciscor (3 *dep*)
venial *use phr*, cui ignosci pŏtest **(that can be pardoned)**
venison fĕrīna căro, *f*
venom vēnēnum, *n*
venomous vĕnēnātus
vent *nn*, spīrāmentum, *n*
vent *v.t*, **(pour out),** effundo (3)
ventilate *v.t*, ventĭlo (1); **(discuss, etc.),** *use vb*, prōfĕro (*irreg*) **(to bring out)**
ventilator spīrāmentum, *n*
ventricle ventrĭcŭlus, *m*
venture *nn*, **(undertaking),** rĕs, *f*, inceptum, *n*
venture *v.t*, pĕrīclĭtor (1 *dep*)
venturous audax
veracious vērus
veracity vērĭtas, *f*
veranda pŏdĭum, *n*
verb verbum, *n*

verbal *nn, see adv,* **verbally**

verbally per verba **(by means of words)**

verbatim *adv,* tŏtĭdem verbis **(with the same number of words)**

verbose verbōsus

verdant vĭrĭdis

verdict (of a person or jury) sententĭa, *f;* **(of a court),** iūdĭcĭum, *n*

verdigris aerūgo, *f*

verge *nn,* ōra, *f,* margo, *c;* **(on the — of)** *use phr.* minimum abest quin ... **(it is very little wanting that ...)**

verge *v.i,* vergo (3)

verger appārĭtor, *m*

verification prŏbātĭo, *f*

verify *v.t,* prŏbo (1)

veritable vērus

vermilion mĭnĭum, *n*

versatile vărĭus

versatility ăgĭlĭtas, *f*

verse versus, *m*

versed in *adj,* exercĭtātus

versify *v.i,* versus făcĭo (3)

version *use vb,* converto (3) **(turn)**

vertebra vertĕbra, *f*

vertical rectus

vertigo vertīgo, *f*

very *adj, use emphatic pron,* ipse

very *adv, use superlative of adj. or adv, e.g.* — **beautiful,** pulcherrĭmus; — **quickly,** cĕlerrĭmē; *otherwise* maxĭmē, valdē, admŏdum

vessel (receptacle) vās, *n;* **(ship),** nāvis, *f*

vest *nn,* tūnĭca, *f*

vest *v.t,* **(invest, impart),** do (1)

vestal virgin vestālis virgo, *f*

vestibule vestĭbŭlum, *n*

vestige vestīgĭum, *n;* **(mark),** nŏta, *f,* indĭcĭum, *n*

vestry aedĭcŭla, *f*

veteran *adj,* vĕtĕrānus; **(— soldier),** vĕtĕrānus mīles, *m*

veterinary vĕtĕrīnārĭus

veto *nn,* intercessĭo, *f*

veto *v.i,* intercēdo (3) *(with dat)*

vex *v.t,* vexo (1), sollĭcĭto (1)

vexation indignātĭo, *f,* dŏlor, *m*

vexatious mŏlestus

vial lăgēna, *f*

viands cĭbus, *m*

viaticum vĭātĭcum, *n*

vibrate *v.i. and v.t,* vĭbro (1)

vibration ăgĭtātĭo, *f*

vicarious vĭcārĭus

vice turpĭtŭdo, *f*

viceroy lēgātos, *m*

vicinity vīcīnĭtas, *f*

vicious vĭtĭōsus; **(fierce),** fĕrus

vicissitude vĭces, *f.pl,* vĭcissĭtūdo, *f*

victim hostĭa, *f,* victĭma, *f*

victor victor, *m,* victrix, *f*

victorious victor

victory victōrĭa, *f*

victual *v.t, use phr,* rem frūmentārĭam prōvĭdĕo (2) **(to look after the supply of provisions)**

victuals cĭbus, *m*

vie with *v.i,* certo (1) cum *(with abl)*

view *nn,* aspectus, *m,* conspectus, *m;* **(opinion),** sententĭa, *f*

view *v.t,* conspĭcĭo (3); **(consider),** *use* sentĭo (4) **(to feel)**

vigil pervĭgĭlātĭo, *f*

vigilance vĭgĭlantĭa, *f*

vigilant vĭgĭlans

vigorous impĭger

vigour vīs, *f,* vĭgor, *m*

vile turpis

vileness turpĭtŭdo, *f*

vilify *v.t,* infāmo (1), dētrăho (3)

villa villa, *f*

village pāgus, *m*

villager pāgānus, *m*

villain hŏmo scĕlĕrātus

villainy prāvĭtas, *f,* scĕlus, *n*

vindicate *v.t,* vindĭco (1); **(justify),** purgo (1)

vindication purgātĭo, *f*

vindictive *use phr,* ăvĭdus iniūrĭae ulciscendae **(eager to avenge a wrong)**

vinegrower cultor, *(m)* vītis

vine vītis, *f*

vinegar ăcētum, *n*

vineyard vīnĕa, *f*

vintage *nn,* vindēmĭa, *f*

vintner vīnārĭus, *m*

violate *v.t,* vĭŏlo (1)

violation vĭŏlātĭo, *f*

violator vĭŏlātŏr, *m*

violence vīs, *f* vĭŏlentĭa, *f*, impĕtus, *m*

violent vĭŏlentus, impŏtens

violet *nn*, vĭŏla, *f*

violet *adj* **(— colour)**, ĭanthĭnus

viper vīpĕra, *f*; *adj*, vīpĕrīnus

virago vĭrāgo, *f*

virgin *nn*, virgo, *f*

virgin *adj*, virgĭnālis

virginity virgĭnĭtas, *f*

virile vĭrīlis

virtually *adv* re ipsā

virtue virtus, *f*, hŏnestas, *f*; **(by — of)**, *use abl. case of noun alone, or use* per *(with acc)*

virtuous hŏnestus

virulent ăcerbus

viscous lentus

visible (noticeable) mănifestus; *or use nn*. conspectus, *m* **(view)**

vision visus, *m*; **(phantom, apparition)**, ĭmāgo, *f*, spĕcĭes, *f*

visionary vānus

visit *nn*, **(call)**, sălūtātĭo, *f*; **(stay)**, commŏrātĭo, *f*

visit *v.t* vīso (3)

visitor sălūtātŏr, *m*, hospes, *m*

visor buccŭla, *f*

vista prospectus, *m*

visual *use phr. with* ŏcŭlus, *m*, **(eye)**

vital vītālis; **(important)**, grăvis

vitality vīs, *f*, vīvācĭtas, *f*

vitiate *v.t*, vĭtĭo (1), corrumpo (3)

vitreous vĭtrĕus

vituperation vĭtŭpĕrātĭo, *f*

vituperate *v.t*, vĭtŭpĕro (1)

vivacious ălăcer

vivacity ălăcrĭtas, *f*

vivid vīvus

vivify *v.t*, ănĭmo (1)

vixen vulpes, *f*

vocabulary verba, *n.pl*

vocal vōcālis

vocation offĭcĭum, *n*

vociferate *v.i*, clāmo (1)

vociferous clāmōsus

vociferously *adv*, magno clāmōre

vogue mos, *m*, **(custom)**

voice *nn*, vox, *f*

voice *v.t*, dīco (3)

void *nn*, ĭnāne, *n*

void *adj*, ĭnānis; **(— of)**, văcŭus *(with abl)*

volatile lĕvis

volcano mons qui ēructat flammas **(a mountain which emits flames)**

volition vŏluntas, *f*; **(of his own —)**, sŭa sponte

volley (of javelins) tēla missa, *n.pl*

volubility vŏlūbĭlĭtas, *f*

voluble vŏlūbĭlis

volume (book) lĭber, *m*; **(of noise)**, magnĭtūdo, *f*

voluminous cōpĭōsus

voluntarily *adv*, sponte **(of one's own accord)** *with appropriate pron*, mĕā, tŭā, sŭā

voluntary vŏluntārĭus

volunteer *nn*, mīles vŏluntārĭus, *m*

volunteer *v.i*, **(of soldiers)**, *use phr*, ultro nōmen dăre **(enlist voluntarily)**

voluptuous vŏluptārĭus

voluptuousness luxŭrĭa, *f*

vomit *nn*, vŏmĭtĭo, *f*

vomit *v.i. and v.t*, vŏmo (3)

voracious ĕdax, vŏrax

voracity ĕdācĭtas, *f*

vortex vertex, *m*

vote *nn*, suffrāgĭum, *n*, sententĭa, *f*

vote *v.i*, suffrāgĭum fĕro *(irreg)*; **(to — in favour of)**, in sententĭam īre *(irreg) (with genit)*

voter suffrāgātŏr, *m*

voting-tablet (ballot paper) tăbella, *f*

vouch for *v.t*, praesto (1), testor (1 *dep*), testĭfĭcor (1 *dep*)

voucher (authority) auctōrĭtas, *f*

vow vōtum, *n*; **(promise)**, fĭdes, *f*

vow *v.t*, prōmitto (3), vŏvĕo (2)

vowel vōcālis littĕra, *f*

voyage *nn*, nāvĭgātĭo, *f*

voyage *v.i*, nāvĭgo (1)

voyager pĕrĕgrīnātŏr, *m*

vulgar vulgāris, plēbēius, sordĭdus

vulgarity (of manner, etc.) *use phr*, mōres sordĭdi, *m.pl*

vulgarize *v.t*, pervulgo (1)

vulnerable ăpertus

vulture vultur, *m*

W

wadding *use* lānūgo, *f*, **(woolly down)**

wade *v.i, use phr*, per văda īre (*irreg*) **(to go through the shallows)**

wafer crustŭlum **(pastry)**

waft *v.t*, fěro (*irreg*)

wag *nn*, **(jester)**, iŏcŭlātor, *m*

wag *v.t*, quasso (1)

wage (war) *v.t*, gěro (3) (bellum)

wager *nn*, sponsĭo, *f*

wager *v.i*, sponsĭōnem făcĭo (3)

wages merces, *f*

waggish făcētus

waggon plaustrum, *n*

wagtail mōtăcilla, *f*

wail, wailing *nn*, plōrātus, *m*, flētus, *m*

wail *v.i*, plōro (1) flěo (2)

waist mědĭum corpus, *n*

waistcoat sŭbūcŭla, *f*, **(undergarment)**

wait *v.i*, mănĕo (2); *v.t*, **(to — for)**, exspecto (1); **(serve)**, fămŭlor (1 *dep*.); **(— in ambush)**, insĭdĭas făcĭo (3) (*with dat*)

wait *nn*, mŏra, *f*

waiter fămŭlus, *m*

waiting exspectātĭo, *f*, mansĭo, *f*

waive *v.t*, rěmitto (3)

wake *v.t*, excĭto (1); *v.i*, expergiscor (3 *dep*.)

wakeful vĭgil

wakefulness vĭgĭlantĭa, *f*, insomnĭa, *f*

walk *nn*, ambŭlātĭo, *f*; **(gait)**, incessus, *m*; **(— of life, occupation)**, quaestus, *m*

walk *v.i*, ambŭlo (1), grădĭor (3 *dep*.), incēdo (3)

walker pĕdes, *m*

walking *nn*, ambŭlātĭo, *f*

wall mūrus, *m*; **(ramparts)**, moenĭa, *n.pl*; **(inner —)**, părĭes, *m*

wall *v.t*, mūnĭo (4) **(fortify)**

wallet saccŭlus, *m*

wallow *v.i*, vŏlūtor (1 *pass*)

walnut (tree and nut) iūglans, *f*

wan *adj*, pallĭdus

wand virga, *f*, cādūcěus, *m*

wander *v.i*, erro (1), văgor (1 *dep*.)

wanderer erro, *m*

wandering *nn*, error, *m*

wane *v.i*, dēcresco (3)

want *nn*, **(lack)**, ĭnŏpĭa, *f*, pēnūrĭa, *f*; **(longing for)**, dēsīděrĭum, *n*; **(failing)**, dēfectĭo, *f*; **(in —)**, *adj*, ĭnops

want *v.i*, **(wish)**, vŏlo (*irreg*); *v.t*, **(to lack)**, cărĕo (2), ĕgĕo (2) (*with abl*); **(long for)**, dēsīdĕro (1); **(desire)**, cŭpĭo (3)

wanting (to be —, to fail) *v.i*, dēsum (*irreg*)

wanton *adj*, lascīvus, lĭbīdĭnōsus

wantoness lascīvĭa, *f*

war bellum, *n*; **(civil —)**, bellum cīvīle, *n*; **(in —)**, *adv*, bello; **(to make — on)**, bellum infěro (*irreg, with dat*); **(to declare — on)**, bellum indīco (3) (*with dat*); **(to wage —)**, bellum gěro (3)

warble *v.i*, căno (3)

warcry clāmor, *m*

ward pūpillus, *m*, pūpilla, *f*; **(district)**, rěgĭo, *f*

ward off *v.t*, arcěo (2)

warden cūrātor, *m*

warder custos, *c*

wardrobe vestĭārĭum, *n*

warehouse horrěum, *n*

wares merx, *f*

warfare mīlĭtĭa, *f*

warily *adv*, cautē

wariness cautĭo, *f*

warlike *adj*, bellĭcōsus, mīlĭtāris

warm călĭdus; **(to be —)**, *v.i*, călěo (2)

warm *v.t*, călěfăcĭo (3)

warmly (eagerly) *adv*, věhementer

warmth călor, *m*

warn *v.t*, mŏnĕo (2)

warning *nn*, **(act of —)**, mŏnĭtĭo, *f*; **(the warning itself)**, mŏnĭtum, *n*

warp *nn*, stāmen, *n*

warp *v.t*, **(distort of mind, etc.)**, dēprāvo (1)

warrant *nn*, mandātum, *n*; **(authority)**, auctōrĭtas, *f*

warrant *v.t*, **(guarantee)**, firmo (1), praesto (1)

warranty sătisdătĭo, *f*

warren lěpŏrārĭum, *n*

weed

warrior mīles, *c*, bellātor, *m*
wart verrūca, *f*
wary prōvĭdus, prūdens
wash *v.t*, lăvo (1); *v.i*, lăvor (1 *pass*)
wash, washing *nn*, lăvātĭo, *f*
washbasin ăquālis, *c*
wasp vespa, *f*
waspish ăcerbus
waste *nn*, damnum, *n*; **(careless throwing away),** effūsĭo, *f*; **(— land),** vastĭtas, *f*
waste *adj*, vastus, dĕsertus
waste *v.t*, consūmo (3), perdo (3); **(— time),** tempus tĕro (3); *v.i*, **(— away),** tābesco (3)
wasteful prŏfūsus
wastefulness prŏfūsĭo, *f*
watch (a — of the night) vĭgĭlĭa, *f*; **(watching on guard),** excŭbĭae, *f.pl*
watch *v.t*, **(observe),** specto (1); **(guard),** custōdĭo (4); *v.i*, **(not to sleep),** excŭbo (1)
watchful vĭgĭlans
watchfulness vĭgĭlantĭa, *f*
watchman custos, *m*
watchword tessĕra, *f*
water ăqua, *f*; **(fresh —),** ăqua dulcis, *f*; **(salt —),** ăqua salsa, *f*
water *v.t*, rĭgo (1), irrĭgo (1)
water-carrier ăquārĭus, *m*
water closet lātrīna, *f*
water snake hydrus, *m*
waterfall ăqua dēsĭlĭens, *f*, **(water leaping down)**
watering place ăquātĭo, *f*; **(resort),** ăquae, *f.pl*
waterworks ăquaeductus, *m*
watery ăquātĭcus
wattle crātis, *f*
wave *nn*, unda, *f*, fluctus, *m*
wave *v.i*, undo (1), fluctŭo (1); *v.t*, ăgĭto (1)
waver *v.i*, fluctŭo (1) dŭbĭto (1)
wavering *adj*, dŭbĭus
wavering *nn*, dŭbĭtātĭo, *f*
wavy (of hair) crispus
wax *nn*, cēra, *f*; *adj*, cērĕus
wax *v.i*, cresco (3)
way vĭa, *f*; **(journey),** ĭter, *n*; **(pathway),** sēmĭta, *f*; **(course),** cursus, *m*; **(manner),** mŏdus, *m*;

(habit), mos, *m*; **(system),** rătĭo, *f*; **(in the —),** *adj*, obvĭus; **(in this —),** *adv*, ĭta, sīc; **(out of the —)** *adj*, āvĭus; **(to give or to make —),** *v.i*, cēdo (3); **(to get one's own —),** vinco (3)
wayfarer vĭātor, *m*
waylay *v.t*, insĭdĭor (1 *dep.*) (*with dat*)
wayward pertĭnax
we *pron*, nos; *often expressed by 1st person plural of vb, e.g* **we are,** sumus
weak infirmus, dēbĭlis; **(overcome),** confectus; **(of arguments, etc.),** lĕvis
weaken *v.t*, infirmo (1), dēbĭlĭto (1); *v.t*, languesco (3), dēfĭcĭo (3)
weak-hearted pŭsilli ănĭmi **(of weak heart)**
weakness infirmĭtas, *f*, dēbĭlĭtas, *f*, lēvĭtas, *f*
weal (the common) bŏnum pūblĭcum, *n*; **(on skin),** vībex, *f*
wealth dīvĭtĭae, *f.pl*, ŏpes, *f.pl*; **(large supply),** cōpĭa, *f*
wealthy dīves, lŏcŭples
wean *v.t*, lacte dēpello (3) **(remove from the milk)**
weapon tēlum, *n*; **(pl)** arma, *n.pl*
wear *v.t*, **(rub),** tĕro (3); **(— out),** contĕro (3); **(— a garment),** gĕro (3); *v.i*, **(last),** dūro (1)
weariness lassĭtūdo, *f*
wearisome lăbōrĭōsus
weary *adj*, fessus, fătīgātus
weary *v.t*, fătīgo (1); *v.i*, **(grow —),** dēfătīgor (1 *pass*)
weasel mustēla, *f*
weather *nn*, tempestas, *f*
weather *v.t*, **(endure, bear),** perfĕro (*irreg*)
weave *v.t*, texo (3)
weaver textor, *m*
web tēla, *f*
wed *v.t*, **(of the husband),** dūco (3); **(of the wife),** nūbo (3) (*with dat*)
wedding *nn*, nuptĭae, *f.pl*; **(— day),** dĭes (*m*) nuptĭārum
wedge *nn*, cŭnĕus, *m*
wedlock mātrĭmōnĭum, *n*
weed *nn*, herba ĭnūtĭlis, *f* **(harmful plant)**

weed *v.t*, runco (1)
week *use phr*, spătĭum septem dĭērum **(a space of seven days)**
weep *v.i*, lăcrĭmo (1)
weeping *nn*, flētus, *m*
weeping willow sălix, *f*
weevil curcŭlĭo, *m*
weigh *v.t*, pendo (3), penso (1), **(consider)**, pondĕro (1); **(— down)**, grăvo (1)
weight pondus, *n*; **(a —)**, lĭbrămentum, *n*; **(influence, etc.)**, *use adj*. grăvis **(important)**
weightiness grăvĭtas, *f*
weighty grăvis
weir (dam) mōles, *f*
welcome *adj*, grātus, acceptus
welcome *nn*, sălūtātĭo, *f*
welcome! salve! *(pl*. salvēte!*)*
welcome *v.t*, excĭpĭo (3)
weld *v.t*, ferrūmĭno (1)
welfare bŏnum, *n*, sălus, *f*
well *adv*, bĕnĕ; **(very —)**, optĭmē
well *nn*, pŭtĕus, *m*
well *adj*, **(safe)**, salvus; **(healthy)**, sānus, vălens; **(to be —)**, *v.i*, vălĕo (2)
wellbeing *nn* sălus, *f*
well-born nōbĭlis
well-disposed bĕnĕvŏlus
well-favoured pulcher
well-known nōtus
well-wisher *use adj*, bĕnĕvŏlus **(well-disposed)**
welter *v.i*, vŏlūtor (1 *pass*)
wench pŭella, *f*
west *nn*, occĭdens, *m*
west *adj*, occĭdentālis
westward *adv*, ad occĭdentem (sōlem)
wet *adj*, hūmĭdus, mădĭdus
wet *v.t*, mădĕfăcĭo (3)
wether vervex, *m*
wet nurse nūtrix, *f*
whale bālaena, *f*
wharf nāvāle, *n*
what *interrog. pron*, quid? *interrog. adj*, qui, quae, quod; *relative pron*, quod, *pl*, quae; **(— for, wherefore, why)**, quārē; **(— sort)**, quālis?
whatever *pron*, quodcumque; *adj*, quīcumque

wheat trītĭcum, *n*
wheel *nn*, rŏta, *f*
wheel *v.t*, circŭmăgo (3)
wheelbarrow păbo, *m*
wheeling *adj*, circumflectens
whelp *nn*, cătŭlus, *m*
when? *interrog*, quando? *(temporal)*, cum *(with vb, in indicative or subjunctive mood)*, ŭbĭ *(vb. in indicative)*
whence *adv*, undĕ
whenever *adv*, quandōcumque
where? *interrog*, ŭbĭ?; *(relative)*, quā; **(— from)**, undĕ; **(— to)**, quō; **(anywhere, everywhere)**, *adv*, ŭbīque
whereas *adv*, quŏnĭam
wherever quācumque
wherefore *adv*, quārē
whereupon *use phr*, quo facto **(with which having been done)**
whet *v.t* **(sharpen)**, ăcŭo (3)
whether *conj. (in a single question)*, num, nĕ; *(in a double question,* **whether ... or***)*, ŭtrum ... an; *(in a conditional sentence)*, sīve ... sīve
whetstone cōs, *f*
whey sērum, *n*
which *interrog*, quis, quid; *(relative)*, qui, quae, quod; **(which of two)**, ŭter
while *conj*, dum *(often foll. by vb. in present tense indicative)*
while *nn*, tempus, *n*, spătĭum, *n*; **(for a little —)**, *adv*, părumper; **(in a little —)**, brĕvi (tempŏre)
while away *v.t*, fallo (3), tĕro (3)
whim lĭbīdo, *f*
whimper *v.i*, vāgĭo (4)
whimsical rĭdĭcŭlus
whine *v.i*, vāgĭo (4)
whinny *v.i*, hinnĭo (4)
whip *nn*, flăgellum, *n*
whip *v.t*, verbĕro (1), flăgello (1)
whirl *v.t*, torquĕo (2); *v.i*, torquĕor (2 *pass*)
whirlpool *m*, gurges, *m*
whirlwind turbo, *m*
whirr *nn*, strīdor, *m*
whirr *v.i*, strīdĕo (2)
whiskers *use* barba, *f*, **(beard)**
whisper *nn*, sŭsurrus, *m*

whisper *v.i*, sŭsurro (1)
whispering *adj*, sŭsurrus
whistle, whistling *nn*, sībĭlus, *m*
whistle *v.i*, sībĭlo (1)
white *adj*, albus; **(shining —)**, candĭdus
white *nn*, album, *n*
whiten *v.t*, dĕalbo (1); *v.i*; albesco (3)
whiteness candor, *m*
whitewash *nn*, albārĭum, *n*; v.t, dĕalbo (1)
whither *(interrog. and relative)*, quo
whiz *v.i*, strīdĕo (2)
whiz, whizzing *nn*, strīdor, *m*
who *interrog*, quis? *(relative)*, qui, quae
whoever *pron*, quīncunque
whole *adj*, tōtus; **(untouched)**, intĕger
whole *nn*, tōtum, *n*, ūnĭvĕrsĭtas, *f*, or use adj, tōtus, e.g. **the — of the army**, tōtus exercĭtus, *m*
wholesale trader mercātor, *m*
wholesale trading mercātūra, *f*
wholesome sălūbris
wholly *adv*, omnīno
whoop *nn*, ŭlŭlātus, *m*
whom *acc. case of rel. pron*, quem, quam; *pl*, quos, quas
whore mĕrĕtrix, *f*
whose *genit. case of rel. pron*, cūius; *pl*, quōrum, quārum
why *adv*, cur, quārē
wick ellychnĭum, *n*
wicked scĕlestus, mălus, imprŏbus
wickedness scĕlus, *n*, inprŏbĭtas, *f*
wicker vīmĭnĕus
wide lātus; **(— open)**, pătens
widen *v.t*, dīlāto (1); *v.i*, sē dīlātāre (1 *reflex*)
widow vĭdŭa, *f*
widower vĭdŭus vir, *m*
widowhood vĭdŭĭtas, *f*
width lātĭtūdo, *f*
wield *v.t*, tracto (1)
wife uxor, *f*
wig cāpillāmentum, *n*
wild indŏmĭtus, fĕrus; **(uncultivated)**, incultus; **(mad)**, āmens

wilderness dēserta lŏca, *n.pl*
wildness fĕrĭtas, *f*
wile dŏlus, *m*
wilful pervĭcax
wilfully *adv*, pervĭcācĭter; **(deliberately)**, consultō
wilfulness pervĭcācĭa, *f*
wiliness callĭdĭtas, *f*
will (desire) vŏluntas, *f*; **(purpose)**, consĭlĭum, *n*; **(pleasure)**, lĭbīdo, *f*; **(decision, authority)**, arbĭtrĭum, *n*; **(legal)**, testāmentum, *n*
will *v.t*, **(bequeath)**, lēgo (1)
willing *adj*, lĭbens
willingly *adv*, lĭbenter
willingness vŏluntas, *f*
willow sălix, *f*
wily callĭdus, vāfer
win *v.i*, vinco (3); *v.t*, consĕquor (3 *dep*), ădĭpiscor (3 *dep*)
wind ventus, *m*; **(breeze)**, aura, *f*
wind *v.t*, volvo (3)
winding *nn*, flexus, *m*
winding *adj*, flexŭōsus
windlass sŭcŭla, *f*
window fĕnestra, *f*
windward *use phr*, conversus ad ventum **(turned towards the wind)**
windy ventōsus
wine vīnum, *n*
wine cask dōlĭum, *n*
wine cellar ăpŏthēca, *f*
wine cup pōcŭlum, *n*
wine merchant vīnārĭus, *m*
wing āla, *f*; **(of army, etc.)**, cornu, *n*
winged pennĭger
wink *nn*, nictātĭo, *f*
wink *v.i*, nicto (1); **(overlook)**, cōnīvĕo (2)
winner victor, *m*
winning *adj*, **(of manner)**, blandus
winnow *v.t*, ventĭlo (1)
winter *nn*, hĭems, *f*
winter *adj*, hĭĕmālis
winter *v.i*, hĭĕmo (1)
wintry hĭĕmālis
wipe *v.t*, tergĕo (2)
wire fīlum, *n*, **(thread)**
wisdom săpĭentĭa, *f*, prūdentĭa, *f*
wise *adj*, săpĭens, prūdens
wisely *adv*, săpĭenter, prūdenter

wish　*nn*, **(desire)**, vŏluntas, *f*; **(the wish itself)**, optātum, *n*; **(longing)**, dēsĭdĕrĭum, *n*

wish　*v.t*, vŏlo (*irreg*), cŭpĭo (3), opto (1); **(long for)**, dēsīdĕro (1)

wishing　*nn*, optātĭo, *f*

wisp　mănĭpŭlus, *m*

wistful　cŭpĭdus **(longing for)**; **(dejected)**, tristis

wit　ingĕnĭum, *n*; **(humour)**, făcētĭae, *f.pl*; **(out of one's —s)**, *adj*, āmens

witch　sāga, *f*

witchcraft　ars măgĭca, *f*

with　*prep*, cum (*with abl, but when denoting the instrument, use abl. case, alone*); **(among, at the house of)**, ăpud (*with acc*)

withdraw　*v.i*, cēdo (3), sē rĕcĭpĕre (3 *reflex*); *v.t*, dēdūco (3), rĕmŏvĕo (2)

withdrawal　regressus, *m*

wither　*v.i*, languesco (3); *v.t*, **(parch)**, torrĕo (2)

withered　flaccĭdus

withhold　*v.t*, rĕtĭnĕo (2)

within　*adv*, intus

within　*prep*, **(time and space)**, intrā (*with acc*); **(time)**, use abl. case alone, e.g. **within three days**, trĭbus dĭēbus

without　*prep*, sĭne (*with abl*); **(outside of)**, extrā (*with acc*); *when* without *is followed by a gerund* (e.g **I returned without seeing him**) *use a clause introduced by* nĕque, quīn, ĭta … ut: *e.g.* rĕgressus sum, nĕque ĕum vīdi

without　*adv*, extrā

withstand　*v.t*, rĕsisto (3) (*with dat*)

witness　*nn*, **(person)**, testis, *c*; **(testimony)**, testĭmōnĭum, *n*

witness　*v.t*, testor (1 *dep*), testĭficor (1 *dep*); **(to see)**, vĭdĕo (2)

witticism　făcētĭe, *f.pl*

witty　făcētus; **(sharp)**, salsus

wizard　măgus, *m*

woad　vĭtrum, *n*

woe　dŏlor, *m*, luctus, *m*

woeful　tristis

wolf　lŭpus, *m*

wolfish (greedy, rapacious)　răpax

woman　fēmĭna, *f*, mŭlĭer, *f*; **(young —)**, pŭella, *f*; **(old —)**, ănus, *f*

womanish, womanly　mŭlĭĕbris

womb　ŭtĕrus, *m*

wonder　mīrātĭo, *f*; **(a marvel)**　mīrācŭlum, *n*

wonder　*v.i*. and v.t, mīror (1 *dep*)

wonderful　mīrus, mīrābĭlis

wont, wonted　*adj*, sŭētus

wont　*nn*, mos, *m*

woo　*v.t*, pĕto (3), ămo (1)

wood (material)　mātĕrĭa, *f*; **(forest)**, silva, *f*

wood-collector　lignātor, *m*

wooded　silvestris

wooden　lignĕus

woodland　silvae, *f.pl*

woodpecker　pīcus, *m*

wooer　prŏcus, *m*

wool　lāna, *f*

woollen　lānĕus

word　verbum, *n*; **(promise)**, fĭdes, *f*; **(information)**, nuntĭus, *m*; **send word**, *v.t*, nuntĭo (1)

wordy　verbōsus

work　*nn*, ŏpus, *n*; **(labour)**, lăbor, *m*

work　*v.i*, ŏpĕror (1 *dep*)

work　*v.t*, exercĕo (2); **(handle, manipulate)**, tracto (1); **(bring about)**, effĭcĭo (3)

worker　ŏpĭfex, *c*, ŏpĕrārĭus, *m*

workman　ŏpĭfex, *c*, ŏpĕrārĭus, *m*

workmanship　ars, *f*

workshop　officīna, *f*

world　mundus, *m*, orbis (*m*) terrārum; **(people)**, hŏmĭnes, *c. pl*

worldliness　use phr, stŭdĭum rērum prŏfānārum **(fondness for common matters)**

worm　vermis, *m*

worm-eaten　vermĭnōsus

worm (one's way)　*v.i*, sē insĭnŭāre (1 *reflex*)

wormwood　absinthĭum, *n*

worn (— out)　*adj*, trītus; **(as clothes)**, gestus

worry　*nn*, anxĭĕtas, *f*

worry　*v.t*, vexo (1); *v.i*, cūrā affici (3 *pass*) **(to be affected by worry)**

worse *adj*, pēior

worse *adv*, pēius

worship *v.t*, vĕnĕror (1 *dep*), cŏlo (3)

worship *nn*, vĕnĕrātĭo, *f*, cultus, *m*

worshipper cultor, *m*

worst *adj*, pessīmus

worst *adv*, pessĭmē

worst *v.t*, vinco (3)

worth *nn*, **(price)**, prĕtĭum, *n*; **(valuation)**, aestĭmātĭo, *f*; **(worthiness)**, virtus, *f*, dignĭtas, *f*; **(— nothing)**, nĭhĭli; **(to be — much)**, *v.i*, multum vălĕo (2); **(adj)** dignus

worthiness dignĭtas, *f*

worthless vīlis

worthy **(with noun)**, dignus **(with abl)**; **(with phr)** dignus qui (ut) **(with vb. in subjunctive)**; **(man)**, prŏbus

wound *nn*, vulnus, *n*

wound *v.t*, vulnĕro (1), saucĭo (1)

wounded vulnĕrātus, saucĭus

wrangle *v.i*, rixor (1 *dep*)

wrangle, wrangling *nn*, rixa, *f*

wrap *v.t*, involvo (3)

wrapper invŏlūcrum, *n*

wrath īra, *f*

wrathful īrātus

wreak vengeance on *v.t*, ulciscor (3 *dep*)

wreath *nn*, serta, *n. pl*

wreathe *v.t*, torquĕo (2)

wreck *nn*, naufrăgĭum, *n*

wreck *v.t*, frango (3)

wrecked naufrăgus

wren rĕgŭlus, *m*

wrench away, wrest *v.t*, extorquĕo (2)

wrestle *v.i*, luctor (1 *dep*)

wrestler luctātor, *m*

wrestling *nn*, luctātĭo, *f*

wretch perdĭtus, *m*

wretched mĭser

wretchedness mĭsĕrĭa, *f*

wriggle *v.i*, torquĕor (2 *pass*)

wring *v.t*, torquĕo (2)

wrinkle rūga, *f*

wrinkled rūgōsus

wrist *use* bracchĭum, *n*, **(forearm)**

writ (legal —) mandātum, *n*

write *v.t*, scrībo (3)

writer scriptor, *m*; **(author)**, auctor, *c*

writhe *v.i*, torquĕor (2 *pass*)

writing scriptĭo, *f*; **(something written)**, scriptum, *n*, ŏpus, *n*

wrong *adj*, falsus; **(improper, bad)**, prāvus; **(to be —)**, *v.i*, erro (1)

wrong *nn*, nĕfas, *n*, peccātum *n*; **(a —)**, iniūrĭa, *f*

wrongly *adv*, **(badly)**, măle; **(in error)**, falso

wrong *v.t*, fraudo (1), iniūrĭam infĕro (*irreg*) (*with dat*)

wrongful iniustus

wroth īrātus

wrought confectus

wry distortus

Y

yacht cĕlox, *f*

yard (measurement) *often* passus, *m*, **(5 ft/1.5 m approx.) (court —)**, ārĕa, *f*

yarn (thread) fīlum, *n*; **(story)**, fābŭla, *f*

yawn *nn*, oscĭtātĭo, *f*

yawn *v.i*, oscĭto (1)

year annus, *m*; **(a half —)**, sēmestre spătĭum, *n*; **(space of six months)**

yearly *adj*, **(throughout a year)**, annŭus; **(every year)**, *adv*, quŏtannis

yearn for *v.t*, dēsīdĕro (1)

yearning dēsīdĕrĭum, *n*

yeast fermentum, *n*

yell clāmor, *m*, ŭlŭlātus, *m*

yell *v.i*, magnā vōce clāmo (1)

yellow flāvus

yellowish subflāvus

yelp *v.i*, grannĭo (4)

yelping *nn*, gannītus, *m*

yeoman cŏlōnus, *m*

yes *adv*, ĭta

yesterday *adv*, hĕri; *nn*, hesternus dĭes, *m*

yet *adv*, **(nevertheless)**, tămen; **(with comparatives)** ĕtĭam, *e.g.* **yet bigger**, ĕtĭam māior; **(of time; still)**, ădhuc

yew   taxus, *f*
yield   *v.i*, cēdo (3) (*with dat*);
  (surrender), sē dēdĕre (3 *reflex*)
yielding   *nn*, concessĭo, *f*
yielding   *adj*, **(soft),** mollis
yoke   *nn*, iŭgum, *n*
yoke   *v.t*, iungo (3)
yoked   iŭgālis; **(— pair),** ĭugum, *n*
yolk   vĭtellus, *m*
yonder   *adv*, illic
yore   *adv*, ōlim **(once, in time
  past)**
you   *pron, often not expressed,
  e.g.* **you come,** vĕnis; *pl*, vĕnĭtis;
  otherwise use appropriate case of
  tu; *pl*, vos
young   *adj*, iŭvĕnis, parvus;
  (child), infans; **(— person),**
  ădŏlescens
young   *nn*, **(offspring),** partus, *m*
younger   iŭnĭor, mĭnor nātu **(less
  in age)**
young man   iŭvĕnis, *m*
youngster   iŭvĕnis, *c*
your, yours   (*singular*), tŭus; (*of
  more than one*), vester
yourself   (*emphatic*), *use* ipse *in
  agreement with pron*; (*reflexive*),
  te; *pl*, vos
youth (time of —)   iŭventus, *f*,
  ădŏlescentĭa, *f*; **(young man),**
  ădŏlescens, iŭvĕnis, *c*; **(body of
  young persons),** iŭventus, *f*
youthful   iŭvĕnīlis

Z

zeal   stŭdĭum, *n*
zealous   stŭdĭōsus
zenith   *use* summus, *adj*, **(top of)**
zephyr   Zĕphy̆rus, *m*, Făvŏnĭus, *m*
zero (nothing)   nĭhil
zest   ălăcrĭtas, *f*
zodiac   signĭfer orbis, *m*,
  (sign-bearing orb)
zone   lŏcus, *m*